The Menshevik Leaders in the Russian Revolution

Studies of the Harriman Institute
Columbia University

Founded as the Russian Institute in 1946, the W. Averell Harriman
Institute for Advanced Study of the Soviet Union is the oldest research
institution of its kind in the United States. The book series *Studies of the
Harriman Institute*, begun in 1953, helps bring to a wider audience some
of the work conducted under its auspices by professors, degree
candidates and visiting fellows. The faculty of the Institute, without
necessarily agreeing with the conclusions reached in these books,
believes their publication will contribute to both scholarship and a
greater public understanding of the Soviet Union. A list of the *Studies*
appears at the back of the book.

The Menshevik Leaders in the Russian Revolution: Social Realities and Political Strategies

ZIVA GALILI

PRINCETON UNIVERSITY PRESS

Published by Princeton University Press, 41 William Street,
Princeton, New Jersey 08540
In the United Kingdom: Princeton University Press,
Guildford, Surrey

This book has been composed in Linotron Palatino

Clothbound editions of Princeton University Press books are printed on
acid-free paper, and binding materials are chosen for strength and durability.
Paperbacks, although satisfactory for personal collections, are not usually
suitable for library rebinding

Printed in the United States of America by Princeton University Press,
Princeton, New Jersey

Library of Congress Cataloging-in-Publication Data

Galili y Garcia, Ziva.
The Menshevik leaders in the Russian Revolution.

(Studies of the Harriman Institute)
Bibliography: p.
Includes index.
1. Socialism—Soviet Union—History. 2. Petrogradskiĭ sovet
rabochikh i krasnoarmeĭskikh deputatov—History. 3. Mensheviks.
4. Soviet Union—History—February Revolution, 1917.
I. Title. II. Series.
HX313.G36 1989   335'.00947   88-32504
ISBN 0-691-05567-x (alk. paper)

To Klara and Lasia Galili
of Kibbutz Afikim

Contents

Illustrations

Unless otherwise indicated, the photographs are from the collections of the Hoover Institution on War, Revolution, and Peace and are reprinted with its permission.

Facing page 3:
Map of Petrograd in 1917 (Rutgers cartography)

Following page 142:
Social Democrats in exile, Irkutsk, 1914–1915

S. L. Vainshtein, L. O. Dan, and I. G. Tsereteli, Irkutsk, 1914–1915

A session of the Petrograd soviet in the early days of the revolution

N. S. Chkheidze addressing sailors at the Tauride Palace, February 1917

Members of the Provisional Government at the burial of victims of the revolution

A session of the All-Russian Conference of Soviets, April 3, 1917 (reprinted from *Vserossiiskoe soveshchanie sovetov rabochikh i soldatskikh deputatov*, Moscow and Leningrad, 1927)

P. A. Garvi, 1915 (reprinted by permission of the Project on Menshevik History)

Iu. O. Martov and F. I. Dan, winter 1917–1918 (reprinted by permission of the Project on Menshevik History)

May Day demonstration in Petrograd, April 18, 1917

A. N. Potresov, 1925

I. G. Tsereteli as minister of post and telegraph, May 1917

Demonstration in Petrograd, June 18, 1917

Presidium of the First All-Russian Congress of Soviets

Acknowledgments

THE DEBTS I incurred in preparing this book make for a long list and one which I am proud to recite. The list begins with those who during my childhood and youth turned my mind to the questions with which this book is ultimately concerned: my parents, who have always struggled to temper ideological commitment with human tolerance and to reconcile national and social justice; and my teachers, who made me aware of this struggle and of earlier attempts at its resolution.

Throughout my academic studies, I was also fortunate to have teachers whose scholarly rigor was matched by their personal dedication to students. Michael Confino, Jonathan Frankel, and Nissan Oren of the Hebrew University opened the doors of Russian and Soviet history to me, then encouraged me in the difficult decision to further my education abroad. At Columbia, Leopold Haimson and the late Alexander Erlich not only made my studies intellectually exhilarating and eased a foreigner's troubles with language and culture, but also eventually launched me on the study of the Mensheviks and the workers in 1917.

The work on my dissertation and eventually on this book led to many new friendships and added more names to my list of debts. The late Anna Mikhailovna Bourguina of the Hoover Institution on War, Revolution, and Peace, and Boris Sapir of the International Institute on Social History in Amsterdam, were generous in sharing documents as well as their own intimate knowledge of Menshevism and its practitioners. Institutional support for work in these archives and in libraries in Moscow and Helsinki came from Columbia University, the International Research and Exchanges Board, and the National Endowment for the Humanities. At the writing stage, I benefitted from the advice of many new friends. Diane Koenker, David Mandel, Reginald Zelnik, and especially William Rosenberg read various versions of my work, and I have drawn enormously from their special knowledge of Russian labor. William Duggan and Alfred Rieber were both helpful and truly gracious about a beginner's mistakes when I expanded this study to include the industrialists. Similarly, Allan Wildman was encour-

aging even in his critique. A special word of gratitude must go to
Ronald Suny, who followed my work from its earliest stages and
has always been willing to read and discuss yet another draft and
to dispense equal measures of criticism and praise, not only because his own research touched on some of the questions I was
studying but out of a true love for the history of the revolution and
a great spirit of generosity.

Members of the History Department at Rutgers University also
gave willingly of their time and knowledge. Seymour Becker, Paul
Clemens, Victoria DeGrazia, John Gillis, and Traian Stoianovich
read large portions of the dissertation, and others in the department's Social History Seminar commented on a shorter version.
All these people deserve much of the credit for what is worthwhile
in this book, but they bear none of the responsibility for its shortcomings.

Ultimately, however, it is to two men that I owe the greatest
debt: Leopold Haimson and Raúl García. As my dissertation ad-
visor, Leopold Haimson would be presumed to have left his stamp
on this book, and this is true enough. But what is less commonly
known is his rare talent for reading one's work, seeing the patterns and the ideas suggested therein but only dimly perceived by
the writer, pointing out possible conclusions, and then leaving
matters at that. If some of his most dearly held notions about Russian history in the revolutionary era reverberate through this book,
it is because his example of thorough scholarship, a comprehensive approach, and an inspired interpretive ability has made it difficult, yet not at all necessary, to escape his influence.

Finally, there is my debt to Raúl García. Every spouse who has
lived with the writer of a dissertation or a book deserves recognition, the more so one who has volunteered assistance and critique.
It is not mere recognition that I seek to note here, but rather Raúl's
actual and crucial contribution to this book. As the editor of every
version of this work, he not only did much to improve its style
but, more fundamentally, he contributed to the very process of
transforming so much research material into a monograph. At
every stage, it was his critique that forced me to develop an argument, organize it clearly, and often rethink it at a later stage. It
was not always easy for two Russian historians of such different
temperaments and convictions to agree, and our editorial sessions
were rarely peaceful, but the benefit was all mine. I cannot imagine writing a book any other way.

Of the people closest to me, only my five-year-old son, Daniel, has had nothing to do with this book. I did learn to appreciate rather than resent his intrusions into my working hours, and perhaps having someone so clearly more important than this book next to me made the writing more tolerable. Daniel is very happy that my book will be "made" at the press where his best friend's father once worked—and so am I. Indeed, my final thanks belong to Loren Hoekzema, and to Gail Ullman, who acquired the book for Princeton University Press.

Author's Note

ALL DATES are given in the Old Style (Julian) calendar, which was thirteen days behind the New Style (Gregorian) calendar and was in use in Russia until February 1918.

The system of transliteration used here is that of the Library of Congress, with diacritical marks omitted and with soft and hard signs not transliterated in geographic names.

Titles of articles published in Russian-language journals are cited in Russian; those that appeared in Russian-language newspapers are translated here into English.

Finally, the reader may find it helpful on occasion to consult appendixes 1, 2, and 3, which provide, respectively, a glossary of political parties and organizations, a glossary of Menshevik factions, and biographical sketches of Menshevik leaders.

Abbreviations

The Menshevik Leaders in the Russian Revolution

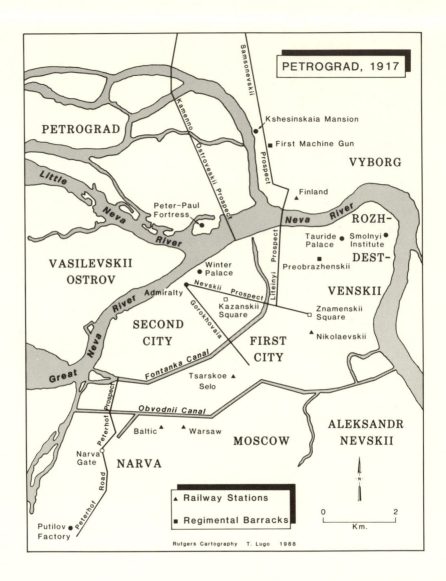

PETROGRAD, 1917

PETROGRAD

VYBORG

Kshesinskaia Mansion

■ First Machine Gun

▲ Finland

Samsonevskii Prospect

Kamenno Ostroveskii Prospect

Little Neva River

Peter-Paul Fortress

Neva River ROZH-

Tauride ● Smolnyi ● Palace Institute DEST-

VASILEVSKII OSTROV

Winter ● Palace

Preobrazhenskii ■

Admiralty

Nevskii Prospect VENSKII

Kazanskii □ Square

Znamenskii □ Square

Liteinyi Prospect

Gorokhovaia

SECOND CITY

Nikolaevskii ▲

FIRST CITY

Fontanka Canal

Great Neva River

Tsarskoe ▲ Selo

Obvodnii Canal

ALEKSANDR NEVSKII

Peterhof Prospect

Baltic ▲ ▲ Warsaw

MOSCOW

Narva Gate

NARVA

Peterhof Road

Putilov ● Factory

▲ Railway Stations

■ Regimental Barracks

0   2
Km.

Rutgers Cartography   T. Lugo   1988

Introduction

AT THE END of February 1917, the tsarist government of Russia collapsed in a whirlwind of demonstrations by the workers and soldiers of Petrograd. Almost immediately, a provisional government was formed by the liberal wing of "census" Russia—that is, the propertied classes of the country and the intelligentsia groups close to them. But even before it was officially established, this government proved dependent on the approval of the Petrograd Soviet, a council of deputies elected by the workers and soldiers of the capital and led by the moderate parties of the socialist intelligentsia, the Mensheviks and the Socialist Revolutionaries (SRs). The history of the February revolution is essentially the history of the relations between the Provisional Government and the Soviet as well as between the two "camps" supporting them, the "bourgeois" and the "democratic" camps.

A period of conditional support for the Provisional Government on the part of the Soviet in March and April (the period of "dual power") ended when the government refused to abide by the Petrograd Soviet's principles on foreign policy. The workers' and soldiers' anger at the bourgeois ministers exploded in demonstrations on April 20 and 21 (the April crisis), which dramatized the government's dependence on the soviet. Then, in order to strengthen the provisional regime and to be better able to push it along the path of reform, the moderate socialist leaders of the soviet agreed to join a coalition government with the bourgeoisie. Thus, a period of closer political cooperation between the leaders of the revolution's two camps was launched in early May.

This cooperation, however, was short-lived, because during May and June Russia experienced social conflicts that undermined the agreement between the socialist and bourgeois ministers on what reforms and policies were needed and eroded the authority of the "conciliationists" (members of the intelligentsia, for the most part) among their respective constituencies. Broadly speaking, the socialists viewed the political and economic betterment of the disadvantaged classes and measures to regulate and improve economic performance as essential to a continued social truce and therefore to the strengthening of the present and future demo-

3

cratic order, particularly in time of war. The central goals of census Russia, on the other hand, were military victory, territorial reward, and the containment of the social transformation begun by the revolution, though significant differences existed within census society concerning the limits of allowable social change. These differences between the two camps of the coalition and their respective adherents led the bourgeois Kadet party to resign from the government on July 2 and resulted in demonstrations by the workers and soldiers of Petrograd on July 3 and 4 (the July Days). Whereas census Russia pressed for the socialists to capitulate on the soviet's goals, the workers and soldiers called unsuccessfully on the moderate leaders of the soviet to abandon coalition and assume full power.

The July Days marked the failure of cooperation between the moderate elements of census Russia and "revolutionary democracy," as the supporters of the Soviets came to be known. The coalition cabinets which succeeded each other in the months leading up to the fall of the provisional regime on October 25 were based on repeated and humiliating concessions forced on the leaders of the soviet. On July 23, the moderate socialists agreed to participate in a second coalition cabinet in spite of its refusal to commit itself to the reforms and policies advocated by the soviet. Then, at the State Conference in mid-August (the closest thing to a constituent assembly during the February revolution), they confined their demands to the most desperately needed social and economic reforms. But their conciliatory motions failed to renew the cooperation between the coalition partners or to stop the mobilization of census Russia for an attack on revolutionary democracy. Indeed, a right-wing alternative to interclass cooperation and coalition—that is, a military dictatorship—was essayed in late August in the form of General Kornilov's attempted coup. This alternative failed because the soldiers, too, were loyal to revolutionary democracy.

By September, the stage was set for an attempt at a left-wing alternative to coalition. The combined pressures of an unrelieved economic crisis, escalating industrial conflicts that more often than not ended in the workers' defeat, and a government policy that continued to pursue military victory at the expense of social change had led the supporters of the soviet to see a "dictatorship of the soviets" as a real possibility, perhaps an inevitable one. The Kornilov affair had added to the threats of counterrevolution and repression felt by revolutionary democracy and further helped cast the social conflicts that workers had experienced in their daily lives into political formulas. Moreover, the parties of the extreme left (the Left SRs and especially the Bolsheviks under Lenin's leadership) contributed to the move toward political extremism by offering the slogan of "all power to the soviets," which promised to put the power of the state at the service of the revolution and the working class—an enticing and forceful vision, even if in reality the state itself was disintegrating with each passing day. The alternative of a "dictatorship of the soviets" would of course mean a civil war, but in the wake of the Kornilov affair, civil war seemed likely even without a soviet bid for power.

Still, the moderate socialists kept hoping to turn things around, and though they declined to have the soviet or its parties represented in the third and last coalition cabinet (announced on September 25), they nevertheless called on the soviet's constituency to support it. Meanwhile, they themselves continued to shape another alternative: one based on interclass cooperation with society's intermediary groups, which they termed "democracy," and located somewhere between census society and their own revolutionary democracy. Even after this initiative had been defeated during the Democratic Conference convened by the soviet in mid-September, the moderate socialists steadfastly rejected the demand of the workers that the soviet seize power, so it was left to the Bolsheviks to lead the workers and soldiers of Petrograd against the Provisional Government. The Bolsheviks then proceeded to establish a "soviet" government, and before the long-delayed Constituent Assembly met, in January 1918, Russia's democratic revolution had given way to a dictatorship by the Bolsheviks in the name of the soviets and the working class.

DURING the period from February to October, the political strategies of the soviets were worked out and implemented by men belonging to the Menshevik party, the moderate wing of Russian Social Democracy. They and the SRs, who generally followed the Mensheviks' political lead, were the acclaimed leaders of the Petrograd soviet from its inception in February, and then of the "all-Russian" network of soviets throughout the country. They retained this latter position of leadership until the overthrow of the provisional regime in October, though they were ousted from the leadership of the Petrograd and Moscow soviets in early September. Whatever the successes or failures of the soviets during the eight months of the February revolution, the Mensheviks were largely responsible for them.

The Mensheviks believed that the working class could not take sole responsibility for governing the country but needed the co-operation of larger, stronger, or better-educated groups in Russian society if the revolution were to survive. The Mensheviks believed also that a premature move toward socialism would lead to the defeat of the working class and bring about a civil war, and for this reason they struggled both to devise political arrangements that would allow the soviets to cooperate with the Provisional Government and guide its policies and also to contain the social processes unleashed by the revolution. It was a group of left-wing Mensheviks and unaffiliated Social Democrats that first negotiated the arrangement of "dual power," and two months later, the centrist Revolutionary Defensist faction of Mensheviks and its SR allies in the Petrograd soviet helped establish a coalition of national unity based on the soviet's program. When the coalition appeared in danger of collapse, the Revolutionary Defensists and the Internationalists sought to avert a dictatorship of the soviets by constructing respectively a "homogeneous democratic" or "homogeneous socialist" government that would be dedicated to social democracy but would link the soviets' constituency to other, broader social groups.

These Menshevik efforts in 1917 put the course of the Russian revolution in a new light and raise an issue hitherto neglected: namely, that Menshevik ideology and political practice made for several viable alternatives between February and July. Western and Soviet studies of the revolution have traditionally focused on the Bolsheviks' victory and for that reason have tended to view urban Russia in 1917 as beset from the start by a bitter, insoluble struggle between the workers and their employers, between city and countryside, and generally between the haves and the have-nots—a struggle that led inevitably to civil war and an eventual Bolshevik dictatorship. This view also presumes that the policies of the Menshevik leaders of the soviet and of other moderate socialists directed toward the prevention of polarization in society were doomed to failure because these policies ran counter to the radical or "extremist" mood of the working class and of the country at large.[1] Finally, this apparent lack of realism in the political

---

[1] This view was elaborated in the first years after the revolution by writers on both the right and the left. Good examples are Miliukov, *Istoriia vtoroi russkoi revoliutsii*, and Trotsky, *History of the Russian Revolution*. But the essential features of this view have been incorporated into much of the historical literature written since. See, for example, two fairly recent works: Liebman, *Russian Revolution*, and Keep, *Russian Revolution*.

thinking of the Menshevik leaders of the soviet has been attributed to their ideology, particularly the doctrine of "bourgeois revolution," which is presumed to have dictated the Mensheviks' choice of strategy in the revolution.[2]

A number of recent studies of workers, soldiers, the Bolsheviks, and the liberals in the Russian revolution have sought to qualify such generalizations through a more careful look at the problems of revolution and democracy in the Russia of 1917.[3] And it is to this purpose that the present work is dedicated: not so much to revise our view of the general course of the Russian revolution in 1917 but rather to clarify the stages and chronology of the process of social and political polarization and thereby outline the "geography" of political opportunities that existed at each stage as well as those that had been missed. The validity and impact of the goals of the Revolutionary Defensist leaders of the soviets are assessed in this broader social and political context. Toward that end, each of the three main periods of the revolution is explored from economic, social, and political perspectives: the period of dual power (March-April); that of the first coalition cabinet (May-June); and the months of search for a third political alternative (July-October). Throughout this study, the emphasis is on the interaction between workers and employers and, more generally, between labor and the commercial-industrial class. It is against this background that the Mensheviks' strategy of cooperation is evaluated—a procedure that draws its rationale both from the principal positions of labor

[2] The history of the Mensheviks in 1917 has been the subject of only one monograph: Basil, *Mensheviks in the Revolution of 1917*. But the general view of the Mensheviks as impractical and doctrinaire, fearful of governmental power and its responsibilities—which is applicable only to a limited degree for the Menshevik Internationalists and not at all for the Revolutionary Defensists—is reflected in almost every study of 1917.

[3] On workers, see Koenker, *Moscow Workers and the 1917 Revolution*; Mandel, *Petrograd Workers and the Fall of the Old Regime* and *Petrograd Workers and the Soviet Seizure of Power*; Rosenberg, "Democratization of Russia's Railroads" and "Russian Labor"; Smith, *Red Petrograd*; and Koenker and Rosenberg, "Limits of Formal Protest" and "Strikes in Revolution." On the soldiers, see Wildman, *Russian Imperial Army*, and a forthcoming sequel by the same author on the period from June to October 1917. On the Bolsheviks, see Rabinowitch, *Prelude to Revolution*, and *Bolsheviks Come to Power*; and on the liberals, Rosenberg, *Liberals in the Russian Revolution*. Three recent studies touch more closely on questions pertaining to the moderates' leadership and strategy: Ferro, *Russian Revolution of February 1917*; Hasegawa, *February Revolution*; and Wade, *Russian Search for Peace*. Also see the historiographical essay by Suny, "Social History of the October Revolution."

and the urban entrepreneurial class and from the respective claims these classes had on the revolution.

Several conclusions emerge from this confrontation of the revolution's political and social aspects. First, it is apparent that, in spite of the mutual suspicion with which Russian workers and their employers had traditionally regarded each other, the process of social polarization was not initiated with full force immediately on the collapse of the old regime. During March and April, a relatively peaceful interaction between workers and employers in industry was the rule. This interaction was based both on the desire of each side to prevent the polarization that had proven so destructive to their respective interests in the past and on the timely and remarkable leadership of various moderates (from both groups) steeped in the traditional values of the Russian intelligentsia and its view of what a social and political revolution meant. Only in June, and particularly after the July Days, did the features of intransigent, conflict-ridden industrial relations develop. This change in the collective behavior and political attitudes of Russia's principal urban social groups resulted from the concurrence of a number of factors, such as long-standing social hostilities, the pressures generated by the war and the economic crisis, and the expectations and misconceptions created by dual power and coalition government. Clearly, even if the social conflicts that made for the final outcome of the revolution reflected fundamental divisive forces of long duration, they were gravely, perhaps critically, exacerbated by the specific revolutionary conjuncture and by the political choices of the intelligentsia leaders.

Second, the Revolutionary Defensists, far from being helpless, unresponsive, and doctrinaire, were characterized by a sense of practicality that had been an integral part of their political culture and that enabled them to act during the early, "peaceful" months of the revolution as social mediators even while they advocated strictly proletarian programs and policies. However, after the deterioration in social relations that occurred in July, the Revolutionary Defensists responded very differently: they turned rigidly defensive, refused to abandon the strategy of coalition, even when they themselves could see it had failed, and entertained groundless hopes for a new political solution that would retain the shape of the revolution as they had conceived it.

Ideology cannot be the sole explanation for this change in Menshevik posture, for the doctrines of Marxism and Russian Social Democracy were too vague to provide prescriptions for actual political strategy. More often, the impact of ideology was indirect or negative: in precluding certain heterodox solutions; in facilitating the apprehension of social and political realities; and, as in the summer of 1917, when ideology could no longer explain reality, in weakening the Mensheviks' ability to respond to the changing circumstances of the revolution. Ideological language, moreover, was often used by the Mensheviks to rationalize political choices affected more immediately by other, less abstract and more personal factors: the memory of past revolutionary episodes, when working-class militancy had led either to isolation or to the Bolsheviks' political advantage, and the burden of the responsibilities shouldered by the Revolutionary Defensists in the soviets and the government during 1917.

Beyond these specific conclusions, the very approach of this work in confronting and combining a social and a political examination directs attention to the interaction between these two aspects of the revolution: how the political solutions elaborated by the leaders of the soviets were informed and shaped by contemporary social realities, and how political conditions, in turn, affected the relations between classes and their respective attitudes toward the existing political order. Some of these political conditions—the absence of a parliamentary tradition, for example, and the presence of strong radical parties—were deeply embedded in the Russian polity. Other conditions resulted from the conjuncture of war and revolution and the unbearable pressures they forced on the state. There were also the conditions created by the political leaders themselves, the Mensheviks included: the changing terms of the soviet's support for the Provisional Government under dual power, the composition of the cabinets, and the failure to convene the Constituent Assembly more promptly. All these elements and changes in the political circumstances of the revolution formed a framework within which the process of social polarization unfolded.

Indeed, if there is any conclusion about revolutions in general to be drawn from this study of the Russian revolution in particular, it must take the form of a cautionary note: that the explosive force of revolutions blurs the distinctions between otherwise separable areas of life and expression and for this reason the study of revolutions requires not an artificial isolation of one area from another but insofar as possible a broad examination of contemporary expression in all areas of public life. Equally important, however, is an examination of the revolution's impact on public expression

9

and representation, so as to distinguish between rhetoric and real motivations, between the political designs of competing leaderships and the aspirations of social groups, and, finally, between the underlying attitudes of these social groups and the temporary shifts in sentiment caused by the dramatic circumstances of revolution.

Other dimensions, less directly connected to the interaction between the social and the political spheres, also bear consideration. The spatial or geographical dimension played an important role in shaping the contemporary perceptions of the revolution, because support for the moderates' strategies of cooperation lasted longer outside Petrograd than in it. Time was another key factor: the attitudes of social groups could change more quickly than the leaders' assessment of such attitudes, and the time lost by the misapprehension of the sentiments of one's constituency or one's political counterparts meant lost opportunities. Such factors are of course present in all historical situations, but the intensity of revolutions and the abnormal sense of accelerated time which they create makes these external factors especially important.

Although this work seeks to integrate various aspects of the revolution, it leaves many areas untouched or only roughly sketched. Differences within the working class along the lines of location, branch of industry, gender, and age are discussed only where they become directly relevant to the leaders' political choices. The peasantry is left out entirely, both because the Mensheviks and the soviets in general concerned themselves principally with urban affairs and because the fate of the February revolution (though not that of October) was determined in Russia's urban centers. The military, too, are discussed only at certain key points.[4] Geographically speaking, the story told here concerns mostly Petrograd, where the leaders of the soviets worked, though events occurring elsewhere are treated insofar as they informed and helped shape the perceptions and the responses of leaders and workers in Petrograd.

Finally, the chronological structure of the book might appear somewhat lopsided: most of it is devoted to the first four months of the revolution, while the four months from July to October are covered in just one chapter. This structure grows out of my belief that the fate of the democratic revolution begun in February—as

[4] For more information on the army's role in the February revolution than is presented here, see Wildman, *Russian Imperial Army*.

well as the fate of the Revolutionary Defensists and the moderate socialists generally—had largely been sealed by the time of the July Days. The months that followed simply exacerbated the social conflict and further eroded the authority of the government. These later months saw the extreme right and left play their last political cards, while the moderates were left with relatively little to do. For this reason, the activity of the moderates during the four months preceding October does not require the elaborate attention that it does for the revolution's first four months.

A note on sources. The picture of urban social relations drawn here is based almost entirely on the contemporary press and whatever other documentation is available in print. In regard to workers, the extensive but tendentious portrayal in documentary collections that have been published in the Soviet Union is balanced by the daily newspaper reports of the Petrograd soviet and the Menshevik party (*Izvestiia Petrogradskogo soveta* and *Rabochaia gazeta*). In general, though, workers' attitudes and collective behavior are among the most thoroughly studied aspects of the Russian revolution.[5] By contrast, the history of the Russian commercial-industrial class has received little attention and, in the case of Soviet historians, it has been badly biased.[6] This lacuna led me to attempt a more extensive coverage of the entrepreneurial press during the war years and the revolution.

Elucidation of the Mensheviks' history in 1917 was handicapped by the fact that nothing from the party's archives for the revolution has ever been made available to either Western or Soviet scholars. The Mensheviks' motives and actions are reconstructed here from

[5] Among Western works, see especially those by Koenker, Mandel, Rosenberg, and Smith cited in n. 3. The most helpful of the Soviet studies was Volobuev, *Proletariat i burzhuaziia*. Also useful were Gaponenko, *Rabochii klass Rossii v 1917 godu*; Pushkareva, *Zheleznodorozhniki Rossii*; and Stepanov, *Rabochie Petrograda*. In addition, a number of Western studies are devoted to specific aspects of the workers' experience in 1917: Avrich, "Russian Revolution and the Factory Committees"; Devlin, "Petrograd Workers and the Workers' Factory Committees"; Boll, *Petrograd Armed Workers Movement*; and Wade, *Red Guards*.

[6] Rieber, *Merchants and Entrepreneurs in Imperial Russia*, though an otherwise excellent study, covers 1917 in just half a chapter. Soviet studies include Lozinskii, *Ekonomicheskaia politika Vremennogo Pravitel'stva*; Volobuev, *Proletariat i burzhuaziia* and *Ekonomicheskaia politika Vremennogo Pravitel'stva*; Laverychev, *Po tu storonu barikad*; Shatilova, "Petrogradskaia krupnaia burzhuaziia"; and Reikhardt, "Russkaia burzhuaziia."

several different sets of data: their writings, correspondence, and memoirs from 1905 to 1917; their public pronouncements in 1917; the record of their actual activity, especially in the soviet's Economic and Labor departments and in the Ministry of Labor; and finally, their retrospective reflections on and analyses of the events of 1917.

The February Revolution and Its Leaders

T HE UPHEAVAL in Petrograd during the last days of February 1917 was paradoxically both spontaneous and long in preparation. It began, escalated, and spread through the autonomous initiative of workers, with no apparent planning or central guidance from the political parties of the intelligentsia that had made themselves leaders and spokesmen for the Russian working class. Yet the political direction the demonstrations soon took, the sense of solidarity the workers drew from other social groups, even the inadequate response to them on the part of the tsarist government—all of these factors were the result of a prolonged, cumulative process.

Once the tsarist forces collapsed—under the pressure of a massive protest movement and as an immediate result of the defection of the Petrograd garrison—the political initiative in the revolution was usurped by two groups of political activists who had been on the scene since at least 1905: the liberals in the State Duma and the moderate socialists. In a matter of days, these two groups of leaders, articulating several alternative views of Russia's future, were in command of the two camps into which Russian urban society was divided: that of the propertied classes, politically organized in several more or less liberal parties and in the so-called "public organizations"; and that of the lower, working classes, led by the Soviet of Workers' and Soldiers' Deputies with the socialist intelligentsia at its head. While the initial victory of the revolution was determined by the largely spontaneous actions of the masses, the political disposition to which the revolution gave rise was the creation of these self-appointed leaderships. It was a disposition that took shape as a result of the new realities created by the revolution, yet one that also bore the marks of earlier experience in political-revolutionary work and the ideas and ideologies through which that experience had been comprehended and rationalized.

13

REVOLUTION IN THE STREETS

The demonstrations that overtook the tsarist forces in February 1917 had been preceded by labor unrest in the second half of 1915 and 1916.[1] The war had made it more difficult for workers to take collective action, but it had done little to modify the major condition that had led to earlier displays of labor unrest (in 1905–1907 and 1912–1914)—namely, the workers' generally hostile feelings toward the regime and census society. In the factories, discipline was enforced through the threat of military conscription, while outside them workers were deprived of even the most limited forms of organization and political expression available in the immediate prewar years. Unions were disbanded, the labor press was closed down, the Bolshevik deputies to the State Duma were arrested, and the Menshevik deputies were no longer allowed to hold meetings with their constituents. While skilled metalworkers in the preferred war industries were able to improve their pay, wartime inflation eroded the real value of most workers' wages.[2]

The war, moreover, provided new issues around which workers' dissatisfaction could crystalize and served to mobilize some of the better-off sectors of Russian society, if not to action, at least to a new kind of oppositional rhetoric. By the fall of 1916, rising prices and occasional shortages of foodstuffs, and to a lesser degree the increasing frequency of work stoppages on account of inadequate supplies of fuel and materials, had become the focal points around which diverse oppositional groups united. These issues were publicized on the floor of the Duma and at other public meetings, making the workers' complaints about these matters seem more legitimate. Moreover, the defeats inflicted on the army, as well as repeated public accusations that the state was mishandling the war effort, further undermined the authority of the re-

[1] This section draws on studies by Soviet historians of Russian labor during the war: Leiberov, "O revoliutsionnykh vystupleniiakh petrogradskogo proletariata"; Miller and Pankratova, eds., *Rabochee dvizhenie v 1917 godu*, 14–20; Grave, *K istorii klassovoi bor'by v Rossii*, part 2 and appendixes; and Shliapnikov, *Kanun semnadtsatogo goda*, an excellent collection of the author's own memoirs, historical research, and documents. Also see the survey of Soviet scholarship on the workers of Petrograd during the war, in Hasegawa, *February Revolution*, chap. 5.

[2] The index of prices for all foodstuffs more than doubled between January 1914 and July-August 1916, and an even more rapid rate of increase was evident in the fall of 1916; see Struve, ed., *Food Supply in Russia during the World War*, 256, and Kondrat'ev, *Rynok khlebov*, 60–71. For a summary of the effects that rising food prices had on the real value of workers' earnings, see Smith, *Red Petrograd*, 44–48.

gime among workers, compounding their generally negative attitude toward the war.[3]

The period between October 1916 and February 1917 was marked by several massive strikes and demonstrations. On October 17, sixty thousand workers from the machine-building factories of the Vyborg district started a political demonstration that was eventually joined by workers from some textile factories and by the soldiers of the 181st Infantry Battalion. On January 9, the twelfth anniversary of Bloody Sunday, two hundred thousand workers from all over the city demonstrated. On February 14, eighty thousand workers went into the streets to demonstrate their support for the Duma on the day it was reconvened (though this turnout was much smaller than the Menshevik organizers had expected). Finally, on February 22, strikes at the Putilov works led to a lockout of over thirty thousand workers.[4]

Members of the moderate socialist intelligentsia in Petrograd watched the rise of labor unrest with both hope and apprehension. They were encouraged when a group of five Putilov strikers, apparently seeking contacts with the Socialist deputies to the Duma, appeared in the offices of the populist monthly *Severnye zapiski* on February 22 and asked for A. F. Kerenskii, who was a Socialist deputy to the Duma, from the Trudoviki group. The workers said that another group of strikers was trying to meet with N. S. Chkheidze, a Georgian who was chairman of the Social Democratic (Menshevik) faction in the Duma. These workers wanted to tell the moderate socialists in the Duma that the strike in their factory concerned not merely economic demands or the difficulties with the food supply but also some "very serious" pos-

[3] "Politicheskoe polozhenie Rossii nakanune fevral'skoi revoliutsii" and "V ianvare i fevrale 1917 g." See also the testimony of the former minister of the interior, A. D. Protopopov, before the Extraordinary Investigation Commission of the Provisional Government, Shcheglov, ed., *Padenie tsarskogo rezhima* 4:83, 92; Blok, "Poslednie dni starogo rezhima" (based on documents collected by the commission); and, for the best overall description of this process, Burdzhalov, *Vtoraia russkaia revoliutsiia*, 26–118.

[4] By one count, "economic" strikes amounted to 23.4 percent of the 530 strikes reported between September 1916 and February 1917: Leiberov, "O revoliutsionnykh vystupleniiakh petrogradskogo proletariata," 73. However, wartime conditions made the distinction between "economic" and "political" strikes even more problematic than usual, as noted in Smith, *Red Petrograd*, 49, and Haimson and Brian, "Three Strike Waves in Imperial Russia." Also see Shliapnikov, *Kanun semnadtsatogo goda* 2:37, 46–47; Shliapnikov, *Semnadtsatyi god* 1:73, 269–78, 310–15; and Burdzhalov, *Vtoraia russkaia revoliutsiia*, 57–58, 89–92, 107–9, 115–16.

sibility, which might happen momentarily.[5] In fact, on the next day, February 23, thousands of men, women, and youth took to the streets with a demand for bread, and they then turned swiftly to other, larger issues.

This action began five days of strikes and demonstrations, which led to the collapse of tsarist rule in Petrograd.[6] With each day, the scope of the movement expanded, and the demonstrations soon spilled over from the working-class districts into the center of the capital.[7] There, along the Nevskii Prospekt, the workers marched in throngs, carrying banners reading "Down with the war" and "Down with autocracy." Workers from metal-processing factories in the Vyborg and Petrograd districts played a critical role in this dramatic escalation: they "took out" factories that had hesitated to join the movement, helped organize the masses of workers in their respective districts, and guided them across the frozen canals into the center of the city.[8] The spontaneous resolve shown by so many workers to reassemble after having been dispersed by the Cossacks largely accounted for the failure of the authorities to keep the demonstrators away from the center and provided the conditions leading to the soldiers' revolt on February 27.[9]

[5] Zenzinov, "Fevral'skie dni," 34:196–98.

[6] For a detailed account of the evolution of the street movement, see Burdzhalov, *Vtoraia russkaia revoliutsiia*, chap. 2, and Hasegawa, *February Revolution*, part 3. See also the police and Okhrana reports reprinted in Shliapnikov, *Semnadtsatyi god* 1:77–86, 91–101, 110–18, 128–31, and 315–28; and "Fevral'skaia revoliutsiia i okhrannoe otdelenie."

[7] According to various sources, the numbers of strikers on February 23 was close to 100,000; on February 24, 200,000; and on February 25, 200,000 to 300,000. See "Fevral'skaia revoliutsiia i okhrannoe otdelenie," 167; Burdzhalov, *Vtoraia russkaia revoliutsiia*, 143n; Leiberov, "O revoliutsionnykh vystupleniiakh petrogradskogo proletariata," 65.

[8] Burdzhalov names Staryi Lessner, Novyi Lessner, Aivaz, Erikson, Reno, Feniks, Promet, and Rozenkrants, all in the Vyborg district, as the most active factories. Leiberov adds Langenzippen and Vulkan, in the Petrograd district. These were factories with long traditions of strike activity and strong Bolshevik influence, which had continued during the war. Burdzhalov, *Vtoraia russkaia revoliutsiia*, 119–20, 125; I. P. Leiberov, "Vtoroi den' fevral'skoi revoliutsii," in *Sverzhenie samoderzhaviia*, ed. Mints et al., 100–104; Leiberov, "O revoliutsionnykh vystupleniiakh petrogradskogo proletariata, 75–77. According to Astrakhan, 37 factories participated in "taking out" other factories, but the majority of factories (144 of 218) joined the movement of their own accord. Kh. M. Astrakhan, "O taktike 'sniatiia s raboty' v Petrograde v pervye dni fevral'skoi revoliutsii 1917 g.," in *Sverzhenie samoderzhaviia*, ed. Mints et al., 120–30.

[9] The authorities commanded close to 200,000 troops; however, only 12,000 of

Weary of the war and fearful of being sent back to the front, many soldiers of the Petrograd garrison felt greater sympathy with the workers' grievances than with the disdainful response to these grievances on the part of the authorities.[10] At first, they were left to observe the growing movement without being forced to take a very clear position on either side, but on February 26, an order was given to fire on the demonstrators.[11] The soldiers obeyed, because the nature of military discipline left them with revolt as the only alternative, and they were as yet unprepared to take this step: "the soldiers could take part in an act against the autocratic regime only on condition that they would not be obliged to return to their barracks until victory had been won."[12] When the soldiers did fire, they saw the workers' lines regroup and resurge after every volley. They also noted that many of their comrades aimed away from the demonstrators, and they concluded that "victory" was now within reach.[13] On the morning of February 27, the Volynskii Regiment set the example, by refusing to obey its commanding officers and seizing the regiment's arms. By nightfall, almost seventy thousand soldiers of the Petrograd garrison had gone over to the side of the insurgents, and the tsarist regime could no longer enforce its authority in the capital.[14]

As the soldiers came out into the streets in defiance of their of-

---

them were considered reliable: Shcheglov, ed., *Padenie tsarskogo rezhima* 4:46, 93. For explanations of this disparity, see Wildman, *Russian Imperial Army*, 123–25.

[10] Miller, *Soldatskie komitety*, 18, states that "the Petrograd garrison was basically ready to follow the proletariat" by February 1917. Wildman divides the soldiers into three groups according to their degree of "revolutionary preparedness" and concludes that the majority were likely to join the revolt once it became clear there were no units left to repress the rebels: *Russian Imperial Army*, 105–15, 154–58.

[11] Although detailed plans had been prepared in early February for the suppression of any revolutionary threat, the military commanders in Petrograd failed to act on them because they judged the demonstrations of February 23–25 to have been "bread riots." See Shcheglov, ed., *Padenie tsarskogo rezhima* 1:184–85 and 4:45–46, 93–96; Shliapnikov, *Semnadtsatyi god* 1:293–303; and Burdzhalov, *Vtoraia russkaia revoliutsiia*, 104–6, 133–34.

[12] These were the words reported by N. D. Sokolov, who met with a group of soldiers on the eve of the February demonstrations; see his "Kak rodilsia Prikaz no. 1." A sergeant of the Volynskii Regiment explained later that "to not carry out the order [to shoot] was impossible—we might have been killed": Kirpichnikov, "Vosstanie l.-gv. Volynskogo polka," 8.

[13] Kirpichnikov, "Vosstanie l.-gv. Volynskogo polka," 10–16.

[14] For official reports and depositions recording the dramatic change in the local authorities' evaluation of the situation during the afternoon and early evening of February 27, see "Fevral'skaia revoliutsiia 1917 g.," 8, 15–16, 20–21; Shcheglov, ed., *Padenie tsarskogo rezhima* 1:197–206; and Blok, "Poslednie dni starogo rezhima," 37.

17

ficers, they were transformed from military units into a mass of disaffected and armed citizenry. They urgently needed leadership to legitimize their rebellion and to turn it from a punishable breach of discipline into an act of participation in a national rebirth.[15] By the early afternoon of February 27, columns of soldiers had begun approaching the gates of the Tauride Palace, where the State Duma met. The socialist deputies of the Duma who came out to meet the soldiers were immediately confronted with the questions of authority and governmental structure: "Where is the new authority?" the soldiers asked. "Give us leaders, we need leaders!"[16]

Workers, too, massed at the Duma in search of leadership, though their demands were less pressing and their attitude toward the Duma far more complicated. Given the Duma's disproportionally large representation of propertied groups, its failure to enact significant social reforms, and, most recently, its lack of resolve in opposing the regime, the Duma appeared more concerned with the protection of privilege than with a fight for freedom. The lack of support for the Duma shown by the workers on February 14 was testimony to the low repute the national assembly had among them.[17] In fact, the February demonstrations against the war and the autocracy had been staged in spite, if not in actual defiance, of the Duma's claim to exclusive authority to "dictate to the country the terms of the struggle against the government," which P. N. Miliukov, the leader of the Kadet faction, frequently asserted.[18]

Yet, except for the most politicized among them (whether Bolsheviks or Mensheviks), the workers had only a dim notion of how a new government was to be formed should their revolt be successful.[19] Guidance could come only from those with a world

[15] See the impressions reported in Mstislavskii, *Piat' dnei*, 7–17.

[16] Skobelev, "Gibel' tsarizma," and Burdzhalov, *Vtoraia russkaia revoliutsiia*, 206.

[17] At the end of October 1916, a police report sent to the minister of the interior said that "judging by reports from the localities, the attitude of the masses toward the State Duma changed seriously in recent months, because the Duma's activity in its last session deeply disappointed them." Grave, ed., *Burzhuaziia nakanune fevral'skoi revoliutsii*, 138. On this point, also see Mandel, *Petrograd Workers and the Fall of the Old Regime*, 78–79.

[18] Grave, ed., *Burzhuaziia nakanune fevral'skoi revoliutsii*, 180–84. The workers' mistrust of Russia's privileged groups extended beyond the Duma; as noted in a report in late 1916, there was among them a tendency toward isolated activity and a "shift toward pure autonomy" (cited in Mandel, *Petrograd Workers and the Fall of the Old Regime*, 19).

[19] Like the Social Democrats who laid claim to the political leadership of Russian labor at the time, historians speak of two roughly distinguished groups of workers: one characterized by relatively high levels of skill, literacy (even education), and

view or ideology that articulated the meaning of the current momentous events and could also capture this meaning in specific formulations that would be not only comprehensible to the masses but also acceptable to them as a true representation of their own experience in the making of the revolution thus far. In Petrograd, in the third year of war, there were few groups and individuals to whom the workers could turn for such guidance. Hardly any legal labor organizations had survived the wartime assault on them. The only exceptions were the workers' sickness funds (established by state law in 1912), a handful of consumer cooperatives, and the Labor Groups that had sprung up in late 1915 and early 1916 under the auspices of the War-Industrial Committees (WICs), public organizations through which Russian industrialists attempted to take responsibility for war production. In spite of their potential as national legal labor organizations, the Labor Groups had failed to gain the support of most workers, because they were so closely associated with the war effort and the industrialists.[20] Of the underground organizations built among workers before the war by the more radical Social-Democratic factions (Bolsheviks, Mezhraiontsy, Menshevik-Initsiatory), only the Bolshevik Vyborg Committee, which was relatively strong in that district's machine-building factories, had maintained an active presence during the war.[21]

---

urbanity and which is generally identified with the male workers of the metal-processing and machine-building industries as well as printers; the other characterized by relatively low levels of skill and literacy and identified more with female workers, especially in the textile industries (where women were concentrated), and with workers whose ties to the countryside had not been severed, particularly those who still lived in rural settings. Social Democrats saw the first group as the "vanguard" or "cadres" of the proletariat, though historians generally call them simply the "skilled workers." In contrast, workers in the second group were often referred to (especially by the Mensheviks) as "less conscious," "dark," or "ignorant" and are generally thought by historians to have been less prone to collective action, especially of an overtly political kind. Of course, many more variables than those listed here affected the behavior and attitudes of workers, though a statistical analysis shows that the three most important factors in making for workers' greater participation in strikes in 1912–1914 and 1915–1916, and especially in political strikes, were all consonant with the profile of urbanized metalworkers: concentration in large urban centers and in large enterprises, and a relatively high average wage: Haimson and Brian, "Three Strike Waves in Imperial Russia."

[20] Two studies, written and assembled respectively by a Bolshevik and a Menshevik, contain a rich record of workers' attitudes toward the Labor Groups and the war effort in general: Shliapnikov, *Kanun semnadtsatogo goda*, and Maevskii, *Kanun revoliutsii*.

[21] Its activity is documented in Shliapnikov, *Kanun semnadtsatogo goda*.

It was, indeed, the Bolshevik Vyborg Committee that had first attempted to guide the workers' revolt. On the morning of February 27, it issued a call for a new, exclusively proletarian center of political authority. Workers were instructed to elect deputies to a "soviet" or council and to send them to the Finland Station in the Vyborg district; this soviet would then establish a "Temporary Revolutionary Government."[22] Some of the workers from the Vyborg district did follow these instructions and assembled at the Finland Station, but by the afternoon of February 27, the soldiers had made the Duma the center of their revolt and most workers had followed them there.[23] The turn of the workers to the Duma was understandable. There were socialist deputies in the Duma—Mensheviks, Socialist Revolutionaries (SRs), and Trudoviki (the Bolshevik deputies had been arrested at the beginning of the war). These were the only socialists of any stature on the scene, and the only deputies who could be claimed by workers as "theirs" by virtue of their having been chosen by the workers' electoral assemblies. Indeed, M. I. Skobelev, a Menshevik deputy from Baku, had been besieged in the days before February 27 by workers asking for advice and seeking "orientation."[24] The fact that the workers sought out the Duma's socialists greatly enhanced the latter's confidence in their ability to lead the workers.

As we shall see, the moderate socialists were in fact eager to take over the political leadership of the street movement and to impart to it their view of the revolution. But the appearance of thousands of soldiers and workers in the courtyard of the Tauride Palace on the afternoon of February 27 also had the effect of forcing into action another group of deputies who had remained aloof from the revolutionary street movement during the preceding days and ignored the calls of the socialists for action by the Duma. These were the men generally known as "liberals" and associated with the large Progressive Bloc, in which all the Duma factions except the extreme right and the socialists had united in 1915. Notwithstanding their initial coolness, they soon claimed political authority for

[22] *RD posle sverzheniia samoderzhaviia*, 5. Also see Burdzhalov, *Vtoraia russkaia revoliutsiia*, 210.

[23] Burdzhalov, *Vtoraia russkaia revoliutsiia*, 210–11.

[24] Skobelev, "Gibel' tsarizma." Also see the recollections of a deputy, S. P. Mansyrev, "Moi vospominaniia o Gosudarstvennoi Dumy," 265, and of a Bolshevik worker (and member of the Vyborg Committee), V. Kaiurov, "Shest' dnei fevralia," 70; and the discussion in Burdzhalov, *Vtoraia russkaia revoliutsiia*, 203–4.

themselves in the new Russia and became the political counterparts with whom the moderate socialists would have to contend.

The Liberals

The idea that the Duma was the legitimate source of national leadership and the natural successor to the tsar was not far from the minds of the deputies of the Progressive Bloc and other liberals. However, the history of the bloc gave little indication of any readiness to seriously challenge the tsar's power, let alone place itself at the head of an armed revolution. Indeed, it was the specter of revolution, or rather the rural and urban anarchy of 1905, that Russian liberals expected from revolution and that kept them from openly defying the state.[25] This specter was all the more troubling when contemplated in the context of a war in which Russia's congenital anarchy—affecting the economy, transportation, and administration—was already responsible for several serious reverses. For this reason, Miliukov, the leader of the bloc's largest faction, had appealed to the workers of Petrograd on February 14 not to demonstrate in support of the Duma, because in doing so they would be playing into the hands of the German enemy.[26] For this reason, too, the leaders of the Progressive Bloc had shown only one concern on February 25 and 26, when the protest movement in Petrograd was assuming an alarming shape: namely, to bring the unrest to a quick end before it spread to the army.[27] Thus, they now entreated the tsar and his ministers with the greatest urgency to institute those personnel changes in the cabinet for which the bloc had been pleading all along, in the hope that the demonstrators might still be placated.[28]

The events of February 27 ended all such hopes, and the fear of anarchy that had previously inspired caution now forced the lib-

[25] For studies of Russian liberalism during the war, see Pearson, *Russian Moderates*; Diakin, *Russkaia burzhuaziia i tsarizm*; Grave, *K istorii klassovoi bor'by v Rossii*, part 3; and Duggan, "Progressists."

[26] Shliapnikov, *Semnadtsatyi god* 1:49–50. See also Rodichev, "Vospominaniia o 1917 g.," 2, and Miliukov, *Vospominaniia* 2:282–85.

[27] The liberals in the Duma adopted this position in spite of the socialists' repeated calls for decisive action by the Duma. See "Chastnoe soveshchanie"; Avdeev et al., eds., *Revoliutsiia 1917 goda: Khronika sobytii* 1:33 (hereafter cited as *Khronika*); Skobelev, "Gibel' tsarizma"; Kerensky, *Catastrophe*, 11–12; and Burdzhalov, *Vtoraia russkaia revoliutsiia*, 161–62, 228–29.

[28] Rodzianko, "Gosudarstvennaia Duma," 56–57; Shul'gin, *Dni*, 120; and "Fevral'skaia revoliutsiia 1917 g.," 5–6; Burdzhalov, *Vtoraia russkaia revoliutsiia*, 164.

erals in the Duma into hurried attempts to reestablish order even if it meant taking responsibility for a victorious insurrection. The decision was not an easy one. As late as 2:30 P.M. on February 27, when a "private" Duma meeting convened (the tsar had officially dissolved the Duma the night before), Miliukov and the Duma's president, M. V. Rodzianko, had urged against taking any decisive action before a clearer picture of the balance of forces had emerged. Then, as the voices of soldiers in the courtyard and the halls grew louder, everyone except the extreme right-wing deputies acquiesced in the formation of a "Provisional Committee of Duma Members for the Restoration of Order."[29] When the committee issued its first public announcement, at 2:30 A.M. on February 28, it was short and understated: "The Provisional Committee of the State Duma finds itself compelled to take responsibility for restoring national and public order."[30]

The establishment of the Provisional Committee signaled a significant, if ultimately deceptive, shift in the balance of forces within the Duma and Russian liberalism at large. Indeed, the composition of the committee implied an admission of what had been so dramatically demonstrated by the columns of workers and soldiers approaching the Tauride Palace: that the old structure of constraints was gone; that Russia's various social groups would now claim a role in the shaping of a new order; that even the least privileged and educated of these groups, perhaps more so than all others, would demand this right; and, finally, that the establishment of any new regime would require the participation in it of those who could bring these unchained forces to accept it.

The Provisional Committee included in its membership some of the old leaders of the Progressive Bloc. After some hesitation, Rodzianko and Miliukov joined it, and each in his turn would dominate its political course. The original ten members also included two socialists—Chkheidze and Kerenskii—and three liberals who enjoyed relatively good rapport with the moderate socialists and favored revolution as a lesser threat to Russia than that of the tsarist government's continued failings. These three were A. I. Konovalov and V. A. Rzhevskii, whose Party of Progressists had left the Progressive Bloc a few months earlier in protest over the irreso-

[29] "Chastnoe soveshchanie," 4; *IzvRN*, February 27, 1917 (no. 1), 1; Shul'gin, *Dni*, 130–32, 158–62; and Mansyrev, "Moi vospominaniia o Gosudarstvennoi Dumy," 265–67.

[30] *IzvRN*, February 28, 1917 (no. 2), 1. See also Miliukov, *Istoriia vtoroi russkoi revoliutsii* 1:42.

luteness of its opposition to the tsarist government; and N. V. Nekrasov, a critic of Miliukov in the left wing of the Kadet party.

Not only did the Provisional Committee give greater weight to the socialists and the more "progressive" liberals than had been the case in the Duma, or even in the Progressive Bloc, but its composition also hinted at the important role the "public organizations" were to play in the political disposition of the revolution. These organizations were represented in the original committee by Konovalov, who was deputy chairman of the Central War-Industrial Committee, and Nekrasov, who was a leading figure in Zemgor, the wartime executive of the Unions of Cities and of Zemstvos. A day or two later, several more activists of the public organizations were given positions on the Provisional Committee (and they were also subsequently included in the Provisional Government): A. A. Bublikov, A. I. Guchkov, M. I. Tereshchenko, and A. A. Manuilov, all of the WICs, and A. I. Shingarev and Prince G. E. L'vov of the Union of Zemstvos.

It was through these public organizations that "society" had wrested an unprecedented measure of economic and organizational power from the state in the years immediately preceding the revolution and had gained an arena outside the Duma for efforts to unite a disparate set of social forces for a final showdown with autocracy.[31] And it was these organizations that made the state's failure to secure orderly food supplies the issue around which the opponents of autocracy might coalesce. In the spring of 1916, Nekrasov and Konovalov had used this failure to launch a campaign for the establishment of a central "public organization for supplies," which they hoped would serve for the political mobilization of society, much as the Union of Unions had done in 1905.[32] Simultaneously, Konovalov had attempted to build direct contacts with both workers and moderate socialists through the WICs and their sponsorship of the Labor Groups as well as other institutional frameworks for worker-employer discourse.[33] Before his fel-

[31] For studies of the public organizations, see Gleason, "All-Russian Union of Towns"; Siegelbaum, *Politics of Industrial Mobilization*; Duggan, "Progressists"; Katkov, *Russia, 1917.*

[32] Departament politsii, "Obzor politicheskoi deiatel'nosti."

[33] Grave, *Burzhuaziia nakanune fevral'skoi revoliutsii,* 140–41. In this initiative, too, Nekrasov collaborated with Konovalov: he chaired the Labor Section of the Second Congress of WICs that passed resolutions prepared by the Labor Group of the Central WIC calling for the establishment of various worker-employer organizations. For a discussion of Konovalov's ideas and activities during this period, see chap. 3.

low industrialists, Konovalov had repeatedly expressed his confidence that a workers' revolution could be contained by an alliance of progressive industrialists and moderate socialists.[34]

Not all the activists of the public organizations shared Konovalov's views. The Unions of Cities and of Zemstvos had insisted, as late as December 1916, that the Duma was the legitimate national body around which all efforts to challenge the autocracy should be organized.[35] Moreover, in all of the public organizations, it was usually the technically educated professionals in charge of the day-to-day work, not the men of property elected to lead the organizations, who initiated the daring strategies of political mobilization and social cooperation. Not only did these professional *intelligenty* have no proprietary rights to defend, but they often welcomed the opportunities to use their expertise, expand their economic and administrative operations, and unite the country's social groups as only the intelligentsia could.

Notwithstanding these distinctions, on the eve of the February revolution, the worsening condition of food supplies and the military situation had brought all the leaders of the public organizations to accept the necessity of decisive action against the autocracy.[36] Even Guchkov, a Moscow industrialist, who was chairman of the WICs and was far less sanguine than Konovalov about accommodation with the lower classes, recommended such action as the only way of preventing a dangerous mass revolution.[37] With their confidence in their ability to lead the country, their resources of economic and administrative expertise, and the relatively good rapport they enjoyed with the socialists, the leaders of the public organizations could at least hope that any "spontaneous anarchy"

[34] Grave, *Burzhuaziia nakanune fevral'skoi revoliutsii*, 95, 140–41.

[35] See the December 9, 1916, resolution of the Union of Cities in ibid., 157–59. See also Rodzianko, "Gosudarstvennaia Duma," 47–49. For the more radical position of the WICs see Grave, *Burzhuaziia nakanune fevral'skoi revoliutsii*, 164–65, and Shliapnikov, *Semnadtsatyi god* 1:280–82.

[36] A meeting of "public activists" on January 29 called for "the establishment of a public organization that would be able to take on the general leadership of the political struggle" and the creation of a "central *organ* for informing the broad masses of measures taken by the public organizations." Grave, *Burzhuaziia nakanune fevral'skoi revoliutsii*, 180–84.

[37] Departament politsii, "Obzor politicheskoi deiatel'nosti"; "Iz vospominanii A. I. Guchkova," *PN*, September 9 and 13, 1936 (nos. 5647 and 5651); "Dopros A. I. Guchkova," in Shcheglov, ed., *Padenie tsarskogo rezhina* 6:261–62, 277–80; Denikin, "Ocherki russkoi smuty," 192; Miliukov, *Istoriia vtoroi russkoi revoliutsii* 1:35–36; and Miliukov, *Vospominaniia* 2:284–85.

resulting from their actions could be stemmed and that they, "as people with experience in state affairs," would be called on to "manage the country."[38]

In the first of many twists, however, as the Duma liberals meeting in the right wing of the Tauride Palace neared the decision to assume leadership of the revolt and take their place as successors to the autocracy, another institution was taking shape in the building's left wing—the Soviet of Workers' Deputies. It would soon become the only repository of the workers' loyalty and a strong contender for that of the soldiers as well. By virtue of its hold over the masses, the soviet would have to be taken into consideration in resolving any crisis of governmental authority; indeed, it was soon encroaching on the responsibilities that had hitherto seemed to be the Duma's.

THE LEADERS OF THE SOVIET

The power of the soviet rested entirely on the support of the masses in the capital. It was the readiness of workers and soldiers to obey the directives of the soviet and their view of it as the keeper of the revolutionary flame that allowed its leaders to claim the right to sanction the new political arrangements and thereafter to monitor what they saw as the "bourgeois" Provisional Government. Yet the initiative for the establishment of the soviet did not have any apparent basis of legitimacy, not even revolutionary legitimacy deriving from mass support, because this "Soviet of Workers' Deputies" was called into existence not by the workers but by the intelligentsia activists of the socialist parties. To them, the workers' and soldiers' revolution was at one and the same time a moment of "incomparable spiritual celebration," when the dream of generations of Russian intelligenty was finally realized, and a source of torment for having revealed their own "passivity" and "isolation."[39] They were attracted to the powerful currents of revolutionary energy in the streets, and they yearned to throw themselves into the "bosom of the revolution," yet they also sought to harness these spontaneous forces and shape the course of revolutionary activity.[40]

Reaching back in their experience for organizational and political

---

[38] "Iz vospominanii A. I. Guchkova," *PN*, September 9, 1936 (no. 5647). See also Miliukov, *Istoriia vtoroi russkoi revoliutsii* 1:43.

[39] Sukhanov, *Zapiski o revoliutsii* 1:19, and Zenzinov, "Fevral'skie dni," 210.

[40] Sukhanov, *Zapiski o revoliutsii* 1:27, and Ermanskii, *Iz perezhitogo*, 144.

forms that had proven attractive to workers in the past, these men attempted to revive the institution that had emerged as a sort of workers' self-government in the 1905 revolution—the soviet. On February 23 or 24, and again on February 25 and 26, private assemblies of socialists, especially the Mensheviks involved in the remaining legal labor organizations, issued calls to the workers of the capital to elect deputies to a new soviet.[41] Even before the workers had responded to this summons, some thirty or forty veteran socialists met in the hope of keeping pace with the movement in the streets, and they elected from among themselves a "Temporary Executive Committee of the Soviet of Workers' Deputies"— in effect appointing themselves to lead the workers' revolution.[42] This gathering took place on February 27, thirty minutes after the Duma had begun its own "private" meeting. Who were these men who professed to speak in the name of the Petrograd workers?

The temporary committee was made up of some seven or ten Mensheviks—mostly *praktiki* (activists) of the legal labor organizations, but also two Duma deputies—and two or three "Independent" Social Democrats (i.e., Social Democrats with no clear organizational ties to either the Bolshevik or the Menshevik party). Later the same evening, about fifty workers' deputies joined the forty-odd intelligenty in the first session of the Petrograd Soviet and elected a standing executive committee, which replaced the temporary committee without changing its makeup in any significant degree.[43] The majority still consisted of Menshevik "legals": two Duma deputies, Chkheidze and Skobelev; two leaders from the Labor Groups, K. A. Gvozdev and B. O. Bogdanov; and five other representatives of the Menshevik praktiki: K. S. Grinevich, G. G. Pankov, I. G. Volkov, E. Sokolovskii, and N. Iu. Kapelinskii. On February 28, the executive committee was joined by two more Mensheviks (also praktiki), B. S. Baturskii and V. N. Krokhmal', as well as by two representatives of the Jewish Bund, which had been in close collaboration with the Menshevik party since 1907— G. M. Erlikh and M. Rafes. The latter was replaced shortly after-

[41] Zenzinov, "Fevral'skie dni," 34:207–10 and 35:215; Sukhanov, *Zapiski o revoliutsii* 1:34–35, 51; M. Rafes, "Moi vospominaniia," 186; Iurenev, "Mezhraionka, 1911–1917 gg.," 2(25):138, and *Bor'ba za edinstvo partii*, 13; Chernov, *Great Russian Revolution*, 101–2; Leiberov, "Vtoroi den' fevral'skoi revoliutsii," 118; Katkov, *Russia, 1917*, 476.

[42] Shliapnikov, *Semnadtsatsyi god* 1:144–45; Sukhanov, *Zapiski o revoliutsii* 1:85–88; Zenzinov, "Fevral'skie dni," no. 35:215–18; Burdzhalov, *Vtoraia russkaia revoliutsiia*, 212–14.

[43] Shliapnikov, *Semnadtsatyi god* 1:147–48.

ward by M. I. Liber. The membership also included five moderate Populists: three Trudoviki—Kerenskii, L. M. Bramson, and V. B. Stankevich—and one SR, V. M. Zenzinov, and one People's Socialist, A. V. Peshekhonov.[44]

Thus, two-thirds of the early executive committee (eighteen out of twenty-seven) belonged to a group that may be described as "legal democracy": moderate socialists who had spent the war years in Russia in "legal" work, often in institutions and organizations where they came into contact with the liberals and their public organizations. Most important, however, the political initiative within this moderate majority in the committee belonged to the Mensheviks, and when the time came to decide the question of power, which is to say the shape and makeup of Russia's new government, most of the Populists deferred to the Mensheviks, who became in effect the unchallenged leaders of the soviet.[45]

That the Mensheviks were able to play such a role was the result partly of the extreme weakness in those early days of the soviet's left wing. By February 28, the executive committee did include four Bolsheviks (A. G. Shliapnikov, P. A. Zalutskii, K. I. Shutko, and V. M. Molotov), one Mezhraionets (I. Iurenev), one Left SR (P. A. Aleksandrovich), and three Independent Social Democrats (P. A. Krasikov, N. D. Sokolov, and N. N. Sukhanov). But, with the exception of the last two (especially Sukhanov), the influence of the radical wing was hardly felt in the soviet, even though whatever leaders there had been in the street movement of the February days had been Bolsheviks from the Vyborg district and the militant workers who had followed them. The reason for the left wing's absence at the moment when the nature of the revolution was being shaped, its political consequences determined, and the workers being guided to accept these arrangements, was that the radical leaders and thinkers, notably Lenin, were abroad or in exile. Moreover, those Bolsheviks who were still active in Petrograd were confused or in disagreement among themselves.[46] Indeed, as we have seen, it was the Vyborg organization of the

[44] No one source provides a full, reliable list of the members of the Executive Committee during the first days of its existence. I used accounts by Zenzinov, Sukhanov, Shliapnikov, and others and compared them with the general list of the committee's members (throughout 1917) in *Petrogradskii Sovet*, appendix.

[45] This judgment is confirmed by both the leader of the SRs and their historian. See Chernov, *Great Russian Revolution*, 116–17, and Radkey, *Agrarian Foes of Bolshevism*, 103, 135–37.

[46] Shliapnikov, *Semnadtsatyi god* 1:202–4, 223–30.

party, in which most members were factory workers, rather than the hierarchically superior city committee, that issued the call for the establishment of "revolutionary headquarters" in the Finland Station. It further weakened the radicals' position that, in presenting workers with this militant "proletarian" alternative, the Vyborg Bolsheviks appeared to deny the "all-national" character which the revolution had begun to assume once the soldiers had joined in and which encouraged many workers to believe the movement would be successful. Finally, many Bolsheviks and Mezhraiontsy had a decidedly negative attitude toward the liberals as well as a sense of estrangement from the legal socialists, and they concentrated their energies on the workers' uprising and subsequently on the organizing of life in the working-class districts and gave little thought to general political questions.[47]

Thus, while the influence of the Bolsheviks and Mezhraiontsy was felt in Vyborg and other factory districts, it was the Mensheviks who called the soviet into existence, guided it through the early days of uncertainty, and formulated its position on the "question of power." To all these tasks, the Mensheviks brought very particular ideas—on Russian society as a whole, the transformation the revolution might bring, the roles to be played by the major social groups (proletariat, bourgeoisie, and peasantry) as well as by the Social Democrats, and the courses of action the Social Democrats could take. These views and expectations of the Mensheviks (though the label "Menshevik" conveys far more unity than the party ever enjoyed) shaped, if not actually determined, their responses to the tasks and decisions that lay ahead in the early hours of the revolution.

MENSHEVIK VIEWS AND EXPECTATIONS

From the outset, the Social Democrats who became Mensheviks were attracted to both the analytical framework and the predictive powers of Marxism but above all to the promise that Russia would

[47] Shliapnikov would later admit, somewhat defensively, that discussion of the political shape of the revolution was just off because of "practical matters"; ibid., 119. On the attitudes of Bolsheviks and Mezhraiontsy, also see ibid., 1:108, 154–55, 265–68, 303–6; Zalezhskii, "Pervyi legal'nyi Pe-ka," 135–36; Iurenev, Bor'ba za edinstvo partii, 13, and "Mezhraionka, 1911–1917 gg.," no. 2: 122–35. On the Bolsheviks' organizational work, see Shliapnikov, Semnadtsatyi god 1:141–43, 181–83, 203–4; Zalezhskii, "Pervyi legal'nyi Pe-ka," 139; Kaiurov, "Shest' dnei fevralia," 158–69; Kondrat'ev, "Vospominaniia o podpol'noi rabote," no. 7:63–69.

follow the Western course of political, social, and economic developments from feudalism to capitalism, to "bourgeois democracy," and to socialism, and in this way would rejoin the main body of European society and culture. This attraction was the combined result of personal preferences, education, and the fact that the two largest constituent groups of Mensheviks came from minority nationalities within the Russian Empire—the Jews and the Georgians. The Jews who became Marxists were at first from among the well-to-do, educated, and Russified Jews of St. Petersburg, and later from the small towns of the Pale of Settlement, whereas the Georgians were mostly the intelligentsia descendents of the national nobility, which had something of a tradition of educating itself in seminaries. Whether Jewish, Georgian, or Russian, however, most Mensheviks had some kind of higher education or were otherwise educated in student circles, as was often the case with young Jews from the Pale as well as worker-intelligenty whom the party recruited in significant numbers after 1905. As a rule, Mensheviks were also urban, both in background and orientation, and this urbanism, coupled with their membership in national minority groups, found resonance in Marxism's cosmopolitan point of view and promise of a universalistic society.[48]

Of course, the Mensheviks' interpretation of Marxism tended toward those aspects of the doctrine that most closely corresponded to their own particular requirements. For example, although all Russian Marxists shared a view of the countryside and the peasantry as bastions of the "semifeudal relations" that had been artificially prolonged in Russia, among the Mensheviks—particularly the urban Jews, less so the Georgians—this view developed into a deep-rooted mistrust of the peasantry, who were seen as a symbol of Russia's backwardness, and into disdain of its near inability to become a conscious social and political actor. More important, the Menshevik faction of Russian Social Democracy was bound by the notion of prescribed stages of development to a far greater extent than were Lenin and his followers. To be sure, neither of the Social Democratic factions questioned the correctness of the scheme worked out by G. V. Plekhanov in the 1880s, according to which a bourgeois revolution would precede a capitalist, and later a social-

[48] This profile of the Menshevik party emerges from the many memoirs, interviews, biographical sketches, and contemporary periodicals collected by the Project on Menshevik History, now housed at the Harriman Institute, Columbia University. See also Haimson, Introduction to Haimson, Galili y García, and Wortman, eds., *Making of Three Russian Revolutionaries*.

ist, transformation of Russia.[49] Indeed, by the early 1900s, the requirement that a bourgeois regime replace autocracy seemed a matter not merely of doctrine but of obvious necessity, for without the political freedoms that the bourgeois phase supposedly entailed, no political party of any substantial size could have developed in Russia.

On the other hand, Mensheviks as well as Bolsheviks did not plan to leave the matter of this first stage of the revolution to the bourgeoisie alone. In preparing for Russia's "first" revolution (1905), they had assigned a position of "hegemony" to the working class and its Social Democratic party.[50] Yet they never tired of quoting Marx in arguing that political formations rested on socioeconomic processes, certain developments had to wait their turn, and human will—even that of the working class and its party— could not change the laws of history. Nor did they ever resolve these contradictions, however much they may have recognized or acknowledged them. Thus, while their deterministic theory could be a source of patience and spiritual sustenance during long revolutionary ebbs, it was also a potential limit on the range of their political choices during times of rapid political change.

IN 1905, when both Bolshevism and Menshevism underwent their revolutionary initiation, the deterministic interpretation of Marxist doctrines had not appeared to be a source of weakness. In light of the general course the revolution followed, especially in St. Petersburg—initial victory through the concerted action of all social groups, followed by frustration, attack, and defeat as social conflicts crippled political unity—the Mensheviks' cautious implementation of "proletarian hegemony" and their general admonition against unilateral action on the part of the workers appeared to have been the most judicious approach. Looking back on 1905, the Mensheviks blamed themselves for only one mistake: having briefly forsaken their caution during the heady days following the October Manifesto and ignoring all that they had known and believed about Russia's unpreparedness for a social revolution. They

[49] The Bolshevik M. Olminskii wrote in his retrospective account that it had been "the official opinion of the [Bolshevik] party" until February 1917, and even for sometime longer, that the prospective Russian revolution "could only be bourgeois" and would merely "lay the groundwork for the struggle for socialism": *Iz epokhi "Zvezdy" i "Pravdy,"* 156.

[50] The doctrine of the "hegemony of the proletariat" in the Russian revolution was formulated as early as 1898 in Axelrod, *Istoricheskoe polozhenie*.

blamed themselves for their failure to restrain the workers from launching an attack against their employers in quest of immediate and radical economic reforms (such as the institution of an eight-hour workday) and thereby having allowed the Russian bourgeoisie to retreat into a protective alliance with the autocracy.[51]

In examining the 1905 experience through the prism of their ideological beliefs, the Mensheviks found that it vindicated their doctrine. Moreover, their attachment to these tenets of ideology was now invested with the full emotional power of that experience: the fervent expectations of October and November 1905, when Russia lived through those few "days of freedom" and the Soviet of Workers' Deputies acted as a government of the working class in St. Petersburg; then the shattering of all hope during the next eighteen months, when the state, with the growing support of the propertied groups, moved to crush the revolution and many of the freedoms it had generated.

Yet if 1905 had not shaken the basic Menshevik interpretation of Marxism, or had even deepened its mistrust of political voluntarism, the revolution's lessons as well as the political conditions that prevailed after 1905 prompted many Mensheviks to rethink the prospects of revolution in Russia and to formulate a uniquely Menshevik program of action. Four issues occupied the center of all Menshevik discussions, correspondence, and journalistic writing during the period between 1905 and 1917: (1) the prospects, even the necessity, of another revolution to complete Russia's bourgeois transformation; (2) the role the Russian bourgeoisie might be expected to play in such a transformation, whether it be by revolution or by reform; (3) the preparation of the working class for its own tasks in this process, which would require the self-restraint and political maturity so patently absent in 1905; and (4) the functions of the Social Democratic party vis-à-vis the bourgeoisie and the working class itself.

It was the last of these issues that was the first to emerge in the conditions of the new, limited opportunities for legal activity that existed after 1905. In the spring of 1906, A. N. Potresov, one of the leading Menshevik thinkers and publicists, sounded an urgent call to transform Social Democracy "from a party of the formerly revolutionary intelligentsia . . . into a party of the masses," and to do so by "destroying the walls of the underground, whatever the

[51] See L. Martov, "Facing a New Battle," *PI*, February 7, 1906 (no. 1), for the earliest example of this argument.

price." Potresov called on the Mensheviks to exchange their roles as conspirators and manipulators of the masses for those of publicists and propagandists.[52] In effect, he proposed a program of what Lenin would later call "liquidationism": that is, liquidating the party underground and with it the notion of the revolutionary party as the activator of social forces.[53] Social forces, he argued, must be allowed or taught to act in their own right.

Potresov and other Menshevik publicists—the so-called *literatory*—poured their energies into the legal press in an effort to establish Menshevism as an "ideological trend" accessible in the national marketplace of political ideologies and to direct the attention of a Europeanized, mature working class to the State Duma, wherein the emerging social classes might construct political alliances (such as socialists with liberals) for the purpose of containing the arbitrary power of autocracy and fighting for greater political freedoms.[54] At the same time, other Mensheviks adapted Potresov's liquidationism to the practical work of labor organizing. In their search for ways of helping workers become actors in their own right and achieve political maturity, these praktiki developed the notion that open, legal labor organizations and *samodeiatel'nost'* (self-activity) by workers could serve as schools for democratic political action. To this end, the praktiki made themselves into bookkeepers, secretaries, and organizers in otherwise worker-run trade and industry unions, cooperatives, and cultural clubs.[55] In the process, they also found a place for themselves at a time when legal possibilities, on the one hand, and police penetration, on the other, had diminished the relevance of the underground.

As might be expected, there was disagreement over how much

[52] A. N. Potresov, "Neotlozhennaia zadacha," *Otkliki sovremennosti*, 1906, no. 2; Potresov to Martov, January 19 and March 3, 1908, Correspondence between Iu. O. Martov and A. N. Potresov, Nicolaevsky Collection of the Hoover Institution (hereafter cited as Martov-Potresov correspondence).

[53] Nikolaevskii, ed., *Potresov*, 51–53. The term "liquidationist" was coined by Lenin in 1909 and applied by his followers to the Mensheviks, whom they accused of advocating the "liquidation" of the Social Democratic party as a revolutionary organization. Among Mensheviks, the term was used to describe those Mensheviks who completely rejected underground activity and held an optimistic view of Russia's chances for an "organic" transition to democracy (see appendix 2).

[54] Potresov to Martov, January 19 and March 3, 1908, Martov-Potresov correspondence; A. N. Potresov, "O tom, pochemu pustiaki odoleli," *NZ*, 1910, no. 2:50–62.

[55] See, for example, interviews nos. 4 and 5 with Solomon Schwarz, and Garvi, "Unpublished Memoirs, 1906–1912," in the collections of the Project on Menshevik History. See also Bonnell, *Roots of Rebellion*, 338–44.

of the party should be "liquidated." In the spring of 1907, for example, while some groups of praktiki denounced the "party regime" in Russian Social Democracy and declared their preference
for "organized masses without Social Democracy over Social Democracy without organized masses,"[56] others, as well as most of
the leaders of the party (Potresov included), argued that the party
was still needed to guide the legal labor organizations along the
political line derived from its "Marxist heritage."[57] Later on, the
attack on the liquidationism of both the praktiki and the literaty
came mostly from those Menshevik leaders, notably Iu. O. Martov
and F. I. Dan, who had passed the "years of reaction" (1907–1912)
in emigration.

At first, the attack from abroad was directed at the praktiki for
their rejection of politics and their narrowly practical conception of
labor organizations. "What will happen to our Menshevik squir-
rel?" Martov wrote to Potresov. "Will there be anything left of the
old Marxist intelligentsia" or only "a few old bones in the form of
bookkeepers of cooperatives and [workers'] societies?"[58] On a
more serious note, he argued against the liquidation of all elements of politics and against the loss of "party-mindedness,"
which alone could give some direction and unity to the fragmented, "kustar' [handicraft] work" of the praktiki.[59]

This disagreement found a resolution of sorts on the eve of the
World War, as more and more praktiki joined the work of local
Initiative Groups, which combined work in open workers' organizations with involvement in a revived Menshevik underground.
(The first such group was established in 1911 in St. Petersburg by
Iu. Larin and S. O. Ezhov.) Although the praktiki held on to their
belief in the political and educational value of samodeiatel'nost',
these practical-minded men could see the advantages of continuity
and overall direction derived from a central, shielded underground organization. Unlike the Bolsheviks, however, they put
the underground organization in service to the aboveground

---

[56] From a statement of a group of praktiki to the Fifth (London) Congress of
RSDRP: *Piatyi (londonskii) s'ezd RSDRP*, 501). See also "Resolution of the Petersburg
Mensheviks concerning the Workers' Congress," *Delo zhizni*, April 5, 1907 (no. 8).

[57] "Takticheskaia platforma k predstoiashchemu s'ezdu, vyrabotana Marty-
novym, Danom, Staroverom, Martovym i dr., pri uchastii gruppoi men'shevikov
praktikov," in the collections of the Project on Menshevik History.

[58] Martov to Potresov, November 3, 1907, Martov-Potresov correspondence.

[59] Martov to Potresov, June 17, 1909, Martov-Potresov correspondence. See also
letters of February 13, 1908, and March 20, 1909.

one—i.e., the open or legal labor movement.[60] Still, the restoration of unity on this issue glossed over a conflict that would gradually become apparent in 1917: a conflict between the commitment to, if not adulation of, self-activity and the urge to direct and even restrain the workers, especially in times of crisis.

Unity was even harder to achieve on the issues that later divided the emigre critics from both the Initiative Groups and (to a greater degree) the Liquidationists of the literator type. The literary remained unconvinced of the value of the underground and celebrated the success of the open labor organizations in fostering self-discipline and "political tact" in the Russian working class, the more so because these organizations had now been "liberated" from the Social Democratic party.[61] Moreover, the liquidationism of the literary involved not only the role of the Social Democratic party but the very nature of the historical processes expected to unfold in Russia. By 1908, Potresov was privately charging that Social Democracy had played a duplicitous game with the Russian liberals, by paying "extraordinary attention" to possible liberal allies but using the concept of "hegemony" to establish "a real dictatorship of Social Democracy in the Russian revolution."[62] As Russia passed from reaction to the political revival of 1912–1914, Potresov and other Liquidationist publicists (E. Maevskii, V. O. Levitskii, F. A. Cherevanin, B. I. Gorev) became enamored of the prospect of avoiding a revolution altogether and any "loosening of the social fabric" that could risk an outbreak of the social anarchy that had doomed the revolution in 1905. In place of revolution, they now posited the possibility of an "organic" reshaping of autocracy into a constitutional monarchy and replacing the "gentry dictatorship" with a bourgeois one. However, no Menshevik, not even the most right-wing Liquidationist, was prepared to see the

[60] See, for example, Dan, "Sotsial Demokratiia i rabochee dvizhenie," in the collections of the Project on Menshevik History. See also Bonnell, Roots of Rebellion, esp. 343–44, 391–93.

[61] V. O. Levitskii, "Na temy dnia: Likvidatsiia ili vozrozhdenie," NZ, 1910, no. 7:91–103; A. Mikhailov [I. A. Isuv], "Letnee stachechnee dvizhenie i ocherednye zadachi rabochikh organizatsii," NZ, 1911, no. 12:41–43; B. Gorev, "Demagogiia ili marksizma?" NZ, 1914, no. 6:30–41.

[62] Potresov to Martov, April 7, November 18, and December 9, 1908. These exchanges arose from Potresov's conflict with Plekhanov over Potresov's interpretation of Russian Marxist thought in his contribution to L. Martov, P. Maslov, and A. Potresov, eds., Obshchestvennoe dvizhenie v Rossii v nachale XX-go veka, 4 vols. (St. Petersburg, 1909–1912). See also A. Potresov, "Kriticheskie nabroski: O Plekhanove," NZ, 1910, no. 10:87–100.

Russian bourgeoisie as the sole mover of revolutions. Indeed, in an ironic reversal of roles, it was often Potresov who criticized Dan for his "optimistic prognosis" regarding the oppositional potential of the bourgeoisie, though Dan had always indicated that his optimism had been born of the working class's necessity "to get out of its forced isolation" by joining with other oppositional groups.[63]

The Liquidationists' own optimism was partly based on such examples as they were able to observe of the gradual Europeanization of Russian society and state, as well as the increase in the relative weight of the urban sector.[64] More significant, this optimism was also derived from the emergence of a new sociopolitical group that, from the Liquidationist point of view, could replace or at least prod the recalcitrant bourgeoisie. This new group was the "intermediary strata of the city"—i.e., educated professionals, white-collar employees, students: all those elements that stood between the propertied upper strata of the city and its lower strata of workers and laborers.[65] Potresov and Levitskii called this group the "democratic intelligentsia"; Cherevanin referred to it as "urban democracy." But all Liquidationists agreed that the group's intermediary social position and its urbanism, together with its broad affiliation with the intelligentsia, made it both ideally open to the Social Democratic demand for the fullest measure of democracy in any future bourgeois regime and also capable of constructing an alliance with other forces, mainly the "progressive" bourgeoisie, opposed to the "asiatic rule" of gentry and autocracy.

In evaluating the prospects of such an alliance of "the vital forces of the country" (a term that would assume great significance in 1917), Cherevanin was the most optimistic and specific of the Liquidationists, for he believed he could identify Russia's progressive bourgeoisie with Moscow's "young industrialists": the leaders of the Party of Progressists who, in their criticism of the regime, sought to guide Russia's emerging capitalist class toward an awareness of its potential political role and who had already

[63] See, for example, Potresov to Martov, April 7, 1908, Martov-Potresov correspondence; F. D. [Dan], "Sovremennoe polozhenie i zadachi SD fraktsii," NZ, 1913, no. 7/8:100–5; and idem, "Burnye dni," NZ, 1914, no. 4:94–101.

[64] Levitskii, "Na temy dnia: Likvidatsiia ili vozrozhdenie"; "Na temy dnia: Na povorote," NZ, 1910, no: 11/12:59–69; "Vozrozhdenie burzhuaznoi oppozitsii," NZ, 1911, no. 3:54–63; "Politicheskoe samoupravlenie russkoi burzhuazii," NZ, 1913, no. 1:45–56; and "God bor'by," NZ, 1913, no. 4/5:49–55.

[65] The allusion to this group and its general definition are found in Cherevanin's speeches and writings (see n. 67).

proven willing to collaborate with elements from the intelligentsia in pursuing these goals.[66] Together, the urban coalition of democracy and the progressive bourgeoisie could constitute a counterweight to the agrarian interests that supported autocracy. Under pressure from this coalition, and because of the general processes of Europeanization, a bourgeois government might emerge in an "unrevolutionary" way and then be prompted to institute the fullest measure of political democracy. And should a revolution prove unavoidable, a possibility Potresov feared but could not deny, this same coalition would be the only force capable of saving Russia from the abyss of social anarchy.[67]

None of this Liquidationist approach to revolution was acceptable to Martov and the other critics in European exile, such as A. S. Martynov, S. Iu. Semkovskii, and, for a while, Dan. Martov had always thought that the Russian bourgeoisie was incapable of fulfilling the revolutionary role assigned to it by history, nor could he see how a "gentry dictatorship" could be "organically" transformed into a bourgeois dictatorship without revolution. Even during the political revival on the eve of the war, when an oppositional bourgeois center seemed to be in the making, Martov emphasized that the groups involved in this enterprise wanted to have a "constitution without democracy"—that is, they wanted to exclude the lower strata of society. For this reason, he did not see that urban democracy had any chance of obtaining hegemony over the revolution; nor did he believe that this group could act independently of the bourgeoisie and its parties. Indeed, he could envision no ally at all for the working class (having rejected, like all other Mensheviks, the peasantry) and was forced to conclude that the proletariat was isolated in its quest for truly democratic freedoms in Russia.[68]

---

[66] See the discussion of these men in chap. 3.

[67] Potresov to Martov, April 7, 1908, and April 15, 1909, Martov-Potresov correspondence; and N. Cherevanin, "Pered novoi sessii Dumy," NZ, 1913, no. 9:66–76; "Ekonomicheskii pod'em i politicheskii krizis," NZ, 1914, no. 2:42–50; "Krizis obostraetsia," NZ, 1914, no. 4:101–10; and "Oppozitsiia v Dume i strane," NZ, 1914, no. 5:83–90. See also Gol'denberg, "Sotsial'no-politicheskoe soderzhanie likvidatorstva," 235–45.

[68] Martov to Potresov, April 4, 1909, Martov-Potresov correspondence, and L. Martov, "Neskol'ko slov o nechistoi sovesti," NZ, 1911, no. 6:69–72; "Osnovnyia polozheniia izbiratel'noi platformy," NZ, 1911, no. 7/8:42–54; "SD fraktsiia II-oi Dumy," NZ, 1911, no. 12:3–11; "Pered vyborami," NZ, 1912, no. 3:67–76; "Rabochaia fraktsiia v IV Dume," NZ, 1913, no. 1:3–10; "Bor'ba obshchestvennykh sil v

While Martov and the Liquidationists were sharply divided in their expectations from the bourgeoisie and urban democracy, and the praktiki of the Initiative Groups shared Martov's doubts about the bourgeoisie though they were perhaps less suspicious of the democratic intelligentsia, all Mensheviks held similar assumptions on the participation of the working class in state power during the stage of bourgeois revolution. These assumptions were formulated by Martov and adopted by the party in the spring of 1905, and Mensheviks had accepted them as reflecting the essence of Marxism. Martov emphasized that a transfer of power could come about only through a process of social change. The Social Democrats could organize and prepare the workers for such a transfer, but they could not decide the moment at which this change would occur. Moreover, whatever provisional regime would replace tsarist rule would be concerned with both the elimination of all the remnants of autocracy and the building of a bourgeois order. Because of this last point, Martov cautioned against unconditional support for such a government and, even more, against participation in it, for participation could either limit the independent, proletarian policy of the Social Democrats or, what would be worse, result in the Social Democrats' suddenly finding themselves in sharp opposition to the proletariat. Accordingly, the First Conference of Menshevik Activists, which met in Geneva in May 1905, adopted a resolution, "On Seizing Power and on Participation in a Provisional Government," which stipulated that "Social Democracy must not aim at seizing or sharing power in a provisional government but [must] remain the party of the extreme revolutionary opposition."[69]

The events of the last months of 1905 had intensified the Menshevik fear of raising the workers' hopes and creating expectations not commensurate with Russia's level of development and well beyond the capacity of a socialist leadership to achieve at that point. Thus, the experience of 1905 reinforced the ideological strictures against coalition government with particular cogency for Martov and many other Mensheviks, and their suspicions about bourgeois liberalism only grew in the years following. Martov himself turned to the international socialist movement as the force

---

1913 godu," *NZ*, 1914, no. 1:95–100; "Otvet Bulkinu," *NZ*, 1914, no. 3:64–70; and "Taktika 'levogo bloka'," *NZ*, 1914, no. 5:54–62.

[69] L. Martov, "Next: The Workers' Party and the Seizure of Power as Our Immediate Task," *Iskra*, March 17, 1905 (no. 93), 2–5; *Pervaia Obshcherossiiskaia konferentsiia partiinykh rabotnikov*, supplement to *Iskra*, May 15, 1905 (no. 100), 23–24.

that could rescue the Russian working class from the political impasse imposed on it by the country's backwardness.[70] This internationalism would be his first and most enduring answer to the problems his party faced in 1917.

In focusing on the international labor movement, as in many of his other observations, Martov proved to have been almost prophetic, for "internationalism" and "defensism" would become the poles between which Russian socialists, the Mensheviks included, would array themselves during the years immediately preceding the revolution in 1917. At one extreme of the Menshevik party would be the Internationalist emigres, such as the old critics of liquidationism who stood at the center of the antiwar Zimmerwald movement (whereas Lenin and Trotskii occupied its left wing). These Internationalists held to a tripartite doctrine regarding the war: first, that it was imperialist in origin and nature; second, that socialists must not participate in it, not even under the banner of defense; and third, that it had to end with a universal, just peace, to be imposed on the warring governments by the European socialist movement.[71] Sharing practically the same views was a small group of Petrograd publicists, centered around Maksim Gorkii's journal *Letopis'*, which included the Independent SDs Krasikov, Sokolov, Sukhanov, and V. A. Bazarov and the Menshevik O. A. Ermanskii. Their internationalism, like that of Martov, derived largely from a deep suspicion of "national liberalism" and therefore an overriding concern not to sacrifice the international solidarity of the proletariat, and its class point of view, to the interests of national defense.[72]

At the other extreme of Menshevism stood the Defensists—Potresov, Levitskii, and other Liquidationist publicists. (Plekhanov

---

[70] Martov, "Next: The Workers' Party and the Seizure of Power"; Martov to Potresov, April 7, 1908, and April 15, 1909, Martov-Potresov correspondence.

[71] *Pis'ma P. B. Akselroda i Iu. O. Martova*, 312, 325–26 (hereafter cited as *Pis'ma*); L. Martov, "Russian Imperialism and the War" (letter to a group of publicists in Petrograd), *Nashe slovo*, May 29 and 30 and June 1, 1915 (nos. 100, 101, and 102); idem, "Reviving the International," *Izvestiia zagranichnogo sekretariata organizatsionnogo komiteta RSDRP*, June 14, 1915 (no. 2); idem, "Opposing Trends in the August Bloc," ibid., February 5, 1916 (no. 3); A. Martynov, "A Patriotic Epopee," ibid. On Martov's differences with Lenin and Trostky, see Getzler, *Martov*, 140–42.

[72] A. Er—skii [Ermanskii], "Where Does Danger Lie?" *Golos*, September 2, 1916 (no. 1). See also Ermanskii, *Iz perezhitogo*, 121, 129–30, and *Marksisty na rasput'ia*; S. Dubnova-Erlikh, *Obshchestvennyi oblik zhurnala "Letopis'*," 5–7, 22–36; and the collection of Sukhanov's articles in *Letopis'* published under the title *Pochemu my voiuem?*

had practically removed himself from Social Democracy with his declaration that an Allied victory in the war would be a triumph of history's progressive forces.) While Potresov and his followers objected to the war in principle, they nevertheless insisted that the tasks of self-defense demanded the participation of all the "vital forces" of Russia, the socialist intelligentsia included. More important, they held that the anti-tsarist alliance that had failed to emerge during the immediate prewar crisis might still be forged around these tasks.[73]

BEHIND the formulation of both the Internationalist and the Defensist positions, we again see questions concerning the Russian bourgeoisie, its role in any future transformation of the country, and the possibility as well as permissibility of socialist alliances with it. In regard to these questions, significant shifts of attitudes had taken place among many (though not all) of the Mensheviks who had spent the war years in Russia, shifts that both reflected and increased the ambiguities and disagreements inherent in Menshevism. Potresov's views struck a responsive chord among various kinds of Mensheviks—Duma deputies, publicists in Petrograd and Moscow, those who worked as statisticians, economists, and the like in the public organizations, and finally those who belonged to the fairly homogeneous intelligentsia of provincial (or Siberian) Russia by virtue of their education and professions. They agreed that the defects and economic failures of the tsarist state required the mobilization of all groups in Russian society that could contribute to the national effort; and indeed, members of the intelligentsia, of every political persuasion, seemed to be the only ones capable of facilitating this coming together and defining the supraclass national interest.[74] Moreover, this unique role not only afforded the intelligentsia in general, and the socialists in particular, a heightened sense of relevance and importance but also presented them with a practical opportunity to reestablish their he-

[73] See the collection of articles by Potresov and his followers published in 1916 under the title *Samozashchita*; and Potresov's regular articles for the Defensist monthly *Delo*, during 1916.

[74] One Menshevik publicist explained later that the "legal" socialists felt themselves to be the "bridge between the bourgeois, educated, and upper-class people and the lower peasant-worker masses": Aronson, *Rossiia v epokhu revoliutsii*, 10. Also see Denike, interview no. 7, pp. 17–21 (Project on Menshevik History); P. Garvi, "Unpublished Memoirs, 1915–1916," 29–31, 40–41; B. I. Nikolaevskii, "Gruppa 'Sibirskikh Tsimmerval'distov'," typescript lent to me by Anna M. Bourguina; and Galili y García, "Origins of Revolutionary Defensism," 460–70.

gemony over the social forces on the side of progress in Russia. At the Second Congress of WICs, for example, men from various sectors of the intelligentsia joined hands with the most progressive industrialists and with the Menshevik leaders of the Labor Groups to press successfully for a program of militant political action and significant social reforms.[75]

Thus, those Mensheviks whose work involved contacts with the public organizations of liberal Russia, even those who had not shared the optimism of the literaty before the war, became hopeful that an alliance of the "vital forces" might be feasible and might serve to protect the now visibly approaching revolution from both the counterrevolutionary instincts of certain segments of the bourgeoisie and the inherent weakness of the working class. They founded their hopes on the socialist-liberal cooperation that they themselves engaged in during the war, as well as on the political disagreements that had appeared among the propertied groups—between the Progressive Bloc of the Duma and the public organizations, and among the various commercial-industrial circles.[76]

Somewhat different attitudes existed among the praktiki of the legal labor organizations, especially in Petrograd and Moscow, for several reasons. First, they were far less enthusiastic about socialist participation in national defense. As workers' patriotism subsided, even the Labor Groups of the WICs, particularly the central group in Petrograd, attempted to dissociate themselves from the essentially military function of their parent organization. Second, because they were more convinced than other Mensheviks of the irreconcilable nature of the conflict between labor and capital and had had to confront the essentially antilabor stance of powerful groups within the commercial-industrial sector, most praktiki were skeptical of the chances for unhindered cooperation. It was impossible and even harmful to speak of "social peace" in Russia, the Menshevik leader of the Central Labor Group wrote to the chairman of the WICs; the most that moderates on both sides could hope for was "some measure of regulation of economic relations

[75] *Trudy vtorogo s'ezda predstavitelei voenno-promyshlennykh komitetov*, 282–378, 359–97.

[76] See, for example, the resolution passed by a conference of Labor Groups in December 1916, which called for a provisional coalition government in which "democracy" would cooperate with the "progressive wing of the Duma": Maevskii, *Kanun revoliutsii*, 7, 82. At other times, the Labor Groups emphasized their role in pressuring moderates into more resolute opposition to the autocracy: ibid., 37–38, 69–70, 82–83, and Shliapnikov, *Semnadtsatyi god* 1:143–55.

between social classes with contradictory interests."[77] If the praktiki had chosen to guide the workers into participation in the
WICs, it was principally because the Labor Groups provided the
working class with a unique opportunity to organize its ranks, articulate its demands, and influence the public organizations.[78]
They insisted, moreover, that "the representatives of the working
class, on the one hand, and the representatives of the [bourgeois]
majority in the WICs, on the other, act as equal *partners*, with *equal*
rights."[79] However hollow these words may sound in retrospect,
and even if they were contrived to induce workers into participating in the war effort, the thoughts reflected the same logic that had
led the Menshevik labor praktiki in their attempt to exploit other
legal opportunities in the prewar years.

Even so, the work in the public organizations exerted the same
kind of pull on the praktiki as it had on the technical specialists
among them. Representatives of the Labor Groups, holding their
own conference at the Second Congress of WICs, declared, after
having called for the convocation of a separate "workers' congress," that "the task of self-defense . . . had created conditions
more favorable than ever before for coordination of the efforts of
the proletariat and the progressive-bourgeois segments of Russian
society in the decisive struggle [and] for the transfer of power to a
government established by the people and responsible to it."[80] In
the fall of 1916, when meetings were organized by Konovalov,
Nekrasov, and others to promote such coordination, the Mensheviks from the Labor Groups as well as from the Duma were regu-

[77] Open letter from K. A. Gvozdev to A. I. Guchkov, which appeared in *Izv-MVPK* early in March 1916, as cited in *Gvozdevshchina v dokumentakh*, 229–30.

[78] From the outset, Labor Groups everywhere made it clear that they consented to participate in the WICs mainly for these "organizational opportunities" and that the realization of these opportunities required that the Labor Groups be allowed to operate autonomously, to maintain an independent voice within the committees, and to meet freely with their worker constituency. For evidence from the Central Labor Group in Petrograd, see the "Projected Program and Organizational Regulations for an All-Russian Workers' Congress" drawn up by the Central Labor Group, in *IzvTsVPK*, March 25, 1916 (no. 77), 4. For evidence from Moscow, see *IzvMVPK*, 1915, no. 6/7:1–2; no. 8:43–44; no. 9/10:54–56; no. 11:50. For evidence from Kiev, see ibid., 1916, no. 14:75; and from Samara, *IzvTsVPK*, February 10, 1916 (no. 58), 5, and April 16, 1916 (no. 83), 6. See also the statement of a meeting of representatives from all Labor Groups in November or December 1916, in *Izv-MVPK*, 1916, no. 33:194.

[79] Maevskii, *Kanun revoliutsii*, 58.

[80] Ibid., 28–31.

larly among the participants.[81] The war and the wartime public organizations indeed generated centripetal forces that had made
many Mensheviks inside Russia more willing than ever to enter
into political alliances with at least the most progressive groups of
educated Russia.

The leaders of the Labor Groups combined, as it were, two
views of themselves and their role, each of which corresponded to
a different long-established tendency in Menshevism. During the
war, these veteran praktiki came to share the hopes of the publicists and the technical intelligentsia regarding cooperation with
the most progressive of the Russian propertied groups. Yet they
continued to view themselves as the organizers of the working
class and the facilitators of its struggle for economic, civic, and political betterment. How, then, could their self-image as the leaders
of labor be reconciled with the position the progressive bourgeoisie had come to occupy in their conception of the revolution? Before examining the answers Menshevik doctrine afforded to these
troubling ambiguities, it must be said that among the Mensheviks
living in Russia during the war years, there were some who had a
far more pessimistic view of the Russian bourgeoisie. Although
the Mensheviks from the Labor Groups, the public organizations,
and the Duma were the most visible leaders of the soviet in 1917,
it was the more pessimistic activists of the Initiative Groups who
dominated the Menshevik party organizations, particularly in Petrograd and Moscow.

Individual activists from the Initiative Groups of Petrograd and
Moscow had from the start expressed grave reservations regarding
the workers' participation in the WICs, not only because participation implied "defensism" on the part of the workers but also
because they believed that the Labor Groups' ties to the industrialists compromised their Menshevik leaders in the eyes of the
workers.[82] In the fall of 1916, the Petrograd Initiative Group,
driven by the expectation of an impending political crisis and the
perception of a growing militancy among the workers, and determined not to miss the opportunity of guiding the workers in the
resolution of a potential crisis, issued a public condemnation of the

[81] Departament politsii, "Obzor politicheskoi deiatel'nosti"; Duggan, "Progressists," 337–43.

[82] Letter from Sergei O. Ezhov to his brother Iu. O. Martov, in the Axelrod Ar-
chive, IISH. The letter is undated but carries a postmark of October 19, 1916, when
Martov, in Paris, forwarded the letter to Akselrod. Also see Garvi, "Unpublished
Memoirs, 1915–1916," 40–41; Shliapnikov, *Semnadtsatyi god* 1:258.

Labor Groups, though it later participated in the semilegal "support groups" set up by the Labor Groups in response to the same expectation and perception.[83]

Still, these differences between two groups of praktiki—in Menshevik parlance, the *likvidatory* (those who were close to the liquidationists) and the *initsiatory* (their critics from the Initiative Groups)—were probably not as great as those separating both of them from the Internationalists, both Menshevik and especially Independent. Here again, the argument concerned not so much the war (which the Labor Groups only implicitly condoned and the Initiative Groups actively condemned) as the "social content" of the approaching revolution. Internationalists like Sukhanov, Ermanskii, or Bazarov looked toward the social revolution that would follow the political overthrow; the praktiki, even those who were deeply suspicious of any cooperation with the bourgeoisie, had their sights fixed on achieving the political freedom necessary for the organization of the working class.[84] Indeed, the Internationalist conception of autocracy's end as the freeing of Russia's social forces to test themselves against each other contrasted sharply with the "legal" Mensheviks' hope of safeguarding the revolution through some measure of interclass accommodation.

With all these disagreements and ambiguities, Menshevism could not be said to possess a unified view of the revolution, let alone a practical solution to the question of power that would be created by the revolution. The one strategy prescribed by party doctrine (in 1905) and accepted by all factions was of negative value only: socialists should not partake of state power prematurely or before "objective" conditions permitted the implementation of socialist policies. This was a stricture against coalition with the bourgeoisie as well as against a socialist takeover; it allowed the Social Democrats to continue and even increase their efforts at organizing and educating the working class but left ill-defined their relationship to the country's propertied groups and to the government they were likely to establish. A bourgeois revolution could mean different things: political freedom for all but greater economic power for the capitalists; or an increase in the working

[83] Ezhov to Martov; Shliapnikov, *Kanun semnadtsatogo goda* 2:67–70, and *Semnadtsatyi god* 1:45–47; Rafes, "Moi vospominaniia," 179; Maevskii, *Kanun revoliutsii*, 5–7, 9–10. The support groups organized political meetings of large numbers of workers (up to five hundred at a time) in the headquarters of the Central Labor Group.

[84] This was the issue as seen by Petr Garvi, a veteran of the Petrograd Initiative Group; see his *Zapiski sotsial demokrata*, 233–34.

43

class's share of political power combined with protection against economic exploitation and perhaps even a first step on the road to socialism. Accordingly, Social Democrats could either tend to their own organizational work, tacitly supporting the new bourgeois order for an indefinite length of time; or they could exert pressure on the bourgeois government to introduce social reforms. In the years between 1905 and 1917, Menshevism did not formulate a clear doctrinal answer to these questions, nor had the various factions in the party been able to agree on the attitudes toward the Russian bourgeoisie on which any political strategy would have to rest.

What unifying and distinguishing qualities the Mensheviks did possess lay, first, in their fundamental conception of history as the unfolding of a process that was rationally comprehensible yet not immediately alterable by human action; and second, in the creation, on the part of the Mensheviks who had stayed in Russia in the years prior to 1917, of a "political culture" that involved work in legal labor organizations and in the public organizations. This political culture fostered a penchant for, and a belief in, practical work among the laboring masses, which would serve the Mensheviks well during the early days of the February revolution. True, by temperament and worldview the Mensheviks were more disposed to reflect on the course of events and react to it than to attempt to change it. But with the revolution's victory on February 27, their attention, energies, and hopes once again focused on the workers and on the definitive working-class organization, the soviet. Through their practical experience in the soviet in the early hours of the revolution and their confrontation with the military, economic, and organizational exigencies of revolutionary Petrograd, the members of the executive committee would develop a more specific comprehension of the revolution and of their role in it, leading them in a few days to the resolution of the question of power.

The Origins of Dual Power

I T WAS a lifelong commitment to guiding the Russian lower classes in their quest for freedom and justice and the goal of securing their latest revolt that had prompted the small group of socialists in Petrograd to establish themselves as the executive committee of the Petrograd Soviet of Workers' Deputies in the hopeful hours of February 27. As yet, they possessed no clear idea of who should establish a new government to replace the crumbling edifice of autocracy or how this might be done. Nor, in fact, were they certain that the tsarist forces had been decisively defeated. In those first hours and days, their thoughts and energies were devoted to safeguarding whatever gains seemed to have been made: to feed and organize the masses of soldiers and workers on whose support they counted, and to defend the capital from counterrevolutionary attacks.

Not only did the members of the executive committee display remarkable resourcefulness in their response to the challenge of events, but through their decisions and responses to various problems they also charted a political strategy that dealt with the relations between the two contending political centers of the revolution and became the cornerstone in the structure of power that emerged from the revolution. It has often been argued that this strategy—which came to be known as "dual power"—was dictated by doctrine alone, or that it reflected the socialists' fear of power and responsibility, but in any case did not correspond to the political and social realities of Russia at the moment of the revolution's victory.[1] Actually, as this chapter will demonstrate, the socialists on the executive committee, including the Mensheviks,

---

[1] Trotsky, *History of the Russian Revolution*, 238–44, especially stresses the Mensheviks' presumed fear of the masses and their reluctance to take responsibility and assume power. Liebman, *Russian Revolution*, 115–16, agrees with Trotsky both on the unsuitability of dual power to the existing social and political constellations and on the Mensheviks' motives in pursuing this strategy. Hasegawa, *February Revolution*, 421–27, provides important corrections to this interpretation, though he too sees in the more assertive aspects of dual power the result of the masses' pressure on the Menshevik leaders, who would otherwise have left all power to the bourgeois government.

proved remarkably creative in balancing their ideological precepts and the practical needs of the moment. Moreover, the strategy they finally agreed on not only was appropriate to the balance of political forces but also was responsive to the strongest sentiments of most workers and soldiers, at whose head the moderate socialists had placed themselves. This was the Mensheviks' finest hour in 1917, even if their later memories of the time were mostly of confusion and fear.

THE REALITIES OF REVOLUTION

An incident during the soviet's first meeting late on the night of February 27 demonstrated the extreme uncertainty about the revolution's victory. Someone announced that the Tauride Palace, where the meeting was being held, was surrounded and shooting had been heard in the vicinity. Panic broke out; everyone rushed to the doors and took cover, stepping over each other. It continued like that for a few minutes until Chkheidze, standing on a chair, called the soviet to order and reminded it of its revolutionary duty: "We came here for a struggle that involves life and death, and if necessary, we'll die. There cannot be any room among us for fear."[2]

While in retrospect the soviet's edginess might appear ludicrous, even pathetic, firsthand accounts of the revolution's earliest days in Petrograd, especially the one given by Iu. Steklov just four weeks after the events, in a speech to the First All-Russian Conference of Soviets, testify to great apprehension regarding the stance that the Russian army outside Petrograd, and the country as a whole, would take toward the revolution. Such accounts convey the deep anxiety created by the complete disorganization of those hundreds of thousands of excited but inexperienced "revolutionaries" who looked on the members of the executive committee as their leaders. In Steklov's words:

You, comrades, who were not here in Petrograd and did not experience this revolutionary fever cannot imagine how we lived: surrounded by various soldiers' units that did not even have noncommissioned officers; we had not yet succeeded in formulating any political program for the movement and at the same time learned that the [tsarist] ministers were still

[2] Rafes, "Moi vospominaniia," 191. According to Sukhanov, *Zapiski o revoliutsii* 1:200, this incident took place during the second meeting of the soviet, on February 28.

free and convening either in the Admiralty or in the Marinskii Palace. We had no information about the attitudes of the troops [outside Petrograd]. . . . There were rumors that five regiments were marching on us from the north and that General Ivanov was leading twenty-six echelons [against us]. Shooting resounded in the streets, and we could only conclude that the weak forces surrounding the Tauride Palace would be routed. From minute to minute we expected that they would arrive and if not shoot us, take us away.[3]

These fears and anxieties were mixed with euphoria to give the context of events a quality eerily reminiscent of the 1905 catastrophe, nor was there any assurance that this time the outcome would be different. On March 2, an editorial in the soviet's newspaper reminded its readers that, in 1905, people had "talked too much, expected too much, conferred, discussed, convinced each other and themselves that everything would go well and rejoiced at every insignificant piece of favorable information." The lesson of 1905, the editorial warned, was "not to surrender oneself to illusions" and not to overestimate the revolutionary forces.[4] Later, Ermanskii also drew parallels with 1905, pointing out another similarity and another lesson: that a revolution in times of military defeat may win an easy victory in the short run but may still be crushed in the long run. For this reason, the ease with which the initial victory had been achieved and the absence of any serious confrontation made the triumph somewhat illusory.[5]

Contemplation of the makeup of the revolutionary masses was not reassuring, either. The Mensheviks' attention was drawn to the fact that what had begun as a workers' revolution had won its victory as a "*soldiers'* revolution"—that is, only the support of the soldiers had ensured the victory. Still further, as Ermanskii observed, this fact brought to the foreground the question of the peasantry and its "cultural and political backwardness."[6] No Menshevik—whether Internationalist or Defensist, praktik or one who merely regarded himself as a member of the intelligentsia—could envision the peasant-soldiers as an asset in a new configuration of social and political relations, let alone accept them as trusted allies of the working class. On this point, the Mensheviks remained true

[3] *Vserossiiskoe soveshchanie*, 112. See also Skobelev, "Gibel' tsarizma." On the state of disorganization in the Petrograd garrison, see Mstislavskii, *Piat' dnei*, 21–22, 29–34, 46.

[4] *IzvPS*, March 2, 1917 (no. 3), 1.

[5] Ermanskii, *Iz perezhitogo*, 153–54.

[6] Ibid., 154 (emphasis in the original).

47

to their Marxist doctrine and their urban bias. In addition, the armed, hungry, and homeless masses of soldiers represented a real threat to the efforts of the executive committee in organizing and feeding its supporters. In these circumstances, as Sukhanov explained later, the attention of the committee was diverted from "high politics" to "technical questions."[7]

Indeed, the earliest actions of the executive committee in the face of perceived threats to itself and the revolution were concerned with making itself the "organizational center of Democracy," around which the masses were called to organize.[8] In part, this concern followed from the faith that these veteran socialists, especially the Mensheviks, put in organizational work. In the words of an editorial in the soviet's newspaper, "Let us not waste time on words now—we know what we want, so let us take up everywhere the work of organizing the proletariat."[9] To a remarkable degree, however, this organizational impulse was not centrally directed so much as it was spontaneously and unconsciously determined by the two factions of the revolution and their establishment of the Duma committee and the soviet. Again, here is how Steklov described it:

During these two or three days of uncertainty, the revolutionary forces of Petrograd scattered through the various districts were gradually drawn to the Duma [building] and gradually regrouped around the Soviet of Workers' and Soldiers' Deputies on the one hand and around the Provisional Committee of the Duma on the other. In these first moments, neither we nor the bourgeoisie were thinking of creating a government (*vlast'*). Each of us was trying to regroup our forces and to gather all the forces that were flowing toward us from various sides.[10]

This process of "self-determination" was crucial to the evolution of the soviet's political strategy, inasmuch as the revolutionary forces that infused the left wing of the Tauride Palace presented the executive committee with problems of two kinds: those whose solution necessitated cooperation with the Duma committee, and those that forced the executive committee to confront the Duma committee with solutions of its own.

The self-appointed temporary executive committee had already taken steps on the afternoon of February 27 (even before the sovi-

[7] Sukhanov, *Zapiski o revoliutsii* 1:87–89.
[8] Ibid.
[9] "Less Talk, More Action," *IzvPS*, March 2, 1917 (no. 3), 1.
[10] *Vserossiiskoe soveshchanie*, 107.

et's plenum had met for the first time) to deal with the two most pressing needs, defense and provisions. It had nominated the Mensheviks Volkov, V. G. Groman, and Frankorusskii to a supply commission, and it had called on S. D. Mstislavskii, an army officer with SR-Internationalist leanings, to come to the Tauride to organize its defense.[11] The first meeting of the plenum, convening at around nine or ten o'clock in the evening, triumphant if disderly, also gave immediate attention to the issues of defense and food supplies. The question of cooperation with the Duma on these two issues was discussed at the second plenum meeting on February 28. At that time, the soviet decided that its military and supply commissions should work independently of the corresponding commissions established by the Duma committee, although keeping in contact with them.[12] Even while this noncommittal, balanced mandate was being voted on, the soviet's commissions were already experiencing pressures in quite contradictory and conflicting directions.

The problem of supplying essential foodstuffs for the population of the capital clearly required close cooperation with the Duma committee. Alone, the soviet's supply commission could neither guarantee the cooperation of railroad personnel in shipping food to Petrograd nor gain access to whatever reserves were still in the city. The Duma committee controlled the railroad's telegraphic service (through Bublikov, its commissar of transportation) and was therefore capable of both declaring itself the interim power and communicating its orders to loyal railroad workers, who could thus control the movement of supplies (and troops) to Petrograd.[13] Of no less importance was the pressure from the Central Cooperative of Wholesale Buyers in Petrograd, which offered its services to the soviet but then demanded that the soviet's supply commission be merged with its Duma counterpart. On February 28 or at

[11] *Khronika* 1:40–41; Mstislavskii, *Piat' dnei*, 17; Sukhanov, *Zapiski o revoliutsii* 1:88; Tokarev, *Petrogradskii sovet*, 50–51, 54–55.

[12] The soviet's handling of the supply question during these early days is discussed in Rafes, "Moi vospominaniia," 190–91; Sukhanov, *Zapiski o revoliutsii* 1:121–53; and Peshekhonov, "Pervye nedeli," 261.

[13] See Bublikov's telegram of February 28, entitled "Appeal to the Railroad Workers," in which the country was informed of what had transpired in Petrograd and of the intention of the Duma committee to establish a new government: *IzvRN*, February 28, 1917 (no. 2), 1. Bublikov also ordered the railroad officials to disrupt a military attack being made on Petrograd, and an aide of Bublikov's instructed workers in several stations to block all train movement to Petrograd by removing the switches from the junctions: Lomonosov, *Vospominaniia*, 33–44.

the very latest March 1, the soviet did reverse its earlier decision and established a common supply commission with the Duma committee.[14] This was a decision of great political import, and it was clearly made in reaction to pressing reality rather than according to rigid doctrine. In explaining the soviet's actions on defense and food supplies several years later, Rafes made the observation that, in the debates on these questions, the mutual relations between the two organs "were haphazardly outlined" and new groupings appeared inside the soviet: "The Menshevik 'Internationalists' . . . gradually began . . . to unite with the Menshevik 'Defensists'."[15] Thus, even the Internationalist members of the executive committee, who would otherwise have objected to any contact with the suspect bourgeoisie, were impelled by the urgency of the supply situation into cooperation with its political leadership.

On the major issue of the military defense of the revolution and the question of the army's loyalty, matters were far more complicated, though here too, cooperation seemed unavoidable at first. Arguably, the balance of forces in the country at large favored the Duma committee.[16] Not only was it in a position to control the movement of troops on the railroads leading to the capital, but—as became apparent after a short series of telegraphic exchanges with the army's headquarters—only the Duma committee (and especially those Duma deputies from the parties of the propertied classes that had supported the war) could claim the loyalty of the tsar's generals in command of the army on the front. Reassured by the Duma's expressed concern for maintaining order and continuing the war effort, the fronts' commanders urged Gen. N. Iu. Ivanov to halt his attack on Petrograd and, on March 2, also recommended the tsar's abdication.[17] To them, as well as to military

[14] According to *IzvPS*, February 28, 1917 (no. 1), supplement, the decision to unite the supply commissions of the soviet and the Duma was adopted by the soviet on February 28, whereas Rafes, "Moi vospominaniia," 190–91, places it a day later.

[15] Rafes, "Moi vospominaniia," 190–91.

[16] The best overall discussion of the general balance of forces is Mel'gunov, *Martovskie dni*, 22, 36. For a more recent analysis of the strength of the army on the front and of the Petrograd garrison, see Wildman, *Russian Imperial Army*, 105, 124. In considering the balance of power, the political leaders in 1917 were concerned not only with the question of who might win a military confrontation but also with the horrifying specter of civil war. See, for example, Guchkov's testimony before the Investigation Commission, in Shcheglov, ed., *Padenie tsarskogo rezhima* 6:262.

[17] "Iz dnevnika Gen. V. G. Boldyreva"; "Fevral'skaia revoliutsiia 1917 g.," no. 2

observers inside Petrograd, it was of paramount importance that the revolution "not affect the war effort adversely" or be allowed to degenerate into a "digraceful civil conflict." Support of the Duma committee not only would serve this purpose but also would strengthen the moderate wing of the revolution.[18] In fact, the appearance of the soviet on what ranking officers saw as the "extreme left" of the revolutionary forces contributed to the end of the generals' support of the tsar, just as the army's acceptance of the Duma committee, in turn, imposed on the soviet's leadership the imperative of cooperation.

The Duma committee also held the key to the support of the officers of the Petrograd garrison, which numbered some 180,000 men. Signals of loyalty to the Duma on the part of the officers were coming in from everywhere: first, a telephone call from the officers of the Preobrazhenskii Regiment to Rodzianko late on the night of February 27; then, the surrender of the Peter and Paul Fortress to V. V. Shul'gin, a Nationalist deputy to the Duma, on February 28; and finally, a resolution passed by two thousand officers gathered in Army and Navy Hall on March 1.[19] It was essential for the soviet to "neutralize" the officers and obtain their cooperation, for only they could organize the soldiery into units capable of defense or at least prevent the army's becoming a source of "general anarchy."[20] To assure itself of such cooperation, the soviet would have to recognize the Duma's authority in military matters, as the following incident clearly demonstrated. During the night between February 27 and 28, Rodzianko appeared in Room 42 of the Tauride Palace and presented to the military commission of the soviet the "new commander of Petrograd," Col. B. A. Engel'gardt. When Sokolov, a commission member, refused to accept the Duma's authority in this matter, all the officers present who had previously offered their services to the soviet left the room in protest.[21]

Indeed, with respect to both the military question and that of food supplies, it was not only their own estimate of the balance of

---

(21):42, 52, 55–59, 68–70, 72, 75, and no. 3(22):7, 25–29, 31, 33–42; Lukomskii, "Iz vospominanii."

[18] This was the opinion of two colonels from the Petrograd garrison who went to Tsarskoe Selo on the evening of March 1 to report to General Ivanov, perhaps as unofficial envoys of the Duma committee: Perets, *V tsitadeli russkoi revoliutsii*, 67.

[19] Shul'gin, *Dni*, 164–65, 179–80, 176; Shidlovskii, *Vospominaniia* 2:68.

[20] Sukhanov, *Zapiski o revoliutsii* 1:161–63 (report of his conversation with Mstislavskii).

[21] Mstislavskii, *Piat' dnei*, 29–31.

forces that persuaded the socialist leaders of the soviet to cooperate with the Duma committee. Such cooperation was insisted upon by those with specialized knowledge, and who were otherwise sympathetic to the revolution, as a condition of their participation in the soviet's work. This had been the case with the representatives of the Central Cooperative in regard to the supply commission as well as with the officers in regard to the military commission.[22]

IT IS NOT SURPRISING, then, that the executive committee's first manifesto to the soldiers, issued on February 28, was careful not to undermine the authority of the officers or the Duma, though in fact its purpose was to counter another of Rodzianko's attempts to establish the Duma's hold over the soldiery—his "Order to the Troops" that they obey their officers. The soviet's manifesto declared:

The executive committee of the Soviet of Workers' Deputies does not recommend that soldiers refuse to preserve their regular organization or refuse to obey the orders of the military commission [of the Duma] and its officials. At the same time, it advises all military units to immediately elect representatives to the soviet . . . for the establishment of one, united will for all of the . . . working class.[23]

The restrained language of this document is worth noting, for it stands in striking contrast to the soviet's second appeal to the soldiers, the Order No. 1, issued just one day later. The events surrounding the issuance of these two documents were indicative of the changing pressures on the executive committee as well as of the leadership's quick response to the challenge from its growing constituency, particularly that of the ideologically mistrusted soldiery.

Between February 28 and March 1, a new problem arose, as soldiers in one unit after another refused to allow the return of their officers even after the latter had declared their support for the revolution. In effect, the soldiers were declaring that they would no longer tolerate the relationship of unquestioning obedience that

---

[22] Sukhanov later explained that "the officer corps in the capital at that time was far from being the Old Guard 'regulars': it was overflowing with 'ensigns,' which meant all sorts of 'third elements' [i.e., nonpropertied elements] ready to join the revolution not out of fear but out of conscience": *Zapiski o revoliutsii* 1:161–63.

[23] Burdzhalov, *Vtoraia russkaia revoliutsiia*, 292.

had existed between officer and soldier under the old regime.[24] At first, the Social Democrats in the executive committee interpreted these acts as reflective of the unreliable, unorganizable nature of the peasant-soldier, so that even as the executive committee called on the soldiers to elect their deputies to the soviet, it also sought to convince them to accept their officers' authority.[25] But when units responding to the committee's call began sending deputies to the soviet, the leaders were forced to conclude that, as long as the Duma committee supported traditional relationships in the army, the soldiers were likely to remain opposed to its authority as well as to that of their immediate officers.[26] Indeed, it was this challenge from the soldiers' barracks (rather than the workers' quarters), which was narrowly focused on the issue of authority within the garrison units, that compelled the executive committee to abandon its emphasis on cooperation in favor of open defiance of the Duma committee.

The first soldiers' deputies appeared at the soviet plenum on March 1, and they took the floor immediately to voice their grievances before the sympathetic audience.[27] Emotional though their addresses were, more and more specificity was apparent in the words of each succeeding speaker, as if the very setting—an assembly of the revolutionary masses and their executive leaders—was emboldening the soldiers to formulate practical demands. One soldier began: "Was it for this that we have made the revolution? For the State Duma to again seat the officers on our shoulders?" Then, almost as an afterthought, he added: "Now that we have our soviet, and we all realize that in all our units, too, we should introduce committees to manage supplies, let's allow these committees to also watch over the officers."[28]

Here, in a soldier's simple language, was the notion of "institutionalized suspicion" that would become part of the soviet's strategy for its relations with the Duma committee and the Provisional Government. A short resolution hurriedly scribbled by Sokolov

[24] Shidlovskii, *Vospominaniia* 2:67–70; Stankevich, *Vospominaniia*, 72.

[25] Sukhanov, *Zapiski o revoliutsii* 1:191.

[26] Ibid., 163–69.

[27] The most informative memoirs of this episode are Taras-Rodionov, *February 1917*; Sokolov, "Kak rodilsia Prikaz no. 1"; Skobelev, "Gibel' tsarizma"; and Shliapnikov, *Semnadtsatyi god* 1:206ff. Good historical treatments are V. I. Miller, "Nachalo demokratizatsii" and *Soldatskie komitety*, 25–35; Burdzhalov, *Vtoraia russkaia revoliutsiia*, 292–97; Wildman, *Russian Imperial Army*, 182–92; and Hasegawa, *February Revolution*, 390–404.

[28] Taras-Rodionov, *February 1917*, 205.

when the soldiers had finished speaking was immediately adopted. It stated for the first time the principle of a conditional acceptance of authority: "The soldiers' masses [will obey] the Soviet of Workers' and Soldiers' Deputies. The opinion of the military organization [i.e., the military commission of the Duma] will be accepted only to the extent that it does not conflict [with the guidance of the soviet]."[29]

In spite of the apparent discrepancy between this resolution and the position taken by the executive committee in its manifesto of the night before, the committee raised no significant objection to another resolution, brought before it by a deputation of ten soldiers. Instead, the committee entrusted this deputation with the final working out of an order (*prikaz*) that the soviet was to issue to the soldiers of the Petrograd garrison. This Order No. 1 was thus the creation of the soldiers themselves but enjoyed the full sanction of the executive committee. The order consisted of three main points: the civil equality of soldiers and officers; a separate self-administration for the soldiers in all but purely military matters (that is, administration of the unit's daily life by elected committees and of political matters by the soldiers' representatives to the soviet); and the conditioning of the soldiers' loyalty to the Duma committee *and* to the officers on fulfillment of the first two points.[30]

The demands of the soldiers bore a remarkable resemblance to those the workers soon started to send to the soviet. In its handling of these demands the executive committee showed itself ready to respond to the needs and aspirations of those groups that were its natural constituency, to coax them to political expression, and to represent them vis-à-vis the Duma committee. In return, the soldiers, whose political allegiance had been sought by the Duma committee, now began to ally themselves with the soviet.[31] Suddenly, the leaders of the executive committee perceived that the soviet possessed genuine authority.[32]

Still, it was not yet a complete victory. The fate of the soviet, at least from the Social Democratic point of view, depended on the workers. From the earliest hours of the revolution, intense orga-

[29] Miller, "Nachalo demokratizatsii," 33.

[30] Full text is in *Petrogradskii sovet*, 290–91.

[31] In the many eyewitness accounts of February 27 and 28, the soldiers are reported as cheering both Rodzianko and Chkheidze. See, for example, Ermanskii, *Iz perezhitogo*, 150.

[32] Sokolov, "Kak rodilsia Prikaz no. 1."

nizational activity was under way in the working-class quarters of Petrograd, to which the executive committee responded in its first official meeting on February 28, when it called on the workers to organize soviets, "defense centers," and elective "workers' militias" in their districts.[33] If this organizational effort did not seem to occupy much of the committee's time over the next few days, it was only because the work was advancing without major confrontations. The executive committee found it easy, for example, to respond to a call from a group of socialist students for contact between the command structures of the "workers' militia" and that of the "democratic city militia." Not only were these students (one of the intermediary "third" elements) often themselves the commissars of the workers' militia, but there was as yet no sustained opposition to such cooperation among the workers. In fact, in their districts, workers often joined collaborative bodies on their own initiative, working together with soldiers, cooperatives, and committees of ordinary city dwellers (*obyvateli*) to establish order and ensure food supplies. They saw no contradiction between these bodies and the soviet.[34]

Given the uncertainty of the moment, the still-looming presence of the tsar's army on the front, and the fear of repression, most workers appeared to agree with the assembly of the Geisler factory that the success of the revolutionary movement depended on the "unity of all classes of the people that took part in the revolutionary uprising and who sympathize with it."[35] It was not that workers were less suspicious than soldiers were of the privileged members of Russian society but rather that with few exceptions they apparently did not feel they had to defy the authority of these groups, which seemed so much less ominous after the disappearance of the tsarist police. Instead, most workers concentrated on strengthening their bases of support in the factory and the community, though they, too, balanced the summons for unity with a warning that the new powers "be watched."[36]

[33] References to the organizational activity of workers are abundant in the accounts of the Bolsheviks active in the Vyborg district: Kaiurov, Zalezhskii, Kondrat'ev, and Shliapnikov (who was named by the executive committee as its commissar for Vyborg). The February 28 meeting was reported in *IzvPS*, February 28, 1917, supplement.

[34] The committee of the city dwellers of the Moscow district, for instance, declared that it had been formed to help the soviet: *IzvPS*, March 5, 1917 (no. 6), 4.

[35] This resolution was adopted on March 1: Burdzhalov, *Vtoraia russkaia revoliutsiia*, 285.

[36] On February 28, the workers of the Zibel factory adopted a resolution in which

MUTUAL dependence and suspicion, cooperation and separate independent action—these were the poles between which the members of the executive committee were pulled during the first few days of activity as they came into contact with workers and soldiers and sought to solve the immediate, practical problems of life in revolutionary Petrograd. Time and again they discovered that neither they nor the men in the Duma committee could act by themselves. If the Duma alone could appeal to the loyalty of the generals still in command of the army, the soviet had already become the supreme authority for the soldiers of the Petrograd garrison. Moreover, the committee's cooperation was demanded as a condition of service by those groups that straddled the two camps of the revolution—the engineers, students, noncommissioned officers, food specialists, and others without whose services no government could function (and in Russia, expertise was still relatively rare). As the Menshevik-Liquidationists had foreseen, these "democratic intelligenty" were at once sympathetic to the masses' yearnings for freedom and justice and yet bound by their culture and values to educated, propertied Russia.

In the executive committee, the Defensists, the publicists, and the activists of the public organizations were particularly susceptible to sentiments for unity, but like others in the committee, they also responded to the contradictory pressures emanating from the soviet's expanding following. Having made themselves the leaders of an ostensibly mass organization, they attempted to tie the dispersed masses to this body and offered to provide workers and soldiers with a means of communication, articulation, and revolutionary authority separate from those dominated by the propertied groups. This slowly gathering self-image, as well as their view of their role and of their followers, increasingly corresponded to reality, and in consequence they persuaded themselves that they were capable of defying the Duma committee on behalf of their constituency.

But what would be the formal division of political authority between the soviet and the Duma committee? The solution to this question of power was initially intimated in the responses of the soviet's leadership to the pressing matters of supplies and defense. Yet, as of March 1, the broader principles on which a new

they expressed concern about the composition and activity of the Duma committee yet called on other workers "not to rise against other classes of the population": Burdzhalov, *Vtoraia russkaia revoliutsiia*, 285.

political authority might be established were still unformulated. Whereas in regard to the practical problems facing them, the Mensheviks found no ready-made solutions in either their previous experience or their doctrine—indeed, where doctrine proved too limiting even in its broadest terms, they disregarded it, as in their calling on the peasant-soldiers to join the Soviet of Workers' Deputies—the question of power engaged their general view of the historical moment more immediately and was shaped by ideology and the long experience of its application in Russia.

IDEOLOGY AND EXPERIENCE

All Social Democrats, and indeed all Russian socialists, began from the assumption that Russia was finally going through its "bourgeois revolution." Disagreements and uncertainty concerned three interrelated issues: the length of the period before the socialist transformation could be attempted; the extent to which social change was possible during the transitional phase; and the roles of the bourgeoisie and the proletariat during this transition. Different answers were likely to be given to these questions by groupings of Mensheviks in Petrograd, according to their preferred areas of activity and the ideological conceptions they had developed in the past. Yet by all accounts, the Mensheviks in the executive committee responded in unity to the question of power, especially on the most important question before the committee: that of socialist participation in government. The Mensheviks led the soviet in its rejection of a coalition government and even carried the votes of the Populists, who otherwise favored coalition.

Coalition was rejected not only by the Petrograd Initiative Group (and Chkheidze, the most popular of the Mensheviks) but even by the arch-Defensist Baturskii, who had been thought by some in Petrograd to have favored the closest cooperation with the "progressive bourgeoisie."[37] They all knew their party's established stricture: socialists should never participate in a bourgeois government. Only one veteran Menshevik in the executive committee, the Defensist Bogdanov, dared propose such a hybrid creation, though it must also have been favored by Potresov's followers, whose staunch defensism and preference for publicistic work

[37] Rafes, "Moi vospominaniia," 194; Sukhanov, *Zapiski o revoliutsii* 1:240–41, 255; Shliapnikov, *Semnadtsatyi god* 1:219 (wherein he reports his conversations with Chkheidze, Skobelev, and Grinevich); Skobelev, "Gibel' tsarizma." On Baturskii's position, see Shliapnikov, *Kanun semnadtsatogo goda* 2:67–70.

had excluded them from the early executive committee. Two other associates of the party also advocated coalition, the Bundists Erlikh and Rafes (both of Defensist orientation), but they apparently envisioned a provisional government as short-lived and engaged principally in the task of liquidating all remnants of the old regime. A temporary coalition of this sort, they hinted, was not a government in the full sense of the word and would not be involved in the making of social policies.[38] Even so, their careful explanations betrayed the anguish that all SD-Defensists were surely experiencing in trying to reconcile their ideologically rooted rejection of socialist participation in a bourgeois government with their current notions on the positive contribution of the "progressive bourgeoisie" in administering the country and the pivotal role the soviet was expected to play in articulating and directing the "voice of the people."

The Mensheviks on the executive committee, however, did not have the opportunity for leisurely contemplation of these issues. They were occupied with a host of immediate concerns and new experiences: the necessity of dealing with numerous problems of a political, military, and economic nature; the burden of responsibility for the fate of the revolution and the conduct of the masses; the frequent moments of fear and the many occasions for pride, euphoria, and, increasingly, command. Their opposition to any form of coalition during the executive committee's initial discussion of the question of power on March 1 was not so much the outcome of a considered analysis of the situation as it was a resort to the formulas of their party's ideology. This position also conformed to their experiences of the past two or three days—of the conflicting urge both to cooperate and to remain on guard. Yet it was the ideological constancy of the Mensheviks that set them apart from the Populists with whom they shared the work of the executive committee. The Populists—the SRs and especially the Trudoviki among them—were experiencing the same conflicting urges as the Mensheviks, but they favored coalition, though at this point they lacked the numbers and leadership necessary to influence the soviet in that direction.[39]

[38] Rafes, "Moi vospominaniia," 194.

[39] Of the twenty-three original members of the executive committee, only six were Populists. Their number may have been higher on March 1, but they were still in the minority and completely overshadowed by the SDs: Radkey, *Agrarian Foes of Bolshevism*, 133, 136. Of the six known Populists, only Aleksandrovich, a Left SR, was solidly against coalition; three Trudoviki actively advocated coalition,

Otherwise, the Mensheviks' stand on coalition brought them into agreement with a handful of Internationalist SDs whose solution to the question of power, if not the analysis on which it was based, the executive committee was to adopt as its own, largely through the votes of the Mensheviks. Among these Internationalists were the Independents Steklov and Sukhanov as well as the Menshevik Ermanskii. They, too, assumed that the present revolution was bourgeois, and though they insisted it had to be a *"thorough* social revolution" and that the only active revolutionary force in Russia was the urban proletariat, they nevertheless agreed with other Mensheviks that Russia was *"not yet mature* in the Marxist sense" for a socialist revolution.[40] Indeed, so mindful were these Internationalists of Russia's backwardness that they postulated a priori that its transition to socialism could begin only, as Sukhanov put it, "against the background of a socialist Europe and with its help." Such expectations entailed certain responsibilities, he added, for it made the Russian revolution a matter of importance to international socialism—a point that he was at pains to emphasize:

Europe is entering a new period in its historical development, that of the *liquidation of capitalism*, and we must view the course of our own revolution in the light of this fact. . . . Because of the character of the present overthrow, it must be conplemented with enormous and hitherto unseen *social content*. [Although] the revolution has not resulted in immediate socialism, [it] must lead toward it by a *direct road* and safeguard the full freedom of socialist construction in Russia. To this end it is necessary to establish immediately the appropriate *political preconditions*: to safeguard and strengthen the *dictatorship of the democratic classes*.[41]

The practical question, then, was how to preserve the young, fragile revolution as well as to expand and deepen it. On this point, there was full agreement between the Internationalists (both Mensheviks and Independents) and all other Mensheviks in the executive committee. Sukhanov, in considering the "real balance of power," reached the same conclusions as others on the executive committee: namely, that the organizationally weak and politically isolated "camp of democracy" had to establish a modus

---

while two moderate SRs (Zenzinov and Peshekhonov) favored coalition but did not actually advocate it. For the earliest official SR statement on the issue of coalition, see "The Great Overthrow and the Party," *DN*, March 15, 1917 (no. 1), 1.

[40] Ermanskii, *Iz perezhitogo*, 151–52 (emphasis in the original).

[41] Sukhanov, *Zapiski o revoliutsii* 1:229–30 (emphasis in the original).

vivendi with the "bourgeois camp," because "state agencies, the army, the zemstvos, and the cities . . . might obey [the Kadet] Miliukov, [but] they would not obey [the Menshevik] Chkheidze," and also because, on most issues, though not on that of the war, the bourgeois camp could be pressured into more accommodating positions. For these reasons, Sukhanov argued, Democracy would initially have to hand power over to its "class enemy," but the soviet, as the organization of the revolutionary masses, should retain the "fullest *freedom of struggle*" against these enemies.[42]

These positions did not preclude a coalition government, and though it was unacceptable to more orthodox Russian Marxists, the possibility of coalition was recognized and advocated by the Independent-Internationalist Bazarov:

The energy and unity of revolutionary democracy have already forced the bourgeoisie to take a number of steps beyond the line the ruling class was originally unwilling to cross. . . . But in order to prevent the transformation of this revolutionary path into [one of] counterrevolution, the democratic [camp] should participate energetically in the Provisional Government to prevent it from stopping halfway [and] push it further and further . . . ; of course, the attainment of this goal [the furthering of the revolution] also requires a powerful independent organization from democracy in the form of the Soviet of Workers' and Soldiers' Deputies, for only by operating on this basis of strength will the democratic members of the Provisional Government be able to command the proper respect from their bourgeois colleagues in the ministries.[43]

This was not a call for the establishment of a soviet government. Bazarov shared the view that democracy was "not yet capable" of carrying out the responsibilities of state. In fact, no one on the executive committee advocated that the soviet assume full authority, and this was so not only because Lenin (who would later win over the Bolshevik party to just this strategy) was still abroad. It was as if familiarity with the conditions of the revolution's first days discouraged extreme political alternatives and made unthinkable a dictatorship either of the bourgeoisie or of democracy. Bazarov's emphasis, like that of Sukhanov's, was on the pressure that democracy could bring to bear on the leaders of the propertied classes in order to use political freedoms for the achievement of social change. Bazarov's assumption, however, was that such pressure could be effective only if it worked from inside the gov-

[42] Ibid., 20–33, 80–84, 115–19, 231 (emphasis in the original).
[43] *IzvPS*, March 2, 1917 (no. 3), 2.

ernment—an opinion Sukhanov and many others would endorse, albeit briefly, two months later.

Given the ideological prohibitions to which the Mensheviks were more subject than were the Independents, it was Sukhanov's position around which Mensheviks coalesced, giving their votes first to the rejection of coalition and then to a program of demands on the bourgeois government that included only the civil and political rights necessary to "safeguard the freedom of struggle."[44] A broad consensus on this "minimum program" emerged among the Social Democrats on the executive committee, especially among the veterans Mensheviks and those, like Sukhanov, Bazarov, and Steklov, who would join the Internationalist wing of the party a few months later. However, this consensus obscured profound differences among the various factions of Menshevism in their attitudes toward the progressive bourgeoisie. The more conciliatory members of the executive committee were reassured by the minimalist nature of the soviet's program, as seen in its exclusion of "unrealizable" demands, such as the eight-hour workday, the redistribution of land, and the creation of a democratic republic. In comparison, Sukhanov's interpretation of his proposed demands was more radical because it aimed at "the establishment of such conditions of political life as would enable 'democracy' to immediately develop its program in the areas of domestic, foreign, social, and economic policy."[45] Some of these differences had already surfaced at the March 1 meeting, when Sukhanov brought up another element in his scheme for the first time: namely, a formula for conditional support of the Provisional Government.

At first sight, the opposition raised by the more conciliatory members of the executive committee seemed surprising. After all, by putting forth a "program," a list of demands to which the government in the making would have to consent before it received the soviet's support, the committee was declaring its own power and its intention to dictate at least some of the new government's policies. Yet many members of the committee, including some of the Mensheviks, were uneasy about the pointed implication of suspicion toward the bourgeoisie contained in Sukhanov's formula.[46] In the end, however, these objections dissolved, partly because of the influence the Internationalist SDs exercised in the ex-

---

[44] Sukhanov, *Zapiski o revoliutsii* 1:256.
[45] Ibid., 231–32.
[46] Ibid., 227–28, 239–40, 260–61.

ecutive committee and partly under the weight of the "spontaneous course of the revolution," to use an expression of the time.

Three events heightened the Menshevik leaders' sense of power and led them to use it as leverage over the new governments. The first of these was the soldiers' appearance (in the midst of the executive committee's discussion of the question of power late on the night of March 1) to ask the committee's support for what would later become Order No. 1. The second was the report of the negotiators sent by the executive committee to the Duma committee on the night between March 1 and 2. Three of the four negotiators were Internationalists—Sukhanov, Steklov, and Sokolov (Chkheidze was the fourth). Surprisingly, they encountered almost no opposition to their demands. "Our program," Steklov later recalled, "was accepted by everybody as being unquestionable and unavoidable."[47] Finally, there was the incident on March 2, just before the soviet's final discussion of the question of power, when a large crowd assembled in the Catherine Hall reacted with hostility to a speech by Miliukov defending monarchy. Sukhanov and Steklov were reassured by the apparent belief of the crowd that "democracy was within reach of a republican structure and a solution to the land question."[48] Thus, the "logic of events" helped the Internationalist SDs impress on the more ambivalent Mensheviks the imperative of making their support of the government conditional.

To recapitulate, the self-appointed leaders of the soviet found themselves fundamentally divided in their expectations of the revolution; the Mensheviks among them struggled to resolve the long-standing ambiguities of their party's ideology and practice and also attempted to understand a baffling array of new phenomena. Yet, in a process that defies precise documentation, these divisions and conflicts were temporarily suspended if not resolved as the reality of revolutionary Petrograd—apprehended by the members of the executive committee through their dealings with both their rivals on the Duma committee and their supporters in the streets—passed through the prism of Marxist ideology (whose basic precepts the Independents and the Mensheviks shared) and

[47] *Vserossiiskoe soveshchanie*, 114. Sukhanov, *Zapiski o revoliutsii* 1:271–346, provides the most exhaustive account of these negotiations. Different points of view are presented in Miliukov, *Istoriia vtoroi russkoi revoliutsii* 1:46–49, and *Vospominaniia* 2:305–7; and Shul'gin, *Dni*, 185–91.

[48] *IzvRN*, March 2, 1917 (no. 6):1; Sukhanov, *Zapiski o revoliutsii* 1:236.

modified some of the specifically Menshevik interpretations of this ideology. Mensheviks and Independents alike found their expectations altered and had to accept the notion that, in the present revolution—because of society's division into upper and lower strata, the presence of the soldiers among the latter group, and the declared loyalty of the soldiers to the soviet—the soviet, an essentially working-class institution, had to assume a greater and more precisely defined responsibility for the course of the bourgeois revolution than Menshevik-Marxist doctrine seemed to allow. In time, the differences between the Internationalists, the Independents, and the more ambivalent Mensheviks would become apparent, but for the moment, the executive committee of the soviet appeared unified in its support of the political solution of "dual power."

THE DUAL-POWER ARRANGEMENT

In the historiography of the revolutions of 1917, the term "dual power" (*dvoevlast'*) usually refers to the division of political authority that existed in different forms between the Provisional Government and the Soviet of Workers' and Soldiers' Deputies between February and October. Here, however, the term will be used to denote the specific political agreement that was concluded on March 2 between the executive committee of the Petrograd soviet and the temporary committee of the State Duma. The agreement was published in the form of joint statements: one by the Provisional Government, which listed its program of promised reforms; the other by the soviet, which called on the masses to "lend support" to the new government "as long as . . . it fulfilled these obligations and struggled resolutely against [remnants of] the old regime."[49] The eight points of the Provisional Government's program guaranteed civil and political equality for all as well as complete freedom of political activity. Except for the particular case of Kerenskii, there was to be no participation by the soviet in the government, nor were any institutional ties established between the two bodies. The ministers of the Provisional Government were drawn from the parties and the public organizations of liberal, propertied, and "loyal" Russia.[50]

[49] *IzvPS*, March 3, 1917 (no. 4):1.
[50] The ten members of the first cabinet, other than Kerenskii, came from the Kadet, Octobrist, Progressist, and Center parties; six of them had been in the leadership of the public organizations.

In its most basic sense, dual power was a division of authority and responsibility between the two contending social and political forces. As such, it reflected their mutual recognition that the suspicion separating their respective bases of support in society as well as the balance of strength existing between their forces made it impossible for either the Duma or the soviet to establish by itself the political order that was to replace the tsarist regime. While the March 2 agreement left all formal state authority in the hands of the liberal bourgeoisie, this did not signal an unconditional surrender on the part of democracy or its abdication of its right to influence the course of the revolution.[51]

By deliberately refusing to participate in the cabinet, the socialists of the executive committee secured the soviet's existence as a separate entity, as well as its right to engage in the work of organizing its followers into a united political force. By insisting that, in return for their support, the Provisional Government accept a program designed to create "full political freedom and absolute freedom of organization and agitation in Russia,"[52] the soviet's leaders created a legal framework not only for their organizational work but also for the utilization of the soviet's growing force to ensure the realization of democratic and social reforms through pressure on the government from without. Finally, by urging their followers to support the Provisional Government only "insofar as [postol'ku, poskol'ku]" it abided by the obligations undertaken in relation to the soviet, the socialists made clear their conditional support for the government—i.e., for a dualistic form of authority in revolutionary Russia.

The essence of dual power, then, lay in the division of political authority between the soviet and the Provisional Government (representing, respectively, the lower classes and the upper classes), the conditional support by the soviet for the Provisional Government, and the retention of the soviet's right to mobilize its constituency for political action. Clearly, dual power would not have worked, nor would it have been morally valid, if it had not corresponded to the attitudes of the workers and soldiers on whose support the soviet's authority and strength rested. It was therefore with some trepidation that the framers of the dual power

[51] The accusation that the agreement was a capitulation to the bourgeoisie is frequently made by Soviet historians and was the basis for the famous statement about the "paradox" of the Russian revolution in Trotsky, *History of the Russian Revolution*, 186–92.

[52] Sukhanov, *Zapiski o revoliutsii* 1:232.

agreement submitted it to the plenum of the soviet for ratification on March 2. They found reassurance in the results of the vote as well as in the general thrust of the discussion. Only ten out of some four hundred deputies present voted against the resolution proposed by the executive committee, and only nineteen voted for the Bolshevik-sponsored counterresolution, which called on the soviet to support a "Revolutionary Provisional Government" rather than the existing "antipeople" Provisional Government. At the same time, the Bolsheviks' insistence on the "three-tail" minimum program of Social Democracy (the eight-hour workday, confiscation of the gentry's land, and a democratic republic) was met with "stormy applause."[53]

Insofar as these proceedings reflected the attitudes of the Petrograd working class, they suggested that for the moment most workers in the capital supported the strategy of dual power as well as the leadership that proposed to implement it but also that this support rested on the belief that the leaders were dedicated to the realization of the social and political changes symbolized in the "three-tail" program. The analysis that underpinned dual power might not have been apparent to the delegates from the factories, nor could they have known of the "minimalist" interpretation given to it by some members of the executive committee. Indeed, there were many reports of confusion even about the identity of the contending bodies—the Duma, the soviet, and the Provisional Government.[54] Workers may have also been swayed by the ap-

[53] *Khronika* 1:54–55; Shliapnikov, *Semnadtsatyi god* 1:240–41; Sukhanov, *Zapiski o revoliutsii* 1:320–21; Rafes, "Moi vospominaniia," 196–97. About half of the Bolshevik deputies voted against the Bolshevik resolution; according to Shliapnikov, this was because they were aware of the great animosity on the part of the majority of deputies for the idea of a "revolutionary government" based on the soviet. Bolshevik apologists as well as various historians have explained the vote by claiming that workers in small enterprises, who were less "politically conscious," predominated in the soviet; see, for example, Anweiler, *Soviets*, 108–9. Burdzhalov, however, has shown that in the earliest days of the soviet's existence the majority of workers' deputies came from large and medium-size plants: *Vtoraia russkaia revoliutsiia*, 366–67. The influx of soldiers, which would bring the number of deputies to twelve hundred by March 5 (and reduce the Bolsheviks' share of the assembly to 2.4 percent), did not begin until March 2 and so could not have had an impact on the vote for dual power. See Andreev, *Mestnye sovety*, 22.

[54] One Bolshevik worker described how the workers in two metalprocessing factories (in the Vyborg district) in which he was active gave their support to one party and then, on the next day, under the influence of other speakers, to another: K. Kondrat'ev, "Vospominaniia o podpol'noi rabote," no. 7:64–65, 69. Burdzhalov cites similar examples of confusion: *Vtoraia russkaia revoliutsiia*, 223.

pearance of the only socialists whose names they knew—the Menshevik Duma deputies. Above all, as the Bolshevik Shliapnikov recognized, workers were more interested in their own organizational work in the districts than in the plenum's debates over questions of government.[55]

But if the vote on March 2 does not appear as conclusive to the historian as it did to the leaders of the executive committee at the time, the workers' powerful impulse to organize indicated certain attitudes that made dual power eminently acceptable to them. The workers seemed resolved to take responsibility for the essential aspects of their lives and to ensure their freedom to do so. Meetings held on March 2 in the Rozhdestvenskii district and at the Shlissel'burg-Porokhov, Staryi Parviainen, and Aivaz factories created their own food committees and workers' militias in addition to electing delegates to the soviet.[56] Behind this resolve there was a deep suspicion of the propertied classes, in whom power and economic privilege continued to reside. The resolution adopted on March 5 by the workers of the Second Moscow military equipment factory shows that they were conscious of this suspicion and of the consequent need for separate organization, though its language also suggests the involvement of a politically experienced agitator:

The Provisional Government that emerged from the revolution speaks for the interests of the bourgeoisie, and therefore the working class can support this government only insofar as [postol'ku, poskol'ku] its policy will not run against the interests of the broad toiling masses. At the same time, the working class must organize itself for the defense of its class interests and the consolidation of all the achievements of the revolution.[57]

The defensive stance of this resolution, no less than the mistrust it expressed, was born of the direction the workers' organizational activity assumed. Shliapnikov recounted that a group of Putilov workers told him after a few days of "ruling" the district around their factory that they had decided to stop doing so because it was too "dictatorial."[58] True, the workers sought no alliance with the suspect census society. But apart from a small group in Vyborg— the most militant of the working-class districts—workers did not appear ready to take responsibility for the country as a whole.[59]

[55] Shliapnikov, Semnadtsatyi god 1:146, 150.

[56] IzvPS, March 4, 1917 (no. 5), 6.

[57] RD posle sverzheniia samoderzhaviia, 463.

[58] Shliapnikov, Semnadtsatyi god 1:252.

[59] This conclusion is inadvertently supported by the Soviet editors of the collec-

Rather, they seemed disposed to assert autonomy in their own lives, watch their employers carefully for any attempt to encroach on this newly gained autonomy, and leave it to the leaders of the soviet (the only leaders present in Petrograd) to exercise *kontrol'* over the bourgeoisie at large. In political terms, this attitude meant a form of dual power resembling Sukhanov's more radical, dynamic version. A general assembly of workers and employees at the Petrograd cable factory made this clear on March 3, when it solemnly stated that "the most urgent business of the moment [is to establish] strict *kontrol'* over the ministers appointed by the State Duma . . . who [do] not enjoy the people's trust. [Such] *kontrol'* must be composed of workers' and soldiers' deputies who are represented in the soviet."[60]

Dual power provided not only a formula that captured these diverse feelings—insecurity, suspicion, the desire for equality—but also a framework within which both workers and leaders might acquire political experience while avoiding responsibilities for which they felt themselves unready; a framework, moreover, that allowed for the goals and the limits of revolutionary change to be determined at each stage according to the balance of forces, the level of organization of "revolutionary democracy," and the political development of the masses; and a framework, finally, that was thought to be flexible enough to accommodate both the state of relative social peace necessary for the strengthening of the revolution and the heightened social conflict that some leaders of the soviet anticipated with fear and others with assurance.

In retrospect, only Sukhanov and a few others grasped the full implications of dual power, though all of the members of the executive committee seem to have been aware of the dangers lurking behind the concept of a separate, autonomous arena for the activity of the lower classes. Much of the success of dual power and of the February revolution itself would depend on the ability of the Mensheviks in the executive committee to organize their followers

tion *RD posle sverzheniia samoderzhaviia*. The section entitled "The Workers' Movement" contains very few resolutions (mostly from factories in the Vyborg district) in which workers called on the soviet to assume full power.

[60] *RD posle sverzheniia samoderzhaviia*, 458. In Russian, the term *kontrol'* connotes the overseeing of a certain body or process, rather than the exercise of directional authority. The term was used in this sense throughout 1917, as well as to refer more narrowly to the workers' supervision of certain aspects of factory life. Because of this difference, the Russian term will be retained here instead of using the English cognate.

into a powerful and disciplined force. To accomplish this, the leaders had to ensure that the masses' most pressing demands and aspirations were fulfilled. They had to keep pressure on the country's new rulers and yet prevent the pressure from below from destroying the delicate political arrangement that had been worked out between the soviet and the Provisional Government. To what extent they succeeded is the subject of the next chapter.

Dual Power Tested: Workers, Industrialists, and the Menshevik Mediators

THE POTENTIAL for tension between the leaders of the soviet and their mass following was greatest in the areas closest to workers and soldiers. Order No. 1 had eased the pressure from the garrison but had done nothing to satisfy the demands of the workers, who were, after all, the only legitimate constituency of the soviet from the Menshevik perspective. Indeed, for a few days, the executive committee tried to hold the line on workers' demands and in so doing came close to creating a crisis of trust and understanding between itself and its working-class constituency.

The problem lay not only in the role of the soviet as a labor organization (the Menshevik praktiki wanted a rejuvenated trade-union movement to lead the workers in their struggle for economic betterment) but, more important, in what contemporaries called the "social content" of the revolution. This involved three different sets of issues. The first of these was the extent of change that workers could expect in their economic situation: their material condition, their dealings with their employers, perhaps even their participation in economic decision making. Second, and of more immediate concern to Mensheviks, was the degree to which those who wielded economic power—the commercial-industrial bourgeoisie—could be pressed into conceding labor's demands. Finally, there was the danger of a social polarization that could fatally weaken the revolution. These issues were fundamental to the Menshevik assessment of the revolution's success and its future direction. As such, their resolution would play a crucial role in determining the Mensheviks' continued adherence to dual power and their eventual decision to abandon this strategy.

THE THREAT OF LABOR CONFLICTS

The fear of a social conflict, especially one that would pit workers against employers, loomed large in the minds of the leaders of the Petrograd soviet in the early days of the revolution. Sukhanov, the architect of dual power, expected that Russia's propertied classes would yield on economic issues only under heavy pressure from the soviet and its mass following, but he was concerned that a premature eruption of this struggle might endanger the modus vivendi just established among the disparate forces that had declared their support for the revolution.[1] Similar assessments were made by the Menshevik praktiki in Petrograd, who tried to impress the workers with the necessity of avoiding controversial economic demands. One of their organs, for example, reminded its readers that the revolution had been only a "political revolution"; what had been destroyed was the "bastions of political autocracy," but the "foundations of capitalism" still remained standing.[2]

Yet, as they tried to guide the workers away from a confrontation with the capitalists, the Mensheviks sensed the futility of attempting both to distinguish between political and economic gains and to urge the workers to deny themselves the satisfaction of their economic demands. In presenting an executive committee recommendation for ending the ten-day revolutionary strike on March 5, Chkheidze emphasized that workers would be ready to "go into the streets . . . at any given moment" and promised that in the meantime the soviet would draw up "a program of economic demands."[3]

Even so, and despite the plenum's overwhelming vote of support (1,170 to 30) for the committee's recommendation, the decision to end the strike before any economic demands had been met provoked angry responses in working-class quarters. A meeting of representatives of twenty-one factories in the Petrograd district on March 8 accused the soviet of "ignoring the sentiments of the broad proletarian masses" and demanded that, in the future, such decisions be taken only after "serious consideration" of workers' sentiments. The soviet was called upon to "work out and imple-

[1] For that reason, he avoided all mention of economic issues in his negotiations with the Duma deputies of the propertied groups: Sukhanov, *Zapiski o revoliutsii* 1:230.

[2] *RG*, March 7, 1917 (no. 1), 2. The editors of the soviet's newspaper, among whom there were both Mensheviks and Independent SDs, had made more militant demands from the outset: "If in the [course of the] Russian revolution someone has to yield, it should not be the working class.": "Who Should Yield," *IzvPS*, March 5, 1917 (no. 6), 6.

[3] *IzvPS*, March 6, 1917 (no. 7), 1–2. On March 9, the executive committee issued an appeal to the workers to return to work and warned the industrialists not to abuse "those who fought for the freedom of our country": *IzvPS*, March 9, 1917 (no. 10), 1.

ment *radical reforms in the field of economic life*," and the agitation against the workers' unilateral implementation of an eight-hour workday was declared to be *"harmful to the general cause."*[4] It was evidently with deep resentment that most workers submitted to the soviet's authority (there were cases of defiance), and they did so only because they believed that their leaders would support them in completing "their" revolution.[5]

In the workers' minds there was apparently no division between political and economic aspirations.[6] There was one revolution, and it encompassed all aspects of life. "A new life has begun! We have to create a new order for ourselves," declared a meeting of construction workers, and the tailors called on their brethren to work "for our workers' interests, for freedom, for life."[7] If there was a distinction to be drawn, it was between the national, somewhat abstract level of relations between classes and the more concrete relations at the factory. The thrust of the workers' campaign in March was to obliterate other distinctions. Most workers' resolutions mixed expressions of support for the soviet with specific demands (addressed to the employers) for changes in the conditions of life and work in the factories.[8]

The demand workers voiced most frequently and urgently in the early days of March was the institution of an eight-hour workday.

[4] *RD posle sverzheniia samoderzhaviia*, 229–31 (emphasis in the original).

[5] A meeting of the soviet's workers' section on March 7 heard reports from twenty-two factories; in eight of them, the workers had refused to work until their demands had been met by the employers; in three, such concessions had already been achieved; and in two, the workers themselves had instituted new regulations. Workers in the other factories had declared their readiness to submit to the soviet's authority but pleaded that it intervene with the employers on their behalf. *IzvPS*, March 10, 1917 (no. 11), 30.

[6] For a recent analysis of workers' demands that does break them down into economic and political categories, see Ferro, *Russian Revolution of February 1917*, esp. 115–17. For an analysis that is closer to that offered in this chapter, see Mandel, *Petrograd Workers and the Fall of the Old Regime*, chap. 5, and Smith, *Red Petrograd*, 2–3. See also Volobuev, *Proletariat i burzhuaziia*, 116–47.

[7] *IzvPS*, February 28, 1917 (no. 1), supplement, and March 4, 1917 (no. 5), 6.

[8] The workers of the Skorokhod factory, for example, passed a resolution on March 5 supporting the soviet and its political program and at the same time presented the factory management with demands for an eight-hour workday, a wage increase of 100 percent, and other improvements: *Pravda*, March 7, 1917 (no. 2), 2; *RD posle sverzheniia samoderzhaviia*, 490–91, 573. See also the resolution adopted by the workers of the Sestroretsk armament factory on March 9, in which they expressed their support for the soviet but demanded, among other things, the immediate establishment of "an eight-hour workday [and] a democratic republic . . .": ibid., 478–79.

It was regarded as a symbol of the revolution's grant of civic equality—a free citizen should have time to rest and to engage in public affairs—and had been a fundamental part of the workers' political agenda for over a decade. It had been one of the three "tails" of the Social Democratic minimum program, the one provision of the program that pertained directly and exclusively to workers.

Almost as popular as the eight-hour workday were two demands that touched on the structure of relations in the factory: that workers who had been blacklisted and sent off to the army (usually for strike or political activity) be rehired, and that managerial representatives from the factory who had abused their authority in the past, or were resented by the workers for other reasons, be dismissed. These two demands reflected the workers' perception that in the factory, too, "autocracy" should be abolished and replaced with a "democratic order."[9] Because most workers doubted their employers' willingness to establish such an order, they moved in many cases to form autonomous organizations to control those aspects of their lives not directly connected with production.[10] Moreover, they demanded that the employers recognize these "factory committees" and remunerate their members for time spent away from the benches.

In mid-March, the workers added a demand for higher wages, partly to offset the decline in real wages during the inflationary war years,[11] but also as a symbol of their claim to civic equality. That the latter was even the more important stimulus for wage demands was shown in several ways: by the campaign for a minimum wage, beginning immediately after February and continuing

[9] By one count, 83 percent of all workers' pronouncements in March and April 1917 demanded the purging of factory administrations: M. Fleer, "K istorii rabochego dvizheniia v 1917 g.," *KL*, 1925, no. 2(13):242.

[10] On March 11, a meeting of one thousand textile workers adopted a resolution that said, "We must immediately take up the establishment of factory committees in our factories, in the majority of which the remnants of serfdom still exist": *RG*, March 17, 1917 (no. 10), 4.

[11] Average real wages declined by February 1917 to between 70 and 75 percent of the prewar level in Petrograd, to as low as 50 percent in the Urals, and to 60 percent in the Donbas: Volobuev, *Proletariat i burzhuaziia*, 89–95. Workers in factories engaged in defense production generally fared better, but a study of wages in the chemical-artillery Parviainen plant showed that a 340 percent increase in the cost of living during the war years had considerably reduced the real value of workers' wages; during 1916 alone, the real average hourly wage had declined from 27.8 to 22.9 kopeks an hour, although the nominal hourly wage had increased from 48.4 to 72.1 kopeks. In the Moscow industrial region, real wages in the second half of 1916 stood at 76 percent of the 1914 level. Strumilin, *Zarabotnaia plata*, 13–14.

for several months; by the fact that the skilled and better-paid workers put their organizational force behind the demand for a minimum wage from the outset, thus helping the lowest-paid, usually unorganized workers; and by the wording of the resolutions passed in many factories, such as one that declared, "Now that we have political freedom in the country, we have also to try to destroy the economic slavery that has survived until now in the area of labor-capital relations."[12]

Indeed, even though the immediate object of all these demands was the individual factory, the frequency and uniformity of their appearance indicated that they should not be considered as merely isolated, economic manifestations. For the workers, these demands signified their rights to freedom from arbitrariness, to control over their own lives, and to a sense of personal worth earned by virtue of their having brought about the revolution. In short, the worker saw these demands as proof of his right to live as was "deserving of a worker and a free citizen."[13]

In VIEW of the breadth and power of these sentiments, a sharp social conflict involving the conditions of life and work in the factories seemed likely during the first two weeks of March—a conflict that could have split the democratic camp between its leaders and its followers. However, the second half of March saw a dramatic change in the general picture of labor relations and a shift in both the mood of the workers and the policies of their Menshevik leaders in the soviet. Essentially, this change reflected a new readiness by both workers and employers to make concessions in order to avoid a disruptive social conflict. That such moderation existed among both parties is evident from such statistical data as are available on labor relations for March and April 1917.

On the workers' side, there was an abrupt decline in strike activity, which was at a low level throughout the second half of March and most of April. Of the 101 factories in Petrograd reporting to

[12] Resolution adopted by one thousand textile workers on March 11, in *RG*, March 17, 1917 (no. 10), 4. Workers in various factories came up with different ways of effecting the general principle. The workers of Promet, for instance, decided that they themselves would negotiate a minimum wage with their employers. At the Putilov shipyard, the local conciliation board referred the issue of higher wages to the Central Conciliation Board but declared that, meanwhile, 20 percent of the total yearly payroll was to be allocated to compensate the lowest-paid workers. *RG*, March 10, 1917 (no. 4), 4, and March 19, 1917 (no. 12), 3.

[13] *Tekstil' nyi rabochii*, 1917, no. 2:6, as cited in Volobuev, *Proletariat i burzhuaziia*, 125.

the Society of Industrialists at the end of March, the majority had resumed operations between March 7 and 10; only two remained struck after March 13. Figures compiled by the Factory Inspectorate for all of Russia, though grossly inadequate, show a similar trend.[14] Moreover, workers in the better-organized factories, in particular, showed their moderation in other ways: in efforts to raise labor productivity, in a frequent use of arbitration, and in a willingness to forgo the immediate implementation of some of their demands.

For their part, the industrialists appeared ready during these first two months of the revolution to meet many of the workers' most pressing demands. In Petrograd and other industrial centers, the principle of the eight-hour workday was established, and special rates were paid for overtime work. Although statistical data are hard to come by, the Soviet historian Volobuev estimates that the average workday in Petrograd's factories declined during March from 10.1 hours to 8.4, while wages rose by 35 percent; for the country as a whole, the average nominal wage rose by 50 percent during the first three months of the revolution.[15] In the Donbas mines, nominal wages rose by 50 percent and overtime wages (at a rate half again higher than the new wages) gave the workers an additional increase of about 30 percent.[16] In addition, agreements on a minimum wage were signed by many of the largest employers' organizations (in Petrograd and the Donbas region, for example), while the workers' right to be represented through their factory committees appears to have been accepted by many own-

[14] *RD posle sverzheniia samoderzhaviia*, 569–74, 592–95; *RD v aprele*, 476–79. The number of strikes registered declined from 152 (114,304 strikers) in March to 41 (12,392 strikers) in April. As these figures indicate, the average size of the striking enterprise was smaller in April (302 workers) than it was in March (752 workers). The Factory Inspectorate did not collect strike statistics for workers in mining, transportation, or state-owned factories, and, more important, only aggregate figures have been published, making it extremely difficult to determine the cause, course, and significance of strikes. However, the general picture implied by the inspectorate's figures is borne out by the preliminary findings of a new study of strike statistics, which has data on twice as many strikers as were contained in the inspectorate's reports: Koenker and Rosenberg, "Strikes in Revolution," 17.

[15] Volobuev, *Proletariat i burzhuaziia*, 121, 126–28. Volobuev based his calculations on statistical data collected and published in 1918; the same data show that gains were registered in every sector of the Petrograd working class, though working conditions continued to vary. *MST*, 1918, no. 1:56. The universality of the principle of the eight-hour workday is evident also in a resolution of the SSPPit to use the eight-hour day as the basic pay unit: *PiT*, May 13, 1917 (no. 16/17 [256]), 320.

[16] *Konferentsii rabochikh*, 61–64; *FO*, April 22, 1917 (no. 13/14), 17–18.

ers, especially of medium- and large-size factories.[17] The demands to rehire blacklisted workers and to oust objectionable managerial representatives were so widely implemented that the demand itself soon disappeared.[18]

As might be expected, the moderation shown during March and April by significant segments of the working class and commercial-industrial circles affected the political mood of the cities in crucial ways. It was responsible for what Soviet historians sardonically call "the honeymoon" of the revolution, and it prepared the ground for the soviet's eventual entrance into a coalition government with the bourgeoisie in early May. Yet the reasons for this moderation, and even its very existence, have not received due attention from historians, who have more frequently focused on the process of social polarization that underlay the Bolshevik challenge and the October revolution.

These reasons had to do with political and structural developments during the decade prior to 1917, the expectations of workers and industrialists of the revolution's progress (which, in the case of the latter, had undergone drastic change during the two and a half years of war), and the manner in which economic, political, and organizational factors interacted with the particular conditions created by the revolution. But what was probably most important in explaining the predominance of conciliatory gestures on both sides of labor relations was the mutuality of this response. Let us turn first to the industrialists.

THE PROGRESSISTS

In the years preceding the February revolution, there had been a rapid, though uneven, expansion in the economic and political power of Russia's commercial-industrial class.[19] Between 1910 and 1914, investment in industry had risen impressively after a long period of stagnation, with the balance between foreign and native

[17] Smith, *Red Petrograd*, 80, calculates that over half of the factories in these categories (i.e., with two hundred workers or more) were represented at the First Petrograd Conference of Factory Committees, which was held at the end of May.

[18] Volobuev, *Proletariat i burzhuaziia*, 139–40; Fleer, "K istorii rabochego dvizheniia," 242.

[19] The use of the term "commercial industrial class" (or "industrial class" or "entrepreneurial class") is not intended as an assertion of the existence of a bourgeois class in Russia; rather, it is a term of convenience that draws its legitimacy from its widespread use in the period under discussion, often by the entrepreneurs themselves.

capital shifting somewhat in favor of the latter.[20] Moreover, an array of commercial-industrial organizations had increased the power of the entrepreneurial class, if not its unity. In addition to the old local exchange societies, these included raw material syndicates, antilabor societies, and associations of representatives from various regions and industries, as well as a nationwide Association of Trade and Industry (SSPPiT).[21] The last-named of these organizations was dedicated to lobbying the government on behalf of industrial interests in general. All of this pointed toward the creation of a national bourgeoisie. Yet social, economic, and cultural divisions undermined concerted action by the commercial-industrial elements, and separation from both rural Russia and the working and professional classes of the city further diminished their political effectiveness.[22] They had attempted to force the alliance of autocracy and nobility that had dominated Russian life since 1907 to concede some of its power and privileges, but the effort had been in vain.

It was against this background of inchoate change that the spectacular rise of a group of "Progressist" industrialists began. This group, named for the Party of Progressists they helped found in 1912, descended from the Moscow merchantry ("native" Russian entrepreneurs) and held immense fortunes and considerable economic power. But more to the point, they were conscious of being the vanguard of a bourgeois class destined for the leadership of Russia's economic and political life. For them, both liberal and Marxist theories spelled out this destiny plainly, while the West European bourgeoisie provided a living example. They also saw, however, that the European experience as well as the dogged resistance of autocracy and gentry indicated that, to realize their bold vision, they would have to embark on a fundamental restructuring of Russia's society and government. The old, state-sanctioned social estates and privileges would have to give way to a society of universal citizenship—a goal that both required and fa-

[20] The precise balance between foreign and domestic capital is difficult to determine and remains the subject of historical debate, in part because foreign investors were forced to use Russian-owned banks for their operations during this period.

[21] Berlin, *Russkaia burzhuaziia*, 260–63; Vanag, "K metodologii izucheniia finansovogo kapitala," 24, 40–41. See also Roosa, "Russian Industrialists and 'State Socialism.' "

[22] Vanag, "K metodologii izucheniia finansovogo kapitala," 42–46. Recently, two independent studies by Western scholars have documented the divisions within Russia's commercial-industrial class, whose very existence as a class they reject: Duggan, "Progressists," and Rieber, *Merchants and Entrepreneurs in Imperial Russia.*

cilitated the formation of coalitions with other social groups, notably the academic and professional intelligentsia and the working class. On the eve of the war, two Progressists, A. I. Konovalov and P. P. Riabushinskii, had been actively searching out such contacts while also campaigning, with some success, for support within their own class for this strategy.[23]

THE WAR presented the commercial-industrial class with fresh opportunities, which the Moscow Progressists exploited with their customary confidence and energy.[24] They made themselves the strongest advocates of complete, patriotic industrial mobilization and thus ensured their selection to head the WICs.[25] The Central WIC was entrusted to Konovalov and A. I. Guchkov (the latter still officially with the Octobrists party but a close collaborator of Konovalov for the balance of the war), while Riabushinskii headed the Moscow WIC, which acted as a clearinghouse for the WICs of the central industrial region.[26] The responsibilities and economic functions which these positions involved enhanced their claim to the leadership of their class and of society at large. But in addition, the struggles they waged against the state and its bureaucracy—for the power to distribute industrial orders as well as for the right of "society" (*obshchestvo*) to have its voice heard in the councils of state—established their position as the vanguard of the antiautocratic forces and made them the center around which diverse elements, especially the public organizations, could unite. Indeed, as the Progressist S. A. Smirnov would later explain, the WICs made themselves the core of social coalitions which brought together entrepreneurs, the elected representatives of workers, and the tech-

[23] For studies of the Moscow entrepreneurial group and its politics before the war, see Owen, *Capitalism and Politics in Russia*; Ruckman, *Moscow Business Elite*; Rieber, *Merchants and Entrepreneurs in Imperial Russia*, chaps. 4, 5, and 7; Laverychev, *Po tu storonu barikad*, chap. 2; and Haimson, "Social Stability in Urban Russia," 4–8.

[24] This section on commercial-industrial circles during the war draws on Rieber, *Merchants and Entrepreneurs in Imperial Russia*, chap. 8; Laverychev, *Po tu storonu barikad*, chaps. 3 and 4; Diakin, *Russkaia burzhuaziia i tsarizm*; Tarnovskii, *Formirovanie gosudarstvenno-monopolisticheskogo kapitalizma*; Siegelbaum, *Politics of Industrial Mobilization*; and Duggan, "Progressists." The last two were particularly pertinent.

[25] See, for example, the response to Riabushinskii's speech at the Ninth Congress of the SSPPit (May 1915), in *Promyshlennaia Rossiia*, May 31, 1915 (no. 6/7), 5–7. Duggan, "Progressists," 81–87, and Siegelbaum, *Politics of Industrial Mobilization*, 44–45, 48–49, give accounts of this congress's decision to establish the WICs.

[26] On the formation of the WICs in the summer of 1915 and their first congress (July 1915), during which the Moscovites won their victory, see Siegelbaum, *Politics of Industrial Mobilization*, 56–68, and Duggan, "Progressists," 135–51.

nological-scientific intelligentsia, to whom the committees offered the vision of a more efficient and more rational economic structure as well as a practical means of influencing the country's economy.[27]

The Progressists also built important bases of support within their own class, though they suffered some setbacks, especially in the summer and fall of 1916. From the outset, they could count on the resentment of small and medium industry and the provincial WICs toward the traditionally favored magnates of Petrograd industry.[28] Moreover, this animosity (typically expressed in patriotic rhetoric) was coupled with a quite obvious economic interest, particularly in the early period of the Central and Moscow WICs, when they obtained a large number of state orders. At that time, small and medium plants in the provinces, which had never produced for the state, were encouraged and helped to convert to military production, so they were able to share in the wartime opportunities.[29] For a while, it seemed to the Progressists as if they had

[27] *IzvMVPK*, 1917, no. 45/46:6–8. The most prominent representatives of the technical intelligentsia in the WICs were the "engineer-managers" from the south, who had been active in the SSPPiT and had taken over the technical sections of the Central WIC when it was first organized by the SSPPiT. They continued to work on these sections under the leadership of the Muscovites even after the association had broken with the WICs in the spring of 1916. Siegelbaum, *Politics of Industrial Mobilization*, 56–58. The themes of efficiency and technical development appeared regularly in the publications of the Moscow WIC, *IzvMVPK* and *Proizvoditel' nye sily Rossii* (The Productive Forces of Russia). The importance of the intelligentsia "third element" in the WICs was explored in F. Platonov, "The Social Character of the WICs," *IzvMVPK*, 1916, no. 31/32:53–55. For characterizations of the economic and technical intelligentsia before the revolution, see Bailes, *Technology and Society under Lenin and Stalin*, chap. 1; Sanders, "Union of Unions," 218–31, 434–59, and 465–87; and Rieber, *Merchants and Entrepreneurs in Imperial Russia*, 354–57.

[28] The press representing middle and small industry was filled with attacks on Petrograd's entrepreneurial giants and especially praised the Moscow industrialists for their independence from the large banks of the capital: *Promyshlennaia Rossiia*, April 15, 1915 (no. 1), 1–3; May 7, 1915 (no. 4/5), 1–2; May 31, 1915 (no. 6/7), 1–3, 5–7; June 28, 1915 (no. 10/11), 1–5; and July 26, 1915 (no. 14/15), 3–4; *VVTiP*, 1915 (no. 5):6–7, (no. 7):1–6, (no. 8):1–6, 7–8; *Vestnik kustarnoi promyshlennosti*, 1915, no. 7[29]:1–13 (reprint of a memorandum submitted to the Ministry of Trade and Industry, which dwelt on the importance and the needs of small industry in wartime) and 24–41.

[29] The Progressists' takeover of the Central WIC coincided with the selection of Gen. A. A. Manikovskii as the new minister of war and with changes in the Special Conference on Defense that led to a greater reliance on the public organizations and on the WICs in particular; see Siegelbaum, *Politics of Industrial Mobilization*, 70–72. Although the bulk of orders still went to large enterprises, the WICs were the only source for orders, advances, and technical expertise for the small and medium pro-

gained not only the organizational loyalty of many entrepreneurs but also their faith in the vision of the bourgeois Russia for which the Progressists had been campaigning. This was particularly true in the summer of 1915, when the state appeared so inept in performing its economic and military functions. In fact, in September 1915, electors to the commercial-industrial group in the State Council voted unanimously for Riabushinskii and Guchkov as their "political" representatives and defeated all the candidates of the more sedate, "apolitical" SSPPiT.[30] Two months later, Konovalov was given serious consideration as the new head of the SSPPiT itself.[31] At the Second Congress of WICs, which met in late February 1916, the representatives of 192 local and 34 regional committees resoundingly approved the Progressists' program of extensive labor reforms, which included freedom for workers to organize and measures of democratization in local and central government.[32]

A good deal of this strength was lost later in 1916, when the Progressist leadership of the WICs became involved in a controversy concerning the labor program at the Second Congress and the shape Russian society was to take when autocracy was destroyed. During that summer and fall, the two most important societies of industrialists in the country, those of Moscow and Petrograd, repeatedly blocked the WICs' efforts to implement the

---

ducers in the provinces. See, for example, the reports from Odessa, Kursk, and Kharkov, in *IzvTsVPK*, August 29, 1915 (no. 2), 3; October 13, 1915 (no. 15), 4; and March 8, 1916 (no. 68), 6; and the report on a conference of regional WICs held in Petrograd on April 18–19, 1916, in ibid., April 23, 1916 (no. 86), 2.

[30] Diakin, *Russkaia burzhuaziia i tsarizm*, 123–24; Duggan, "Progressists," 235–36. What made the election even more significant was the publication of two programmatic articles in Riabushinskii's newspaper, *Utro Rossii*, at the beginning of September, which amounted to a declaration of the bourgeoisie's right to become the ruling class. These articles are quoted in Diakin, *Russkaia burzhuaziia i tsarizm*, 146–47.

[31] Diakin, *Russkaia burzhuaziia i tsarizm*, 147–50.

[32] *Trudy vtorogo s'ezda predstavitelei voenno-promyshlennykh komitetov*, 329–37; see also the speeches of S. S. Raetskii (engineer from the Moscow WIC), A. E. Shiriaev (Perm), A. I. Churkin (Samara), and M. M. Belov (grain merchant from Nikolaev), in ibid., 45–46, 50–51, 318, 573–77. A Soviet historian has argued that Konovalov "manipulated" the congress into accepting his labor program: Laverychev, *Po tu storonu barikad*, 133. But it was more likely the general mood created in the WIC by the intelligentsia members of the individual committees (especially in provincial towns) and the advocacy of a progressive labor policy by the leaders of the Petrograd, Moscow, Kiev, and Odessa committees that made it hard for the delegates to publicly oppose the Central Labor Group's program prepared for the congress; see S. N. Tret'iakov's report on his visit to the Central WIC on February 6–7, 1916, in *IzvMVPK*, 1916, no. 15/16:103.

provisions of the program calling for establishing citywide conciliation boards, factory-based elected councils of "elders," and, in
Petrograd, dining halls to ease the effects of food shortages on the
workers.[33] Some of the opposition's support came from the new
Association of Metalprocessing Industries, established in February
1916 by the largest of Petrograd's and Moscow's owners in an attempt to regain their monopoly of state orders.[34] More generally,
however, the attack was inspired by the tsarist government itself,
which forbade the WICs to engage in public political work and
deprived them of the state orders that had been one source of their
increasing prestige.[35]

Most damaging of all, however, were the divisions that appeared among the Progressists' own ranks as they passed through
the crucible of war and approaching revolution. In one respect, the
debate was over Konovalov's invitation to workers to elect representatives to the WICs and his offer of full autonomy to their Labor
Groups. Riabushinskii, S. N. Tret'iakov, and probably other Mos-

[33] The publications of the Moscow and Central WICs were filled with reports of
the meetings held with representatives of the PSI and its Moscow counterpart at
which such opposition was regularly offered, especially toward the end of the summer of 1916. For reports from Petrograd, see *IzvTsVPK*, January 23, 1916 (no. 52),
4; March 12, 1916 (no. 70), 3–6; August 23, 1916 (no. 136), 1–2; August 30, 1916 (no.
139), 3–4; September 13, 1916 (no. 144), 2–3; September 24, 1916 (no. 149), 3; October 11, 1916 (no. 156), 1–2; and *IzvMVPK*, 1916, no. 27/30:278. For reports from
Moscow, see *IzvMVPK*, 1916, no. 14:53; no. 21/22:172–80, 204–5; no. 23/24:155–73,
176–77, 191; no. 25/26:153–75; no. 27/30:191–201, 281–82.

[34] Diakin, *Russkaia burzhuaziia i tsarizm*, 177–78, has argued that the metalprocessing association made the labor policy of the WICs its primary target, but at the
association's first congress, held in Petrograd at the end of February 1916, the main
issues were the WICs' strategy of political opposition and their incursion into the
area of state orders, which had previously been the exclusive domain of the large
enterprises represented in the association; see especially the keynote speeches of
V. P. Meshcherskii and M. A. Tokarskii and the speeches of Iu. P. Guzhon of Moscow and A. I. Putilov of Petrograd, in *Trudy pervogo s'ezda predstavitelei metalloobrabatyvaiushchei promyshlennosti*, 19–39.

[35] On these decisions by the government, see Diakin, *Russkaia burzhuaziia i tsarizm*, 182–87, and Siegelbaum, *Politics of Industrial Mobilization*, 114–18. Also, see the
reports from various meetings of regional WICs and the bureau of the Central WIC
on the effects of these decisions on the Central WIC's ability to distribute orders,
its authority over local and district committees, and its prestige in the commercial-
industrial class in general: *IzvTsVPK*, April 26, 1916 (no. 86), 2; May 24, 1916 (no.
99), 4–5; May 26, 1916 (no. 100), 2–3; June 14, 1916 (no. 108), 2–4; July 1, 1916 (no.
114), 7; July 21, 1916 (no. 122), 3; November 8, 1916 (no. 167), 3; November 17, 1916
(no. 170), 3; December 20, 1916 (no. 183), 1–2; January 1, 1917 (no. 186), 1–2; and
IzvGK, August 1, 1916 (no. 23), 146–47, 154–55; and August 15, 1917 (no. 24), 88,
100.

cow entrepreneurs refused to countenance such demands for autonomy, though Riabushinskii supported other, more paternalistic
measures to improve labor relations—higher wages, conciliation
boards, and the institution of an elected workers' representation
at the factory level.[36] More broadly, the dispute involved Konovalov's articulation of his social vision for Russia, one of broad social
coalitions led by the "enlightened" entrepreneurs and their intelligentsia allies in the WICs.[37] Konovalov's was an unreservedly
"modern" view, in which the good of the state, equated with the
good of society at large, would be determined by all social groups
in free political interaction through their parliamentary parties.
Riabushinskii's perception was less consistent. He had joined with
Konovalov in the prewar period in advocating a modern party system and had freely used the rhetoric of "class," but the war and
the threat of defeat had impressed him with the importance of
identifying the bourgeoisie with the state's interest. In a word, he
was returning to the traditional Russian view of social groups as
comprised of hierarchically ordered estates, among which the merchant-entrepreneurs were now to be ranked highest. Indeed, with
the Russian state in mortal danger, Riabushinskii no longer
seemed willing to tolerate the public discussion of conflicting social
interests that a modern party system would have entailed.[38]

Clearly, there was formidable attitudinal resistance as well as
political opposition in commercial-industrial circles to Konovalov's
progressive ideas. Yet, by the time of the February revolution, the
weaknesses that had troubled the Progressist leadership of the

[36] For examples of Konovalov's cooperation with the Central Labor Group, his
struggle to secure freedom of action for all the labor groups, and his effort to convince Riabushinskii of the need for workers' autonomy in the WICs, see *IzvTsVPK*,
January 15, 1916 (no. 49), 6; January 17, 1916 (no. 50), 4; February 10, 1916 (no. 58),
5; February 26, 1916 (no. 63), 3–5; April 19, 1916 (no. 84), 7; and *IzvMVPK*, 1916,
no. 13:46–54, and no. 15/16:103. Riabushinskii's position emerged during the debate that took place at the Moscow WIC on December 23, 1915, and in an open
letter to the Moscow Labor Group; see *IzvMVPK*, 1916, no. 13:46–55, and no. 14:1–2.

[37] Konovalov elaborated his labor program in an article entitled "Some Observations on the Present Labor Movement and the Measures Needed for Its Regulation," which was circulated to local WICs in June 1916. It is reprinted in "K istorii
'Rabochei gruppy,' " 72–84.

[38] This analysis of Riabushinskii's ideas draws mainly on his statements during
the debate over the demand of the workers' representatives for autonomy (see n.
36 above). Similar differences between Riabushinskii and Konovalov arose when
the Moscow WIC discussed the question of whether the projected war-commercial
departments should be "public" or purely "merchant" in makeup and orientation:
IzvGK, August 15, 1916 (no. 24), 104–6.

81

WICs were turned into advantages as a result of the generally rising tide of revolution and of one specific circumstance. Early in 1916, Riabushinskii and Tret'iakov, both pleading poor health and a commitment to organizing a commercial-industrial congress (itself a part of the Progressist scheme for the mobilization of society), terminated their involvement in the Moscow WIC, leaving it in the hands of a new coalition of the technological, scientific, and "public-minded" intelligentsia with a few of the most progressive industrialists. (Smirnov, for example, became the new deputy chairman of the Moscow WIC.)[39] For the rest of the year, the Moscow and Central WICs worked jointly to promote Konovalov's labor program, which called for full organizational freedom for workers as well as improvements in working conditions.[40] In the publications of the two committees and in the public meetings Konovalov organized in his mansion, industrialists were promised that organized and well-paid workers would be more peaceful and efficient. Alternatively, those industrialists whose willingness to

[39] Riabushinskii remained the titular head of the Moscow WIC but ceased to be actively involved in its work after he fell ill early in 1916. Tret'iakov had resigned in April 1916, ostensibly to concentrate on preparations for the projected All-Russian Trade and Industry Union, though the Moscow Labor Group accused him of deserting the committee while under attack from the state: *IzvMVPK*, 1916, no. 21/22:172–80. Both Riabushinskii and Tret'iakov made the Moscow Exchange Society (of which they were chairman and deputy chairman, respectively) the base of their activity in 1916, and by the end of that summer there was apparent tension between this committee and the WIC; see the exchange of letters between Smirnov and Tret'iakov, in *IzvMVPK*, 1916, no. 27/30:211–12, and no. 31/32:168. During the debates over the Moscow WIC's labor policy, Smirnov and a coalition of workers' delegates and professional men—among them the Menshevik economists Groman and P. P. Maslov, the Kadet economist Manuilov, the Kadet jurist A. E. Borms, and the engineers N. P. Nochevkin and S. G. Gurevich—usually outvoted the opposition from the Moscow Society of Industrialists led by Guzhon and Iu. P. Poplavskii: *IzvMVPK*, 1916, no. 17/18:133–34; no. 21/22:172–80, 204–5; no. 23/24:155–73, 176–77, 191; no. 25/26:153–75; and no. 27/30:191–201, 281–82.

[40] See, for example, the reports from the meetings of the WICs' representatives at factory conferences and those held by the Central WIC with local committees and the Petrograd and Moscow Societies of Industrialists, in which engineers defended the workers' demands and the progressive labor program: *IzvMVPK*, 1916, no. 23/24:155–73, and no. 25/26:173; and *IzvTsVPK*, August 23, 1916 (no. 136), 1–2; and August 25, 1916 (no. 137), 1–2. See also the report from a meeting of the Central WIC with the State Duma and State Council in *IzvGK*, August 1, 1916 (no. 23), 148–50, and the many articles advocating labor reforms written by academics in the service of the WICs: *IzvTsVPK*, January 31, 1916 (no. 55), 2–3; February 5, 1916 (no. 25), 2; February 10, 1916 (no. 58); February 24, 1916 (no. 62); and March 22, 1916 (no. 74), 2; *PSR*, November 15, 1916 (no. 1), 1–3, 14–18; and *Torgovo-promyshlennyi iug*, July 15, 1916 (no. 14[102]), 11–16.

accept that argument was restrained by contempt for the Russian worker were warned that labor organizations and a moderate socialist leadership would be their only defense against the anarchic masses, because the government was not to be depended on.[41]

Gradually, Konovalov, his intelligentsia collaborators, and a few other progressive industrialists created a new set of terms for the public discussion of entrepreneurial behavior, especially in regard to labor, which they would offer to the commercial-industrial class at large after the revolution.[42] Meanwhile, Konovalov's informal coalition was attempting to mobilize a broad array of social forces around a call to allow "society" more power and responsibility. In the spring of 1916, and again on the eve of the February revolution, in conferences with the intelligentsia activists of the Union of Cities, the Labor Groups, and the cooperative movement, plans were made for a campaign to put pressure on the tsarist government.[43]

[41] See esp. N. Kablukov, "The Interests of Labor and the Productive Forces of Russia," *PSR*, November 15, 1916 (no. 1), 14–18; Konovalov, "Some Observations on the Present Labor Movement"; and Konovalov's addresses to meetings of entrepreneurs during September, October, and December 1916, in Grave, ed., *Burzhuaziia nakanune fevral'skoi revoliutsii*, 140–41. See also the Central WIC's protest against the arrest of its Labor Group: Shliapnikov, *Semnadtsatyi god* 1:280–83.

[42] F. Platonov described these progressive industrialists as having "risen above the dominant sentiment of their environment, sometimes even sharply contradicting the traditional ideology and biases of their class": "The Social Character of the WICs," *IzvMVPK*, 1916, no. 31/32:53–56. Indeed, during the summer of 1916, the industrialists who resisted the progressive program were regularly portrayed in the journal of the Moscow WIC as conservative and generally unfit for the new role of industry in Russia's political life; Riabushinskii's *Utro Rossii* retorted by mocking Smirnov and the WIC for their self-righteous preaching. See *IzvMVPK*, 1916, no. 19/20:43–44; no. 29/30:44–48, 95–101; and no. 31/32:168. Platonov's judgment, for whatever it is worth, was that, in spite of their small numbers, the progressives had become the most influential segment of the industrial class.

[43] During the second congress of WICs in February 1916, steps were taken to mobilize various social groups around the issue of food supplies and to organize them into individual unions as well as a "union of unions" (a strategy that had worked well in 1905), but the scheme was eventually foiled by the authorities; see Department politsii, "Obzor politicheskoi deiatel'nosti." In the fall of 1916, a loose alliance of oppositional groups and individuals took shape, with Konovalov and Guchkov at its center and probably involving the Labor Groups as well; Riabushinskii and the Moscow merchantry, the Union of Cities, the left Kadets, and other "public" men and organizations participated in at least part of its activity. See *IzvTsVPK*, December 17, 1916 (no. 182), 1–2; Grave, ed., *Burzhuaziia nakanune fevral'skoi revoliutsii*, 141–42, 155–60, 164–65, 180–84; Shliapnikov, *Kanun semnadtsotogo goda* 2:128–32; Shcheglov, ed., *Padenie tsarskogo rezhima* 6:277–78; and Duggan, "Progressists," 335–36.

Ultimately, circumstances would again help Konovalov and his associates. The collapse of the tsarist regime raised the influence of the Progressists to a new height, undermined (at least for a while) the position of those industrialists who had relied on state support to counter the WICs, and vindicated Konovalov's warnings and vision. Moreover, the men of the WICs began to exercise state power and the authority to speak for the new government of a free Russia. Konovalov was appointed minister of trade and industry; Guchkov, of war and navy; and M. I. Tereshchenko (a wealthy sugar-industry magnate and chairman of the Kiev WIC), of finance. It was to them, and to the intelligentsia writers and speakers who helped shape the progressive view, that the suddenly disoriented commercial-industrial circles turned for leadership in February.

FOR A PERIOD of two months after the February revolution, the groups that had united around the WICs' labor program dominated the business press. Basing themselves on the experience of the revolution, utilizing the social and political strategies of the WICs, and relying heavily on the ministerial prestige of Konovalov, these groups expounded the economic and labor programs of the WICs (now enlarged to include the workers' new demands) as the standard of behavior for the commercial-industrial class at large. Their arguments varied but together had the effect of offering the disparate commercial-industrial elements a coherent formula for apprehending the confusing new circumstances, a formula around which these elements could unite. It embodied a view of the commercial-industrial class and of the revolution that reinforced the entrepreneurs' sense of their own importance and magnanimity even as it prepared them for concessions to labor in the name of their new responsibilities.

At the heart of this coalition again stood Konovalov, who continued to develop his program in a series of addresses, press conferences, and ministerial decisions. First, he sought to emphasize the "exceptional importance" of the labor question and to use the state apparatus to carry out an immediate reconstruction of labor relations on principles of "law and justice." Thus, in an "open letter" to workers, he stressed that the expansion of trade unions was "one of the chief prerequisites of Russia's economic survival" and that conciliation boards were "urgently needed" to establish proper relations between labor and capital, and he promised "every effort to promote the growth of labor legislation."[44] Ideally, he believed this task should be entrusted to a ministry of labor, headed by a socialist, but until this could be done, Konovalov made himself the patron of labor legislation, established a Department of Labor in his own ministry, appointed Professor M. V. Bernatskii, a former Menshevik as its head, and invited the Petrograd soviet to send representatives to the department's advisory committee.[45] Under Konovalov's guidance, both the new department and the Labor Group of the Central WIC set out to develop legislative projects for a variety of labor organizations (unions, factory committees, conciliation boards), to set down certain industrial procedures (for employment, collective bargaining, and strikes), and to plan for a program of social benefits, such as the workers' most urgent demand—that of the eight-hour workday.[46]

Second, Konovalov attempted to use his position as the highest-ranking "citizen-industrialist" to convince entrepreneurs to sacrifice some of their economic advantages so that the workers' "spiritual and material needs" could be satisfied. To bolster this appeal, he reminded the commercial establishment that the old regime had not only inhibited entrepreneurial activity but also had fostered suspicion among classes by failing, for example, to regulate the economy and by allowing the sort of wartime profiteering that had turned the population against the commercial-industrial class. In fact, he pointed out, the repressive methods of the tsarist government were themselves responsible for the workers' present insistence in pursuing their demands. However, in the new Russia, he promised, there would be no place for "false fears, anxieties, or doubts." "Direct, open contact" would flourish among social groups, and in these conditions the commercial-industrial estab-

---

[44] *VVP*, March 7, 1917 (no. 2), 1–2. See also the report of Konovalov's press conference in *VVP*, March 31, 1917 (no. 21), 4.

[45] *Khronika* 1:80, and *Den'*, March 17, 1917 (no. 11), 3. See also *Edinstvo*, March 31, 1917 (no. 3), 3, and *RG*, April 1, 1917 (no. 22), 3. Konovalov's offer was discussed by the soviet's executive committee on March 16, and it was decided to send Gvozdev, Pankov, Baturskii, Vinokurov, Zalutskii, Krasikov, and two others as delegates. Of those whose names are known, the first three were Mensheviks, the other three were Bolsheviks. *Petrogradskii sovet*, 56

[46] *FO*, March 29, 1917 (no. 11/12), 16; *Khronika* 1:102. Konovalov was probably responsible for the Provisional Government's decision to establish the eight-hour workday in all of the enterprises run by the Ministry of War and Navy and for the cabinet's instructions to his own ministry to work out the legislative means for the institution of the shorter workday in all of Russia's industry: *RG*, March 19, 1917 (no. 12), 3; *RD posle sverzheniia samoderzhaviia*, 434.

lishment's readiness to make sacrifices for the "general good" would overcome the legacy of suspicion and allow the commercial-industrial class to take its rightful place of "great significance" in the country. Clearly, in arguing the need for a "new psychology" before Russia's entrepreneurs, Konovalov was also attempting to entice them with the prospect of hegemony over "a new and great Russia." The benefits he promised, then, were not merely spiritual. And indeed, government restrictions on joint-stock companies were eased on March 10, and work was begun on plans for a nationwide network of self-governing chambers of commerce as well as on such measures conducive to domestic industrial growth as a steady flow of credits and state orders, protective tariffs, and the expansion of ports and the merchant marine.[47]

That this program was not merely a reflection of the aspirations of the class to which Konovalov belonged was evident from the variations in the appeals be used to his fellow industrialists, by turns admonitory, exhortative, and enticing. The success of the progressive program depended on Konovalov's ability to have entrepreneurs accept the authenticity of the view he was offering: of themselves as belonging to a class, a bourgeoisie. Yet his was by no means a lonely voice. There were other industrialists—a handful in Moscow, a few more in Petrograd, some in the south—who greeted the revolution with similar expectations; namely, that the commercial-industrial class would come to dominate the country's economy and also become a partner in an urban coalition of the country's "vital forces" (in contrast to its backward-looking rural or reactionary forces), which would effect Russia's transition to parliamentary democracy and free capitalism. In Moscow, S. A. Smirnov of that city's WIC led these "forward-looking" industrialists.[48]

[47] See reports of a press conference by Konovalov, in *TPG*, March 30, 1917 (no. 65), 4, and *VVP*, March 31, 1917 (no. 21), 4; and his address to the Moscow Exchange Society in *IzvOS*, 1917, no. 3:88–93. The text of the Provisional Government's decision to ease restrictions on joint-stock companies is in Volobuev, ed., *Ekonomicheskoe polozhenie Rossii*, 1:215–16 (hereafter cited as *EPR*). In late March, Konovalov proposed to transfer the oversight of provisions from his ministry to Zemgor and of fuel and metal production to the WICs. At about this time, Guchov invited the same organizations to participate in the distribution of state orders for military production: *FO*, March 29, 1917 (no. 11/12), 20–21.

[48] See his speech at the First Congress of Trade and Industry, which took place in Moscow on March 19-22, in *Pervyi vserossiiskii torgovo-promyshlennyi s'ezd*, 34–39, and a speech on October 1 on the occasion of his joining the cabinet in the position of state controller, in *IzvMVPK*, 1917, no. 45/46:6–8.

In Petrograd, the newspaper *Finansovaia zhizn'* (Financial Life) was the best representative of this view. One typical article urged the Russian bourgeoisie, which it said had become for the first time "a bourgeoisie in the West European sense" and a political force, to rise above its "narrow, egotistic class interests." This was necessary, the author explained, for reasons of self-preservation, for "otherwise, the bourgeoisie would raise strong feelings against itself among working people and sharpen the class differences that might lead to strife and dissension." Moreover, he continued, broad-mindedness and social generosity were the prerequisites of a class that sought to lead its country's economic and industrial life. Such leadership belonged to the bourgeoisie "by right," but leadership required that this class "renounce its sins, the dark pages of its past, and show enough political maturity" to preserve the necessary degree of unity.[49]

Impressive as these sentiments of repentance were, especially when expressed in an editorial in a journal that was proud to call itself "bourgeois," they surely did not reflect the feelings of the average industrialist. In 1917, as in 1916, the economically oriented intelligenty—men who wielded considerable influence in ministries and industrial organizations—often tried to impose their own values and views on the industrialists, if not actually to speak for them.[50] In a veritable barrage of articles and speeches, they attempted to invoke the industrialists' sense of social responsibility and at times to manipulate a potentially guilty conscience. For example, Bublikov (a railroad engineer, Progressist Duma deputy, head of the transportation section of the Central WIC, and a member of the management of several companies) made the rounds of entrepreneurial meetings to advocate that industrialists adopt a "state point of view"—i.e., that they show a readiness to make sacrifices and to accept the workers' various demands, for the sake of orderly production and increased national output.[51] Similarly, the newspaper *Torgovo-promyshlennaia gazeta* (Commercial-Indus-

[49] "The Revolution and the Commercial-Industrial Class," *FZh*, March 9, 1917 (no. 9/10), 141–43. See also "The Labor Question," *FZh*, March 9, 1917 (no. 9/10), 144–45, and "Employers and Workers," *FZh*, March 16, 1917 (no. 11), 168–69.

[50] In an article welcoming the Congress of Trade and Industry that was convening in Moscow, the editors of *Financial Life* insisted that the commercial-industrial class should be represented in the projected Constituent Assembly "by industrialists and merchants themselves and not by men foreign to that class": *FZh*, March 9, 1917 (no. 9/10), 143–44.

[51] *Pervyi vserossiiskii torgovo-promyshlennyi s'ezd*, 143–46; and Drezena et al., eds., *Burzhuaziia i pomeshchiki*, 31–33, 46–47.

trial Gazette), which was written and edited by employees of the Ministry of Trade and Industry, appealed for concessions to labor: "The new government [and] the people's ministers must have their counterpart in a new [kind of] industry, moved by national and public sentiments and open to the aspirations of the workers."[52] Although the emphasis here was on the state's social rather than economic functions, demands and obligations were again balanced by promises of material rewards, as it was observed that enlightened legislation and a departure from "old prejudices" would produce a more orderly, even "peaceful" labor force.[53] Indeed, contributions to the *Commercial-Industrial Gazette* argued that the newspaper's recommendations had already been realized by a mature working class and a moderate socialist leadership. One writer praised the working class for having played a major role in the political revolution and returning to work on the following day, thus furnishing "a remarkable example of the power of internal discipline derived only from the free self-organization of the broad masses of workers [in] an industrial democracy."[54]

THAT such bold assertions and high-minded admonitions could be addressed to commercial-industrial circles and be expected to have an effect was a tribute to the impact the February revolution had had on the perceptions and self-perceptions of entrepreneurs as well as on the alignment of forces within and among entrepreneurial organizations. To be sure, even in the flush of self-congratulatory pride for their role in the revolution, old feelings of social

[52] "The New Government and Industry," *TPG*, March 10, 1917 (no. 50), 2.

[53] G. Kasperovich, "A Ministry of Labor"; B. Seliber, "Agreement between Workers and Employers"; A. Bykov, "The Future Ministry of Labor and Its Structure"; G. Gol'dberg, "The Organization of Labor"; and A. Bykov, "Industrial Courts," in *TPG*, March 7, 1917 (no. 47), 2; March 11, 1917 (no. 51), 2; March 15, 1917 (no. 54), 2; March 17, 1917 (no. 56), 2; and April 15, 1917 (no. 77), 2. Essentially the same promise was made by an engineer writing in a liberal newspaper: "The more the workers' desires are satisfied, the smaller the chances that they will turn from a peaceful mood to a hostile one": "Workers and Entrepreneurs," *RV*, March 8, 1917 (no. 53), 3.

[54] G. Gol'dberg, "The Organization of Labor," *TPG*, March 17, 1917 (no. 56), 2. See also B. Seliber, "Agreement between Workers and Employers"; A. Bykov, "Trade Unions" and "Conciliation Boards"; G. R., "The Soviet of Workers' and Soldiers' Deputies and the Labor Question"; and G. S., "The Revolution and the Working Class," in *TPG*, March 11, 1917 (no. 51), 2; March 21, 1917 (no. 59), 1; March 29, 1917 (no. 64), 1–2; April 9, 1917 (no. 72), 3; and April 14, 1917 (no. 76), 1; and M. I. Sirinov, "A Program for the Labor Question," *IzvTsVPK*, April 8, 1917 (no. 213), 2.

resentment and perhaps simple greed among entrepreneurs were engaged in battle with those of civic pride. The pressure from Konovalov's coalition of forward-looking industrialists and technical intelligentsia was most effective among the more modern, cosmopolitan entrepreneurs of the capital and the south, whereas among the more parochial merchantry of Moscow and the provinces as well as among the most privileged group of industrial and financial magnates of Petrograd, Konovalov's message often provoked the same sort of strong resentment that had been voiced from the earliest days of the revolution, though for a while this feeling had been overshadowed by the enthusiasm of industrial progressivism.

Leading the opposition to Konovalov's social program was his old ally, Riabushinskii. At the First Congress of Trade and Industry, which convened on March 19, he sought to exploit feelings of injured pride and resentment to rally commercial-industrial circles around his own positions: that the defense of the state required a united effort, which precluded the satisfaction of the demands of any single class, even that of the workers; that the commercial-industrial class had to stand "as a mighty wall" around the government to protect it from the pressure of the "elemental masses"; and that it was to the commercial-industrial class that belonged the task of "organizing the country's economy." The vision Riabushinskii offered his fellow merchants and entrepreneurs was again a contradictory one. He spoke of the "bourgeoisie" as the ascendant class, berated the old regime for suppressing private enterprise and personal freedom, and even quoted Engels to prove that capitalism was required in Russia before socialism could take effect. But he then turned from such expressions of a modern worldview to assertions that the state was the supreme "harmonizer" of social relations and that society was to organize itself in functional "unions" rather than political parties. Even in his more traditionalist arguments, Riabushinskii was a champion of the commercial-industrial class and assigned it the role of what might be termed the "state's class," a role similar to the historical one of the Russian service nobility.[55]

In Petrograd, too, there was opposition to imposing the demands of workers—the "passive," purely physical force in industry—on the "brains" of the economy (i.e., the entrepreneurs).[56]

[55] *Pervyi vserossiiskii torgovo-promyshlennyi s'ezd*, 7–19.
[56] *PiT*, April 15, 1917 (no. 12/13), 241–45.

Petrograd industrialists criticized social reforms in the name of a presumed "national" interest. They charged, for example, that a shorter workday would raise production costs, render Russian products uncompetitive on the international market, and so undermine the national economy.[57] More dubious, but doubtless effective in stirring up old hatreds and suspicions, was the allegation that the eight-hour workday would deprive the army of needed supplies.[58] The new measure of national responsibility was used by some to claim for the commercial-industrial class the right to define national goals and determine "correct" behavior for all classes.

In March and April, these voices of commercial-industrial belligerence were largely isolated and ineffectual, at least in Petrograd, largely as a result of a temporary shift in commercial-industrial circles. With the collapse of the autocracy, the magnates of the metalprocessing industry and the banks that had financed their operations lost confidence and strength. The more progressive members of the Petrograd Society of Industrialists (PSI), who gained in prestige and support when Konovalov took over the Ministry of Trade and Industry, ousted the society's old leadership and elected a provisional committee.[59] Also indicative of this shift in forces, though less significant, was the decision of the SSPPiT to name N. N. Kutler its new chairman. This decision ended an

[57] FO, March 18, 1917 (no. 9/10), 4–6, and March 29, 1917 (no. 11/12), 5–6; IzvSSPPiT, April 23, 1917 (no. 3), 1; and PiT, April 29, 1917 (no. 14/15), 265–69.

[58] Evidence from state agencies and entrepreneurial organizations suggests that in June 1917 the army still had enough munitions for six months of fighting. See, for example, ZhOS, July 1, 1917, 174, and "The Tasks of Our Association," PiT, June 24, 1917 (no. 22/23).

[59] The only direct evidence of this change comes from Shliapnikov, Semnadtsatyi god 2:126, but it is corroborated by frequent references to the provisional committee in March. On April 15, a general assembly of the PSI elected a new chairman, A. A. Bachmanov, and five other committee members and adopted new regulations: PiT, April 29, 1917 (no. 14/15), 293; and FO, 1917, no. 15:24. Evidence of disagreement among the membership of the PSI concerning labor policy had surfaced at the second congress of WICs, when the society's representative, B. A. Efron, under pressure to explain its opposition to conciliation boards, declared that it lacked the unanimity to make arbitration binding: Trudy vtorogo s'ezda predstavitelei voenno-promyshlennykh komitetov, 313–18, 552–53. During the summer of 1916, in spite of the PSI's official opposition to the labor program of the Central WIC, specific initiatives received support from individual owners in Petrograd as well as from the PSI's Commission on Workers' Lives and its Commission on Improving the Conditions of Workers in the Textile Industry; see IzvTsVPK, August 30, 1916 (no. 139), 3–4; September 10, 1916 (no. 143), 3–4; September 13, 1916 (no. 144), 2–3; and September 16, 1916 (no. 145), 3–4.

eighteen-month stalemate between the two main groups in the association: the Petrograd "oligarchy" and the more dynamic group of engineer-managers from the south to which Kutler belonged. The southern managers had worked closely with Konovalov in the Central WIC and shared his optimism and activist approach even if they remained doubtful about his social vision.[60]

In the country as a whole, the opponents of social and economic reform were divided by the traditional rivalry between Moscow's aggressive merchant-entrepreneurs and the Petrograd oligarchy and weakened by the parochialism of their largest source of support, the provincial merchantry.[61] In contrast, Konovalov and his ministry served as a rallying point of sorts for those who saw the revolution both as a source of economic and political opportunity for the commercial-industrial class and as the origin of certain duties and obligations.

In addition to the influences of such structural changes as the revolution had brought and of the social rivalries that had survived from past decades, the attitudes of the commercial-industrial circles were affected by the dynamics of the revolution. The peculiar manner in which the revolution created great hopes for the future and combined them with the compelling realities of the moment predisposed the majority of entrepreneurs in Petrograd, the south, and many provincial centers to accept the sacrifices urged on them by Konovalov and his colleagues. The revolution had created a sense of confidence and pride among the men of business: the bourgeoisie's long-standing contribution to the nation had finally been recognized; its leading representatives were now ministers of the state, in charge of all economic agencies; the Provisional Government was its own ("our regime," Riabushinskii called it); and the socialists did not even attempt to claim a share in state power. In short, the entrepreneurial interest was well represented.[62]

[60] In early March, the SSPPiT decided to entrust the preparation of a labor reform to the more neutral WICs, a concession which Konovalov immediately seized on; see the minutes of the SSPPiT meetings of March 5 and 9, as cited in Volobuev, "Politika burzhuazii," 128–29.

[61] These limitations were manifested at the First Congress of Trade and Industry in the absence of the Petrograd oligarchy and the tendency of provincial merchants to concentrate on specific local issues. The men from the provinces complained that Riabushinskii's political platform did not take their dependence on the peasantry into account. *Pervyi vserossiiskii torgovo-promyshlennyi s'ezd*, 51–58, 78–119, 136–38.

[62] *Financial Life* described a gala meeting held in Petrograd on March 3 in honor of the three ministers from the WICs as a gathering of people who "for centuries

But the revolution had also brought about a dramatic change in the balance of industrial forces. Workers were now free to organize and strike, and employers had lost the protection of the police and the army.[63] Sometimes, concessions to labor's demands were made under the impression of the workers' superior power. In Moscow and a number of provincial towns, for instance, entrepreneurs were forced to accept the principle of the eight-hour workday after local soviets had decreed the measure, because from the entrepreneurs' point of view it was the only way to end several prolonged strikes.[64]

In other instances, it was the adverse impact that industrial conflict could have on the perceived national interest at this crucial moment in the revolution and war that compelled industrialists to make unprecedented concessions or at the very least provided a way to rationalize painful material losses. It was in these terms that the Omsk Exchange Society attempted to prevail on its members to accept the need to satisfy their workers' demands:

Taking into account that at the present time . . . many enterprises work exclusively for national defense . . . the Omsk Stock-Exchange Committee . . . turns to all the entrepreneurs of the town and region with the earnest request [that they] adopt the conditions worked out by the Omsk Soviet

had borne the responsibility for a national industry and commerce": *FZh*, March 16, 1917 (no. 11), 165–66. V. I. Timiriazev, speaking at the same meeting on behalf of the Association of Commercial and Agricultural Exchanges, expressed gratitude to the new ministers, whom he called "the sons of commercial-industrial Russia," for the "incomparable deed [of replacing the tsarist government], so simply yet so grandly accomplished." Similar sentiments were expressed by others, together representing all of the important industrial organizations in Russia; see *IzvTsVPK*, March 13, 1917 (no. 208), 2–3; *TPG*, March 9, 1917 (no. 49), 3–4; and *VVP*, March 10, 1917 (no. 5), 2–3.

[63] At a meeting of industrial leaders with Konovalov on March 16, Efron of the PSI insisted that the industrialists' concessions were only "temporary," made necessary "for the purpose of establishing order in the labor situation of the capital": *RD posle sverzheniia samoderzhaviia*, 438.

[64] On the events in Moscow, see Miller and Pankratova, eds., *Rabochee dvizhenie v 1917 godu*, 44–47; *EPR* 1:159–61; Laverychev, *Po to storonu barikad*, 183, 232; and Volobuev, *Proletariat i burzhuaziia*, 161, 175. Soviets in other cities and towns followed the example of Moscow either because the industrialists put up strong opposition to the eight-hour demand or more often because there was no industrial organization with which to negotiate. For an example of the former, see the reports from Saratov in *RG*, March 26, 1917 (no. 17), 4, and *Pravda*, March 28, 1917 (no. 18), 4. For an example of the latter, see the accounts of events in Kazan in Miller and Pankratova, eds., *Rabochee dvizhenie v 1917 godu*, 49; and in Denike, "Men'sheviki v 1917 godu," 12–13, 22, and interview no. 8, pp. 24–26, both in the archives of the Project on Menshevik History.

of Workers' and Soldiers' Deputies on March 4 for the introduction of . . . an eight-hour working day. . . .

The committee believes that the industrialists would rather sacrifice a part of their interests and not be guilty of aggravating the class struggle at this exceptionally important historical moment.[65]

The patriotic argument carried particular weight in those provinces where the war had been the cause of intensified economic activity. However, many other entrepreneurs recognized that "only social peace could save both industry and the state," as S. S. Novoselov, chairman of the Society of Leather Manufacturers, put it.[66] Similar thinking guided the organized mineowners of the Donbas when they agreed, in a joint conference with their workers in Kharkov in late March, to the eight-hour workday and wage increases and offered to improve living conditions with the proviso that a network of conciliation boards would be established to handle all labor conflicts.[67]

This stipulation underscores an important aspect of industrial relations in early 1917: a readiness to accept arbitration of disputes with workers. The industrialists had not deluded themselves that industrial strife would disappear as a result, but many of them were willing to test Konovalov's premise that it could be contained within "familiar frameworks."[68] Faced with new and unfamiliar conditions of industrial employment, employers were more willing than they might have been in normal times to comfort themselves with Konovalov's vision of a "Europeanized" Russian in-

[65] *RD posle sverzheniia samoderzhaviia,* 50. That the position expressed by the Omsk Exchange enjoyed wide support in commercial-industrial circles is evident from the election of A. A. Skorokhodov of the Omsk Exchange Society to the Permanent Council of the All-Russian Union of Trade and Industry during its first congress: Rieber, *Merchants and Entrepreneurs in Imperial Russia,* 386.

[66] *VVOKZ,* May 15, 1917 (no. 32), 199–200. This newspaper, published biweekly by the Society of Leather Manufacturers, reported regularly and approvingly on the work of Konovalov's advisory committee on labor legislation and the Central Conciliation Board; see, e.g., *VVOKZ,* May 1, 1917 (no. 31), 192; May 15, 1917 (no. 32), 222–23; and June 15, 1917 (no. 33/34), 269.

[67] *Konferentsii rabochikh,* 61–64. At a meeting of the heads of industrial organizations with Konovalov, N. F. fon Ditmar of the Association of Southern Mineowners stressed that social peace was essential for economic recovery: *FO,* March 29, 1917 (no. 11/12), 7–8.

[68] From a June 1916 article by Konovalov, cited in "K istorii 'Rabochei gruppy,' " 76. In this article, Konovalov argued that "European experience" had shown that the general level of "civic consciousness and responsibility" could be raised "by raising the cultural level of workers and turning the formless mass of individual workers into an organized, public-minded, productive class."

93

dustry: a free capitalist economy complemented by an organized, moderate working class. It was repeatedly urged upon them that the establishment of labor organizations was not a concession to socialist pressures but a measure for the general welfare of the country as much as for themselves.[69]

Nowhere was acceptance of this message as evident as in Petrograd, where it exercised a direct influence on the political leaderships of both the bourgeois and the democratic forces. Only a few days after the provisional committee of the PSI had been created, it issued a statement of willingness to pay workers for time spent in "revolutionary" strikes, and on March 9, it then invited the Petrograd Soviet of Workers' and Soldiers' Deputies to send representatives to negotiate new working conditions for all the city's workers.[70] An agreement reached between the two organizations on March 10 provided for the institution of an eight-hour workday with no reduction in pay and the establishment of workers' committees and conciliation boards in all of the capital's factories.[71] Thus, the agreement provided for all of the reforms the PSI had so vehemently opposed throughout 1916. A few days later, a meeting of three hundred owners of Petrograd's largest factories unanimously approved the actions of the provisional committee and agreed to pay time-and-a-half for all work done in excess of eight hours a day.[72] It would seem, then, that the "new spirit" within and without the PSI forced even the members of the Association of Metalprocessing Industries, owners of the largest factories in Petrograd, to accept in fact, if not in principle, important elements of Konovalov's labor program.

The provisional committee of the PSI interpreted its agreement

[69] See, for example, "The Labor Questions," *FZh*, March 9, 1917 (no. 9/10), 144–45, and the articles in *TPG* cited in n. 53 above. At a meeting of Mensheviks from Vyborg factories, it was reported that wage demands were at least partially satisfied whenever they were submitted through factory committees: *RG*, March 17, 1917 (no. 10), 3.

[70] *FZh*, March 9, 1917 (No. 9/10), 144–45; *IzvPS*, March 10, 1917 (no. 11), 3; *Petrogradskii sovet*, 31.

[71] *IzvPS*, March 10, 1917 (no. 11), 1. At the same time, the PSI entrusted a commission with preparing a program for the "regulation and improvement of working conditions in Petrograd's factories": ibid. For examples of workers' success in obtaining similar concessions from employers outside Petrograd, see the reports from Odessa, Nizhnii Novgorod, Kharkov, Nikolaev, Iaroslavl, Simferopol, Saratov, Rostov, Perm, and Ekaterinburg, in *RG*, March 21, 26, 28, 29, and 31, 1917 (nos. 13, 17, 18, 19, and 21); and Miller and Pankratova, eds., *Rabochee dvizhenie v 1917 godu*, 48–49.

[72] *TPG*, March 16, 1917 (no. 55), 3.

with the soviet in the progressist spirit: "The eight-hour workday has been established as one of the best ways of ensuring the further spiritual growth of the working class. It will allow workers time for self-education and the development of professional organizations whose goal must be the establishment of correct, orderly relations between labor and capital." The committee was not purely idealistic; it admitted that the adoption of the eight-hour principle was predicated on the assumption of higher productivity as well as on the workers' readiness to work overtime. But its commitment to the new principles was demonstrated in its simultaneous warning to industrialists that any arrangement for overtime work must have the consent of the factory committees, to which proof must be shown of the necessity for the work.[73] A few days later, the committee informed owners of their obligation to pay workers for time spent in the activities of the soviets, trade unions, and factory committees.[74]

Further signs of a conciliatory mood can be seen not only in the actions of the provisional committee but also among the professional sections and the member factories of the PSI, as well as among the owners of small shops not active in the society. The Leather and Footwear Section, which met on March 17 to elect four representatives to a Central Conciliation Board about to be formed in Petrograd, recommended that they, and all leather manufacturers, pay "special attention" to the workers' requests that they make compromises "whenever possible."[75] On March 14, employers in the woodfinishing industry (probably small owners unaffected by the March 10 agreement) agreed to institute the eight-hour day and to settle wage disputes through a conciliation board. On the same day, at the Frolik factory, the employer's representatives to the conciliation board agreed to pay workers for days lost during the "revolutionary" strike and for time spent in labor organizing, and they promised a 100 percent wage increase (125 percent for female workers) beginning on April 1 (but retroactive to March) if production delays were corrected by then.[76]

The turn to arbitration, which was the mark of entrepreneurial response to labor conflicts all over Russia during the first two months of the revolution, derived as much from the hopes raised by the revolution as from the urgent needs it created or the limits

[73] Circular no. 247 (March 14, 1917), in *EPR* 1:511–13.

[74] Circular no. 293, cited in "Petrogradskaia krupnaia burzhuaziia," 55.

[75] *VVOKZ*, May 1, 1917 (no. 31), 192.

[76] *RG*, March 15, 1917 (no. 8), 3, and March 17, 1917 (no. 10), 2–3.

it placed on the arbitrary power of employers. Most entrepreneurs found little to dampen their optimism or lessen their new sense of civic responsibility during the early weeks of the revolution. When the first issue of the PSI's newspaper appeared on June 1, the lead editorial declared that Russia had just entered the capitalist stage, and it was incumbent on Russian industrialists to adjust to life under these new conditions. "We don't shut our eyes to the inevitable class struggle; but now, it can, and must, proceed under normal conditions. . . . We believe that *the free citizen-industrialist and the free citizen-worker will find a common language in which to communicate [and] will find normal forms of mutual relations.*"[77]

If the industrialists could be so confident yet ready to adjust, it was because the workers, though far less optimistic than their employers, had demonstrated no less moderation during most of March and April than the men on the other side of the barricade. Moreover, the workers' behavior seemed to indicate a readiness to accept the limits of a bourgeois revolution—that is, to recognize the principles of private enterprise and proprietary prerogatives as well as the primacy of production over all other considerations.

THE WORKERS' MODERATION

The curious dualism that characterized the workers' behavior during the early part of 1917—their determination to pursue what they considered to be rightful demands and their self-restraint and concern for the continuation and even improvement of production, especially in defense-related enterprises—was not the same everywhere. As Steven Smith has shown, workers in Petrograd engaged in a variety of collective actions: factory committees in state-owned enterprises were considerably ahead of their private-industry counterparts in practicing self-management and control; women were more likely to insist on a literal implementation of the eight-hour workday than men; and whereas the well-organized, skilled workers in large and medium factories were generally patient and measured in advancing their demands, the generally unorganized, inexperienced, and poorly paid workers of low skill lurched from aggression to resignation and back to aggression.[78]

[77] As quoted in Shatilova, "Petrogradskaia krupnaia burzhuaziia," 50–51 (emphasis in the original).

[78] Smith, *Red Petrograd*, 60–73. The distinctions drawn by Smith for the Petrograd working class of 1917 are not unfamiliar to historians of Russian labor and roughly conform to the distinctions drawn by the Social Democratic leaders of the labor

All these variations notwithstanding, moderation appears to have been the norm among workers in labor conflicts, in their daily work at the factory, and in regard to those of their demands that could affect production.

The majority of workers responded to their leaders' appeals and submitted their cases to arbitration however strongly they may have resented the delay involved.[79] The case of the wage demands of workers in the Skorokhod shoe factory in Petrograd is a good example of the hesitancy of most workers to carry their struggle to its potential limits. The administration's rejection of a 100 percent wage increase and other improvements for these poorly paid workers resulted in a confrontation between five hundred angry workers and the director of the factory on March 20, yet the workers had remained at their jobs since March 10, when they had submitted the issue to arbitration, and only one-sixth of them participated in the confrontation. As a result of the confrontation, the PSI advised the director to accept all the workers' demands.[80]

Other signs of the workers' concern for the proper functioning of the factories were the prompt resumption of normal production and the reports of rising labor productivity. In April, state agencies reported normal or above-normal production in the Ural mining region and in Petrograd, and the PSI itself reported that all of the factories on which it had information were working "regularly."[81]

movement at the time. Although the latter used "consciousness" as their conceptual yardstick, they often in practice based their categories on the skill, urbanity, and organization of the workers.

[79] A typical workers' resolution, that at the I. G. Kebke sailcloth factory, was to accept a partial satisfaction of their wage demands and allow the executive committee of the soviet to negotiate for a citywide argeement with the PSI: *IzvPS*, March 29, 1917 (no. 26), 7. On April 14, a group of workers who described their working conditions as "horrible" nonetheless appealed to the Central Conciliation Board to arbitrate their complaints: *RD v aprele*, 378.

[80] *RD posle sverzheniia samoderzhaviia*, 490–91; Mandel, "Development of Revolutionary Consciousness," 179–80.

[81] *FO*, 1917, no. 15:22, 24; *TPG*, April 14, 1917 (no. 76), 2. Even where productivity declined, most observers agreed that it was not the workers' fault. The first report of the Committee for a Normal Course of Work (whose establishment by the Union of Engineers in early April indicated some concern with low productivity) blamed the decline in production in several important factories on shortages of raw materials; in two other cases, it cited poor management; in only one case did the committee cite "a poor understanding of the importance of the moment" and low wages among women workers. The report also listed six factories in which production was continuing "exceptionally well." *TPG*, April 11, 1917 (no. 73), 2. A much-publicized exception to this rule was the survey conducted by the Ministry of Trade and Industry in seventy-five of Petrograd's large factories (with five hundred or

Indeed, during the summer months of 1917, entrepreneurs and others who watched economic developments closely would speak wistfully of the brief period in March and April when labor productivity and factory output had been on the rise, promoting hopes that the economic crisis that had struck the country on the eve of the February revolution might be ending.[82]

Signs of moderation could be found even in the way workers tried to obtain their most cherished demands as well as those that were clearly "political" in intent or affected the structure of relations in the factory. Workers were generally ready to forgo strict implementation of the eight-hour workday as long as their right to shorter hours was recognized in principle and higher rates were paid for overtime work.[83] Thus, for example, the highly organized workers of the Donbas mining region declared at a conference with their employers that the institution of the eight-hour workday was, for them, a "tactical demand" and that under the new conditions of freedom they would perform any overtime work needed "for the welfare of the country," provided they were paid at time-and-a-half of their regular rates.[84]

more workers), which altogether employed about 55 percent of all factory workers in the capital. The survey showed that in textile and food-processing factories, production between March 10 and 24 was 20 to 30 percent lower than in a two-week period in January, and that in metalprocessing factories the decline had reached as much as 60 percent: *TPG*, April 25, 1917 (no. 84), 2. These figures were repeated in *IzvSSPPiT*, May 3, 1917 (no. 4), 2; and *IzvMVPK*, 1917, no. 35:15. M. Tugan-Baranovskii, an economist and author of the major study, *The Russian Factory*, commented that he found the results reassuring, because in twenty-one of the factories the decline could be shown to be the result of shortages in raw materials and the decline in the fifty-four other factories could be explained either by the shorter workday or by the revolution's generally unsettling effects. He viewed the figures as disproving the widespread belief that the Russian worker disliked labor. *IzvMVPK*, 1917, no. 35:15.

[82] At a meeting devoted to criticism of socialists and workers in August 1917, Bublikov spoke wistfully of how railroad workers had worked "with uncommon energy" during the first two weeks of the revolution: *Otchet o moskovskom soveshchanii*, 94–97. Reporting to Konovalov on the agreement reached between Donbas mineowners and workers, fon Ditmar complained about the financial burden but noted with satisfaction that productivity had improved: *FO*, April 22, 1917 (no. 13/14), 17–18. Later, he stated that production had been higher between January and April 1917 than during the corresponding months of 1916: *FG*, August 12, 1917 (no. 476), 8–10. P. I. Pal'chinskii made the same point at a meeting of the Special Conference on Defense, noting that coal production in the Donbas for April 1917 was two million puds higher than that of April 1916: *ZhOS*, 585–86.

[83] Volobuev concedes that in the resolution of "almost all soviets and the majority of workers' assemblies" overtime work was specified for the duration of the war: *Proletariat i burzhuaziia*, 123.

[84] *Konferentsii rabochikh*, 63–64.

Some of the workers' demands could adversely affect production and cause alarm among industrialists, particularly the frequent insistence that foremen and management representatives unacceptable to the workers be removed from the factory. Spontaneous "purges" of personnel in the first days of March had eliminated forty management representatives from the Putilov works and fifty from the Treugol'nik plant. Dismissals were especially numerous in state-owned enterprises and railroads where management was directly connected to the old regime.[85] However, the workers' own factory committees, which held themselves responsible for the workers' conduct and for productivity, opposed any tide of forceful evictions of hated personnel. "Let us not give rise to the charge that tsarist tyranny has been replaced with the tyranny of the proletariat," the Aivaz factory committee urged the workers.[86] The twenty-five members of the Putilov factory committee who described their attempts to conduct an orderly "purge" to a delegation of the executive committee assured the delegation of the workers' "discipline" and their readiness to submit to the factory committee.[87]

Indeed, recent studies have shown that, during these early weeks, the factory committees acted as instruments of moderation and responsibility and urged workers both to await the outcomes of arbitration procedures and to work harder to increase productivity.[88] Moreover, with the exception of state-owned enterprises in the defense industries, this concern for orderly production did not as yet involve the demand for the right of *kontrol'* over production, which would become increasingly attached to it after May 1917. What mattered most to the workers was the creation of their own autonomous entity within the factory walls, which would serve both to strengthen their unity and to secure their welfare and rights vis-à-vis their employer.[89] Thus, the right to *kontrol'*,

[85] Volobuev, *Proletariat i burzhuaziia*, 140, and Pushkareva, *Zheleznodorozhniki Rossii*, 336–37.

[86] *RG*, March 22, 1917 (no. 14), 4.

[87] *RG*, March 26, 1917 (no. 17), 4. Factory committees often made themselves the guardians of productivity. The Porokhov district soviet, acting as a factory committee of the large Okhta gunpowder mill and explosives factory, declared that workers found drunk or absent from work would be sent to the army: *Raionnye sovety Petrograda* 3:185–86. For other examples, see *RG*, March 17, 1917 (no. 10), 3, and March 31, 1917 (no. 21), 3.

[88] See esp. Smith, *Red Petrograd*, chap. 4.

[89] In a call to the workers of the Putilov plant to organize shop committees, the factory committee emphasized the value of having the workers' practice "initia-

when asserted in privately owned enterprises, was applied almost exclusively to matters concerning hiring and firing.[90]

A telling example of how workers understood the functions of their factory committees is found in the statement of intentions issued by the provisional factory committee of the Radio-Telegraph factory of the Navy Department, a state-owned enterprise but one in which Menshevik Defensist workers predominated. The task of the committee, the statement read, was to "work out norms and principles for the *internal life of the factory*." "Internal life" was defined to include conditions of employment (the length of the working day and wages); the workers' general welfare (labor insurance, medical aid, mutual aid funds, and food supplies); the workers' relations with their employer (hiring, dismissals, and labor conflicts); the workers' autonomous organization ("rights, duties, elections"); and measures to ensure orderly production (labor discipline, security measures).[91] Although the assumption that only their own autonomous organizations could secure their welfare testified to the workers' deep suspicion of their employers, the committee's activity, as defined here, did not directly challenge managerial authority.

Doubtless, the seeds of future conflicts were being sown. Even the careful definition adopted by the workers of the Radio-Telegraph factory posited some degree of responsibility for the factory's productivity, so they had unwittingly prepared themselves to invoke the right of *kontrol'* over production. In other state-owned enterprises (and railroads), cases were reported of workers actually taking over production, though they insisted that the takeover was temporary, until the new regime named directors and managers to replace the former servitors of the tsar.[92] Still, generally

---

tive," "autonomous activity" (*samodeiatel'nost'*), and "self-government" (*samoupravlenie*). (*RD v aprele*, p. 418).

[90] *RD v aprele*, 343, 353, 419–20.

[91] *RD posle sverzheniia samoderzhaviia*, 491–92 (emphasis added). See also similar resolutions adopted by the Petrograd cartridge factory and the Putilov factory: ibid., 358–60, 417–18. The factory committee of the 1886 Electrical Light Company set up three commissions charged with attending to food, the militia, and "internal order"; the last of these organized work in accordance with managerial directives: Amosov et al., eds., *Oktiabr'skaia revoliutsiia* 1:47–48.

[92] At the Petrograd cartridge factory of the Artillery Department, a provisional factory committee exercised managerial authority from March 8 to 30, at which time it returned all responsibility to the newly appointed director, Major General Doronin: *RD v aprele*, 575–77. See also Pushkareva, *Zheleznodorozhniki Rossii*, 338–40; and Taniaev, *Ocherki dvizheniia zheleznodorozhnikov*, 53.

speaking, it was labor moderation that prevailed. In fact, a reluctance to take over management's functions was in evidence everywhere, even in state-owned enterprises. When representatives from all state-owned enterprises in Petrograd met on April 15 to issue regulations for the workers' committees in their factories, the emphasis was again on matters pertaining to "internal order." Although committees were also expected to monitor the activity of the factory management "in the administrative, economic, and technical spheres," this was to be achieved by assigning committee members to merely advisory roles in the various sections of the administration, with specific instructions not to assume "responsibility for the technical and administrative organization of production."[93]

Workers continued to refrain from the conflicts that outright *kontrol'* would have provoked even as new factors began to affect their attitudes toward the employers and their definition of the committees' functions. Beginning at the end of March, and increasingly in April, shortages of fuel and raw materials hampered production in many factories and threatened industry with work stoppages. At the same time, the nonsocialist press was carrying on a campaign of vilification against the soviet, the workers, and their "excessive" demands. In response, some factory committees demanded the right to inspect financial and supply records to verify an owner's claimed inability to operate at full capacity, though more commonly they would ask the Soviet to conduct such inspections in their behalf.[94] But most workers did not resort to even this milder form of *kontrol'*. Instead, they were likely to express concern about production and to declare their faith in the soviet's power to correct the situation. Thus, a resolution adopted by the general assembly of Novyi Parviainen, a machine-building factory in the Vyborg district, affirmed the workers' commitment to "full production" and pointed out that general economic problems, especially shortages of raw material, constituted a "substantial obstacle" to this goal; but it concluded by expressing the workers' hope

[93] *RD v aprele*, 383–86.
[94] See, for example, the resolutions adopted by a workers' assembly in the I. G. Kebke sailcloth factory and by the committee of the Petrograd railcar factory, in *RD v aprele*, 342, 346. A resolution at the Nevskii shipbuilding and machine-building factory that insisted on the committee's right to respond to workers' reports of falling productivity with *"kontrol'* over the course of work" in the factory was an exception even among state-owned factories producing for the war effort: ibid., 387.

that the Soviet of Workers' and Soldiers' Deputies "would give [these problems] the necessary attention and make appropriate recommendations."[95]

Again, what is most striking about even these examples of "intervention" is the workers' moderation, concern for order, and readiness to accept the authority of both a rehabilitated management and the soviet. Most significant, the workers' commitment to productivity during March and April did not usually lead to interference in management's sphere of competence or to *kontrol'* over its practices and decisions. Insofar as there was a struggle in the factories at this early stage, it did not involve any attempt by workers to take over the functions of management, but rather the far less troublesome demand for autonomy. Thus, PSI chairman A. A. Bachmanov later stated that, at the beginning of their activity, the factory committees "had not provoked any protest" on the part of the industrialists.[96] Indeed, the workers' definition of their committees' authority corresponded closely to the sentiment expressed at a meeting of the Association of Ural Mining Industries held in Petrograd on March 9, at which the mineowners declared themselves prepared "to meet any of the demands of the workers in regard to their organization. . . . but under no circumstances to allow intervention in the management of the factory."[97]

THE MODERATION shown by workers during the first two months of the February revolution has yet to be fully explained or even adequately acknowledged. The workers' restraint in realizing their goals contrasted sharply with their view of these goals as an integral result of their having made the resolution. This contrast was a consequence of a basic ambivalence that characterized the workers' attitudes: suspicion of the propertied classes and hope for an accommodation with them, a sense of the revolution as something of their own making and an equally deep appreciation for the role the soldiers had played in it.

In the first days of the revolution, when the workers were still confused about questions of political power, their sentiments had been expressed in terms of self-defense. Their feverish activity to organize themselves in factories and working-class districts was conducted under the slogan "the working class must organize it-

[95] *RG*, March 26, 1917 (no. 17), 4.
[96] Volobuev, *Proletariat i burzhuaziia*, 175.
[97] *RD posle sverzheniia samoderzhaviia*, 479–80.

self for the defense of its class interests," and it had sprung from a deep suspicion of the propertied classes and a strong resolve not to be overpowered by them. Even so, the workers did not seem willing to shoulder the task of establishing their own, defiant proletarian government. Their reluctance derived not only from a sense of disorganization and unpreparedness, which the workers shared with their leaders, but also from an overriding concern with the achievement of the broadest possible support for the revolution.[98] Thus, the workers' urge to achieve full citizenship and dignity through changes in the structure of human relations within the factory conflicted with the fear of being rebuffed and isolated by the bourgeoisie and with an almost desperate search for unity with the soldiers, whom they saw as their natural allies.[99] Even the most proletarian of the soviets, that of the Vyborg district, urged workers to end their strikes and "all violent acts" against management lest they "play into the hands of the old regime and its evil forces."[100]

That the workers' desire for accommodation with the propertied classes and unity with the soldiers acted powerfully to impose restraint upon them became clear during the last days in March, when it seemed that the campaign against the soviet that was being waged in the nonsocialist press and by Duma deputies touring the front might turn the soldiers against the workers.[101] Workers announced not only their intention to work "at full strength" but also their condemnation of any "negligence or excessive wage demands," and they resolved to increase production and "to sacrifice as much of our time to work as is necessary."[102] The socialist press was filled with similar resolutions.[103]

[98] Koenker, *Moscow Workers and the 1917 Revolution*, 107, says that "it was the lack of any feeling of great urgency and the need above all for revolutionary unity which characterized this first period of the revolution."

[99] One resolution typical of the time declared that "the revolutionary struggle was not over yet," so it was necessary "to have a strong and durable organization of the whole working class *and* the revolutionary army": *Pravda*, March 14, 1917 (no. 8), 3 (emphasis added).

[100] *RG*, March 18, 1917 (no. 11), 3.

[101] This episode will be discussed at greater length in chap. 4. See also Wildman, *Russian Imperial Army*, 291–320.

[102] *IzvPS*, March 25, 1917 (no. 24), 7, and March 31, 1917 (no. 29), 6.

[103] See, for example, *RG*, March 26, 1917 (no. 17), 4; March 31, 1917 (no. 21), 3; April 6, 1917 (no. 24), 3, as well as the column, "Workers and Soldiers," that was published in all of the issues of *RG* from March 31 to April 10. Also see *IzvPS*, March 22, 1917 (no. 21), 6; March 29, 1917 (no. 27), 7; March 30, 1917 (no. 28), 3;

Although these resolutions usually made reference to the army's need for munitions, what moved the workers to make the extra effort was not so much the prospect of national victory in the war as the fear of alienating their soldier comrades, especially those at the front, whose deputations appeared daily before the soviet to urge its leaders to support the war effort and keep the workers at their benches. For example, seventeen hundred workers at the railcar department of the Putilov works responded to the critical attacks on the soviet with a vow to work through the Easter holiday to prove the "provocation" wrong.[104] If these attacks deepened the suspicion workers had entertained from the outset toward their employers and the propertied groups in general, their impact was, at least for a while, to increase workers' determination to avoid a rift with the soldiers and prevent the isolation of the soviet. The fear of estrangement was much greater among the workers because they could more easily detect the hand of the bourgeoisie behind the antisoviet campaign than could the less experienced peasant-soldiers.

While fears of isolation were paramount during the first month or so of the revolution, there was another, increasingly strong attitude among workers that also mandated caution and restraint. The workers felt great pride and solidarity with the soviet, and these feelings were used by the socialist leadership to urge moderation on the workers. The desire to be a part of this larger revolutionary collective compelled delegates from the factories of the Petrograd district to insist, even as they condemned the soviet's call to end the strike on March 6, that the workers of the capital "show class solidarity and submit to the Soviet of Workers' and Soldiers' Deputies by resuming work as soon as possible."[105]

The importance that the workers attributed to organizing and to uniting around the soviet was shared by the Menshevik leaders. For followers and leaders alike, the soviet represented a safeguard against the suspect propertied classes as well as an arena for the growth and political maturation of the working class. "On our re-

---

March 31, 1917 (no. 29), 5; and April 2, 1917 (no. 31), 6; *Pravda*, March 31, 1917 (no. 22), 4; and *Raionnye sovety Petrograda* 3:185–86.

[104] See *IzvPS*, March 31, 1917 (no. 29), 5, and similar resolutions in *RG*, March 31, 1917 (no. 21), 3; April 5, 1917 (no. 23), 2; April 6, 1917 (no. 24), 2, and April 28, 1917 (no. 42), 2–3; in *IzvPS*, March 30, 1917 (no. 28), 6; and in *RD v aprele*, 334, 336–37, 339.

[105] *RD posle sverzheniia samoderzhaviia*, 229–31.

turn to work," declared the workers of the Sestroretsk armament factory on March 9,

we call on all workers to follow the political events in the country and to be ready, at the first signal from the Soviet of Workers' and Soldiers' Deputies, to halt [work] again and undertake an active struggle for the realization of the goals and tasks of the Russian proletariat. At the same time, we call on all our comrade workers to begin the immediate establishment of labor organizations of every sort: political [organizations], professional unions, workers' clubs, etc.[106]

This point of view corresponded closely to that which the editors of the soviet's newspaper propounded just one day later, when they described the "latest victories" as "the first act in a long struggle" and called on workers to defend them, above all, through the construction of political parties, trade unions, and consumer associations.[107] To be sure, there is evidence here that workers entertained a vision of the immediate future that differed significantly from that informing the strategies of the Mensheviks on the executive committee. Whereas *Izvestiia* emphasized the defense of the gains already made, the Sestroretsk armament workers focused on the struggle for the realization of further gains; and through improvement of the workers' situation was not altogether absent from the Menshevik vision, it was perceived as a prolonged process. But such differences were as yet barely noticeable; meanwhile, the moderate leaders and their working-class constituency joined in a perception of unity.

Indeed, the premises on which the existence of the soviet and its relationship to the Provisional Government were based—separateness, autonomy, and conditional support, which were expressed in the arrangement of dual power and which secured the soviet's freedom to engage in organizational work and to exert pressure on the government of the propertied classes from without—these premises corresponded closely to the workers' own ambivalent feelings about the powerful, educated class of their employers.[108] After all, were not the socialist leaders in the soviet

---

[106] Ibid., 478.

[107] *IzvPS*, March 10, 1917 (no. 9), 2. An article in *RG*, March 10, 1917 (no. 4), 1, explained the purpose of professional unions as a means of raising the workers' consciousness and organization and in this way allowing them to match the strength of the employers.

[108] The following resolution, adopted by a meeting of ironsmiths employed in small shops on March 13, is typical of the workers' understanding of conditional support: "Support the government insofar as [*postol'ku, poskol'ku*] its measures

(self-proclaimed leaders, to be sure) handling the Provisional Government with the same mixture of suspicion and restraint that the workers in the factories practiced toward management? For this reason, the slogan, "Unite around One Revolutionary and Organizational Center—the Soviet of Workers' and Soldiers' Deputies," remained the most popular one among the workers of Petrograd throughout March and April.[109]

Moreover, as the employers' newly acquired willingness to make concessions became manifest in labor's tangible gains, the workers' patience with the soviet's mediation efforts grew, while the tensions that had accompanied their quest for unity with its leadership in early March began to disappear. Thus, within the context of dual power and with the help of a relatively successful labor struggle, many workers were able to reconcile their goal of human and political achievement with the perceived necessity (emphasized by the soviet's leaders) to accommodate other groups and classes in Russian society.

THE MENSHEVIKS AS MEDIATORS

It was only natural that the Menshevik leaders of the soviet should seek to take an active part in managing labor relations. As Social Democrats, they expected the revolution to improve the workers' lives, and they also feared that sharp labor conflicts could doom the whole revolutionary undertaking to defeat. Moreover, the Menshevik praktiki, possessed of long experience in the legal labor organizations, were dedicated to practical work among the workers. Gvozdev and Bogdanov, chairman and secretary respectively of the Labor Group of the Central WIC, put the group's secretarial staff at the disposal of the executive committee and set about to organize the committee's labor section. Both were Menshevik praktiki par excellence: Bogdanov, a labor organizer from the ranks of the intelligentsia as well as a contributor to the labor press; Gvozdev, an educated and Europeanized metalworker and a union leader. They were joined in the labor section by G. G. Pankov, a veteran organizer of workers' cooperative associations in Petrograd, and somewhat later by P. A. Garvi, formerly a member of the Petrograd Initiative Group, who had returned from exile

---

agree with the resolutions of the soviet, the revolutionary tribunal of Russia": *RG*, March 16, 1917 (no. 9), 4.

[109] Ibid.

in mid-March.[110] Under the leadership of these Menshevik praktiki, the soviet's labor section handled all aspects of labor relations
in the capital, at least until a ministry of labor (in which some of
the same men held high positions) was established in early May.[111]

From the outset, the major goal of the labor section was to prevent collisions between workers and industrialists. This goal was
adopted for somewhat different reasons by two different groups
of Mensheviks. On the one hand, there were the praktiki, men like
Pankov and Garvi, who believed that the workers' premature extremism, the extension of their struggle into the sphere of industrial relations, had been partly responsible for a counterrevolutionary backlash in 1905; they were anxious that this mistake not be
repeated. Their position was vividly expressed in an article in the
Menshevik newspaper *Rabochaia gazeta* (Workers' Newspaper):
"Remember 1905! . . . At the end of October 1905, the Soviet of
Workers' Deputies decided unilaterally to introduce a universal
eight-hour workday. And it did. But by November 6, this same soviet had been forced to revoke its earlier resolution. . . . The capitalists in Petrograd launched their policy of lockouts, closed their
factories, and left the workers exhausted . . . and isolated."[112] On
the other hand, there were the Mensheviks whose wartime work
in the public organizations—usually in the capacity of professionals, but in the cases of Bogdanov and Gvozdev as representatives
of members of the WICs, where they had become acquainted with
Konovalov—had led them to a vision of a progressive bourgeoisie
that would be willing to cooperate with the socialist leaders of the
workers to secure the country's transition to full democracy. The
fulfillment of this vision required that labor conflicts be curbed.

[110] *Petrogradskii sovet*, 31, and Sukhanov, *Zapiski o revoliutsii* 2:16, 22, 160. Sukhanov was elected to the section on March 9, but never visited its offices. For
biographical sketches and references to these four men, see Nikolaevskii and Bour-
gina, *Biographical Dictionary* (Project on Menshevik History); *Bol'shaia Sovetskaia Ent-
siklopediia* (Moscow, 1929), 14:746–47; Garvi, "Iz vospominanii o fevral'skoi revoliutsii," 48; Tsereteli, *Vospominaniia o fevral'skoi revoliutsii* 1:49; Sukhanov, *Zapiski o
revoliutsii* 2:16, 22; and Ascher, Introduction to Garvi, *Zapiski Sotsial Demokrata*. See
also appendix 3 of this book.

[111] Rarely did any labor issue come to the attention of the full executive committee. One notable exception in early March concerned disputes between the bakers
and the draymen, which threatened to leave the city without bread supplies; see
Petrogradskii sovet, 49, 68.

[112] "1905–1917," *RG*, March 9, 1917 (no. 3), 1 (emphasis in the original). During
the early weeks of the revolution, this position was similar to that of the Menshevik
Internationalists, whose attention was otherwise centered on questions of state
power and the war; see Sukhanov, *Zapiski o revoliutsii* 1:230 and 2:99, 184–85.

Whatever their motives for trying to avert an escalation of labor conflicts, the Mensheviks in the leadership of the soviet and its labor section initially used the same tactics: drawing the workers into larger organizational frameworks and using the prestige of such organizations, particularly that of the soviet, to press restraint on the workers. *Rabochaia gazeta* warned the workers of the dangers of failing to heed the soviet's authority: refusal to follow its directives—in this case, to end the strike that had begun during the February days—would "weaken the revolution . . . [and] weaken the power and authority of the great moving force behind the revolution—the Soviet of Workers' and Soldiers' Deputies."[113] The workers were urged to limit their demands to the introduction of the "principle of constitutional relations between workers and management"; in other words, to concentrate on organizational safeguards, even organizational autonomy, and to avoid economic demands.[114] Both *Rabochaia gazeta* and *Izvestiia* reminded the workers of the importance of organization and of acting in a manner that was "orderly" (*zakonomerno*) rather than "spontaneous" (*stikhiino*) or, worse yet, "coercive" (*zakhvatno*).[115]

The attitudes and conceptions that underlay these appeals to restraint and organization were fundamental to the Menshevik vision of revolution, which included not only the desire to avoid social and political polarization but also the hope, if not always the confidence, that involvement in open, democratically run organizations would educate the workers in mature, political action. Yet a conflict continued between the role the Menshevik praktiki performed as guardians of the precarious gains made by the revolution and the other self-assumed mission to which they had dedicated their best years and of which they were particularly proud: their championship of the working class and its interests.

By THE LATTER part of March, the Mensheviks appeared to have resolved the conflict in their revolutionary strategy as well as the

[113] "The Question of Resuming Work in the Factories in the Name of the Revolution," *RG* March 11, 1917 (no. 5), 2.

[114] "The Resumption of Work," *RG*, March 7, 1917 (no. 1), 2.

[115] See the labor section's admonition to the Langenzippen factory committee, in *RG*, March 19, 1917 (no. 12), 3 , and the articles on the merits of collective bargaining, labor exchanges, and labor organizations in *RG*—"Organize Trade Unions," March 10, 1917 (no. 4), 1, "The Great Victory of the Working Class," March 12, 1917 (no. 6), 1, and "The Struggle for the Eight-Hour Workday," March 14, 1917 (no. 7), 2; and in *IzvPS*—"Organize!" March 8, 1917 (no. 9), 2, and "The First Great Economic Victory" and "Collective Agreement," March 11, 1917 (no. 12), 1, 2.

confrontation it had created, however circumspect, between themselves and the workers. They came to accept the workers' economic demands as a legitimate and natural part of the revolution,
and they thus reversed their earlier rejection of such demands and
even defended them against attacks from the bourgeoisie. It was
then that the editors of *Rabochaia gazeta* admitted that a certain
amount of tension had existed in the early days of March between
the two tasks the Mensheviks had sought to accomplish:

Time and again we warned the workers against an unorganized economic
struggle. . . . We cautioned the workers against thoughtless steps; we
urged on them restraint and organization in the interests both of their
class and of the struggle for economic and political freedom being conducted by the proletariat.

But in making these comradely appeals we were also well aware of how
unavoidably disorganized and chaotic the struggle would be during this
early period. One has only to remember how the industrialists exploited
the helplessness of workers laboring under wartime regulations and
squeezed them of their remaining strength. . . . After having made a revolution, can one blame such workers for also wanting to attain a more
humane existence?[116]

It appears, then, that between roughly the second and fourth
weeks of March, there occurred a remarkable transformation in the
positions taken by the moderate leaders of the soviet in general
and the activists of the labor section in particular, in regard to both
their role and their opportunities in the new revolutionary situation. It was as though after an initial period of trial, tension, and
uneasiness, they had found a style of work with which they could
feel comfortable, found the proper way to combine the goal of improving the workers' lot with the task of mediating labor conflicts.
This change not only grew out of an urge to resolve the conflict
between their several tasks but also was a response to an entirely
new situation created by dual power and the realities of labor
relations.

The first indication of this new situation came on March 9, with
the previously mentioned invitation to the soviet from the PSI to
negotiate new working conditions for Petrograd's workers.[117] In
the aftermath of these negotiations, which were successful, the la-

[116] "The Attack against the Working Class," *RG*, March 31, 1917 (no. 21), 1.

[117] The soviet's representatives in the negotiations were Gvozdev and Pankov,
who promised to use the soviet's authority against the "coercive introduction [by
workers] of reforms in factory life": cited from the newspaper of the PSI for March
10, 1917, in Volobuev, *Proletariat i burzhuaziia*, 107.

bor section found its mediation services in great demand among both workers and employers, and its members threw themselves into this unfamiliar work with great energy. Even Sukhanov, who was not a supporter of the moderate Mensheviks, spoke admiringly of how they "labored in the sweat of their brow, between the hammer and the anvil [sic] . . . worked out the terms of labor agreements and resolved conflicts and endlessly tedious disagreements."[118]

Articles in the contemporary press leave no doubt that the efforts of the praktiki contributed significantly to the atmosphere of conciliation in the factories. The following report from the Frolik plant is quite typical:

The conflict in our factory was resolved by a conciliation board assembled with the help of the labor section of the Soviet of Workers' and Soldiers' Deputies. On March 14, the board held a meeting which issued the following directives:
1. On the question of being paid for the days of revolution: It was decided that the owner will pay [each worker] the average daily pay for six days.
2. On the question of raising wages for men by 100 percent and for women by 125 percent: It was determined to leave the discussion of this question in abeyance until March 31; to take the most decisive measures to ease the pressure of [the backlog of] orders; and, in the event that these measures succeed, to pay all workers the additional sum as of March 1.
3. On the question of payment to workers who have organizational responsibilities: It was decided that the owner will pay these workers for the time that they are away from work.[119]

If at first the praktiki simply reacted to urgent situations as they arose—visiting factories where the workers had been unable to secure their demands, helping them to get organized, and setting up conciliation boards—by the end of March their role in the labor arena had become more regularized, even institutionalized.[120] The labor section was by then a crucial link in the economic life of the war-torn country; as the industrialists themselves acknowledged, it was contributing greatly to the restoration of normal produc-

---

[118] Sukhanov, *Zapiski o revoliutsii* 2:160.

[119] *RG*, March 15, 1917 (no. 8), 3.

[120] On March 26, the labor section announced that the executive committee was organizing a Central Conciliation Board to take care of any unresolved conflicts. Every Petrograd factory was asked whether it had a conciliation board, whether there was a conflict in the factory at present, and if so, what its source was. *IzvPS*, March 26, 1917 (no. 25), 3.

tion.[121] Similarly, reports of resolved conflicts coming from the workers of one or another factory often contained expressions of gratitude to the labor section. For example, the workers of the Petrov machine-building factory wrote to *Rabochaia gazeta* that not until a representative of the soviet had come to the factory and organized elections to a factory committee and a conciliation board had their employer agreed to change his "pharaoh-like" treatment of them.[122]

The emphasis of this last report, and that of many others at the time, was on the gains made by the workers as a result of the soviet's intervention. The activists of the labor section, carried forward by the momentum of early victories, had apparently begun to expand their role. No longer were they content to serve merely as mediators between labor and capital to facilitate orderly production and greater social peacefulness; they were now intent on also serving as the advocates of the workers' needs and demands, and they would do so no less effectively. Perhaps the most dramatic demonstration of this shift was the decision of the labor section, taken during the last week in March, to begin negotiations with the PSI on the establishment of a minimum wage. This was one of the issues Bogdanov and others had initially considered premature and even a threat to the revolution's political gains.[123] Yet it was also an issue of immense importance to workers and one on which they expected their leaders to act. "You understand the situation of all the workers," one factory representative said at the March 20 meeting of the soviet, turning to the activists of the labor section, "and you will probably tell [the industrialists]: 'No! You oppressed the workers, you fleeced them and in the future you have to pay that which labor is worth'."[124] On March 31, the labor section pre-

---

[121] After having heard reports of continued conflicts and work stoppages, a meeting of Petrograd owners on March 17 voted to appeal to the soviet to influence the workers to return to work and submit their complaints to arbitration: *TPG*, March 19, 1917 (no. 58), 3. On several other occasions, the PSI asked the soviet to extend and regularize its arbitration work: *Khronika* 1:102–3; *VVP*, March 23, 1917 (no. 16), 3.

[122] The conciliation board negotiated an agreement securing the eight-hour workday and a promise not to resort to layoffs should production drop; a dispute over wages was referred to the Central Conciliation Board: *RG*, March 31, 1917 (no. 21), 1. The executive committee reported numerous requests from workers asking it to intervene in conflicts and improve their lives: *IzvPS*, March 22, 1917 (no. 21), 6.

[123] See the citations from the minutes of the soviet's plenary meeting on March 20 in Mandel, "Development of Revolutionary Consciousness," 178.

[124] Ibid., 177. See similar appeals to the executive committee by the Peterhof dis-

sented the Central Conciliation Board with a plan for a minimum wage of five rubles a day for male workers and four for women. In spite of considerable opposition from the industrialists, the negotiations eventually led to the establishment of a minimum wage for the whole of Petrograd on April 24.[125]

The Mensheviks displayed increasing confidence in their dealings with labor issues, reflecting not only the success of their mediation efforts but several other lessons drawn from their experience in industrial relations in March and April. First, there was the irrefutable evidence of the soviet's power vis-à-vis the employers and of its sway over the workers, which brought many Mensheviks to the conviction that in the framework of dual power, and as a result of their own organizational efforts among the workers, the soviet had become a mighty force indeed. On March 12, two days after the soviet had concluded the agreement on the eight-hour day with the industrialists, *Rabochaia gazeta* declared: "This valuable *economic* gain was achieved through an organized *political* struggle. Mass political force compelled the representatives of capital to give up one of their economic positions without a struggle . . . through the efforts of the spokesmen for this united will—the Soviet Workers' and Soldiers' Deputies." The newspaper went on to suggest that immediate efforts be made to carry out "economic demands" that would include the institution of an eight-hour workday throughout Russia. In this struggle, it was necessary again to act in an "organized way" and to fight "as one force against another."[126]

Second, there was the unexpected and unprecedented record of managerial concessions and proletarian moderation. The dual fears of workers' extremism and counterrevolutionary backlash, which had been paramount during the revolution's earliest days and were evident in the repeated references to the failures of 1905, were reduced, if not actually replaced, by a mood of hopefulness. The conciliatory behavior of so many employers as well as Konovalov's declared dedication to an extensive program of new labor legislation and cooperation with the soviet indicated that the Menshevik strategies of averting social polarization corresponded to

---

trict soviet and the Porokhov district soviet in *Raionnye sovety Petrograda* 2:102–3 and 3:185–86, and see also Mandel, *Petrograd Workers and the Fall of the Old Regime*, 90–91.

[125] Volobuev, *Proletariat i burzhuaziia*, 127–28.

[126] "The Great Victory of the Working Class," *RG*, March 12, 1917 (no. 6), 1 (emphasis in the original).

the realities of the moment and would be effective in securing the betterment that the workers had the right to expect from the revolution. "One can rest assured," *Rabochaia gazeta* asserted, "that a peaceful resolution of the justified and economically realizable demands of the workers will redound to the advantage of the workers, and with less of an inconvenience for society as a whole, than one [wrought] through thoughtless strikes."[127] And again:

Democracy *grew up* during the last ten years. The crumbs of freedom that were left in Russia after the struggle of 1905—the shadow of popular representation, the pitiful freedom of the press—slowly but steadily did their educative work.

If not for that [work], Democracy could not have proven itself . . . in the days of the revolution. But now that it has—there is hope for the future.[128]

To many Mensheviks—praktiki, former Liquidationists, and members of the intelligentsia who joined the party in 1917—the generally subdued tenor of labor relations and their own success in managing them were a strong argument in favor of closer cooperation between moderate socialists and the progressive elements in the entrepreneurial class. Moreover, Mensheviks like Bogdanov and Gvozdev—who were already functioning, in Sukhanov's words, as a "de facto ministry of labor" in harmony with Konovalov and his Ministry of Trade and Industry[129]—could see no reason (apart from their party's ideology) for remaining outside the government. Eventually, the Menshevik involvement in managing labor relations would help form a new consensus in the party and in the soviet's executive committee in favor of a coalition government with the bourgeoisie.

IT IS IRONIC that the political conclusions drawn from the experience of labor relations in March and April actually contributed to the Mensheviks' eventual acceptance of coalition. For it was precisely the dual nature of power during these two months—with the separate organization and role it allowed for each of the camps of the revolution—that enabled the contending social forces to accept concessions and accommodations in the present while remaining adamant about their respective goals for the future. In this sense, the dual structure of power, which accurately reflected

---

[127] "The Revolution and the Economic Struggle," *RG*, March 26, 1917 (no. 17), 3.
[128] "A Great Day," *RG*, March 25, 1917 (no. 16), 1 (emphasis in the original).
[129] Sukhanov, *Zapiski o revoliutsii* 2:22.

the divergence of these social goals, was responsible for at least a temporary lessening of the danger of social polarization.

If the successful application of dual power in the area of labor relations nevertheless did contribute to the abandonment of this strategy in favor of coalition, it was for two reasons: First, this success created the impression that the social and economic issues that hung in the balance between the lower and upper classes could be resolved without recourse to violence and within the context of a bourgeois revolution. Second, this impression diminished the strength of earlier ideological strictures (namely, the Mensheviks doctrine warning against socialist participation in a bourgeois government) and freed the Menshevik leaders of the soviet to respond in what seemed the most effective way to the problems resulting from the implementation of dual power in various spheres of contemporary life—the economy, the army, war policy, and the question of political authority. In this sense, dual power fostered a political flexibility among the Mensheviks that had not been typical of them in the past.

Dual Power Reexamined: The Questions of the Economy, the War, and Political Power

IF DUAL POWER was responsible for the lessening of social tensions, the same cannot be said of its impact on the relations between the two political bodies that shared that power, the soviet and the Provisional Government. In the weeks that followed the establishment of the new regime, the threat of counterrevolution rapidly diminished, but in its place there developed a more sharply defined division, at least in Petrograd, between the two camps of the revolution. The political parties and the public organizations of the propertied and educated groups rallied to the support of the Provisional Government and together with the officer corps called on all Russians to concentrate on the task of winning the war and to postpone an extensive reform program until victory had been won.[1] For their part, the socialist leaders of the soviet attempted to construct a network of organizations (local soviets, political parties, trade unions, and soldiers' committees) through which workers and soldiers could be drawn into sustained support of the soviet. Much to these leaders' surprise, the most important conflicts in which they found themselves involved during March and April did not concern their constituency, whose demands they had momentarily satisfied, but rather their relations with their counterparts in the dual-power agreement, the ministers of the Provisional Government. What was surprising was, first, that the Provisional Government should balk at certain initiatives of the soviet which had seemed so unobjectionable to the moderates on the executive committee; and second, that even the most right-wing members of the executive committee should challenge the government's exclusive exercise of state authority. These unexpected reactions emerged in a series of conflicts between the executive committee and the Provisional Government over problems

---

[1] See the discussion of these efforts in Rosenberg, *Liberals in the Russian Revolution*, 70–74, 78–83, and the proceedings of the First Congress of Trade and Industry, at which speakers called for the "preservation of the existing social order": *Pervyi vserossiiskii torgovo-promyshlennyi s'ezd*, 139–41, 167–68.

caused more or less directly by the continuation of the war and requiring immediate resolutions.

These conflicts—over the regulation of food supplies, the nature of military authority, and the definition of Russia's war aims—were important per se, because they affected the pricing and distribution of essential foodstuffs, the army's discipline, and the nation's commitment to the goal of military victory. But what is of greatest concern here is the way in which the disposition of the issues both rested on the outcome of the political conflict between the Provisional Government and the soviet and also continuously fueled this conflict, so that both sides were pushed to define the political contours of the February revolution down to the last detail—the daily balance of forces each side commanded or was prepared to use for its respective purposes.

As we shall see, the leaders of the soviet, particularly the Mensheviks among them, responded enthusiastically to the new opportunities afforded them by dual power and made full use of the soviet's strength to solve the immediate and practical problems the revolution posed. In doing so, the Mensheviks often allowed the circumstances of the moment to redefine the party's traditional principles. This flexibility became apparent especially in the areas of food supplies and the soviet's relations with the soldiers (as it already was in labor relations), because, whatever conflicts had developed in these areas during March between the soviet and the Provisional Government, these conflicts had not yet made dual power unworkable. It was dual power that enabled the various Menshevik interpretations of the bourgeois revolution to coexist in an ideologically acceptable environment.

In contrast to their stand on practical problems, the Menshevik leaders of the soviet showed far greater reluctance to discuss the more principled question of political power, whose resolution required above all a firm and precise definition of the nature of the revolution. Disagreements with the Provisional Government over Russia's war aims, as well as the appearance of a new group of Menshevik leaders in the soviet, finally forced the Mensheviks to a partial resolution of the question of power during the last week of March, though even then this resolution was obscured by their continued formal adherence to dual power. At the end of March, dual power still stood as the soviet's political strategy—altered, challenged, but perhaps ultimately irreplaceable—and this served as a reflection of both the strength and the weaknesses of the Menshevik leaders of the soviet.

The Beginning of Economic Planning

The problem of food supplies was perhaps the most pressing one in March. After all, the revolution had ostensibly been launched as a protest against food shortages, and the disorganization of the early days did not improve the situation much.[2] The procurement and orderly distribution of food supplies were among the most frequently discussed issues in the district soviets and the factory committees and came up frequently before the executive committee itself.[3] A supply commission had already been established, on February 28, through the joint initiative of the Duma and the soviet, and the Menshevik Groman had been elected as its head.

At first sight, the question of food supplies did not seem to have the potential of causing a conflict between the soviet and the Provisional Government. The men who had been drawn to the work of the supply commission (and later the soviet's economic section) from the outset were former Liquidationists, the most moderate of the Mensheviks. Indeed, their interest in this question had begun during their work for the public organizations of census society; Groman, a widely respected zemstvo statistician, had served as the head of the Economic Department of the Union of Cities and as its representative to the Special Conference on Food Supplies, while his right-hand man, Cherevanin, also a statistician, had been in charge of the department's Petrograd bureau.[4] Moreover,

[2] There seems to be general agreement among historians that in the early months of 1917 there was less grain than usual in the heavily populated central areas and that the problem was not merely one of transporting the grain but of getting producers (mainly the well-to-do peasants) to market it. See, for example, Volobuev, *Ekonomicheskaia politika Vremennogo Pravitel'stva*, 383–89.

[3] See the announcements and protocols of the factory committee of the Radio-Telegraph factory and the Moskovskii, Rozhdestvenskii, Vasileostrovskii, and Petrogradskii district soviets in *RD posle sverzheniia samoderzhaviia*, 491–92; *IzvPS*, March 6, 1917 (no. 6), 4; *RG*, March 14, 1917 (no. 7), 4; *Raionnye sovety Petrograda* 1: 72–87 and 2:93–94. See also Smith, *Red Petrograd*, 86–88. On the discussions in the executive committee, see *Petrogradskii sovet*, 12, 30, 51, 56, 309.

[4] Groman and Cherevanin were also members of the Commission to Combat the High Cost of Living. For biographical details on the two men, see [Aronson], "Sud'ba V. G. Gromana," and appendix 3 of the present work. The Economic Department had been formed in February 1915 to combat the rising cost of living. It collected data on the prices of essential commodities and goods from two hundred cities and towns, organized conferences, and was at the center of the public campaign to force the tsarist government to adopt a more responsible economic policy: *IzvVSG*, 1916, no. 23:148–55. The Special Conference had been established in August 1915 and included representatives from the Unions of Zemstvos and of Cities,

on behalf of the public organizations, Groman had developed a plan for dealing with Russia's supply difficulties. It was toward the implementation of this plan that his activities in the soviet's supply commission and the economic section were now directed.[5]

Drawing on the experience of other European countries, especially Germany, in managing their wartime economies, Groman's plan essentially called for regulating all aspects of the economy—supplies, production, and prices—in both the agrarian and the industrial sectors, through a Commission for the Organization of the National Economy and Labor. His observations of the wartime regulatory conferences that operated in Russia had further convinced him that any attempt to regulate only part of the economy would merely accentuate the economic distortions caused by the war and give rise to monopolistic conditions and to speculation and, more seriously, would discourage production in the agrarian sector. He concluded that only comprehensive regulation could improve economic performance and that this task was beyond the ability of the public organizations alone, for it required an administrative apparatus with the full authority of a government behind it.[6]

The plan was an ambitious one, but it had been received with enthusiasm by the public organizations, in which Groman had a reputation for political moderation because of his insistence that the public organizations cooperate with the regulatory agencies of

---

the State Duma, the State Council, and relevant governmental departments: Struve, ed., *Food Supply in Russia during the World War*, 9–13.

[5] Volobuev, *Ekonomicheskaia politika Vremennogo Pravitel'stva*, 61, contends that the soviet's economists merely borrowed their plan from the projects already worked out by the Union of Cities; he fails to mention Groman's crucial contribution to the development of those early projects. Other specialists who had worked in the economic sections of the public organizations paid tribute to Groman's radical conceptions. See K. I. Zaitsev's contribution to Struve, ed., *Food Supply in Russia during the World War*, 46n, 358n; Jasny, *To Live Long Enough*, 20; N. D. Kondrat'ev, *Rynok khlebov*, 81. In a speech to the executive committee on March 16, 1917, Groman himself referred to his wartime plan as the source of the ideas he was bringing before the committee: *Petrogradskii sovet*, 310.

[6] Groman had presented an earlier version of his plan to a conference organized by his Economic Department in July 1915: *IzvVSG*, 1916, no. 23:21–22, 148–49. A more detailed version was presented to the Fourth Congress of the Union of Cities in March 1916, and it was expanded again on the eve of a projected Supply Congress in October 1916: *IzvVSG*, 1916, no. 31/32:179–92, and no. 37:113. The final form of the plan was described by Groman in a conversation with Sukhanov on March 4, 1917: Sukhanov, *Zapiski o revoliutsii* 2:73–74.

the tsarist state.[7] Indeed, during the war years, Groman, like other former Liquidationists active in the economic departments of the public organizations, had come to believe that the regulation of the economy offered an ideal opportunity for cooperation between labor organizations and the public and commercial-industrial organizations. Moreover, because Groman was confident that government intervention had saved the capitalist economies of other warring countries, he expected that, at the very least, enlightened Russian capitalists, such as Konovalov, would understand the necessity for similar measures in Russia.[8] The record of his activity during the early weeks of the revolution made his views seem plausible.

On March 4, Groman brought an initial proposal for improving food supplies before the executive committee. It called for grain rationing, requisitioning grain from owners of more than fifty *desiatinas*, and entrusting the oversight and management of supplies to a network of bodies made up of representatives of commercial-industrial and public organizations and of the newly organized soviets of workers, soldiers, and peasants. All of these components were to be coordinated by a National Supply Commission, into which the existing Duma-Soviet supply commission would be incorporated.[9] The proposal was given unanimous approval by the executive committee, and the idea for a National Supply Commission was adopted without opposition by the Duma-Soviet supply commission and by Shingarev, the minister of agriculture.[10] In the weeks following, the most moderate of socialists gave Groman's further plans for a state monopoly on grain and state-regulated prices their full support.[11] The reaction of entrepreneurial circles

[7] *IzvVSG*, 1916, no. 31/32:179–92; Jasny, *Soviet Economists of the Twenties*, 100. Most of Groman's colleagues had rejected such cooperation, because they felt the management of food supplies was secondary to the task of assuming responsibilities for the social and economic reforms that the tsarist government had failed to institute. A similar approach was evident in the Union of Zemstvos; see Fallows, "Politics and the War Effort in Russia."

[8] V. Groman, "A Renewal of Order in the Administration of Industrial Affairs," *TPG*, March 16, 1917 (no. 55), 2. The same hopeful evaluation was made by other socialists; see N. Orlov's opinion in *Letopis'*, 1917, no. 2/4:392, and "To What the Old Regime Has Brought the Country," *RG*, March 8, 1917 (no. 2), 1.

[9] *Petrogradskii sovet*, 12–13; *IzvPS*, March 6, 1917 (no. 7), 4; Sukhanov, *Zapiski o revoliutsii* 2:112–13.

[10] *Petrogradskii sovet*, 13–14, 295; *RG*, March 8, 1917 (no. 2), 3; N. D. Kondrat'ev, *Rynok khlebov*, 87–88; Shliapnikov, *Semnadtsatyi god* 2:190.

[11] A. V. Peshekhonov, for example, a Defensist Populist, called on the executive committee to instruct its supply commission to declare a monopoly on grain with-

was generally tolerant, though it ranged from outright opposition to guarded support.[12] On March 25, the minister of agriculture signed into law the measures called for by Groman's food-supply proposal.[13]

The process of obtaining this legislation, however, had not been easy. It provoked several conflicts between the soviet's economists, and their Duma counterparts in the National Supply Commission, and the Ministry of Agriculture. There were disagreements over the makeup of the local committees and over the issue of grain prices. The socialist economists complained that Shingarev had undercut the effectiveness of the grain monopoly by staffing the grain committees in the countryside and the supply committees in the cities with landowners and grain merchants.[14] One specific blow was Shingarev's decision to raise grain prices by an average of 60 to 70 percent over those that had been set in the

out regard for Shingarev's objections: *Petrogradskii sovet*, 46 (and see ibid., 309–12, for other examples). See also "How to Obtain Grain," *RG*, March 11, 1917 (no. 5), 1.

[12] Entrepreneurial attitudes toward economic regulation have usually been described as negative on the basis of the resolution on food supplies adopted in March 1917 by the First Congress of Trade and Industry; see, for example, Volobuev, *Ekonomicheskaia politika Vremennogo Pravitel'stva*, 393–95; and Rieber, *Merchants and Entrepreneurs in Imperial Russia*, 402. This resolution did denounce Groman's planned state monopoly on grain as "dangerous," but it also recognized that inflation and shortages made it impossible to realize the goal of full freedom in the grain trade and it demanded only that merchants be allowed to play an important role in the projected supply committees: *Pervyi vserossiiskii torgovo-promyshlennyi s'ezd*, 230–31. Moreover this resolution was the result of a compromise into which the congress's delegates were pressured or even manipulated by Riabushinskii and V. D. Sirotkin after the congress's supply section found itself deadlocked on the issues of commercial freedom and the public supervision of commercial activity: ibid., 78–110, 183–212, 221–31. Entrepreneurial associations in Moscow and the south actually appealed to "their" ministers in the Provisional Government to undertake the regulation of raw materials in order to supply factories with their necessities. See, for example, Tret'iakov's letter to Konovalov, in *TPG*, March 17, 1917 (no. 56), 2, and Prodamet's letter to Guchkov, in *EPR* 1:246–47. See also chap. 6 below.

[13] A Soviet historian and a Kadet leader agree that the measure on the grain monopoly was dictated to the Provisional Government by the soviet: Volobuev, *Ekonomicheskaia politika Vremennogo Pravitel'stva*, 395–96; and Manuilov, "Shingarev."

[14] "How to Obtain Grain," *RG*, March 11, 1917 (no. 5), 1; "The Food Supply Crisis in Petrograd," *RG*, March 30, 1917 (no. 20), 1; "On the Struggle With Economic Destruction," *IzvPS*, April 1, 1917 (no. 30), 1–2; M. Smit, "Problemy s snabzheniia," *Letopis'*, 1917, no. 5/6:338. Historians writing from the point of view of the Provisional Government argued the impracticality of the monopoly in the conditions of administrative disintegration that obtained in 1917; see Struve, ed., *Food Supply in Russia during the World War*, 104; and Manuilov, "Shingarev."

fall of 1916 by the then minister of agriculture, A. A. Rittikh.[15] This decision also demonstrated the problems inherent in Groman's ideas regarding the role of the soviet in economic affairs.

Groman had argued before the executive committee that the soviet should not limit itself to providing political leadership for the masses, because the "vital question of supplying the front and the rear" required the imposition of economic regulation. He saw in the soviet, and more particularly in the executive committee, an organization that shared many of the goals of the public organizations, though it was more democratic, more powerful, more efficient, less given to the pressures of private interests, and therefore more suitable as the institutional basis of a regulatory machine.[16] Thus, Groman's view of the executive committee was at once both moderate, in the tradition of prewar Menshevik Liquidationism—the public-minded leadership of a mature working class and its instrument for cooperation with the other "vital forces" of Russian society—and yet activist, even radical, in that he assigned to the executive committee and to the intelligentsia leadership of the public organizations the role of directing the nation's social and economic life. (The importance of the intelligentsia in Groman's conception of the revolution had become increasingly clear during the war years.)

Groman's expanded definition of the soviet's function was fraught with political implications, because it cast the executive committee as the principal initiator of economic planning for the country and thus brought confrontation both with the economic interests that were to be regulated and also with the Provisional Government's declared authority over the country's economic life.[17] The Provisional Government was subject to pressure not only from the soviet but from its constituency of propertied groups as well.[18] Meanwhile, the executive committee was increasingly

---

[15] Volobuev, *Ekonomicheskaia politika Vremennogo Pravitel'stva*, 397.

[16] Sukhanov, *Zapiski o revoliutsii* 2:73–74.

[17] The two aspects of Groman's "radicalism" were emphasized, respectively, by Shliapnikov, *Semnadtsatyi god* 2:190, and Sukhanov, *Zapiski o revoliutsii* 2:113.

[18] At a meeting of the Duma-Soviet supply commission on March 10, two grain merchants from the Kalashnikov Exchange in Petrograd, who were known to represent "the extreme trend in the commercial class," argued vehemently against Groman's advocacy of regulation. Shingarev, who chaired the meeting, agreed that prices should be fixed and distribution regulated, but he balanced these concessions to Groman with a call for merchants to become involved in the regulatory work and for an increase in the fixed prices for grain: *TPG*, March 15, 1917 (no. 54), 4. See the sharp attack on Shingarev and his alleged surrender to the interests of agrarian producers in *RG*, March 17, 1917 (no. 10), 1–2.

compelled to exercise its own authority in order to ease economic problems, as was demonstrated by the steps the committee took in regard to the supply situation in Petrograd.[19] However, the national economy required nationwide measures, and these the soviet's economists could obtain only by working with the National Supply Commission and the cabinet, although their efforts to do so were not always successful.[20]

In addition to these problems of implementation, it was not at all clear which measures could in fact improve the economy or even guarantee food supplies. Groman's plans had called for comprehensive price regulation, and this was evidently deemed necessary by other economists as well, but no one had actually worked out a pricing system.[21] Groman asked the executive committee to form a special commission that would be attached to the cabinet and would, "in a month's time," present an accurate assessment of the state of the economy, work out the general principles of regulation, and fix prices for all products of mass consumption.[22] Some contemporary observers considered Groman's plan overconfident and unrealistic.[23] That it could not have been realized in the short time he allowed is abundantly clear in light of the later soviet experience with economic planning. In any case, the push for state regulation of the economy, touching as it did on the fundamental interests of landowners and entrepreneurs and confronting the government with the unpleasant prospect of alienating its strongest supporters, was bound to cause conflict in the coming months.

IN MARCH, the economists had been the strongest supporters of dual power, in part because they had not yet tried to take on the

[19] On March 24, the executive committee put into effect a rationing system worked out by its supply commission, and on several later occasions it threatened the owners of bakeries and the operators of carts with requisitioning: *IzvPS*, March 2, 1917 (no. 3), 2, 4; March 3, 1917 (no. 4), 5; March 25, 1917 (no. 24), 1–2; March 26, 1917 (no. 25), 1–2; March 28, 1917 (no. 26), 3; *RG*, March 26, 1917 (no. 17), 4; March 28, 1917 (no. 18), 3; *Petrogradskii sovet*, 69–70.

[20] Manuilov, "Shingarev," is emphatic in describing the pressure put on Shingarev by Groman but adds that often the majority in the National Supply Commission went along with the minister against the men from the soviet. The same impression is conveyed in Jasny, *To Live Long Enough*, 30–33, and idem, *Soviet Economists of the Twenties*, 98–99.

[21] Sukhanov, *Zapiski o revoliutsii* 2:271–74.

[22] *Petrogradskii sovet*, 311–12.

[23] Jasny, *To Live Long Enough*, 30–33; idem, *Soviet Economists of the Twenties*, 98–99.

regulation of industry or perhaps because the calm in industrial relations suggested that state regulation could be imposed without undue opposition. Moreover, through their experience in setting up the monopoly on grain, even Groman and Cherevanin, the moderates in the economic section of the executive committee, had come to see the soviet's ability to pressure the government as a key factor in the campaign for economic regulation. As for the more radical Internationalist economists—Bazarov, Sukhanov, and N. Orlov—they were attracted to the economic section precisely because it had become a major instrument of pressure on the Provisional Government and they were satisfied that within the context of dual power even a Liquidationist of Groman's standing could produce a program that was at once politically daring and socially radical.[24] Looking to the future, the moderates still placed some hopes on the progressive industrialists and the "public men" in the cabinet, whereas the more pessimistic radicals continued in their efforts to find specific forms of pressure on the government. To this extent, dual power suited the purposes of both groups, though its cumulative effect on the ultimate question of political authority was already becoming apparent in the case of the army and on the issue of war and peace.

THE STRUGGLE OVER THE ARMY

Dual power proved less effective as a formula for the soviet's handling of its following among the soldiers and the concomitant issue of whether the soviet or the Provisional Government was to exercise final authority over the soldiery. From the outset, the question of Russia's involvement in the war was a source of great uneasiness among Social Democrats. For them, the Russian revolution had always been portrayed as an essentially social revolution—and an urban one at that—but an accident of history had brought the revolution in the midst of a war and had distorted both the composition of the social forces supporting it and the central concerns of its leadership. The war became the source of a crisis with which the leaders of the soviet would grapple throughout the summer and fall of 1917 and also the reason for the unexpected political influence of the peasant-soldier on the outcome of the revolution. Moreover, the soldiers' centrality in the revolution would necessarily affect the balance of forces between the camps

---

[24] Sukhanov, *Zapiski o revoliutsii* 2:113.

of the revolution and thus the relations between the soviet and the Provisional Government. The loyalty of the soldiers was torn between these two contending forces, and in seeking the soldiers' allegiance and support, the soviet would thus ipso facto challenge the government. But before this drama could be played out, the Social Democrats in the soviet would have to overcome their reservations about serving as leaders of the soldiery. Although the garrison's revolt had guaranteed the victory of the workers' demonstrations in February, most Social Democrats still expected the peasant-soldiers to act in future as the revolution's reactionary wing.[25]

In spite of the soviet's consent on March 1 to be prolocutor of the Petrograd garrison, the executive committee had responded with anxiety to the subsequent news of widespread disobedience and violence against officers in the army on the front and in the navy.[26] Fearing that the army might turn into a mob, the executive committee agreed with Minister of War Guchkov and the army's commanders on the necessity of restoring discipline in the armed forces.[27] At the same time, the executive committee demanded that the new government of "free Russia" effect a fundamental change in the structure of relations in the army, though it suspected that these changes would not go unchallenged.[28] To complicate matters further, the soviet's discussions of the disturbances in the naval bases of Kronstadt and Helsinki placed the executive committee under menacing pressure from the soldiers. At a meeting of the soviet on March 6, the full force of the soldiers' rebellion against the officers' authority was made plain for the first time.[29] After Sukhanov had spoken in opposition to the soldiers' de-

[25] Ibid., 138–39.

[26] Wildman, *Russian Imperial Army*, chap. 6, and S. S. Khaisin, "Russkii flot i sverzhenie samoderzhaviia," in Mints et al., ed., *Sverzhenie samoderzhaviia*, 186–89.

[27] Steklov explained at the time that the executive committee's concern to prevent the "battleworthy revolutionary army" from turning into a "scattered mob," rathern than real agreement with Guchkov, had brought about its cooperation: *Vserossiiskoe soveshchanie*, 111.

[28] Sukhanov, *Zapiski o revoliutsii* 2:158. On a number of occasions during the first week of the revolution, General Alekseev, the commander of the army, demonstrated his hostility to the soviet and to the "democratization" of the army: *RD posle sverzheniia samoderzhaviia*, 619; Shliapnikov, *Semnadtsatyi god* 2:65–66, 83.

[29] For contrasting explanations of the soldiers' revolt against their officers, see Trotsky, *History of the Russian Revolution*, 264–75 (where the revolt is treated as an extension of the peasants' revolt against the landed gentry); Wildman, *Russian Imperial Army*, chap. 6, esp. 239–40; and Ferro, "Russian Soldier in 1917."

mands that they be allowed to elect their officers, a soldier blocked his way from the rostrum back to his seat and brandished his fist as he screamed with rage about "gentlemen who had never been in a soldier's skin." Like other Social Democrats, Sukhanov feared that the soviet would be taken over by these "impenetrable muzhiks in their grey overcoats."[30] The dilemma confronting the executive committee was how to satisfy the soldiers' demands and at the same time restrain them and persuade them to accept the need for discipline.[31]

During the first days of the dual-power arrangement, the response of the executive committee to these conflicting pressures was quick, self-assured, and unprovocative. On March 6, the committee issued Order No. 2 to the Petrograd garrison, confirming the basic stipulations of Order No. 1 but adding a new formulation that allowed the soldiers' committees "to object to the appointment of any officer" while the soviet continued to consider the more radical demand for elected officers.[32] The executive committee also named a delegation that was to demand of Guchkov that he add his signature to Order No. 2, accept the principle of election of officers, and institute reforms in the army along the lines set forth in Order Nos. 1 and 2.[33] An indication of how strongly the executive committee felt about its overall policy can be gained from the fact that the delegation did not retreat on its demands even when an enraged Guchkov threatened to resign and agreed to moderate its stand only when Guchkov finally put the whole matter into the hands of two generals who were known to be sympathetic to the soviet.[34] On the advice of these generals and that which Gen. N. V. Ruzskii had telegraphed from the front,[35] the executive committee issued Order No. 3, to the soldiers on the

[30] Sukhanov, *Zapiski o revoliutsii* 2:145–46.

[31] *Petrogradskii sovet*, 12, 21, 28, 37–38, 53; Shliapnikov, *Semnadtsatyi god* 2:84–87; and Sukhanov, *Zapiski o revoliutsii* 2:51–52, 139, 145–46.

[32] *Petrogradskii sovet*, 11, 16, 296–97. For a discussion of Order No. 1, see chap. 2.

[33] *Petrogradskii sovet*, 16–19; *Khronika* 1:71. The delegation consisted of Skobelev, Sokolov, Gvozdev, Steklov, Iu. A. Kudriavtsev, V. N. Fillipovskii (an SR officer), and possibly also the Bolshevik soldier A. I. Paderin.

[34] These were Gen. N. M. Potapov, of the Duma Military Committee, and Gen. A. A. Polivanov, head of a commission to review military rules. See Guchkov, "Iz vospominanii," September 6, 1936, and Shliapnikov, *Semnadtsatyi god* 2:101–4.

[35] Shliapnikov, *Semnadtsatyi god* 2:104. Ruzskii was known to have favored Nicholas's abdication in the early days after the revolution's victory; see Wildman, *Russian Imperial Army*, 208–13.

front.[36] This order explained that the preceding orders had been meant only for Petrograd and promised the immediate implementation of new rules for the army at large. In the meantime, it called on soldiers and officers to show each other mutual respect.[37] In return for this last pronouncement, Guchkov grudgingly pledged prompt reforms in soldier-officer relations.[38] While this compromise was being negotiated, the executive committee decided to establish control over the army in Petrograd, and eventually elsewhere, in the form of commissars to be dispatched to all units.[39]

By this series of measures, the executive committee established policy along several lines which fell within the framework of dual power but also expanded its application into the crucial sphere of military affairs. The soviet had brought the government to grant soldiers some basic civil rights and had claimed for itself the right to control over the military and had further declared itself the political leader of the soldiers in Petrograd and their autonomous committees.[40] When Guchkov wrote to Gen. M. V. Alekseev on March 9 that the government "did not have any real power over the Petrograd garrison," he was not merely playing the pessimist; the soldiers' committees in the capital had declared that they would instruct soldiers not to obey any orders that had not been approved by the soviet.[41] By applying pressure where necessary and cooperating where it was both possible and acceptable to their followers, the leaders of the Petrograd soviet had succeeded—or so it seemed at the moment—in securing the basic rights of soldiers and in containing their potentially destructive revolt, to the soviet's own political advantage.

However, as the Mensheviks in the executive committee were to

[36] *Petrogradskii sovet*, 18; *Khronika* 1:71.

[37] *Petrogradskii sovet*, 397–98.

[38] *Khronika* 1:71.

[39] *Petrogradskii sovet*, 19–20. The task of the first of these commissars was to oversee the activity of Gen. L. G. Kornilov, the commander of the Petrograd district. On the commissars' uneasy relations with Kornilov, see ibid., 34–36; Shliapnikov, *Semnadtsatyi god* 2:96; and Sukhanov, *Zapiski o revoliutsii* 2:193–94. On the authority invested in the commissars, see *Petrogradskii sovet*, 45, 61–62.

[40] A commission appointed by Guchkov and headed by Polivanov worked over the next month, in close contact with the executive committee, to revise the military rules concerning the "internal life of military units," including regulations for electing committees at all military levels. See Browder and Kerensky, eds., *Russian Provisional Government* 2:854 (hereafter cited as *RPG*): Shliapnikov, *Semnadtsatyi god* 2:106–8 and 3:180–81, 312–30; and *Khronika*, 1:92–93, 138.

[41] Shliapnikov, *Semnadtsatyi god* 2:236–37.

discover shortly, their success in early March was not a guarantee either of the army command's continued cooperation in democratizing the army or of the soldiers' support for future policies of the soviet, especially of the soldiers at the front. The first sign of continuing problems was Guchkov's resistance to the soviet's initiatives on military reform. For example, he refused to sight a Declaration of Soldiers' Rights which had been drafted by the soviet in consultation with his own commission on military rules, and he encouraged the commanders on the front to take a similar stance.[42] At issue here was not only the commanders' authority or the battleworthiness of the army—though Guchkov regarded both of these issues as very important—but the duality of power itself: that is, the soviet's implied or actual intervention in state affairs. The issue of the war and the fear of defeat were exploited in a public campaign the bourgeois forces launched against the soviet in mid-March. Statements by the government, declarations from the Duma, newspaper reports quoting the commanders on the front, and editorials in the nonsocialist press all warned of immediate military danger, and these warnings were given force by the defeat of the Russian forces at Stokhod on March 22. Antisoviet voices lost no time in relating this defeat to the general harmfulness of dual power, and they called on the soldiers to submit to military discipline for the sake of the motherland and on the workers to forgo their economic demands (especially the shortening of the workday) and to give all their strength to the war effort.[43]

What was particularly worrisome to the leaders of the soviet was the apparent effect that the campaign was having on the soldiery, though this perception of change was only partially correct, because it also rested on the Social Democrats' persistent mistrust of the peasant-soldier; it would in any case be reversed within weeks. Until the middle of March, the only tension between the soldiers and the executive committee involving the war had concerned the reluctance of units of the Petrograd garrison to serve

[42] *Vserossiiskoe soveshchanie*, 116–17.

[43] The campaign began with a series of appeals by Duma deputies and Guchkov and in the second half of March was carried on independently by all the nonsocialist newspapers. Speaking to his soldiers in the Petrograd garrison, Colonel Engel'gardt called on the soviet to limit itself to workers' affairs and to allow the Provisional Government to be the "one power." For contemporary and retrospective discussions of this episode, see Shliapnikov, *Semnadtsatyi god* 2:139–43, 273–82, and 3:36, 46–60, 168–70; Sukhanov, *Zapiski o revoliutsii* 2:189–94, 217–19; V. A. Bazarov, "Pervye shagi russkoi revoliutsii," *Letopis'*, 1917, no. 2/4:383; and Wildman, *Russian Imperial Army*, 303–4.

on the front, where they would be beyond the soviet's protection of their new rights and of course exposed to the dangers of combat.[44] As we shall see, on this issue, the leaders too had their reservations. Chkheidze, for example, could hardly bring himself to sign Order No. 3, saying, "How can I call on soldiers to continue the war, to stay at the front?"[45]

Yet, as Wildman has shown, the soldiers as a whole, especially those on the front, neither had formed a clear view of what the revolution meant for the execution of the war nor were they aware of the soviet's differences with the Provisional Government on this score.[46] Most soldiers were not enthusiastic about fighting as such, and those on the front often argued that they had done their duty and it was now someone else's turn (be it a worker or a soldier of the rear garrison); they expected the revolution to bring about immediate victory, peace, and demobilization.[47] Moreover, in contrast to the soldiers' revolt against military authority in Petrograd—and the soviet's swift response to it, which had had the effect of forming a bond of loyalty between the garrison and the soviet—the revolution had taken a different path on the front. There, officers had usually been rejected when suspected of pro-German or pro-tsarist sentiment; the soldiers' committees had quickly been recognized by the command, in an effort to both restrain them and integrate them into the existing structure of authority; and the officers of "democratic" social origins and of noncommissioned rank (many of them Menshevik Defensists) exerted the greatest influence in the soldiers' committees, helping to articulate a mood of patriotism based on the premise that a "new nation" had been born of the revolution.[48] For these reasons, soldiers

[44] Sukhanov, *Zapiski o revoliutsii* 2:173 reports that in early March this issue replaced that of elected officers as the most urgent item on the agenda of the soldiers' section. The executive committee does not appear to have acted consistently on this question; some units were sent away, while other were allowed to stay in Petrograd in spite of orders to move to the front; see *Petrogradskii sovet*, 23, 28, 41, 55–56; Shliapnikov, *Semnadtsatyi god* 2:167; and Peshekhonov, "Pervye nedeli," 278–85.

[45] Stankevich, *Vospominaniia*, 98.

[46] Wildman, *Russian Imperial Army*, chaps. 7 and 9, esp. 294–302. For assertions that in March the soldiers were thoroughly patriotic, see Shliapnikov, *Semnadtsatyi god* 3:166 and Ermanskii, *Iz perezhitogo*, 160. Desertion was not a major problem at this stage; indeed, soldiers denounced it as an act of betrayal: Wildman, *Russian Imperial Army*, 235–36. See also Sobolev, "Pis'ma v petrogradskii sovet," 163–65.

[47] Kakurin, ed., *Razlozhenie armii*, 11, and Ferro, "Russian Soldier in 1917," 486.

[48] Wildman, *Russian Imperial Army*, 236–40, 248; Ferro, "Russian Soldier in 1917," 486–87, 490–91. See also Kakurin, ed., *Razlozhenie armii*, 58; Shliapnikov, *Semnadt-*

on the front were slow to turn against the war, and this fact was both encouraged and exploited by the Duma deputies touring the front, as well as by the nonsocialist press, which channeled the soldiers' vague misgivings against the soviet and especially against the workers' demands.[49]

Beginning around the middle of March, the court of the Tauride Palace became the scene of many demonstrations staged by military units from Petrograd and elsewhere proclaiming (as did the Semenov Regiment on March 15), "The Preservation of Freedom Means Victory over Wilhelm." On March 16, the soldiers of the Guards' Reserve Artillery Battalion promised to sacrifice themselves for the Provisional Government, and on March 17, the Izmailov Regiment called for the continuation of the war to victory, while the Guards' Petrograd Regiment appeared with banners declaring "War for Freedom," "Soldiers to the Trenches," "Workers to the Benches," and "Confidence in the Provisional Government."[50] Such demonstrations were seen daily at the Tauride Palace for the next two weeks, but in the last week of March, following the defeat in Stokhod, the slogans suddenly became hostile to the workers and the soviet. On March 27, a meeting of delegates from the front called on workers to work overtime, and a meeting of eighty-nine of Petrograd's garrison units demanded that workers forsake the eight-hour workday. On March 28, a deputation from the First Army (59 officers and 145 soldiers) pleaded with the soviet to strengthen its solidarity with the Provisional Government in order to ensure military victory.[51] At one point, Skobelev, who was by no means an Internationalist, was nearly lynched by the soldiers for expressing reservations about the war.[52]

For a while, it seemed to the Social Democrats on the executive committee as if the bourgeois camp would succeed in turning the soldiers against the workers, the soviet, and dual power and altering the balance of forces between the two camps of the revo-

---

satyi god 2:67–70, 251–72, and appendix 24; and Miller, Soldatskie komitety, 36–37. For a biographical sketch of a Menshevik leader of an army organization, G. D. Kuchin, see appendix 3 of the present work.

[49] That the soldiers' antagonism toward the workers was aroused by the press campaign is indicated by the fact that previous soldiers' demonstrations sometimes carried banners calling for an eight-hour day for the workers as well as for victory in the war: Sukhanov, Zapiski o revoliutsii 2:214–15.

[50] IzvPS, March 17, 1917 (no. 17), 1; Den', March 17, 1917 (no. 11), 2, and March 19, 1917 (no. 13), 3; RG, March 18, 1917 (no. 11), 2.

[51] RG, March 29, 1917 (no. 18), 3, and March 29, 1917 (no. 19), 2–3.

[52] Sukhanov, Zapiski o revoliutsii 2:222; see also ibid., 306–7.

lution. Mistrust of the soldiers had made these Social Democrats slow to recognize the shakiness of the progovernment mood in the army. In fact, once the soldiers had come face to face with the workers, heard their complaints, and taken note of the divisions between the soviet and the Provisional Government, they invariably sided with "democracy."[53] Nevertheless, however short-lived the threat, it did check the growing power of the soviet, kept the soviet and the Provisional Government in mutual dependence, and prolonged the dual-power arrangement. Most important for the immediate future, it was the soldiers' behavior that rendered unthinkable, at least to the Social Democrats on the executive committee, any possibility that the soviet would join a coalition government or assume responsibility for the army and the war effort.

The Emergence of Revolutionary Defensism

At the outset, there was a surprising degree of accord among the members of the executive committee on the question of the war, even among the Mensheviks who had been so deeply divided between Internationalists and Defensists up to 1917. The conception of the war as having originated in the imperialist schemes of the tsarist regime was accepted by all as a proven fact. But the necessity of defending the revolution from the German Imperial Army was also taken as axiomatic, although no suggestions for practical measures toward that end were deemed appropriate or even needed. The essence of that attitude was expressed in a resolution adopted unanimously on March 6 by Mensheviks from all over Petrograd and in the executive committee's acceptance on March 11 of a declaration authored by Sukhanov and entitled "An Appeal to All the Peoples of the World."[54] The appeal was approved with

[53] Wildman, *Russian Imperial Army*, 319–21.

[54] The meeting on March 6 was attended by two hundred Mensheviks and declared itself the "Constituent Assembly of the Petrogard Organization of the RSDRP [Russian Social Democratic Workers' Party]." Potresov told the assembly that continuation of the war was "unacceptable," whereas Ermanskii argued the need for the army to continue defending the revolutionary country. Their differences concerned the extent to which "defensism" or "internationalism" should be emphasized in the party's public pronouncements. See the report of the meeting, entitled "The Establishment of the RSDRP Organization," in *RG*, March 8, 1917 (no. 2), 2, and Ermanskii's letter to *RG*, March 10, 1917 (no. 4), 4. Also see Nikolaevskii, "RSDRP," 16–17; Tsereteli, *Vospominaniia o fevral'skoi revoliutsii* 1:42; and *Petrogradskii sovet*, 27, 39–40, 300–1. On the circumstances surrounding the passage of the

much ceremony by the full soviet on March 14. Both the resolution and the appeal contained two basic points: the repudiation of the war in general and of annexations in particular, and the recognition of the need to defend the revolution until peace should come. Neither of these documents, however, prescribed any specific steps.

The absence of practical recommendations underscored the shakiness of the consensus on the war, which consisted of two separate expectations. First, the Mensheviks, always the most European-oriented of Russian socialists, expected that European socialists, especially the German Social Democrats, would recognize their duty to the young Russian revolution and "force their governments to conclude peace."[55] Second, there was the hope, more broadly shared, that the new government would renounce all expansionist goals and dedicate its efforts to the pursuit of a democratic peace. It was the collapse of the second of these expectations, almost as soon as it was expressed, that gave the war issue a centrality for the soviet that it had not had during the first weeks of the revolution. This is an important point both for the timing of crucial developments in the executive committee and more generally for the consequences that the war's continuation would have for the Menshevik view of the revolution.

Beginning with the second week in March, Miliukov, the minister of foreign affairs, expressed the government's steadfast adherence to Russia's earlier war aims and to military cooperation with the allies in a number of statements.[56] On March 23, the Kadet newspaper printed an interview with Miliukov in which he

---

"Appeal," see Sukhanov, *Zapiski o revoliutsii* 2:50, 148–49, and Shliapnikov, *Semnadtsatyi god* 2:145.

[55] "The Russian Revolution and the International Proletariat," *RG*, March 8, 1917 (no. 2), 1. See also "We and They on the War," *RG*, March 14, 1917 (no. 7), 1; "A Significant Step" and "Toward the Democratization of Europe," *RG*, March 15, 1917 (no. 8), 1; "At Long Last," *RG*, March 16, 1917 (no. 9), 1; "War and Revolution," *RG*, March 17, 1917 (no. 10), 1. When the German SDs spoke in the Reichstag against the defense budget, the editors of *RG* saw it as a vindication of their expectations: *RG*, March 18, 1917 (no. 11), 4. However, the Mensheviks in Petrograd were shocked to hear the Swedish SD leader Karl Hjalmar Branting argue that the German workers should not be expected to rise up against the war: Garvi, "Iz vospominanii o fevral'skoi revoliutsii," 49; Stankevich, *Vospominaniia*, 107–9. Mensheviks in the provinces had apparently been more doubtful and had recognized the need for active defense much earlier; see the March 9 resolution of the SDs in Minsk, as reported in *RG*, March 17, 1917 (no. 10), 4, and Denike, interview no. 8, pp. 29–30.

[56] Wade, *Russian Search for Peace*, 9–14; Medlin and Parsons, eds., *Nabokov*, 105–25; and Rosenberg, *Liberals in the Russian Revolution*, 74–77.

labeled the soviet's slogan of "peace without annexations" a "German formula" and reiterated his own dedication to Russia's annexation of Constantinopole and the Bosporus and the Dardanelles.[57] When the soviet's liaison committee tried to have the cabinet repudiate the annexation plans in public (at a meeting on March 24), the cabinet took two days to discuss the request, then presented the soviet with a statement coauthored by Miliukov and V. D. Nabokov (head of the Provisional Government's chancellery and a close collaborator of Miliukov's in the Kadet party), which the latter described as a "Machiavellian exercise" in satisfying the soviet without binding the cabinet to any concessions on its territorial goals. Moreover, when this statement was issued, on March 26, it was not as the diplomatic note the soviet had demanded but rather as a declaration to the Russian people, wherein democratic phrases had been used but the issue of annexations had not been addressed.[58]

Clearly, the war issue had the makings of a major confrontation between the two camps of the revolution: between Miliukov's view that the soviet had no legal standing and the soviet's view that the renunciation of annexations was integral to Russia's democratic revolution as well as the precondition to any negotiated peace.[59] Miliukov was able to resist the soviet's demands much more consistently than was Guchkov because on the issue of war, unlike that of military authority, the soldiers appeared to be on the government's side. In short, the issue of the war confronted the soviet for the first time with a potentially divisive choice: either to make good on its threat of rousing the workers against the government, or to retreat from its declared goals. Thus, the conflict over war aims touched directly on questions of political strategy and state power. But the problem of the war itself also caused a difficult personal struggle for many of the Mensheviks. Although to them the notion that Russia should continue to seek territorial and economic rewards from the war was unacceptable, they also felt that Germany could not be allowed to occupy Russian territory

[57] RPG 2:1044.

[58] Medlin and Parsons, eds., Nabokov, 116. See also RG, May 6, 1917 (no. 49), 1, and Milinkov, Istoriia vtoroi russkoi revoliutsii 1:86.

[59] Miliukov's view is described in Rosenberg, Liberals in the Russian Revolution, 100. For a discussion of the conflict in the soviet's press, see "War for Freedom," IzvPS, March 17, 1917 (no. 17), 1; "Secret Diplomacy," IzvPS, March 18, 1917 (no. 18), 1–2; "Two Positions," ibid., 2; and "Unresolved Contradictions," RG, March 26, 1917 (no. 17), 1–2.

and threaten the revolution. A new sense of responsibility, along with the influence of their Populist colleagues on the committee and the soldiers' demonstrations of patriotism, helped to undermine the negative attitudes that had characterized the Mensheviks' wartime discussion of military defense.

Indeed, even while the question of power remained largely undiscussed, the Mensheviks on the executive committee had much to say about the issue of the war, though what they said was often contradictory. Miliukov's rejection of the demand to modify Russia's war aims provoked even Mensheviks of long-standing Defensist convictions to support the Internationalists' call for a "broad, national campaign" around the "Appeal to All the Peoples of the World."[60] In fact, a number of them on the executive committee had signed a draft resolution to this effect drawn up by Sukhanov and Larin.[61] And yet, most Mensheviks, even those who had in the past prided themselves on their "internationalism," appeared to be growing uncomfortable with the Internationalists' blanket denunciation of the war. Ironically, the strength of the Defensist sentiment became apparent at the March 14 meeting of the soviet, when it ratified the "Appeal to All the Peoples of the World." Steklov, the official speaker, ended his otherwise standard Internationalist speech with a warning to the German people that "Russian freedom" would be defended to the last drop of blood. Chkheidze expanded on that message, exclaiming with great fervor: *"We make this offer with weapons in our hands. The slogan for the revolution is 'Down with Wilhelm!'"*—words he would repeat frequently over the next two weeks.[62]

Steklov and Chkheidze were arguing that the soviet must make defense its responsibility, but the force of the old wartime divisions, their Internationalist self-image, and their awareness of the war's unpopularity among workers all combined to deter most

[60] Editorials in *RG* denounced Miliukov and appealed to the workers and the soldiers to demand, "by unanimous declarations in meetings and organized assemblies," that he reverse his course: "Impossible to Keep Silent," March 25, 1917 (no. 16), 1, and "The Imperialists—The Foes of Russia," March 26, 1917 (no. 17), 1.

[61] Sukhanov, *Zapiski o revoliutsii* 2:271, 333–34, and Stankevich, *Vospominaniia*, 100–1. Larin, who had just returned from Stockholm, was a staunch Internationalist who would soon leave the Menshevik party, and eventually joined the Bolsheviks.

[62] See *IzvPS*, March 16, 1917 (no. 16), 4, and March 18, 1917 (no. 18), 4–6; Sukhanov, *Zapiski o revoliutsii* 2:148–50 (emphasis in the original). For reports of Chkheidze's subsequent speeches to the soldiers, see *IzvPs*, March 17, 1917 (no. 10), 1, and *RG*, March 18, 1917 (no. 11), 2, and March 21, 1917 (no. 13), 3.

Mensheviks on the executive committee from articulating this sentiment in terms that were both consistent and practical. Such articulation had to await the arrival in Petrograd of I. G. Tsereteli, who came to address the March 21 meeting of the executive committee on the war issue. Armed with a set of well-defined ideas on the questions of war and state power which later came to be known as "revolutionary defensism," Tsereteli was able not only to avert an imminent confrontation between the soviet and the Provisional Government but also to draw all the Defensists and the doubting Internationalists into a new majority, first in the executive committee and later at the Conference of Soviets, that would assume the leadership of the soviets for the next seven or eight months. The significance of this change in leadership and strategy was enormous and eventually led the soviet into participation in the forming of a coalition government.

Up to this time, Tsereteli had been known mostly for his oratorical skill as leader of the Social Democratic deputies to the Second Duma and for the many years he had spent in prison and exile (see his biographical sketch in appendix 3). Those familiar with his articles of the war years and with the writings of other Social Democrats who had shared his exile in Irkutsk and were collectively known as the Siberian Zimmerwaldists assumed that Tsereteli was a thoroughgoing Internationalist.[63] Like other Internationalists, he had insisted that the Social Democrats remain neutral in the war and had called for a general peace to be achieved through pressure from the international labor movement. No one, it seems, had paid much attention to the fact that for the first two years of the war Tsereteli had based his denunciation of socialist participation in military activities on the role the autocracy had played in Russia's and the Entente's conduct of the war. In fact, Tsereteli had not embraced the standard Internationalist analysis of the war as "imperialist" until the second half of 1916, and even then he had posited that, if the war were to change from being "imperialist" into one of national "self-preservation," the socialists would then

[63] Sukhanov later recalled (*Zapiski o revoliutsii* 2:277–78, 288–91) that Larin had urged him to organize a large reception for Tsereteli upon his arrival in Petrograd because Larin believed (as did Sukhanov) that Tsereteli and his group would strengthen the Internationalist wing in the soviet. For contemporary evaluations of the Siberian Zimmerwaldist position, see *Pis'ma*, 319–21, 323; L. M. [Martov], "Sibirskie marksisty o voine," *Nashe slovo*, February 26, 1915 (no. 25); Nikolaevskii, "Gruppa 'Sibirskikh Tsimmerval'distov' "; and Levin, "Sotsialisticheskaia pechat'," 211–12.

be justified in joining the battle against the "militaristic" aggressor.[64]

To be sure, Tsereteli considered himself an Internationalist and believed that Russia's revolutionary, democratic forces had a special role to play in the regeneration of an international socialist solidarity and the reestablishment of a general peace. But it was precisely this "Russian" perspective which convinced him that Russia should not be made to pay the price of a separate peace. Indeed, his version of internationalism made it easy for the Siberian Zimmerwaldists, who had come to lead both the soviet and the Committee of Public Organizations in Irkutsk after the February revolution, to assume actual responsibility for aspects of the military effort.[65] They had accepted defense for the sake of securing the revolution from outside aggression, a point that Chkheidze (a fellow Georgian) had made in a speech on March 14.[66] For Tsereteli, however, as well as for his comrade in exile V. S. Voitinskii, an independent, practical-minded former Bolshevik, the task of defense was also mandated by the importance of a stable political structure, particularly during a time of unsettling social change. As "masters of a revolutionary country," the soviets, Tsereteli believed, had the duty to strengthen this structure. Such had been his experience in Irkutsk—and this was more or less the route to the idea of revolutionary defensism.

It was Tsereteli's hope that the soviet could appeal to an international socialist solidarity to end the war with a "just and universal" peace and yet ensure the survival of the revolution. Over the next few months, revolutionary defensism would gain widespread popularity in the soviets, for it not only articulated the new mood

[64] For a fuller discussion of the wartime writings of Tsereteli and other Siberian Zimmerwaldists, see Galili y García, "Origins of Revolutionary Defensism," 461–70. See also the group's two single-issue journals, *Sibirskii zhurnal* (December 1914) and *Sibirskoe obozrenie* (January 1915), and the occasional articles by Tsereteli and Dan (the second most important figure in the Siberian group) published in the Samara-based "legal" Menshevik newspaper *Golos* (also published under the titles *Nash golos* and *Golos truda*).

[65] For example, Tsereteli ordered the railroad workers in Irkutsk to let pass a train loaded with military supplies for the front: Tsereteli, *Vospominaniia o fevral'skoi revoliutsii* 1:24. For a discussion of this episode, see Galili y García, "Origins of Revolutionary Defensism," 472–73.

[66] That Georgian Social Democrats tended to appreciate the prerogatives of power more than other Mensheviks (except Dan and Potresov) is demonstrated in letters exchanged during the war between Tsereteli and A. I. Chkhenkeli (another Georgian Menshevik Duma deputy), in which the latter advocated "an active defense in the case of revolution": Tsereteli, *Vospominaniia o fevral'skoi revoliutsii* 1:7.

of "defensism" but promised to free the Social Democrats from the necessity of choosing between "internationalism" and "defensism."[67] Most important, Tsereteli's formulation had converted a pressing task into a revolutionary strategy, albeit one compromising the principles of internationalism.

Just how appealing Tsereteli's ideas were became clear on March 21, when he spoke at an executive committee meeting for the first time, after Sukhanov had presented the internationalists' draft resolution.[68] Tsereteli argued forcefully that the political condition of the revolution had changed the nature of defense, so that it could no longer be compared to "social-patriotism." Moreover, he declared, the strength of the democratic camp and its "principled opposition to imperialism" guaranteed that Russian foreign policy would be directed toward peace. The problem posed by the war, he said, lay in the fact that no one beside the soviet—not even the government—was capable of organizing the country for the defense of the revolution.

> Who would take upon themselves the task of organizing the defense of the country until peace is achieved? The circles beyond . . . the soviet are not up to the task . . . that means that we must renounce the policy of an *irresponsible opposition*. We must stop viewing the defense of the country as something foreign to us or as a *compromise*. . . . We must advance it as one of the *basic tasks of the revolution*, without the accomplishment of which the attainment of peace would be impossible.[69]

The effect of Tsereteli's words was immediate and dramatic. Only two Mensheviks (Larin and Grinevich) continued to advocate the Internationalists' resolution,[70] while those who had signed it—Erlikh, Bogdanov, Gvozdev, Liber, Chkheidze, and Skobelev—now rallied to revolutionary defensism; their speeches were, as Sukhanov peevishly put it, a veritable bacchanalia of "defensist," "statist," and even "coalitionary" sentiments. Indeed, Tsereteli's

---

[67] There is ample evidence that Tsereteli did not abandon his internationalist views. They were expressed in strong terms during his meeting with Branting and other European socialists shortly after Tsereteli's return to Petrograd; see Garvi, "Iz vospominaniia o fevral'skoi revoliutsii," 49, and Stankevich, *Vospominaniia*, 108.

[68] No minutes were taken at this meeting, but it has been described by Sukhanov, Tsereteli, and Shliapnikov.

[69] Tsereteli, *Vospominaniia fevral'skoi revoliutsii* 1:46–47 (emphasis in the original). See also Sukhanov, *Zapiski o revoliutsii* 2:338.

[70] Other Internationalists who spoke against Tsereteli were Sukhanov, Iurenev (a Mezhraionets), and the Bolsheviks Stuchka and Shliapnikov: Sukhanov, *Zapiski o revoliutsii* 2:340–41, and Tsereteli, *Vospominaniia o fevral'skoi revoliutsii* 1:47–48.

speech seemed to remove a deep inhibition against the "heretical thoughts" that many Mensheviks in the Soviet's leadership had obviously come to have in the past three weeks, as speaker after speaker expressed himself.

Bogdanov emphasized that the conditions of the revolution had made the disagreements over the war "history." Like Tsereteli, he was sure that the peace program of the soviet "would become the program of all revolutionary Russia and its government." Gvozdev argued that the slogans of defense were the only ones capable of placating the soldiers, and Liber depicted the danger that "German imperialism" represented to the revolution. Skobelev spoke of the "state and revolutionary responsibility" now weighing on the leaders of "democracy," and he referred to his experience in pacifying the military units in Kronstadt and Helsinki. He proposed bringing the same "state and governmental-revolutionary considerations" to bear on the soviet's war policy by "rejecting the extreme revolutionary formula of immediate peace in favor of a realistic struggle that would bring [peace] closer."[71] Suddenly, the old majority of Mensheviks and Internationalists which had gathered around the arrangement of dual power (and which had been holding strong in spite of internal doubts and pressure from other groups) was in shambles.

The immediate effect of this realignment was to delay for a month the confrontation between the soviet and the Provisional Government over the question of Russia's war aims. In the hours after his first speech to the executive committee, Tsereteli rethought the Defensist position he had advocated, and on March 22 he brought before the committee a resolution that balanced defense with peace and so won the support of both the unrepentant Defensists (the Populists Fillipovskii, Stankevich, and Bramson) and the staunchest of the Internationalists.[72] However, while the

---

[71] Tsereteli, *Vospominaniia o fevral'skoi revoliutsii* 1:49–51.

[72] Ibid., 53–54; Sukhanov, *Zapiski o revoliutsii* 2:343–44, 348. A similar realignment took place in the Mensheviks' Petrograd organization. A citywide meeting of a thousand members on March 26 adopted a resolution that combined a call for pressure on the government to renounce annexations and initiate peace talks with warnings on the danger "to the Russian revolution and international democracy" which would result from any attempt to "disorganize defense." Only Ermanskii and a few others voted against the resolution. See *RG*, March 25, 1917 (no. 16), 4, and March 28, 1917 (no. 18), 3–4; Nikolaevskii, "RSDRP," 18. See also the reports of the March 26 meeting of 120 Menshevik representatives of factories in the Petrograd district and the March 27 meeting of Mensheviks from the Moscow district, *RG*, March 28, 1917 (no. 18), 4, and March 31, 1917 (no. 21), 3; the editorial "What

executive committee was again united on a position regarding the war, the position labeled "revolutionary defensism," its members were still at odds on the question of pressuring the Provisional Government. A small group of Internationalists proposed calling for a massive campaign of support for the peace slogans included in the resolution just adopted, but Tsereteli and the majority preferred to negotiate the renunciation of annexations directly with the Provisional Government.[73]

If this preference was not sufficiently indicative of where the burden of Tsereteli's ideas lay, then Tsereteli's making himself a member of the soviet's negotiating team (the liaison committee which met with the cabinet on March 24) and his attempt to convince the ministers that a universal, democratic peace was Russia's safest defense were clearer indications.[74] He remembered later having detected an opportunity to divide the cabinet, given the sympathetic hearing he had received from three of its ministers, Kerenskii, Tereshchenko, and Nekrasov. Hence, even after the cabinet had united around the Miliukov-Nabokov statement of March 26, Tsereteli insisted on continuing to negotiate, telling the ministers that the statement was unacceptable.[75] For the moment, he did not have to choose between exerting pressure on the government and negotiating with it, because the cabinet yielded and on March 27 issued an altered version of the statement. It contained five new words declaring that the goal of "free Russia" was not the "forcible occupation of foreign territories," but it was still in the form of a declaration to the Russian people alone.[76]

Tsereteli's evaluation of this episode, which he offered to the First Conference of Soviets on March 29, was revealing. In his key-

---

Should Not Be Forgotten," *RG*, March 25, 1917 (no. 16), 2; and Liber's statement to the conference of Soviets, in *Vserossiiskoe soveshchanie*, 95–96.

[73] Tsereteli, *Vospominaniia o fevral'skoi revoliutsii* 1:54–55; Sukhanov, *Zapiski o revoliutsii* 2:344–46.

[74] Again, no minutes were taken at these meetings, and we have to rely on the participants' accounts. The fullest reports are in Tsereteli, *Vospominaniia o fevral'skoi revoliutsii* 1:60–72, and Sukhanov, *Zapiski o revoliutsii* 2:349–54, 360–65, and supplementary information is in Medlin and Parsons, eds., *Nabokov*, 114–15, and Miliukov, *Istoriia vtoroi russkoi revoliutsii* 1:84–87. Also see Wade, *Russian Search for Peace*, 26–27, and Roobol, *Tsereteli*, 96–99.

[75] The executive committee meeting of March 27, at which the question was discussed, is related in Tsereteli, *Vospominaniia o fevral'skoi revoliutsii* 1:72–74, and Sukhanov, *Zapiski o revoliutsii* 2:365–68.

[76] A full text of the statement in English translation can be found in Golder, *Documents of Russian History*, 329–31.

note address, he was only cautiously optimistic and seemed to imply that the soviet might have to apply more pressure on the Provisional Government in the pursuit of its goals for peace.

I do not want to overestimate the significance of [the modified Miliukov-Nabokov statement]. It does not fully satisfy all of our wishes. . . . We consider it necessary that the Provisional Government also enter into negotiations with the Allies in order to work out a general platform for all the Allies on the basis of the principles [of the March 27 declaration]. . . . But, comrades, once our government has taken a decisive step on that road, its further steps in this direction are unavoidable.[77]

Nonetheless, he was more pleased with his negotiating approach than he cared to reveal, as is suggested by an impromptu response to a criticism of his speech: "We have already accomplished the main thing!" he said[78]—meaning that the Provisional Government had accepted the soviet's approach to peace. But the government had not. In fact, Tsereteli derived his optimism not from any promise the government had made and not from the soviet's power to impose its will while avoiding an unsettling confrontation but from his belief that distinctions could be made among the bourgeoisie. The bourgeoisie at large, he admitted, had been guided in the past by its "narrow class interests in foreign policy," and some elements in its political leadership (presumably including Miliukov and Guchkov) persisted in their attachment to these goals. However, there was also the "responsible representation of the bourgeoisie" in the Provisional Government, which "out of consideration for the opinion of democratic Russia has recognized that . . . it had to renounce the narrow class policy into which it had been pushed and is still being pushed by certain circles within the bourgeoisie."[79] The conclusion that Tsereteli drew from the March 27 declaration was that the soviet should strive toward co-

---

[77] *Vserossiiskoe soveshchanie*, 40. Tsereteli's supporters differed in their own evaluations of the episode. Compare, for example, the very optimistic assessment in the SR newspaper *DN*, March 28, 1917 (no. 11), 1, and the more guarded one in *RG*, March 29, 1917 (no. 19), 1, and March 30, 1917 (no. 20), 1. There is consensus among memoirists that the soviet's "victory" was deceiving. See, for example, Miliukov, *Istoriia vtoroi russkoi revoliutsii* 1:86–87; Medlin and Parsons, eds., *Nabokov*, 116; Sukhanov, *Zapiski o revoliutsii* 2:369–70; Nikolaevskii, "RSDRP," 21; and Voitinskii, "God pobed i porazhenii," 38. Tsereteli himself continued to see the March 27 agreement as an "abrupt turnabout in the views held by the bourgeoisie": *Vospominaniia o fevral'skoi revoliutsii* 1:72–74.

[78] *Vserossiiskoe soveshchanie*, 87.

[79] Ibid., 39.

operation with these moderate, "responsible" segments of the propertied and educated classes, which Tsereteli identified with the "public men" who had made themselves the leaders of the progressive Russian bourgeoisie.[80]

THE SIGNIFICANCE of the idea of cooperation with the bourgeoisie was immense. A principal figure of Menshevism in Petrograd had not only set it forth; he had tied it to the war issue and had thus used it to promote a remarkable degree of unity among the leaders of the soviet and to create the conditions for a change in the soviet's stand on the question of political power. Under Tsereteli's leadership, the two largest groups in the soviet, the SRs and the Mensheviks, united to form the new Revolutionary Defensist block, which replaced the Menshevik-Internationalist majority in the executive committee and left the most committed proponents of dual power and the peace campaign isolated.[81] Moreover, the goal of defending both the revolution and the country provided a platform on which the soviet and the Provisional Government could now—indeed, were now forced to—cooperate.[82]

It was the issue of the war, then, more than any other the soviet had to confront during the first month of its existence, that was responsible for the move at the Conference of Soviets to abandon the strategy of dual power. Whereas the satisfaction of labor's demands and the regulation of the economy had seemed obtainable in the context of dual power, and the struggle for the soldiers' loyalty had made every member of the executive committee recognize that the soviet could neither increase its pressure on the government nor shoulder the responsibilities of power, the issue of the war presented the socialists with a clear choice: either they would have to pressure the Provisional Government to initiate peace negotiations, or they would have to cooperate with it on the task of defense. The majority of Mensheviks preferred the latter course, especially because Tsereteli's new formulations allowed defense to coexist with the soviet's peace slogans. The principles of dual

[80] Tsereteli later remembered being most impressed by Nekrasov, who argued that the government's document should be understood as a demonstration of the cabinet's desire to accommodate revolutionary democracy and make possible "a policy of unity": Tsereteli, *Vospominaniia o fevral'skoi revoliutsii* 1:70–71. See also the discussion of this episode and its lessons in Roobol, *Tsereteli*, 96–101.

[81] It was precisely at this time that a separate "internationalist bureau" was formed within the Menshevik Petrograd organization: Nikolaevskii, "RSDRP," 23.

[82] Voitinskii, "God pobed i porazhenii," 38.

power were therefore seriously undermined, though, as we shall see shortly, the arrangement survived into the second month of the revolution and outlived its perceived usefulness. Finally, it was the war issue that had forced an open discussion of the question of power, which the Mensheviks had been trying to avoid in the weeks since dual power had been established.

THE QUESTION OF POWER

The experience on which dual power had been based—namely, the executive committee's dealings with the Provisional Duma Committee and the events of the revolution's first three days—was only partially indicative of what was to follow. The members of the executive committee could not have foreseen the enormous responsibilities that were to be theirs by virtue of both their sway over so much of the population of urban Russia and their own boldness of action. As the importance of their organization grew, so did their dissatisfaction with dual power, which kept them one step removed from the actual exercise of state power.

Yet there was a reluctance—if not an inability—on the part of the socialists on the executive committee to discuss and resolve the inadequacies of dual power. This reluctance was readily apparent to Menshevik visitors from the provinces, who commented on the "confusion" and "disorientation" in the committee's position on the question of power, in sharp contrast to its activism in regard to the problems of the war, the economy, and labor relations.[83] In part, the reluctance could be attributed, especially during the first two or three weeks of March, to the plethora of issues the committee was called on to resolve and the chaotic conditions in which it had to work. The unceasing turmoil left the soviet's leaders little time for thought or planning and exhausted even the most energetic of activists.[84] By now, the soviet included some two thousand soldiers and one thousand workers, and Sukhanov remembered how Bogdanov used to preside over interminable meetings, "brandishing a bell in one hand and majestically conducting with the other."[85] There was also the newness of the situation. "New ques-

[83] Ibid., 27; Garvi, "Iz vospominanii o fevral'skoi revoliutsii," 48; Denike, interview no. 8, p. 18.

[84] Sukhanov reported "unbearable fatigue" during most of March and considered it the most difficult time in all of 1917: *Zapiski o revoliutsii* 2:195.

[85] Ibid., 15. The soldiers were overrepresented in the soviet by comparison to the workers; the former sent one delegate for each unit, the latter one delegate for

tions arose in such numbers and in such an unprecedented way," Stankevich recalled, "that anyone who did not confine himself blindly to some dogma but wanted to act according to the circumstances was utterly confused."[86]

The executive committee itself was in a state of flux, as changes in personnel and attitudes eroded the consensus that had once united the committee behind dual power. By mid-March, the Populists, who had earlier followed the Mensheviks' lead without much opposition, seemed to have found their own voice and now admitted that they had accepted dual power specifically as an instrument of support for the Provisional Government. It was this aspect that they now emphasized in their constant warnings of the danger inherent in vying with the Provisional Government for greater authority.[87] Moreover, the Populists' gained new strength as a result of changes in the membership of the executive committee. By the middle of the month, almost half of the committee was composed of representatives from the soldiers' section of the soviet, from the soviet of officers, and from the citywide unions, not those of workers but of white-collar employees, porters, domestic servants, and shoemakers—that is, the very groups that the Social Democrats had identified as the "urban petty bourgeoisie." These groups favored the Populists' call for closer cooperation between the soviet and the Provisional Government.[88] Furthermore, other groups of sympathizers from outside the soviet—students and professional organizations, cooperatives, consumer associations—echoed this sentiment.[89]

---

every thousand workers. Attempts to change these ratios failed: ibid. 225–27; *Petrogradskii sovet*, 48; *RG*, March 21, 1917 (no. 13), 2; Shliapnikov, *Semnadtsatyi god* 3:167–74; and Anweiler, *Soviets*, 107–8.

[86] Stankevich, *Vospominaniia*, 90.

[87] According to an editorial in *DN*, March 15, 1917 (no. 1), 1, the party was united in its support of the Provisional Government and its conduct of the war. Also see ibid., 4, and Stankevich, *Vospominaniia*, 188.

[88] Sukhanov, *Zapiski o revoliutsii* 2:259–60. See also Shliapnikov, *1917*, 2:2. Lists of meetings, resolutions, and announcements of these new unions appeared in all the socialist newspapers. One good example of the views they reflected is found in a report of the March 22 meeting of the Union of Bank Employees: *IzvPS*, March 26, 1917 (no. 25), 4.

[89] See the appeal to the soviet and the Provisional Government by a meeting of deputies from twenty-six railroad unions, in *IzvPS*, March 12, 1917 (no. 13), 6, and the resolutions adopted at a meeting of artillery technicians, in *RG*, March 11, 1917 (no. 5), 3; by a conference of cooperatives in the Petrograd region, in *Den'*, March 9, 1917 (no. 4), 2; and by an assembly of students, in *IzvPS*, March 22, 1917 (no.

Social Democrats in exile, Irkutsk, 1914–1915. Seated: I. G. Tsereteli (l.) and V. S. Voitinskii. Standing at their left is A. R. Gots; standing at their right is F. I. Dan. Below, S. L. Vainshtein (l.), L. O. Dan (c.), and I. G. Tsereteli, Irkutsk, 1914–1915.

At the left, a session of the Petrograd soviet in the early days of the revolution. Lower left, N. S. Chkheidze addressing sailors at the Tauride Palace, February 1917. Below, members of the Provisional Government at the burial of victims of the revolution. Front row, center, l. to r.: A. I. Shingarev, Prince G. E. L'vov, I. V. Godnev, P. N. Miliukov. Behind Shingarev and to his right: A. I. Konovalov. Between Prince L'vov and Godnev: N. V. Nekrasov.

Upper right, a session of the All-Russian Conference of Soviets, April 3, 1917. Front row, l. to r.: K. A. Gvozdev, V. N. Filippovskii, N. Iu. Kapelinskii, Iu. M. Steklov, B. O. Bogdanov, M. I. Skobelev, G. V. Plekhanov, N. S. Chkheidze, I. G. Tsereteli. Above, P. A. Garvi, 1915. At right, Iu. O. Martov (l.) and F. I. Dan, winter 1917–1918.

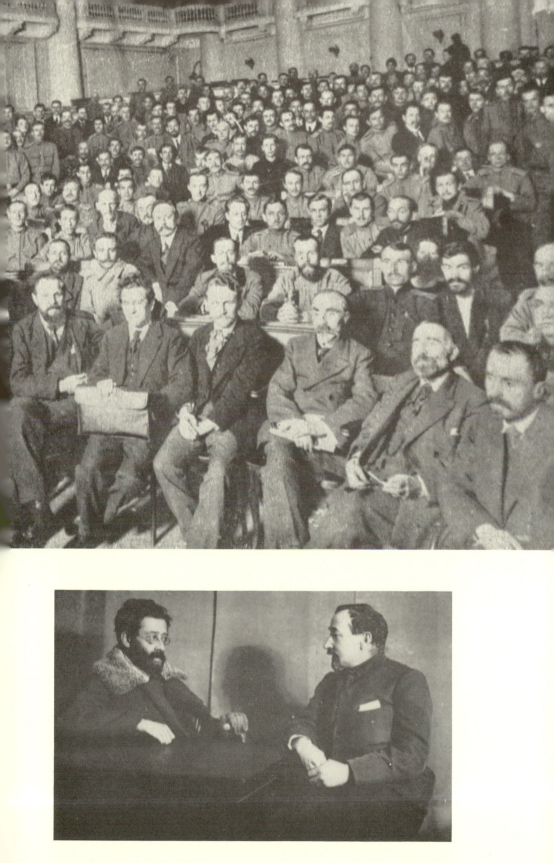

May Day demonstration in Petrograd, April 18, 1917. Far right, I. G. Tsereteli as minister of post and telegraph, May 1917. Below, A. N. Potresov, 1925.

Демонстрация in Petrograd, June 18, 1917. Below, Presidium of the First All-Russian Congress of Soviets. L. to r.: M. I. Skobelev, N. S. Chkheidze, G. V. Plekhanov, I. G. Tsereteli.

Still, the single most important factor in preventing the executive committee from taking up the issue of dual power was the subtle change taking place within the Menshevik party itself and its associated circles. In Petrograd, the newspaper *Den'* expressed the opinions of Potresov's Defensist followers, who were not outside the party and were calling for closer cooperation between the soviet and the Provisional Government. They argued that it was the alliance of democracy and the liberal bourgeoisie that had secured victory in February, and that if this alliance were to continue to safeguard the revolution and not undermine general political authority, the soviet would have to refrain from questioning the government's exercise of its authority under the dual power arrangement.[90] Outside Petrograd, the tendency to interpret dual power in a spirit of support for the Provisional Government was apparent even among mainstream Mensheviks; it was the interpretation offered by the Menshevik party organizations of Moscow and other cities, where Mensheviks faced even less of a challenge from the left than they did in Petrograd.[91] By and large, these Mensheviks were more concerned with the preservation of a semblance of order in the provinces, where peasants and garrison units predominated, than with exerting pressure on the Provisional Government.[92]

In Petrograd, however, the Mensheviks resisted any rethinking of the issue of governmental authority until the latter part of April. With the exception of Potresov, even the former Liquidationists in Petrograd, who recognized and feared the country's potential for anarchy, clung to their belief in the efficacy of educational and organizational work and were not convinced that a strong govern-

---

21), 6. *RG* called these groups the "true allies" of the proletariat, in an editorial entitled "Is Everyone for Freedom?" March 8, 1917 (no. 2), 1–2.

[90] P. Iushkevich, "The Soviet of Workers' Deputies and the All-National Tasks," *Den'*, March 21, 1917 (no. 14), 1; V. Kantorovich, "An Incorrect Course," *Den'*, March 22, 1917 (no. 15), 1.

[91] Resolutions adopted by the Menshevik organizations of the cities of Moscow, Kiev, Kharkov, and Samara, and by the Kiev soviet all urged support of the Provisional Government: *RG*, March 16, 1917 (no. 9), 3; March 19, 1917 (no. 12), 4; March 30, 1917 (no. 20), 3; March 31, 1917 (no. 21), 4.

[92] In Irkutsk, much of the effort of the Committee of Public Organizations (headed by Tsereteli) was directed toward restoring order in the town and the province and especially toward gaining control of the local garrison; see Voitinskii, "God pobed i porazhenii," 12–18; Tsereteli, *Vospominaniia o fevral'skoi revoliutsii*, 20–22; and Serebrennikov, "Vospominaniia," 1:11–12, 28. For a discussion of Denike's experience in Kazan, see chap. 5.

ment was required for the maintenance of social order. Thus, an article in *Rabochaia gazeta* warned that anarchism and maximalism "could again cast their shadow on our revolution, as they had in 1905–6." The article explained that "a people that had lived in slavery for centuries could not suddenly become free and restrained." The only remedy, it concluded, was organization: "It is necessary to direct the agitated sea of the popular masses into channels of organized political life: an organized class struggle, . . . trade unions, councils of elders, and conciliation boards among the workers, and public organizations in the cities and the villages."[93]

Although all Mensheviks theoretically shared this emphasis on organization, the concept implied quite different strategies to the two main strains within the party. Whereas the more activist among them sought to exploit the growing organizational force of democracy for the revolutionary tasks still ahead,[94] former Liquidationists were troubled by the possibility that a bourgeois democratic Russia would turn against the working class, and so they advised caution in pressuring the Provisional Government and looked on the new organizational opportunities as a means of restraint. But not even the most moderate of Mensheviks in Petrograd questioned the basic premise of dual power—that the socialists should maintain a separate, independent organizational base and not join the government. Thus, the Menshevik newspaper continued to reiterate the general principles of dual power even when two of its five editors (Cherevanin and Baturskii) were staunch Defensists.[95] Party doctrine had made this formula the least objectionable to all shades of Menshevism, and continued party unity required strict adherence to it.[96] Even though many Mensheviks feared the consequences of the strategy of pressure implicit in dual power, they remained silent, though their attitude was known and precluded a consistent and deliberate application of pressure.

This dilemma obviously paralyzed the executive committee, and Sukhanov finally proposed, on March 4, that dual power be recon-

[93] "Anarchy and Organization," *RG*, March 19, 1917 (no. 12), 2.

[94] "Strike While the Iron Is Hot," *RG*, March 21, 1917 (no. 13), 1–2; "An Absolutely Urgent Task," *RG*, March 18, 1917 (no. 11), 1.

[95] See, for example, "The Provisional Government," *RG*, March 7, 1917 (no. 1), 1. The other three members of the editorial board were B. Gorev and A. N. Smirnov, representing the "center," and Ermanskii for the Internationalists: *PI*, July 15, 1917 (no. 1), 4.

[96] Nikolaevskii, "RSDRP," 15–16.

sidered. He suggested that the executive committee create institutional channels through which the soviet's pressure on, and *kontrol'* of, the Provisional Government might be implemented in a planned, consistent manner. First, the committee should elect a commission to prepare social legislation that the government would be expected to adopt, perhaps after some negotiations; second, it should name "delegations" to be attached to the government's ministries, where they would exercise *kontrol'* and pressure and also learn the business of state; and third, it should form a "shadow cabinet" made up of representatives of these ministerial delegations for the purpose of "applying pressure and *kontrol'* in the sphere of general policy."[97]

The Mensheviks were not yet prepared to embrace either Sukhanov's proposals or the Populists' critique of the formula of conditional support for the government.[98] A "legislative commission" was set up, and a shadow cabinet was elected, in which the supporters of pressure and cooperation were carefully balanced. But the legislative commission never met, and the shadow cabinet, which became known as the liaison committee, did nothing to enhance the efficacy of *kontrol'* over the Provisional Government.[99]

Clearly, the support of the Mensheviks was needed if a new consensus was to be built around a more precisely defined or entirely different political arrangement. But not until mid-March did the Mensheviks begin to face their own central dilemma: They were eager to exploit all the practical possibilities of the strength that leadership of the soviet had conferred on them, but they were reluctant to draw any of the logical political conclusions. Many inside the executive committee had come to see that dual power was no longer consonant with the soviet's growing burden of responsibility. Both the overall success and the occasional failure of the executive committee in employing the principles of dual power had involved the soviet in new spheres of activity and made untenable its insistence on remaining an "outsider" or a separate entity. The Conference of Soviets at the end of March provided the

[97] Sukhanov, *Zapiski o revoliutsii* 2:81–85.

[98] Ibid., 89.

[99] Of the commission's members, Sukhanov and Steklov were advocates of pressure, and Skobelev and Fillipovskii, of cooperation. The fifth member, Chkheidze, appeared to be in a state of depression and was not very active in the commission's work. See ibid., 85–87; *Petrogradskii sovet*, 15, 26–27; Medlin and Parsons, eds., *Nabokov*, 126–29; and Steklov's report on the liaison commission to the soviet's plenum, in *IzvPS*, March 12, 1917 (no. 13).

first opportunity at which the dilemma could be discussed fully and with the participation of the provincial delegates.

THE CONFERENCE DEBATE on the relationship to the Provisional Government began on March 31 (after the debate on the war) and lasted two days.[100] Steklov, the executive committee's official spokesman, restated and acclaimed the principle of dual power.[101] Almost immediately afterward, delegates from the provinces and from military units began to attack it. With great urgency, they gave vent to their disbelief and anger. Some had come to Petrograd ready to demand an end to dual power, which they viewed as unsuitable to the situation created by the revolution. The task of defending the country, some Populist army delegates insisted, required a government of authority and will, not one that was divided or of a dual nature. They accused the Petrograd soviet and the Social Democrats of promoting a "narrow party and class view" that divided the citizenry.[102] Other provincial delegates betrayed a fundamental misunderstanding of dual power and the concept of *kontrol'*. Stachkov, a delegate from the Twelfth Army who identified himself as a Menshevik, said that the soldiers in his organization understood the existing political order as an "unwritten constitution" that provided for a chamber of representatives, the soviet, and an executive organ, the Provisional Government. "The majority of us," he added, "consider that the government expresses the will of the soviet; but Steklov's statement here has caused enormous confusion in our minds."[103]

Clearly, the leadership in Petrograd had failed to explain its po-

[100] The proceedings of this debate occupy eighty pages of the conference protocols: *Vserossiiskoe soveshchanie*, 106–89. Shorter but reliable reports are provided in *Khronika* 1: 151–58 and Shliapnikov, *Semnadtsatyi god* 3:229–44.

[101] *Vserossiiskoe soveshchanie*, 106–24. For excerpts from Steklov's speech, see chap. 2.

[102] See *Vserossiiskoe soveshchanie* for statements by the following: P. P. Usov, an SR from the Berdichev garrison, 167–69; Adamov-Frenkel', from Pskov, 127–30; Donetskii, from the Ekaterinoslav garrison, 144; Kokhno, 144–47; A. E. Skachkov, a Menshevik delegate from the Twelfth Army, 161–63; and D. N. Titov, an SR from Ufa, 164–65. Also in *Vserossiiskoe soveshchanie* are calls for support of the Provisional Government by an SR delegate from Moscow, M. Ia. Gendel'man, 155–58; the Tenth Army SR delegate, Kotliarev, 166; and, with some qualification, two Mensheviks, the army delegate G. D. Kuchin, 169–71, and P. F. Istratov, from Tambov, 175–76.

[103] *Vserossiiskoe soveshchanie*, 161–63. An SR from Chita, N. P. Pumpianskii, spoke in defense of the existing soviet policy and against coalition and said that dual power did not exist and was only a bourgeois lie: ibid., 152–53.

litical strategy to its less sophisticated adherents in the provinces. That task was made more difficult by differences in the balance of social and political forces between the capital and the rest of the country. In garrison towns and in those near the front, soldiers were often a soviet's only constituency, as the delegate Kamenskii, from Ekaterinoslav, pointed out in describing the likely result of his taking Steklov's proposals back home in his "little suitcase" to the soldiers: they would send him back to Petrograd with instructions to "go and bring back another one." At the very least, the soldiers, as well as many others in the provincial soviets, wanted their representatives to support the Provisional Government fully and without qualification, and that meant without mentioning the bourgeois nature of the government.[104] But if possible, they wanted their leaders to join a coalition government, so that "mistakes could be avoided" and the government "wouldn't collapse from weakness" and would be "deserving" of their confidence.[105]

The strength of the soviet and the responsibilities it had already assumed had evidently convinced the provincial delegates that it was capable of achieving such a coalition; "after all, among us there are such famous, nationally known names as Chkheidze, Skobelev, and Tsereteli."[106] The provincial delegates were baffled that their leaders in Petrograd should decline to join the cabinet yet give formal sanction to the cooperation between the soviet and the government. The reason why the situation in the capital made no sense to them was that in their own localities social divisions ran along different lines: between soldiers and civilians, town and country, forces of order and those of anarchy. The term "bourgeois" meant little to them, while the term "democracy" meant everyone but the supporters of the old regime.

After the first hours of the debate, then, it was clear that a desire for a reformulation of dual power prevailed in the provinces. Yet Steklov's statement, as well as the draft resolution the Menshevik organizational committee had prepared for the party's faction at the conference, merely restated the principles of dual power without modification. The draft resolution endorsed the tactics of pressure and *kontrol'* and conditioned the soviet's "recognition" and

---

[104] Ibid., 146–47. See also the address by Dobychikov, in ibid., 135–37, for a similar outlook.

[105] Ibid., 173.

[106] From a speech by the delegate Kamenskii: ibid., 146–47.

support of the Provisional Government on the latter's continued adherence to the soviet's political program.[107]

At this point, when the provincials were at loggerheads with their leaders' doctrinal obstinacy, Tsereteli stepped in, ostensibly to clarify differences between Steklov's position and that of the executive committee's new Revolutionary Defensist majority but in fact to suggest a new political strategy for the soviet. In the process, he provided a bolder reinterpretation of Social Democratic doctrine than his Revolutionary Defensism had seemed to imply.

TSERETELI'S IDEAS regarding the political shape of Russia's revolution had been formulated at the same time as his revolutionary defensism—that is, during the war and in the weeks following the February revolution, though their premises went back to Tsereteli's Georgian origins and his early experiences in revolutionary politics as a student activist in Moscow University from 1900 to 1902 and as leader of the Social Democratic faction in the Second Duma in the spring of 1907.[108] Two ideas were central to Tsereteli's political worldview: first, that all social groups and classes in Russia, with the exception of the tsarist bureaucracy, were "progressive" in the sense that they sought political democracy; and second, that the socialists and, in the case of Georgia, the Marxists had a special role to play in uniting these disparate forces and transforming Russia's political system. Tsereteli had held these ideas throughout his intermittent political career, even in the aftermath of 1905 and during the political revival of 1912–1914, when other Mensheviks had come either to doubt the workers' readiness to follow a "mature" political strategy or to suspect that the bourgeoisie was essentially counterrevolutionary.[109]

During the war, and despite his disappointment at the collapse of international socialist solidarity, Tsereteli had become even more sanguine about the prospects of a democratic reconstruction

[107] RG, April 7, 1917 (no. 25), 2.

[108] For discussions of these early experiences and their impact on Tsereteli's political ideas, see Galili y García, "Origins of Revolutionary Defensism," 456–60; Nikolaevskii, "Tsereteli"; and Roobol, Tsereteli, chaps. 1–2.

[109] Such doubts can be seen in many of the contributions to the Menshevik newspaper Nasha zaria. Tsereteli's optimism was expressed in a letter to P. B. Akselrod, June 2, 1914 (Collections of the Axelrod Archive), in which he stated his faith in the "universal victory of the Menshevik principle" and the "normalization of the labor movement" in Russia. For a discussion of Menshevik interpretations of the strike movement of 1912–1914, see L. H. Haimson, "Social Stability in Urban Russia," 23:619–42.

in Russia. He believed firmly (as did other Siberian Zimmerwald-ists) that the public organizations contained the bourgeoisie's "healthy, progressive" elements, that these were already forming the kind of cooperation with the working class essential for Russia's safe transition to democracy, and that the working class was ready to participate in such an alliance. Moreover, the intimate ties he and his closest followers in Irkutsk had formed with a number of SRs (notably A. R. Gots) convinced Tsereteli that even the peasantry, or at least the Populists who purported to speak for it, could be trusted to follow the political lead of Social Democracy.[110] In sum, Tsereteli's vision of a prospective revolution was far more optimistic than that of his fellow Mensheviks in Petrograd, in the provinces, or abroad, because he judged the divisions separating urban Russia from its rural hinterland as well as those that cut through urban society itself (census society and the lower classes) to be surmountable, especially under the unifying guidance of the socialist intelligentsia.

Indeed, Tsereteli had seen his expectations fulfilled in every way during the revolution's first three weeks. His experience as the chairman of the Irkutsk Committee of Public Organizations and the responsibilities entailed by that role had prompted him to formulate a comprehensive concept of the revolution and define the specific strategies this new conception mandated for the Social Democrats in the soviets.[111] He saw the Russian revolution as a democratic, national revolution carried out by the "vital forces of the country," among which he counted not only the soviet's socialist leadership, the workers, and the soldiers but also the peasantry and the progressive bourgeoisie. Although he believed that Russia's revolution was an "all-national" one, he felt the country's backwardness required the socialist intelligentsia both to promote the alliance of the "vital forces" on the one hand and to safeguard freedom and the revolutionary spirit on the other.[112] In addition, and apart from his concept of the social makeup of the revolution-

---

[110] Galili y García, "Origins of Revolutionary Defensism," 465–66, 469–70.

[111] Ibid., 470–73.

[112] Tsereteli described the evolution of his ideas on the revolution in a series of fifty-seven articles written in French under the general title of "Souvenirs sur la révolution russe" (Nicolaevsky Collection of the Hoover Institution on War, Revolution, and Peace) and published between 1927 and 1929 in the Swedish newspaper *Ny tid*; see esp. articles 3 and 24. Also see Tsereteli's telegram of March 3 to the Provisional Government and the one sent later to Chkheidze, in *IzvPS*, March 6, 1917 (no. 7), 5, and March 7, 1917 (no. 8), 3.

ary forces, Tsereteli saw the necessity of a stable political structure at a time of unsettling social changes (this had also been one of the reasons for his support of military defense) and assigned this task as well to the soviets.[113]

Tsereteli did not question the political strategy pursued by the executive committee; he simply interpreted dual power in the spirit of his own ideas, as an "agreement with the bourgeoisie for long-term political reconstruction," and he complained only that it was not being implemented with sufficient constancy.[114] Nevertheless, his statement to the Conference of Soviets was strikingly different from the language used by other Social Democratic leaders of the Petrograd soviet. At the outset, he declared that the soviet had been strong enough to seize power, as if agreeing with those who spoke before him, but soon his emphasis shifted to the need for an "all-national unity" of the "vital forces of the country." He praised the workers for their wisdom in accepting this requirement and for understanding that it could be achieved only so long as the revolution adhered to its bourgeois limits. He thanked them for making "the democratic republic" their single most important political slogan and added that it provided the platform for an "all-national agreement" that could unite the proletariat, the peasantry, and "all the strata of the bourgeoisie that understood the national tasks of the day." Finally, he reassured his listeners that the "vast majority of the bourgeoisie" belonged to these responsible strata.[115]

This last point was particularly important, first, because in its assertion of bourgeois progressivism it exceeded the expectations of even the most confident Mensheviks in Petrograd; and second, because it was immediately qualified by Tsereteli himself. The antisoviet campaign in the press had begun to assume a threatening tone at the time of Tsereteli's return to Petrograd, so he could not have failed to mention the existence of "irresponsible circles" within the bourgeoisie, to which he attributed the attack. Yet, by drawing a distinction between these circles and the majority of the

[113] Voitinskii, one of Tsereteli's closest collaborators in Irkutsk and Petrograd, has written in his memoirs that both he and Tsereteli saw the "consolidation and strengthening of the state apparatus" as one of democracy's most important tasks; the interests of the state and of the revolution were "inseparable." Voitinskii, "God pobed i porazhenii," 20.

[114] See Tsereteli, *Vospominaniia o fevral'skoi revoliutsii* 1: 28, and his first speech to the Petrograd soviet, in *IzvPS*, March 21, 1917 (no. 20), 2–3.

[115] *Vserossiiskoe soveshchanie*, 147–50.

bourgeoisie (as he had already done in his statement on the question of the war) and by pointing to the readiness of the Provisional Government—"the responsible organ of the bourgeoisie"—to meet the soviet's demands, Tsereteli was able both to claim that the "vital forces" were indeed united and to imply that *kontrol'* was not at all necessary.[116]

As might be expected, Tsereteli's address was received with great enthusiasm by the majority of Mensheviks, by most of the other delegates at the conference (including the Populists), and especially by those from the provinces, partly because he had given expression to the significance of the soviets' strength and the burden of national responsibility, which the provincials felt they were already carrying, but more important because in his formulation strength did not translate into risky confrontation. For all these reasons, as well as for the sake of party and socialist unity, the Menshevik faction withdraw its original draft resolution in favor of one prepared by a "compromise commission" (drawn from the executive committee). This latter resolution was modified and then adopted by a joint meeting of the conference's Menshevik and SR factions.[117] This event signaled the formation of the new SR-Menshevik Revolutionary Defensist bloc that would dominate the soviets until October 1917.

The new alliance was not consummated at the conference, however, in part because, although it had the votes and the political stature to support a new strategy, it lacked the necessary unity and resolve.[118] Indeed, the compromise resolution itself at once weakened the notion of separateness on which the strategies of pressure and *kontrol'* were based (by calling for a "union with the other progressive forces") and yet obligated the soviets to pursue that strategy.[119] Essentially, the problem was that Tsereteli's goal of cooperation and unity not only did not match the revolutionary conceptions of some key Mensheviks but also, and more importantly, it required a united coalition government, not one based on dual power. That is, Tsereteli's proposition required the abandonment of a doctrinal point on which all Mensheviks had agreed since 1905.

---

[116] Ibid.

[117] Sukhanov, *Zapiski o revoliutsii* 2:398; and Dan's explanation to the Conference of Soviets, in *Vserossiiskoe soveshchanie*, 188. The compromise resolution adopted by the conference is reprinted in *Vserossiiskoe soveshchanie*, 292–93.

[118] Radkey, *Agrarian Foes of Bolshevism*, 134–37.

[119] *Vserossiiskoe soveshchanie*, 292–93.

For this reason, the first manifestation of opposition to Tsereteli came on the point of his "revolutionary conception" and emanated mostly from Petrograd Mensheviks and from former labor *praktiki* from elsewhere. L. M. Khinchuk, for example, the Menshevik chairman of the Moscow soviet and a veteran labor organizer, dismissed Tsereteli's "revolutionary conception" as unsuited to the relationship between revolutionary democracy and the Provisional Government. "No coalition government, no conciliatory opinion, no cooperative work" was necessary for the realization of the soviet's goals, he declared; it required only "organized pressure" by the forces of revolutionary democracy.[120]

Of greater significance to Tsereteli both personally and politically, because so much of the history of Menshevism was tied to it, was the opposition of F. I. Dan. Dan was the most prominent Menshevik in Petrograd by virtue of his having been the party's "chief of staff" for so long as well as Martov's closest confidant (he was Martov's brother-in-law). Moreover, his mastery of factional politics and his ability to deliver the votes of his followers were needed if Tsereteli's ideas were to gain a solid base of support within the Menshevik party. In the past, Dan had collaborated with Tsereteli in the Siberian Zimmerwaldist circle in Irkutsk, but there had been disagreements between the two men.[121] These disagreements reappeared when they met at the conference after a separation of several months. (Dan had returned to Petrograd only at the start of the conference.) Dan's main concern had always been to use every opportunity to turn his party into an active, participatory political entity, and in this he resembled Tsereteli. But his experience in the practical application of Menshevik doctrine under very changeable political conditions had led him to be deeply suspicious of the principal social actors in a projected rev-

[120] Ibid., 163–64. Another delegate echoed this sentiment when he stated that the tasks of the soviet were "to establish organization in the localities, to strengthen that which we have conquered, and to pressure the Provisional Government": ibid., 165–66.

[121] On the collaboration and the differences between Dan and Tsereteli, see Galili y García, "Origins of Revolutionary Defensism," 467–70. Tsereteli himself is the main source of information regarding these differences (*Vospominaniia o fevral'skoi revoliutsii*, 9–10), but fragments of information suggest that the Siberian Zimmerwaldists were quite divided over these issues, with Dan being supported by N. A. Rozhkov (a former Bolshevik) and Tsereteli by Voitinskii and by S. L. Vainshtein and K. M. Ermolaev (Mensheviks of Liquidationist leanings). See Dan's letter to Akselrod, January 3, 1916 (Collections of the Axelrod Archive), and Nikolaevskii, "Gruppa 'Sibirskikh Tsimmerval'distov'," 11–12.

olution, particularly the bourgeoisie, and therein lay his differences with Tsereteli.

During the war, Dan had been pessimistic about the possibility
of creating a "broad revolutionary movement" in Russia, for he
believed that, in the struggle for bourgeois democracy, the liberals
would rather seek the protection of the autocracy than oppose it.[122]
Consequently, he had argued that the economic, social, and political transformation Russia so urgently needed could be brought
about only by the independent action of the proletariat, and he
had in fact cited the opportunities for Social Democratic organizational work as the only justification for workers' participation in
the public organizations.[123] Now, at the Conference of Soviets,
Dan spoke in the name of the Menshevik delegates to underscore
two of their principal positions in regard to the question of power:
first, that the soviet should not participate in the exercise of state
power but should strive to influence policy through pressure on,
and *kontrol'* of, the government; and second, that "for the moment" the Provisional Government should be recognized as "a
fact" and not be destroyed.[124] Clearly, Dan's vision of the revolution excluded Tsereteli's new concept of the "vital forces" and instead placed the emphasis on the temporary and qualified nature
of the soviet's acceptance of the Provisional Government. In other
words, he affirmed the concept of dual power in most essentials.[125]

However, the problem besetting the Mensheviks was more complex than was indicated by the disagreements between Dan and
Tsereteli. It stemmed from the ambiguities with which they had to
contend as they attempted to respond to changing political realities. For example, Dan was at once suspicious of the men in the

[122] F. D. [Dan], "Dve voiny," *Sibirskoe obozrenie*, 12–18; idem, "Vnutrenniaia politika v 1915 godu," *Nash golos*, January 10, 1916 (no. 16), 1; letter from Martov to
Akselrod, January 3, 1916 (*Pis'ma*, 355), in which Martov reports the views expressed in a letter he had received from Dan; Tsereteli, *Vospominaniia o fevral'skoi
revoliutsii* 1:9.

[123] Nad [Dan], "Rabochie i voenno-promyshlennye komitety," *Nash golos*, November 17, 1915 (no. 10), 1; "Deklaratsiia russkikh internatsionalistov-Menshevi-
kov," *Izvestiia zagranichnogo sekretariata organizatsionnogo komiteta RSDRP* [Zurich],
February 5, 1916 (no. 3), 7–8.

[124] *Vserossiiskoe soveshchanie*, 188.

[125] Two commentators of otherwise different opinions—Sukhanov, and the Menshevik Boris Sapir—speculated later that, if Dan had chosen to ally himself with
Martov rather than Tsereteli, political divisions within the Menshevik party in 1917
might have followed a pattern different from what they actually did. Sukhanov
called Dan "the only giant figure" in the Revolutionary Defensist leadership of the
executive committee. See Sukhanov, *Zapiski o revoliutsii* 3:132–38; and Sapir, "Theodor Dan," 12. For a biographical sketch of Dan, see appendix 3 of the present work.

cabinet yet appreciative of the ways in which governmental authority could be used (an uncommon recognition among veteran Mensheviks). Furthermore, he was eager to take every opportunity to influence the course of the revolution, and this mandated an activist approach for the soviets and a measure of responsibility so large it could not be reconciled with remaining separate from state affairs. Conversely, Tsereteli was wholly committed to the soviet's role as the unifier of the nation's "vital forces," and yet he could not overcome his party's ideological stricture against coalition. For these reasons, no resolution to the question of power could be reached at the conference, though an open split between Tsereteli and Dan was avoided.

Indeed, Menshevik doctrine proved to be the greatest obstacle to the soviet's realignment behind a strategy of coalition (though there were also "objective" factors, which will be discussed in chapter 5). At the Conference of Soviets, the entire Menshevik faction denounced the Trudoviki for even proposing the idea, and at the faction's meetings the usually mild Chkheidze was vehement in his attack on the proponents of coalition and accused them of "disorganizing the conference." Even Tsereteli, who had come close to advocating coalition, avoided the issue altogether during his public appearances and argued against it in the faction's private meetings.[126]

All this presents us with a curious spectacle. To explain Tsereteli's retreat, we must look at his early encounters and renewed contacts with his party. At the Conference of Soviets, the Menshevik leaders of the executive committee were warned not to forget, "in their inebriation with their present power," that political arrangements must reflect the relations of existing social forces. In words that recalled the arguments of the previous decade, they were reminded of the dangers of participating in a bourgeois government: "Even if you send Chkheidze, Tsereteli, etc., to the cabinet, the situation will remain much the same as it is now, as long as there is no social revolution. By sitting in the cabinet, Chkheidze and Tsereteli will only end up taking upon themselves the responsibility for that which the bourgeois ministers do."[127] When it came to the question of power and the related question of the nature of the revolution, the Mensheviks seemed not to be able

[126] Voitinskii, "God pobed i porazhenii," 101–2; Sukhanov, *Zapiski o revoliutsii* 2: 384.

[127] *Vserossiiskoe soveshchanie*, 176, 165.

to comprehend it in terms other than those provided by the ordered scheme of their ideology. It was as if their boldness, their sense of the practical, ably demonstrated in their varied work in the executive committee, had failed them when the abstract question of power was raised.

As THE FIRST MONTH of the revolution drew to a close, the Menshevik leaders of the soviet faced a painful problem. The revolutionary reality they had helped create required that they take an increasingly direct part in the process of decision making and perhaps even in the exercise of governmental authority. But how could this be done? The most extreme solution would have been for the soviet to assume full governmental authority, but not even the Bolsheviks were ready to embrace this course (the Bolshevik faction at the Conference of Soviets voted for the compromise resolution), nor were the majority of workers in Petrograd.[128] Although the soviet could attempt to make the Provisional Government its instrument by applying more pressure and *kontrol'* on it, as was provided for in the concept of dual power, that course depended ultimately on the government's recognition of the legitimacy of the soviet or the soviet's readiness to risk an open, even violent confrontation with the government. But the negotiations over the question of the war had shown that the government was not prepared to accord recognition to the soviet, while the Mensheviks who embraced revolutionary defensism judged the strategy of open confrontation to be ill-suited to the circumstances that obtained by late March—i.e., the moderation in labor relations and the soldiers' attacks on the soviet. Moreover, a confrontation would have further eroded governmental authority, a matter of the gravest concern to the Menshevik leaders of the provincial soviets.

Finally, there was the course of coalition. Everything that Tsereteli said and did as well as the sentiment of the delegates to the Conference of Soviets pointed in that direction, yet most Mensheviks would not hear of it, and without their support no change of strategy was possible. The Conference of Soviets essentially ended in the same political stalemate in which it had begun, and a whole month would elapse before the stalemate could be broken.

[128] Before the vote was taken on the compromise resolution, spokesmen for the various factions expressed their willingness to vote for it in order to preserve unity: ibid., 89, and Shliapnikov, *Semnadtsatyi god*, 3:264.

Toward a Coalition Government

IF THE FIRST MONTH of the revolution was a time of testing the strategy of dual power and the social and political concepts on which it was grounded, then April was spent by the leaders of the soviet in trying to deal with some of the contradictions and shortcomings that seemed to undermine the validity of this arrangement, in order that it might still be salvaged. These efforts were conducted largely behind the scenes, directed at compelling the government to follow the soviet's policies in regard to economic matters and the war, though in connection with this goal the executive committee also made an open bid for the soldiers' loyalty. To ensure careful implementation of this reinterpretation of dual power—emphasizing negotiations with the Provisional Government over pressure, and cooperation over *kontrol'*—the leadership of the new Revolutionary Defensist bloc sought to discipline the executive committee and the soviet in general. Meanwhile, however, certain developments gradually forced the executive committee to abandon dual power, and by the end of the month, following a two-day paroxysm of strikes and demonstrations—the "April crisis"—the Mensheviks became convinced, despite profound doubts, that they must accept coalition.

Historians and memoirists have stressed the effect of the April crisis (the revolution's first major political crisis) in bringing about the formation of a coalition government. By exposing the government's essential weakness, it created enormous pressure on the socialists to swallow their ideological objections and enter the cabinet to strengthen its authority with the masses. This result involved two sorts of developments: those that helped the Mensheviks overcome their doctrinal reservations and those that impressed all socialists with the urgency of their participation in the government. Increasingly, the leaders of the soviet came to feel that only their presence in the councils of government could guarantee the implementation of policies vital to the fate of the revolution.

Once the ideological resistance to coalition had been overcome, the executive committee appeared to be united around a new political consensus. Nevertheless, there remained crucial, though often hidden, differences in the significance that various members and factions attached to the new political arrangement. Coalition, like dual power, could be a framework for either cooperation or pressure, and the shape the revolution would take in the months to follow would depend partly on the victories within the executive committee and within the Menshevik party of one or the other view. The central goals of this chapter are, first, to explain how various groups of Mensheviks and their allies on the executive committee resolved the issue of coalition, and, second, to explore the outlines of the new political arrangement as defined by the Revolutionary Defensist leadership. Inasmuch as the resolution reached in early May and the divisions that appeared in the executive committee during its discussion of the new political arrangement were a response to the April crisis, it is with that crisis that we must begin.

The April Crisis and Its Aftermath

The first half of April was a time of renewed hope among the Revolutionary Defensist leaders of the Petrograd soviet. The truce in the factories held up. Production was increasing in many plants, and though Lenin's return to Petrograd on April 4 again gave rise to anxiety about the "danger on the left," this was largely allayed by the record of workers' resolutions published in the socialist press, which seemed to indicate that few workers were ready to embrace Lenin's slogan of "All Power to the Soviets."[1] Moreover, the soldiers, who had only recently threatened the leaders of the soviet politically and even physically, now began to issue declarations of loyalty. Meetings of representatives from front-line units encouraged their fellow soldiers to disobey orders that might lead to "political action not in accordance with their civic convictions"

---

[1] The theme of "extremism," absent from the pages of *Rabochaia gazeta* since mid-March, reappeared in the days following Lenin's return to Russia. The editors expressed fears that the "Leninists' " promises of "full and immediate economic liberation" might have a detrimental impact on the less conscious workers. Nonetheless, these articles insisted that the majority of workers subscribed to "healthier" attitudes. See "Danger on the Left Wing," *RG*, April 6, 1917 (no. 24), 1; report by Ivan Kubikov, a labor praktik, on his visit to the Shlissel'burg gunpowder works, *RG*, April 8, 1917 (no. 26), 2–3; and "The Revival of Anarchism and Maximalism," *RG*, April 9, 1917 (no. 27), 2. The editors' confidence seemed justified by the tenor of workers' resolutions printed in their daily "Soldiers and Workers" column and in the "Workers' Life" column in *IzvPS*.

157

and asserted that the only guarantee against civil war lay in the soldiers' exclusive loyalty to the soviet.[2]

By mid-April, the executive committee and the soviet had become more efficient, if less active, instruments, under the leadership of Tsereteli and the group of old friends who now held important positions in either the soviet or the Menshevik and SR organizations. Every morning, this leadership group would meet in Skobelev's apartment to go through the day's agenda, to draft resolutions to be presented to the executive committee for approval, to outline its positions in negotiations with the Provisional Government, and to debate required changes in strategy.[3] Although the members of this informal "presidium," derisively labeled the "star chamber" by its enemies, came from different parties and factions, they were characterized by a more practical approach to the situation than that taken by other, more doctrinaire socialists. Above all, these practical politicians appreciated the importance of a strong, unified leadership, and their unity as well as their control of the soviet's two largest factions enabled them to predetermine all the major political decisions of the executive committee and the Petrograd soviet.[4] Who were these powerful men?

First in importance was Tsereteli—by then the most popular man in the soviet, its current theoretician, and its chief negotiator with the Provisional Government. Then, in descending order of importance, were three former collaborators of Tsereteli in the Siberian Zimmerwaldist group: Dan, the chief editor of *Izvestiia*; Voi-

[2] These formulations were adopted by a meeting of soldiers that took place on April 7 in the Tauride Palace, with representatives from the Fourth, Fifth, Sixth, Seventh, and Eighth Armies and the First and Tenth Grenadier Divisions in attendance: *Khronika* 2: 20.

[3] The best description of these meetings and the composition of the group was left by Voitinskii, "God pobed i porazhenii," 58–60. Also see Sukhanov, *Zapiski o revoliutsii* 3:132–39, 151–53, and 4:44–46. References can also be found throughout Tsereteli's memoirs.

[4] A proposal brought by the "presidium" before the executive committee on April 14 called for the creation of a "bureau of the executive committee" to consist exclusively of the factions making up the majority. Although in the end the elections to the bureau were held on the basis of participation in the committee's twelve functional sections, not of factional affiliation, the Revolutionary Defensists held twenty of its twenty-nine seats: *Petrogradskii sovet*, 107–9. This result might be explained by the tendency of the Bolsheviks and other radicals to avoid the practical, "petty" work of the sections. Voitinskii attributes the origins of Tsereteli's idea of a "majority bureau" to the Bolsheviks' increasingly vocal opposition: "God pobed i porazhenii," 58–59.

tinskii, the soviet's best troubleshooter in dealing with workers and soldiers; and Gots, the group's liaison with the SR party. These four men were usually joined by Chkheidze and Skobelev, both of whom had been, like Tsereteli, Duma deputies from the Caucasus. On the periphery were four other Siberian Zimmerwaldists who were now members of the executive committee or of the Menshevik organization: N. A. Rozhkov, and three Menshevik praktiki, V. A. Anisimov, S. L. Vainshtein, and K. M. Ermolaev.[5] Sometimes the "presidium's" meetings would be joined by Gvozdev, Bogdanov, or Liber as well as by a few Populists: V. M. Chernov, the SR leader who had returned from Europe in early April, or N. D. Avksent'ev, a right-wing SR who served as chairman of the Soviet of Peasants. Together, these men could reasonably claim to embody the unity of the three constituent groups of "democracy" (workers, soldiers, and peasants), and for this reason throughout most of April the discipline they sought to enforce on the soviet did not cause tension between leaders and followers. Questions persisted, of course, concerning the extent to which the unity of democracy and its precarious accommodation with the bourgeois camp would survive confrontation with the Provisional Government. However, various developments were encouraging, none more so than the turnabout in the soldiers' loyalty to the soviet.

There were several reasons for this change in the soldiers' position. First, the soviet's public stand on defense now reassured the soldiers that they would not be betrayed by a defeatist leadership. Second, the government's seeming acceptance of the slogan of a "democratic peace" gave an aura of national acceptability to the soldiers' desire for a prompt end to the war. Third, the crisis of late March had forced the executive committee to improve its lines of communication with the soldiery through its commissars, the soldiers' committees, and daily discussions with delegations from the front. Finally, and perhaps most decisive, was the course of the confrontation between soldiers from the front and the Petrograd workers. The workers' restraint had the effect of undermining the soldiers' belief in the bourgeois press's stories about the workers' "excessive" demands, so that the numerous delegations sent from the front to report on events in the capital returned from

---

[5] On their return to Petrograd, Rozhkov and Ermolaev were elected to the Menshevik Central Committee, and Anisimov and Vainshtein were members of the soviet's executive committee. For biographical sketches of these men, see appendix 3.

their visits to the factories expressing sympathy for the harsh conditions in which the workers had long been forced to live and for their demands, as well as appreciation of the workers' expressed readiness to continue serving the war effort.[6]

The favorable effect of these developments seemed to be confirmed when the new leadership sent its highest-ranking members to the First Congress of the Western Front, held in Minsk from April 7 to April 16. Not only did the congress adopt verbatim the resolutions on war and state power passed by the Conference of Soviets and demand that the Provisional Government grant financial support to the Petrograd soviet, but the soldiers also expressed unqualified support for an eight-hour workday.[7] Addressing the congress, Tsereteli assured the soldiers that "such unity among all elements of Russia" had never existed before.[8] Indeed, this sense of unity seemed to be felt for a moment by many elements of the population as workers and soldiers marched together down the capital's avenues on May Day (April 18), with banners calling for "The Peace and Brotherhood of Nations," while crowds of the "upper strata" of Petrograd, dressed up and in a festive mood, watched from the sidewalks.[9] *Rabochaia gazeta* commented with satisfaction that in Russia, the "holiday of class struggle against existing society" had become, at least in that year, an "all-national holiday."[10]

The soviet's contacts with the Provisional Goverment also augured well during the first half of the month, though the war issue itself remained intractable. The soviet demanded that the government restate in clearer language than was the case in its "Declaration to the Russian People" (March 27) a renunciation of annexations and indemnities, and Miliukov agreed to this demand. However, he did not act on it immediately, even though he was under pressure to do so from within the cabinet as well as from

---

[6] Wildman, *Russian Imperial Army*, 311–20. See Sukhanov, *Zapiski o revoliutsii* 3:62–126, for a detailed discussion of the soviet's campaign for the soldiers.

[7] *IzvPS*, April 14, 1917 (no. 40), 5, and April 17, 1917 (no. 43), 3–4; *Khronika* 2:22, 28, 32–33, 37–38, 40, 42; Tsereteli, *Vospominaniia o fevral'skoi revoliutsii* 1:77–83; Sukhanov, *Zapiski o revoliutsii* 3:82–85. The soviet's delegation to the congress consisted of Tsereteli, Chkheidze, Skobelev, and Gvozdev.

[8] Tsereteli, *Rechi*, 35–36.

[9] Particularly moving is the description of this day in Sukhanov, *Zapiski o revoliutsii* 3:242–46. In order to emphasize the international solidarity of workers, Russian workers celebrated May Day on the day it was celebrated in the rest of Europe, which was April 18 by the Julian calendar.

[10] *RG*, April 20, 1917 (no. 32), 1.

the visiting delegation of Allied socialists, which included Albert Thomas, the French minister of munitions.[11]

To be sure, not everyone shared Tsereteli's optimism about the government's willingness to comply with the demand. There were skeptics even in the presidium group, but they too were confident of the ultimate outcome, for they had found a new weapon with which to pressure the government: the Freedom Loan. This loan had been proposed by the government to help meet the costs of the war and of the new social programs, but it was not popular among workers, who believed such expenses should be covered by increased taxation of the rich, especially of their infamous and much rumored "war profits."[12] Taking their cue from the workers, most Mensheviks (especially Chkheidze) objected to Tsereteli's favorable presentation of the loan and moved the soviet to condition its support of the loan on the issuance of Miliukov's promised diplomatic note.[13] It was in this context that the three thousand deputies of the soviet were informed about Miliukov's promise and about Tsereteli's trust in its fulfillment.

On April 18, as all of Petrograd was celebrating May Day, Miliukov finally sent the promised note to the Allies, but it was hardly what Tsereteli had anticipated. It was merely appended to the text of the former "Declaration," thus in effect negating the latter's very essence: It promised that Russia would continue the war to a "decisive victory" and together with the other "leading democracies" establish "guarantees and sanctions"—terms suspiciously reminiscent of the objectionable "annexations and indemnities." To make matters worse, in the soviet's view, the entire cabinet (including Nekrasov, Tereshchenko, and Kerenskii) had approved the offending document.[14]

[11] See Tsereteli, *Vospominaniia o fevral'skoi revoliutsii* 1:84–85; Sukhanov, *Zapiski o revoliutsii* 3:204; and Radkey, *Agrarian Foes of Bolshevism*, 157–58, on the meeting of the soviet's liaison commission with the cabinet on March 11, at which Chernov, just back from Europe, presented the demand to Miliukov. For discussions of the pressure put on Miliukov by Kerenskii (who leaked the whole matter to the press), see *RPG* 2:1096; Kerensky, *Catastrophe*, 134; Miliukov, *Istoriia vtoroi russkoi revoliutsii* 1:92; Medlin and Parsons, eds., *Nabokov*, 121–22; and Buchanan, *My Mission to Russia* 2:119. On the visit of the Allied socialists, see Tsereteli, *Vospominaniia o fevral'skoi revoliutsii* 1:169–214; Sukhanov, *Zapiski o revoliutsii* 3:181–91; *RPG* 2:1097. Also see Wade, *Russian Search for Peace*, 35–37.

[12] For examples of workers' condemnation of the Freedom Loan, see *RG*, April 4, 1917 (no. 23), 2, and April 25, 1917 (no. 39), 4; *IzvPS*, March 30, 1917 (no. 28), 6, and April 15, 1917 (no. 41), 3–4; *RD v aprele*, 353–54, 386, 419, 439.

[13] *Petrogradskii sovet*, 90–91, 111, 316–17; Sukhanov, *Zapiski o revoliutsii* 3:216–28.

[14] *RPG* 2:1097–98; Kerensky, *Catastrophe*, 135; Miliukov, *Istoriia vtoroi russkoi revoliutsii* 1:92; Medlin and Parsons, eds., *Nabokov*, 122–23.

Everyone on the executive committee, Internationalists and Revolutionary Defensists alike, was distressed by the note, and they spent the night of April 19 discussing it. Tsereteli declared that this act "had destroyed the compromise that had made cooperation with the government possible," and Bogdanov admitted that it had been a blow aimed precisely at themselves, the leaders of the majority.[15] In spite of the general dismay, however, the executive committee could not agree on any course of action. The three leading Siberian Zimmerwaldists (Tsereteli, Dan, and Gots) recommended quiet negotiations with the government, because that course of action had worked in late March and they hoped that it would again prove efficacious, with the soviet now in a stronger position. But most of the old leaders, such as Bogdanov and other moderate Mensheviks who had recently joined the Revolutionary Defensist block, insisted on calling on the workers and soldiers to demonstrate against the government's declaration.[16] The disagreement in the executive committee seemed to have involved political tactics rather than strategy, but in fact it reflected a fundamental difference in political approach: The Siberians were essentially "state-minded" (*gosudarstvennye*), hesitant of causing disorder or undermining authority, and preferred to act as members of a "loyal opposition," whereas their fellow socialists were more likely to feel hostile toward those in power.

In any case, events beyond the control of the leadership did not allow this crisis to follow the outlines of the less serious one of late March. Having been alerted by earlier discussions in the soviet of their leaders' position on the question of the war, as well as of Miliukov's promise, and having found out in the morning papers of April 20 that the promise had in effect been violated, thousands of workers and soldiers came out to demonstrate, not against the government as such but against its refusal to accept the demand of the soviet.[17] Their banners were either those left over from May Day, which called for peace and brotherhood, or new, hastily pre-

[15] The best source on this meeting is Tsereteli, *Vospominaniia o fevral'skoi revoliutsii* 1:86–90. It is reported at second hand in Sukhanov, *Zapiski o revoliutsii* 3:251–58.

[16] These differences were reported by Chkheidze in a speech he made to the Petrograd soviet the next day: *NZh*, April 21, 1917 (no. 3), 1. See also Voitinskii, "God pobed i porazhenii," 66, and Stankevich, *Vospominaniia*, 113.

[17] Throughout the first half of April, the workers had expressed support for the peace slogans of the soviet. See, for example, the resolutions adopted by three thousand workers of the Treugol'nik plant (after having heard a statement by a representative of a Menshevik district committee) and by a similar number of workers of Skorokhod: *RG*, April 15, 1917 (no. 12), 2–3.

pared ones with the slogan "Down with Miliukov and Guchkov." The more radical Vyborg district workers—a small part of the demonstrators—advocated the resignation of the entire cabinet.[18]

By the second day of the protest, April 21, the mood of the demonstrators had changed somewhat. A sense of betrayed trust and a renewed belligerency seemed apparent, perhaps as the result of a counterdemonstration organized by the Kadet Central Committee and attended by thousands of well-to-do citizens, intelligenty, and shopkeepers, who had come out to defend "their government" and repel its attackers. The city was suddenly divided, and many workers—such as those of the Putilov works for example, who had previously heeded their leaders' advice to stay off the streets—could no longer avoid taking sides in this social and political confrontation.[19]

In a curious way, the effect of the masses' spontaneous action in demonstrating against Miliukov's note was to align the executive committee behind Tsereteli. When the first demonstrators arrived in front of the Tauride Palace early on April 20, the committee's bureau immediately resolved to appeal to the masses of the city, through the socialist press and through the committee's most popular speakers (who were dispatched to factories and military units), to avoid demonstrations that were not authorized by the soviet. The point was not that the leaders disagreed with the political goal of the demonstrators (though a conflict between a radicalized constituency and its moderate leadership did appear later). Rather, the Revolutionary Defensists were once again concerned with avoiding an unorganized, "anarchic" display of force and were quite realistically fearful that an open attack on the government would further undermine its already shaky authority and provoke violent clashes in the streets. For this reason, when, on April 21, news arrived of just such clashes and of Kornilov's order to the troops to come to the defense of the government, the executive committee, at Skobelev's behest, issued a "proclamation" to

[18] For a sample of resolutions adopted by soldiers on the same day, see *RD v aprele*, 728; *RG*, April 21, 1917 (no. 36), and April 22, 1917 (no. 37). There is general agreement that the Bolsheviks had little to do with the initial demonstrations on April 20: Rabinowitch, *Prelude to Revolution*, 44–45; Tsereteli, *Vospominaniia o fevral'skoi revoliutsii* 1:192–93; and Voitinskii, "God pobed i porazhenii," 73–76.

[19] *DN*, April 25, 1917 (no. 32), 4. For general descriptions of this day's events, see *RG*, April 22, 1917 (no. 37), 2; *Khronika* 2:54–55; and Sukhanov, *Zapiski o revoliutsii* 3:29–192. On the Kadet demonstration, also see Rosenberg, *Liberals in the Russian Revolution*, 108–9.

the troops which forbade them to follow any government order without the soviet's sanction—an open challenge to the government's authority. At the same time, however, the full soviet accepted Dan's proposal to ban all demonstrations in Petrograd for two days, and in this way the leadership indicated its right to censure its constituency.[20]

This episode tended to confirm the impression that the Revolutionary Defensist leadership of the executive committee, when faced with a crisis, was likely to act not as a contender in a political dispute but as the country's self-appointed authority, fully cognizant of the burden of national responsibility. This had been and continued to be the meaning of its policy of restraint, as Stankevich put it very clearly in a speech to the full soviet on the evening of April 20, which drew the deputies' enthusiastic applause. Agreeing with earlier speakers that Miliukov's note had destroyed the basis of the agreement between the soviet and the government, Stankevich nevertheless objected to undertaking any specific action against the government:

Why, comrades, do we need "action"? At whom will we shoot? Against whom shall we employ our forces? After all, the only forces are you and the masses behind you . . . Whatever you decide, will be. . . . Look, it is five minutes to seven; we will call them on the phone and within five minutes the government will hand over its authority. By seven o'clock [the government] will no longer exist. Force, action, and civil war—why do we need this?[21]

Significantly, the sense of power and responsibility that pervaded Stankevich's speech did not lead him, nor for that matter most of the people who applauded him, to the conclusion that the soviet should form a government but rather to the idea of coalition. Stankevich argued that the soviet should demand the "exclusion of certain persons" from the cabinet (voices from the hall were heard calling, "Away with Miliukov!") and added, "then—a coalition government." Yet even now, Stankevich's Menshevik colleagues, some of whom otherwise shared his analysis of the situation, could not accept his political conclusions.

[20] *Petrogradskii sovet*, 116–18, 318; "A Call for Calm," *IzvPS*, April 21, 1917 (no. 46), 1; Sukhanov, *Zapiski o revoliutsii* 3:260–61; Tsereteli, *Vospominaniia o fevral'skoi revoliutsii* 1:95, 105; Voitinskii, "God pobed i porazhenii," 66–68, 72; Stankevich, *Vospominaniia*, 114, 117–18.

[21] The details of the meeting including the excerpts from the speeches are drawn from *NZh*, April 21, 1917 (no. 3); Sukhanov, *Zapiski o revoliutsii* 3:271–77; and Tsereteli, *Vospominaniia o fevral'skoi revoliutsii* 1:96–98.

This April crisis was eventually resolved through negotiations between the executive committee and the Provisional Government in a nightlong session. Tsereteli and Nekrasov, the two men who personified the intelligentsia's mission to unite and lead Russia's "vital forces," composed a short text in which annexations were again repudiated and the offending terms "guarantees" and "sanctions" were explained as being references to international tribunals, limitations on armaments, etc.[22] The executive committee discussed the text for five hours on the afternoon of April 21, and though no one, not even Tsereteli, would call it a "victory," most of the members of the committee's majority argued in favor of accepting the new document as being the least disruptive of the current modus vivendi. That this was the thought behind the Revolutionary Defensists' support of Tsereteli's compromise, and that the new note was not deemed truly satisfactory, was made clear by a provision added to the resolution of the executive committee (probably at the Mensheviks' insistence) that the soviet should increase its *kontrol'* over the conduct of foreign policy. Only after this addition did thirty-four members of the executive committee vote with Tsereteli, though nineteen still voted against accepting the "clarificatory note."[23]

There was considerably less opposition in the plenum of the soviet, where 2,000 votes were registered later that evening in favor of accepting the compromise as a "great achievement for democracy" and only 13 against.[24] Moreover, the next day the same body overwhelmingly approved the presidium's proposal to lend its support to the Freedom Loan; the vote was more than 2,000 to 112.[25] For the most part, the deputies appeared willing to abide by

[22] Details of the meeting are in *RG*, April 22, 1917 (no. 37), 2; *Den'*, April 22, 1917 (no. 40), 1–2; Sukhanov, *Zapiski o revoliutsii* 3:280–89; Tsereteli, *Vospominaniia o fevral'skoi revoliutsii* 1:98–104; Stankevich, *Vospominaniia*, 114–16; Shliapnikov, *Semnadtsatyi god* 3:103–9. A good summary is available in *Khronika* 2:51.

[23] *RG*, April 22, 1917 (no. 37), 2; *Petrogradskii sovet*, 118; Sukhanov, *Zapiski o revoliutsii* 3:300–6; and Voitinskii, "God pobed i porazhenii," 70. The Menshevik origin of the provision on *kontrol'* is evident in its resemblance to resolutions adopted by the Menshevik organizational committee and the committee of the Menshevik Petrograd organization; see *RG*, April 22, 1917 (no. 37), 3.

[24] *RG*, April 22, 1917 (no. 37), 3. According to this report, there were 125 or 150 votes against the resolution, but Avdeev gives the number as 13: *Khronika* 2:56. Also see Tsereteli, *Vospominaniia o fevral'skoi revoliutsii* 1:104–5, and Voitinskii, "God pobed i porazhenii," 71.

[25] *IzvPS*, April 23, 1917 (no. 48), 2–4; Sukhanov, *Zapiski o revoliutsii* 3:313–14. In the executive committee, the question of the Freedom Loan showed roughly the

the recommendations of their leaders, the more so because they must have derived some sense of pride and strength from the soviet's authoritative conduct during the crisis, especially in its challenge of Kornilov's order. On this basis, Skobelev could ask the deputies to support the loan both because "we know we are masters now" and because democracy was strong enough to force the bourgeoisie into serving the interests of the revolution.[26]

To be sure, there developed at just this time a discrepancy between the sentiments expressed by workers and soldiers in the streets and those of the soviet deputies toward the initiatives of the Revolutionary Defensist leadership.[27] The deputies elected in early March no longer reflected the mood of the workers, particularly in regard to the issue of the loan, and soon many of them would be replaced by more militant deputies. Yet during the April crisis and for the next two weeks, these differences were not deep enough, and the political conclusions the workers drew from the new situation were not sufficiently clear, to cause real tensions.

As the crisis ended, then, the Revolutionary Defensist leaders of the soviet could claim to have averted the frightening prospects of a radicalized constituency becoming unruly, of counterrevolutionary intrigue taking hold in the army, and of society's falling into civil war and anarchy and aborting the revolution and the first growths of civic society. An editorial in the soviet's newspaper very likely reflected their evaluation of events in its exultant statement that "no government in the world could have achieved such a decisive and swift victory."[28] There was reason for the members of the executive committee to be proud: They had had the courage to stand up to both the demonstrators and their potential opponents and had done so for the sake of safeguarding the revolution.

The soviet's new measure of confidence and prestige did not immediately lead to a new political strategy, however. In at least three of their public pronouncements, the Revolutionary Defensists argued neither that dual power should be abandoned nor that a coalition government should be established. Tsereteli simply reasserted that the "vital forces of the nation could and must

---

same division as had the question of the note: 33 voted for it, 16 against: *Petrogradskii sovet*, 119–20; Sukhanov, *Zapiski o revoliutsii* 3:310–12.

[26] *IzvPS*, April 23, 1917 (no. 48), 4.

[27] See, for example, Voitinskii, "God pobed i porazhenii," 67, and Trotsky, *History of the Russian Revolution*, 351–52.

[28] "A Demonstration of Strength," *IzvPS*, April 23, 1917 (no. 48), 2. On the same theme, see Sukhanov, *Zapiski o revoliutsii* 3:264–66, 293–94.

march together again." Dan pointed to the emergence of a new "structure of power" during the crisis but described it in terms too similar to those of dual power to suggest anything really new; the soviet was said to have been the only force capable of preventing a civil war, yet its strength was also sufficient guarantee for the Provisional Government's implementation of the necessary reforms.[29] And while the more cautious Mensheviks, such as Baturskii, who had spent the war years in Petrograd did see proof in the April crisis that a bourgeois revolution entailed a fundamental conflict of interest between the bourgeoisie and the proletariat, they nevertheless argued that the revolution's success depended on cooperation between these two forces and that democracy could maintain its strength only by shunning state power.[30] But these statements and restatements of old conventions led nowhere. In the aftermath of the crisis, the Menshevik leadership had still to find its way to a resolution of its central political problem.

IN THE DAYS following the April crisis, a striking contrast developed between the Mensheviks' reaction to it and that of the non-Menshevik circles in the soviet and the partisans of democracy outside the soviet. The events of April 20 and 21 had aroused a widespread desire for a formal expression of unity, especially among those intermediary social and political groups that hoped to prevent the polarization of society. Intelligentsia organizations, locally elected governments, soldiers' and officers' organizations, and peasant soviets all appealed to the Petrograd soviet and the Provisional Government to form a coalition. Indeed, within days, a campaign advocating coalition assailed the Provisional Government and the circles close to it. Meanwhile, the cabinet of the Provisional Government called on the soviet to add its "active and creative force" to the "responsible work" of government and hinted at the cabinet's weakness. Similar appeals were made by the Moscow Committee of Public Organizations, the Moscow Ka-

[29] Tsereteli's words were in his speech to the soviet plenum on the evening of April 21: *RG*, April 22, 1917 (no. 37), 3. Dan's position is deduced from editorials in *IzvPS*, of which he was the chief editor: "Irresponsible Acts" and "Conflict or Misunderstanding," April 26, 1917 (no. 50), 1–2.

[30] See, for example, "Crisis," *RG*, April 22, 1917 (no. 37), 1, and "The Lessons of Two Days," *RG*, April 23, 1917 (no. 38), 1. Both these articles were probably written by Baturskii.

dets, Kerenskii, Nekrasov, and finally the prime minister himself, Prince L'vov.[31]

The April crisis had demonstrated that a change in the soldiers' loyalties had deprived the Provisional Government of the single most important instrument of governmental authority.[32] Even inside the soviet, many who had previously been content to practice cooperation within the framework of dual power were moved by their concern for both a sound structure of governmental authority and the continuation of the war effort to ponder the demand for coalition. The Trudoviki had been propagating this idea with considerable success in the garrison's barracks for some time, and now the SRs as well made it part of their party's official strategy.[33] The right-wing Social Democrats, who were gathered around the newspaper *Den'*, doubled their efforts to impress a sense of the nation's imminent jeopardy on their fellow Social Democrats.[34] In fact, under the influence of the *Den'* group, the Menshevik faction of the soviet, made up largely of new recruits to the party, had already on April 21 voted in favor of coalition, though the deputies conditioned the implementation of their resolution on its approval by their leadership.[35]

[31] *VVP*, April 26, 1917 (no. 40), 1; *RPG* 3:1249–52; *Khronika* 2:67; *NZh*, April 27, 1917 (no. 8), 2; and *RV v aprele*, 833–34. There are good discussions of the campaign for coalition in Sukhanov, *Zapiski o revoliutsii* 3:385–89; Tsereteli, *Vospominaniia o fevral'skoi revoliutsii* 1:108, 135; and Rosenberg, *Liberals in the Russian Revolution*, 110.

[32] Guchkov later estimated that only 3,500 of the troops would have come out against the soviet in defense of the Provisional Government: "Iz vospominanii," September 23, 1936.

[33] For the position of the Trudoviki, see the text of the resolutions passed at their congress of April 8–9: *DN*, April 11, 1917 (no. 21), 4, and Sukhanov, *Zapiski o revoliutsii* 3:385. The SRs' Second Petrograd Conference on April 4 had decided against coalition, but in the aftermath of the April crisis, their newspaper advocated it as the only "responsible resolution" to the crisis of governmental authority: *DN*, April 7, 1917 (no. 18), and April 26, 1917 (no. 33), 1. Also see the reports of resolutions in favor of coalition adopted at a meeting of SRs of the Moscow district, and by the Western Front Committee of Soldiers' Soviets, in which 26 SRs defeated the opposition of 25 Social Democrats: *Khronika* 2:84.

[34] "A Government of National Trust," *Den'*, April 24, 1917 (no. 41), 3; "A Ministry of Public Salvation," *Den'*, April 25, 1917 (no. 42), 1; P. Iushkevich, "Unavoidable Solution," *Den'*, April 23, 1917 (no. 40), 1; and "Without Delay," *Den'*, April 27, 1917 (no. 44), 1.

[35] The vote, taken on April 21, was 51 in favor, 6 against, and 9 abstentions: *RG*, April 23, 1917 (no. 38), 3–4. Of the seven members of the faction's bureau at the time, one, Sokolovskii, was identified as an Internationalist, and three were staunch Defensists: M. I. Broido, F. A. Iudin, and Kantorovich, who belonged to the *Den'* group. No affiliation was given for the other three (Sevast'ianov, Kramer,

The Menshevik leadership, however, held firmly to its rejection of coalition. In a round of meetings between April 21 and 25, the party's Petrograd organization, its district committees, the organizational committee, and the editorial board of *Rabochaia gazeta* all agreed that the pressure for coalition had to be resisted. Toward that end, Dan drafted a resolution summarizing the Menshevik view on coalition. It was the fullest Menshevik statement to date on the subject, a list of the expected detrimental effects of coalition:

1. The soviet . . . will lose all its influence and the ability to lead the masses.
2. The responsibility for all the social conflicts inevitable in the course of the revolution will fall on the socialist members of the government. . . . As members of a government facing revolutionary elements (*stikhiia*), they will be in objective opposition to the [masses].
3. [Coalition] will strengthen . . . social maximalism and give credence to the illusion that extremist demands may be fulfilled [and] will increase anarchy on the left.
4. [Coalition] will tie the soviet to the government and will destroy the role of the soviet as the organ of revolutionary democracy that exercises *kontrol'* over the government; it will undermine the revolutionary stature of the soviet and will turn it into a regular governmental department.
5. [Coalition] will create an extremely unstable situation . . . and could cause an unavoidable collapse of the government, the result of which will lead either to a victory of the counterrevolutionary forces or to a dictatorship of the proletariat that would be doomed to defeat at this time.[36]

The plodding, doctrinaire style of Dan's statement should not mislead us. Dan saw clearly the consequences of the pending political decision. Indeed, over the next few months he would see his prophecies realized in almost every detail.

Dan's vision of the catastrophe that would result if a coalition were to be established at that point was shared by the other Menshevik members of the soviet's informal presidium. On April 28, when L'vov's letter of invitation to join the cabinet was discussed by the presidium during its regular morning meeting at Skobelev's apartment, the Mensheviks present were faced with a "rebellion" by their SR allies. Avksent'ev and Gots sought to change the Men-

---

and Piatov). The Menshevik faction of the Petrograd soviet was continuously at odds with the Petrograd organization: *PI*, July 15, 1917 (no. 1), 13–14; Sukhanov, *Zapiski o revoliutsii* 3:359–60.

[36] *RG*, April 29, 1917 (no. 43), 3–4. For reports on the meetings leading up to the resolution, see also *RG*, April 22, 1917 (no. 37), 3, and April 26, 1917 (no. 40), 3–4.

sheviks' views on coalition, but the only Social Democrat to concede the necessity of coalition was Voitinskii, a recent recruit to the party. Tsereteli, Chkheidze, Dan, Skobelev, Liber, Gvozdev, and Bogdanov all objected.

Their objections were of various sorts. Tsereteli's derived from a practical political consideration: Would not the loss of the soviet's unique role as broker diminish its influence over both the masses and the government? Skobelev's lay in his self-image; he could not see himself addressing workers in the capacity of a government minister. For Bogdanov, there were doubts about the social composition of the more enthusiastic supporters of coalition; they were peasants and soldiers rather than the "advanced workers who had undergone party schooling." Most characteristic of the Menshevik attitude toward coalition, however, was Chkheidze's warning. He introduced it with the frank admission that he had often used his position as chairman of the soviet to avoid expressing his own opinion but would not do so on this occasion, for he feared that if the soviet joined the government, it would lose the "authority that had allowed it to give an organized character to the movement of the masses as well as support for the construction of a democratic order in the country." Chkheidze's explanation rested on the same doctrinal assumptions as Dan's, but the language was more personal, even pained.

When we defend a government that is not ours, a bourgeois government, and we explain that no government could bring peace and institute fundamental reforms all at once, then the masses listen to us with trust, and [they] conclude that under such conditions the socialists should not join the government. But if we join the government, then we will raise hopes in the masses for something entirely new and different, hopes we cannot carry out.[37]

Another representative expression of Menshevik doubts, of the dilemma of reality and ideology, can be found in B. I. Gorev's articles in *Rabochaia gazeta*. His was the voice of doctrine. The "logic" of history, he wrote, mandated that every bourgeois government, even the most democratic one, "would sooner or later act against the social demands of the proletariat" and, further, that "socialist measures could not be pursued in a bourgeois revolution." He admitted that, since his earliest article on this issue, he had had to overcome some powerful heretical considerations. Nowadays, he

[37] The speeches are quoted from memory by Tsereteli in *Vospominaniia o fevral'skoi revoliutsii* 1:127–31. No other record of the meeting exists.

declared, socialists were inclined to place the interests of "the *revolution as a whole*" above those of "the soviet's parties," and he, too, in developing his argument against coalition, had to address these considerations. But even from this vantage point, he saw that socialist participation in government would be "inexpedient," for it threatened to unleash anarchist demagoguery and deprive the soviet of its influence on the "destiny of the revolution."[38] Yet in an article two days later, Gorev seemed compelled to concede much more to the voice of reality. Only "collaboration" between the soviet and the government (though not a formal coalition) could "soften the terrible social conflict" now threatening the country; only the "revolutionary energy and courage" of "democracy" would ensure the necessary reforms.[39]

The Menshevik members of the Revolutionary Defensist presidium searched desperately for a way to both strengthen the authority of the cabinet and gain greater leverage over its work even as they rejected a formal coalition. During the meeting of April 28, Chkheidze proposed that the SRs—as the party of the peasantry and the urban petty bourgeoisie—join the government. When Gots refused, Tsereteli suggested that nonparty "democratic elements" sympathetic to the soviet join the government and be assured that democracy would support them.[40] With this possibility in mind, twenty-four members of the executive committee voted later that day against coalition, barely defeating the twenty-two supporters, among whom there were now several Internationalists as well as most of the Populists. Eight members announced they were abstaining, and many others refused to take any position at all.[41] The effort, however, was doomed from the start, for as L'vov made clear to Tsereteli that evening, what the ministers actually wanted was for the soviet to renounce the formula of conditional support and so give up its separate power, its separate authority.[42]

[38] "Coalition Ministry," *RG*, April 25, 1917 (no. 39), 1–2 (emphasis in the original).

[39] "The Activity of the Government and the Tasks of Democracy," *RG*, April 27, 1917 (no. 41), 1.

[40] Tsereteli, *Vospominaniia o fevral'skoi revoliutsii* 1:128–29, 131.

[41] These are the figures given in Tsereteli, *Vospominaniia o fevral'skoi revoliutsii* 1:131–33, and in Nikolaevskii, "RSDRP," 24–25. The newspaper *Edinstvo*, April 30, 1917 (no. 27), 1, gave almost identical figures (23 in favor, 22 against, and 8 abstentions), and Avdeev's account is the same as that except for saying there were only 2 abstentions: *Khronika* 2:82. Also see Sukhanov, *Zapiski o revoliutsii* 3:397–400.

[42] Tsereteli, *Vospominaniia o fevral'skoi revoliutsii* 1:133–34.

Three days later, the government formally turned down Tsereteli's proposal.

Meanwhile, the leaders of the executive committee did all they could to lend the government some of the soviet's strength. A resolution to support the Freedom Loan (April 22) was one such act, significant both because it refrained from conditioning this support on the government's continued pursuit of peace and because it signaled acceptance of a measure that workers and socialist economists alike had rejected.[43] Next, the executive committee searched for ways of restoring discipline in the garrison. At Tsereteli's behest, and over the objections of Steklov and other Internationalists, the committee published an announcement on April 26 that not only acknowledged General Kornilov's authority but did not demand implementation of the promised plan of reorganization and glossed over the conflict that had surrounded Kornilov's order to mobilize the troops against the demonstrators on April 21. It was a measure of the soldiers' disaffection from the government that even after the publication of this statement some units refused to obey Kornilov's orders without the authorization of the executive committee, precipitating his resignation on April 30.[44]

Aware of the futility of most of their efforts to help the government regain its hold on the situation yet unable to pursue any other course, the Revolutionary Defensist leaders turned to the constituency of the soviets and to the population at large with a series of appeals published between April 30 and May 2. There were appeals to the peasants to market their grain and not to seize land before a Constituent Assembly had had a chance to discuss the problem. Another appeal, drafted by Voitinskii, was addressed to the soldiers and went beyond any earlier commitment of the soviet's leadership to the continuation of the war. It declared that there were times "when only offensive action can repel, or prevent, an attack by the enemy." In introducing this appeal at the soviet's meeting on April 30, Tsereteli expressed his concern for the strength of the army and said nothing of the struggle for

[43] For the opinions of various Mensheviks during the debates on this issue, see *Khronika* 2:67–68 (speech by Chkheidze); G. Baturskii, "On the Question of the 'Freedom Loan,' " *RG*, April 25, 1917 (no. 39), 2; and Ermanskii, "For or Against the 'Freedom Loan,' " *RG*, April 26, 1917 (no. 40), 1–2. The soviet's economists had argued that the loan put an unjust financial burden on the lower classes and could not take the place of a tax on war profits.

[44] *Petrogradskii sovet*, 214–15; Sukhanov, *Zapiski o revoliutsii* 3:318–22.

peace.[45] To be sure, the Revolutionary Defensists had not reneged on their slogan of "democratic peace." In fact, on April 30 they brought the text of yet another appeal before the soviet, this one calling on the European socialist parties to convene an international socialist conference for peace.[46] What this series of appeals demonstrated was the growing sense on the part of the soviet's leaders that the government's weakness, its inability to enlist the support of the broadest segments of population in the execution of its most essential functions, posed an imminent danger to the revolution.

This sense of danger had been increasing ever since the April crisis, but it assumed urgency with an event that finally proved decisive in forcing the Menshevik Revolutionary Defensists to accept coalition. On April 29, Guchkov announced his resignation from the post of minister of war, citing the threat of anarchy, especially in the army, as his reason.[47] Immediately, the soviet was flooded with telegrams from soldiers' committees and personal appeals from officers sympathetic to democracy that it join the government to prevent the further disintegration of the army. Tsereteli remembered it as the moment when he concluded that it was "necessary to give the country a new government, [and] not to delay by even one minute."[48]

Guchkov's resignation provoked a change in Menshevik strategy for several reasons. It underscored the deterioration of authority and order, and it served to hasten two related political developments: a division within the first cabinet of the Provisional Government, and the emergence of a "counterrevolution"—that is, an organized political opposition to the soviet and to the processes of democratization which it championed. The first of these developments had already been perceived in mid-March, in the intransigence shown by the two key ministers, Guchkov and Miliukov. At first, their position was thought to have resulted simply from sensitivity for their respective areas of concern—military

[45] These appeals were published in *IzvPS*, May 2, 1917 (no. 55), 1–3. The speeches at the April 30 meeting were reported in the same issue, 5–6. Also see *Khronika* 2:91–93, 269–71, and *Den'*, April 30, 1917 (no. 47), 4.

[46] This appeal was written by Dan and introduced by Skobelev: *RG*, April 26, 1917 (no. 40), 3–4, and April 29, 1917 (no. 43), 4; *Petrogradskii sovet*, 127–28, 322–24; and *Khronika* 2:91–93, 267–69. Also see Tsereteli, *Vospominaniia o fevral'skoi revoliutsii* 1:126–27, and Sukhanov, *Zapiski o revoliutsii* 3:322–28, 335–40.

[47] *RD v aprele*, 835–36.

[48] Tsereteli, *Vospominaniia o fevral'skoi revoliutsii* 1:135. Also see Sukhanov, *Zapiski o revoliutsii* 3:228–34.

173

and foreign affairs, respectively—but they soon made clear their belief that the cabinet alone spoke for Russia's national interests, whereas the soviet was merely a "partisan" institution not deserving of special influence over state policy.[49] At the same time, it also became clear that there were men in the cabinet, and in Miliukov's Kadet party, who were, in Rosenberg's words, "ready and willing to work closely with a broad spectrum of political leaders,"[50] though the Kadet "left wing" had suffered defeat at the party's congress in late March. Still, the left wing's representative in the cabinet, Nekrasov, had acted independently of the congress's resolutions and in concert with three other cabinet ministers who shared his receptiveness to collaboration with the moderate socialists: Konovalov, an old ally from the public organizations; Kerenskii, the popular Trudovik who was fond of describing himself as "democracy's hostage" in the government; and Tereshchenko, the nonparty "repentant capitalist," as Nabokov called him.[51]

To be sure, Konovalov, Nekrasov, and Tereshchenko shared the cabinet's principal concern that the erosion of political authority

[49] For retrospective assertions of this attitude, see Guchkov, "Iz vospominanii," September 20, 1936, and Miliukov, *Istoriia vtoroi russkoi revoliutsii* 1:84, 102. Also see Rosenberg, *Liberals in the Russian Revolution*, 70–74, and Mel'gunov, *Martovskie dni*, 375–77.

[50] Rosenberg, *Liberals in the Russian Revolution*, 59–63. On the local level, the best example of this willingness was provided by the Moscow Kadets, who were leading the Moscow Committee of Public Organizations, a coalition group and the archetype for similar groups all over Russia. See the introduction to *Sbornik materialov komiteta*, part 1. For criticisms of Miliukov from the left Kadets, see Vinavera, "Vospominaniia" (manuscript collection of the Hoover Institution), 94; Boris A. Gurevich, "Krasnyi sfinks" (Bakhmetev Archive, Columbia University), esp. 239–58.

[51] On developments within the Kadet party, see Rosenberg, *Liberals in the Russian Revolution*, 83–93. Because all four men were widely believed to have been Freemasons (as were Prince L'vov and Chkheidze), it has been tempting for those who disagreed with them to argue that their common position had been dictated by forces outside Russian political life; see Miliukov, *Vospominaniia* 2:311–12, 329, 332–33; Mel'gunov, *Na putiakh*, 163–98. However, the reality behind this speculation appears more mundane. With its goals of uniting moderates of various political persuasions for a common effort to establish parliamentary democracy in Russia, the "political" or "Russian" Masonry to which the five ministers and some socialists may have belonged differed little from other coalition efforts in the years prior to 1917. Moreover, whatever importance it had held in earlier years as a safe, nonpolitical forum for such efforts had been diminished by the establishment of political freedom in February 1917. In support of this view, see the letters from E. D. Kuskova, a veteran of Russian Masonry, to Grigorii Aronson, who published them with his own interesting observations in *Rossiia nakanune revoliutsii*, 119–21, 126, 138–42.

might render the government powerless. But they sought to overcome what they saw as the harmful effect of dual power not through confrontation with the soviet but through co-opting its moderate leaders into the cabinet. From the very beginning of their ministerial work, they had taken steps to involve the soviet in its various aspects: Konovalov had cooperated with the soviet's "laborists" in mediating industrial relations and reforming labor legislation; Tereshchenko had invited the economists to help rework the tax system; and Nekrasov had called for the democratization of the staff of his Ministry of Transportation as well as participation by worker and employee organizations in ministerial decisions.[52] Naturally, the confrontation between democracy and the Provisional Government during the April crisis had sharpened disagreements in the cabinet. Whereas Miliukov and Shingarev had been ready to consider Guchkov's proposal to suppress the demonstrations by force and thereby break the soviet's strength—if troops could have been found to carry this out—Tereshchenko had announced that he would rather resign than authorize such bloodshed.[53] In any case, by April 24 Kerenskii had been able to assure the executive committee that Guchkov and Miliukov had been "isolated" in the cabinet.[54]

Indeed, to make up for this isolation and as the first step toward mobilizing the forces of the right against the soviet and its supporters, Guchkov had attempted to revive the Duma and its Provisional Committee.[55] Moreover, at a meeting of the members of all four dumas which the Provisional Committee convened on April 27, ostensibly to commemorate the convocation of the First Duma, Guchkov attacked the soviet in the strongest words yet. Its sponsorship of dual power and "multi-power" had resulted, he declared, in "no power" and this threatened the country with civil

[52] Medlin and Parsons, eds., *Nabokov*, 93; Sukhanov, *Zapiski o revoliutsii* 2:275–77; *Den'*, March 10, 1917 (no. 5), 2; *RG*, March 28, 1917 (no. 18), 3.

[53] Guchkov, "Iz vospominanii," September 23, 1936; Miliukov, *Vospominaniia* 2: 329–33; and Medlin and Parsons, eds., *Nabokov*, 86–88, 98–99.

[54] *Petrogradskii sovet*, 216–18. This impression was corroborated by Guchkov, who recalled a cabinet meeting summoned by Prince L'vov during Miliukov's and Shingarev's absence from the capital at which it was decided to remove Miliukov from the Ministry of Foreign Affairs: Guchkov, "Iz vospominanii," September 30, 1936. Also see Tsereteli's report of his conversation with Prince L'vov regarding these disagreements: Tsereteli, *Vospominaniia* 1:108–9. Tsereteli kept in daily contact with the liberal ministers: *Petrogradskii sovet*, 123; Sukhanov, *Zapiski o revoliutsii* 3:404–5.

[55] Guchkov, "Iz vospominanii," September 23, 1936.

war.[56] It was evident that the April crisis had set in motion a re-alignment of forces within the bourgeois camp which would lead to the emergence of a counterrevolutionary alliance a few months later. Yet, as Tsereteli had emphasized in his speech to the Duma's commemorative meeting, for every attacker the soviet had a bour-geois defender. If Rodzianko rejected the soviet's *kontrol'* of the government, Nekrasov stressed that "the goal of the Russian rev-olution was not to replace one autocrat with twelve"; where Shul'gin's sights were fixed on the war, Prince L'vov saw the rev-olution's legacy of freedom.[57]

Seen in this broader perspective, Guchkov's resignation marked the crystalization of the antidemocratic or even counterrevolution-ary forces as well as their departure from the Provisional Govern-ment. When news of the resignation reached the soviet's presid-ium during its morning meeting on May 1, together with an invitation to Tsereteli to discuss the new situation with Prince L'vov, Tsereteli and his colleagues agreed to accept coalition if no other solution to the political crisis could be found.[58] Ideology had apparently finally given way to reality or at least to the reality per-ceived by the Revolutionary Defensist leaders through their expe-rience in the executive committee. And yet, as we shall see, ide-ology and the attitudes derived from it would still play a role in defining the nature of the new political arrangement, the necessity of which could not longer be denied.

The Decision for Coalition

The formal decision to open negotiations for a coalition with the Provisional Government was taken at a meeting of the executive committee that lasted the night from May 1 to 2. The final vote was forty-four in favor of coalition, nineteen against, and two absten-tions.[59] Earlier that evening, the committee's Menshevik faction met with members of the Menshevik Organizational Committee

[56] The speeches delivered at the meeting were reported in full in *Den'*, April 28, 1917 (no. 45), 1–3, and April 29, 1917 (no. 46), 1–2. Partial reports and commentary appeared in *NZh*, April 28, 1917 (no. 9), 4; *RG*, April 30, 1917 (no. 44), 1–2; and Sukhanov, *Zapiski o revoliutsii* 3:345–54. A few days after his resignation, Guchkov repeated these accusations to a private meeting of the Duma's Provisional Com-mittee and demanded the soviet's "submission" to the Provisional Government: *IzvVKGD*, May 14, 1917 (no. 5), 4; *VVP*, May 5, 1917 (no. 48), 1–2.

[57] Tsereteli, *Rechi*, 50–60.

[58] Tsereteli, *Vospominaniia o fevral'skoi revoliutsii* 1:134–36.

[59] *Khronika* 2:95; *RG*, May 3, 1917 (no. 46), 3.

and had voted in favor of coalition government; only three of those present—the Internationalist Sokolovskii and the labor prak-tiki Grinevich and Pankov—persisted in their opposition.[60] A com-parison between the votes taken on April 28 and in the early hours of May 2 demonstrates the Mensheviks' role in reversing the com-mittee's stand on coalition. The negative votes had declined only slightly (from twenty-two to nineteen), for Bolsheviks, Anarchists, Left SRs, and some Independent SDs continued to oppose coali-tion. But this time there were fewer abstainers (two instead of eight) and nonvoters; thus, the additional twenty-two votes in fa-vor of coalition came mostly from those Mensheviks who had pre-viously declined to vote because of doctrinal doubts and party loy-alty.

The majority of the executive committee again appeared united around a new political strategy. Whereas the new majority ex-cluded the extreme left of the committee, it included the extreme right, which had not supported dual power. Most important, the Independent Internationalists and the Mensheviks had again joined in sponsoring a political arrangement, though their reasons for doing so as well as their interpretations of it were markedly different. In the days immediately following its May 2 decision, the executive committee was faced with two conceptions of the coalition strategy: that of Tsereteli, which emphasized cooperation between democracy and the progressive bourgeoisie in fulfilling the promises of a bourgeois-democratic revolution; and that of the Independent Internationalists, who hoped coalition would en-hance the socialists' ability to pressure the bourgeoisie to begin transcending the limits of a bourgeois revolution. Tsereteli's con-ception attracted the Populists and a majority of Mensheviks— who, however, supported it for different reasons, which can be identified with three different groups: the Defensists, the praktiki, and the more pessimistic Revolutionary Defensists of Dan's type. Still other Mensheviks—the Internationalists who now favored co-alition and the soviet's economists—viewed coalition in terms sim-ilar to those of the Independent Internationalists.

Tsereteli's conception of coalition was for him essentially the ideological path of least resistance: Coalition saved the soviet from the far less acceptable alternative of establishing its own "soviet"

[60] Nikolaevskii, "RSDRP," 25–26, 29; Sukhanov, *Zapiski o revoliutsii* 3:408. The Menshevik faction had been formed on April 13, ostensibly to counter Bolshevik influence in the committee but actually to cement Menshevik unity: *RG*, April 14, 1917 (no. 31), 1.

government. (Prince L'vov had presented Tsereteli this alternative, obviously effectively, in the form of an ultimatum on May 1.) Tsereteli expected coalition to allow the soviet to consummate the unity of the "vital forces" and neutralize the influence of the more intransigent elements of the bourgeoisie on their progressive brethren, an assumption derived from Guchkov's resignation and seemingly confirmed by Miliukov's departure two days later. In addition, and in spite of Tsereteli's trust in his future cabinet partners, he appreciated the tactical advantage contained in an arrangement that would give the soviet direct access to the deliberations on state policy, especially in the area closest to Tsereteli's heart, that of war and peace. But above all, Tsereteli, like all who accepted his conception of coalition, insisted that it was made unavoidable by the "utterly exceptional conditions" of war under which the revolution had taken place. "Life itself imposed new tasks each day," he explained on May 5 to the All-Russian Conference of Mensheviks.

Decisive action was required in the struggle against the collapse of internal supplies and against the manifestations of disintegration on the front, which grew disturbingly more noticeable because of the revolutionary army's uncertainty about the government's foreign policy. A strong revolutionary authority was needed that could be one with the people's aspirations and enjoy its fullest support. . . . We tried other ways of supporting [the government], but they did not turn out. For all practical purposes, the government left, and we were faced with the choice of either the soviet's seizing power or our joining a Provisional Government on coalitionary principles.

We could not choose the first [path], for we would have committed the mistake against which Engels warned when he spoke of the tragic situation befalling a proletariat that takes power into its hands when the objective conditions for the implementation of a proletarian program do not yet exist. . . . [Thus], there was only one thing we could do—enter the Provisional Government.[61]

Tsereteli's summons to the progressive forces of Russia to unite and his emphasis on a stable state structure received the support of various groups in the executive committee for different reasons, as mentioned. Kantorovich, who represented the staunch Defensists on the executive committee, had abstained from the vote on April 28 but nonetheless had published an editorial that same day in which he sought to prove the existence of dangerous social

[61] *RG*, May 9, 1917 (no. 51), 7.

"contradictions" that could destroy the very fabric of society unless it were held together "by a strong and united leadership"—in other words, by a coalition.[62] A strong government was also Voitinskii's goal, though his main concern was for the army's defensive capabilities. As a recent convert to Menshevism, he could disregard doctrine, and in fact he had already voted for coalition on April 28.[63] This was the "minimalist" interpretation of coalition, but on the whole it reflected a sense of strength rather than weakness. Kantorovich and Voitinskii as well as other Defensists (Liber and Erlikh, the Menshevik-Bundists, for example) worried about the potential for strife and anarchy, but like Tsereteli they all looked to themselves—to the socialist leaders of democracy—as the nucleus of that unity and order that alone could forestall catastrophe.[64]

The second source of Tsereteli's supporters—the praktiki who were involved in the work of the soviet's labor section, especially Gvozdev and Bogdanov—were just as confident about their success in government. Their sense of strength and importance had by now overridden any fear or doubt, for in the apparent moderation of both workers and employers they had found assurances that their task as social arbiters was within their power, the more so because events had also vindicated the estimates of Konovalov and Nekrasov, whom the praktiki chose to see as the "conscience" of the Russian bourgeoisie.[65] Moreover, having taken responsibility for peace in the country's industrial centers, the leaders of the labor section could see no practical sense in remaining outside the government. Indeed, this newly found sense of national responsibility tended to obscure the very facts that might have given them pause—the increasingly frequent expressions of workers' mistrust of the bourgeoisie and the rise in strike activity following

[62] "In Defense of a Coalition Ministry," *Den'*, April 28, 1917 (no. 45), 1. See also the earlier articles in the same newspaper by Stepan Ivanovich, "Coalition Ministry," April 1, 1917 (no. 24), 1; April 6, 1917 (no. 26), 3, and April 8, 1917 (no. 28), 1.

[63] Voitinskii, "God pobed i porazhenii," 101–2; B. I. Nikolaevskii, "Voitinskii," 169.

[64] Erlikh and Liber aired their views in their speeches to the Bund conference in Petrograd on April 4, though at the time they still opposed coalition: *RG*, April 27, 1917 (no. 25), 3.

[65] Tsereteli had apparently drawn on the same experience for his confidence. In his first speech before the soviet, he had declared that the "responsibility," "maturity," and "understanding" shown by the workers had made it possible for him to believe in the "unity of the vital forces": *IzvPS*, March 21, 1917 (no. 20), 2–3.

the April crisis—and only strengthened their resolve to influence and bolster the moderate, "mature" majority of the working class against the small element of "extremism."[66] A socialist ministry of labor, they believed, would enhance their prestige among workers as well as increase their influence on state policy concerning labor.

The opportunity for direct influence on state policy was the argument that convinced the third group of Mensheviks, notably Dan, who were more reluctant than the former Defensists or the praktiki in accepting coalition.[67] Tsereteli consciously used this argument to win the support of his own group. On May 1, he brought to the executive committee a program, later known as the soviet's "May 2 Principles," that not only helped to reverse this body's stand on coalition but that Tsereteli himself viewed as both the condition and the platform for socialist participation in government. Prominent among these principles was the Revolutionary Defensist position on war. The first point stipulated that the government should seek an opportune peace without annexations, and the second called for making every effort to restore the army's defensive and offensive capabilities. In connection with the war effort, the program also provided for some regulation of industrial and agricultural production and for tax reforms.[68] In Tsereteli's presentation (to the executive committee on May 1 and the soviet on May 2), the purpose of the soviet's joining the cabinet was justified not only to lend strength and popularity to a weak national government at a time of national crisis but also to influence the

[66] The April crisis signaled a turning point of sorts in the workers' political mood. The work of organizing Red Guard detachments, which had earlier met with considerable opposition, finally succeeded (a clear victory for the Bolsheviks) as workers became fearful of the prospects of counterrevolution. See the reports in *IzvPS*, April 22, 1917 (no. 47), 5–6, and *RD v aprele*, 412–14, 420, 430–31, 435–39. In labor relations, too, there appeared new strains, as the economic situation took a turn for the worse and the debate on the Freedom Loan focused attention on the capitalists' war profits. Thus, strike activity in Petrograd increased considerably during the last third of April: Koenker and Rosenberg, "Strikes in Revolution," 17.

[67] On Dan's attitude, see Sapir, "Theodor Dan," 15, and L. Dan, interview no. 22, p. 21.

[68] *RG*, May 4, 1917 (no. 47), 2, and Tsereteli, *Vospominaniia o fevral'skoi revoliutsii* 1:138–39, 151. Articles in *IzvPS* during these days reflected Tsereteli's confidence that the progressive ministers who had stayed in the Provisional Government were in agreement with the soviet or could be forced to follow its dictates: "Toward the Establishment of a Revolutionary Power," May 3, 1917 (no. 56), 1, and May 4, 1917 (no. 57), 1–2. Information on Tereshchenko's stand in regard to the war partially justifies this confidence: see Medlin and Parsons, eds., *Nabokov*, 96–98, and Wade, *Russian Search for Peace*, 75–77.

conduct of national policy. Indeed, even the most moderate Mensheviks recognized that only through the accomplishment of the latter could the soviet hope to retain its hold over its mass constituency.

In practice, it was Tsereteli's insistence on three points that united his Menshevik supporters and distinguished his conception of coalition from that of the Internationalists who supported it: that the socialists should constitute only a minority of the cabinet; that they should limit their programmatic "conditions" to the issues of war and peace; and that the soviet should declare full confidence in the government.[69] What was striking about this approach was the degree to which it was rooted in Menshevik ideology. In stipulating a socialist minority in the cabinet (a point opposed even by the SRs), the Mensheviks were in fact reiterating their earlier reservations about coalition: that it would raise false hopes among the workers and that the role of the Social Democrats in the bourgeois stage of revolution was to press the bourgeoisie into action and not replace it. In the case of Dan and other veterans, the former objections had also been that the soviet's claim to too great a share of power for itself would hasten the formation of a counterrevolutionary party within the bourgeoisie.[70] Thus, at the very moment that the Mensheviks were breaking with their long-held ideological strictures in order to respond to a new reality—testimony to the sense of strength and responsibility they had derived from their role as leaders of the Petrograd soviet—they demonstrated their continued perception of this reality in terms of their Marxist-Menshevik view of history and revolution. They had used these terms in the past to make sense of the changing structures of Russian society and politics as well as to reassure themselves that political democracy, and later socialism, would follow the dark years of reaction, and they were now unwilling to dispense with these conceptual devices or incapable of doing so. Only a few could cast aside the old doctrinal formulas that no longer seemed to explain reality, and for the most part these were men who had not participated in the party's work during the years of expectations and disillusionment—men such as Voitinskii and to a lesser degree even Tsereteli.

[69] Tsereteli, *Vospominaniia o fevral'skoi revoliutsii* 1:138–43; Sukhanov, *Zapiski o revoliutsii* 3:408–17.

[70] Tsereteli, *Vospominaniia o fevral'skoi revoliutsii* 1:141; A. Panin, "The Choice Has Been Made," *RG*, May 3, 1917 (no. 46), 1–2; L. Dan, interview no. 22, p. 21; Sapir, "Theodor Dan," 15.

In contrast to the position of most Mensheviks, doctrinal heterodoxy was the hallmark of the other, more "radical" conception of coalition held by the Independent Internationalists, especially Sukhanov and Bazarov. There was, to be sure, a link between this conception and that of Tsereteli: namely, the view of coalition as an opportunity for greater influence on government policy. For Bazarov and Sukhanov, however, this opportunity was not merely a way of overcoming doctrinal objections; rather, it was the very essence of their innovative reinterpretation of Marxist doctrine. Prompted by the April crisis to rethink the soviet's strategy, they argued, as early as April 26, that the "narrow class character" of the Provisional Government which had mandated the strategy of dual power in early March had been so exacerbated by the crisis and the resulting development of the masses' "political consciousness" that the soviet could no longer avoid the "shift in power to 'democracy.' " For both practical and doctrinal reasons, they still advised against a "soviet government" but insisted that formal expression be given to the soviet's actual strength through socialist participation in government. Most important was their demand that henceforth the soviet should be represented in the cabinet not as "opposition" but as the source of the government's authority.[71]

In terms of Social Democratic doctrine, this conception of the Independent Internationalists meant that coalition was not merely a temporary measure for strengthening a weak bourgeois government or for forcing this government to carry out policies that would earn it the support of workers and soldiers but that coalition was a step on the road toward a socialist revolution. In practical terms, the position led to three demands: that the soviet have the majority of ministers in the cabinet; that it pursue an aggressive "peace policy" (including publication of the secret treaties) and establish full government control over production, distribution, pricing, and profits; and that the soviet's support of the coalition cabinet be made conditional on the acceptance of this program.[72]

---

[71] "The Political Crisis," *NZh*, April 26, 1917 (no. 7), 1; Sukhanov, "Coalition Ministry," *NZh*, April 27, 1917 (no. 8), 1; Sukhanov, "In Search of a Way out," and V. Bazarov, "The Reconstruction of the Provisional Government," *NZh*, April 30, 1917 (no. 11), 1. Also see Sukhanov's retrospective discussion of the evolution of his ideas in his memoirs: *Zapiski o revoliutsii*, 3:354–58, 393–96. Other Independent SDs who are known to have supported this position were Steklov and Gol'denberg; see Tsereteli, *Vospominaniia o fevral'skoi revoliutsii* 1:140.

[72] Tsereteli, *Vospominaniia o fevral'skoi revoliutsii* 1:138–43; Sukhanov, *Zapiski o revoliutsii* 3:408–17.

Two groups of Mensheviks responded to the Independent Internationalists' view of the new political arrangement by dropping their opposition to coalition, and of them the Menshevik Internationalists were less of a surprise, for they were generally close to the Independents in both analysis and temperament. Certainly, the possibility of imposing policy on a reluctant bourgeoisie seemed more realistic to them as a result of the soviet's recently demonstrated strength in the area of labor relations. Moreover, without undue contortion the Independents' conception could be made to fit the doctrinal formulations the Mensheviks had adopted in 1905, according to which socialist participation in power was at least permissible in situations where the "historically confined limits" of the bourgeois revolution might be transcended (though the Mensheviks had envisioned such a possibility only if a socialist revolution occurred in the industrially developed countries of Europe).[73] On the basis of these arguments, at least three Menshevik Internationalists reversed themselves on the issue of coalition: L. G. Shapiro, a delegate from the Eighth Army to the Conference of Soviets, where he was elected to the executive committee; D. Iu. Dalin, who had just returned from exile in Stockholm; and B. I. Nikolaevskii, who, like Dalin, was a member of the Petrograd organization.[74]

The second group of men who joined in the Independents' radical interpretation of coalition did present something of a surprise: these were Groman and Cherevanin—both former Liquidationists and public organization employees who had taken over the soviet's economic section. Their support for coalition as a means of forcing measures on the cabinet resulted from the combined impact of their attempts to implement economic regulation and the erosion of their earlier confidence, during April, that the soviet could dictate to the government the measures essential for alleviating the supply crisis. Their victory in establishing a state monopoly of grain had been overturned by the staffing of local supply committees with landowners and merchants and later by Shingarev's refusal to act on the recommendation of the All-Russian Supply Commission that special emissaries be sent to the provinces to oversee the marketing of grain. In fact, the executive committee had been forced to name its own emissaries "to organize grain reserves," armed with nothing more than letters of authorization

[73] "Pervaia konferentsiia," supplement to Iskra, May 15, 1905 (no. 100), 23–24.

[74] Sukhanov, Zapiski o revoliutsii 3:199; RG, May 4, 1917 (no. 47), 3–4; Nikolaevskii, "RSDRP," 26.

from Groman, the chairman of the supply commission.[75] Clearly, the soviet's economists were ready to challenge what they felt was government obstructionism, but in so doing, their expectations, and their preferred strategy, had been altered.[76]

In effect, the economists had had their hopes frustrated by governmental and entrepreneurial resistance to the idea of economic regulation, and they were now becoming more alarmed by mounting economic difficulties: rising prices, chronic shortages of industrial goods, and, toward the end of the month, an increasing frequency of work stoppages because of shortages of fuel and raw materials.[77] Their sense of urgency was reflected in a series of articles by Cherevanin in *Rabochaia gazeta*, beginning on April 30. In the first of these, he argued that what was needed was a "courageous" and far-reaching intervention in the economy, which could be done only through the state apparatus. Moreover, he declared that his past experience and thought on these matters had convinced him that only one group in Russia was prepared for this and the other tasks of democratizing the country: the technical intelligentsia.[78] Yet, as Cherevanin recognized, time was running out, so he concluded that under the circumstances the "ideological representatives of the proletariat" (meaning the socialist intelli-

[75] *Petrogradskii sovet*, 120–21; *IzvPS*, April 23, 1917 (no. 48), 1–2; Sukhanov, *Zapiski o revoliutsii* 3:196.

[76] Another example of how the economists were being pushed to radical solutions was provided when the executive committee formed a new Central Supply Commission for the city of Petrograd (April 5) and made it, on Groman's suggestion, a "coalitionary" body by adding three representatives of the workers, two of local cooperatives (*obyvatel'* organizations, in the contemporary phrase), and one each of the merchants and the city government. When the municipal authorities, in concert with Shingarev, tried to prevent the new commission from taking over the city's food provisions, Groman thwarted their efforts but returned to the executive committee to ask that the representatives of the city government and the merchants be replaced by representatives of the *"obyvatel'* district committees," presumably because the former had collaborated with the commission's opponents: *Petrogradskii sovet*, 85, 96; *IzvPS*, April 12, 1917 (no. 38), 3.

[77] "On Whom Should the Expenses of War Rest?" *RG*, April 13, 1917 (no. 30), 2; "A Plan Is Needed," *RG*, April 28, 1917 (no. 42), 1; "Supplying the Population With Industrial Goods," *IzvPS*, April 30, 1917 (no. 45), 4; V. Bazarov, "The Fatherland in Danger" and "Imperialism and Hunger," *NZh*, April 18, 1917 (no. 1), 1, and April 25, 1917 (no. 6), 1.

[78] N. Cherevanin, "The Crisis of Power," *RG*, April 30, 1917 (no. 44), 2. Cherevanin himself belonged to the technical intelligentsia by virtue of his profession, and he had cooperated with its representatives in the public organizations. More broadly, he had in mind the "urban democratic bourgeoisie," a term he had coined years earlier (see chap. 1).

gentsia) should take it upon itself to force the necessary economic reforms by entering the cabinet. (Incidentally, it appears that Cherevanin was the first Menshevik in 1917 to speak of the soviet's Social Democratic leaders as "intelligentsia," though Groman had earlier hinted at this definition in his economic plan.) Cherevanin's advocacy of coalition preceded his party's decision by a day or two, and as he made clear in an article written after the party had in effect endorsed his position, his view of coalition was closer to Sukhanov's than Tsereteli's, because Cherevanin had insisted that in order for the soviet to carry out its "intervention" in government work and force the "necessary" measures, the soviet would have to hold a majority in the cabinet.[79]

Thus, as the executive committee prepared to begin negotiations with the Provisional Government on May 2, its members were divided between Tsereteli's "minimalist" demands and the "radical" demands of the Internationalists and the economists. These differences reflected the variety of Social Democratic interpretations of the revolutionary experience that had nevertheless converged to produce the committee's support of coalition. The nature of the new political arrangement could not be determined until one or the other position had been adopted. As it turned out, the executive committee's decision that a coalition should be negotiated in the first place began a chain of events that seemed inexorable and culminated in the soviet's overwhelming ratification of the minimalist position.

IT QUICKLY BECAME clear that Tsereteli's conception of coalition was ensured a majority in the executive committee, made up as it was of the Revolutionary Defensist bloc and the Populist-Defensists. Moreover, it was only natural that the process of negotiations between the executive committee's delegation and the Provisional Government (these lasted three days and encountered several minor obstacles) should result in a further dilution of the "May 2 Principles," although despite this dilution at least two Mensheviks would feel compelled to join the cabinet as an indication of the soviet's full support.[80] Nevertheless, enough of Tsereteli's princi-

[79] N. Cherevanin, "A Question Requiring an Immediate Answer," *RG*, May 4, 1917 (no. 47), 1–2.

[80] On the negotiations, see the accounts in Stankevich, *Vospominaniia*, 128–32; Tsereteli, *Vospominaniia o fevral'skoi revoliutsii* 1:143–46, 156–63; and Sukhanov, *Zapiski o revoliutsii* 3:411–39. The soviet's delegation included three "minority men" (Sukhanov, Iurenev, and the Bolshevik Lev Kamenev), but the ministers naturally

ples on peace, defense, and democratic reform survived to make it possible for Skobelev to ask the Petrograd soviet on May 5, a few hours after the negotiations had ended and the new cabinet had been established, to approve the program and lend the government its "full confidence" and "complete authority."[81]

There seemed to be nothing further in the way of coalition. The socialists felt reassured by Miliukov's resignation from the cabinet on May 2, which left the foreign affairs portfolio for Tereshchenko, while Kerenskii took over the Ministry of War and Nekrasov the Ministry of Finance. With Skobelev as minister of labor, Chernov as minister of agriculture, and Tsereteli representing the soviet's general political line (his specific assignment was the Ministry of Post and Telegraph), the executive committee felt that the new cabinet would be dedicated to the social and political democratization that they perceived as both the task of the revolution and a prerequisite for the government's stability.[82] At the soviet plenum on May 5, Gots assured the deputies that their representatives would not serve in the cabinet as the "prisoners of the bourgeoisie" but would use their position "to advance the trenches of the revolution forward."[83]

In their own camp, too, the leaders faced little opposition. A meeting on May 2 had confirmed the decision to open negotiations by a vote of over two thousand to about one hundred.[84] At the

---

preferred to deal with Tsereteli's group, which included, beside himself, four other Mensheviks (Dan, Voitinskii, Chkheidze, and Bogdanov) and six Populists (Gots, Avksent'ev, Peshekhonov, Fillipovskii, Stankevich, and Bramson). See *Khronika* 2:95, and Sukhanov, *Zapiski o revoliutsii* 3:411. The ministers also insisted that Tsereteli personally join the cabinet.

[81] The text of the government's declaration on the outcome of the negotiations, written jointly by Tsereteli and Nekrasov, was printed in all of the newspapers on May 6; it is reprinted in *Khronika* 2:271–73, and in *RPG* 3:1277. The soviet's plenary meeting is reported in detail in *Khronika* 2:110–12.

[82] The other socialists in the cabinet were the moderate Populists Peshekhonov (Supplies) and P. N. Pereverzev (Justice). The nine nonsocialist ministers included the members of the first cabinet (with the exception of Guchkov and Miliukov) and the Moscow Kadet I. D. Shakhovskoi.

[83] It may be that Gots was trying to allay his own fears—fears raised by Miliukov's statement a day earlier that the Kadet party would support the government "insofar as [*postol'ku, poskol'ku*]" it fulfilled the tasks outlined in a resolution of the party's executive committee; see *Khronika* 2:118–19; *IzvVKGD*, May 14, 1917 (no. 5); Miliukov, *Istoriia vtoroi russkoi revoliutsii* 1:113–14. Tsereteli was assured by Nekrasov that Miliukov's stand did not reflect the thinking of the party's majority: Tsereteli, *Vospominaniia o fevral'skoi revoliutsii* 1:155–56.

[84] *Khronika* 2:98–99; Sukhanov, *Zapiski o revoliutsii* 3:420.

May 5 meeting, which Tsereteli later remembered as the most "moving and inspired with hope" of all the soviet's meetings he attended in 1917, only one man stood up to speak against the new political arrangement—the radical Internationalist Lev Trotskii. Indeed, the sentiment for coalition was so strong that Grigorii Zinov'ev, who was scheduled to speak for the Bolsheviks, decided not to address the meeting.[85] When the workers' section of the soviet held a separate meeting on May 13 to hear the reports of Tsereteli, Skobelev, and Chernov concerning their work in the cabinet, no more than thirty Bolsheviks (out of nearly one thousand deputies) voted for Trotskii's motion of "no confidence" in the government.[86] Meanwhile, in the factories of Petrograd, workers were adopting resolutions of support for the leaders' new political strategy.[87]

Only on closer examination does it become apparent that the workers' attitudes toward the new cabinet and their expectations of it were at odds with the interpretation the executive committee had adopted, because not many workers shared Tsereteli's trust in the progressive bourgeoisie. Only rarely had a resolution expressing confidence in the government ever gained approval at a workers' meeting.[88] The typical resolution at these meetings alluded only to the socialist ministers. For example, that adopted by the workers of the Russian Society of Telegraph and Telephone on May 10 declared, "As long as you, comrades, are in the government, we are convinced that all its activity is directed toward the further strengthening of the revolution's achievements."[89] The seven thousand workers of the Admiralty shipyard also reflected this confidence when they greeted the "socialist comrades" on joining the government, wherein they would "carry out the finan-

[85] Tsereteli, *Vospominaniia o fevral'skoi revoliutsii* 1:165; *Khronika* 2:110–12. The Bolshevik faction instead ordered a little-known member, Sundukov, to deliver a one-sentence statement repeating the party's opposition to coalition. On sentiment in favor of coalition, see also Voitinskii, "God pobed i porazhenii," 103.

[86] *Khronika* 2:148–51.

[87] Between May 7 and 18, *RG* published a daily column, "For Coalition Government," which featured the texts of such resolutions as well as long lists of factories and meetings whose resolutions could not be printed for lack of space.

[88] One such resolution was adopted at the Putilov works on May 14, after Dan and Skobelev had addressed a large meeting: *RG*, May 16, 1917 (no. 57), 4.

[89] *RG*, May 13, 1917 (no. 55), 3. See also the resolutions adopted by three thousand workers of the state-owned Orudiinyi factory on May 4 and by the workers of the Westinghouse plant: *RG*, May 7, 1917 (no. 50), 4, and May 12, 1917 (no. 54), 4.

cial reform worked out by the economic section of the soviet." The shipyard workers' resolution said they supported the Provisional Government but stated their intention that the soviet should "consciously and unswervingly" bring about "an increased socialist influence" on the government.[90] Clearly, the workers expected the leaders who represented them in the cabinet to use the authority of the soviet to advance the goals of peace, democracy, and social reform.

The workers' interpretation of coalition, then, was closer to the Internationalists' than to Tsereteli's. Generally speaking, their support of coalition derived from two perceptions of the revolutionary change of the past two months. On the one hand, they were confident that the socialists in the cabinet would act in their behalf against the expected opposition of the bourgeois ministers, a confidence based on the tangible gains they had made in the early months of the revolution and on the role played by the leaders of the soviet, especially the Menshevik activists of the labor section, in securing these gains. On the other hand, the workers' sense of economic injustice was beginning to grow again toward the end of April, with rising food prices and the demand that workers contribute to the Freedom Loan. Also, the press campaign in late March against democracy and the Kadet demonstrations of April 21 had reawakened the workers' suspicion of counterrevolution, as shown by their sudden organizing of "Red Guard" detachments in the factories, as the Bolsheviks had been demanding for some time (unsuccessfully up to this point).[91] Thus, while the workers had observed the restrictions of dual power,[92] they also evinced a growing desire—evident in their resolutions throughout April—to exercise greater *kontrol'* over the government. It was for this reason that they viewed the prospect of socialists joining the government as something of a triumph.

The Menshevik leaders of the soviet naturally rejoiced in this expression of confidence and in the fact that the Bolsheviks' slogan of "all power to the soviets" had not spread beyond a few factories in Vyborg, where the Bolsheviks had had support from the very beginning. Few of the Mensheviks paid close attention to the

[90] *RG*, May 25, 1917 (no. 64), 3.

[91] See n. 66 above, and Wade, *Red Guards*, 79–90.

[92] Examples of support for dual power abounded during April. See *RG*, April 5, 1917 (no. 23), 2; April 6, 1917 (no. 24), 2; April 25, 1917 (no. 39), 2; April 26, 1917 (no. 40), 2; April 28, 1917 (no. 42), 2–3; *IzvPS*, April 23, 1917 (no. 53), 6; and *RD v aprele*, 333.

echoes of the old "pressure" formula that reverberated through the workers' new resolutions.[93] The main concern of the Menshevik leaders of the soviet in early May was for the response of their own party. As they were well aware, their own acceptance of this "heavy sacrifice" (to use Dan's words at the soviet plenum on May 5) had come about as a result of the role they had undertaken as the guardians of democracy. Their practical work in the executive committee and its sections—work for which their Menshevik political culture had prepared them but which sometimes put them in conflict with the ideological facet of this culture—had both forced them and allowed them to overcome the ideological prohibition against coalition. The immediate question before them now was whether their fellow Mensheviks, those outside Petrograd and those not active in the soviet, would approve this unorthodox move.[94]

THE MAY CONFERENCE

By coincidence, the first nationwide Menshevik gathering since the revolution was scheduled to meet just two days after the coalition government had been formed and approved by the soviet. As party organizations all over the country prepared to send their delegates to Petrograd, positions were discussed and votes taken, and resolutions were published that could not but raise anxiety in the Revolutionary Defensist leadership. At a meeting in Moscow on April 28, the second largest Menshevik organization declared itself against coalition and, more broadly, against the very notion of a national constituency. The participants approved, by a vote of 56 to 23, a resolution proposed by the veteran praktik I. A. Isuv stating that a coalition cabinet did not correspond to the actual alignment of social and political forces, and it voted 60 to 1 to not even consider Potresov's proposal to create a national forum

[93] For examples of the handful of resolutions favoring a transfer of power to the soviet, see *IzvPS*, April 15, 1917 (no. 41), 3, and *RD v aprele*, 392–93. This latter collection, in spite of its pro-Bolshevik bias, lists only three such resolutions for all of April. In early May, several new factories joined the short list of those voting for soviet power; only in these factories did workers vote against coalition. See, for example, the resolutions adopted by the United Cable factories and the Military-Horseshoe factory: *Pravda*, May 5, 1917 (no. 49), 4.

[94] Sukhanov remembered this concern being discussed during the breaks in the negotiations with the Provisional Government: *Zapiski o revoliutsii* 3:418. See also A. Panin, "Confidence in the New Government," *RG*, May 6, 1917 (no. 49), 1–2.

("state conference") for the exchange of political ideas.[95] In Tiflis, Noi Zhordania, one of the founding fathers of Georgian Menshevism, condemned his Petrograd colleagues' decision to join a coalition government. A resolution he drafted for the Tiflis soviet called for a congress of all the soviets to be convened promptly in order to make a "competent decision" on the political questions of the day as well as to create a nationwide soviet leadership that would express the "will of all the Russian proletariat." The resolution, which was adopted, went on to express conditional confidence in the coalition government in words similar to those used in the case of the old cabinet.[96]

Most worrisome of all, however, was the response of the Petrograd organization of the party, the largest one and the one most distinguished by famous Menshevik names. The first citywide conference of the Petrograd organization, meeting from May 3 to 5, rejected the proposals and ultimatums of the extreme Internationalists as well as those of the Defensists and fashioned its final resolutions to accommodate as large a majority of the participants as possible.[97] The majority that formed around the compromise resolutions, however, was clearly more Internationalist and radical than was the Revolutionary Defensist leadership of the Menshevik Organizational Committee and the soviet's executive committee. This majority was comprised of Menshevik veterans and Petrograd literaty; the former shared Dan's suspicion of the bourgeoisie, and the latter gravitated toward the internationalism of Ermanskii.[98] Thus, the conference adopted several of Ermanskii's resolutions: on the general question of the war (by a vote of 63 to 40); on the revival of the Socialist International (68 to 14); and, in spite of an appeal from Dan and Skobelev, a condemnation of so-

[95] RG, May 3, 1917 (no. 46), 4. There were 135 participants in the meeting, but only 110 of them had voting rights.

[96] Tifliskii listok, May 9, 1917 (no. 102); Zhordania, Moia zhizn', 77.

[97] The desire to preserve Menshevik unity was evident in a resolution passed by the bureau of the Menshevik Internationalists a few days before the conference, which condemned Larin's efforts to create an Internationalist bloc of Mensheviks, Bolsheviks, and Mezhraiontsy around his newspaper, Internatsional; see "The Declaration of Mensheviks-Internationalists," RG, April 26, 1917 (no. 40), 4, and Nikolaevskii, "RSDRP," 23–24.

[98] The meetings of the conference were reported in RG, May 4, 1917 (no. 47), 3–4; May 5, 1917 (no. 48), 4; and May 6, 1917 (no. 49), 4. See also a general report on the conference presented on May 10 to a general assembly of the Moscow district of the Menshevik Petrograd organization, in RG, May 13, 1917 (no. 57), 3. The conference was attended by 117 delegates, representing 7,200 members.

cialist participation in coalition (59 to 55, with the Internationalists who subscribed to the radical interpretation voting with the losing side).[99] This was a great embarrassment for the Menshevik ministers and would have been more so had not the conference finally decided in a last-minute move to partially reverse itself and give them "full and energetic support."[100]

The Revolutionary Defensists' apprehension was all the greater because a large group of Menshevik emigres was expected to arrive in Petrograd at any moment and to add to the strength of the Internationalist wing. Two of the returnees were the most revered leaders of Menshevism: Akselrod and Martov. In earlier communications, they had expressed their opposition to coalition (Martov had called it "intolerable," though Akselrod had declared it only a lesser evil than a fully socialist government), and they had implied that the present Menshevik leadership of the soviet, "those comrades to whose lot it fell to be the immediate leaders of the movement," might be a transient one.[101] *Rabochaia gazeta* argued against such doubts and appealed to the party that secondary issues not be allowed to divide it precisely at the historic moment when it was finally possible to realize the Menshevik dream of a "European-type Social Democratic party," and especially when such a party was urgently needed to guarantee the success of the revolution. The newspaper offered two principles as a platform for party unity, neither of which, it argued, could be objectionable to any Menshevik because each was consistent with a wide range of strategies: the search for peace, and the definition of the revolution as "bourgeois democratic."[102] But Tsereteli and Dan were determined to have their strategies adopted by the party at large before the emigre Internationalists had had a chance to join the debate.[103]

The All-Russian Conference of the RSDRP (Mensheviks) opened on May 7 with the customary series of reports and congratulatory speeches. As new ministers and "respected leaders," Tsereteli and

[99] Draft resolutions voted down included an enthusiastic support of coalition proposed by S. Schwarz, an ambiguous statement by M. Panin, a radical version of coalition by Nikolaevskii and Dalin, and a rejection of coalition by Larin. In addition, Chernov, G. O. Binshtok, and Grinevich spoke against coalition, and Potresov, Iudin, and Kantorovich spoke for it.

[100] See Gorev's commentary in "After the Crisis," *RG*, May 5, 1917 (no. 48), 1–2.

[101] *RG*, April 18, 1917 (no. 34), 3; May 5, 1917 (no. 48), 2; and May 6, 1917 (no. 49), 4.

[102] "The All-Russian Conference," *RG*, May 6, 1917 (no. 49), 1.

[103] Sukhanov, *Zapiski o revoliutsii* 4:23–24; "Akselrod's View on the Question of War," *IzvPS*, May 6, 1917 (no. 50), 7.

Skobelev addressed the conference and used the opportunity to defend the decision on coalition.[104] Cautiously and systematically, Tsereteli presented coalition not as part of his strategy for uniting the "vital forces" but as the only alternative to the assumption of full power by the soviet and for this reason as a "tremendous victory for the realistic tactics" Menshevism "had always championed." Later, he promised that the socialist ministers would follow "Menshevik tactics," though in defining these he hinted at his remarkably "un-Menshevik" optimism and serenity. The socialists, he expected, would lead that part of the bourgeoisie that could follow them in pursuing an "increasingly decisive policy on both domestic and foreign questions" while "casting away" and isolating those who could not.[105]

When the conference turned to a discussion of the party's relations to the Provisional Government, caution was again the watchword.[106] Gorev presented coalition as unavoidable; he emphasized the opportunity it provided the soviet to influence government policy, but he also emphasized that the ministers should be responsible to the party as well as to the soviet. Not unexpectedly, his presentation evoked opposition from the extreme Internationalists (Larin, Piletskii, Chernov), who wanted their fellow Mensheviks out of the cabinet, with its "limited" and "unproletarian" program. The moderate Internationalists (Ermanskii and Grinevich) were just as adamant, though they limited themselves to calling for conditioning the soviet's support of the government on the implementation of "democracy's program." The counterattack was made by Dan and Erlikh and by Khinchuk, Ezhov, and Isuv, who occupied a position in Moscow similar to that of the Mensheviks in the Petrograd soviet. All defended coalition as a burden of responsibility placed on the soviet and its Menshevik leaders by the revolution. For Isuv, who had led the Moscow soviet in its rejection of coalition barely a week earlier, the decisive factor was the

[104] The details of the first session of the conference have been pieced together from reports in *RG*, May 9, 1917 (no. 51), 3; *Edinstvo*, May 9, 1917 (no. 34), 3; and *Den'*, May 9, 1917 (no. 54), 2–3. A file of newspaper reports on the conference prepared for the Project on Menshevik History was of great help in reconstructing the proceedings.

[105] *RG*, May 9, 1917 (no. 51), 7.

[106] This debate began during a late-evening session on May 7 and was concluded at the morning session on May 8. The reports in *RG*, May 9, 1917 (no. 51), 3, and *Den'*, May 9, 1917 (no. 54), 2–3, provided only one-sentence summaries of the many speeches.

contrast in tone between the new ministers and the extreme Internationalists.

What was especially surprising was the depth of feeling demonstrated by these new defenders of coalition, particularly at the suggestion of returning to dual power. Gorev, for example, reserved his bitterest criticism for Ermanskii's defense of dual power: even the full soviet power advocated by Lenin was preferable, he declared.[107] At bottom was a sentiment best captured in the reply that either Khinchuk or Isuv made to Ermanskii: "We are the governing party!"[108] As such, the Mensheviks had the right and the obligation not to hold themselves above responsibility either by pulling out of the government or by granting it only conditional support. When the final vote was taken on the organizational committee's resolution (in wording devised by Dan, Gorev, Isuv, and Ezhov), the sentiments in favor of coalition proved to be dominant, especially among the delegates from the provinces, who made up the majority of the conference and whose views on the revolution had been virtually unknown to the leadership until that moment. The resolution, expressing strong support of coalition, was passed by a vote of fifty-one to twelve (with eight abstentions). No sooner had it been adopted than a supplementary resolution from the floor was proposed, and accepted, which stressed the need for a strong government and condemned anyone who discredited the present cabinet, especially its socialist ministers.

The debate on the question of the war followed much the same pattern.[109] Dan spoke for the organizational committee; many amendments from the floor were proposed, and the final resolution was considerably more "defensist" than were most of the Revolutionary Defensists in Petrograd. Not only did this resolution call for the defense of the country until a universal, "democratic" peace had been secured, but it also described the goal of peace as one that was fully acceptable to the new cabinet and added a sharply worded condemnation of fraternization on the front. Again, a strong vote in favor of the resolution (fifty-three to

[107] Two days earlier, Panin had written that "whatever happens, the formula of *postol'ku-poskol'ku* had to be put into the archives of history": "Confidence in the New Government," *RG*, May 6, 1917 (no. 49), 1–2.

[108] Ermanskii, *Iz perezhitogo*, 161.

[109] The debate began during the evening session on May 8 and ended on the morning of May 9; the reports in the press were again laconic: *RG*, May 10, 1917 (no. 52), 2; *NZh*, May 10, 1917 (no. 19), 4; *Den'*, May 10, 1917 (no. 55), 2.

ten) was immediately followed by an amendment offered from the floor and adopted that specifically mentioned the need to preserve the army's fighting capacity and made defense a "national task" transcending "class lines." Thus, by the time the returning Internationalist leaders appeared before the conference, early on the evening of May 9, the two most important issues had been settled and Revolutionary Defensism had been recognized as the party's strategy.

WHAT the first two days of the deliberations revealed was that the Menshevik party at large—or at least its representatives to this first "open" conference—was far less inhibited and uneasy in its support of coalition than were both the Internationalists and the Revolutionary Defensists in Petrograd. In fact, the majority of the delegates to the conference displayed an enthusiasm for coalition government that was greater than even Tsereteli's and indicated that they were ready to go further than their leaders in the soviet toward the assumption of national tasks and national responsibility. Above all, they responded to the new image of Menshevism as a "governing party" with pride and a sense of relief. Who were these delegates who gave Revolutionary Defensism such a victory? And what was the source of their unambiguous acceptance of coalition and defense?

The eighty-eight voting delegates represented fifty-four organizations (of which twenty-three called themselves "United SD") with a total membership of 44,830.[110] The largest Menshevik organization, that of Georgia, with approximately 40,000 members, as well as twenty-three other organizations already in contact with the Menshevik Organizational Committee, refused to send delegates to a separate Menshevik conference because they thought the time was right for the reunification of Russian Social Democracy.[111] A questionnaire distributed to the delegates by the organizational committee, as well as other information gathered at the conference, revealed three principal facts about the delegates, at least one of which goes a long way toward explaining the striking difference of attitude between the all-Russian conference and the Petrograd organization.

[110] *RG*, May 10, 1917 (no. 52), 3, and *PI*, July 15, 1917 (no. 1), 27. The latter lists only fifty organizations with a total membership of 41, 250.

[111] Reports on reservations regarding the convocation of a separate Menshevik conference are in *RG*, April 6, 1917 (no. 13), 3, and April 25, 1917 (no. 39), 4; Nikolaevskii, "RSDRP," 27; and Kin, "Bor'ba," 33–34.

First, many of the eighty-seven respondents to the question-naire appear to have been long-time veterans of Social Democracy. Sixty-nine had been active from at least 1905 (and of them, twenty-eight had an even longer record of activity), though it is impossible to know whether they were active during the 1907–1912 lull in revolutionary activity. Eighty had been arrested at least once, and the average respondent had been arrested 3.5 times and had spent 2 years in prison and 2.5 years in exile.[112] Second, these Mensheviks were prominent in local centers of power: fifty-eight were members of soviets, thirty were members of the executive committees of their soviets, and seven served on local "commit-tees of public organizations." In their activism, both before and during 1917, the conference delegates were not markedly different from Mensheviks in Moscow or Petrograd.

The greatest difference lay in the third characteristic: the high percentage of delegates from provincial towns and cities, espe-cially among the voting delegates. Most of the party's famous leaders attended the conference as nonvoting "consulting dele-gates" (thirty-five were listed in this category), and the Petrograd and Moscow Mensheviks accounted for slightly less than one-quarter of the voting delegates. Perhaps as many as another quarter of the voting delegates came from towns with relatively large Menshevik organizations (such as Kharkov, Kiev, Saratov, Nizhnii Novgorod, and Riga), each of which was allocated two or three votes, and the rest, approximately half of the delegates, came from provincial towns that sent one delegate each to the con-ference.[113]

The Mensheviks in the larger cities or towns that served as in-

[112] *RG*, May 31, 1917 (no. 68), 4.

[113] The Moscow organization was assigned five votes, plus two for its faction in the Moscow soviet, and the Petrograd organization was given five for its Interna-tionalist majority, four for its Revolutionary Defensist minority, and five for its fac-tion in the Petrograd soviet, the organizational committee, and *Rabochaia gazeta*. In general, the system of representation allowed one delegate for every five hundred party members and additional delegates for any organization divided between Rev-olutionary Defensists and Internationalists: *RG*, April 20, 1917 (no. 35), 3–4. As often happens, the smaller organizations were overrepresented. Eleven of the eighty-eight voting delegates came from Menshevik organizations of less than 400 members, and twenty-three other organizations (all United SD), with a combined membership of about 10,000 (less than 25 percent of the membership represented at the conference), sent twenty-six delegates; thus, together, these two groups ac-counted for 42 percent of the voting delegates: *PI*, July 15, 1917 (no. 1), 27. The names of the voting delegates and the organizations they represented are listed in *RG*, May 16, 1917 (no. 53), 3.

195

CHAPTER FIVE

dustrial, administrative, or educational centers where workers, intelligentsia, and commercial-industrial elements could meet played a role similar to that of their counterparts in Petrograd: they had their own organization, separate from the local Bolshevik organization, if such existed, and they served as leaders of a soviet of workers' deputies, where they pursued the moderate labor policies that were identified with Menshevism and that seemed suitable to their tasks. These provincial delegates were likely to look at Russia's political situation in much the same way as would Dan, Garvi, or Ezhov.[114]

However, the largest single group of delegates came from towns that served as administrative and perhaps educational centers but had no sizable amount of industry. Although these towns may have had a substantial intelligentsia (professionals, city and zemstvo employees, students, and teachers), they had a relatively small number of industrial workers and no commercial-industrial organizations to speak of. In these towns, the soviets were likely to include many more soldiers and nonindustrial laborers than factory workers. Also, there was usually only one Social Democratic organization, and it was essentially Revolutionary Defensist, whether it called itself "United SD" or "Menshevik." The experience of Mensheviks in these nonindustrial towns differed significantly from that of their fellow party members in Petrograd and informed their attitudes toward the questions before the May conference.[115]

By far the most perceptive participant in and observer of this provincial scene was Iu. P. Denike, who had been a Bolshevik ag-

[114] The tendency of separate Menshevik organizations to exist in larger centers is evident from the fact that sixteen purely Menshevik organizations represented at the conference had a combined membership of over 25,000, which is to say that they were relatively large organizations: PI, July 15, 1917 (no. 1), 27. The register of Social Democratic organizations drawn up by Kin ("Bor'ba," 66–70) also shows separate organizations in large industrial centers, whereas United organizations appear mostly in nonindustrial towns and in Siberia. A survey of the socialist press in the provinces for May and June 1917 also found separate Menshevik or Bolshevik newspapers only in large industrial centers: A. Kudriavtsev, "Revoliutsiia i provintsial'naia pechat'," Letopis', 1917, no. 5/6:26–28.

[115] There was a third type of town, in which there was likely to be only a Bolshevik organization—namely, the industrial center located in a rural area, where workers were cut off from all other groups of society except the peasantry. Ivanovo-Voznesensk was one such town, and it did not send any delegates to the Menshevik conference. Another example was Sormovo, where a United organization did send a delegate to the conference but later forced him to apologize for having supported coalition in spite of the organization's opposition to it: RG, May 11, 1917 (no. 53), 4.

itator in 1905 but had left political activity to study history at Moscow University and pursue an academic career.[116] The revolution had caught him in his hometown of Kazan (a university town as well as the seat of the provincial government, but not an industrial center of any significance), where he had spent the war years in journalistic work.[117] Reacting to the announcement of a change of government, Denike and other former Social Democrats—there seems to have been little difference here between Bolsheviks and Mensheviks—joined with other intelligentsia elements in founding a "committee of public safety," while worker veterans of the legal labor organizations took the initiative in organizing elections for a soviet. The soviet soon became the representative organization of the 40,000-strong garrison as well, and the Social Democrats assumed its leadership while also continuing their work in the committee for public safety. Denike himself served as deputy chairman of both bodies until the committee closed down in mid-April, and he was also the editor of the soviet's newspaper (which included a Menshevik section entitled *Rabochaia gazeta*).[118] In a word, he was, one might conclude, the real "power" in Kazan. Like other former Bolsheviks, he joined the newly established United SD organization, which in Kazan adopted resolutions along Revolutionary Defensist lines.

What made the experience of Mensheviks in Kazan and in other provincial towns of the same type so different from that of Petrograd, or of Moscow and other industrial centers, was the realization that there was no one capable of replacing the old regime except the socialist intelligentsia. In fact, there were not even any other contenders. Whatever sense of "society" existed in these towns was embodied in the intelligentsia, and those among it who were eager to fulfill their mission as the successors of autocracy joined revived socialist organizations, such as the soviets, because only they could claim the leadership of the masses. As Denike explained, the choice usually fell on the Menshevik party because

---

[116] Denike's experience and observations are described in interview nos. 9–11, Project on Menshevik History. For a discussion of the transition from Bolshevism to Menshevism in the life of another former Bolshevik, see Haimson, preface to Schwarz, *Russian Revolution of 1905*, viii–xiii.

[117] Before the war, there was only one factory in Kazan, making footwear. During the war, it was retooled and expanded, and in 1917 it employed about ten thousand workers, mostly women. A larger, "evacuated" munitions factory was relocated to Kazan: Denike, interview no. 10, pp. 8–10, and no. 11, pp. 1–2.

[118] The combination of the *Izvestiia* of a soviet with an SD newspaper was very common in provincial towns: Kudriavtsev, "Revoliutsiia i provintsial'naia pechat'," 26–28.

the intelligentsia activists in the provinces viewed themselves first and foremost as "democrats" and perceived in Menshevism the most "European," most "democratic" strain in Russian socialism, the one most capable of introducing European parliamentary democracy and correcting the wrongs in Russia's social system.[119]

Given their disposition, it is not too surprising that the greatest fear of these provincial socialist leaders was that their islands of order and authority might be engulfed by the sea of "rural anarchy" around them. Denike found dual power and the Petrograd strategies of pressure and conditional support appalling both in their undermining of governmental authority and in the divisiveness they introduced into the ranks of the democratic intelligentsia—the only social element capable, he felt, of leading the country through the period of transformation. Indeed, he compared the leaders of the Petrograd soviet to the inmates in the Kazan insane asylum, who had been invited by the attendants to "rebel" against the medical staff and establish their own soviet. Moreover, because many of the provincial Mensheviks were new to the party or had been reintegrated into it only after years of separation, party doctrine as such meant little to them. Given the great tasks of reconstruction and defense, coalition seemed to them the only possible and correct strategy, the one they themselves would have carried out in their localities if faced with the same situation as in Petrograd.

The victory of this "provincial" view at the May conference was an event of momentous importance in the history of Menshevism. It reflected a dramatic change in the very nature of the party, resulting from the introduction of political freedom. Prior to 1917, no party in Russia had ever been subject to the rigorous process of delegate selection, open debate, and majority rule on fundamental doctrinal issues or matters of political strategy. Party leaders had never fully depended on majority votes. Those who were considered leaders of the Mensheviks had won this recognition or popularity through long association with the party, the articulation of its principles, and, more recently, through work in the Petrograd soviet. They now found themselves outnumbered by the provincial delegates, some of whom had never been members of the party while others had drifted away from its activities and had re-

[119] Again, Kudriavtsev's findings confirm that Denike's experience was typical. His data show that the SD press was most widespread and most "vital" in the provinces and that in the nonindustrial towns the SD newspaper was usually a United one, which propagated a Revolutionary Defensist position: ibid.

turned less committed to the party as such or to its ideological legacy.

For the moment, the provincials' support of Revolutionary Defensism tended to obscure the meaning of these new conditions of party life. However, a hint of the provincials' impact on the alignment of factions in the party appeared when the emigre leaders finally joined the conference early on the evening of May 9. They were met with the usual "stormy ovation," but the mood changed drastically when the newcomers took the floor to attack the Revolutionary Defensist leadership for its departures from Social Democratic doctrine and to warn against the view of Menshevism as a "governing party."[120] The new ministers, who had only recently succeeded in resolving the conflict between their commitment to the party's ideology and the pressures of perceived reality and actual responsibility, were obviously hurt. Skobelev retorted that "even teachers can make mistakes" and that the revered leaders should first study the "actual situation."[121] The provincial delegates, many of whom were seeing the emigres for the first time, found their foreign clothes alienating, their flamboyant manners ridiculous, and their views lacking any shred of realism—elements of estrangement that would not disappear even when the experiment with coalition fell apart and the Internationalists' ideas gained in popularity among Mensheviks in Moscow and Petrograd.[122]

Years of fragmentation had left the party divided, and the different ways in which the revolution was experienced by Mensheviks in the capital, the provinces, and emigration accentuated the elements that each of these groups chose from the common legacy of party ideology. The depth of these divisions became apparent during the conference's last session in a variety of ways: the newly arrived men (with the exception of Akselrod) were denied seats on the organizational committee; the Internationalists' announcement (in the name of the seventeen voting delegates) that they could not be responsible for policies they felt were "contradictory to the vital

---

[120] Den', May 10, 1917 (no. 55), 2; NZh, May 10, 1917 (no. 19), 4. See also Garvi, "Unpublished Memoirs, 1917," 83–84.

[121] Skobelev's attack was directed especially at Martynov. The other emigre Internationalists who arrived with him, Martov, and Akselrod included Semkovskii, R. A. Abramovich, I. S. Astrov, and the Polish SD, P. Lapinskii.

[122] See the description of the Internationalists' appearance during the August congress of the Menshevik party in Denike, interview no. 11, pp. 14, 27; and Sukhanov, Zapiski o revoliutsii 4:25.

interests of the proletariat" evoked shouts of "Disgrace!" from the floor; and finally, when Martov took the rostrum to read a note from Akselrod, he was met by the pounding of desktops and shouts of "We don't want to listen to him!" and "Down with him!" After he had finished, one delegate said: "When I left for the conference, everybody envied me, for I was going to see our leaders. Now I have seen them and I envy those who are far away from here."[123]

Claims of ideological purity and of responsible realism clashed and hatreds flared at the May conference, yet the party did not split apart largely because among the veterans of Menshevism there was a desire for unity on all sides: on the part of those Revolutionary Defensists who had been close to Martov and Akselrod in the past, and on the part of the two Internationalist leaders who at least wanted to win back their "lost" comrades.[124] Both factions even managed to agree on a resolution regarding the forthcoming socialist conference on peace.[125] Nor were the Revolutionary Defensist leaders, whose position in the party had just been affirmed, eager to expel their Internationalist opponents. The bitterness and estrangement expressed by the provincial delegates allowed the Revolutionary Defensists to look on the May conference as a vindication of their strategy, for it could be claimed that the Internationalists were too detached from the actual situation and could not offer any new or practical alternative to coalition. The Mensheviks who shared the task of leading the soviets, whether in Petrograd, Moscow, or the provinces, seemed united around the Revolutionary Defensist strategy and firmly in control of the party's organizational committee. Of the seventeen members elected to the committee, only two, Ermanskii and Akselrod, were Internationalists.[126] Otherwise, the results of the Conference were clear.

[123] *RG*, May 12, 1917 (no. 54), 4, and May 14, 1917 (no. 56), 3; *Den'*, May 12, 1917 (no. 57), 2, and May 13, 1917 (no. 58), 2–3; *NZh*, May 13, 1917 (no. 22), 2.

[124] Sapir, "Theodor Dan," 14; Garvi, "Unpublished Memoirs, 1917," 82–83; "The Declaration of Menshevik Internationalists," *Letuchii listok Menshevikov-Internatsionalistov*, May 15, 1917 (no. 1), 1–5. Also see Ascher, *Axelrod*, 421–24; Getzler, *Martov*, 150.

[125] *RG*, May 11, 1917 (no. 53), 2, and May 12, 1917 (no. 54), 3; *Den'*, May 11, 1917 (no. 56), 2, and May 12, 1917 (no. 57), 2.

[126] *RG*, May 13, 1917 (no. 55), 3. Of the seventeen, four were from Moscow (Khinchuk, Isuv, A. Romanov, and S. M. Zaretskaia) and thirteen from Petrograd (Ermanskii, Akselrod, Ermolaev, Garvi, Gorev, Smirnov, Dan, Ezhov, Baturskii, Panin, Iudin, Bogdanov, and Krokhmal'). *Rabochaia gazeta*, the Bund, and the Lithuanian and Caucasian organizations were each invited to send one member.

THE MENSHEVIK PARTY had given its blessing to the decision of the executive committee of the Petrograd soviet to establish a coalition government with the bourgeois parties of Russia. The decision was a momentous one: the two opposing camps of Russian society had formally declared their intention of working together toward the survival and transformation of the country; they had agreed to join in the military defense of the country from German aggression; and the Social Democratic leaders of the soviet, by ending their abstention from formal state power, had broken with their own ideological legacy. Indeed, it was remarkable with what little trepidation the Mensheviks embraced the new strategy. The mood at the closing of the May conference was confident, even triumphant.

Yet beneath the repeated declarations of optimism, there must have been some uneasiness. Had not coalition been proposed originally only as an unavoidable necessity? Had it not elicited visions of anarchy, extremism, and perhaps defeat? Had not all the important groups in the party—the organizations of Petrograd, Moscow, and Tiflis, and the Internationalist wing (about 20 percent of the delegates at the May conference)—looked on coalition with deep reservations if not actual opposition? Of all those who supported or acquiesced in coalition, only Potresov gave expression to the fears that must have been on the minds of others. Russian democracy, he warned at the conference and elsewhere, had inherited from Russian autocracy the fearsome legacy of the *bunt*, the unrestrained protest that sought to correct the wrongs of centuries immediately and without concern for the survival of the "organism" of the state, without which no social system could function.[127] But his warning went unheeded. For the most part, the recent experience of mustering the masses in the factories and the streets and the victories achieved under dual power, as well as the failures that made the Mensheviks on the executive committee feel they needed a better hold over the state machine, and in general the sense of strength as well as responsibility—all these made most Mensheviks willing and able to forget their earlier anxieties as they began a new chapter in their revolutionary activities. Moreover, they were relieved to have found a solution of sorts to what must have been a painful paralysis because of the fear that the revolution would go awry; relieved because they had at last broken with the ideology that had failed to predict the course of

---

[127] These ideas were expressed most fully in an article by Potresov in the Moscow Defensist journal *Delo*, 1917, nos. 3–6:112–24.

the revolution, let alone prescribe an appropriate political strategy; relieved, finally, because they were now following what to them were the dictates of "reality" itself.

But for coalition to succeed, several conditions would have to be met. First, the truce between the major groups of Russian society, especially urban society, would have to be preserved, which in turn required that the political leaderships of these groups—drawn so far largely from among the intelligentsia or imbued with its ideals—continue to see and use the revolution to meet the fundamental needs and interests of their constituencies, that they be politically effective, and that the objective conditions, especially the economic ones, be propitious. In addition, the socialists in the cabinet would have to be able to fulfill the specific promises and expectations that had won for coalition the support of many workers and soldiers: a prompt peace, extensive changes in the legal and material conditions of peasants and workers, and the reordering of priorities for the purpose of ending economic disorganization. The fulfillment of these promises depended, at least partly, on the ability of the state apparatus to handle all of its pressing tasks.

This was a formidable challenge, but it did not appear at the outset as inconsistent with coalition even in the minimalist form adopted by the soviet. Tsereteli's strategy in allowing the socialists only a minority in the cabinet ultimately depended on the goodwill of the nonsocialists in this coalition of "vital forces," but it provided an unprecedented opportunity for the socialists to design and implement social policies in the areas under their control. As the month of May began, then, the question before the Menshevik leaders of the soviet concerned the extent to which they would actually use the new possibilities, and this question subsumed others: How broadly would they define the social transformation possible at that state of the revolution? How would they respond to their followers' aspirations and demands? How ready were they to risk the collapse of this new political agreement with the bourgeoisie should it prove to constrain unduly the freedom of Social Democracy? Above all, there was the question of the revolution itself—that is, the direction in which the relations among the revolution's principal social and political groups would develop. In this area, dual power had proven unexpectedly beneficial, its vagueness and contradictions helpful in lessening social tensions. Would coalition now change the situation and actually exacerbate social strife?

Labor Relations under Coalition: Social Conflict and Economic Crisis

H ISTORIANS GENERALLY AGREE that the formation of the coalition government in May 1917 coincided with a sharp increase in social discord in general and industrial conflict in particular and that the increasing social polarization of this period
eventually made coalition untenable. It is usually assumed that the
polarization was an unavoidable consequence of the revolution itself, which destroyed the authority of the state and undermined
the social order over which it presided. However, the complexity
of the issues, events, and developments involved should caution
us against any assumptions about inevitability. It would be well to
recall that in the immediate aftermath of the February revolution
there was a reduction rather than an increase in the tensions that
had divided Russian urban society. As we saw in chapter 3, the
combination of euphoric expectations, uncertainty about the new
social and political order, and mutual fear impelled workers and
employers to accept temporary sacrifices in the name of the revolution that both groups claimed as their own. Consequently, they
had found the arrangement of dual power acceptable, though
most workers and industrialists could not quite see themselves as
part of the "united vital forces" hailed by their intelligentsia leaders. Implied in the arrangement was a promise that the social truce
could be preserved without the surrender of anyone's fundamental interests.

In contrast to the initially more or less untroubled relationship
between leaders and followers, the tenor of labor relations in May
and June was dramatically changed by a "revolt" of both workers
and entrepreneurs against their respective self-appointed leaderships (the moderate socialists and the progressists) and against the
conceptions of unity and accommodation which now appeared to
entail the sacrifice of basic interests. This revolt followed the workers' and industrialists' increasing awareness of their specific class
interests and derived more or less directly from the actual confrontation and juxtaposition of labor's and industry's expectations.
This confrontation was generated, first, by the "objective" condi-

203

tions of war and economic crisis and by the political arrangement of coalition, and, second, by the long-standing attitudes through which these circumstances were perceived and interpreted.

The purpose of this chapter is to trace this complex web of interactions in order to explain the processes of social polarization that developed at the inception of the coalition's work. It will first consider the ways in which workers and industrialists responded to the economic and political realities of May and June and how these responses affected their relationship. The concluding section of the chapter will explore the solutions offered by the Menshevik economists and by industrialists and workers to the economic crisis that was threatening the vital interests of both industry and labor.

THE WORKERS UNDER COALITION

Between the time the first coalition was formed in early May and the time it collapsed amidst political crisis in early July, the behavior of the workers in Petrograd changed dramatically. The political evidence for this transformation is familiar enough: the workers who had supported the Revolutionary Defensist leadership in its decision to join a coalition government in early May were by early July marching under the Bolshevik banner "All Power to the Soviets." In the workplace, the change had been both more rapid and less uniform in its manifestations and therefore less apparent as a distinct development. The general impression, however, is of a labor force that had abandoned mediation and self-discipline in favor of repeated if erratic confrontations with the owners of industry.

Strike activity was clearly on the rise.[1] The factory committees no longer limited themselves to acting as intermediaries between workers and factory administrations, while with growing frequency workers demanded the right to supervise and even deter-

[1] While there is no single, complete set of strike statistics for this period (or 1917 in general), there are strong indications of this rise in the partial figures that are available. The Factory Inspectorate's data show 78 strikes in May and 76 in June, compared with 41 in April; similarly, the number of striking workers rose, from 9,802 in May to 17,336 in June. From these and other figures, A. M. Lisetskii deduced that there were 35,500 strikers in April, 73,700 in May, and 174,700 in June (cited in Gaponenko, *Rabochii klass Rossii v 1917 godu*, 378). Another indicator of the rise in strike activity is that strikes accounted for only 4 percent of all actions taken by workers in March and April, but for 41 percent in May and June: Fleer, "K istorii rabochego dvizheniia," 242.

mine managerial practices directly connected to the economic functioning of enterprises, such as securing orders and financing and ensuring the orderly supply of raw materials and the distribution of finished products. In addition, the productivity of labor declined precipitously over the summer months. Although reliable data are difficult to come by, the trend was unmistakably reflected in the many complaints from both employers and factory committees.[2]

These changes do not by themselves prove that workers were becoming more radical.[3] As we shall see presently, many of the labor conflicts in May resulted from the dynamics of unionization, and in June the majority of conflicts reflected the impact of inflation on workers' earnings. Similarly, workers' *kontrol'*, discussed later in this chapter, was often exercised in response to a real or perceived threat to production and therefore to the workers' very livelihood. But if specific forms of workers' collective behavior might be explained in terms of the conditions of May and June— and these will remain in the foreground of the scene described here—the overall pattern of these two months was also shaped by two powerful sets of attitudes and expectations held by workers at the outset of the coalition period.

First, there was the suspicion of the bourgeoisie which was part of the workers' historical memory and which the intelligentsia

[2] See *VVOKZ*, August 15, 1917 (no. 38), 397–99, for figures collected by the Ministry of Trade and Industry from some of Petrograd's best-equipped factories, which show a significant decline in production even though these factories did not suffer shortages or important labor turnover. Also see *FO*, 1917, no. 16:22, for a report on a meeting of the Union of Engineers in May, at which a "recent" 25 percent decline in productivity was discussed and blamed largely on the shorter workday and the lack of work discipline; and Smith, *Red Petrograd*, 88–98, for a discussion of the factory committees' complaints about the reluctance of workers to accept discipline or to make efforts to produce more. The productivity of Russian labor had always been relatively low, but during the war it declined further because of the influx of women and youth, and in some industries prisoners of war, into the work force. According to a study by the Special Conference on Defense, women and youth made up 10.7 percent, and prisoners of war 26.3 percent, of the Donbas work force on the eve of the February revolution: *Biulleteni statisticheskogo otdela*, 1917, no. 5:4. See also D. P., "The Labor Question in the Mining Industry of Southern Russia," *PiT*, April 29, 1917 (no. 14/15 [255]), 278–80.

[3] In their pioneering study of strike and nonstrike activity among Russian workers in 1917, Koenker and Rosenberg, "Limits of Formal Protest," 18, argue that the strikes of May and June reflected the workers' expectation of being able to use the new bourgeois order to redress their grievances, rather than a direct challenge to this order.

leaders of the soviet had seeming legitimated in their formulation of dual power, even if it was later temporarily put aside. This suspicion grew throughout April, was deepened by Miliukov's note and the Kadet demonstration on April 21, and was now being articulated ever more clearly by the Bolshevik party under Lenin's restored leadership. Indeed, this reinforced suspicion and the determination to make sure that the bourgeois ministers followed the economic and peace policies outlined by the soviet had been behind the workers' support for the soviet's participation in the government. Second, a sense of political and revolutionary strength, through which the moderate leadership had attempted to unite all workers around the soviet, had become an important element in the workers' perception of the revolution and was further increased by the fact of coalition itself, for in it the workers thought they were seeing evidence of this strength confirmed, and they expected their leaders would soon force the bourgeoisie to yield to the soviet's superior force. It was in this political setting that labor conflicts evolved in May and June, a setting that disposed workers to interpret entrepreneurial resistance and production difficulties as aggressive actions and also made labor's defeats and the economic crisis itself all the more unacceptable to workers.

STRIKE ACTIVITY began rising in the last third of April, in an apparent response to the April crisis, and continued in an only slightly diminished degree in May.[4] To a large extent, these strikes concerned wage demands.[5] What distinguished them, especially those of May, from those that preceded and followed them was the makeup of the strikers and the nature of their demands. The strikers came from the weaker, less organized groups of the work-

[4] Koenker and Rosenberg, "Strikes in Revolution," 17, counted 1 or 2 strikes daily for the six weeks from the signing of the PSI-Soviet agreement on March 10 to the April crisis, and a total of 45 strikes for the ten days between April 20 and May 1. During May and most of June, their figures show between 20 and 30 strikes weekly.

[5] Higher wages were the major demand in 75 out of the 78 strikes registered by the Factory Inspectorate in May: *RD v mae-iiune*, 294–97, 324–27. Koenker and Rosenberg, "Strikes in Revolution," table 3, show wage demands to have caused 123 strikes out of 216 in May and 98 out of 154 in June (57 percent and 64 percent, respectively). In the same months, demands for better "conditions" caused 49 and 26 strikes, respectively, and when these strikes are added to those concerning wages, the percentage of strikes provoked by economic demands rises to 80 percent. Organizational issues and questions of workers' "dignity" accounted for the other 20 percent.

ing class—laundresses, pharmacy employees, shop assistants, factory employees, and workers from shops and small factories.[6] Their demands were for the wages "already paid in other factories"—that is, in larger factories, where workers had been able to fight for themselves without having had to await the organization of citywide unions.[7] These strikes contributed to some extent to the radicalization of the workers, because the employers to whom the wage demands were presented were on the whole less capable of meeting them. Small entrepreneurs often argued that they could not compete with the improvements granted to the workers of the larger factories,[8] and for this reason they often rejected offers of mediation by the soviet's labor section.[9] One report demonstrated that some of these claims had been made in good faith. It told of several small metalprocessing plants where work had stopped and the workers' inspections of the books had discovered that the entrepreneurs had indeed been operating at a loss.[10]

Another factor contributing to the labor conflict in May, and

[6] According to the Factory Inspectorate figures, the average size of the work force in striking factories in May was 126, compared to 752 in March, 302 in April, and 228 in June: RD v mae-iiune, 294–97, 324–27. These findings are corroborated by Gaponenko (Rabochii klass Rossii v 1917 godu, 377), who examined some of the strikes more closely and found that, whereas in April about half of them occurred in large factories (500 workers and up), in May this figure was only 10 percent. Gaponenko studied factories from the textile, typographical, food-processing, and woodworking sectors but not the six metalprocessing factories and the five mineral and chemical factories for which strikes were registered in May and for which the inspectorate's data shows a total working force of 2,645 and 360, respectively.

[7] The quoted phrase is from an announcement by the coopers at the Glukhverskii cement factory, where a strike began on May 24, after the director had rejected the workers' wage demands: RG, May 31, 1917 (no. 68), 4. The coopers at the small Smirnov shop began a strike on May 30: RG, June 3, 1917 (no. 71), 4. See also the list of current strikes in RG, May 18, 1917 (no. 59), 4. One of the most bitter conflicts of April was between the Union of Pharmaceutical Employees and the Society of Pharmacy Owners; it was settled only after a lengthy mediation effort by the soviet's labor section and a strike; see NZh, April 25, 1917 (no. 6), 3, and April 26, 1917 (no. 7), 3; and RG, April 25, 1917 (no. 39), 4. An equally bitter struggle involved widely dispersed shop assistants and culminated in a strike at the end of May: RG, May 27, 1917 (no. 66), 4.

[8] See, for example, the argument made by the owners of glass shops, who restated their inability to yield to their workers' demands even after two weeks of a strike: RG, May 31, 1917 (no. 68), 4.

[9] IzvPS, May 14, 1917 (no. 66), 4. At a meeting called in May by the Petrograd Committee of Small and Medium Industry, small owners were urged to organize themselves to be better able to confront the soviet: FO, 1917, no. 16:21–22.

[10] In this instance, the workers even found themselves agreeing to the dismissal of some of their number: NZh, May 10, 1917 (no. 19), 5.

more so in June, was the demand presented by the organization- ally strongest groups of Petrograd workers, the printers and the metalworkers, for wage contracts that would cover all of the city's workers in the respective industries, rather than only workers in individual factories. Such wage agreements had been one of the goals for labor organizations set by Social Democrats a decade ear- lier, and because the appearance of this demand in May followed the formation of citywide unions, it must be seen as the result of the dynamics of unionization rather than a sudden burst of mili- tancy. In fact, by establishing procedures for industrywide bar- gaining, the union leadership tried to stem the "spontaneous," "disorganized" campaigns for higher wages in individual facto- ries. Still, the struggle for wage contracts both exposed and con- tributed to a decline in the readiness of both workers and employ- ers either to commit themselves to mediation or to accept its results. Increasingly, both sides reacted sharply to even temporary setbacks. The typographical section of the PSI, for example, re- jected the labor section's arbitration offer throughout the second half of April and early May, and the Union of Printers responded in mid-May with a decision to launch a citywide strike. In this case, a strike was averted when the Union of Owners of Typo- graphical Enterprises broke from the PSI, agreed to arbitration, and signed a wage agreement with the printers. However, the PSI's actions indicated how a "second line" of labor demands was going to affect the industrialists' handling of the labor organiza- tions.[11] Indeed, the course of wage negotiations in Petrograd pro- vides a good record of the deterioration of labor relations during the summer months, and for this reason a detailed consideration of the three most important agreements negotiated in Petrograd between June and October will be instructive.

The Union of Metalworkers represented the largest and best-or- ganized group of workers in Petrograd, and it is to be expected that the metalworkers would follow the printers' example and seek a citywide agreement, though the task was greatly compli- cated by the enormous variety of skills and specialties in the met- alprocessing industry. In fact, it required a month for the union's rates commission to divide all the categories of workers into four groups and work out pay scales for each one. During the ensuing

[11] *RG*, April 16, 1917 (no. 33), 3–4, and April 25, 1917 (no. 39), 4; *IzvPS*, April 17, 1917 (no. 43), 5; "Bor'ba za tarif rabochikh pechatnogo dela," 15–16; Volobuev, *Pro- letariat i burzhuaziia*, 128–29.

negotiations, the union acted to develop a militant sense of class solidarity among workers as well as to impose restraint on them. It apparently prevented 180 strikes from taking place, but when the leadership recommended acceptance of the PSI's offer, a meeting of the union's factory delegates on June 25 rejected it because the proposed wages for unskilled workers fell far short of the union's demand and because the membership opposed the productivity clauses. Then, just as the crisis of the July Days weakened the membership's opposition to the productivity clauses, the PSI changed its team of negotiators and categorically rejected the demand on pay for unskilled workers. Furthermore, the PSI negotiators refused a compromise worked out by the government's conciliation board, whereupon the union decided to call a citywide strike, which was averted only through efforts by the Ministry of Labor at conciliation and by the union leadership at convincing the delegates to compromise. On August 7, an agreement was finally signed, though individual owners attempted to delay its implementation and provoked local conflicts. In any case, by October 14 the union decided to press for a new contract that would adjust wages to the rising cost of living.[12] The metalworkers of the Donbas and Ural regions followed the example of their Petrograd comrades and entered into agreements on September 5 and October 10, respectively, and other unions did the same.[13]

The Union of Woodworkers decided on October 1 not to allow any change in its proposed contract because it would be nearly identical to the one the metalworkers had already obtained, and on October 16 the woodworkers went on strike. Before that, however, the union had spent months in drawing up its proposed pay rates and negotiating with the increasingly intransigent employers. Throughout the negotiations, the union leadership attempted to prevent local strikes and continued to do so even after leaving the bargaining table on August 28 and after weeks of awaiting the results of the Ministry of Labor's mediation.[14]

What stands out in the cases of both the metalworkers' and the woodworkers' negotiations is the hardening of the employers' po-

[12] "K istorii tarifa metallistov," 4–8; Bulkin, *Soiuz metallistov*, 181–83. Also see the appeal for restraint by the Bolshevik union leader Shliapnikov: *RG*, July 15, 1917 (no. 107), 4.

[13] Bulkin, *Soiuz metallistov*, 184. The course of wage negotiations in Moscow paralleled almost precisely that in Petrograd, except that a short strike took place in early July: Koenker, *Moscow Workers and the 1917 Revolution*, 319–20.

[14] "Bor'ba za tarif derevoobdelochnikov," 28–32.

sition in regard to collective agreements after the July Days. This change was apparent also in the way the owners of typographical enterprises prepared for the expiration of the printers' wage agreement on August 1. They established antistrike funds, refused to negotiate, and in effect pushed the workers into declaring a strike in mid-August.[15] As we shall see, the industrialists' behavior, like the workers', evolved in stages, fueled by both intensified labor conflicts and various political changes.

IF THE DYNAMICS of unionization gave rise to relatively minor labor disturbances in May and to a few well-defined conflicts in June and July, which led to strikes only at the end of the summer, this was not the case with inflation, which was the second source of industrial conflict during these months. Beginning in late May and continuing well into June, an increasing rate of inflation gave rise to a second wave of wage demands that led to many conflicts, some of which occurred in very large factories and involved well-organized workers who had already won significant wage increases in March and April.

Inflation had been a constant wartime problem, and its root causes did not disappear with the February revolution but rather were augmented. Goods shortages were exacerbated by a decline in transport and later by lower production, and the government itself contributed to inflation by printing money as a means of balancing a budget heavily weighed down by war expenditures and a failing tax system. According to one source, the rate of inflation was 6.4 percent in March (when it was already over three times that of 1913), 13.4 percent in April, 18.4 percent in May, and 28 percent in June.[16] Wages also rose rapidly in March and April, so that by May real wages are estimated to have been about 50 percent higher than in January 1917. However, during May and June wages rose much more slowly, and in June they actually declined.[17] This erosion in the workers' gains brought new wage de-

---

[15] "Bor'ba za tarif rabochikh pechatnogo dela," 16–23; RG, August 3, 1917 (no. 123), 4.

[16] Volobuev, Proletariat i burzhuaziia, 219.

[17] Ibid., 136. This pattern is confirmed in other sources. The average hourly pay of workers in the Parviainen factory in Petrograd rose by 64 percent between March and May, and purchasing power rose by 51.9 percent, but in June the real value of wages began to decline: Strumilin, Zarabotnaia plata, 13. See Stepanov, Rabochie Petrograda, 54–55, for wage data collected from six Petrograd factories in the metal-processing, textile, and tobacco industries and from the Petrograd Labor Exchange. For data on similar trends in Moscow, see Mindin, "Rabochee vremia."

mands. Inflation had its most serious effect on the less skilled workers. Because of their generally low earnings, these workers were particularly vulnerable to the rapid rise in the cost of grain staples that followed the March 25 decree that set higher prices for them.[18] By June, the uneven race between food prices and wages had made survival itself difficult for these workers.[19] Yet because of their relatively large numbers and low productivity, their demands were resisted the more strenuously by employers.

The importance of the inflation-related wage conflicts of June was as much in the way they shaped the workers' perception of a society divided by irreconcilable hostilities as in their impact on workers' earnings. As the inflation figures show, the wage demands were grounded in a reality of actual economic deprivations, but they resulted also from the workers' feelings that these demands represented their real and well-deserved gains from the revolution, gains that were now endangered not only by the economic crisis and inflation but by entrepreneurial action as well.

According to one source, fewer than 50 percent of the strikes in June ended in full or partial success, a sharp drop from the 95 to 97 percent rate of success reported for March to May.[20] Even if this contrast is overdrawn, June was clearly a month of more protracted strikes and more difficult gains.[21] Mandel has shown that the struggle itself and the employers' frequent rejection of the workers' demands most affected the less skilled workers—those

[18] In Petrograd, the price of the standard daily food ration for an unskilled worker rose sharply just before the February revolution (35.6 percent in January-February 1917), remained more or less stable in March (2.7 percent rise), then increased again in April (20 percent): *MST*, 1918, no. 1:62.

[19] Figures collected by the Petrograd Labor Exchange show that the average nominal wage of unskilled workers rose from 97 rubles a month in January to 111 in April and 122 in June. However, real wages for these months (calculated in 1913 rubles) were 28, 24, and 20 rubles. Thus, the average real wage of unskilled workers was almost 30 percent lower in June than it had been in January: Stepanov, *Rabochie Petrograda*, 54–55. In the metalprocessing industry, in which unskilled workers were most active, the situation was different, because the workers had successfully demanded that wage differentials be narrowed.

[20] A. M. Lissetskii, cited in Gaponenko, *Rabochii klass Rossii v 1917 godu*, 385.

[21] The Factory Inspectorate recorded a much smaller drop in the rate of full or partial strike victories, from 86 percent in May to 82 percent in June: *RD v mae-iiune*, 294–97, 324–27. However, the 76 strikes recorded by the inspectorate in June lasted a total of 402 days, compared with 298 days for the 78 strikes in May. Of the 100 conflicts the Ministry of Labor mediated from mid-May to mid-June (out of 557 disputes brought to its attention), one-third remained unresolved at the end of July: see the report to the Economic Council in *SOZES*, July 26, 1917 (no. 4), 6–7.

who earlier had been the most willing believers in the image of the revolution offered them by the moderate leadership.[22] But for all workers, especially for those who read the newspapers and followed events outside their factories, the employers' growing resistance appeared as a familiar pattern of antilabor activity, an impression that was reinforced by verbal attacks on labor in the industrialists' petitions to the government and in the bourgeois press as well as in a few notable conflicts that made the industrialists look threatening even to the many workers who did not personally experience entrepreneurial mistreatment.[23]

One such conflict took place in the Donbas in May. This conflict was discussed in the cabinet (and later by a special committee of three ministers) and became the subject of an unsuccessful mediation effort by the minister of labor; in fact, it dominated the socialist press in mid-May. The owners of the Donbas mines and metallurgical plants refused to raise the minimum wage of their workers to four rubles (which was still below the Petrograd minimum wage).[24] The soviet did not accept the employers' plea of financial difficulties because, it claimed, Russia's strongest raw-material syndicates, Prodamet and Produgol, had made enormous profits during the war.[25] In June, the attention of the press turned to Moscow, where a monthlong conflict between Iu. P. Guzhon, owner of 85 percent of the region's metalprocessing capacity, and his workers provoked the first large-scale lockout. Arguing insufficient funds, Guzhon closed down his factory in late May, refused to accept an arbitrator's decision on higher wages for his workers, and, in conjunction with the owners of Moscow's other important metalprocessing factories, announced the complete shutdown of

[22] Mandel, *Petrograd Workers and the Fall of the Old Regime*, 142–44.

[23] It should be pointed out that, even with the rise of strike activity in June, the number of strikes was still far below the level it had reached in 1905–1907 and 1912–1914: Iakovleva, "Zabastovochnoe dvizhenie," and Grave, *K istorii klassovoi bor'by v Rossii*, 66–67. Also, the number of unemployed workers rose only slowly during the summer of 1917; on August 19, the Petrograd Union of Metalworkers (140,000 members) reported 2,800 of its members were out of work: *PiT*, September 16, 1917 (no. 34/35), 157–62.

[24] The workers were also demanding wage increases of 50 to 250 percent: *Konferentsii rabochikh*, 7–38.

[25] "The Industrialists' Address to the Provisional Government," *IzvPS*, May 13, 1917 (no. 65), 2–3; "Who Destroys Industry?" *IzvPS*, May 17, 1917 (no. 68), 2; "Danger to the Country," *RG*, May 14, 1917 (no. 56), 1–2; Iu. M. Steklov, "The Industrialists' Complaints," *NZh*, May 13, 1917 (no. 22), 1; V. Bazarov, "The Conflict in the Don Basin," *NZh*, May 16, 1917 (no. 24), 1; P. Arskii, "Higher Wages and the Collapse of Industry," *NZh*, May 28, 1917 (no. 34), 2.

all these factories effective July 1.[26] *Rabochaia gazeta* called Guzhon's actions "sabotage" and declared that his intention was to block the workers' demands, which it said were "partially justifiable" because of both inflation and the unusually high profits accrued by the metalprocessing industry in earlier years.[27] The soviet's economic section adjudged Guzhon's claim that the shutdown was financially necessary as "spurious"; its economists argued that an entrepreneur of Guzhon's scale could have secured the necessary credit to continue operating his plants.[28] Moreover, the fact that Guzhon was foreign in manner and social standing— though Russian-born, he was of French origin—must have made many workers see in him the very incarnation of the feared bourgeois: so powerful that he could afford to keep his factories idle while the workers starved and so contemptuous of the notion that workers' productivity improved under better conditions. He said of Russian workers that "the more you pay them the less they work."[29]

Taken as a whole, the lessons of the escalating labor conflicts in June were probably the same for all workers, whether skilled or unskilled, politically active or only dimly aware of the larger design of events.[30] As transmitted and elaborated through the network of labor organizations, meetings, and the socialist press, these lessons were, first, that the bourgeoisie was determined to deny the workers any redress of injustices; second, that the employers were likely to exploit their advantages in the struggle with workers, especially their familiarity with, and control of, the financial and contractual operations of enterprises; and third, and most alarming, that the entrepreneurs were willing to use the tactic of

[26] *EPR* 1:432–45; *RG*, June 27, 1917 (no. 91),1.

[27] "It's Necessary to Hurry Up," *RG*, June 27, 1917 (no. 91), 1.

[28] *RG*, June 30, 1917 (no. 94), 4; *IzvPS*, June 29, 1917 (no. 104), 11.

[29] The quote is from a speech by Guzhon at a conference of war industries: *IzvMVPK*, 1916, no. 23/24:155–73. He repeated this statement at other such conferences. A similar assertion was made by the Guzhon management in a letter of June 20 to the Moscow Factory Conference, which said that a few days after most of the workers' demands had been granted by the arbitrators in the dispute, production had dropped to 50 or 60 percent of the normal level: *EPR* 1:442.

[30] Smith, *Red Petrograd*, 14–36, 190–200, and Mandel, *Petrograd Workers and the Fall of the Old Regime*, 9–43, discuss important differences in the propensity of various groups of workers (defined by industry, skill, education, gender, age, and responsibility in the factory or the labor movement) to draw political conclusions from their experience, and differences as well in their responses to these experiences. But there is nothing in these studies to suggest that those workers affected by the wage conflicts of June differed in their fundamental perception of their meaning.

stopping production in order to defeat labor. A meeting of five thousand workers voted on June 25 to demand that the Provisional Government establish a state- and employer-funded unemployment insurance program (a Bolshevik formula), justifying such a measure by referring to the "conscious disorganization of production through lockouts or stoppages on the part of the capitalists."[31] The resolution had probably been drafted by the Bolsheviks—one of their speakers helped rouse the crowd with descriptions of impending catastrophe—but what is important is that the recent conflicts had made the Bolsheviks' descriptions of social reality seem closer to the workers' own experience and observations than those still propagated by the moderates. S. N. Gessen, a Bolshevik active in the Narva district, reported to the Bolshevik Petrograd committee that the newfound popularity of the party among the Putilov workers stemmed from the workers' "militant mood," which had "deep economic causes" and conformed to the workers' sense of having been "deceived."[32]

WE CAN now retrace the early stages of the radicalization of workers. The political setting was that of coalition, which workers understood as a framework for increased *kontrol'* by the soviet's leadership over the Provisional Government and the bourgeoisie in general. In this setting, there were three waves of labor conflicts: those involving workers in small enterprises, unionized workers, and workers seeking to recoup their losses from inflation. In all of them, wage demands were made, and all encountered some resistance, partly due to the economic crisis which both provoked and impeded the workers' struggle. Although at the outset of each conflict, the workers seemed calm and confident of their leaders and of their own organized force, the resistance they encountered, and their interpretation of this resistance, aroused increasing militancy and helped give it political definition. It was this interaction between the political and the economic, between expectations and reality, between hope and anxiety that accounted for the workers' radicalization and the concomitant decline in the political fortunes of the Mensheviks.

[31] *RD v mae-iiune*, 322.

[32] Ibid., 558. The words "We Have Been Deceived" appeared on a banner carried by Putilov workers in a demonstration organized by the soviet on June 18; and at the Second Conference of Petrograd Factory Committees, a Putilov worker also spoke of the "deception" perpetrated against him and his fellow workers: Amosov et al., eds., *Oktiabrskaia revoliutsiia* 1:210.

At least two separate elements can be discerned in this process of radicalization as it would play itself out over the next few months. First, there was a growing rift between workers and the better-off groups of urban society that expressed itself in the workers' pervasive suspicion of their employers and the Provisional Government. "We have seen with our own eyes," declared one Putilov worker (a Bolshevik), "how the present Provisional Government refuses to take resolute measures against the capitalists. The interests of the capitalists are dearer to it than the interests of the working class."[33] If this perception led the workers to accept the Bolshevik vision of a divided society, there remained a difficulty in acting on the political conclusion to be drawn from it. The workers' sense of identity and strength continued to be manifested through the soviet, and the moderate leadership of the soviet had committed itself to a coalition strategy. Hence, a break with this leadership and its policies had to precede the workers' acceptance of the Bolshevik slogan, "All Power to the Soviets."

The second element in the workers' radicalization was indeed a sense of estrangement from the soviet's moderate leadership, which began during the term of the first coalition in May and June. The specifics of this development will be discussed in later chapters. What is important here is that workers directly involved in labor disputes felt that the "neutral" posture of the Menshevik mediators, their concern for production and the national economy in general, was a betrayal of the working class, whose interests the Mensheviks were supposed to be representing. During May and June, the workers came to differ with the Menshevik leaders over the causes of labor conflicts and the ways of resolving them, and these differences turned into disagreements over the nature of the revolution and the appropriate strategy for the working class. While most workers still hesitated to challenge the well-known intelligentsia leaders in matters of high politics, they had by now developed definite views on what was needed in the factories. Even more than the labor conflicts of May and June, it was the question of regulating the economy that seemed to focus all the elements of worker discontent and to give this discontent a political direction. Before taking up this question, however, a parallel discussion of the industrialists' role in labor relations during this period is needed.

[33] Cited in Smith, *Red Petrograd*, 124.

The Industrialists under Coalition

The industrialists, like the workers, also exhibited signs of a change in attitude during May and June, though it was a change that for most of them was no more than a return to attitudes typical of their positions as proprietors of industry and employers of labor. Generally speaking, the industrialists now rejected the optimistic element of Konovalov's view that in March and April had resulted in a flurry of revolutionary rhetoric as well as investment activity,[34] and they dropped the Progressist labor policy they had at first embraced with varying degrees of enthusiasm or resignation. In May and June, they abandoned any belief in the beneficial value of higher wages and shorter hours for workers and began to resist labor's demands and then to attempt a reversal of earlier concessions.

In fact, the progressist coalition practically disappeared as a distinct voice, especially after Konovalov's resignation from the Provisional Government in mid-May. Some of the newspapers and individuals who had helped transmit the Progressist vision of the revolution or impose it on the commercial-industrial class joined new entrepreneurial organizations dedicated to the defense of this class's interests.[35] Others continued to advocate moderation and reason but without exhibiting confidence that these strategies held any promise.[36] Still others, notably Konovalov, seemed for a moment lost in confusion and inaction.

Soviet historians reject the notion that any attitudinal change occurred either in early March or in early May and instead describe the shifts in commercial-industrial strategy as essentially "political" in nature, provoked by the strength the soviet had shown during the April crisis and the socialists' entry into the Provisional Government and intended as a restoration of the bourgeoisie to its

[34] According to two articles in the *Commercial-Industrial Gazette*, investment activity that had been spurred during the early months by a "new spirit of enterprise" began to decline only in July: cited in *EPR* 1:35–39.

[35] Bublikov, for example, addressed a meeting of Duma members on May 12 with words of sympathy for the plight of the industrialists whose resources were in danger of being wiped out by workers' wage demands and higher taxes: Drezena et al., eds., *Burzhuaziia i pomeshchiki*, 31–47. By early August, when he spoke to the Moscow Conference of Public Activists, he was denouncing both workers and their socialist leaders and Nekrasov as well: *Otchet o moskovskom soveshchanii*, 94–97.

[36] See, for example, I. Brashin, "The Revolution and the Bourgeoisie," *TPG*, May 18, 1917 (no. 102), 2.

natural place as the predominant economic and political force.[37] Alternatively, the shift has been attributed to the strengthening of entrepreneurial organizations and their recovery from the position of powerlessness into which the revolution had initially thrown them.[38] Actually, both of these explanations can be seen as aspects of a complex process of "reawakening" of class interests that the commercial-industrial class underwent in the months following February. This reawakening—a process of clarification and even vindication to some, of disappointment to others—quickened its pace during the first weeks of coalition government. Social, economic, and political developments converged to account for the scope and swiftness of the shift in enterpreneurial attitudes.

THE INDUSTRIALISTS' sense of their own class interests in the revolution grew, like that of the workers, in response to perceived threats to those interests, as manifested specifically in the industrialists' relations with the workers and the Provisional Government. The most obvious conflict concerned labor's demands for higher wages and shorter working hours. Aside from the immediate effect that meeting these demands would have on profits, they raised anxieties about the economic viability of individual enterprises (accustomed now to operating at unusually high profits); about Russia's attractiveness to foreign investors and its ability to compete on the international market at war's end; and, finally, about unstated goals, including perhaps the workers' intention of expropriating the profits of private entrepreneurs if not their factories.[39] That labor's demands seemed to be endless, with one wave following another, must have made the last of these fears appear more reasonable than the earlier promises of the Progressists.[40] In addition, the industrialists watched in alarm as the factory committees gradually expanded their sphere of activity. The committees' intervention in matters of supplies, finances, and mana-

[37] See, for example, Reikhardt, "Russkaia burzhuaziia," 5–47.

[38] Volobuev, *Proletariat i burzhuaziia*, 164.

[39] See, for example, "On the Road to Bankruptcy," FO, 1917, no. 15:3–4; "Unfair Accusations," *PiT*, May 27, 1917 (no. 18/19), 351–54; "On the Eight-Hour Day," *VVOKZ*, May 15, 1917 (no. 32), 202–4; V. T. T—ov, "Higher Wages, Lower Productivity," *VVOKZ*, June 15, 1917 (no. 33/34), 239–42; and the statement issued on May 4 by the Union of Owners of Mechanized Woodprocessing Plants in Petrograd and the southern industrialists' petition of May 27 to the Provisional Government in *EPR* 1:514–17, 173–80.

[40] This particular point was not made as often as one might expect, but see, for example, "A Sobering," *VVOKZ*, July 15, 1917 (no. 36), 333–34.

gerial decisions threatened the industrialists' image of themselves as owners and entrepreneurs.[41]

The conflict with the government was less apparent, possibly because it was more difficult to admit. To be sure, some industrialists had questioned Konovalov's enthusiastic support of economic regulation by the government and the public organizations, and most of them did not really share his trust in the moderation of labor and the socialists. Men as different as Riabushinskii in Moscow and Putilov in Petrograd must have begun to doubt whether Konovalov was one of their own, or one of the intelligentsia men of the public organizations, or even one of the soviet's moderate socialists. Yet such disagreements were rarely aired, and if they were then only in private, for we have little evidence of public discussion of these questions. In May, however, there were two important turning points: the establishment of the coalition government and the resignation of Konovalov.

The coalition government espoused policies that might have aroused some objections, because of the material sacrifices they required, even under a purely bourgeois government. However, because of the presence of representatives of the soviet in the cabinet, the government was in addition suspected of actually aiming at the destruction of capital.[42] Regulatory measures, tax reforms, labor legislation—legal and administrative changes to which the commercial-industrial class had in fact shown little opposition when demanded by "their" ministers—were now viewed as the harbingers of socialism and so provoked broad opposition from the industrialists.[43] Moreover, ever-wider functions were being assumed by locally elected authorities, by local and regional regulatory agencies, and by various other public bodies in which the intelligentsia predominated.[44] This extension of governmental

[41] See the complaint on this score made on June 2 by the Association of the Metalprocessing Industry to the minister of trade and industry, in *EPR* 1:184–85.

[42] See V. Shtein, "The Realization of Socialism—Is It Possible?," *PiT*, May 13, 1917 (no. 16/17), 312–16, which expressed the fear that the soviet's victories would produce a "typically Russian ideological maximalism" and give rise to the belief that socialism was timely.

[43] G. Mertsalov, "On the Question of the Fuel Monopoly," *PiT*, May 13, 1917 (no. 16/17), 305–9.

[44] See S. Rozov, "The New Bureaucracy," *PiT*, July 22, 1917 (no. 26/27), 50–52, for a complaint about the cost of all the new regulatory agencies, which the writer characterized as "intelligentsia creations." Also see *Biulleten' Komiteta iugo-zapadnogo fronta* (published by the Union of Zemstvos), July 2, 1917 (no. 80), 1, for an assessment of the role of a "third element": the "supraclass" intelligentsia in the

capacities to democratic organizations contributed to the merchants' and entrepreneurs' feeling both a sense of virtual persecution (as they found themselves subject to all sorts of supervisory agencies that were more often useless than efficacious) and a sense of desertion on the part of a government that had supposedly been "theirs."[45] Put differently, what made the industrialists pessimistic was not only the change in the makeup of the central government but also the erosion of the central government's traditional authority, on which they, especially the Petrograd industrialists, had customarily depended.

In the background of all these conflicts there was the economic crisis, which embodied the failure of the revolution's promise and made every demand addressed to the entrepreneurs, every restriction on their freedom of action, seem more and more ominous. This crisis interfered with the employers' ability to respond to their workers' demands or even ensure them continuous employment. The prices of raw materials were rising; there were frequent shortages; and higher wages, sometimes paid for idle time, were depleting the liquid assets of the less profitable enterprises and cutting sharply into the profit margin of even the industrial giants.[46]

The labor conflict, the presence of socialists in the cabinet, the actual and imagined economic difficulties—all these stimulated the change in perception and attitude that took place largely during the first coalition government. But the shift was not uniform throughout the commercial-industrial class. Each of the major con-

---

zemstvo and city governments. According to the article, the revolution had transformed these men from "hired employees" into "responsible leaders" of the public organizations.

[45] See "Citizens of the First and Second Order," *PiT*, July 8, 1917 (no. 24/25), 12–14, for a complaint of this kind. When the workers strike, the article said, the government merely appeals to them, but when Guzhon, "the largest metal producer in Moscow," rejected the workers' demands, the government allowed the Moscow Factory Conference and the Special Conference on Defense to sequester his factory.

[46] The journals of the Special Conference on Defense show a marked increase during May in the number of defense contractors claiming insolvency because of the rising cost of raw materials and labor: *ZhOS*, May 3, 20, 24, 27, and 31, and June 3, 1917 (nos. 159, 162–66), 362, 343–52, 357–58, 372, 380–83, 393–95. It is extremely difficult to determine whether these claims were made in good faith. The socialist press argued repeatedly that extraordinary war profits in 1915 and 1916 made it possible for entrepreneurs to absorb subsequent financial losses. The *Commercial-Industrial Gazette* had indeed warned in April that the profits then being reported by joint-stock companies should not be distributed in dividends because entrepreneurs would be called on to pay higher wages and higher taxes: "The Dividend Policy of Joint-Stock Companies," *TPG*, April 11, 1917 (no. 73), 2.

stituent groups responded to the new factors in accordance with its own self-image and habits, so that even as the bourgeoisie in general moved in the same direction—toward greater conflict with the workers and other social groups—its ranks did not unite for effective action in behalf of its class interests. This failure of the commercial-industrial groups to unite seems to undermine the contention of Soviet historians that a well-coordinated "offensive" against workers got under way in May and June.[47] In fact, there was a variety of entrepreneurial attitudes and responses to the social and political realities and a variety of labor policies on the part of the major industrial organizations in Moscow, Petrograd, and the south, and these will be considered in the following pages.

IT WAS to the coalition of technologically oriented intelligentsia and forward-looking industrialists around Konovalov that the events of late spring dealt the hardest blow. Their vision of Russia as a European society, complete with modern capitalism and parliamentary democracy, was destroyed by what they perceived as signs of economic "backwardness" and of the "sectarianism" of the socialists, the "maximalism" of the workers, and the "egotism" of the industrialists themselves. In mid-May, the engineer K. Dembovskii, the manager of a leather factory, still professed confidence that "mutual and correct" labor relations were both "necessary and possible," that in spite of excesses on both sides the majority of workers and employers genuinely wished to establish such relations, and that, while "terrible words" were being heard all around, "terrible deeds were few and far between."[48] But such expressions of confidence soon disappeared from the very periodicals that had promoted the progressive message in March and April. By early July, the editor of the newspaper of the Central WIC lamented the "gulf of misunderstanding" separating workers and industrialists and seemed to be resigned to this "tragedy."[49] In Moscow, the journal *Productive Forces of Russia*, which served as an advocate for the academic and technical intelligentsia, remained silent on the labor question until September, when a sharp note of despair that had probably long been felt was suddenly

[47] Reikhardt, "Russkaia burzhuaziia," 29–31; Volobuev, *Proletariat i burzhuaziia*, 137–38, 159, 163–70, 180–83; Volobuev, *Ekonomicheskaia politika Vremennogo Pravitel'stva*, 49; Laverychev, *Po tu storonu barikad*, 235–38.

[48] K. Dembovskii, "The Social Revolution and Industry," *TPG*, May 13, 1917 (no. 98), 1–2.

[49] "On Opposing Sides," *IzvTsVPK*, July 3, 1917 (no. 242), p. 2.

sounded. The journal's contributors had taken pride in Russia's economy and for the part they had played in its development, but they now saw it as being ruined, and they fixed the blame for this on both the workers' low productivity and the moderate socialists' betrayal of the promise to transform Russian labor into a reasonable and productive force.[50]

The tendency to blame the workers and their leaders was particularly observed among the engineers who had actually worked in the factories, had witnessed at firsthand the decline of productivity, and had often served as targets of the workers' anger. At the Third Conference of Southern Industrialists in September, the situation of plant managers and technical personnel was described as "unbearable," because they, not the stockholders or the board of directors, had faced the daily struggle with workers. Moreover, they could no longer rely on the factory committees for help in organizing production; the workers had become so impatient that any committee member who opposed them was likely to be recalled by the workers' general assembly.[51]

This disillusionment with the workers could be noted among the employees of the Ministry of Trade and Industry even before Konovalov's resignation. One contributor to the *Commercial-Industrial Gazette*, the newspaper published by these employees, had expressed dismay at information reaching the ministry in mid-May about a second wave of wage demands in Petrograd's metalprocessing factories, about declining productivity, and about general "disorder" in the factories, all of which indicated to him the "shallowness of revolutionary discipline" among the workers.[52] With Konovalov's resignation, the ministry had ceased to serve as the focal point of his coalition, and by June it had come under the influence of groups that spoke for entrepreneurial interests.[53]

---

[50] Editorial in *PSR*, September 19, 1917 (no. 13/14), 1–2; M. N. Sobolev, "The Crisis of Labor Productivity," ibid., 3–4; N. Gorbachev, "The Decline in Labor Productivity," ibid., October 15, 1917 (no. 15/16). In an address to the Moscow Conference of Public Activists, Bublikov also criticized both workers and "our friends on the left" for failing to see that Russia's economy could not support all their demands and aspirations: *Otchet o moskovskom soveshchanii*, 94–97.

[51] See addresses by fon Ditmar and Priadkin in *Tret'ia konferentsiia promyshlennikov*, 1–6, 9–12.

[52] I. Derevenko, "The Fate of Factories in Russia" and "Industrial Breakdown in Russia," *TPG*, May 13, 1917 (no. 98), 2, and May 25, 1917 (no. 107), 1–2. See also V. Shimanovskii, "Fixed Prices for Labor," *TPG*, May 19, 1917 (no. 103), 2.

[53] This was reflected in the ministry's intervention on behalf of the industrialists to block labor legislation proposed by the Ministry of Labor (see chap. 7).

Another kind of response from the intelligentsia specialists—mostly those working outside a factory setting and especially the engineers and the economists who had become involved in the work of overseeing industry—was to blame both the working class and the industrialists for having displayed "immaturity": the workers because they preferred immediate and local action over a collective, coordinated approach to the economic crisis; the industrialists because they failed to follow the social and economic programs developed by the Progressist alliance on the eve of the revolution.[54] This analysis led some among the technical intelligentsia to the conclusion that they alone were capable of saving Russia and the revolution, because not only did they stand for progress in general, but also, and more important, they stood above class interest and thereby for the nation itself.[55] Clearly, there was nothing in this analysis that would encourage the industrialists to see themselves as the enlightened, powerful people they had deemed themselves to be during the early weeks of the revolution. On the contrary, the technical intelligentsia, who had held up this ideal to them, were now condemning them for failing to live up to that ideal.[56]

Not only was the coalition of progressive entrepreneurs and intelligentsia dissolving, but the coalition's goals and its strategy for realizing them were being discredited. For example, the newspaper *Financial Life*, which had warmly embraced the Progressist vision in March and April, now complained that the revolution that had begun as an "all-national revolution" had been turned into a "class revolution" and had in fact put trade and industry under "a

[54] At the Third Congress of WICs in mid-May, Bublikov actually came to the workers' support by stating that their demands were often justified, and he criticized the industrialists for being more concerned with profits than with the state of the national economy: *IzvTsVPK*, May 22, 1917 (no. 231), 1–2. Of course, in saying so he contradicted his own statement of a few days earlier (see n. 35 above).

[55] I. Brashin, "The Revolution and the Bourgeoisie," *TPG*, May 18, 1917 (no. 102), 2. See also the letter of May 30 from the Central Committee for the Restoration and Support of a Normal Course of Work in Industrial Enterprises (established in early April by the Union of Engineers) to the minister of war and the navy, which set forth an absolute need for centralized *kontrol'* of industry: *EPR* 1:180–81.

[56] See, for example, the bitter response in the newspaper of the Association of Leather Manufacturers to an article in the journal of the Unions of Zemstvos and Cities, in which a certain Panov advised the government not to listen to the industrialists' appeals that it "curb the workers' appetites" but instead stop industrialists from shutting down their factories and force them to operate on less generous profits than they had been used to: "The Labor Question: Harmful Tendencies," *VVOKZ*, July 1, 1917 (no. 35), 299–300.

socialist siege," though it should have been bourgeois in nature.[57] In essence, the newspaper held the workers and their leaders responsible for the revolution's difficulties and implied that the industrialists should no longer be conciliatory in meeting labor's demands.

Among industrialists at large, the conflicts of May and June seemed to elicit a curious sense of relief, almost glee, which can be read in the letters of complaint they addressed to the government and the press. A letter of May 9 from the PSI is a particularly good example of this new tone of reproach and self-righteousness:

Neither in the name of the industrialists' interests nor self-interest but from a feeling of responsibility before the motherland, the Society of Industrialists sees itself obliged to turn the attention of the Provisional Government to the unusually difficult situation in which the industry of the Petrograd district now finds itself. . . .

After the attainment of the political goals of the revolution . . . the Society of Industrialists thought an internal conflict would affect the interests of defense adversely . . . and took the only correct road—the road of conciliation with the organized representation of the working class. . . . The industrialists made very significant concessions at great sacrifice. . . . Yet [now] the demands of the workers and employees have gone beyond the limits of the possible and a catastrophe for industry advances at a dizzying pace.[58]

In this and similar appeals, figures were supplied that cannot be confirmed, though it is clear that in many cases they were exaggerated for inflammatory effect. Nevertheless, they were later repeated in newspaper articles as slogans rather than as the basis for dispassionate economic discourse.[59]

In the late summer and the fall of 1917, the industrialists became as concerned as everyone else with what clearly had become an economic catastrophe, even though some still attempted to make a profit out of the disaster or to save what they could of their fortunes regardless of the harm caused to the operations of their factories (see chap. 9). But during May and June there was a sense

---

[57] "Defending Trade," *FZh*, May 25, 1917 (no. 20), 370–72, and "A Sobering Up," ibid., 373–74.

[58] *EPR* 1:166–68.

[59] The newspaper of the leather manufacturers claimed that workers and their families made up 5 percent of Russia's population but consumed one-third of its national income: *VVOKZ*, July 1, 1917 (no. 35), 299–30. A financial journal made the claim that workers' demands in Petrograd alone had cost industrialists 1,000,200,000 rubles by May: "On the Road to Bankruptcy," *FO*, 1917, no. 15:3–4.

of vindication in the complaints of many industrialists. What had been perceived as "irresponsible" behavior on the part of workers was taken as a justification by the industrialists both for deflecting whatever moral pressure had been directed at them by the Progressists and for reaffirming their trust in their own earlier impulses. From this point on, the industrialists were inclined to reject concessions to labor and to reassert their belief that their own class interests could just as well have been claimed as one of the state's paramount interests and deserving of the government's protection. Therefore, the *Financial Review*, in which Konovalov's ideas had not been welcome before, could now assert that the workers were "ignorant," "lacking in consciousness," and conducting an "egotistic class struggle," while praising the commercial class for its past and present contributions to the national economy and demanding that the government pledge to resist any "socialist measure."[60]

But even if most industrialists had come to share these self-righteous notions, their responses to the resumption of pressure from the soviet still differed considerably. Moscow's men of business again demonstrated both their self-reliance and the limitations of their nationalism and of their "Moscow centrism." On May 19—that is, shortly after the formation of the coalition government and Konovalov's resignation—Moscow's textile manufacturers demanded that no question touching on the "vital interests" of trade and industry be decided in the government without the direct participation of the concerned groups.[61] This demand may have reflected the fear of all entrepreneurs that the government would now act under the pressure of the soviet, but the reaction of the Muscovites was considerably more swift and decisive than that of other entrepreneurial groups. "Organized industry," they warned, would offer "resolute counteraction." Moreover, it is apparent that their anger had not been provoked merely by the action against which they were warning—Skobelev's promise to the soviet (on May 13) that industrialists would be taxed "up to 100 percent of their profits"—for the Moscow Exchange Committee itself had begun to prepare for a self-imposed limit on profits.[62] What the Muscovites were objecting to most was the refusal of the "state" to listen to "society."

[60] "Gratifying Circumstances," *FO*, 1917, no. 17/18:4–6.
[61] *EPR* 1:171–72.
[62] A subcommittee headed by S. I. Chetverikov was discussing plans to set the permissible rate of profit at 5 or 10 percent: *FO*, 1917, no. 15:24.

That the Moscow entrepreneurs should have set themselves up as an alternative voice to that of the government was not surprising. From the beginning of the revolution, Moscow's stance had been that the bourgeoisie was the class best embodying Russia's interests at its present stage of history. Such Moscow industrialists as Riabushinskii and Tret'iakov had sought to organize others of their class in an All-Russian Union of Trade and Industry and alert them to the new responsibilities and rights attending their role in the state.[63] Moreover, the new definition that Riabushinskii had devised for the Russian state and its bourgeoisie, though ridden with contradictions, had set him apart from Konovalov and the Progressist program and had led to a conflict between the Moscow entrepreneurial group and the Provisional Government that surfaced only in May. Over the summer, the Muscovites' disappointment with the Provisional Government had steadily mounted, and at the Second Congress of Trade and Industry, held in early August, Riabushinskii explained why: "The present revolution is bourgeois . . . and from this follows a completely logical conclusion. The persons who direct the government must think and act as bourgeois." Instead, he complained, men of business had been discouraged from participating in the determination of government policy by the "charlatans" who had taken over the Russian state.[64]

Meanwhile, more and more industrialists outside of Moscow were coming to share the Muscovites' outrage at the perceived failure of the government to represent their interests, but even as they took positions similar to Riabushinskii's, they nevertheless declined to accept Moscow's leadership in their struggle against labor and the government. The Muscovites were left to fight on their own, and they did so with characteristic brazenness. As we have already seen, the first lockout took place in June at Guzhon's and other metalprocessing factories in Moscow province.[65]

[63] Riabushinskii's base of influence was the Exchange Committee. This committee, the Moscow Society of Industrialists (MSI), and the Association of Textile Manufacturers were the forces behind the Moscow Commercial-Industrial Committee. Guzhon and Poplavskii, the two principal figures in the MSI, did not share Riabushinskii's conception, but neither did they disagree with him; they believed, as Poplavskii put it (in a typically crude manner), that "the class that produces fifteen billion rubles a year" must have a say in how the money is spent: *Pervyi vserossiiskii torgovo-promyshlennyi s'ezd*, 127–29.

[64] *EPR* 1:196–201.

[65] In the latter part of May, the Moscow-based Union of United Industry made a decision to stop work from June 15 to September 15: *EPR* 1:404–5.

The response of industrialists outside Moscow to the realities of May developed more gradually. The entrepreneurial organizations of Petrograd and the south had not joined in confrontation with the Provisional Government. Instead, their first response was to relapse into their traditional position of dependence on the state and to appeal to the government for help by calling on its authority against the workers' superior strength.[66] Their goal, as stated in these appeals, was "defensive," in that they attempted to stop rather than reverse labor's gains. Most often, the government was asked to fix a ceiling on workers' wages or to rewrite contracts on state orders so as to compensate the industrialists for the higher wages.[67] The industrialists used the economic crisis and the war to advantage by claiming that the "national interests" required curbing the workers' wages.[68]

By late May and early June, however, the entrepreneurs of Petrograd and the south were expressing disappointment with the Provisional Government's accomplishments as well as disapproval of its overall direction and specific actions. A letter of May 27 from the Conference of Southern Industrialists to the Provisional Government spoke bitterly of the failure to uphold the law and instill respect for the rights of proprietors.[69] A meeting of thirteen of the largest entrepreneurial organizations in the country, which took place in Petrograd on June 1 and 2 and was labeled by the socialist press the "Conference of the Big Bourgeoisie," was even more hostile, blaming the government for anarchy in general and the workers' demands in particular. The assembled magnates of industry argued, in terms similar to those later used by Riabushinskii, that the government did not understand the essential role capitalism was destined to play in Russia. Consequently, they sought to establish strong entrepreneurial organizations—the

[66] The SSPPiT, for example, continued to act as a lobbying organization concerned with influencing government economic policy in "nonpolitical" ways, though it made a concession to the new conditions by seeking to draw into its ranks the smaller industrialists, because "under democracy, numbers count": "The Tasks of Our Association," *PiT*, June 24, 1917 (no. 22/23).

[67] The first request of this sort actually came on April 5 from the Association of Metalprocessing Industries, an organization with close ties to the old regime: *EPR* 1:163–65. Similar appeals were made in May by the southern industrialists, the SSPPiT, and the PSI: *TPG*, May 28, 1917 (no. 110), 3–4; *EPR* 1:165–71, 403–4. In June, requests for rewriting state contracts became prevalent: *EPR* 1:338–42.

[68] See, for example, the statement by SSPPiT in *TPG*, May 28, 1917 (no. 110), 3–4.

[69] *EPR* 1:173–80.

meeting gave birth to a Committee of United Industry and to a Petrograd-based Union of Trade and Industry—both to force the government to adopt new policies and to influence the manner of their implementation.[70]

The disappointment of the Petrograd and southern entrepreneurs with the government had at least three consequences. First, the industrialists decided to organize and strengthen themselves in order to force the cabinet to stand up to the challenges from labor or, failing that, to be able to confront the workers on their own. To be sure, differences of interest and temperament made unity an elusive goal. The various organizational efforts initiated by the Petrograd industrialists—at the "Conference of the Big Bourgeoisie," at an earlier meeting of industrial organizations called by Putilov on May 25, and in a PSI initiative in mid-June—demonstrated that Riabushinskii had failed to turn his brainchild, the Moscow-based Union of Trade and Industry, into a truly all-Russian organization.[71] Nor would the new ventures fare any better, because none of the Moscow industrial organizations was present at the Petrograd meetings.

Still, the renewed activity of Putilov and other members of the Association of Metalprocessing Industries marked the return to the scene of the former clients of the tsarist state who had been temporarily thrown off balance by the revolution. In the major industrial associations in Petrograd, the PSI and the SSPPiT, strength again shifted away from the Progressists, who had lost their principal protector in the Ministry of Trade and Industry, Konovalov, to the former leaders, who had offered a narrower definition of commercial-industrial goals. Eventually, the new or transformed organizations would become springboards for more intransigent entrepreneurial policies in regard to the two main issues in the industrial sphere: labor relations and the regulation of economic activity.

A second development that followed from the industrialists' disillusionment with the government's protection of their interests was a growing recklessness in the struggle against labor. Confrontations with the workers had become virtually unavoidable in May

---

[70] The meeting was held behind closed doors; two resolutions are reprinted in *EPR* 1:181–84. See *PSR*, August 15, 1917 (no. 12), 18, for a report on the first meeting of the Committee of United Industry.

[71] The meeting on May 25, probably attended only by representatives of organizations based in Petrograd and perhaps serving as a preparatory session for the meeting of June 1 and 2, was reported in *FO*, 1917, no. 16:3–4, 7–8.

because of the workers' insistence on their demands, the socialists' ability to block any attempt in the cabinet to set legal limits on wages, and the government's loss of any means of protecting proprietary rights. Nevertheless, the employers' response in May had been mostly one of passive resistance, for they were not yet ready to cripple their factories' productive capacity for the sake of defeating labor. The best example of this was in the mines and factories of the Donbas. The well-organized workers there had followed earlier gains (increased wages and a shorter workday) with demands, made during parallel conferences of industrialists and workers meeting from April 29 to May 2, for higher wages and a new minimum wage for unskilled workers. The industrialists rejected the demands, declared the issue a "governmental and national question," and submitted it to the Provisional Government.[72] They also rejected a compromise proposal of the government's arbiter, Labor Minister Skobelev, at the risk of a general regional strike, but they nevertheless declared their resolute opposition to a policy of lockouts.[73] A similar stance was typical of small owners in May, particularly in Petrograd. Most large industrialists in Petrograd continued to show a greater readiness to accept mediation.

By June, however, a strategy of rejecting outright both the workers' demands and the decisions of the government's arbiters became quite universal among the owners of both small and large enterprises. There was also a transition to more "offensive" strategies, particularly through the organization of a united front against the workers. As one speaker at the "Conference of the Big Bourgeoisie" explained: "The workers hold us in their hands, intervene in the management of [our] affairs, and arbitrarily dismiss [our] employees. We have been preparing and are now prepared to rebuff the attack on private property. . . . You must defend yourselves by establishing . . . unity."[74] Indeed, the PSI seemed to be following this suggestion when it asked on June 13 that all its members sign a "convention" obligating them to consult with the society before responding to their workers' demands.[75] Lockouts

---

[72] *Konferentsii rabochikh*, 7–8.

[73] *EPR* 1:169–71, 403–4.

[74] Quoted in Reikhardt, "Russkaia burzhuaziia," 26.

[75] Ibid., 29–31. The PSI had already been under some pressure from its Vyborg district members (mostly owners of metalprocessing plants) to initiate such "radical measures"; they considered the rewriting of government contracts only a temporary solution: see the minutes of their meeting of May 26 in *EPR* 1:335. A circular

were still relatively rare in June (Moscow was the exception), but they became common in July and especially August.[76] Moreover, the warnings issued by industrial organizations about the prospects of unemployment and the hunger that would result from labor's "excessive" demands helped create the impression that every shutdown was in fact a deliberate lockout.[77]

A third consequence of the new attitude among the Petrograd industrialists concerned the government's legislative work. Although entrepreneurial resistance to labor legislation did not have the immediate inflammatory effect of lockouts, it was detrimental to the workers' past and future gains and contributed much to undermining their support of the soviet's coalition strategy. From the first meeting of the Commission on Labor Legislation attached to the Ministry of Labor, the industrialists' representatives demonstrated a reluctance to see measures they had accepted on an ad hoc basis made into law,[78] and in the following weeks they strongly opposed the ministry's various proposals and often demanded that they be sent back for reworking. When outvoted in the commission, they would call on the Ministry of Trade and Industry to pressure the Ministry of Labor into withdrawing the proposals, or they would call on the nonsocialist majority in the cabinet to vote them down. A law on the freedom to strike, for example, was held up in the commission for nearly a month while the industrialists worked out a "counterproject." When draft legislation was finally submitted to the cabinet over the industrialists' protest, it was sent back to the Ministry of Labor for reworking.[79] Similarly, legislative proposals on the eight-hour workday, a minimum wage, and unemployment insurance were defeated by en-

sent by the PSI to its members on June 3 explained the need for a new policy to meet the "new wave of economic demands . . . conducted by separate groups of workers in individual factories": *EPR* 1:523. A similar effort to establish entrepreneurial solidarity was made in the Donbas: *EPR* 1:523–24.

[76] According to a government study, only 57 of the 586 shutdowns that occurred between March 1 and August 1 were due to workers' demands or disagreements between owners and workers; the rest of the shutdowns were attributed to shortages (about two-thirds), repairs (22), or other causes: *EPR* 2:44–46.

[77] One such warning was issued by the Donbas industrialists on June 28: *EPR* 1:407–8.

[78] The meeting took place on June 13 and was reported in *IzvPS*, June 14, 1917 (no. 91), 10.

[79] *VMT*, 1917, no. 1/2:26–27; Auerbakh, "Revoliutsionnoe obshchestvo," 15. The counterproject sought to limit the freedom to strike considerably while legalizing lockout.

trepreneurial opposition and its supporters in the Ministry of Trade and Industry, and the same alliance joined to make significant changes in laws on workers' sickness insurance and on the Central Insurance Council.

Opposition to new labor legislation had emerged even earlier. On April 20, L. I. Shpergaze, a representative of the PSI to the Committee on Labor Legislation in Konovalov's Ministry of Trade and Industry, used this argument against a proposed law on the eight-hour workday: "A law on the eight-hour day should not be passed, not because the present situation does not allow the application of this principle in the majority of enterprises (the reality of its application contradicts this) but because once the law is established, and when postwar conditions later make it impossible to submit to it, it will be hard to abolish."[80] In June, however, the opposition was based on other reasons as well. The proposals of the Ministry of Labor were deemed objectionable also because they were the work of socialists. Moreover, opposition to them was morally and politically easier after Konovalov's departure from the Ministry of Trade and Industry. The new leaders of the ministry were not inclined to serve as a conscience for the commercial-industrial class, and their concept of entrepreneurial interests focused on economic rather than political power. In addition, the rewriting of labor laws became one of the weapons in the industrialists' struggle against the workers' immediate gains, while the workers' repeated demands were used to support the industrialists' case that the government should establish limits on workers' wages and on labor's freedom of struggle in general.[81] Finally, the economic crisis made it possible for industrial organizations and their spokesmen in the government to employ the rhetoric of "national interest" in their own behalf, so that entrepreneurial intransigence could be made to appear as a response to the country's needs, in implicit contrast to the merely selfish demands of the

[80] Quoted in Volobuev, *Proletariat i burzhuaziia*, 186. Pankov and Gvozdev, two of the soviet's representatives on the Committee on Labor Legislation, complained that cooperation between the representatives of the employers and those of the public organizations put the workers' representatives in the minority and blocked legislation on unions, strikes, and the eight-hour workday: Lozinskii, *Ekonomicheskaia politika Vremennogo Pravitel'stva*, 184–85. Similar information appeared in the press: *RG*, April 1, 1917 (no. 22), 3, and April 20, 1917 (no. 35), 2–3; *Den'*, April 17, 1917 (no. 36).

[81] On June 8, Pal'chinskii brought a proposal to set a ceiling on workers' earnings before the cabinet: *EPR* 1:546. See chap. 7.

workers.[82] However, the true test of the entrepreneurs' concern for the national economy lay in their response to initiatives for state regulation of the economy—an issue of the greatest importance for Russian industry and for the revolution itself.

Regulating the Economy

One of the principal goals of the soviet in joining a coalition government had been to ensure that the cabinet implemented a plan for state regulation of the economy that the soviet's economic section had worked out and the Conference of Soviets had adopted on April 3. If the government accepted the plan, the soviet would score a political victory and at the same time take the first step toward accomplishing its self-assumed task of saving the economy from ruin. As sketched out by Groman, the plan consisted of two parts: a social section, which provided for a limit on entrepreneurial profits and guarantees for minimum standards of work and living conditions for the workers; and an economic section, which called for state planning and regulation of production, commerce, transport, and distribution.[83] The Provisional Government committed itself to these principles in its declaration of May 6.[84]

Regardless of how binding the coalition partners felt this commitment really was, the issue of economic regulation was forced on both the government and the soviet by the conditions of economic crisis: the rapidly rising cost of raw materials and manufactured goods; the financial difficulties of workers, industrialists, local governments, and the Provisional Government itself; and the shortages of raw materials and fuel caused by declining production and the near-collapse of the transport system.[85] In mid-May,

[82] See, for example, Kutler's address to the Economic Council, in Lozinskii, *Ekonomicheskaia politika Vremennogo Pravitel'stva*, 187–88. Kutler demanded that, instead of a law establishing an eight-hour workday, there should be measures for imposing longer hours on workers. He declared that, during the summer months, workers had begun to insist on adherence to the eight-hour principle.

[83] For Groman's presentation of this plan at the conference, see *Vserossiiskoe soveshchanie*, 203–5, 257–61. Also see Schwarz, "Materialy o razvitii programm" (Project on Menshevik History), 2–3, and "On Whom Should the War Expenditures Fall?," *RG*, April 13, 1917 (no. 30), 1.

[84] *VVP*, May 6, 1917 (no. 49), 1; *Khronika* 2:271–73. The declaration promised "systematic establishment of governmental control of production, transport, exchange, and distribution of commodities, and in necessary cases . . . the organization of production."

[85] In April, it was reported that Petrograd was expected to receive 3 million puds

P. I. Pal'chinskii, chairman of the Special Conference on Defense, estimated that Petrograd industry was operating at 40 or 50 percent below capacity, mostly because of shortages; and a government study later concluded that shortages had affected two-thirds of the 586 factories in Petrograd that had been forced to close down between March and July.[86]

Finally, if all these problems had not been sufficiently urgent, there erupted, during the first week of the coalition's existence, the labor conflict in the Donbas which was alluded to earlier in this chapter. Because of the magnitude of this conflict and the importance of the industry involved (the mines and metallurgical plants in the region that was Russia's main source of coal and iron), and because both workers and industrialists used the economic problems of the moment to support their claims—the workers citing inflation in demanding higher wages, the industrialists threatening to raise the price of fuels and metals sharply if the workers won their demands—the Donbas conflict became the springboard for two attempts to work out regulatory measures, one originating in the Provisional Government, the other in the soviet.

On May 10, the Donbas industrialists presented their case directly to the cabinet, and the ministers accepted Konovalov's suggestion that he, Skobelev, and Tereshchenko be appointed to a committee to discuss measures for the regulation of worker-employer relations as well as the "economic side of industrial life."[87]

---

of liquid fuel a month and 5.5 of hard fuel—far less than the current monthly consumption of the region's industry, which was 4 million puds of liquid fuel and 14 of hard fuel: *ZhOS*, April 5, 1917 (no. 152), 276 (1 pud = 36 lbs.). Figures compiled by the Special Conference on Fuel show that the problem was caused by transport, not production. In the country as a whole, 1,036,929 puds of hard fuel were produced from January to July 1917, compared with 2,096,194 during all of 1916. But the amount of hard fuel being shipped to the centers of industry declined sharply, from 56,414 puds in February, to 55,727 in March, 45,690 in April, 44,280 in May, and 41,433 in June. See *Biulleteni statisticheskogo otdela*, 1917, no. 5:4. Reporting to the Third Conference of Southern Industrialists in September, Ia. D. Priadkin noted that production of coal was actually higher in January–April 1917 than in the corresponding months of 1916 (568 and 558.2 million puds, respectively) but declined rapidly in the second third of the year (to 485.5): *Tret'ia konferentsiia promyshlennikov*, 9–12. A similar decline in production affected the metallurgical industry of the region, but transport was so slow that stockpiles of iron ore continued to grow in the Krivorog region, from 65 million puds on January 1, 1917, to 98 million puds on August 1: ibid., 13.

[86] *IzvPS*, May 20, 1917 (no. 71), 4, and *TPG*, October 1, 1917 (no. 213), as cited in Volobuev, *Proletariat i burzhuaziia*, 218.

[87] *RD v aprele*, 362–65; *EPR* 1:173–74; Reikhardt, "Russkaia burzhuaziia," 15; Tsereteli, *Vospominaniia o fevral'skoi revoliutsii* 1:434.

Although this committee held only two meetings, it represented the Provisional Government's most ambitious attempt to use regulatory measures to alleviate the economic crisis, and for this reason both the extent and the limits of what the ministers accomplished were of great significance to the success of the coalition government.

The one issue on which the committee acted immediately and with no apparent disagreement during its first meeting on May 11 was that of taxation.[88] The ministers proposed a tax program that would demonstrate the government's evenhandedness in its distribution of the national financial burden (for which it was repeatedly hailed by the soviet's leaders),[89] while also helping the treasury meet the budgetary obligations that the Freedom Loan had not met.[90] When finally decreed by the Ministry of Finance on June 12, the tax program was declared a great victory for the camp of democracy. It instituted three progressive tax scales—a regular income tax, a special levy on incomes of more than ten thousand rubles, and a tax on increases in income that were due to the war—that together could add up to a 90 percent tax rate. Even the most ardent socialists agreed that any higher level of taxation would be harmful to industry, and their only criticism was that the program did not extend to property taxes.[91]

The transformation in entrepreneurial attitudes also affected their position on taxes. Whereas in May many industrialists (the Donbas owners among them) had professed a willingness to see their profits largely taken by the treasury,[92] in June their journals

[88] The meeting was reported in detail in *NZh*, May 12, 1917 (no. 21), 3, and is described also in *Khronika* 2:141–42.

[89] See, for example, Skobelev's report to the soviet on May 13, reported in *IzvPS*, May 14, 1917 (no. 66), 2; and *Khronika* 2:149.

[90] There was apparently great enthusiasm for the loan in the early weeks after its issuance, according to reports in the government press: *VVP*, May 4, 1917 (no. 47), 3, and May 6, 1917 (no. 49), 4. But the terms of purchase for large buyers were so favorable, and the required down payments so small, that although some 2.5 billion rubles in face value had been sold by late April, the treasury had actually received only 250 million rubles: S. [D. Iu.] Dalin, "Our War Finances," *NZh*, April 28, 1917 (no. 9), 2. Naturally, entrepreneurs became less willing to invest in government bonds after doubts had arisen about the economic and political stability of the country.

[91] For the text of the new law, see *VVP*, June 16, 1917 (no. 81), 1. For a discussion of the law in the socialist press, see "A First Step," *IzvPS*, June 17, 1917 (no. 94), 4; N. Ch. [Cherevanin], "A Better Beginning," *RG*, June 17, 1917 (no. 83), 2; D. Kuzovkov, "A Financial Reform 'Without Precedent,'" *NZh*, June 22, 1917 (no. 55), 1; and S. Dalin, "Financial Experiments," *NZh*, June 25, 1917 (no. 58), 1.

[92] For the position of the Donbas industrialists, see the report on their May 10

attacked the new tax laws as a socialist conspiracy to expropriate capital through a combination of high wages and high taxes and as spelling the doom of Russian industry. Higher taxes, it was argued, could not make up for the government's mismanagement of the country's finances yet would prevent reinvestment for technological improvement and would deter new investors.[93] In Moscow, the industrialists resorted to the step of refusing to allow Tret'iakov to replace Konovalov in the Ministry of Trade and Industry until the new taxes had been abolished.[94] Later on, in August, the Moscow Conference of Public Activists called for the imposition of indirect taxes on basic necessities, a regressive measure which only the most intransigent of entrepreneurs had advocated previously.[95] Under such pressure, the government eventually relented, and in the fall the tax decrees were considerably modified.[96] Still, the June 12 tax program stands as the most radical measure undertaken by the Provisional Government.

In other respects, though, the record of the ministerial committee was one of timidity and conflict. At their first meeting, the ministers agreed that the government should establish procedures for the arbitration of major industrial conflicts at the cabinet level (see chapter 7) and also that it must "intervene" in the economy.[97] A distinction was drawn, however, between intervention in specific cases, when financial, supply, or labor difficulties threatened the production of essential commodities, and the broader goal of regulating economic life in general, which the committee seemed re-

---

meeting with the cabinet, in *IzvPS*, May 13, 1917 (no. 65), 2–3. Also see "Limiting War Profits," *FZh*, May 4, 1917 (no. 16/17), 289–90.

[93] *TPG*, May 28, 1917 (no. 110), 3–4; "The Ruble in Danger," *FZh*, May 25, 1917 (no. 20), 369–70; "Industry and the New Taxes," *PiT*, July 8, 1917 (no. 24/25), 1–4; A. Eliasson, "The Money Circulation and the Compulsory Loan," *FG*, July 16, 1917 (no. 473), 7–11; and S. V. Kotliarov, "Essential Shortcomings in the Taxes of June 12, 1917," *FG*, September 9, 1917 (no. 480), 8–10.

[94] Laverychev, *Po tu storonu barikad*, 205.

[95] *Otchet o moskovskom soveshchanii*, 72–89. See also the endorsement of this idea by the SSPPiT in "Our Financial Situation," *PiT*, August 5, 1917 (no. 28/29), 61. An equally regressive, though technically simpler, measure had been advocated by Putilov since May: the exchange of all fiscal notes (except stocks) over twenty-five rubles, with the value of the new currency set at 25 percent of the old: *FO*, 1917, no. 16:3–4, and *VVTiP*, 1917, no. 4/5:6–8.

[96] The ceiling on the tax on growth of war profits was lowered from 80 percent to 50 percent, and payment was due at the end of 1918 instead of 1917. The proposal was made by the ministry on September 11 and approved by the cabinet on October 13: Lozinskii, *Ekonomicheskaia politika Vremennogo Pravitel'stva*, 113–14.

[97] *NZh*, May 12, 1917 (no. 21), 3.

luctant to tackle. During the committee's two meetings, Gvozdev apparently argued for the necessity of comprehensive regulation, whereas Konovalov and Tereshchenko insisted that the mandate from the Provisional Government was merely to protect the operations of individual enterprises. In fact, the three measures approved by the committee at its second meeting, on May 12, fell far short of comprehensive regulation. These measures were, first, to establish government *kontrol'* over certain individual enterprises through the appointment of special commissars who would function alongside consultative bodies of workers' representatives; second, to make special loans and credits available to entrepreneurs in financial difficulty; and third, to name an ad hoc commission to study and resolve the problems in the Donbas mining industry.[98]

The unwillingness of the government to institute a broad program of economic regulation prepared the stage for a confrontation on the issue between it and the soviet. To the soviet's economists, the conflict in the Donbas appeared not only as dangerous in its immediate implications, but also as emblematic of the overall economic problems of the country. To deal with it, some of them advocated organizing the crucial metal and mining industries of the south into compulsory state trusts or even nationalizing them.[99] Moreover, the economists moved on to an effort on behalf of a new economic plan.

This plan, the most detailed one to have come out of the soviet's economic section, offered an organizational framework for the regulation of the economy as well as specific recommendations for economic policies. The plan, generally attributed to Groman, envisioned two networks of local and central bodies: one, advisory and representative in nature, was to be entrusted with studying the state of the economy and suggesting broad policies; the other was to possess executive authority to plan and carry out the regulation of economic life. The plan recommended the establishment of state monopolies, compulsory trusts, and a ceiling on profits in

[98] There is some confusion about who participated in the second meeting. *Novaia zhizn'* lists Skobelev, Konovalov, and Tereshchenko but attributes the statement about comprehensive regulation to Gvozdev, while Volobuev mentions Shingarev rather than Tereshchenko as the representative of the minister of finance: ibid.; Volobuev, *Proletariat i burzhuaziia*, 200.

[99] "What Does the New Provisional Government Want?" *RG*, May 11, 1917 (no. 53), 2–3; "The Country Is in Danger," *RG*, May 14, 1917 (no. 56), 1–2; Iu. Steklov, "The Industrialists' Complaints," *NZh*, May 13, 1917 (no. 33), 1; V. Bazarov, "The Conflict in the Don Basin," *NZh*, May 16, 1917 (no. 24), 1; B. Avilov, "The Essence of Economic Ruin," ibid., 2.

crucial areas; government control of all credit and financial institutions; rationing of available supplies; and active intervention by the Ministry of Labor in worker-employer relations.[100] Clearly, this was an ambitious plan (in fact, it was quite similar to what Lenin would advocate several months later) but not a great deal more radical than measures implemented in other warring countries. When the executive committee met to discuss it on May 16, there was general agreement that measures of this scope were indeed necessary. Most of the economists were on hand to back Groman's presentation (Cherevanin, Bazarov, B. V. Avilov, G. V. Shub, and A. I. Bukovetskii), and Sandomirskii offered support in the name of the Donbas workers. The ensuing discussion centered on three points: that similar measures had already been taken in Germany; that the plan employed *kontrol'* rather than the actual takeover of enterprises; and that its goal was to save the national economy, not socialize it.[101]

If there was any objection to the plan in the executive committee, it was political. Speaking for the Revolutionary Defensists, Bogdanov warned the committee that the program "may be unacceptable to the cabinet as a whole." Then he posed several questions: Did the socialist ministers have any means of forcing the government to carry it out? And if they did, could they predict the political consequences?[102] Bogdanov was in effect expressing his group's overriding commitment to the principle of coalition and a recognition that the majority of nonsocialist ministers would not let the soviet impose the regulatory plan upon them.

The economic cogency of Groman's plan, however, was so strong that the executive committee endorsed it as a "practical guideline" for the committee itself and for the "comrade ministers." The committee authorized an expanded economic section to prepare the organizational scheme and the substantive measures for the regulation of economic life and to draft the legislative proposals the cabinet would be asked to adopt. The socialist ministers were instructed to maintain communications between the section and the cabinet and to have the latter immediately establish an advisory Economic Council on which revolutionary democracy would have the majority of seats.[103] Thus, the executive committee was

[100] *IzvPS*, May 11, 1917 (no. 63), 3–4; *Petrogradskii sovet*, 144–49.

[101] *Petrogradskii sovet*, 146–52, 332–38.

[102] Bogdanov's statement does not appear in the meeting's protocol but is cited from memory in Sukhanov, *Zapiski o revoliutsii* 4:111–13.

[103] *Petrogradskii sovet*, 150–51; Volobuev, *Ekonomicheskaia politika Vremennogo Pravitel'stva*, 139. This resolution refutes Volobuev's assertion (ibid., 67) that the execu-

making regulation an issue of confrontation between itself and the Provisional Government. Meanwhile, the socialist press insisted that the plan was not to be interpreted as "socialist."[104] On his way out of the meeting, Dan said to Bazarov, "You and your Groman may be worse than the Bolsheviks."[105]

In an address to the First Congress of Soviets in mid-June, Skobelev announced that the cabinet had named six ministers to prepare the organizational scheme for the Economic Council and for an executive Main Economic Committee and that on June 21 these two bodies would be authorized both to oversee the work of all formerly existing regulatory agencies (mainly the "special conferences" established during the war) and to prepare a comprehensive program of economic planning and regulation. These steps, he added, amounted to a victory of the soviet over the Provisional Government.[106] However, the victory proved to be hollow, for when the members of the bodies were named, it turned out that the soviet had only a minority of the seats; even with the cooperatives added, the representatives of democracy accounted for just half of the Economic Council's members.[107] Moreover, by July, when the new regulatory bodies became operative, economic and administrative deterioration had advanced so far as to render any attempt at arresting it futile (see chapter 9).

However, the more important conflict arising from the soviet's pressure for economic regulation was not the political contest between the executive committee and the Provisional Government but the struggle between democracy and the bourgeoisie, and to a certain extent between the latter and the government, over control of the country's economy. The resignation of Konovalov from his post as minister of trade and industry has often been pointed to as the principal event in this struggle, and so it must be studied before examining the positions taken by the commercial-industrial class at large on the issue of regulation.

---

tive committee "trustingly left to the government of the capitalists the grandiose task of saving the country."

[104] F. Cherevanin, "Are We on the Road to Socialism?" *RG*, May 18, 1917 (no. 59), 2; B. Avilov, "The Struggle against Economic Ruin," *NZh*, May 12, 1917 (no. 21), 1; "Our Program for Economic Policy," *NZh*, May 18, 1917 (no. 26), 1.

[105] V. A. Bazarov, "Gromanovskaia kontseptsiia narodnokhoziaistvennogo tselogo," *Planovoe khoziaistvo*, 1927, no. 6:165.

[106] *Pervyi s'ezd sovetov*, 248–49. The cabinet meeting at which the measures were adopted is described in *Khronika* 2:251. The text of the statute establishing the two bodies appears in translation in *RPG* 2:677–78.

[107] *RG*, June 23, 1917 (no. 88), 1.

KONOVALOV'S RESIGNATION, coming just two days after the soviet's decision to press for its plan of economic regulation, seemed to suggest that Konovalov himself had turned against regulation. However, previous actions of his had demonstrated a commitment to regulating entrepreneurial activity whenever it seemed economically necessary. For example, on May 5 he had announced the creation of a central planning body, the Conference on Questions of Developing the Productive Forces; and on May 7 he had requested that the cabinet establish fixed prices on all metals. On May 9, he had issued new guidelines for the distribution of fuel and issued orders to continue with preparations for fixed prices and a state monopoly on fuel in spite of opposition from the industrialists of the Donbas.[108]

At the same time, however, there were signs that Konovalov was finding it increasingly difficult to make his policies acceptable to his fellow industrialists. During his last two weeks in office, he made every effort to make industrialists feel that the Provisional Government was still "theirs" and was deserving of their support. The Conference on Questions of Developing the Productive Forces, for example, was designed to bring together men from the government, the entrepreneurial and public organizations, and the scientific community to discuss, among other things, measures for the protection of Russian industry from foreign competition.[109] A Central Purveying Committee established on May 5 was similar in composition, its purpose being to ensure that state orders were directed to Russian rather than foreign firms.[110] In these efforts, as well as in his support for the extension of special credits to enterprises in financial difficulty, Konovalov seemed to be balancing his self-assumed role as trustee of the national economy with his political goal of gaining support for his policies among those whose support was essential.[111]

[108] *VVP*, May 7, 1917 (no. 50), 2, and May 11, 1917 (no. 52), 2; *EPR* 1:259–64; *RPG* 2:689–92. For socialist criticism of Konovalov's record on regulation, see G. Tsyperovich, "To the Question of the Fuel Monopoly," *NZh*, April 20, 1917 (no. 2), 5; and B. Avilov, "The Struggle against Economic Ruin," *NZh*, May 12, 1917 (no. 21), 1.

[109] On the establishment of the conference, see *VVP*, May 5, 1917 (no. 48), 1–2; *EPR* 1:261–62. Its first meetings were reported in *VVP*, May 30, 1917 (no. 66), 3.

[110] *VVP*, May 7, 1917 (no. 50), 2; *PiT*, May 13, 1917 (no. 16/17), 321.

[111] Konovalov was reported to have asked the Provisional Government to approve a reconsideration of contracts signed by state agencies with the southern industrialists, as well as to fix new fuel prices at a level high enough to compensate industrialists for the increased costs of labor and materials, even while he was fight-

Yet, contemporaneously with these efforts, Konovalov was clearly having some doubts, as one can see in the messages he was sending to the soviet and to his fellow ministers. On May 8, he complained in a letter to Prince L'vov about the Ministry of Interior's failure to enforce the laws forbidding attacks on property and protecting entrepreneurs from interference by all sorts of organizations.[112] During a cabinet meeting on May 15, he raised the issue of the workers' "excessive" demands.[113] Finally, on May 16, in a speech to the Third Congress of WICs, he attacked the socialists directly: the extremists among them for "hypnotizing" the masses with their slogans, and the moderate leaders of the soviet for failing to keep the labor struggle within "legitimate channels."[114] In these complaints, Konovalov was evidently hoping to make himself credible again to his fellow industrialists while also trying to come to terms with what was to him a truly shocking recognition—namely, that Russian society might not, after all, have been ready for democracy and freedom, both because the masses seemed to turn easily to excess and because the superstructures, such as the state, were so fragile.

The latter aspect of Konovalov's analysis was expressed most strongly in his speech to the Congress of WICs. Speaking to his fellow Progressists after he had privately resolved to resign, he began by praising the committees for having brought together "all the vital forces of the country," among which he specifically mentioned workers, industrialists, merchants, scientists, "public men," and the "labor intelligentsia." He then went on to describe their common dream and its demise:

When overthrowing the old regime, we firmly believed that under the conditions of freedom a mighty development of the productive forces lay before the country, but at the present moment it is not so much a question of developing the productive forces as of exerting every effort in order to save those embryos of industrial life that have survived the difficult atmosphere of the old regime from complete destruction. . . . [Today,] the conscious kindling of passions is being carried on systematically and insistently; demands incessantly follow one another, the form of their presentation take an ever more insufferable and inadmissible character. . . . And if in the near future a sobering up of befogged minds does not take

---

ing the southerners' opposition to the very idea of fixed prices: *FO*, 1917, no. 16: 19–20.

[112] Ibid., 21; *VVP*, May 13, 1917 (no. 53), 2.

[113] *NZh*, May 18, 1917 (no. 26), 4; *Khronika* 2:157.

[114] *IzvTsVPK*, May 25, 1917 (no. 230), 1; *VVP*, May 18, 1917 (no. 57), 3.

place, . . . we shall witness the complete paralysis of economic life and enter into a long period of irreparable economic catastrophe during which millions of people will find themselves without work, bread, even a roof. . . . Only then will the masses understand into what an abyss they have let themselves be drawn, but by then it will be too late.[115]

This warning to the workers was curiously similar to the warning Konovalov had issued to the industrialists in September 1916; indeed, the motive behind the two statements was identical. Because all other arguments and measures had failed to secure the social cooperation he deemed essential for Russia's safe transition to democracy, Konovalov had then tried to appeal to basic fears.

Konovalov's actions on the eve of his resignation—the regulatory measures, the appeals for the industrialists' support, and the warnings against anarchy—point to two elements in his decision to resign, neither of which represented a change in his position on the principle of regulation. First, there was his growing despair over the developing social conflict and the erosion of governmental authority. In fact, he made his decision to leave the cabinet on May 11 or 12, just after he had learned the full extent of the problems in the Donbas industries but before the executive committee had adopted Groman's plan.[116] Konovalov himself mentioned the issue of regulation as the one over which he was at odds with Skobelev but studiously avoided any reference to the soviet's "imposing" the program on the government or to the presumed "socialist" nature of the plan.[117] Instead, at the Congress of WICs he complained that the "conditions of unlimited anarchy" had made it impossible for the government to regulate the economy and condemned the "antistate" forces responsible for this situation. He returned to this theme in his letter of resignation, in which he derided the belief that, in conditions of anarchy, "democratic organizations" could be effective in regulating economic life and explained his decision to resign as resulting principally from the government's failure to "manifest its full authority." At the very end of his letter, Konovalov added a peculiar comment: because the present government could not maintain authority, he considered it necessary to "clear the way" and allow the revolution to

[115] RPG 2:668–69, translated from IzvTsVPK, May 25, 1917 (no. 230), 1.

[116] This timing is based on information in IzvPS, May 20, 1917 (no. 71), 5–6, and TPG, May 20, 1917 (no. 104), 4.

[117] In the bourgeois press, Konovalov's resignation was attributed precisely to the "influence of socialist doctrine" on the government: see, for example, FO, 1917, no. 16:1–3.

pass on to the stage of a "homogeneous, socialist ministry."[118] Konovalov was no socialist, but perhaps he had come to the conclusion that only a socialist government stood any chance of reestablishing authority.

However, what was defeated in May was not only Konovalov's vision. The organizational revival among the old Petrograd financial oligarchy and giant metal producers signaled his defeat also in the struggle for the support of the commercial-industrial class, and it is in this struggle that the second cause of Konovalov's resignation is to be found. Information on the conflicts is difficult to come by, but it seems clear that Konovalov had affronted the Donbas industrialists (who were connected to the Petrograd banks through the raw-material syndicates) with his push for fixed prices on fuels. Indeed, one source reported Konovalov's resignation to have been both provoked and celebrated by the directors of Petrograd's largest bank.[119] Tsereteli, who conferred with Konovalov often during those days, considered his resignation to have been caused by entrepreneurial opposition to regulation and called it a "personal tragedy."[120] Indeed, whatever Konovalov's reasons for resigning, it was judged at the time to be a "desertion" of the revolution by the commercial-industrial class and must be viewed now as emblematic of the position taken by the bourgeoisie in regard to the question of economic regulation under a coalition government.[121]

REGULATION of economic operations, by the state or by public bodies, was an issue that was much discussed among entrepreneurs during the war years and one on which there was considerable disagreement. Generally speaking, the positions were related to material interests. The large industrialists of the south and Petrograd, all of which were connected to the syndicate Prodamet, sought to use the regulatory agencies established by the Central WIC to "regulate" their own operations, and as long as they could do so, they supported this form of regulation of the economy. The large metal producers of Moscow province, who often found themselves the victims of Prodamet's exclusionary arrangements

[118] *IzvPS*, May 20, 1917 (no. 71), 5–6; *TPG*, May 20, 1917 (no. 104), 4.

[119] "The Azov-Don Bank," *VVTiP*, 1917, no. 4/5:4–5.

[120] Tsereteli, *Vospominaniia o fevral'skoi revoliutsii* 1:432, 439.

[121] For contemporary comments, see: "Who Is to Blame?" *RG*, May 19, 1917 (no. 60), 1–2; "On Konovalov's Departure," *RG*, May 21, 1917 (no. 61), 2–3; B. Avilov, "On the Departure of A. I. Konovalov," *NZh*, May 21, 1917 (no. 29), 1.

with Petrograd industry, supported instead regulation through the state-sanctioned regional Factory Conferences, controlled by the engineers associated with the Moscow WIC.[122] Opposition to any form of state or public regulation was widespread among small producers, who suspected with some justification that regulatory bodies catered to the interests of large producers; such opposition was especially strong among those producers and distributors who had been the subject of intensive regulatory measures under the old regime, notably the grain merchants and leather manufacturers. Indeed, anyone attending the First Congress of Trade and Industry in mid-March and listening to the charges of excesses and stupidities leveled at the tsarist regulatory bodies would have had to conclude that negative feelings were so strong that any imposition of a regulatory apparatus on merchants and industrialists by the new regime was precluded.[123] Commercial-industrial criticism of regulation, though directed specifically at the tsarist bureaucracy, was based on fundamental sources of opposition to state regulation.

One source of such opposition derived from the fact that, both under the old regime and after the February revolution, regulation was imposed by "outsiders": first the tsarist bureaucracy and later the intelligentsia serving in the public organizations and the Provisional Government.[124] Indeed, one of the complaints heard in the early months of the revolution was that the technical intelligenty in the democratized regulatory bodies were acting in the same high-handed fashion as their tsarist predecessors and paid no attention to the "men of experience" or the actual needs of commerce.[125]

[122] See the reports from the Congress of WICs' representatives to the regional factory conferences held in Moscow on May 8 and 9; from the Conference of Regional WICs held in Petrograd on May 23 and 24, 1916; from the meeting of the metallurgical section of the Central WIC on May 25; and from the conference hosted by the Rostov-on-Don regional WIC in the fall of 1917: *IzvMVPK*, 1917, no. 23/24:155–73; and *IzvTsVPK*, May 26, 1917 (no. 100), 2–4; May 28, 1917 (no. 101), 3–5; June 14, 1917 (no. 108), 2–4; and November 8, 1917 (no. 167), 3. See also Siegelbaum, *Politics of Industrial Mobilization*, 121–39.

[123] See especially the minutes of the debates in the congress's supply section and the plenary session dedicated to the question of supplies: *Pervyi vserossiiskii torgovo-promyshlennyi s'ezd*, 78–119, 183–231.

[124] For a discussion of the conflict during the war years between the technical experts and the merchants and entrepreneurs they sought to regulate, see Rieber, *Merchants and Entrepreneurs in Imperial Russia*, 398–404.

[125] One article said, for example, that the "agronomists and village teachers" running the thousands of local grain committees knew as little about the grain trade as

A related source of opposition was the hostility felt by merchants and many industrialists toward any grandiose design, certainly one that would directly affect their commercial operations. Groman and his plan were often the target of expressions of suspicion, contempt, and outright disgust with the intelligenty and their harmful "utopias."[126] Yet another aspect of this opposition was the conflict between "localist" and "centralist" approaches, which affected men of the intelligentsia as well as merchants. At the May Congress of Supply Committees, for example, Groman and the Central Supply Committee he headed were opposed by a coalition of merchants, bankers, and intelligentsia activists of consumer cooperatives and local self-governments. These groups did not question the need for public planning and oversight of food distribution, but they argued for decentralization and specifically contrasted the uselessness of Groman's grandiose plan to the immediate beneficial effects of "small deeds" by the men on the scene in the localities.[127]

All of these reservations notwithstanding, most commercial-industrial organizations gave guarded support to economic regulation in the early weeks of the revolution, partly because their members were suffering from the effects of the supply crisis, and partly because they expected that the regulatory agencies would reflect entrepreneurial interests and give the representatives of commercial-industrial groups an important role in the implementation of regulation.[128] If little was accomplished during this early

---

their tsarist predecessors, yet they treated the merchants with contempt and barred them from contributing their experience: "Again, the Grain Monopoly," FO, 1917, no. 15:1–3. The same complaint came up repeatedly in the leather manufacturers' explanation of their opposition to a state monopoly on leather, which they would otherwise have accepted as a necessary evil of wartime requirements. The public members of the new regulatory bodies were compared to the old *chinovniki* (tsarist bureaucrats), in that they thought only they knew what was good for Russia and trusted no citizen "who didn't sit on a committee." See reports of various meetings of the Association of Leather Manufacturers during May and June in VVOKZ, May 14, 1917 (no. 32), 242–45; July 1, 1917 (no. 35), 291–98; July 15, 1917 (no. 36), 311–14; and August 1, 1917 (no. 37), 343–46.

[126] *Pervyi vserossiiskii torgovo-promyshlennyi s'ezd*, 85–88, 183–90.

[127] See, for example, the statement by the congress's chairman, A. M. Berkengeim, in *Vserossiiskii s'ezd upolnomochennykh predstavitelei*, 237–39.

[128] See Tret'iakov's statement at the March 16 meeting of industrialists with Konovalov (*Den'*, March 17, 1917 [no. 11], 2; *VVP*, March 17, 1917 [no. 13]); his letter of March 23 to Konovalov (cited by Laverychev, *Po tu storonu barikad*, 198); and the petitions sent by the SSPPiT on March 5 and by Prodamet on March 21 to the minister of war (*EPR* 1:243–44, 246–47).

period, it was the result not so much of outright entrepreneurial opposition but of the fact that the existing agencies (that is, the special conferences on defense, fuels, transport, and supplies) were undergoing a process of reorganization involving a three-way competition for position and influence: the southern engineer-managers who had been put at the head of the conferences after the revolution; the university professors-engineers who were active in the public organizations; and the representatives of democracy who had just been co-opted into the conferences.[129]

There had been opposition to various specific aspects of regulation even during March and April, when Konovalov had been minister of trade and industry. The southern industrialists, for example, had advocated a "rationalization" of the economy but had objected to the setting of fixed prices on the coal they produced, and the grain merchants had never reconciled themselves to the grain monopoly.[130] But it was only in May, after the establishment of the coalition government, that major commercial-industrial organizations began voicing opposition in their trade publications to the very principle of state regulation of the economy. Their arguments usually focused on the soviet's participation in the government, as Riabushinskii did in a speech at the Second Congress of Trade and Industry: "In Europe, when the state intervenes in the sphere of [economic] life, it receives full control, and to this we do not object. We fear, however, that such control is impossible here from the point of view of its usefulness and expediency for the state as a whole, [especially] so long as the government itself continues to be controlled."[131] In regard to the issue of regulation,

---

[129] The southern engineer-managers supported central regulation, unlike the proprietary industrialists in the region. See the report by Priadkin to the Third Conference of Southern Industrialists, in *Tret'ia konferentsiia promyshlennikov*, 9–12. During the fourth congress of regional commissioners of the Special Conference on Fuels (May 12–14), K. V. Kirsh, a professor at Moscow University with ties to the public organizations and also the conference's commissioner for Moscow, and S. V. Bernshtein-Kogan, representing the point of view of the public organizations, repeatedly urged the conference's top officials—Pal'chinskii and Priadkin, who were both representatives par excellence of the southern engineer-managers—to hasten the process of democratization and decentralization. However, they sided with these officials in the decision to bar the soviet's representatives, led by S. G. Petrushkevich, from voting. The soviet's representatives then left the meeting in protest: *IzvOS*, 1917, no. 4:36–42. The same debates occupied the meetings of the conference's Constituent Congress of Regional Representatives, which took place in Petrograd from May 31 to June 2: *IzvOS*, 1917, no. 5:130–40.

[130] *FO*, 1917, no. 16:19, and 1917, no. 15:7–9.

[131] Quoted in Volobuev, *Ekonomicheskaia politika Vremennogo Pravitel'stva*, 35. See

then, more than to any other issue in dispute between workers and industrialists, the formation of a coalition government acted directly to end enterpreneurial willingness—already limited even under a bourgeois government—to submit to the regulation of economic operations by the state. Under these conditions, even the formerly progressive journal *Financial Life* now interpreted the soviet's continued advocacy of *kontrol'* of the economy as an intent to "establish the 'socialization' of factories and mills."[132]

Aware of this interpretation and perhaps even sharing it, the men who led the Ministry of Trade and Industry after Konovalov's resignation took the greatest care to balance their sponsorship of economic regulation with an emphasis on the specific and limited scope of the measures under consideration and sought to remove the representatives of democracy from the actual exercise of regulation and to place it instead in the hands of the organized representation of the industrialists themselves. Indeed, the two fullest statements of the Provision Government's position on regulation, submitted by the ministry's director, V. A. Stepanov, to the cabinet on June 8 called the idea of comprehensive regulation a "utopian adventure" and promised to entrust regulation to those who supported the principle of private enterprise, though Stepanov also pointed out that the country's economic collapse required the subjection of "private interests" to regulatory measures.[133]

The soviet's economists continued to push for the implementation of their plan at every opportunity and appeared at the many conventions of supply and regulatory specialists to advocate comprehensive economic planning and regulation.[134] During the First

also the ambiguous recommendation regarding the "syndicalization" of the metal industries in a letter of July 7 from P. A. Tikston, of the Union of Metallurgical and Iron Industries, to the Moscow metal factory. Although he considered voluntary syndicalization necessary and preferable to compulsory measures, Tikston warned that the promises of the Ministry of Trade and Industry that *kontrol'* over the syndicate would be minimal should not be trusted, because the government was subject to pressures from the left: *EPR* 1:185–87.

[132] "*Kontrol'*," *FZh*, 1917, no. 21/22:403–4.

[133] *EPR* 1:220–27. See also Stepanov's statement to a "private" meeting of the Duma on May 20, in which he argued for the value of regulation and attacked the workers for their "excessive" demands: Drezena et al., eds., *Burzhuaziia i pomeshchiki*, 61–65, 68–69.

[134] Among these conventions were the Congress of Supply Committees held in Petrograd (May 12–14), the Supply Congress in Moscow (May 21–26), and a congress of regional factory conferences in Petrograd (late May). See *Vserossiiskii s'ezd upolnomochennykh predstavitelei*; *Trudy Vserossiiskogo prodovol'stvennogo s'ezda*;

Congress of Soviets, the economic and labor sections further developed the details of the soviet's economic plan and stressed that compulsory syndicalization of whole industrial branches was to be the basic method of organizing the economy.[135] But the economists could not force the Provisional Government to go beyond the limited regulation indicated in Stepanov's documents. Pal'chinskii and Prof. N. N. Savvin, the technical experts who ran the Ministry of Trade and Industry, favored syndicalization but did not dare force it on the reluctant entrepreneurs, who had come to view it as merely another form of *kontrol'* and a threat to their proprietary rights.[136] If there was any chance of comprehensive central regulation, it lay in a socialist ultimatum to the Provisional Government, though for reasons that will be discussed later this option was never employed.[137]

TAKEN TOGETHER, all of these developments—the commercial-industrial opposition to regulation, its victory on this issue over the old coalition of Progressists and technical intelligentsia, and the failure of the socialist ministers to force the cabinet to adopt the soviet's economic program—could not but seriously damage the influence of the moderate socialists among the workers. The damage was the greatest among the most activist workers, who had been drawn to the factory committees and become personally concerned with the operations of their factories. These workers were among the first to break, at least temporarily, with the moderates' coalition strategy, and they did so precisely over the issue of regulation.

F. Cherevanin, "The Question of Organizing the National Economy and Labor at the Supply Congress," *RG*, May 24, 1917 (no. 63), 1–2.

[135] See the statements by Groman, Cherevanin, Bukovetskii, and Bazarov, and the texts of five resolutions proposed by these speakers and adopted by the congress, in *Pervyi s'ezd sovetov* 2:200–18, 231–32. Even the Bolsheviks could not object to this program, except to assert that it would not work unless the soviets assumed governmental power; see the statement and resolution of Vasil'ev, in ibid., 218–20. See also *NZh*, June 15, 1917 (no. 49), 3, and June 16, 1917 (no. 50), 3; *RG*, June 17, 1917 (no. 83), 3; and *Khronika* 3:71.

[136] A. Tiurbert, "Compulsory Trusts or Freedom of Entrepreneurial Agreements," *PiT*, July 22, 1917 (no. 26/27), 45–50, and idem, "From Prohibition to Compulsion (Syndicates)," *FG*, July 29, 1917 (no. 474), 8–9. A matter-of-fact report in a publication of the Moscow WIC told readers that syndicalization was "expected to be removed from the agenda" of the Ministry of Trade and Industry after the SSPPiT had expressed its opposition: *PSR*, August 15, 1917 (no. 12), 18–19.

[137] See B. Avilov, "The Socialist Ministers in the Struggle against Ruin," *NZh*, June 4, 1917 (no. 41), 1.

From the outset, the expectation that the socialist presence in the cabinet would force it to implement regulatory measures had largely accounted for the workers' support of coalition. Articles in the socialist press had played up these expectations and had repeatedly assured its readers that the soviet's economists were committed to an extensive program of regulation intended not only to improve the functioning of the exchange and supply system but also to redistribute the national financial burden.[138] Beyond such expectations, there was the economic crisis itself; the shortages that had caused chronic brief and limited work stoppages, as well as occasional longer shutdowns that affected entire factories, seemed to threaten workers with unemployment or at least reduced earnings.[139] Not only were workers anxious to see the state take measures to ease this situation, but they were naturally dismayed at finding themselves blamed for the decline in production and their wage demands rejected because of crisis. Here again, indisputable objective difficulties commingled with expectations and perceptions to heighten social estrangement and lead to actions that were bound to be perceived as hostile to entreprenuerial interests.

Most immediate was the response of the factory committees. In their desire to ensure the continuous operation of their factories, as well as to dispel suspicions, the committees began to expand their functions. They made efforts to ascertain the availability of fuel and raw materials for their factories and, where these were insufficient, to procure the necessary supplies. In other words, through the factory committees workers began to exercise *kontrol'* by engaging in tasks that were outside the sphere of "internal or-

---

[138] For examples of articles in the socialist press promoting these expectations, see N. Cherevanin, "A Question Requiring an Immediate Answer," *RG*, May 4, 1917 (no. 47), 1–2; and V. Bazarov, "The Present Anarchy and the Future Napoleon," *NZh*, May 24, 1917 (no. 30), 1. The workers of the Admiralty shipyard referred explicitly to the "financial program developed by the economic section" that they expected the socialist ministers to implement: *RG*, May 25, 1917 (no. 64), 3. See also the resolution adopted on May 29 by the Langenzippen workers, in *IzvPS*, June 3, 1917 (no. 82), 7, and the article on the evolution of workers' understanding of the connection between regulation, prices, and wages by B. Avilov, "The Struggle between the Conscious and the Destructive Principles," *NZh*, May 28, 1917 (no. 34), 1.

[139] In its attempt to explain that most shutdowns should not be considered lockouts, the Menshevik press contributed to the impression that production difficulties were the result of the supply crisis. See "On the Question of Closing the Factories," *IzvPS*, June 24, 1917 (no. 100), 7, and Iu. Chatskii, *Kapital protiv truda*, 5.

der" and tied directly to production. In factories in which wage demands had been rejected on the basis of insufficient funds or a declared bankruptcy, some committees claimed the right to inspect the owners' financial records.[140]

As historians have shown, the workers deemed such instances of *kontrol'* to be purely "defensive," in the sense that their aim was to secure the workers' livelihood and the gains they had made in March and April, not to take over the factories and establish socialism or an anarchist utopia.[141] Indeed, production difficulties had already been responsible for the appearance in April of *kontrol'* over supplies in the state-owned defense enterprises as well as the formation, in this sector, of organizations for the coordination of supplies.[142] In May, however, especially in privately owned industries, *kontrol'* was not merely a strategy for "survival" but also an expression of the workers' growing suspicion that these difficulties represented an intentional, perhaps even a collaborative, attempt by the industrialists to disrupt production.[143] V. M. Levin, one of the organizers of the First Conference of Petrograd Factory Committees (May 30–June 5), made those suspicions quite clear in an address to the conference:

[140] Examples of the forms *kontrol'* took in May and June appeared in *RD v mae-iiune*, 269–323; Amosov et al., eds., *Oktiabrskaia revoliutsiia* 1: 28–158 (which includes the protocols of the First Conference of Petrograd Factory Committees); *Fabrichno-zavodskie komitety*, 75-103, 212–25; *RG*, May 18, 1917 (no. 59), 3. Mandel, *Petrograd Workers and the Fall of the Old Regime*, 151, cites a study of eighty-four factories in Petrograd in which some form of *kontrol'* existed in May and June; it showed that in nearly 55 percent of these cases, *kontrol'* was still applied to the internal order, whereas only about 25 percent pertained to some aspect of production and less than 10 percent to factory finances.

[141] Smith, *Red Petrograd*, 145–49; Mandel, *Petrograd Workers and the Fall of the Old Regime*, 151–57.

[142] See the reports on the Conference of Representatives from the Factories of the Department of Artillery, in *RG*, April 9, 1917 (no. 27), 2–3; *IzvPS*, April 11, 1917 (no. 37), 2–3; and *Pravda*, April 9, 1917 (no. 28), and April 11, 1917 (no. 29); on the Conference of Factory Committees in State-owned Factories, in Amosov et al., eds., *Oktiabrskaia revoliutisiia* 1:31–37; and on the Congress of Executive Committees from the Factories of the Department of Navy, in *RG*, May 17, 1917 (no. 58), 2–3, and May 18, 1917 (no. 59), 3; and Amosov et al., eds., *Oktiabrskaia revoliutsiia* 1:37–43. See also the report on the work of the committee of the Petrograd gun factory, which for two months had been concerned with matters pertaining to the internal order of the factory and decided to oversee supplies only after learning that the factory had only a two-to-three-day supply of fuel: ibid., 57–60.

[143] The term "survival" is used by Smith, *Red Petrograd*, 145–49, in the course of his highly persuasive argument that the origins of *kontrol'* did not lie in anarchist or otherwise utopian ideas.

248

After the first weeks of the revolution, strange things began to happen. Here and there, in various factories there was no fuel, raw material, or money. More importantly, the administration took no steps to secure what was necessary. Everyone could see that this was an Italian [i.e., a sit-in] strike. . . . After all, it is no secret that an end to the economic dislocation is not in the interests of capital.

It was as a result of this situation and the suspicions it raised, according to Levin, that factory committees decided to take the matter of supplying the factories into their own hands.[144]

Another example of how the workers' suspicion of the bourgeoisie affected their perceptions of the economic difficulties was their reaction to the government's intention to "unload" Petrograd of as many as 100,000 workers. In mid-May, it was revealed that the government planned this unloading in an effort to ease food shortages in the city, protect essential industries from the German threat to Petrograd, and place them closer to the sources of fuels and raw materials.[145] The plan was supported in principle by the soviet's economists and by some labor organizations, though they considered it to be too ambitious and likely to result in enormous expenses, dislocations, and a weakening of the soviet's strength.[146] Most workers, however, believed the unloading was a "counterrevolutionary" scheme motivated by the "malicious intentions" of the industrialists and the coalition government. They contended that the supply crisis was the result of the "anarchic nature of capitalism," if not actually an effort by the industrialists and capitalists to "aggravate chaos," and they called for extensive regulation of entrepreneurial activity as the only effective means of ending the crisis. The unloading project also provoked workers to describe the bourgeoisie as parasitic, living off the revolution, while the workers were being called on to make all

[144] Amosov et al., eds., *Oktiabrskaia revoliutsiia* 1:112–14. Dmitriev, "Petrogradskie fabzavkomy."

[145] The plan had first been broached in 1916 and then appeared on the agenda of the Special Conference on Defense the next year: *ZhOS*, March 15, 1917 (no. 149), 252.

[146] For the opinion of the soviet's economists, see the report of Dalin's address to a meeting of the workers' section, in *IzvPS*, May 25, 1917 (no. 74), 3, and Dalin, "The So-called 'Unloading of Petrograd,' " *RG*, May 26, 1917 (no. 65), 2–3, and idem, "The Unloading of Petrograd," *NZh*, May 20, 1917 (no. 28), 1. For examples of qualified or full support from labor organizations, see A. Gust'ev, "The Unloading of Petrograd," *NZh*, May 14, 1917 (no. 23), 1, and resolutions adopted by the Congress of Factory Committees of the Naval Department and the Union of Draftsmen, in *RG*, May 31, 1917 (no. 68), 4, and June 6, 1917 (no. 73), 3.

sorts of sacrifices in the effort to keep up production. The workers argued that if Petrograd had to be unloaded, the first to go should be the speculators or the well-dressed idlers strolling on the Nevskii Prospekt or eating in fine restaurants—that would secure the food supply for the toilers of the city.[147] Thus, the unloading issue reflected the workers' sense of isolation from the better-off strata of the city and contributed to their belief that the Provisional Government and the bourgeoisie were conspiring to strip them of their achievements.

Well grounded or not, such perceptions drove some factory committees to undertake *kontrol'*. This response, however circumscribed, caused fundamental disagreements between the Mensheviks and those "responsible" workers on whom they had built their hopes. Even when the soviet's specialists on the economy and labor relations shared the workers' suspicions regarding the role of employers in disorganizing production—indeed, even when these suspicions were aired in the socialist press, encouraging the workers to blame every aspect of the crisis on the industrialists[148]—the ranking members of the soviet, including Mensheviks and Independent Internationalists, nevertheless refused to sanction the exercise of *kontrol'* by factory committees.

There were at least two major reasons for their opposition. First, former Liquidationists, like Groman and Cherevanin of the economic section, objected to the notion that workers could regulate industry on their own. Instead, they called for the establishment of governmental regulatory agencies in which representatives of workers', peasants', and soldiers' organizations, as well as cooperative associations, would cooperate with entrepreneurial and public groups. The second and by far the stronger objection, shared by all of the soviet's economists, was the belief that only comprehensive and coordinated regulatory measures could ease the effects of an economic crisis which they viewed as essentially structural in nature and a consequence of imbalances created before and during the war, even if these imbalances had been inten-

---

[147] The quotations are from resolutions by the Sestroretsk armament factory, the Baranovskii factory, the Kozhevnikov textile mill, and the Putilov gun shop: *RD v mae-iiune*, 280–81; *RG*, June 8, 1917 (no. 75), 3; Smith, *Red Petrograd*, 172. Also see the reports on the discussion of the project in the soviet's workers' section, in *IzvPS*, May 20, 1917 (no. 71), 4; *NZh*, May 19, 1917 (no. 27), 1; *Khronika* 2:169.

[148] See, for example, "On the Coming Conference of Factory Committees," *IzvPS*, May 30, 1917 (no. 78), 2, and "The Struggle against Ruin," *IzvPS*, June 2, 1917 (no. 81), 2.

tionally exacerbated by the entrepreneurs. Such measures would require the use of the state's apparatus, but—because they did not consider Russia ready for a socialist economy—even the Independent Internationalists (who were losing faith in the coalition strategy) insisted that their success was dependent on the cooperation of entrepreneurs.[149]

The political implications of the leadership's position became apparent during the First Conference of Petrograd Factory Committees. Two draft resolutions were proposed by the economists, describing economic regulation as a governmental task that required cooperation across class lines and assigning only a secondary role to the factory committees.[150] Most of the delegates, however, gave their support (297 votes in favor to 21 against, with 44 abstentions) to a resolution drafted by Lenin and presented to the conference by Zinov'ev. It demanded "immediate revolutionary measures" in all areas of economic life and demanded that these be implemented not in "bureaucratic" fashion but through "actual workers' *kontrol'*," a procedure that would necessitate a "transfer" of power to the soviet.[151] Although such steps were not yet supported by the Petrograd working class at large, it is worth noting that, three days earlier, the soviet's workers' section had concluded its discussion of the unloading project with a resolution (again inspired by the Bolsheviks) that branded the project "a bourgeois offensive" and declared that state regulation of the economy would be possible only when the soviet assumed all governmental authority.[152]

These votes were due only in small part to the direct influence of the Bolsheviks among the committees' membership and the

[149] *Vserossiiskoe soveshchanie*, 245–46; *RG*, May 12, 1917 (no. 54), 4; "On the Conference of Factory Committees," *IzvPS*, May 30, 1917 (no. 78), 2; "The Struggle against Ruin," *IzvPS*, June 2, 1917 (no. 81), 2; and the addresses of Cherevanin, Avilov, and Dalin to the First Conference of Petrograd Factory Committees, in Amosov et al., eds., *Oktiabrskaia revoliutsiia* 1:89–90, 95–96, 100.

[150] The draft resolution presented by Cherevanin, Dalin, Groman, and Bukovetskii simply called for the committees to be "drawn into participation" in the network of regulatory bodies, whereas the resolution by the Independent Internationalist Avilov gave them a specific role in overseeing individual factories and called for the formation of branch and regional unions of factory committees: Amosov et al., eds., *Oktiabrskaia revoliutsiia*, 90, 95–96.

[151] Ibid., 107–9. In addition, 45 delegates voted for a radical but vague Anarchist resolution, and 85 for the Revolutionary Defensist and Menshevik Internationalist call for "state regulation." Even with these votes included, the voting figures fall short of the total number of 568 delegates: ibid., 85.

[152] *IzvPS*, June 2, 1917 (no. 81), 4. See also *Khronika* 2:241.

workers' deputies. To be sure, some Bolshevik workers saw the issues in clear-cut fashion. As one of them told the conference, "If one wants to establish government *kontrol'*, then one has first to agree on the class composition of the government that will realize this *kontrol'*," and since coalition government was "more bourgeois than democratic," any regulatory measures it applied would consist merely of "self-regulation."[153] However, the activists of the factory committees in the early months of the revolution, even those most insistent on supervising managerial operations (especially in state-owned enterprises), were more likely to consider themselves Mensheviks or SRs than Bolsheviks.[154]

The Menshevik workers had their own ideas about the revolution's social makeup, and these ideas made the prospect of a "proletarian government" seem highly risky. The worker Tkachenko, for example, urged the delegates to the conference not to forget that the revolution was "bourgeois-democratic" in nature. The workers were the "architects and builders of a new life," but precisely this responsibility required special care in planning their strategy. Workers had to do what was necessary but avoid all that was premature, dangerous, or dysfunctional.

Kontrol' over production and distribution is not frightening. Government *kontrol'* and regulation are necessary . . . and we will realize them on the spot, in our [factories]. What is frightening is that *kontrol'* is being tied to the transfer of power to the soviets. They [Lenin and Zinovev] want to convince us that without the transfer of all power in the country to the workers and to democracy, neither actual *kontrol'* over production nor the equal distribution of goods among the population can be realized. Moreover, they act as if the workers could cope with these tasks without the support of all of democracy and against the obvious opposition of the big bourgeoisie and the intelligentsia.[155]

Tkachenko's fears, his manner of expressing them, and his sarcasm about the Bolshevik leadership all show him to have been a veteran of the Menshevik labor movement. But if at the outset of the revolution these fears had acted as a brake on the radicalism of most workers, this was no longer true by early June. For most of the committees' activists, including those who identified themselves as Mensheviks or SRs, all other considerations had by then

[153] Amosov et al., eds., *Oktiabrskaia revoliutsiia*, 105.

[154] According to Smith, *Red Petrograd*, 160–64, the process of reelection that eventually gave the Bolsheviks a majority on a large number of factory committees began only in June, accelerating toward the end of the month and in July.

[155] Amosov et al., eds., *Oktiabrskaia revoliutsiia*, 104.

paled in comparison with the problems caused by the economic crisis, the inaction of the government, and the failure of the soviet's leadership to implement *kontrol'* as they had expected of the socialists in the cabinet. At the conference, they expressed anger and exasperation at the economists' "naive" belief in the Provisional Government's ability to carry out regulation.[156] A worker named Nemtsov, from the Petrograd metal factory, declared that talk of expropriating the capitalists was premature but asserted that "life itself" had made *kontrol'* over production unavoidable. The executive committee's opposition to intervention by the factory committees seemed strange to him, and he went on to say that *kontrol'* in fact already existed and had been realized by the workers, especially now that owners had been getting ready to cut back production. He ended with the statement that "government *kontrol'* has not touched our lives" and that he would vote for the Bolshevik resolution because it reflected the reality that had developed in his and other factories.[157]

Thus, the Menshevik position on workers' control found no resonance among the workers themselves, however rational it may have been from an economic standpoint (and in fact, the call for central state regulation was made by Lenin as well). Although most workers had not yet resolved to fight for full power in their factories, nor in the country at large, the economic difficulties they experienced as well as their suspicions of the bourgeoisie had led them to conclude, first, that both economic and political survival required that the economy not be entrusted to the employers or the coalition cabinet, and second, that it was up to them to impose *kontrol'* on the entrepreneurs in their own factories. Over the summer months, workers in a growing number of factories expanded the scope of their *kontrol'*. Meanwhile, the increasingly frustrating attempt to overcome economic difficulties on the factory level pushed workers toward accepting the premise of the resolution adopted at the First Conference of Petrograd Factory Committees: that only a transfer of power to the soviets would enable them to deal with the problems and the attacks threatening their very existence as workers.

THERE can be no doubt that during May and June the workers' political attitudes began to change significantly or that economic

[156] Ibid., 97, 106.
[157] Ibid., 97.

developments and labor conflicts played a major role in making for the workers' growing militancy in industrial disputes as well as for the political radicalization of the most activist element in the Petrograd working class. But to what extent had the formation of coalition contributed to these processes? Or, put differently, to what extent was the transition from dual power to coalition responsible for the dramatic, if cumulative, transformation in the tenor of social relations? The answer appears clearest with respect to the issue of regulation. The participation of socialists in the Provisional Government raised the expectations of workers, but it also threatened commercial-industrial interests and reduced their willingness to see their operations monitored by the government. Finally, because the socialists were a minority in the cabinet and feared that the bourgeois ministers might resign, they could not force the cabinet to make a serious effort at regulating the economy. While no such effort was likely to have resulted in any considerable economic improvement so long as the war continued to burden the country's economy, for the workers it was the twin failures of the Provisional Government to end the war and cope with the economic crisis that provided the verdict on the strategy of coalition. For them, coalition seemed to threaten their very livelihood and reinforced their suspicion of the upper classes whether in or out of the cabinet.

As for the socialists, their presence in the cabinet forced them to bear much of the blame for the government's shortcomings, no matter how hard they fought to remedy them, and revealed the differences between their conception of the revolution and that of the workers. Moreover, as we shall see in the next chapter, participation in governmental affairs also left its mark on the Mensheviks, particularly on those who assumed positions in the "Menshevik" Ministry of Labor, and thereby limited the range of responses and policies they could endorse in a social situation that was rapidly undermining their political strategies.

The Menshevik Ministry of Labor: Socialists in a Coalition Government

A T THE BEGINNING OF MAY, the moderate socialists took on a new role which greatly expanded their sphere of activity, transformed their self-image, and changed their relations to their followers. They became ministers of state, had formal authority over certain areas of Russian life, and were expected to collaborate in formulating governmental policies. These socialists were well aware of the advantages and the pitfalls inherent in their newly acquired authority. They had now been provided with an opportunity to realize the aspirations of the masses in whose name they had entered the cabinet and on whose strength and support much of their own prestige rested. But they were now also responsible before their constituency for the policies and actions of the government. From the outset, these expanded possibilities entailed a degree of tension between the commitment to social ideals and the more immediate concern for the preservation of state and society. More fundamentally, participation in government and the sharing of its responsibilities were bound to strain the ambiguity inherent in the Menshevik self-image, particularly that of the Liquidationists, who saw themselves both as champions of the workers and as members of Russia's only truly "national" force, the intelligentsia.

In spite of the daunting aspects of national leadership, the Revolutionary Defensist leaders of the soviet took up their new duties with surprising confidence, relying on what they perceived were certain guarantees of success. First, there was the fact that the new cabinet included only those representatives of the bourgeoisie sufficiently "courageous" to work with the socialists in implementing the program of revolutionary democracy, as seen in the government's May 6 Program, which provided for the "protection of labor," the shifting of the tax burden to the propertied classes, and state *kontrol'* of the economy.[1] Second, the Menshevik Revolution-

[1] "The New Government," *IzvPS*, May 4, 1917 (no. 57), 1–2; "The Conditions Under which Our Comrades Joined the Government," *IzvPS*, May 6, 1917 (no. 59), 1–2; "Revolutionary Power," ibid., 3; "What Does the Provisional Government Want?" *IzvPS*, May 13, 1917 (no. 65), 3. The May 6 Program was printed in all the

ary Defensists who assumed responsibility for the Ministry of Labor—whose actions in the following months would be most critical to their party's stature among workers—believed that "the goal and the spirit" motivating their efforts were sufficiently close to the aspirations of organized labor to turn it into a genuine "workers' ministry."[2] Third, on the basis of their two-month experience in managing labor relations, they expected not only that the most pressing and justified demands of the workers could be made acceptable to the representatives of the bourgeoisie but also that the majority of workers would accept the limits imposed by the bourgeois nature of the revolution.

Within two months, however, the Menshevik Revolutionary Defensists discovered to their bewilderment and despair that a sudden escalation in the labor conflict, coupled with a drastic deterioration of the economy and a rapid disintegration of the state's administration, had made a shambles of their expectations. Plans for progressive labor legislation had ceased to be relevant in circumstances where labor conflicts, shortages of every kind, and collapsing markets had made the very survival of enterprises the real issue. Meanwhile, the dream of politically mature labor organizations was replaced by the nightmare of a seemingly unchecked workers' radicalism.

The conflict that emerged in June 1917 between the Revolutionary Defensists' expectations and the reality confronting them was the more painful because in many respects it was reminiscent of earlier experiences of defeat, particularly the Mensheviks' unsuccessful struggle against workers' militancy in 1913–1914. At that time, support for the Mensheviks had been eroding in the open labor organizations which they had painstakingly built in the years after 1905 and from which they had expected the development of a "mature," disciplined, and restrained labor movement. By 1912, these efforts had given rise to a popular workers' leadership of a generally Menshevik type. But during the next two years of increasing labor militancy (from the April 1912 massacre of workers in the Lena goldfield to the outbreak of World War I), workers had come to disregard the Mensheviks' counsel of caution, and eventually they not only drove the Menshevik leadership out of one labor organization after another but also replaced it with younger, more militant, and often Bolshevik leaders. The general strike in

newspapers; see, for example, *VVP*, May 6, 1917 (no. 49), 1. An English translation is in *RPG* 3:1276–78. *IzvPS* printed the government's program next to the executive committee's program.

[2] Volobuev, *Proletariat i burzhuaziia*, 196.

St. Petersburg which these new leaders sponsored in the early part of July 1914 was a grim reminder to all Mensheviks of how a radicalized working class might cause its own isolation and defeat.[3] Indeed, it was precisely this specter of social polarization and political isolation which the Mensheviks had set out to avoid in 1917 but which now seemed to reappear. In later years, all Menshevik memoirists would look at the months from June to October 1917 as the most spiritually distressing time in their years of political work.

How did the Menshevik Revolutionary Defensists respond to these difficulties and disappointments? The present chapter will examine this question through a study of the Revolutionary Defensists' three main areas of labor-related activity during the first term of coalition government in May and June: labor reforms, mediation of labor conflicts, and the organization of the working class. Significant differences will appear between the response of the former praktiki who had worked in the soviet's labor section, and who were concerned with organizing the workers and acting as their champions, and that of the former Liquidationists who staffed the Ministry of Labor, where the burden of their work was in *restraining* the workers' struggle, either in the name of principles worked out by the Mensheviks in years past (and invoked frequently in the ministry's legislative projects) or on the ground of the "state interest" of which the ministry's mediators were now the guardians. Still, the behavior of the Menshevik Revolutionary Defensists, both in and out of government, was bound to appear to workers as betraying the promises the soviet's leaders had made in joining the coalition. Indeed, the historical significance of the activities to be described lies not so much in the Revolutionary Defensists' achievements or their failures—for these were in line with the general course of events in the summer of 1917—but in the way these activities revealed both the amalgam of principles guiding the Revolutionary Defensists and the gap between these principles and the workers' urgent concerns.

Efforts at Labor Legislation

If coalition made any sense for the Menshevik praktiki, it was because coalition allowed them to take charge of implementing the labor reforms they had been advocating for more than a decade

---

[3] On the radicalization of workers in 1914, see Haimson, "Social Stability in Urban Russia," and Bonnell, *Roots of Rebellion*, 390–438.

both as a minimum program of improvements in the lives of workers and as the conditions necessary for the political maturation of the working class. The list of reforms to which they had committed themselves at the First Conference of Soviets was impressive and included not only the familiar slogans of past years—freedom of association, social insurance, labor inspection, labor exchange, conciliation boards—but also the now popular demands of workers to which the Mensheviks themselves had initially objected in the early days of the revolution: a minimum wage, an eight-hour workday, and unemployment insurance.[4]

To be sure, the usual note of caution had been heard even at the Conference of Soviets, and it resounded both at the Menshevik conference in May and in Skobelev's early pronouncements as the newly appointed minister of labor. Promises of far-reaching changes in workers' rights vis-à-vis their employers and provisions for extensive social protection of labor were tempered with reminders that the workers and the soviet must consider "questions of state," especially the complications created by the revolution's coinciding with war.[5] Moreover, because of their conviction that the war had the highest priority on the national agenda, the most cautious Mensheviks allowed old fears to surface even during this period of general optimism. This is clear from the resolution, "On the Labor Question," which was adopted by the Menshevik Conference in May, warning that the "enemies" of "democracy" could oppose the workers' interests to those of a beleaguered nation and even turn the soldiers (the "nonproletarian segments of democracy") against the working class should the workers pursue their demands to the point of "disorganizing the economy."[6]

At first, this tension did not seem to reduce the ambitions of the Mensheviks who joined the coalition government. When Skobelev held his first press conference as labor minister, he promised in the strongest words to develop and bring before the cabinet the legislation necessary to secure the workers' freedom to organize and pursue their economic demands, to protect them from unfair treatment by employers and from the vagaries of the labor market,

---

[4] *Vserossiiskoe soveshchanie*, 242–45, 247–48, 251–53.

[5] Ibid., 241–42; report from the Menshevik May conference in *RG*, May 12, 1917 (no. 54), 4; Skobelev's addresses to the soviet and to the Union of Glass Workers as reported in *IzvPS*, May 14, 1917 (no. 66), 2, and *RG*, May 16, 1917 (no. 57), 4.

[6] *RG*, May 12, 1917 (no. 54), 4.

and to meet their most deeply felt aspiration, to establish the eight-hour workday in law.[7] This program was influenced by concern for the limitations imposed by the bourgeois nature of the revolution and the conjuncture of war, but it was intended nonetheless to radically transform the conditions of labor in Russia and place them even beyond those of more developed European societies.

THE IMPLEMENTATION of the program required an enormous legislative and administrative effort, which began with the establishment of a Ministry of Labor (long advocated by Konovalov and activists of the labor department in his Ministry of Trade and Industry), the creation of an administrative structure, and the recruitment of personnel. Six departments were established: Labor Market, Worker-Employer Relations, Legislation, Labor Protection, Social Insurance, and Statistics, as well as a Special Commission on Labor Legislation, composed of workers and employers, and, somewhat later, three other committees on the distribution of the labor force, postwar demobilization, and labor conditions in state-owned enterprises.[8] From among the party's labor specialists, Dan selected (presumably in consultation with Skobelev) the departmental chairmen and the deputy ministers. Gvozdev was named deputy in charge of mediating labor conflicts; P. N. Kolokol'nikov, a deputy who assisted in mediation efforts but was primarily responsible for contacts with labor unions and with the Special Commission on Labor Legislation; and A. E. Diubua, a third deputy whose duties are not clear. S. Schwarz headed the Department of Social Insurance; L. M. Pumpianskii, the Labor Market Department; and I. M. Maiskii, just back from years of party literary work in emigration, was put in charge of the Department of Worker-Employer Relations.[9] Only the head of the Legis-

[7] *Nzh*, May 7, 1917 (no. 17), 3.

[8] Volobuev, *Proletariat i burzhuaziia*, 196, 213–14; *IzvPS*, June 14, 1917 (no. 91), 10; "Skobelev on the Distribution of the Labor Force," *IzvPS*, June 23, 1917 (no. 99), 12; "From the Ministry of Labor," *RG*, July 4, 1917 (no. 94), 3; and *SOZES*, July 26, 1917 (no. 4), 8.

[9] Schwarz has provided details on the manner of recruitment of these veteran *praktiki* into the ministry: interview no. 6, pp. 7–8. Some of the persons involved were identified in *Petrogradskii sovet*, 137; *EPR* 1:628; *RG*, July 23, 1917 (no. 114), 3. For biographical details on some of these men, see appendix 3. Neither Schwarz nor any of the other participants mention the possibility that Dan himself might become a minister in the coalition cabinet. This is consistent with his earlier expe-

lation Department, S. O. Zagorskii, was not a party member, though he was close to the Defensist SDs of the newspaper *Den'*.[10]

For all of this apparatus and the devoted efforts of its staff, the ministry's achievements fell far short of expectations, in the number of laws actually passed, the compromises that had to be accepted in exchange for even these laws, and, above all, in the implementation of the new measures. Key elements of the Menshevik legislative program, such as the eight-hour workday, the freedom to strike, the minimum wage, and unemployment insurance, were never enacted. The conciliation boards and labor exchanges were legislated only on August 5 and 19, respectively, and then left largely unrealized. Of the projected 400 exchanges, of which 90 were to be established "immediately," only 27 had been put in place by October.[11] Ironically, the two most important labor laws of 1917—the law on freedom of association and organization and the law on factory committees—had been passed under the sponsorship of Konovalov's Ministry of Trade and Industry in April and remained unchanged under the Menshevik ministry.

On July 25 and October 11, the Provisional Government did decree revisions in the laws governing workers' insurance in case of illness and the structure of local insurance councils, but it did not revise the law on accident insurance. Of the laws under consideration for the protection of labor, only that pertaining to women and children in night work was passed (on August 8), whereas a law regulating child labor was never enacted. The ministry did not even keep its promise to replace the old and mistrusted Factory Inspectorate with a labor inspectorate in which workers would participate along with state officials to ensure that entrepreneurial

---

rience as the party's principal organizer, strategist, and contact with the Duma delegation.

[10] Zagorskii had been deputy chairman of the Labor Department in Konovalov's Ministry of Trade and Industry and was transferred to the Ministry of Labor together with the whole department: *RPG* 2:727. In an article entitled "The Tasks of Labor Policy," in *Den'*, April 26, 1917 (no. 43), 1, he had expressed his conviction that any "bourgeois-democratic" government not only must provide for the complete equality of workers in their relations with employers, but also should intervene where necessary to protect workers from unfair practices, though he had also emphasized the overriding importance of "state interest."

[11] There was to have been an exchange in every town of at least fifty thousand inhabitants. The estimates of the number of exchanges to be established were given by Kolokol'nikov in his report to the Economic Council: *SOZES*, July 26, 1917 (no. 4), 9.

pressure did not compromise standards of safety, hygiene, or interpersonal relations.

How is this poor legislative record of the Ministry of Labor to be explained? Surely, the Menshevik labor program was not merely a ploy in the political struggle for the workers' support, as Soviet historians have charged.[12] This program had long been the ideal toward which the Menshevik praktiki believed Russian social democracy should strive. As members of the government, they felt that they were the fortunate ones chosen to realize a cherished socialist dream. However, of the four factors that eventually frustrated the Mensheviks' legislative program, three were outside of their control, the result of social and administrative circumstances under which they worked: the disorganization of the state apparatus, the employers' opposition to legally establishing those changes they had accepted ad hoc, and the general polarization of society that gradually made cooperative projects impossible. Only the fourth factor was of the Mensheviks' own making: their insistence on being a minority in the cabinet meant that their proposals could be voted down by the nonsocialist ministers.

Having just come into existence, the Ministry of Labor did not have a network of local agencies, and it lacked the administrative resources to develop one. Although a law signed on July 11 provided for regional and local commissars of labor, only twenty of the commissars were in place by the end of August.[13] Thus, the ministry was largely without executive power in the localities and could not even gather the data necessary for planning its work—problems that were particularly detrimental to projects depending on local agencies for implementation.[14] The plans for local labor inspectorates and labor exchanges (plans that had actually been initiated during Konovalov's ministry) were not ready for discussion until August.[15] The heads of several large exchanges that had

---

[12] E.g., Volobuev, *Proletariat i burzhuaziia*, 332.

[13] *VVP*, June 20, 1917 (no. 84), 2; July 9, 1917 (no. 100), 3; and July 19, 1917 (no. 108), 2; and *VMT*, 1917, no. 1/2:8–10, 45. The law called for forty commissars to be named "immediately."

[14] In explaining the shortcomings of the Ministry of Labor to the Economic Council on July 26, Kolokol'nikov stressed that the absence of local agencies "seriously inhibited the development of its activity": *SOZES*, July 26, 1917 (no. 4), 14. The ministry repeatedly asked local zemstvos and municipalities to share whatever information they might have that could help the ministry's work: *VVP*, June 2, 1917 (no. 84), 2, and June 21, 1917 (no. 85), 2; *IzvPS*, June 28, 1917 (no. 103), 7.

[15] For information on Konovalov's and the Mensheviks' positions on labor inspectorates and the project itself, see *VVP*, May 2, 1917 (no. 45), 3; "Factory In-

become operational at the end of the summer complained of the "impossibility of collecting information on the supply of and demand for labor," and the same difficulty beset the work of a later Committee on the Distribution of the Labor Force, which was attached to the ministry.[16] The efforts expended on the organization of an information network, local agencies, and the ministry's departments consumed much of the energy of the new officials and delayed work on legislative projects.[17]

In other ways, too, conditions in the summer of 1917 were not favorable to labor reform. By the time legislative projects reached the Special Commission on Labor Legislation for discussion, they had usually been rendered nugatory by the gathering industrial conflict or the general polarization of society. Indeed, the commission turned out to be the burial ground for many of the Mensheviks' most dearly held projects, such as laws on the freedom to strike, the eight-hour workday, the minimum wage, and unemployment benefits. The activists of the Ministry of Labor had hoped that their new authority would make the commission more hospitable to labor reforms than its predecessor in the Ministry of Trade and Industry had been.[18] But they soon discovered that labor reforms proposed by a socialist Ministry of Labor were mostly unacceptable to the industrialists. Moreover, when the Menshe-

---

spection," RG, May 7, 1917 (no. 50), 1–2, and August 23, 1917 (no. 140), 1–2. On the labor exchanges, see Vserossiiskoe soveshchanie, 306; "The Organization of the Labor Market," RG, March 30, 1917 (no. 20), 2. On the plans of the Labor Department in April, see DN, April 19, 1917 (no. 27), and RG, April 22, 1917 (no. 37), 3, and April 14, 1917 (no. 31), 2. The law on the exchanges was published in VVP, September 29, 1917 (no. 164); an English translation is in RPG 2:744.

[16] VVP, September 21, 1917 (no. 158), 3. The new committee was established in mid-June, after a month of squabbling between the ministry and the Special Conference on Defense; it was supposed to have a strong workers' representation and to be under the executive authority of the ministry, though its plans were to be coordinated with the projected Economic Council. The ambitious plans of the committee's early weeks were all abandoned because of its inability to collect the necessary information: VVP, June 20, 1917 (no. 84), 2, and June 21, 1917 (no. 85), 2; IzvPS, June 20, 1917 (no. 96), 8, and June 23, 1917 (no. 99), 12; SOZES, July 26, 1917 (no. 4), 9; RG, July 4, 1917 (no. 97), 3; Volobuev, Proletariat i burzhuaziia, 213–14.

[17] SOZES, July 26, 1917 (no. 4), 14.

[18] Both Pankov and Gvozdev had complained that cooperation between the representatives of the employers and those of the public organizations had left the workers in the minority on Konovalov's committee on legislation and had blocked legislation on unions, strikes, and the eight-hour workday. See RG, April 1, 1917 (no. 22), 3, and April 20, 1917 (no. 33), 2–3; Den', April 17, 1917 (no. 36); and Lozinskii, Ekonomicheskaia politika Vremennogo Pravitel'stva, 185–84. Schwarz and Kolokol'nikov had also been members of this committee.

viks ignored the employers' objections and brought up their projected legislation for approval by the cabinet, they often found that the Ministry of Trade and Industry had already succeeded in blocking the projects or inserting changes favoring the industrialists.

The Mensheviks had to contend with obstruction from the workers as well, and that was an even greater source of anguish. In many localities, workers prevented the establishment of labor exchanges because they objected to the rule of equal worker-employer representation on the committees entrusted with administering them.[19] Workers and industrialists alike rejected the ministry's program for unemployment insurance based on contributions from employers, workers, and the state and demanded that the state alone supply the necessary funds.[20] From the very beginning, Schwarz, who as head of the Department of Social Insurance was the author of this project, was at loggerheads with the workers who were active on the question of social insurance. He left a frank record of his efforts and the workers' objections to it, which shows how a man deeply committed to the workers' cause came to be considered by them as nothing more than "an artful and experienced bureaucrat in the service of the employers."[21] He also observes that, beyond the defeat of specific reform projects, the former Liquidationists involved in labor legislation lost support through their refusal to endorse the workers' escalating demands.

THE DEBATE over workers' insurance was characterized from the outset by the political overtones deriving from the long-standing

[19] Lozinskii, *Ekonomicheskaia politika Vremennogo Pravitel'stva*, 192.

[20] The draft legislation called for contributions amounting to 2 percent of wages from both workers and employers and 1 percent from the state; payments to the unemployed at two-thirds of the current local wage for unskilled workers; and management of the funds by labor unions, with minority representation for the Ministry of Labor. Opposition was expressed by workers at the Conference of Soviets, the First Congress of Soviets, and the August 23 meeting of the Special Commission on Labor Legislation. See *SRiSP*, 1917, no. 4:16–17; *Vserossiiskoe soveshchanie*, 303–4; *Pervyi s'ezd sovetov* 2:257; Shvarts, *Sotsial'noe strakhovanie*, 114–19.

[21] Cited in Shvarts, *Sotsial'noe strakhovanie*, 64, from a speech by Osipov, the Bolshevik chairman of the Petrograd Insurance Group, at the Second Petrograd Insurance Conference, August 21–23, 1917. Actually, the workers reversed their position after hearing Schwarz's argument that the government was already overburdened with payments to soldiers' families, but entrepreneurial opposition continued and doomed the project: ibid., 119–22; report from September 12 meeting of the SSPPiT, in *EPR* 1:209. For biographical details on Schwarz, the quintessential Liquidationist praktik, see appendix 3.

rivalry between the Mensheviks and Bolsheviks over control of the "sick funds" established by the law of June 23, 1912, to administer workers' sickness insurance. In the repressive conditions of the tsarist regime, the sick funds had provided unique opportunities for organizational efforts among the workers; indeed, the limits the law imposed on the funds created an issue around which workers could be mobilized. The Mensheviks had been the first to realize these opportunities, and they were in the forefront of the "insurance campaign" of 1912–1913.[22] Liquidationists like Schwarz and Baturskii (editors of the journal *Workers' Insurance*) had praised the new funds as ideally suited for the development of workers' self-activity and responsibility.[23] It was to the Bolsheviks, however, that the political fruits of the insurance campaign had fallen, because by the time a workers' delegation had been elected to the Petersburg Insurance Council, in March 1914, they had become aware of the funds' organizational value, had won the workers' support for their militant political program, and had attained a majority among the workers' representatives to the insurance council.[24]

The workers' group of the Petrograd Insurance Council was still under Bolshevik domination in 1917, as shown by the fact that the proposals of Schwarz and Baturskii were defeated by a margin of at least two to one at the insurance conference held on March 25 and 26 in that year.[25] Later, when Schwarz took his place in the Ministry of Labor as head of the Department on Social Insurance, he again encountered the hostility of the workers' group.[26] But this was not the only factor that doomed Schwarz's initiatives. In an effort to circumvent the group, he persuaded the soviet's labor section to convene a meeting of delegates from all of Petrograd's

[22] See Shvarts, *Sotsial'noe strakhovanie*, 15–17, and Korbut, "Strakhovaia kampaniia," for a discussion of the 1912 law and the campaign to change it.

[23] Shvarts, *Sotsial'noe strakhovanie*, 7; Schwarz, interview no. 5, pp. 77–78; Korbut, "Strakhovaia kampaniia," 98.

[24] Shvarts, *Sotsial'noe strakhovanie*, 18–34; Korbut, "Strakhovaia kampaniia," 94–100, 114–15.

[25] *Pravda*, March 28, 1917 (no. 19), 3; *DN*, March 26, 1917 (no. 17), 2, and March 28, 1917 (no. 19), 2; *IzvPS*, April 12, 1917 (no. 38), 10; and *Khronika* 1:123–24. See also Shvarts, *Sotsial'noe strakhovanie*, 43–45. There were 150 delegates at the conference, and they were said to represent 250,000 workers.

[26] Several of these encounters were reported in the Menshevik insurance journal, *Strakhovanie rabochikh i sotsial'naia politika* (Workers' Insurance and Social Policy). Schwarz used these reports in writing his account of the meetings: Shvarts, *Sotsial'noe strakhovanie*, 50–51, 60–62.

sick funds as well as from the Petrograd Bureau of Trade Unions. It was held on May 26, but Schwarz was unable to convince the delegates to adopt his proposals. On this occasion, and again before the workers' section of the First Congress of Soviets, in mid-June, it was only Schwarz's threat to resign that prevented the delegates from replacing his projects with ones he opposed on the ground that they violated the proper principles of workers' insurance.[27] Schwarz viewed the workers' demands as extremely short-sighted; apparently, he failed to see the symbolic and emotional force behind these demands.

Four issues dominated the discussions of illness, accident, and unemployment insurance legislation: who should contribute to the funds and how much; what the level of compensation should be; what categories of workers should be covered; and what should be the composition of the local and central bodies overseeing the funds. In general, both workers and employers wanted to have a majority, or at least parity, on the supervisory bodies, and both preferred not to contribute to the funds at all or to contribute the lesser part. In addition, workers wanted a high level of compensation and coverage for all workers, whereas employers wanted lower compensation for fewer workers. The positions of both sides, especially that of the workers, were not based on purely economic considerations. The "maximalist" slogans of the veteran insurance activists—for the workers' universal right to be insured and without contributing to the funds—derived at least partially from their loyalty to the Bolsheviks. Furthermore, for the majority of workers, these slogans were appealing because they embodied their expectations of the revolution as well as their response to the current labor conflict. Indeed, as the workers' suspicion of the employers mounted, so did their opposition to any workers' contribution to the insurance funds and their demand to have full control of the funds.[28]

[27] For reports on the meeting of sick-fund delegates, see RG, May 31, 1917 (no. 68), 3; Schwarz, interview no. 6, pp. 9–11; and Shvarts, Sotsial'noe strakhovanie, 49. On the meeting of the workers' section of the First Congress of Soviets, see Pervyi s'ezd sovetov 2:257–58; Shvarts, Sotsial'noe strakhovanie, 114–16.

[28] The most striking example of the workers' growing militancy in regard to the insurance legislation came out of the proposed changes in the structure of the Insurance Council. In one meeting of the council, on April 24, the workers agreed to the employers' proposal to divide the council into one section for sickness insurance (in which the employers' contributions were fixed and they were therefore willing to accept a workers' majority in the section) and one dealing with insurance against work-related accidents (in which the two sides would have equal represen-

Schwarz's own position, far more modulated and complex than that of either the workers or the employers, embodied three major considerations. His first concern was to create the conditions for workers' self-activity and responsibility for their affairs, and because of this he sought "full autonomy," meaning that the workers would both administer the sick funds and contribute to them. Otherwise, he argued, the workers could neither claim full authority nor develop a sense of responsibility. Second, Schwarz was determined to make his legislation "realistic," in the sense that no provision having purely symbolic value—that is, one that would not be operable under contemporary conditions—be included.[29] This principle, together with Schwarz's concern for fostering a sense of civic responsibility in the workers by forcing them to accept the limits imposed by the war and economic difficulties, underlay his opposition to the extension of insurance to the workers of small shops, which would have required an enormous organizational effort, as well as his objection to putting the full burden of paying for the insurance on the state. Finally, political considerations—specifically, the survival of coalition government—prevented Schwarz from threatening the cabinet with his resignation, as he had done in confrontations with workers, when the ministers voted to introduce changes he considered harmful to his carefully crafted projects.

The gap between Schwarz's perception of the insurance laws and that of the worker activists was wide indeed. Both were reacting to the circumstances of the summer of 1917 in ways that had been shaped by their past experience and their expectations of the revolution. Whereas the workers were driven by disappointment and suspicion of the bourgeoisie toward ever greater demands, Schwarz insisted that the workers had to accept limits, and these were derived from the ideal of the mature worker as developed by the Menshevik praktiki in the prewar years and now reinforced by the requirements of national responsibility and unity. Not even

tation). But by the time Schwarz presented this same project for discussion, on June 27, and 29 and July 1, it was rejected by both workers and employers. See *SRiSP*, 1917, no. 2/3: 26–28; *Pervyi s'ezd sovetov* 2:257–58; Shvarts, *Sotsial'noe strakhovanie*, 60–64.

[29] This concern was not unfounded. Social insurance in all its forms was radically expanded immediately after the Bolshevik seizure of power, but a year later none of the new provisions had been implemented, and in one report they were said to have served as a political program rather than as practical legislation: I. Rubin, "The October Revolution and Worker Legislation," *Rabochii mir*, November 7, 1918 (no. 16/17), 42–45.

the workers' clear opposition deterred Schwarz from his dedicated but ultimately hopeless struggle, which to him appeared as just another skirmish in the clash between Menshevik "realism" and Bolshevik "adventurism."

TAKEN as a whole, the legislative record of the Mensheviks in the Ministry of Labor revealed the interaction of two fundamental attitudes which were often in conflict. On the one hand, there was the Menshevik commitment to leading the workers to the assumption of new political tasks. Thus, the maturity developed by their activity in the sick funds was intended to prepare them for an independent political role in the era of bourgeois parliamentary democracy. It was a commitment that was perhaps as steadfast as it was futile; only it can explain the repeated struggles to pass legislative projects through hostile committees and cabinet meetings that would have made little difference under the prevailing conditions. On the other hand, there was the approach to revolutionary strategy in terms of historical stages. Their faith in this scheme, the concomitant conviction that there were dangers inherent in the workers' failure to conform to it, and their determination to prevent these dangers from materializing made men like Schwarz appear stubborn, condescending, and alien to the workers. This combination of dedication and paternalism had always marked the attitudes of Menshevik intelligenty toward the working class—and Schwarz was operating very much in that mold—but the revolution and the socialists' entry into the government had given rise to new attitudes, new images of their role, and these would be particularly fateful for the Mensheviks' position as mediators in labor conflicts, the subject to which we now turn.

FROM MEDITATION TO SELF-RESTRAINT

In the weeks before and after the Mensheviks joined the Provisional Government, there was little discussion of the principle of mediation which had been practiced for nearly two months with great success by the soviet's labor section. During the early part of May the labor section continued to mediate the five or six conflicts that came to its attention daily while also taking steps to establish a network of conciliation boards under the auspices of the labor unions and their central bureaus. In Petrograd, for example, a Central Conciliation Board had been established on March 30, and early in May a conciliation board for twenty-five chemical factories

267

of the Main Artillery Administration was organized.[30] The labor section was helped in this activity by the Ministry of Trade and Industry, which throughout April had also considered legislation for the establishment of a nationwide network of conciliation boards.[31]

Although the activists of the labor section could detect a change in the attitude of employers which made compromises more difficult to obtain, they attributed this change to the usually small size of the enterprises involved in the conflicts, and they drew comfort from the fact that the application of additional pressure had led to the resolution of most of the conflicts.[32] A case in point was the dispute between the Union of Laundresses and the Union of Laundry Owners, which had been the subject of unsuccessful mediation by the Central Conciliation Board in late April and had caused a short strike by the laundresses in the second half of May but had nonetheless ended, on May 25, with an agreement worked out by the labor section, which provided for an eight-hour workday, salary increases, and an "annual rest period."[33]

As they had done since the middle of March, the praktiki in the labor section looked into every conflict brought to their attention, usually agreed that the workers had a legitimate complaint, and made every effort to have the demands they considered justified met, though they often showed a greater enthusiasm for demands entailing the establishment of proper institutions and procedures in the factory than for those directed at immediate monetary gains. The Union of Industrial Employees, for example, was asked to withdraw a considerable portion of its economic demands but was supported in its struggle for the right to equal representation on the committees discussing hiring and firing.[34] In any event, voluntary mediation continued to be seen both as the most appropri-

[30] *RG*, April 5, 1917 (no. 23), 3, and May 5, 1917 (no. 48), 4.

[31] *RG*, April 23, 1917 (no. 38), 3.

[32] *IzvPS*, May 14, 1917 (no. 66), 4; *RG*, May 31, 1917 (no. 68), 4, and June 8, 1917 (no. 75), 3. In May, the labor section reported that almost every conflict that had come to its attention had been solved without further complication: *RG*, May 13, 1917 (no. 55), 3.

[33] *RG*, April 15, 1917 (no. 32), 3; April 29, 1917 (no. 43), 3; May 12, 1917 (no. 54), 4; May 17, 1917 (no. 58), 3–4; May 28, 1917 (no. 67), 4; and *IzvPS*, April 30, 1917 (no. 54), 4; and May 5, 1917 (no. 58), 6. See also *Petrogradskii sovet*, 137.

[34] *IzvPS*, May 5, 1917 (no. 59), 6; *RG*, May 4, 1917 (no. 47), 3; May 9, 1917 (no. 51), 4; May 10, 1917 (no. 52), 3–4; May 19, 1917 (no. 60), 3; and May 24, 1917 (no. 63), 4; and *NZh*, May 21, 1917 (no. 29), 3.

ate means of regulating the relations between labor and capital and as an effective way of improving labor conditions.

The only sign that the establishment of coalition government was affecting the Mensheviks' role as mediators appeared in a long editorial in the soviet's newspaper early in May that sought to explain the value of mediation.[35] It noted that, under "ordinary circumstances," conciliation boards played a "relatively insignificant" role and were rarely successful in solving the deep social contradictions "fundamental to the capitalist system." It was the situation of revolution simultaneous with war that made mediation so necessary and effective in Russia, for both workers and employers knew how destructive their respective "weapons"—the strike and the lockout—could be at such a time. The editorial hailed mediation not so much for its importance to class solidarity or for its potential in avoiding the isolation of the working class but rather for its salutary impact on the national wartime economy. If at first glance this difference seems merely semantic, in retrospect it is apparent that the changes in emphasis resulting from the establishment of coalition government, coinciding as they did with the escalation of labor conflicts, were crucial to the manner in which the Mensheviks practiced mediation. Within two months, three new features would give the task of mediation a significantly different character: the direct involvement of the Ministry of Labor in dealing with labor conflicts; the ministry's insistence that its mediation be binding; and a growing tendency to place the burden of concessions on the workers alone. From the workers' point of view, these new features could not but be seen as signs that the Mensheviks were moving from being the supporters of the working-class struggle for economic and civic betterment to becoming its opponents.

How DID the officials of the Ministry of Labor—all veteran labor activists, though mostly of the Liquidationist variety—allow themselves to be seen as the guardians of the bourgeois state? A partial answer is provided in the ministry's response to two labor conflicts in May that Skobelev later cited as having established the practice of "intervention in the struggle and interrelations of labor and capital."[36] The first of these conflicts, in the Donbas mining industry, was brought to the cabinet's attention by employers who were

---

[35] "On Conciliation Boards," *IzvPS*, May 6, 1917 (no. 33) 2.
[36] *Pervyi s'ezd sovetov* 1:231.

seeking the help of the government in resisting the workers' demands for higher wages. The cabinet asked the Ministry of Labor to mediate. During a cabinet meeting on May 10, Skobelev angrily denounced the industrialists' appeal as an expression of "class egotism." He said that the workers of the Donbas had shown great readiness to negotiate and compromise, though their demands had been based on a "completely legitimate" effort to attain "the true value of their labor" hitherto denied them, whereas the employers' intransigence had been particularly unjustified in view of their unusually high wartime profits.[37] In this first instance of Menshevik mediation in the name of the government, the sympathies of the Ministry of Labor clearly lay with the workers, especially because the workers' position was strongly supported by fellow Mensheviks in the soviet's economic section, who helped the delegation of Donbas workers to present its case to the mediation meetings held by Deputy Minister Gvozdev between May 17 and 24.[38] Gvozdev urged the workers to confine their wage demands to the establishment of a higher minimum wage (four rubles) for the lowest-paid workers, but by all indications no undue pressure was put on their delegates, and Gvozdev's purpose in asking for concessions was to secure a compromise satisfactory to all.[39] In the end, this first attempt at mediation on the ministerial level proved a failure, and though at Skobelev's suggestion a special commission was created to study the conflicting claims and to attempt to reach some solution, the two sides remained unreconciled and the Donbas conflict continued for the rest of the year.[40]

The second conflict cited by Skobelev for its impact on the conduct of the Ministry of Labor was resolved in a way that was reminiscent of many earlier, successful mediation efforts by the labor section but was also symptomatic of future problems. This conflict resulted from demands the Union of Industrial Employees (representing some fifty thousand industrial employees, mostly from

[37] *NZh*, May 12, 1917 (no. 21), 3; *IzvPS*, May 13, 1917 (no. 65), 2–3; and *Khronika* 2:136–38.

[38] *RG*, May 17, 1917 (no. 58), 3, and *NZh*, May 24, 1917 (no. 30), 1.

[39] Volobuev, *Proletariat i burzhuaziia*, 211–12, depicts Gvozdev as having given in to the industrialists, but an article in *Den'*, May 25, 1917 (no. 67), 1, which criticized the Ministry of Labor for failing to force the workers into even greater concessions, appears to have been closer to the mark.

[40] The mediation meetings and their outcome were reported in *IzvPS*, May 24, 1917 (no. 73), 7; in a letter of May 24 from the Donbas industrialists to the Provisional Government, reprinted in *EPR* 1:174; and in Skobelev's report to the First Congress of Soviets, in *Pervyi s'ezd sovetov* 1:231.

metalprocessing plants) had presented to the PSI at the end of April. The soviet's labor section had attempted to mediate but had failed, and the ministry's involvement began when the employees threatened to strike and appealed to Skobelev to use his ministerial authority to force the owners to settle. Skobelev was anxious to avert a strike that could have paralyzed many important factories, but he chose to use persuasion rather than exercise his formal authority. To this end, he first had Gvozdev convince the delegates' assembly of the industrial employees to reduce their demands to an eight-hour workday (they had originally sought a six-hour day!) and certain "constitutional" changes. Then he himself secured the PSI's approval of a settlement on those terms.[41]

In the weeks following, the Ministry of Labor continued to undertake the mediation of labor conflicts whenever a strike that could endanger military production or the economy in general seemed imminent.[42] Whether invited by the workers—or, as increasingly became the case, rejected by them—the ministry's mediation was the direct result of the national responsibility the Menshevik Revolutionary Defensists had formally accepted when they joined the government. Speaking for the praktiki in the Ministry of Labor, Kolokol'nikov explained in late July that, though they viewed government intervention in industrial conflicts as "rarely permissible," they had made such intervention "the center of the ministry's activity" because of the "exceptional conditions" of the moment. According to him, the ministry had dealt with no less than 100 conflicts during its first month of existence, out of 557 that had been brought to its attention.[43]

Moreover, the sense of national responsibility that motivated the Mensheviks to involve the ministry in the mediation of labor conflicts also prompted them—though not as soon or as noticeably—to forsake their earlier belief in voluntary mediation and to introduce instead the notion of binding arbitration, because the Revolutionary Defensists had come to view both the workers' struggle

[41] *IzvPS*, May 5, 1917 (no. 58), 6; *RG*, May 4, 1917 (no. 47), 3; May 9, 1917 (no. 51), 4; May 10, 1917 (no. 52), 3–4; May 19, 1917 (no. 60), 3; and May 24, 1917 (no. 63), 4; *NZh*, May 21, 1917 (no. 29), 3.

[42] In his report to the First Congress of Soviets, Skobelev noted that the administration of relations between labor and capital "has taken up all of the time not only of the head of the [appropriate] department and of Deputy Minister Gvozdev . . . but also all that which I have been able to give to the ministry": *Pervyi s'ezd sovetov* 1:230.

[43] *SOZES*, July 26, 1917 (no. 4), 6–7.

for economic betterment and the employers' unbending rejection of the workers' demands as dangerous to the "national interest." The intractability of the employers became apparent during the Donbas conflict, when Skobelev failed to obtain the employers' assent to terms even he himself had considered compatible with the national emergency. Their rejection amounted to a negative judgment of the concept and practice of voluntary mediation, which had served the labor section well for two months and had enabled it both to satisfy the workers' most urgent needs and to nurture the fragile truce in the factories. During June, voluntary mediation still yielded some successful results: of the one hundred conflicts dealt with by the ministry, seventy-two were settled almost immediately.[44] But it was perhaps more significant that the conflicts that were not immediately resolved began to undermine the ministry's authority among workers, because of its failure to force settlements on the employers, and diminished the workers' readiness to accept mediation, which in turn pushed the minister of labor to insist ever more strongly that workers *must* accept his mediation in crucial labor conflicts.[45]

The dispute at the Sormovo metallurgical and mechanical factories illustrated all these developments. In that case, the Ministry of Labor on June 20 declared "the impermissibility from a national and state point of view of idling such a huge factory" and called on both sides to negotiate under its auspices. Ten days later, the negotiations having failed, Skobelev appealed to the workers to submit the case to binding arbitration and return to work. They not only rejected his appeal but refused to participate in the mediation any longer and instead launched a strike and called on Skobelev to take "radical measures" to end it. The ministry replied that those who refused its binding arbitration would be held responsible for the strike and its economic consequences.[46]

However, the only force behind "binding" arbitration, as behind voluntary mediation, was the socialists' moral authority among the workers. The ministry did not have the means of enforcing its

[44] Ibid. See also the reports of successful mediation efforts by Gvozdev in *RG*, June 29, 1917 (no. 93), 3–4, and of the ministry's success in resolving the conflict at the V. A. Lebedev aviation factory in *RG*, July 13, 1917 (no. 105), 3.

[45] *RG*, July 8, 1917 (no. 101), 2.

[46] *EPR* 1:477–80. Not until late July was the strike terminated (and even then the issue of pay for strike days remained unsettled). The Menshevik newspaper gave credit to the Ministry of Labor's commissar for having brought the strike to an end: *RG*, July 27, 1917 (no. 117), 4.

presumed authority nor would the veteran labor activists have consented to forceful measures. The Ministry of Labor had repeatedly made attempts to have the workers' right to strike fixed in law.[47] On the other hand, Skobelev had succeeded on more than one occasion during cabinet meetings in forestalling pressure from the Ministry of Trade and Industry to place a ceiling on workers' earnings by insisting that the government's only proper action lay in appealing to the workers "in the name of the revolution" for "self-restraint."[48] By late June, however, the Mensheviks in the Ministry of Labor had come to view their authority as resting not only on their championing of labor's rights but also, and more significantly, on their responsibility as government ministers.

This striking shift of self-image was accompanied by a third change, one that was even more crucial to the relations between the Mensheviks and the workers. Whereas in their early efforts the ministry's mediators had alternately upheld and attempted to restrain the workers' demands, as they had done when they were members of the soviet's labor section, by the second half of June their emphasis was on restraint. That was the essence of an appeal to the workers that Skobelev delivered on June 28. In addition to summoning the workers to help the government fight the economic crisis at this "critical moment of the revolution" by curbing their demands for the sake of "our final goals," Skobelev sharply condemned those workers who conducted their struggle "without consideration for the condition of the enterprises involved" or the impact this struggle had on "disorganizing industry and depleting the treasury." Moreover, he insisted that irresponsible demands and an "unorganized struggle" (that is, outside the channels es-

[47] A modified bill, restricting the right to strike only of soldiers and workers whose work was "essential for the safety of the state and society," was finally approved by the Ministry of Trade and Industry, but it was defeated in the full cabinet; see Tal', *Ocherki promyshlennogo rabochego prava*, 208–9; Auerbakh, "Revoliutsionnoe obshchestvo," 15; and *VMT*, 1917, no. 1/2:26–28. When the fight to pass the legislation was at its peak, *Rabochaia gazeta* exhorted the workers to demonstrate its support and called on the Mensheviks in the newly elected local governments to ensure this freedom for the workers: "The Industrialists against the Freedom to Strike," *RG*, July 1, 1917 (no. 95), 2; B. Nikolaevskii, "The Freedom to Strike Must Be Secured," *RG*, July 9, 1917 (no. 102), 3.

[48] In May, Skobelev blocked Konovalov's last-minute effort to impose governmentally enforced limits on the workers' "excessive appetites": *NZh*, May 18, 1917 (no. 26), 4. The next month, along with Gvozdev, he engineered the cabinet's rejection of Pal'chinskii's proposal that a ceiling be placed on the wages of unskilled workers in defense-related production: *EPR* 1:546; Volobuev, *Proletariat i burzhuaziia*, 207–8.

tablished by the trade unions) were damaging to the labor movement and were particularly "intolerable" in view of the workers' having achieved "complete freedom" to organize.[49]

Some contemporaries, workers included, saw Skobelev's appeal as proof of his capitulation to the industrialists,[50] though it seems clear that the principal concern of Skobelev and the other Mensheviks in the Ministry of Labor had not been so much to appease their rivals in Trade and Industry as to contain the labor struggle within the confines of what they themselves deemed essential for the preservation of both the country and the revolution. This concern was particularly aroused by the responsibility they felt for the desperate "objective" conditions of the country. But other Mensheviks, among them the praktiki in the labor section, supported the ministry's policies largely because of the important position that proletarian self-restraint had always held in the Menshevik conception of revolution.

To SKOBELEV and his colleagues in the Ministry of Labor, proletarian self-restraint was also necessary because without it the country and the revolution for which these men were now formally responsible could not survive the trials of war and economic crisis. From the middle of May, just a few days after the establishment of coalition, Menshevik mediators, especially those associated with the Ministry of Labor, had tended to judge the workers' demands not only from the point of view of the legitimacy of the demands at the present historical stage but also according to the economic capacity of Russian industry and the general needs of the country. When the representatives of the labor section had sought the support of the soviet's executive committee for the soldiers employed in the factories of the Artillery Administration in their struggle for a minimum daily wage of five rubles instead of three, Bogdanov and others on the committee objected that this would lead to similar demands from all soldiers employed in industry and place an unbearable burden on the treasury.[51] Skobelev explained to the Third Conference of Trade Unions in late June

[49] *VVP*, June 28, 1917 (no. 91), 3.

[50] One commentator noted that Skobelev had directed his demand for sacrifice only to the workers and not to the industrialists: Volkov, "The Appeal of the Minister of Labor," *NZh*, June 29, 1917 (no. 61), 2.

[51] The issue was discussed by the bureau of the executive committee on May 16 and by the full committee on May 23, but it was not settled. See *Petrogradskii sovet*, 158–59, 240–41, and *RG*, May 27, 1917 (no. 66), 4.

that the country was exhausted by the war and "did not possess the resources to effect any real or significant improvement in the living conditions of the workers."[52]

This position obligated the Mensheviks in government to try to determine the objective limits within which they could support the workers' demands. They wanted, as Skobelev put it to the First Congress of Soviets, to be able to tell the workers "in clear conscience": "Here, within such limits it is possible to improve [your] economic situation but beyond these begin the interests of the state, the interests of the whole. We cannot, as the guardians of the interests of the state, allow their destruction and we therefore openly insist: curb your demands!"[53] Toward this end, the Ministry of Labor established commissions of inquiry, as in the case of the Donbas conflict and that of the soldier-workers of the Artillery Administration. This notion of well-defined limits imposed on the workers by the country's economic capacity underlay the Mensheviks' frequent exhortations for self-restraint and sacrifice "for the sake of the revolution" or for "the sake of liberty."[54] Of course, the call for sacrifice was addressed to all Russians, including—and especially—the owners of property,[55] but because the Mensheviks had agreed to join the government as the workers' leaders, it was they who had to ask the workers for self-restraint and sacrifice and who had to make it (as Tsereteli later said) "an essential part of the economic policy of democracy during the period of coalition government."[56] Thus, in their capacity as state officials, the Menshevik Revolutionary Defensists were demanding of the workers the material sacrifices that the cabinet as a whole repeatedly advocated but failed to force on the commercial-industrial class.

Proletarian self-restraint was a concept of long standing among the Mensheviks, ever since December 1905, and was urged on the workers with particular vehemence, even despair, whenever the labor struggle appeared to outstrip the employers' readiness for

---

[52] *TKPS*, 53.

[53] *Pervyi s'ezd sovetov* 1:231.

[54] See, for example, Tsereteli's appeal to the employees of his Ministry of Post and Telegraph, in *RG*, May 10, 1917 (no. 52), 2; Skobelev's address to the Union of Glass Workers on May 11, in *RG*, May 16, 1917 (no. 57), 4; and Vainshtein's address to the workers of the Obukhov factory on May 28, in *RG*, May 31, 1917 (no. 68), 4. See also "The Immediate Task of the Working Class," *IzvPS*, May 14, 1917 (no. 65), 3; *Den'*, May 14, 1917 (no. 59), 3; and *RG*, May 16, 1917 (no. 57), 4.

[55] See, for example, "On Two Fronts," *IzvPS*, May 20, 1917 (no. 71), 2.

[56] Tsereteli, *Vospominaniia o fevral'skoi revoliutsii* 1:442. See also Voitinskii, "God pobed i porazhenii," 110–11.

concessions or had threatened the working class with isolation. The period of increasing labor militancy in 1912–1914 and the first days of the February revolution were cases in point.

At the very beginning of their work in the cabinet, the Mensheviks had been reminded by Liber (a former Bundist, then a Revolutionary Defensist and a close associate of Tsereteli) that the danger of isolation was not past, nor was the dictum of self-restraint irrelevant. In a speech on May 9, he had gone further and declared that Menshevik policies had to avoid the "danger of 1905."[57] Indeed, by the end of May, Liber's observations had become even more pointed, and the Menshevik press and those praktiki whose activity had been centered in the soviet's labor section seemed filled with anxiety about an "entrepreneurial offensive" against the workers, about political isolation, and about the possible repetition of the 1905 disaster.[58]

Expressing the fears of the praktiki, Garvi warned that the "united industrialists" had given up their earlier conciliatory stance, had assumed a "defensive" position, and were preparing to attack the proletariat.[59] The bourgeoisie's best weapon against democracy, he added shortly afterward, was the isolation of the proletariat, and so he urged the workers to do everything possible to prevent the bourgeoisie from turning against the revolution. "The salvation of the revolution," he emphasized, "does not require that the proletariat give up its class goals" but that it "unconditionally subsume group interests to the general interests of the class and the demands of the moment to the general tasks of the revolution." The proletariat must look beyond the shortsighted attitude characterized by the phrase, "may it be mine if only for an hour." This attitude, he and others argued, was leading some workers to take over their factories and, even more often, to engage in an unorganized, unrestrained struggle for the realization of their demands—practices that had already contributed to economic ruin and would create "favorable conditions for the entrepreneurs to carry out their planned offensive."[60]

[57] Gol'dman-Liber, *Zadachi rabochego klassa*, 54–55.

[58] References to 1905 were made in a speech by Vainshtein, reported in *RG*, May 31, 1917 (no. 68), 4, and in the article "On the Question of Factory Closings," *IzvPS*, June 24, 1917 (no. 100), 7.

[59] "The Offensive?" *RG*, May 20, 1917 (no. 61), 1. Although unsigned, this editorial can safely be attributed to Garvi because of the great similarity it bears to the introduction he wrote in June 1917 for his 1914 leaflet, *Kapital protiv truda* (Capital against Labor).

[60] Garvi, "The Beginning of the Break," *RG*, May 24, 1917 (no. 63), 2–3, and M. Kheisin, "Organization and the Right of Seizure," *RG*, June 4, 1917 (no. 72), 2.

To the praktiki and other Mensheviks, the need for proletarian self-restraint followed directly from the conception that the revolution required a degree of cooperation between the working class and at least the most progressive segments of the bourgeoisie. Both the counterrevolutionary tendencies of the bourgeoisie and the working class's potential for extremism could threaten the completion of the revolution.[61] The impulse of the Mensheviks, both in the labor section and in the ministry, was to express their anxiety about the workers' behavior in the same terms they had used under similar circumstances in the past, and to propose the same solutions. In 1913 and 1914, they had explained workers' extremism and the Bolshevik takeover of labor organizations created by the praktiki as the result of new recruits from the countryside having entered the labor force and retarded the development of political consciousness among the workers.[62] Similarly, in the course of June 1917 and especially in the following months, the workers' failure to heed the counsel of self-restraint was ascribed to their political immaturity, particularly on the part of those who had joined the industrial labor force during the war.[63] Suitable examples were not lacking.

At the Lebedev aeronautical factory, the workers decided on June 2 to dismiss the director and take over the factory, but the next day they were told by their factory committee that it was unable to operate the plant for lack of technical skill and money to buy raw materials. The workers subsequently explained that their earlier resolution to take over the factory "should not have been understood the way it was written"; they had wanted merely to oversee production and had taken over the factory only because this was what they thought the workers of Sestroretsk had done. This explanation was noted with ridicule and some satisfaction in

[61] The publication in June 1917 of Garvi's formerly suppressed leaflet *Kapital protiv truda* was symptomatic of the return of the Menshevik praktiki to their earlier concepts and strategies. Written in 1914, this leaflet listed all the Menshevik arguments in favor of restraint and discipline.

[62] See, for example, G. Rakitin [pseud. of V. Levitskii-Tsederbaum], "Rabochaia massa i rabochaia intelligentsiia," *NZ*, 1913, no. 9, 52–60; B. I. Gorev, "Demagogiia ili marksizm?" *NZ*, 1914, no. 6, 30–41; L. M. [Martov], "Otvet Bulkinu," *NZ*, 1914, no. 3. See also Haimson, "Social Stability in Urban Russia," 23:629–39.

[63] See, for example, "How Bolshevik Agitation Is Understood by the Masses," *RG*, June 13, 1917 (no. 79), 1–2; and Garvi, *Professional'nye soiuzy v Rossii*, 12, in which he uses the wartime changes in the composition of the working class to explain "the ease with which the working class fell prey to the social and political demagoguery of the Bolsheviks."

the Menshevik press.[64] Reporting on the dispute at the Putilov works, the Menshevik newspapers pointed out that it was the organized and "responsible" workers from the factory and shop committees, the Union of Metalworkers, and the Central Bureau of Petrograd Unions who had supported Skobelev's insistence (at a meeting on June 22) that no strike take place while collective bargaining was in progress and that demands for higher wages be complemented with increased productivity, whereas the unskilled (and underpaid) workers had been the ones to declare a strike anyway.[65]

In their eagerness to salvage the conception and strategies on which their work over the past decade had been based and to make sense of the events around them, the Menshevik Revolutionary Defensists were quick to seize on such examples of the discipline and self-restraint of the more highly "conscious" workers and to attribute the increasingly numerous instances of militancy to the recently arrived, unskilled, unorganized, and therefore "less conscious" workers.[66] What these Mensheviks failed to note, however, was that the activists of the factory committees as well as the organized metalworkers had also begun to assert not only that workers tend to their productivity, but also that a workers' takeover of the whole economy (rather than of single factories) was urgently required. For example, the Putilov meeting of June 22 declared that the economic crisis could be resolved only when the workers controlled production and distribution, which required that power be transferred to the soviets.

IN THEIR EFFORTS to manage industrial conflicts, as in their work on behalf of labor reforms, the Mensheviks found themselves unable to support the aspirations and demands of most Petrograd workers and thus in opposition to their own constituency. This opposition followed more or less directly from the position Menshevism had always assumed as a party of the intelligentsia dedicated to the advancement of the interests of the working class. The

[64] "Don't Understand It the Way It Is Written," *RG*, June 6, 1917 (no. 73), 2.

[65] *RG*, June 17, 1917 (no. 83), 3, and June 24, 1917 (no. 89), 4; *IzvPS*, June 24, 1917 (no. 100), 11; June 27, 1917 (no. 102), 14; and July 2, 1917 (no. 107), 8. Also see *RD v mae-iiune*, 320–21.

[66] See *RG*, June 1, 1917 (no. 69), 4, for any appeal by the Union of Metalworkers to its membership to avoid "excessive" demands and an unorganized struggle, and for I. Kubikov's enthusiastic endorsement of this appeal and of a similar one by the Union of Printers.

Mensheviks' role as the workers' political guides and the lessons they had derived from past political experiences continued to reinforce their conviction that moderation was the only responsible course. As the industrial conflict escalated, the urgency of this imperative came to be felt more strongly, even as it was clearly running against the workers' mounting belligerence. In short, the social conditions of June 1917 did not provide a hospitable environment for the Mensheviks' favored strategies, nor had the political arrangements of the time allowed them sufficient flexibility. The acumen of the praktiki and their commitment to the cause of the working class had helped to avoid an open conflict between the soviet's leaders and followers in March and April, but by May and June the Mensheviks' freedom of action had been greatly reduced as a consequence of the responsibilities they had assumed in joining the cabinet.

As we shall see further in the next section, the Revolutionary Defensists' two commitments—to the working class and to the national revolution—often came into conflict, and they led to important disagreements between the groups of Mensheviks whose areas of work bore directly on one or the other of these commitments. More important than these differences, however, was the fundamental agreement on the nature of the revolution, especially on what it *could not be*, which would hold the Menshevik party together and make all Mensheviks responsible for the Provisional Government.

THE THIRD CONFERENCE OF TRADE UNIONS

The Mensheviks' remedy for workers' extremism was organization. The plea for organization had been used during the early days of the revolution to draw workers into the soviet and increase its authority, and in later months organization was a significant element in the general call for self-restraint. Its specific forms had become not only an essential part of the Menshevik fund of revolutionary strategies in the years following 1905 but also a basic distinction between themselves and their Bolshevik rivals. The notion of "open" labor organizations run by workers themselves had been developed by Menshevik activists in Russia in response to the newly legal possibilities for organizing workers in the aftermath of the 1905 revolution and had become closely tied to the Menshevik concept of a disciplined, civically responsible labor movement modeled after the mature European labor movements, particularly German Social Democracy and its unions. The open labor organizations were expected to serve not only as barriers to the potentially extreme, spontaneous labor struggle but also, through the experience of self-management and democratic procedures, as "hothouses for cadres of a [genuine] workers' leadership" or as "schools for socialism."[67]

The theme of organization resurfaced as a major concern of the Menshevik praktiki toward the end of March 1917, when a number of them returned from exile, notably Schwarz, Garvi, and D. Kol'tsov. In the articles, leaflets, and resolutions they submitted to the Conference of Soviets, these returnees, and other praktiki who had spent the war years in Petrograd, emphasized the singular quality of labor unions among other forms of organization and specified the "correct" form that unions should take. Only trade unions, they argued, could correctly organize the workers' economic struggle. They acknowledged that political parties, soviets, and factory committees were all important in the mobilization and unification of the working class but emphasized the necessity of separating the workers' economic struggle from their political goals and waging this struggle in the interests of the working class at large. To properly fulfill this function, broadly based workers' organizations were needed, and for that reason, unions had to become the primary form of organization, had to be structured on an industry rather than a trade basis, and had to submit to the guidance of citywide "central bureaus."[68] Evident in these formulations was both the Mensheviks' insistence on the primacy of authentic working-class organizations and their desire to instruct workers in the "proper" ways of organizing, to safeguard them from reckless actions, and to prepare them for their future role in society.

The praktiki relished the new opportunities for organizational

[67] Garvin, "Pamiati pionera."

[68] "Trade-Union Construction," RG, March 22, 1917 (no. 14), 1–2 (probably written by Garvi); "Local Unification of Unions," RG, March 25, 1917 (no. 16), 2; Garvi, Professional'nye soiuzy (a pamphlet written in 1914 but published for the first time in April 1917 with a new introduction by Garvi); and the resolutions "On the Construction of Class Organizations" and "On the Freedom of Association," in Vserossiiskoe soveshchanie, 245–46. According to Garvi, the resolutions were prepared by Schwarz, Kol'tsov, Gvozdev, Baturskii, and himself: Garvi, Professional'nye soiuzy v Rossii, 16. See also the resolution "On Labor Policy," which Garvi offered at the Menshevik conference in May in RG, May 12, 1917 (no. 54), 4, and the appeal of the secretary of the Union of Metalworkers (a Menshevik) to the effect that unions should be organized according to "production, not trade," in RG, May 6, 1917 (no. 49), 3.

work. Although they viewed the soviets as merely temporary substitutes for the unions that had been destroyed during the war years and looked on their involvement in labor disputes as a deviation from the proper course of the economic struggle during a bourgeois revolution, the Menshevik labor organizers in Petrograd and elsewhere concluded that it would be highly beneficial to use the "authority, apparatus, and material means" of the soviets for a reconstruction of the union movement.[69] They entrenched themselves in the soviets' labor sections and from there sought to guide the workers' energies into reviving moribund unions, establishing new ones, and uniting them in central bureaus.[70] By April, Garvi and M. I. Babin of the Petrograd soviet's labor section, and V. Grinevich of Moscow, all veterans of Menshevik union organizing, had begun organizing an all-Russian conference of unions.[71] Meanwhile, other praktiki—Ezhov and Khinchuk in Moscow, and Volkov, Kapelinskii, and M. L. Kheisin in Petrograd—turned their attention to workers' consumer cooperatives, a form of organization that was becoming increasingly popular and was separating itself from the general cooperative movement. Although not a form of organization familiar to the praktiki, the cooperatives were essential to workers' lives at a time of food shortages and high prices as well as highly suitable for the cultivation of the sense of shared responsibility and proper procedure which the Mensheviks considered so crucial to workers' political maturity.[72]

These efforts of the Menshevik praktiki were successful both in that the trade unions and the workers' consumer cooperatives grew to embrace a considerable segment of the working class—1.5 million workers in the former, 500,000 in the latter by midsummer[73]—and in that they were clearly under the Mensheviks' influence, though, as we shall see, less consistently so in the case of the unions than of the cooperatives. Nevertheless, as early

[69] "The Demarcation of Workers' Organizations," RG, May 16, 1917 (no. 57), 2, and Garvi, Professional'nye soiuzy y Rossii, 13, 16.

[70] A central bureau for Petrograd was organized by the labor section of that city's soviet on March 21: IzvPS, March 22, 1917 (no. 21), 6.

[71] Garvi, "Unpublished Memoirs, 1917," 62–65; Vserossiiskoe soveshchanie, 246.

[72] M. Kheisin, "The All-Russian Congress of Cooperatives and the Social Democratic Party," RG, July 21, 1917 (no. 112), 2; Garvi, "Rabochaia kooperatsiia," 14–15.

[73] These figures are based on the number of workers participating in the organizations represented at the unions' conference in late June and the cooperatives' conference in early August; see Miller and Pankratova, eds., Rabochee dvizhenie v 1917 godu, 85, and Garvi, "Rabochaia kooperatsiia," 14.

as June, there were signs that the Mensheviks' steadfast adherence to organizational strategies devised under radically different conditions had begun causing estrangement between them and the workers, especially in the factory committees, which the Mensheviks had initially ignored altogether and later attempted to portray as organizations of secondary importance.[74]

This mistrust of the factory committees requires some explanation, because, of all Russian Social Democrats, the praktiki had been the faction that had always accepted and encouraged workers' initiative, especially when it took an organized and "responsible" form. Indeed, the factory committees had initially seemed to embody the values the Mensheviks had sought to inculcate among workers, and those Mensheviks whose main activity in March and April had been in mediation had found the committees a valuable ally and had often praised them. Yet even before the committees had joined the debate on the regulation of the economy and had advocated a solution repugnant to the Mensheviks not less for its Bolshevik inspiration than for its implied political conclusions, the Mensheviks who were concentrating their efforts on the labor movement refused the committees an important place in their organizational scheme. They contended that the committees were a form of "factory patriotism," which could weaken the solidarity of the workers in their struggle with the employers. In order to avoid that, the committees had to be subjected to the unifying authority of the unions.[75]

By late June, the Mensheviks had further reason to oppose the committees, but by then the issue of the committees had also become central to the struggle between the Mensheviks and the Bolsheviks for influence among the organized workers, and the Mensheviks' rejection of the committees had become a political liability. The Third All-Russian Conference of Trade Unions brought out this weakness in the Mensheviks' position, as well as the considerable strength they still enjoyed in the trade unions.

[74] The program the praktiki prepared for the conference of soviets did not mention the committees, and the resolution "On Labor Policy," adopted by the Menshevik conference in May, insisted that their activity be "coordinated with, and subjected to," the trade unions: RG, May 12, 1917 (no. 54), 4. The committees' proper sphere of activity, explained one article, was "the internal life of the factory": "The Demarcation of Labor Organizations," RG, May 16, 1917 (no. 57), 2.

[75] See, for example, Grinevich's statement to the Third Conference of Trade Unions, in TKPS, 363–66; Garvi, Professional'nye soiuzy v Rossii, 14–15; and Shvarts, "Fabrichno-zavodskie komitety," 1.

Because the conference met at a time of deepening economic crisis and growing workers' militancy in regard to the issue of *kontrol'*, it also revealed divisions that had emerged among the Mensheviks themselves.

IN THEIR PREPARATIONS for the Third Conference of Trade Unions—the last one had been held in 1906—the Menshevik organizers appeared confident that nothing could now prevent the revolution from finally giving rise to mature, legal workers' organizations. The agenda originally consisted of issues that had occupied them since long before the revolution—workers' organization, their struggle for economic betterment, and labor legislation[76]—but by the time the conference convened on June 21, circumstances had forced the addition of the issues of economic regulation and the role of the factory committees. Indeed, two themes prevailed in the speeches of the official speakers: old preoccupations and hopes for the labor movement, and current concerns and fears.[77]

In expressing their hopes for the labor movement, these speakers portrayed the trade unions both as an instrument of progress in general and as the form of organization which, along with the consumer cooperatives, could best prepare workers for their political role as guardians of democracy in the present and "leaders of the economy under socialism" in the future. The Mensheviks' faith in the strength of unions and cooperatives was based on the examples of the proletariat of other countries, the benefits already generated by Russian workers through the unions in the years prior to the revolution, and the educational power of the "self-activity" afforded by the unions.[78] Conversely, the same speakers issued several clear warnings to the assembled unionists: that under the "present capitalist structure" only "disciplined unions" could lead the workers in their fight for economic betterment; "unorganized, syndicalist strikes" had to be avoided at all cost; and

[76] *RG*, April 27, 1917 (no. 41), 4.

[77] The list of official speakers included Grinevich, Kolokol'nikov, Kol'tsov, Cherevanin, Maiskii, Skobelev, and Khinchuk.

[78] See Grinevich's draft resolution, "On the Tasks of the Trade Unions," in Milonov, ed., *Putevoditel' po rezoliutsiiam*, 52–53; Kolokol'nikov's seconding speech, in *TKPS*, 178–79; Kol'tsov's statement on the organizational question, in ibid., 180–88; the resolution offered by Volkov, "On the Workers' Cooperatives," in Milonov, ed., *Putevoditel' po rezoliutsiiam*, 78–79; and a resolution regarding the cooperatives' educational function which the First Congress of Workers' Cooperatives adopted on August 1, cited in Garvi, "Rabochaia kooperatsiia," 15.

arbitration and collective bargaining should always be attempted before a strike was undertaken.[79] Here again was the Menshevik concept of "self-restraint," though as the conference's protocols clearly show, the reasons for reiterating the concept were different for the two principal groups of Mensheviks involved in labor affairs. Whereas the Mensheviks who participated in the government (the *gosudarstvenniki*) urged restraint in the name of the wartime economic emergency, the majority of Menshevik tradeunionists (but also Deputy Minister of Labor Kolokol'nikov) were chiefly concerned about the danger of a backlash from the industrialists.[80]

These divisions grew deeper when the conference took up the issue of economic regulation and the workers' role in it. Apparently seeking to defend their continued participation in the government and to counter the workers' growing inclination to intervene in economic matters, the gosudarstvenniki praised the achievements already realized by the government. They had particular praise for the establishment of the Economic Council, which had been made public on the conference's opening day, and the government's presumed support for regional democratic regulatory agencies such as the Moscow Factory Conference and the Donbas Provisional Committee. On the basis of these claims, Skobelev urged the unions to leave the entire matter of regulation to the government, adding that workers should be included in the regulatory agencies as a matter of course but should not insist on securing a majority in them.[81] In contrast, the unionists emphasized that the defense of the workers' interests required that the unions not only instill self-discipline in the workers but also participate in the new institutions of economic regulation in order to pressure them into action.[82] The unionists' position drew support from the accusations leveled at the Provisional Government by Cherevanin, the party's featured speaker on the question of economic regulation, for its failure to implement essential regulatory

[79] See Grinevich's draft resolution, in Milonov, ed., *Putevoditel' po rezoliutsiiam*, 52–53; and the speeches by him and Kol'tsov, in *TKPS*, 79, 244–48.

[80] For the position of the gosudarstvenniki, see the speeches of Skobelev, Pumpianskii, and Kol'tsov, in *TKPS*, 53–54, 117–20, 238–40, 242–43. For that of the unionists, see the speeches of Grinevich, Kolokol'nikov, and Khinchuk, in ibid., 65, 76, 82, 178–79, and the editorial printed on the day the conference opened, in *RG*, June 21, 1917 (no. 86), 1–2.

[81] *TKPS*, 47–59, 117–20, 357–63.

[82] Ibid., 79–82, 241, 366. See also Garvi, *Kapital protiv truda*, 6.

measures in the face of the industrialists' opposition. The Ministry of Trade and Industry, declared Cherevanin, was a "nest of robbers."[83] Clearly, the unionists were more sensitive to the workers' sentiments and deprivations than were the gosudarstvenniki, who bore state responsibility and had to face the cabinet's denunciations of the workers.[84]

These differences notwithstanding, the Menshevik speakers at the conference were united, first, in their rejection of the factory committees' assertion of the right to intervene in industrial production and distribution, and second, in their criticism of the Bolsheviks' advocacy of this right as part of their general drive to have the soviets assume "all power" in the country.[85] One source of the Mensheviks' unanimous opposition to the exercise of *kontrol'* by individual factory committees was (as it had been during the First Conference of Petrograd Factory Committees) their conviction that unplanned, uncoordinated intervention would not alleviate but rather would worsen the economic chaos which they held responsible for many of the closings and slowdowns occurring in Russian industry. The same conviction motivated the Independent Internationalists' opposition, even though they agreed with the Bolsheviks that the present government was unlikely to implement regulation consistently.[86]

Among the Mensheviks who belonged to the Revolutionary Defensist faction, there was a second and more powerful reason for resisting workers' intervention in production—namely, the fear that it would serve to "discredit the workers' and lead to their isolation.[87] As we have seen, both industrialists and workers considered the issue of *kontrol'* to be vital to their interests, and both had assumed increasingly intransigent positions in regard to it. The Revolutionary Defensists had already become isolated in the cabi-

---

[83] *TKPS*, 304–15.

[84] One Independent Internationalist who was generally critical of the Mensheviks nevertheless praised the unionists for their stand at the conference, which he characterized as antagonistic to any "social peace" and "dedicated to the class struggle": A. L., "The Conference of Trade Unions (Impressions of a Participant)," *NZh*, June 24, 1917 (no. 57), 1.

[85] For the Bolshevik position in the conference on the issues of regulation and the factory committees, see V. Miliutin's speech, in *TKPS*, 293–98, 301–4, and the draft resolution submitted by N. Glebov-Avilov, in Milonov, ed., *Putevoditel' po rezoliutsiiam*, 72–73.

[86] See Riazanov's speech, in *TKPS*, 370–71. In the vote on a draft resolution offered by Miliutin, seventy-nine delegates identified as Internationalists abstained.

[87] From Garvi's speech, in ibid., 333.

net, caught between their worker constituency and their bourgeois fellow ministers, and they would surely have lost additional ground if the workers' behavior could have been shown to have contributed to the crisis. Yet there was something new and noteworthy about the discussion that took place at the trade-union conference. Those Menshevik Revolutionary Defensists who did not serve in the government appeared to have given up on the bourgeoisie altogether and opposed the right of the working class to *kontrol'* out of fear of its being isolated from the larger body of democracy.

What underlay this new concern was nothing less than an effort to adapt Menshevik conceptions of the revolution to the social and political realities of 1917, an effort that drew naturally and heavily on the ideological formulations devised by the Mensheviks in earlier years to account for the twists and turns of revolution, reaction, and political revival. Some Revolutionary Defensists were now driven by their perception of the commercial-industrial class as counterrevolutionary to a concept developed during the revolutionary interregnum which saw urban democracy—now expanded to embrace the whole of Russian democracy—as a social and political force that would be both willing and necessary to sustain the revolution. Men such as Garvi, a unionist, and Cherevanin, an economist, urged the workers to avoid appearing to the peasants as responsible for the high cost of industrial goods, because the peasantry, which these men described as already disposed to blame the workers, might become their partners in a future government, should the soviets be forced to assume power.[88] Cherevanin also reminded the delegates that the workers' most natural ally at this stage of the revolution was the technical intelligentsia, for it shared the same concern for production and could serve as liaison between the workers and the industrialists, whose cooperation was still necessary. The solution Cherevanin proposed to counter the government's otherwise inadequate effort at economic regulation was the formation of regional democratic agencies, modeled on the Moscow Factory Conference, in which the soviets and the technical intelligentsia would cooperate.[89]

The overall effect of the debate on economic regulation, how-

[88] Ibid., 304–15, 329–34.

[89] Cherevanin's proposal called for the soviets to elect one-half of the members of these agencies and the industrialists one-eighth, the remainder to be drawn from the technical intelligentsia such as that of the Union of Cities, in which Cherevanin and Groman had worked during the war: ibid., 309–13.

ever, was not to divide the Menshevik Revolutionary Defensists nor to change their position on the issues discussed. This was because the debate raised not only an important political issue—which social and political groups could be counted on as allies of the proletariat?—but also a fundamental ideological issue: the nature of the revolution itself. On this, the Mensheviks were of one mind and determined to withstand any challenge. The government's failure to deal effectively with the economic crisis posed the possibility that the soviets would assume political power, and this led various Mensheviks to state that such power would necessarily be "democratic"—that is, based on all the nonpropertied groups—rather than "proletarian" and that it would not correspond to economic dictatorship.[90] Against the Bolsheviks' assertions that the "essentially socialist" measures of workers' *kontrol'* would bring Russia to a "transformation into socialism," the Mensheviks insisted that there could be "either capitalism or socialism but nothing 'in between.' "[91] Indeed, this was the real issue between the Mensheviks and the factory committees. The Mensheviks felt that, by their very nature as well as by their recent activities, the committees had helped blur the distinction between what they referred to as the "bourgeois" and "socialist" revolutions and had given rise to expectations among the workers which the Mensheviks considered ideologically incorrect and politically dangerous.

ONCE AGAIN, the Mensheviks demonstrated both the limits and the resources of their political legacy. Their rigid scheme of historical stages, even if essentially correct in its assessment of Russia's capacity for change, prevented them from sympathizing with the workers' struggle for self-reliance under the current conditions. Still, there were precedents in the Mensheviks' practical work as well as in their ideological formulations for innovative and positive solutions to the inadequacies of the revolution. If Cherevanin's vision of an alliance between the working class and the technical intelligentsia could be realized, along with even a minimum of peasant support, the revolution would have a chance of generating both economic development and social democracy. For this vision to be realized, however, not only would Tsereteli and other leading Revolutionary Defensists have to reformulate their defini-

[90] Ibid., 313–14.
[91] Ibid., 304, 189.

tion of the revolution's "vital forces," but also the workers would have to forgo *kontrol'* of the technical personnel and generally demonstrate a more consistent concern for productivity as well as an appreciation of the economic impossibility of having their aspirations promptly fulfilled. The first of these conditions would be fulfilled soon after the trade-union conference ended. The second remained in doubt.

The Third Conference of Trade Unions assured the Mensheviks that their confidence in the maturity of the trade unions had not been misplaced, though in retrospect one can detect omens of eventual disappointment in its proceedings and resolutions. On all issues discussed, even that of regulation, the Menshevik draft resolutions were adopted by a comfortable majority, and at the end of the conference a central council was established with a presidium on which the Mensheviks had a slim majority.[92] Behind this ostensible success, however, there were two potential weaknesses: first, against the 120 supporters of the Menshevik-sponsored Group for the Unity of the Trade Unions, there were some 80 delegates who supported the Internationalist Group led by the Bolsheviks and the Independent Internationalists;[93] and second, much of the Mensheviks' numerical strength came not from Petrograd but from the overrepresented provincial unions[94]—and it was the workers of Petrograd and their unions who were often the vanguard for the working class in other parts of the country, and their political orientation therefore presaged what was likely to follow elsewhere.

Moreover, the alignment of forces at the trade union conference reflected the political outlook of the unions' leadership and not their membership. The delegates had been elected by central bureaus rather than by individual unions, and for this reason the

[92] The majority was so slim that it made the operation of the presidium difficult: Garvi, *Professional'nye soiuzy v Rossii*, 22, and "Pamiati pionera," 254–55.

[93] Zmeul, *Ot fevralia k oktiabriu*, 57. The Group for the Unity of the Trade Unions was supported by Internationalist Mensheviks as well as by Revolutionary Defensists: Garvi, *Professional'nye soiuzy v Rossii*, 18.

[94] This statement is made in Zmeul, *Ot fevralia k oktiabriu*, 55, and is supported by information available on the system of representation at the conference. Provincial central bureaus were allowed one delegate for every five thousand to ten thousand members, but the central bureaus of Moscow and Petrograd, in which union membership was in the hundreds of thousands, were allotted only five delegates each: *RG*, April 27, 1917 (no. 41), 4. On the differences between Petrograd and the provinces at the conference, see "Summing Up the Third Conference of Trade Unions," *RG*, June 30, 1917 (no. 94), 2.

composition of the conference had as much to do with the history of the union movement and its leadership prior to the outbreak of the revolution as with recent developments among unionized workers. In Petrograd, where the Bolshevik takeover of the unions had been most complete in 1913–1914, the Bolsheviks remained prominent in most of the largest unions (the metal, textile, wood, and leather workers) and in the central bureau. The Mensheviks controlled the printers' union, held a majority among the chemical workers, and comprised a strong minority among the metalworkers. They had had parity with the Bolsheviks in the central bureau for a while (partially due to their strength in the soviet's labor section), but by May their own Internationalist wing and the Mezhraiontsy were more likely to vote with the Bolsheviks.[95]

In most other places, however, the initiative and leadership for the revitalization of the unions in 1917 had come from those veteran unionists who had been trained by the Mensheviks in the years after 1905 and had been ousted or at least threatened by the Bolshevik surge of 1913–1914. During the war, the unions had largely disappeared and the militants lost influence or were simply drafted into the army, so that in the relatively calm atmosphere of March and April 1917 the old leadership had stepped into this organizational vacuum and had regained its old position.[96] At the trade-union conference, these veteran provincial unionists generally supported the cautious, moderate stance recommended by the Mensheviks and were very suspicious of Bolshevik militancy in its various forms. Having seen the Bolsheviks question their authenticity as working-class leaders just a few years earlier, these unionists were determined not to be outmaneuvered again. Not only did they oppose the proposal of the Petrograd bureau that the eight-hour workday be extended to all categories of laborers (including the peasants), but they also bitterly condemned the Bolsheviks for their "political factionalism." Miliutin's call for work-

---

[95] See Smith, *Red October*, 109–16.

[96] According to F. Bulkin, the former Menshevik secretary of the Petrograd Union of Metalworkers, when the delegates of thirty-seven unions of metalworkers (representing some 400,000 members) elected a provisional central committee, four of its nine members were Mensheviks—a surprising showing, because the Bolsheviks controlled the largest unions, those of Petrograd (170,000 members), Moscow (50,000 members), Kharkov, and the Urals. Bulkin explained that the Mensheviks still controlled the smaller, provincial unions and in certain cases were elected simply as "old, experienced trade-union activists." Bulkin, *Soiuz metallistov*, 180.

ers' *kontrol'* as well as the Bolshevik slogan of "All Power to the Soviets" were cited as examples of "faction-mongering."[97]

Moreover, at least one delegate, V. Chirikin, a metalworker from Kolomna and a veteran unionist, warned that talk of workers' *kontrol'* might unleash *stikhiia* among the workers, and he added that his anxiety about such unorganized actions was shared by the Bolshevik veterans of the trade-union movement in his town.[98] Indeed, runaway extremism of the unorganized, "less conscious" workers was just as threatening to these men as to the Mensheviks from the intelligentsia, for it undermined their self-image and their position as leaders of the workers. These anxieties further contributed to the provincial unionists' fear of Bolshevik political machinations, and for this reason they steadfastly adhered to the Menshevik vision of the trade unions as the primary unit of the workers' economic struggle.[99]

The support of the trade unionists from the provinces was a source of considerable comfort to the Menshevik praktiki. They viewed it as proof of their success in inculcating "revolutionary realism" among the workers and defeating extremism, which had always been a dangerous potentiality as well as an indication of Bolshevik gains.[100] Also reassuring was the fact that none of the serious disagreements at the conference involved the construction of unions or their relationship to the factory committees, which all unionists, Bolsheviks as well as Mensheviks, wanted subjected to the unions. The problem, however, lay in the divisions over what Grinevich characterized as "political questions" (such as economic regulation) external to the unions.[101] By the beginning of September, the "united" presidium of the union movement had ceased to function, its members stalemated over these political questions. Bolshevik influence was growing in every union except those of the printers and paperworkers, where the Mensheviks retained controls.[102] Yet in late June there still seemed to be grounds for

[97] See an article by a provincial delegate entitled "The Unity of the Trade-Union Movement" and a statement by a group of delegates calling themselves "Supporters of the Unity of Trade Unions," both in *RG*, June 24, 1917 (no. 89), 2–3; and a report on the conference's first day in *IzvPS*, June 23, 1917 (no. 99), 10–11.

[98] *TKPS*, 112–16.

[99] "Unity of the Trade-Union Movement."

[100] "Summing Up the Third Conference of Trade Unions," *RG*, June 30, 1917 (no. 94), 2. Again, the choice of words points to Garvi as the author of this article.

[101] Grinevich, "The Third All-Russian Conference of Trade Unions (A Short Summation)," *Professional'nyi vestnik*, September 1, 1917 (no. 1/2), 3.

[102] Shatilova, "Professional'nye soiuzy i oktiabr'."

optimism, and this, as we shall see in chapter 8, was an important component in the political choices the Mensheviks made during and after the coalition's first two months.

ALL TOLD, and in spite of such support as they found among the trade unionists, the Menshevik Revolutionary Defensists, having been forced into some hard choices, had often met with disappointing results. For the Mensheviks in the Ministry of Labor, the decisions had usually been more difficult and the consequences had followed sooner than for the praktiki in the soviet. As the first socialists in government, they had been expected to perform what would have been, under most circumstances but certainly in the conditions of 1917, a legislative miracle. But if their efforts to reform labor laws had been thwarted largely by objective conditions, this had been less true of their mediation efforts, in which they had allowed themselves to be pressured by their sense of national responsibility, as well as by concern for the survival of coalition government, into a position that gave preference to the presumed national interest over the workers' aspirations. Moreover, the notion of national interest had not been very clearly distinguished among the Menshevik gosudarstvenniki from their concern with maintaining the unity of the "vital forces" of the country. The exercise of power and the experience of participating in coalition government and of enjoying legitimacy had been reinforced and augmented by the Mensheviks' long-standing convictions regarding the shape the revolution in Russia ought to have assumed.

Meanwhile, changes in the Revolutionary Defensists' public image were being magnified by the theatrical quality of public life in 1917, in which rhetoric, gestures, and symbols often counted for more than substantive policies. The very demeanor of the Mensheviks in government frequently served to affront the workers, who had previously viewed them as "their" representatives. Schwarz's legalistic rigidity was matched by Kolokol'nikov's studied neutrality;[103] and Tsereteli, the most popular Menshevik leader, had been noticeably uneasy in confrontations with workers and unwilling to alter his notions of right and wrong to suit the sentiments of the revolutionary masses. Writing in late May to the

[103] As chair of the Commission on Labor Legislation, Kolokol'nikov insisted on being impartial; when the workers' representatives would address him familiarly, by his first name and patronymic, he would "turn his quiet grey eyes up and to the left, look at them over his glasses . . . until they fell silent": Auerbakh, "Revoliutsionnoe obshchestvo," 12.

Congress of Employees of his Ministry of Post and Telegraph, Tsereteli said he spoke "as a minister" possessed of "full authority," and he stated that "under no circumstances" could employees presume to instruct him on his responsibilities.[104] Even Tsereteli's close friend, Garvi, worried that the minister might not find the right words to address the trade unionists' conference.[105] The Group for the Unity of the Trade Unions went so far as to propose that no government official should be eligible for membership on the Central Council of Trade Unions, a proposal that led Kolokol'nikov to cry in anguish: "Didn't I join the government at the insistence of the party and in the interest of the trade-union movement? Why should this act make me a stranger to my trade-union constituency?"[106]

The praktiki in the soviet and the trade unions had fared better during the early months of coalition than had the gosudarstvenniki. They had been more skeptical about the viability of any unity of the "vital forces" and had remained committed to securing the maximum possible gains from the revolution for the workers. They had been well aware of the widening gap between the workers and their presumed representatives in the cabinet and had not hesitated to condemn the government as a whole for its shortcomings. Still, they too had found their ability to act as champions of labor increasingly limited by their fear, shared with other Revolutionary Defensists, that social polarization might lead to political isolation, by their attachment to the specific solutions they had developed in years past to help prevent this threat, and now also by their party's commitment to coalition. Eventually, the praktiki also became transformed in the workers' eyes from their sometimes reluctant champions into demanding disciplinarians, and in the process they lost their moral authority as guides for the workers in their economic and political struggles.

For all Mensheviks, the situation that had emerged by June was an ironic one. The advent of industrial conflict bore out their earlier warnings about bourgeois counterrevolution and proletarian extremism, yet it was also the reason that the traditional Menshevik solutions were now useless. By the end of June, some Mensheviks, notably Cherevanin, had begun to rethink the old ideo-

---

[104] *RG*, June 2, 1917 (no. 70), 3. See also Avilov's criticism of Tsereteli's "professorial style" in his appearance before the First Congress of Soviets: *NZh*, June 4, 1917 (no. 41), 1.

[105] Garvi, "Unpublished Memoirs, 1917," 68.

[106] Cited in ibid., 69.

logical precepts, to try to make them correspond more closely to the social and economic realities of the time as well as to the sentiments of the soviet's working-class following; but it is doubtful that even Cherevanin's "democratic" solution could have halted the workers' radicalization and the process of political polarization or that the Menshevik party as a whole would have embraced the new solution before it had been made obsolete by these processes.

At the Third Conference of Trade Unions, Cherevanin's point was lost in the political and ideological struggle between Mensheviks and Bolsheviks. Meanwhile, a turning point had been reached in the relations between the workers and the Revolutionary Defensists who had sought to guide their economic struggle and their organizational work. For the factory committees, for some of Petrograd's major unions and its central bureau, and for many workers embroiled in industrial conflicts, the "obligatory deference" to the Mensheviks in the Ministry of Labor had become a "yoke" and the Revolutionary Defensists' participation in the "bourgeois cabinet" a sign of betrayal.[107] As chapter 8 will show, this erosion in the Revolutionary Defensists' standing among workers reinforced the changes that had already taken place in the workers' political attitudes. Moreover, not only did this process have critical consequences for the Revolutionary Defensist leadership of the soviets, but workers' militancy itself would become a hindrance to the strategy of coalition.

[107] From a statement of the Central Bureau of Petrograd Trade Unions to the Moscow Congress on Supplies: *NZh*, May 27, 1917 (no. 33), 4.

The Coalition in Crisis

THE DETERIORATION of industrial relations during May and June as well as the growing inability of the Mensheviks to respond to the aspirations of their working-class constituency gradually eroded the social base on which the legitimacy of the political strategy of coalition had been founded. A change in the political attitudes of all urban groups began during June and served as a transition between the industrial crisis (discussed in the last two chapters) and the political crisis of early July which spelled the collapse of the first coalition cabinet. For the Menshevik Revolutionary Defensists, it was the change in the workers' attitudes, and to a lesser extent in the soldiers', which was most important. Yet they spent surprisingly little time discussing questions of ideology or political strategy during these critical months. While the Mensheviks in government tended to the business of state, their colleagues in the soviet appeared content merely to help them muster the support of the workers and soldiers for the principle of coalition and the government's specific policies or to blunt opposition to the leadership's decisions when the need arose. At no point before the July Days did the Revolutionary Defensist leadership come close to reconsidering the strategy of coalition. This apparent complacency raises doubts anew about the effectiveness of the Revolutionary Defensists as leaders of the soviet and of Russia's lower classes. These doubts revolve around three problems.

First, why did the Revolutionary Defensists fail to see the changes occurring in their followers' attitudes? Was it their ideological rigidity that blinded them to the new political situation, or was the oversight the result of a mind-set fixed in the past and reinforced by the experience of governmental responsibility? Second, to what extent did the Revolutionary Defensists' failure to detect the changes in attitude contribute to the process itself? In the political no less than in the industrial sphere, a denial of the changes may have turned the Revolutionary Defensists themselves into principal targets of the workers' anger and undermined the Mensheviks' ability to act as mediators. Moreover, in the context of a revolution that was developing into an ever-deepening social conflict, it was easy to miss the opportunity to restructure political alignments. Third, and most crucial to the Revolutionary Defensists' political destiny, how did they react to their sudden recognition during the July Days that the coalition was in crisis and had lost the support both of their working-class constituency and of their most important partners in the cabinet? Would the reconsideration they were now forced to undertake yield new insights, new initiatives, or a renewed hope for the revolution as they understood it? The fate of the February revolution hung in the balance.

To answer the first two questions, we must study the workers' political attitudes, Menshevik interpretations of these attitudes, and the responses of the Revolutionary Defensist leaders of the soviet to events in Petrograd in late May and early June, to the All-Russian Congress of Soviets (which began on June 3), and to the confrontation between the congress's majority and the workers of Petrograd. Apart from these matters, a consideration of the impact of the Revolutionary Defensists' policies during the first term of coalition on their constituency must include a discussion of their decision to support a new Russian offensive in the war and the rapid transformation that followed in the politics of the soldiery as well as of the workers. Finally, the third question must be answered through an examination of the July Days: what they revealed about the political sentiment of the soviet's constituency in Petrograd, the implications for the strategy and leadership of the Revolutionary Defensists, and their reaction to the crisis.

Changing Political Attitudes

During the first two months of coalition, significant shifts of attitudes occurred among the workers in Petrograd regarding their employers, the propertied classes in general, and the strategy of cooperation between democracy and the bourgeoisie. To be sure, workers did not express their attitudes clearly or consistently, and the collapse of earlier expectations during the summer months left the Petrograd working class more politically fragmented than it had been since the start of the revolution.[1] Nevertheless, the daily experience of workers, shaped by the interconnected processes of economic ruin and intensified industrial conflict, did not accord

---

[1] For a discussion of these political divisions, see Mandel, *Petrograd Workers and the Fall of the Old Regime*, 122–48.

with their initial expectations of the revolution or the hopes that had animated their support for the socialists' participation in government. Increasingly, workers blamed the frustration of their material goals, even the economic crisis itself, on their employers and came to doubt the wisdom of cooperating with them at all. Moreover, the continued participation of the moderate socialists in a coalition government that had failed to meet the workers' expectations and, more specifically, the Mensheviks' opposition to measures the workers considered essential to their own survival—workers' *kontrol'* and the freedom to strike for higher wages—created tensions between the Revolutionary Defensist leaders of the soviet and their Petrograd constituency. This estrangement led a growing number of workers to reject the moderates' advice, first on matters pertaining to factory life, then on the political shape of the revolution.

The most overt sign of this change was the willingness of certain groups of workers to embrace Lenin's slogan of "All Power to the Soviets." This willingness accounted for the Bolsheviks' success in swaying the workers' section of the Petrograd soviet against the government's plan to "unload" the city (see chapter 6) and in having their resolution adopted by the First Conference of Factory Committees.[2] By now, the Bolshevik alternative to coalition was being articulated with greater clarity and force than ever before. Furthermore, just as in February, when the workers' support for dual power had rested on the correspondence between the workers' own anxieties and the slogans of "pressure" and *kontrol'*, so too the workers' disappointment now in the exercise of *kontrol'* and pressure through coalition, as well as the impact of these failures on work and factory, made the more radical political solutions seem attractive. An analysis of the elections in May of delegates to the district and city soviets and to the district dumas in Petrograd shows a shift in workers' support from the moderate socialist parties to the Internationalist parties in general and the Bolsheviks in particular, though at the time these results seemed open to several interpretations.

The elections of deputies to the Petrograd and district soviets were particularly ominous for the Revolutionary Defensists, even if they fell short of establishing Bolshevik majorities in these bodies. Since April, when a Bolshevik-dominated executive committee

[2] The Bolsheviks a 55 percent majority in the workers' section and a 73 percent majority at the factory committees' conference.

had been elected in the Vyborg district, one other small district, Kolomna, had come under Bolshevik control and two others, Vasileostrov and First City, had elected executive committees in which Bolsheviks combined with Internationalists to form a majority.[3] Three of these districts (Vyborg, Kolomna, and Vasileostrov) had a particularly high concentration of metalworkers, noted for their relatively high level of skill, organization, and familiarity with the internal debates of Social Democracy.[4] As Mandel has pointed out, the Bolsheviks' earliest gains were among this "Social Democratic constituency," at the expense of the Mensheviks.[5] Similarly, most of the factories that recalled their deputies from the Petrograd soviet during May and early June were metalprocessing factories in which Menshevik, and less often SR, deputies had been replaced by Bolsheviks.[6]

There were certain elements in the situation that may have prevented the Mensheviks, at least temporarily, from perceiving the developing pattern. First, in June, the district soviets controlled by Bolsheviks or Internationalists still constituted but a small minority of all the district soviets in Petrograd, and Bolshevik and Internationalist deputies remained a small minority in the city soviet.[7] Second, the political significance of the election of such deputies varied. Where Bolsheviks cooperated with Menshevik Internationalists, the friction between the workers and the soviet's moderate leaders could be masked;[8] or the recall of deputies could be prompted, or at least explained, by an estrangement between the workers who stayed in the plant and their comrades whose time was being spent in the soviet;[9] and above all, there was the crucial

[3] *Raionnye sovety Petrograda* 1:11–12, 71, 123, 180, 319, and 3:6.

[4] Stepanov, *Rabochie Petrograda*, 30.

[5] Mandel, *Petrograd Workers and the Fall of the Old Regime*, 124–26.

[6] See the reports from the Sestroretsk armament factory, the Nobel and Feniks machine-building factories, and the Novyi Baranovskii machine and pipe factory cited in ibid., 123.

[7] Sukhanov confirms the belief that the Petrograd soviet continued to support its leadership's coalition policy, though he argues that this was increasingly untrue of Petrograd workers at large: Sukhanov, *Zapiski o revoliutsii* 4:41–42, 57, 199.

[8] In the Vulkan foundry and machine-building factory, for example, such cooperation brought about the election of Internationalist deputies to replace the Mensheviks who had originally represented the factory in the Petrograd soviet: Mandel, *Petrograd Workers and the Fall of the Old Regime*, 123–24, citing *Pravda*, June 27, 1917.

[9] Such estrangement, rather than any political disagreement, was the objection of the Novyi Arsenal workers to S. Samodurov, their Menshevik deputy, although he was eventually retained, with the support of the local Menshevik cell and against the opposition of the factory committee: *RG*, June 7, 1917 (no. 74), 4.

but politically ambiguous role played by the factory committees in translating the workers' vague sense of frustration and bitterness into the terms of party politics.

The members of factory committees were particularly susceptible to the Bolshevik advocacy of a soviet seizure of power (political as well as economic), because the experience of contending with economic uncertainty and entrepreneurial obstruction had made them impatient with the coalition's shortcomings. Moreover, by virtue of their personal activism (which is what had brought them into the committees in the first place) and the responsibility they had taken for their fellow workers and the factory itself, committee members wielded great influence among the workers. In the First City district, for example, it was the prestige of the Central Council of Factory Committees (headquartered in the district and represented in its soviet), rather than any widespread support for the political strategy of the Bolsheviks, that made possible the election of a Bolshevik-dominated executive committee of the soviet on May 27.[10] Yet support for the factory committees, even for the Bolsheviks who championed them, did not always mean support for a soviet government. It was one thing to strike against employers, even to attempt to exercise *kontrol'* over them, and an altogether different thing for the workers to take responsibility for governing the country against the will of census society.

The political fragmentation of the Petrograd working class, the difficulty in interpreting the political behavior of workers, and the undisputable fact of a growing radicalism among them were all demonstrated in the outcome of the elections to the twelve district dumas of Petrograd, held in the last days of May and the first week of June. In general, the vote gave the Revolutionary Defensist bloc a comfortable majority: of the 784,910 votes (nearly 75 percent of all eligible voters), the moderate Socialists received 56.0 percent; the Kadets and other nonsocialists, 21.9 percent; and the Bolsheviks, 20.4 percent. But there were sharp variations from one district to another. It was again in the Vyborg and Vasileostrov districts that the Bolsheviks scored their greatest success, with 58.2 and 34.3 percent of the vote, respectively, compared to the mod-

[10] *Raionnye sovety Petrograda* 1:180. This fact is evident in the minutes of the soviet's meetings, which show that the political disagreement between two deputies, the brothers Nakhimson—the Bolshevik S. M. and the Menshevik F. M.—made debates over political strategy an almost daily affair in this soviet.

erates' 34.9 and 45.2.[11] In contrast, the Mensheviks, who had always courted the support of the more skilled, literate, and politicized workers (generally the metalworkers and printers), now found their Revolutionary Defensist bloc supported largely by the less skilled, less politicized constituency of the SRs.

Where SRs and Mensheviks ran on a single Revolutionary Defensist list, they enjoyed their greatest success in those districts that had little industry, or industry employing less skilled workers, or factories that were mostly state-owned.[12] The difference between the SRs' and Mensheviks' constituencies was demonstrated most clearly in the two districts in which they ran on separate lists: The SRs outpolled the Mensheviks by almost six to one among the mixed industrial workers of the Aleksandr Nevskii district (many of these workers were also residents of the neighboring villages), whereas the Mensheviks maintained a slight edge in the Rozhdestvenskii district—probably with the help of workers from several small metalprocessing and electrical plants and of a large contingent of intelligentsia and white-collar employees. If any general conclusions can be drawn from the aggregate election figures (we do not know such things as the percentage of workers among the eligible voters of each district), they are, first, that the Mensheviks' bases of support among Petrograd's working class had been significantly eroded, particularly among workers in metalprocessing and mechanical factories; and second, that the trend was for these workers to shift their support from the Mensheviks to the Bolsheviks. Of the highly skilled groups whom the Mensheviks viewed as their natural constituency, only the printers still showed solid support for the Revolutionary Defensists and their coalition strategy. Otherwise, the Menshevik party was fast becoming a party of the radical urban intelligentsia.

IF THE ELECTION RESULTS appear in retrospect to have required the Revolutionary Defensists' attention and response, these were not forthcoming. None of the newspaper articles reporting the elec-

[11] Rosenberg, *Liberals in the Russian Revolution*, 162. See appendix 4 of the present work for a district-by-district breakdown of the election results.

[12] On the characteristics of workers in state-owned factories which made for their support of the soviet's moderates, see Mandel, *Petrograd Workers and the Fall of the Old Regime*, 37–38. The Mensheviks were clearly troubled by their electoral association with the SRs and sought to undo the damage by having their own Duma deputies put forward a more radical municipal program: "The First Task of the Menshevik Deputies," *RG*, June 4, 1917 (no. 72), 2.

tions dwelt on the reasons for the relatively strong Bolshevik showing in the Vyborg, Vasileostrov, and Petrograd districts.[13] Instead, they hailed the results as a great victory for the Revolutionary Defensist bloc and as approval of its policies.[14] Insofar as the Revolutionary Defensists admitted that there was reason to be concerned, they explained it in ways that did not call for a reconsideration of their policies. Rather, they defended the wisdom of their political strategy in the face of the workers' changing allegiance. Some of these explanations were retrospective. Those provided by Tsereteli and Voitinskii in their memoirs and correspondence represent differences of perception, already noted in chapter 7, between those Mensheviks who were in the government and those whose activity revolved around the soviet and other labor organizations.

Reflecting the typical perception of the gosudarstvenniki, Tsereteli argued that, although Bolshevik influence had penetrated the sphere of "economic struggle," the Petrograd workers still wholeheartedly supported the "democratic socialism" of the moderates in regard to "general political questions."[15] Tsereteli's disregard for the changing mood of the soviet's constituency was symptomatic of how removed the cabinet men had grown from the soviet. Continuously pressed for quick decisions, these men preferred to work out their solutions in the more congenial and efficient setting of the "star chamber" and to leave the passage of decisions through the soviet to Chkheidze, Dan, or Bogdanov.[16] If at first the ministers were eager to appear before the deputies to report their victories—as Skobelev had on May 13 to celebrate the introduction of the tax reform—this readiness turned to reluctance and eventually to refusal when the cabinet began to reject the soviet's initiatives and questions were raised in the soviet and in the Menshevik party about the ministers' work.[17]

[13] The first election results, on June 1, did not include the Vyborg district; these became known only on June 9. Compare the results reported in *RG*, June 1, 1917 (no. 69), 4; *IzvPS*, June 3, 1917 (no. 82); and *Pravda*, June 9, 1917 (no. 77), 1. The last two are reprinted in *RD v mae-iiune*, 84, 588.

[14] "A Victory for Revolutionary Democracy," *RG*, June 1, 1917 (no. 69), 1; "The Victory Must Be Secured," *RG*, June 2, 1917 (no. 70), 2.

[15] Tsereteli, *Vospominaniia o fevral'skoi revoliutsii* 1:431.

[16] The decisions went first to the bureau of the executive committee and were then presented (usually by Bogdanov) to the full (and more heterogeneous) executive committee. See the minutes of these two bodies in *Petrogradskii sovet*; and see also Sukhanov, *Zapiski o revoliutsii* 4:44.

[17] Tsereteli apparently argued that his mandate from the soviet did not require

The situation was very different for those Revolutionary Defensists outside the government who made themselves the defenders of coalition before audiences of workers and soldiers. Years later, Voitinskii wrote Tsereteli expressing astonishment that the same events could have appeared so differently in their respective memoirs. Voitinskii's explanation for the discrepancy centered on the two men's different activities: "You made policy, whereas I was one of those who personally confronted the waves of hostility."[18] This perception of "hostility" led Voitinskii to suggest to the ministers that they take a day off from their state duties to campaign for coalition among the soviet's followers, for it had become his "grim" impression that "the ground was slipping out from under" the moderates.[19] Yet even in retrospect, Voitinskii was confident that the Revolutionary Defensists had been right in not changing their strategy in response to the expressions of opposition from the workers, for he believed that the real problem had lain in the expectation of "miracles" with which the "raw, ignorant" masses had welcomed the revolution: "The utopian maximalism of the lower classes vs. the real achievements attained by democratic means—this was the essence of the split between the workers and the soldiers of Petrograd and the leaders of the soviet's majority."[20] According to both Tsereteli and Voitinskii, the gap could have been closed by a better, more forceful implementation of the strategy of cooperation and moderation. It was as if the mere mention of the Mensheviks' historic task of fighting "maximalism" could refute the gathering evidence of the workers' turn toward militancy.

Interestingly enough, Voitinskii's retrospective comments are borne out by articles appearing in *Rabochaia gazeta* in late May, in which two related arguments were used to allay any doubts the workers' changing attitudes might have raised about the strategy of coalition. First, it was assumed that all expressions of workers' political radicalization were the result of Bolshevik influence, and this led to increasingly vehement attacks on the Bolsheviks for the

that he report "on every step" of his activity as minister: Sukhanov, *Zapiski o revoliutsii* 4:53–54. He and Skobelev blocked an attempt by the Menshevik Organizational Committee on May 28 to implement the May conference's resolution declaring that ministers must be responsible to the party, though they agreed to report on the activities of the cabinet: *PI*, July 15, 1917 (no. 1), 9.

[18] Voitinskii to Tsereteli, January 4, 1930 (Nicolaevsky Collection).

[19] Voitinskii, "God pobed i porazhenii," 107–10.

[20] Ibid., 106–7, 125–29.

harm they would do to the working class by isolating it or encouraging general anarchy and possibly a counterrevolutionary attack.[21] Bolshevik "romanticism" was compared with the consistently "realistic" positions of the Mensheviks in both the past and the present.[22] These articles alluded to reports of the Bolsheviks' "undemocratic" methods—such as the attacks of Bolshevik workers in Vyborg on Menshevik speakers—to emphasize the fundamental differences separating the two Social Democratic parties.[23] The task of the Mensheviks, then, was not to embrace the workers' demands but to draw their attention to these differences through the educational work of public meetings, debates, and participation in political clubs.[24]

A second Revolutionary Defensist assumption was that the workers who had succumbed to the Bolsheviks' political appeal were "ignorant" and "backward," in contrast to the majority who still supported the moderate leadership in the soviet.[25] As late as the end of June, the Revolutionary Defensists, even the praktiki among them, pointed to their apparent triumph at the Third Conference of Trade Unions to counter examples of militancy among organized workers such as had been demonstrated during the First Conference of Factory Committees in late May. Indeed, against all contrary indications, the Revolutionary Defensists in the government, the soviet, and the trade unions repeatedly ar-

[21] "How the Leninists Fight against Destruction," *RG*, June 1, 1917 (no. 69), 1; M. Broido, "The Fruits of Leninism," ibid., 2.

[22] I. Kubikov, "Party Sectarianism," *RG*, May 31, 1917 (no. 68), 3.

[23] The incident in Vyborg, which occurred during the election campaign for the district dumas, elicited bitter criticism from Mensheviks such as Grinevich (whose name was on the common Bolshevik-Menshevik election list in Vasileostrov). Many compared the Bolsheviks' incitement of the workers to the counterrevolutionary behavior of the infamous Union of the Russian People. See "Pogromists," *RG*, June 4, 1917 (no. 72), 1–2; N. Rostov, "Infamy," ibid., 2; and Rostov's response to Uritskii's denial of the incident, *RG*, June 9, 1917 (no. 76), 3; and letters to the editor by Grinevich, in *RG*, June 3, 1917 (no. 71), 2–3, and by I. Klimov, *RG*, June 9, 1917 (no. 76), 3.

[24] Reporting the success Ermanskii had had debating the Bolsheviks Raskolnikov, Entin, and Roshal before a gathering of workers, soldiers, and sailors in Kronstadt, *Rabochaia gazeta* mentioned that "up until now only the Bolsheviks have organized meetings, whereas the Mensheviks have worked in the soviets": "Kronstadt," *RG*, May 25, 1917 (no. 64), 4. See also "Establishing a Workers' Club," *RG*, June 4, 1917 (no. 72), 2, in which the principal purpose of such clubs was defined as making a clearer differentiation between Bolshevism and Menshevism.

[25] "Unsteady Balance," *RG*, May 24, 1917 (no. 63), 1; "Whom to Believe?" *RG*, May 25, 1917 (no. 64), 2; "Party Sectarianism," May 31, 1917 (no. 68), 3; "How the Masses Understand Bolshevik Agitation," *RG*, June 13, 1917 (no. 79), 1.

gued that maximalist sentiments were marginal among the lower classes and were typically those of the nonproletarian masses in the countryside and the cities, whereas "organized democracy" was "united in will and responsible in action."[26] Accordingly, the way to deal with anarchy and maximalism was to strengthen the "organization and political consciousness" of the workers and to draw all elements of the lower classes into participation in local government and other elected bodies. The second of these tasks was judged to have been launched with the establishment of the coalition government, and the first was now to be given greater attention.[27]

All of these explanations of workers' political radicalism and the suggested responses to it were familiar enough: they were a repetition of the Menshevik rationalizations for workers' militancy during the 1912–1914 period. The result of such self-assuring contentions was that Revolutionary Defensist discussions of the political situation in late May and early June were remarkably calm—more so than they had been during the first days of the revolution or on the eve of the decision to join the coalition government. Nor was there in these discussions the sense of urgency that marked the concurrent debates on economic and industrial policies. The obvious, if uneven, changes in the workers' attitudes, the desertion of the Provisional Government by three of its bourgeois ministers (Miliukov, Guchkov, and Konovalov), and other manifestations of political mobilization on the right—none of these weakened the Revolutionary Defensists' confidence that the majority of the population, including the working class, could be counted on to remain loyal to the revolution and the coalition as long as priority was given to "national tasks." In short, the Revolutionary Defensist strategy was based on the belief that there was no contradiction between the interests of the revolution and those of the proletariat.[28] It was in this frame of mind that the Revolutionary Defensists awaited the opening of the first congress of soviets.

[26] Broido, "Fruits of Leninism."

[27] Gorev, "The Revolutionary Methods of Combating Anarchy," *RG*, May 10, 1917 (no. 52), 1–2; "Unsteady Balance," *RG*, May 24, 1917 (no. 63), 1; "The Government and the Struggle against 'Anarchy,' " *RG*, June 9, 1917 (no. 76), 1.

[28] "The Revolution's Road to Victory," *RG*, June 3, 1917 (no. 71), 2. See also P. Golikov, "Shadows of the Past," *RG*, June 6, 1917 (no. 73), 1; V. I. Talin, "Dull Edge," *RG*, June 9, 1917 (no. 76), 2; N. A., "The Black Hundreds Do Not Sleep," ibid.

The First Congress of Soviets

The First All-Russian Congress of Soviets opened in Petrograd on June 3. In attendance were 1,090 delegates, representing some four hundred organizations with approximately twenty million members.[29] From the outset, this "congress of democracy" was firmly in the hands of the Revolutionary Defensist bloc. Not only could the Menshevik and SR factions count on 571 of the 822 voting delegates (see appendix 5), but within the Menshevik faction the Revolutionary Defensist leadership was supported by the provincial delegates and could effectively neutralize the more radical Petrograd section of the party.[30] Indeed, attempts by the Internationalists to air their differences with the Revolutionary Defensists on the congress's floor were repeatedly censured by the provincial delegates and the faction in general.[31] But if the collaboration between the provincial delegates and the star chamber dominated the Menshevik faction and the congress, it was an unequal partnership, and the Revolutionary Defensist bloc itself was dominated by two men, Tsereteli and Dan. Here is Sukhanov's description of their activities:

I was amazed at seeing how Tsereteli and Dan rushed and flashed in motion-picture speed through difficult and responsible affairs in the command posts of the revolution: there they were at the podium delivering a statement to the congress or at the editorial board [of the Petrograd soviet's *Izvestiia*] writing a lead article; they moved from their party's organi-

[29] *Pervyi s'ezd sovetov* 1:xxvii.

[30] The SRs usually accepted the resolutions proposed by the Menshevik faction without any change: *PI*, July 15, 1917 (no. 1), 10. Under pressure from the provincial Mensheviks, an attempt was made to unite all Social Democrats into one faction, but the motion failed over the questions of war and of power: ibid., and *IzvPS*, June 3, 1917 (no. 82), 4–5. When Menshevik delegates met separately on June 2, they elected a "faction bureau" that included only two Internationalists, Orlov and B. Ber; the other fourteen members of the bureau were Khinchuk, Ermolaev, Voitinskii, Isuv, V. V. Sher, Nikol'skii, A. Romanov, A. N. Smirnov, Vainshtein, Naletov, Sakhvatev, Kliukhin, and Pecherskii (the last three, delegates from the front): *IzvPS*, June 3, 1917 (no. 82), 5, and *RG*, June 3, 1917 (no. 71), 3. For signs of the struggle that had raged in May between the Revolutionary Defensist leadership ratified by the May conference and the majority in the Petrograd organization, see the statements by the Menshevik Organizational Committee, in *RG*, May 17, 1917 (no. 58), 1; by a group of "Menshevik members of the Petrograd organization who support the resolution of the All-Russian Conference," in *RG*, May 24, 1917 (no. 63), 3; by Golikov, in *RG*, June 1, 1917 (no. 69), 3; and by the Committee of the Petrograd Organization on its decision to withhold all contributions to *Rabochaia gazeta*, in *RG*, May 19, 1917 (no. 60), 4.

[31] *RG*, June 9, 1917 (no. 76), 4.

zational committee to the podium of some other public assembly; then into the wings of either the Tauride or the Marinskii Palace [the seats of the Petrograd soviet and the Provisional Government, respectively]; and finally to the presidium [of the congress] or the executive committee [of the Petrograd soviet] for some behind-the-scenes secret diplomacy before reemerging again on the podium.[32]

The delegates to the congress consisted of two fairly distinctive groups, each with its own reasons for accepting the leadership's political course. The first and larger group was that of the army delegates, drawn in most cases from the soldiers' committees, army soviets, and mixed soldier-worker soviets.[33] Among this largely intelligentsia "committee class," as Wildman called it, the patriotic mood of March had survived intact and perhaps even had solidified as the committees had been repeatedly called on by the command to help stem the disintegration of military authority and the spread of antiwar sentiment among the soldiery.[34] In fact, the Menshevik Defensists who headed the committees of several army units had been partly responsible for the increasingly Defensist stance taken by the executive committee of the Petrograd soviet.[35] At the conference, not unexpectedly, they and most other army delegates supported the Revolutionary Defensist policies of national cooperation, especially as it concerned defense.

The second group, more important in terms of the stable (though also largely passive) support it gave to the Revolutionary Defensists, was that of the delegates from provincial town soviets, most of whom were Mensheviks.[36] By and large, their experience had been similar to that of Denike and other provincial Mensheviks who had supported the Revolutionary Defensist leadership during the party's May conference. They still felt that, along with

[32] Sukhanov, *Zapiski o revoliutsii* 4:261.

[33] Eight of the twenty million people represented at the congress were reported to have been soldiers; five million, workers and four million, peasants. Most of the soviets represented were of the "mixed" type, but there were delegates from forty organizations of soldiers only, twenty-four of workers, and four of peasants: L'vov-Rogachevskii, ed., *Sotsialisty i tekushchii moment*, 202–3.

[34] Wildman, *Russian Imperial Army*, 377–78.

[35] Ibid., 360–61. Especially influential were G. D. Kuchin of the Twelfth Army Officers' Soviet and A. A. Vilenkin of the Fifth Army Committee. The latter, together with another Menshevik, Khodorov, came to Petrograd at the end of April to urge the Revolutionary Defensist leaders to speak out against fraternization, resulting in the soviet's April 30 appeal to the soldiers (see chap. 5).

[36] Of the 336 organizations represented at the congress, 313 were town soviets: L'vov-Rogachevskii, ed., *Sotsialisty i tekushchii moment*, 202.

other groups of the democratic intelligentsia, they were responsible for uniting the nation's forces and seeing Russia through the difficult processes of revolution and democratization. For these delegates, the congress, with the divisions that were apparent within it and with its vocal contingent of Bolsheviks, as well as the chaos of Petrograd, provided an almost unbearable contrast to the virtual unanimity still prevalent among the intelligentsia in their provincial towns.[37] Sukhanov portrayed their shocked reaction in the following way:

Back home, in the capital of the province, I am the chairman of the soviet and the executive committee, the editor of the local soviet newspaper, the local party leader, the main organizer, the only agitator, and the most likely candidate for mayor. In practice, I am also the commander of the provincial and the town militias because no official institution can act without the support and sanction of the executive committee. Under such conditions . . . I have every reason to feel overloaded and exhausted. Yet, in comparison to Petrograd with its confusion and anxiety, I recall my work at home as peaceful and quiet. My provincial nerves positively cannot bear the temperature here; I feel a continuous dizziness and nausea and cannot wait to return home.[38]

Given these two groups of supporters, there was little doubt of the outcome of the congress's first and most crucial debate, on relationships with the Provisional Government, nor was there anything new in the speeches of either detractors or defenders. The long debate (some sixty speeches delivered over five days) included strong denunciations of coalition by the Bolsheviks and Menshevik Internationalists: Lenin demanded a transfer of all power to the workers and poor peasants, and Martov called more vaguely for an immediate end to socialist participation in coalition as well as a more energetic pursuit of the soviet's program.[39] Tsereteli and the other socialist ministers treated coalition as an irrefutable fact and ignored all opposition to it. Rather than restate the reasons that had led to coalition, its defenders spoke of its achievements to date and described the "objective" reasons for its shortcomings. Tsereteli's only rebuke was directed at the "anarchism" in Kronstadt during April and May, and he used it to reassert the

[37] Voitinskii later recalled that the provincial delegates "protested hysterically" against being dragged by the Petrograd people into their "domestic quarrels": Voitinskii, "God pobed i porazhenii," 159.

[38] Sukhanov, *Zapiski o revoliutsii* 4:260–66. See also his description of these delegates' behavior during the meetings of the Menshevik faction: ibid., 211.

[39] *Pervyi s'ezd sovetov* 1:76, 116.

need for a "strong government" and for the unity of "all the vital forces of the nation."[40] On June 8, the congress passed the Revolutionary Defensist resolution on this question by a resounding majority (543 to 126). It was not entirely what Tsereteli would have wanted, but the reservations it contained concerning the cabinet and its work had been introduced by Tsereteli's own collaborators, notably Dan. On their insistence, the resolution limited the expression of confidence to the socialist ministers alone but did extend the congress's support to the government's policy.[41]

The outcome of this debate, as well as the strong support Tsereteli received from the provincial delegates among the Mensheviks against the qualifications that Dan and others had introduced, encouraged the Revolutionary Defensist leaders in their conviction that "revolutionary democracy" supported their strategy of coalition. Those who, like Gots and Liber, shared Tsereteli's belief in the unity of the "vital forces" felt no doubt that the congress had embraced this formula.[42] In addition, a series of events in Petrograd while the congress was meeting strengthened the leaders' conviction that whatever opposition to their strategy existed in the capital was narrowly based and in conflict with the will of the larger body of "revolutionary democracy." First, an Anarchist takeover of the Berezin printing plant provoked the delegates' condemnation on June 5. Then, on June 8, the delegates supported Minister of Justice P. N. Pereverzev's action against a group of armed Anarchists who had taken over the dacha of the hated former minister of justice, P. N. Durnovo, located in the heart of the Vyborg district.[43] Finally, there was the response to the political challenge of June 10.

---

[40] Ibid., 54–67 (Tsereteli), 77–83 (Kerenskii), 89–95 (Skobelev), 96–111 (Chernov), and 129–37 (Peshekhonov).

[41] The vote is reported in ibid., 286–88, 291. Fifty-two delegates were reported to have abstained and sixty-five to have been absent from the meeting. The resolution had been drafted by Dan and approved by the executive committee on May 28: *Petrogradskii sovet*, 169. At the congress, an editing committee of four Revolutionary Defensist leaders (Dan, Bogdanov, Isuv, and Liber) and four provincials approved essentially the same resolution: *RG*, June 7, 1917 (no. 74), 4. When Tsereteli, E. P. Gegechkori, and Chkheidze expressed strong opposition, the editing committee met with the Menshevik Organizational Committee and the socialist ministers, and a compromise resolution was worked out: *RG*, June 9, 1917 (no. 76), 4; Sukhanov, *Zapiski o revoliutsii* 4:242–43.

[42] Voitinskii, "God pobed i porazhenii," 119–21, 148–49.

[43] At the same time, the congress insisted that the workers of the Vyborg district be permitted to use the garden surrounding the Durnovo dacha. *Pervyi s'ezd sovetov*

It had become clear that the Bolsheviks intended to call for a massive demonstration against the coalition government on that day. Whether or not the demonstration had been calculated to lead to a takeover of power, the Bolshevik summons represented an assault on the authority of the soviet's leadership.[44] It must therefore have been reassuring when the congress united around an appeal to the workers to ignore the planned demonstrations and indeed to avoid all demonstrations for the next three days. "Let the Leninists be as alone on the streets as they are in the congress," *Rabochaia gazeta* pleaded.[45] The appeal was widely accepted by workers and soldiers in all but the Vyborg and Vasileostrov districts, where about half of the workers reportedly rejected it or accepted it only with resentment.[46] At the last minute, however, the Bolshevik Central Committee itself called off the planned demonstration. Thus, although this incident concerned only the soviet's authority, not its policies, it served to reinforce the majority's confidence.

The congress's discussion surrounding the incident revealed both the cracks in Revolutionary Defensist unity and the arguments that continued to preserve it. Tsereteli and his supporters among the provincial Mensheviks and the gosudarstvenniki, sensing renewed strength in their position and perceiving a threat from both the mounting wave of anarchy and the Bolsheviks' presumed conspiracy to seize power, were emboldened to attempt to "expel" the Bolsheviks from revolutionary democracy.[47] Tsereteli

---

1:120, 260–69. See also Sukhanov, *Zapiski o revoliutsii* 4:283; Tsereteli, *Vospominaniia o fevral'skoi revoliutsii* 2:198–201.

[44] In a rare agreement, both Tsereteli and Sukhanov have asserted that it was the intention of the Bolshevik leaders to seize power: Tsereteli, *Vospominaniia o fevral'skoi revoliutsii* 2:184–87; Sukhanov, *Zapiski o revoliutsii* 4:316–23. After studying these events closely, Rabinowitch concluded that this was the intention of elements that Trotskii called the "hotheads" in the party but that Lenin opposed the move: Rabinowitch, *Prelude to Revolution*, 75, 95.

[45] *RG*, June 10, 1917 (no. 77), 1–2. The same issue of the newspaper carried similar resolutions adopted by the Menshevik Organizational Committee and the Petrograd organization. See *Pervyi s'ezd sovetov* 1:375–83 for the congress's discussion of the appeal. The text was published in all the morning newspapers; for an English translation, see *RPG* 3:1313–14.

[46] Some of the large factories that welcomed the appeal were Putilov, Dinamo, Electrical Society, Skorokhod, Arsenal, Trubochnyi, and Baltiiskii. Almost identical reports to this effect appeared in *RG*, June 11, 1917 (no. 78), 4; *NZh*, June 11, 1917 (no. 46); and *IzvPS*, June 11, 1917 (no. 89), 6–7. See also *RD v mae-iiune*, 500–4.

[47] See Sukhanov, *Zapiski o revoliutsii* 4:302, for a description of the change in the

demanded a change away from "verbal methods of struggle" against the Bolsheviks toward stronger measures, albeit still consistent with the preservation of law and order; specifically, he wanted the soviet to act on behalf of the minister of war, Kerenskii, to disarm all military units that had supported the Bolsheviks.

This demand provoked the first open conflict between Tsereteli and Dan. During a meeting of the star chamber and other Revolutionary Defensist members of the congress's presidium early on the morning of June 11, Dan launched a strenuous attack against Tsereteli and his supporters (Liber, Ermolaev, and Gots), and their proposals were defeated.[48] The debate was resumed before a larger audience when the executive committee of the Petrograd soviet, the congress's full presidium, and representatives of all its factions met on the evening of the same day. On this occasion, Dan labeled the Bolshevik-sponsored demonstration a "political adventure" and proposed that all such demonstrations be banned in the future on the pain of expulsion from the soviet, but he still refused to call for any immediate punishment.[49] Tsereteli did not relent, and he pursued the matter both at this meeting and at that of the congress later that night. The Bolsheviks, he argued, had turned against the revolution and its democratic order and should be fought without regard for one's "revolutionary emotionalism."[50]

The discord that was emerging ran far deeper than the narrow issues might suggest—indeed, deeper than most delegates recognized. It concerned the permissible scope of action revolutionary democracy could take against its lapsed members. Whereas Tsereteli wanted the Bolsheviks expelled as a party and singled out for repression—a task that would have fallen to the soviet—Dan preferred "democracy" to maintain its unity and discipline through moral authority alone and to leave to the government the task of

---

mood of these people on hearing the reports of the delegates returning from the workers' quarters.

[48] Tsereteli, *Vospominaniia o fevral'skoi revoliutsii* 2:226–28. This is the only available account of the meeting.

[49] The meeting was closed to the press, but it was attended by about one hundred people, and so some of what went on became known. A report in *Pravda* is quoted in full by Tsereteli along with his own recollection of the meeting: ibid., 228–43. An incomplete protocol from the executive committee's archives is reprinted in *Petrogradskii sovet*, 191–98, and a detailed account is in Sukhanov, *Zapiski o revoliutsii* 4:302–11. See also *Khronika* 3:56–57.

[50] Tsereteli, *Vospominaniia o fevral'skoi revoliutsii* 2:201–2, 243–50; *Pervyi s'ezd sovetov* 2:20–21, 25–38; Sukhanov, *Zapiski o revoliutsii* 4:310–15.

punishing those individuals guilty of illegal conduct. The controversy thus involved Tsereteli's and Dan's fundamental definitions of the groups that had been entrusted to carry out and shape the revolution. In Tsereteli's view, these stewards of the revolution were the "vital forces of the nation," and their continued cooperation required the elimination of Bolshevism from the ranks of the truly democratic part of "revolutionary democracy." To him, the incident of June 10 was a welcome opportunity for effecting this necessary break. From Dan's point of view, revolutionary democracy was supposed to implement the revolution; Bolshevik "adventurism" was abhorrent to him and his supporters because it threatened to divide the "family of revolutionary democracy," but Tsereteli's proposed measures for dealing with the Bolsheviks were equally abhorrent, for the same reason.[51]

Naturally, such differences over the revolution's social boundaries had serious implications for political strategy. Dan's speech during the congress's debate on relations with the Provisional Government had already revealed how different his definition of coalition was from that of Tsereteli, and how inconsistent he was in his support of coalition, on the one hand, and his equally strong assertion of the independence of revolutionary democracy, on the other. He defended coalition, first, on the ground that the soviet could not assume "full power," both because the social and economic reality did not provide the basis for socialism and because a soviet seizure of power would deprive the working class of the support of not only the "big capitalists" but the middle and petty bourgeoisie as well; and second, on the "deep contradictions in the present revolution" (and he went out of his way to pay tribute to Martov's keen understanding of these contradictions)—that is, on the need to defend the revolution nationally until an international peace could be secured.[52]

Dan was clearly apprehensive about the soviet's cooperation with the men of the "big bourgeoisie," and it was this apprehension that had prompted him to insist that the congress express confidence in the socialist ministers alone. He was not the only

[51] The quoted words are actually Bogdanov's, spoken during a meeting of the executive committee on June 11: *Petrogradskii sovet*, 188–89.

[52] *Pervyi s'ezd sovetov* 1:141–42. Dan's wife, Lydia, later discussed his "instinctive repulsion" for people like the wealthy industrialist Tereshchenko, with whom Tsereteli felt at much greater ease. Intellectually and rationally, she said, Dan believed that coalition was absolutely necessary, but emotionally he felt put off by enforced cooperation with the bourgeoisie: L. O. Dan, interview no. 22, pp. 8–9, 21.

one who was uneasy. In the aftermath of the June 10 incident, there were signs that other Revolutionary Defensists were beginning to fear the pernicious influence of the bourgeois ministers on the socialists in the cabinet and to be anxious both to counteract such influence and to impart greater decisiveness to the coalition's policies. This was the gist of Cherevanin's analysis of the events of June 10, which ended with the demand that the socialist ministers "take revolutionary measures"—specifically, that "everything be done to halt economic disintegration and bring the war to an early end."[53] In the same spirit, the Menshevik Organizational Committee, the party's highest authority, decided on June 14 to require the Menshevik ministers to discuss any governmental action touching on "state-political principles" with the committee.[54]

If there were differences in mid-June between two segments of the Revolutionary Defensist majority in the Menshevik party—Tsereteli and the "new Mensheviks" from the provinces on the one hand, and Dan and his supporters, mostly praktiki, on the other—the discussion of the June 10 incident also demonstrated why the latter would not seriously consider calls from the left to end coalition. For all Revolutionary Defensists, the only conceivable way of avoiding the dangerous domestic and international "contradictions" of the revolution was by some sort of cooperation with forces outside the soviet (though they would soon disagree on the composition of these forces and the degree of cooperation). Not only was the war still Russia's most immediate and serious problem, but the attendant economic difficulties seemed to prove the validity of the Menshevik scheme of historical stages, which posited a purely socialist government only in some distant future. In addition, Bolshevik "adventurism" itself had helped stiffen Menshevik resolve. The effect of the Bolshevik challenge can again be seen most clearly in Cherevanin's analysis. The Bolsheviks, he argued, knew that Russia was not ready for socialism, yet they had tried to prevent a bourgeois-democratic order from being established because their real goal of *international* socialist revolution depended on a socialist revolution taking place first in Russia. Cherevanin had no doubt of the outcome of such a willful distortion of history's prescribed path: it would simply facilitate the coming of the counterrevolution.

[53] N. Cherevanin, "Leninism and Counterrevolution," *RG*, June 11, 1917 (no. 78), 1–2.
[54] *PI*, July 15, 1917 (no. 1), 9.

In fact, as writers for the Internationalists' newspaper observed—even as they joined with the Mensheviks in stressing Russia's unpreparedness for socialism and pressing for economic policies of immediate, practical utility—the Mensheviks' "sectarian" attacks on the Bolsheviks often came in place of a serious consideration of the "real issues" of the moment.[55] Moreover, the frequency of such attacks in *Rabochaia gazeta* indicated that the Revolutionary Defensists' overriding concern with Bolshevik machinations served as a barrier to their cognizance of the growth of radical sentiment among their constituency.[56]

This blindness, and in general the perception—or misperception—of the workers' current and potential attitudes, was what distinguished the Revolutionary Defensists most clearly from their Internationalist comrades at the Congress of Soviets. During the debate on June 11 concerning the Bolshevik demonstration, Martov (who was both Dan's closest friend and his most formidable political foe) as well as F. Bulkin (a veteran worker-intelligent who had been replaced in 1913 by Bolsheviks in the leadership of the metalworkers' union) warned that any measures taken against the Bolsheviks would only further alienate the "more active part of the proletariat" and argued that the attitudes expressed by the Bolsheviks were in fact typical of a "huge mass" of workers. Dan answered with typical Revolutionary Defensist confidence that the "true will" of the laboring masses was expressed in the Congress of Soviets and not in the actions of one or another segment of the Petrograd proletariat; that the congress had agreed that coalition government was provisionally "the best way to surmount the dangers facing the Russian revolution"; and that any opposition to this consensus should be pursued within the soviets.[57] Then Dan boldly repeated a suggestion that had been made on June 9 by the Menshevik Petrograd organization: that the congress organize a mass political demonstration of all the soviet's parties to show support for the leaderrship's strategy, which the delegates had already so overwhelmingly approved.[58]

[55] [N. N. Sukhanov], "The Coalition Cabinet," *NZh*, June 7, 1917 (no. 42), 1; V. A. Bazarov, "Bolshevism as a Psychological Phenomenon," *NZh*, June 11, 1917 (no. 46), 1; idem, "Factional Rage," *NZh*, June 13, 1917 (no. 47), 1. See also Sukhanov, *Zapiski o revoliutsii* 4:186–94, 364–68.

[56] See, for example, "Cowards," *RG*, June 11, 1917 (no. 78), 1; A. Shebunin, "Maximalism in the Russian Revolution," ibid., 2–3; "The Judgment of the People," *RG*, June 15, 1917 (no. 81), 2.

[57] For sources on this meeting, see n. 49 above.

[58] Dan's draft resolution was approved by the congress's presidium and the con-

Any doubts that may have begun to cloud the Revolutionary Defensists' faith in the workers' support for their strategy remained hidden.[59] Tsereteli and Liber registered the only reservations concerning the proposed demonstration, and they did so only because Bolshevik participation in the united venture would have belied their standing as outcasts from revolutionary democracy.[60] Yet even Tsereteli displayed the Revolutionary Defensists' confidence in their standing among the workers when, directing his remarks at the Bolsheviks, he declared, on the eve of the planned demonstration: "Tomorrow, not merely some isolated groups will demonstrate but all of working Petrograd, and not against the will of the soviet but with its blessing. This time we will see whom the majority supports—you or us."[61]

As it turned out, the demonstration, which took place on June 18, did not justify this optimism, but neither did it resolve the question of the political attitudes of the Petrograd workers. The Bolshevik newspaper boasted that the demonstration had revealed "the overwhelming majority" of the industrial proletariat of the capital and its troops to have been "behind the slogans of the Bolshevik party," for the greater number of banners had borne the slogans of the Bolsheviks and not those of the soviet: "Armistice Now!," "Down with the Ten Capitalist Ministers!," and "All Power to the Soviets!"[62] This fact suggested to the Internationalists that a reconsideration of political strategy was in order.[63] The Revolutionary Defensists, however, chose to concentrate on the demonstration's other aspect: its support for the soviet and the marchers' apparent belief that they and their leaders were united behind the same goals.

The demonstration of June 18, though far from a precise gauge

---

gress itself on June 12: *RD v mae-iiune*, 513–14. His proposed slogans for the demonstration—"Unity of Revolutionary Democracy," "A General, Democratic Peace," and "A Prompt Convocation of the Constituent Assembly"—were noticeably less confrontational than those that had been suggested by the Petrograd organization, which had called for a demonstration against the "rise of counterrevolution" and the "prolongation of the war": *RG*, June 10, 1917 (no. 77), 3, and June 15, 1917 (no. 81), 1.

[59] See, for example, N. Rostov, "An Anxious Day," *RG*, June 17, 1917 (no. 78), 1.

[60] Tsereteli, *Vospominaniia o fevral'skoi revoliutsii* 3:243–50.

[61] Quoted in Sukhanov, *Zapiski o revoliutsii* 4:336.

[62] *Pravda*, June 20, 1917 (no. 86). There were, of course, different accounts of the demonstration. Compare, for example, *IzvPS*, June 20, 1917 (no. 96), 2–3; Tsereteli, *Vospominaniia o fevral'skoi revoliutsii* 2:251–52; and Sukhanov, *Zapiski o revoliutsii* 4:337–42.

[63] "On the Lessons of Sunday's Demonstration," *NZh*, June 20, 1917 (no. 53), 1.

of workers' political attitudes, did indicate a potential for a major change. A large number of workers showed themselves to be disappointed with the Revolutionary Defensist strategy of coalition and its attendant policies, even though most of them seemed still to believe that the leadership of the soviets could be persuaded to change its policies, and in this way the unity of the soviets, in which their own strength lay, might be preserved. Even those few workers who may have realized the difficulties involved—the Bolshevik workers of Vyborg and the activists of the factory committees—were evidently not eager to risk disunity in the camp of revolutionary democracy. For the Revolutionary Defensists, these attitudes were sufficient grounds for asserting that the majority of workers in Petrograd would not follow the Bolsheviks and that instances in which they had were merely results of the Bolsheviks' preying on the material suffering of the workers.[64] Events outside Petrograd also provided some comfort. In Moscow, Kiev, Minsk, and other towns in which the soviets had organized demonstrations on June 18, the Bolsheviks did not fare nearly as well as in the capital.[65] In elections to the Moscow city duma, the Mensheviks and SRs won 140 of the 200 seats (although only 24 of these went to the Mensheviks).[66]

According to the Petrograd soviet's newspaper, the "divergence" exposed during the congress between "a well-known section of the Petrograd proletariat" and the rest of democracy had actually served the leadership's cause, for it had reminded those in Petrograd of the "concrete correlation of forces existing in the country."[67] It was considered to be of great significance that the congress had created a new entity, the All-Russian Central Executive Committee (VTsIK), which was invested with supreme authority over revolutionary democracy and thereby institutionalized the superiority of the provinces over Petrograd. In the VTsIK that was elected on June 17, Mensheviks held 104 of the 257 seats and SRs 100, for a total of almost 80 percent (see appendix 5). All told, the Revolutionary Defensists emerged from the First Congress of Soviets confident of the support of the soviet's followers for their political strategy.

[64] N. Cherevanin, "The Lesson of the June 18 Demonstration," *RG*, June 20, 1917 (no. 85), 1–2; "The Results of the June 18 Demonstration," *IzvPS*, June 20, 1917 (no. 96), 5.

[65] *RD v mae-iiune*, 541–43.

[66] *Khronika* 3:122.

[67] "The All-Russian Congress of Soviets of Workers' and Soldiers' Deputies," *IzvPS*, June 25, 1917 (no. 101), 7.

Yet within two weeks, the moderates were facing an even greater challenge, which in retrospect can be seen to have ended their effective leadership of the soviets. Clearly, the Revolutionary Defensists' assessment of the popular sentiment in mid-June was out of touch with reality. To a certain degree, they were victims of spatial and temporal patterns of the revolution of which they were not aware and perhaps could not have been. Manifestations of the workers' changing sentiments were uneven and open to varying interpretations. The distinction between Petrograd and the provinces, for example, was not as consistent or as clear as the Revolutionary Defensists would have it. In the isolated industrial centers of Sormovo and Ivanovo-Voznesensk, for example, workers had already called for a government of the soviets. Most important, however, the Revolutionary Defensists were driven to deny changes in workers' attitudes by their concern to find support for a policy to which they could see no alternative and the success of which depended on popular support. Their past skirmishes with the Bolsheviks had provided them with ready explanations and rationalizations with which to counter the gathering evidence of workers' radicalism.

Meanwhile, the fundamental shift of attitudes among the soviet's followers in Petrograd, which had been in progress since late May, accelerated and reached a turning point. Several events contributed to this shift during the two weeks following the June 18 demonstration. The first of these was the government's attack on the Anarchists occupying Durnovo's dacha (on the night following the demonstration of June 18), which strengthened the Vyborg workers' hostility toward coalition.[68] The second was Skobelev's appeal on June 28 for self-restraint, amidst economic crisis and an escalating industrial conflict. Finally, the beginning of the Russian summer offensive against the Germans on June 18, and its complete failure over the following weeks, was perhaps most decisive, and so it must receive our close attention.

THE OFFENSIVE OF JUNE 18

In late June as in late April, the issues of war, peace, and defense provided a convergence for the antigovernment sentiment among the soviet's followers. These were certainly crucial issues for the soldiers not only on the front but also in the rear garrison units,

[68] Rabinowitch, *Prelude to Revolution*, 107–11; Mandel, *Petrograd Workers and the Fall of the Old Regime*, 132–33, 160–61.

which could be called to battle at any moment. And the soldiers' point of view affected that of the workers, especially in urban settings, where the interaction between factories and barracks was most direct. In addition, the workers were receptive to the Bolsheviks' identification of domestic "capitalism" and international "imperialism," because they had been sensitized by the soviet's moderates to the issue of a just peace and were now increasingly drawn by the realities of factory life into a discussion of political choices.[69] By the end of June, many workers in Petrograd had come to see the Menshevik policy on war and peace as—in the words of a resolution passed at the Novyi Lessner machine-building factory—a "blow to the Russian revolution and the International."[70]

Yet the chance to influence government policy in behalf of a just peace among the warring countries had been one of the reasons for the Revolutionary Defensists' participation in the government. Indeed, they had spared no energy during their first six weeks in the coalition in pursuit of this goal.[71] In addition, through the agency of the soviet, they pressed for the convocation of an international socialist conference that would unite all the socialist parties that were not tainted with the charge of "defeatism" in their respective countries, in an effort to force their governments to negotiate on the basis of the soviet's formula for a "democratic peace." Meanwhile, in the Provisional Government, they sought to direct Tereshchenko, the new minister of foreign affairs, to compel the French and British governments to change the Allies' declared war aims. Neither of these efforts bore fruit, but it was not because of inaction on the part of the Revolutionary Defensists.

The first problem with the proposed socialist peace conference emerged during visits of the leaders of the European socialist parties to Petrograd: They could not be made to understand how urgent peace was for revolutionary Russia.[72] Then, while the Revolutionary Defensists were nevertheless making preparations for

[69] Workers' attitudes on questions of foreign policy and the economy are described in Mandel, *Petrograd Workers and the Fall of the Old Regime*, 134–37.

[70] *RD v mae-iiune*, 567.

[71] Tsereteli, "Souvenirs sur la révolution russe," no. 56, pp. 1–3, 5. "The foreign policy of the new Provisional Government will be the precise expression of the demands of revolutionary democracy": "What the New Provisional Government Wants," *IzvPS*, May 9, 1917 (no. 61), 2.

[72] Tsereteli, *Vospominaniia o fevral'skoi revoliutsii* 1:169–340, esp. 172–73; Dan, "Sozialdemokratie Russlands," 297.

the conference (which was to be held in Stockholm at the end of June), there came the second blow—the refusal of the French, Italian, and U.S. governments to grant passports to their socialist delegates.[73] The difficulties in implementing the other part of the Revolutionary Defensist peace strategy were also created by the Allied governments, not by the moderate socialists or the Provisional Government. Tereshchenko's first diplomatic initiative was an invitation to the Allies to join a conference for a review of the war aims, presumably with the goal of preparing to negotiate peace without annexations or indemnities. Tereshchenko's invitation proved to the Revolutionary Defensists' satisfaction the government's dedication to "the earliest conclusion of peace" and could therefore be construed as demonstrating the value of coalition in allowing the revolution's aspirations to "exert influence" on European affairs diplomatically.[74] Such dedication notwithstanding, Russia's financial dependence on the Allies left the Provisional Government with no further resort when they refused to consider any revision of the war aims.[75]

In their response to these setbacks, the Revolutionary Defensists' dedication to peace appears—and appeared even to themselves—unconvincing. They were angered by the Allies' stubbornness, and they admitted that only an "international struggle of democracy against world imperialism" could overcome it.[76] Yet they did not call on the Russian masses to launch this struggle with demonstrations or with fraternization and a nonbelligerent stance on the front, nor could such a strategy have been expected to convince the socialist parties in the Allied nations. Instead, the Revolutionary Defensists urged workers and soldiers to show their "determination to fight," arguing, first, that such determination would give the Germans an inducement to negotiate, and later, that such determination would enable the Russian revolution to

[73] On this episode, see Wade, *Russian Search for Peace*, 51–73. For the Revolutionary Defensists' hopes regarding the conference, see *IzvPS*, June 2, 1917 (no. 81), 5. For reports on the preparations carried on in the executive committee and the Menshevik Organizational Committee, see *Petrogradskii sovet*, 139, 153–57; *RG*, June 1, 1917 (no. 69), 3; and Shliapnikov, *Semnadtsatyi god* 4:34–35. Tsereteli, Dan, Akselrod, and Chkheidze were particularly active in this area.

[74] *IzvPS*, June 4, 1917 (no. 83), 1. A similar editorial appeared in *RG*, June 4, 1917 (no. 72), 1. The invitation was published in *VVP*, June 3, 1917 (no. 70), 1.

[75] The negotiations are discussed in Wade, *Russian Search for Peace*, 77–87.

[76] For examples of the Mensheviks' angry reaction to the Allies' position, see "The Situation Is Becoming Tragic" and "Italy's Statement," *RG*, May 27, 1917 (no. 66), 2–3, and "In the Struggle for Peace," *RG*, June 6, 1917 (no. 73), 1.

claim that it had "carried the banner of the struggle for peace" and would gain the support of the Allies' socialist parties for peace negotiations.[77] With these arguments, the Revolutionary Defensists sought to justify to themselves and their constituency their support of the Provisional Government's decision, taken under British and French pressure, to launch the offensive against the German army.[78]

Not only was there a touch of the absurd in the launching of a military offensive in the name of peace—much as this might have been anticipated by the original Revolutionary Defensist formula of seeking a universal peace while also defending the Russian revolution—but the validity of its expectations should have been doubtful from the outset. The Revolutionary Defensists, as the Bolsheviks would do after October, exaggerated the influence of the revolution beyond Russia's borders, even among the socialist parties. They also misapprehended the depth of the disruption it would cause in the army. In later years, Dan admitted that the existing balance of forces "had not warranted the strivings of the revolution toward a general democratic peace."[79] Given these misperceptions, the issue of peace was irrevocably tied to that of continuing the war, obscuring the fact that the only practical choice was *between* continued war and a separate peace with Germany.[80]

Moreover, the issues of war and peace were intimately connected to, and often confused with, considerations of the revolution's political shape. Both a separate peace and the vaguer variant of an "immediate armistice" advocated by the Menshevik Internationalists were objectionable to the Revolutionary Defensists principally because they feared that either one would destroy the "unity of the vital forces."[81] In fact, the nonsocialist ministers, especially Tereshchenko and Kerenskii, had used this concern of the Revolutionary Defensists to pressure them into supporting the of-

[77] "Offensive or Preparations for the Offensive?" *IzvPS*, May 17, 1917 (no. 68), 1–2; *IzvPS*, June 4, 1917 (no. 83), 2; I. Kuchin, "Regarding an Offensive," *RG*, May 28, 1917 (no. 67), 1–2.

[78] See the resolution adopted by the Menshevik and SR factions of the Congress of Soviets, in *RG*, June 14, 1917 (no. 80), 3–4; its acceptance by the full congress, in *Pervyi s'ezd sovetov* 2:11–12, 20; and the argument in "The Offensive in the Struggle for Peace," *IzvPS*, June 22, 1917 (no. 98), 8. Voitinskii called the offensive the "last ticket" for peace: "God pobed i porazhenii," 164.

[79] Dan, "Die Sozialdemokratie Russlands," 303.

[80] Voitinskii understood the nature of the choice later; see his "God pobed i porazhenii," 96–97.

[81] Tsereteli, "Souvenirs sur la révolution russe," no. 56, pp. 3–4.

fensive.[82] Had they been free of these considerations, Dan later implied, the Revolutionary Defensists would have seen that the balance of forces had dictated "most emphatically" an end to the war, "even at the heavy price of a sacrifice such as was forced by history on the German Social Democrats in 1918."[83]

It ought not be concluded that the Revolutionary Defensists' stand on the question of a separate peace was utterly blind and wrongheaded, for the military dangers of the moment must be kept in mind. Insofar as an "immediate armistice" might have left Russia fighting alone against the Germany army, it was of course to be feared. The option of peace with Germany could not be counted on, nor was it certain that the Provisional Government could have survived the political effects of such a peace, as the Bolshevik experience of a year later suggests. Then, too, the socialists' membership in the government reinforced the concern shared by Dan, Tsereteli, and other Revolutionary Defensists that the state structure remain sufficiently strong to contain the social explosion of revolution—a concern that further reinforced the moderate socialists in their feeling of responsibility for state order and the defense of the country.[84] Finally, in late May and June, Kerenskii's campaign for "prosecuting the war in order to end it" seemed more promising a policy than that of suing for peace.[85]

The offensive tested the reality of both the renewed optimism about the army's capacity to fight and the hope for diplomatic gain from the mere search for peace. An initial flush of success and the swelling of patriotic feelings among certain groups of workers as well as among the middle class and the intelligentsia gave rise to some enthusiastic rhetoric among the Revolutionary Defensists.[86]

[82] Indications of such pressure as well as the hope that support of the offensive would strengthen the soviet's position in the struggle for domestic reforms can be seen in *IzvPS*, June 22, 1917 (no. 98), 6–7; Dan, "Die Sozialdemokratie Russlands," 299; L. Dan, interview no. 22, pp. 8–9, 24–25; and Voitinskii, "God pobed i porazhenii," 97.

[83] Dan, "Die Sozialdemokratie Russlands," 303.

[84] This point especially was emphasized in the argument over the issue between the Revolutionary Defensists and the Menshevik Internationalists. See, for example, N. Cherevanin, "The Struggle for Peace and Defense," *RG*, May 16, 1917 (no. 57), 1–2, and *RG*, May 27, 1917 (no. 66), 2–4, and June 1, 1917 (no. 69), 2.

[85] Wade, *Russian Search for Peace*, 89; Kakurin, ed., *Razlozhenie armii*, 91; Sukhanov, *Zapiski o revoliutsii* 4:70; and Tsereteli, *Vospominaniia o fevral'skoi revoliutsii* 2:34–36.

[86] See, for example, resolutions supporting the offensive adopted by the workers of the Obukhov factory and some railroad workers and by the factory committees of Arsenal and the Petrograd pipe factory, in *RG*, June 25, 1917 (no. 90), 4; June 27,

Yet even at this moment, the Revolutionary Defensists reasserted their commitment to peace. The offensive, they insisted, had been only a "strategy" subordinated to the revolution's "political tasks," specifically to its "peace policy."[87] Furthermore, they repeatedly attacked Potresov and his colleagues at *Den'* for their unreserved delight in the offensive.[88]

Early success, however, soon turned to defeat, and whatever enthusiasm the offensive had aroused among the soviet's followers vanished. There were reports of soldiers refusing to fight, deserting their units, and even assaulting once-popular emissaries of the soviet. N. D. Sokolov, who had drawn up Order No. 1 (see chapter 2), was one of those beaten by soldiers for his support of the offensive.[89] In Petrograd, the antiwar and antigovernment mood spread quickly from units intended for the front to the garrison at large and finally to the workers.[90] The Revolutionary Defensists' reaction to this turn in popular sentiment was not to admit their mistake but to attack the Bolsheviks.[91] Whatever the Menshevik interpretation of the causes, the offensive had clearly become the symbol of what workers and soldiers in Petrograd believed to have been the government's duplicity and the moderates' acquiescence in it. The political consequences of this mistake would be reaped during the so-called July Days.

1917 (no. 91), 3; June 29, 1917 (no. 92), 4; July 2, 1917 (no. 96), 4. The Petrograd soviet voted 472 to 271 (with 39 abstentions) in favor of the offensive: *IzvPS*, June 2, 1917 (no. 97), 8. The soviet's newspaper declared that the offensive was a "great turnabout," that the Russian army could no longer be considered a "paper army," and that in recognition of this fact the policies of certain Allied governments as well as that of Germany had begun to change: *IzvPS*, June 20, 1917 (no. 96), 5, and June 30, 1917 (no. 104), 5–6.

[87] "The Offensive," *RG*, June 20, 1917 (no. 85), 1. Similar statements were made in "The Offensive and *Pravda*," *RG*, June 22, 1917 (no. 87), 1; in the Menshevik Organizational Committee's declaration, "The Struggle for Peace," *RG*, June 18, 1917 (no. 84), 3–4; and in the resolutions of the Menshevik Moscow and Petrograd organizations, *RG*, June 27, 1917 (no. 91), 4.

[88] Ezhov, "Propaganda as a Weapon," *RG*, June 21, 1917 (no. 86), 2; "Two Potresovs," *RG*, June 23, 1917 (no. 88), 2–3; N. Cherevanin, "Our Fight for Peace," *RG*, June 28, 1917 (no. 92), 1–2; S. Ivanovich, "Are We Frightened of Victory?" *RG*, June 29, 1917 (no. 93), 2–3.

[89] *RD v mae-iiune*, 366–68, 371–75, 377–81.

[90] Rabinowitch, *Prelude to Revolution*, 116–20; Mandel, *Petrograd Workers and the Fall of the Old Regime*, 160–62.

[91] "The Leninists' Verdict on the Offensive" and "He Who Sows the Wind, Must Reap the Whirlwind," *RG*, June 24, 1917 (no. 89), 1–2; *IzvPS*, June 24, 1917 (no. 100), 8.

July Days

The July Days consisted of two crises initiated independently of each other but resolved through nearly the same set of developments. One crisis involved the relations between the soviet's leadership and its followers, who poured into the streets of Petrograd on July 3 and 4 to express their desire for a bold new political initiative by the soviet. The other crisis involved the relations between the representatives of the soviet in the coalition government and the nonsocialist ministers, especially those of the Kadet party. The outcome of both crises depended largely on the Revolutionary Defensist leaders of the soviet, and here again, the Mensheviks took the lead. They provided the explanation for what was clearly a demonstration of widespread opposition to the coalition government. They proposed the political initiatives by which they hoped to restore the workers' support for the government while not altering the coalition policy that had guided the soviet's strategy since early May, and they bore the burden of negotiating with the nonsocialist ministers in behalf of these initiatives. Their success or failure would determine not only the fate of the coalition but also their claim to the leadership of revolutionary democracy and the final outcome of the February revolution.

THE CABINET CRISIS began a day before the street demonstration, when the Kadet Central Committee decided to withdraw its four ministers from the cabinet on July 2, ostensibly to protest the agreement on limited autonomy for the Ukraine just negotiated by Tsereteli, Kerenskii, and Tereshchenko between the Provisional Government and the Ukrainian Central Rada.[92] The agreement, it asserted, had violated two basic Kadet principles: the absolute unity of the Russian state and the equally absolute right of a future Constituent Assembly to determine Russia's political future. The refusal of the negotiating triumvirate to make any changes infuriated many other Kadets. More broadly, however, the agreement was final proof to the Kadets of the coalition's general uselessness; the idea of resignation had been gathering strength among them for some time.[93]

To the Menshevik Revolutionary Defensists, the Kadets' resig-

[92] The resigning Kadets included three ministers (Shingarev, Shakhovskoi, and Manuilov) and one acting minister (Stepanov).

[93] Rosenberg, *Liberals in the Russian Revolution*, 171–75; Miliukov, *Istoriia vtoroi russkoi revoliutsii* 1:232–36.

nation represented the attack on democracy that they had expected. For weeks, *Rabochaia gazeta* had been condemning what it saw as signs of the "bourgeoisie's refusal" to abide by the coalition principle: Konovalov's resignation and the failure of Moscow's "enlightened bourgeoisie" to name a successor to the position of minister of trade and industry; Pal'chinskii's antidemocratic "provocations" in the economic agencies under his authority; and generally, the mobilization of right-wing forces.[94] Yet, paradoxical as it might seem, each of the "desertions" by the bourgeoisie, including especially the resignations of the Kadet ministers, had actually broadened agreement among the Menshevik Revolutionary Defensists about the importance of coalition, because the desertions served to remind them of the ideological principles on which acceptance of coalition had been based in the first place.[95] Even Dan and other skeptics among the Revolutionary Defensists, because they could see no alternative to coalition, seized upon the Kadets' departure as offering an opportunity to reconstruct a new and possibly more workable coalition. *Rabochaia gazeta* explained that certain "democratic elements"—i.e., the "left wing of the bourgeoisie" and its supporters among the "masses of bourgeois democracy in the village and in the city"—had "understood the demands of the revolution" but had hitherto been under the influence of the Kadets and would now come over to the socialists in a new coalition.[96] These were the very groups whose importance to the revolution Cherevanin and others had repeatedly emphasized on the eve of the war and again during the frustrating weeks since coalition.

Finally, adding both to Dan's greater strength within the leadership and to his bond with Tsereteli, the Kadets' resignation allowed the Revolutionary Defensists to admit more openly than they had in the past two months that the program of reforms they had announced at the time of their entry into the coalition had not been carried out. They now felt free to rededicate themselves to the implementation of this program, which in fact served as the basis of agreement among the members of the star chamber when they met on the morning of July 3 to discuss a solution to the crisis. The coalition, without the Kadets, it was decided, would co-opt "those representatives of 'bourgeois democracy' who would

[94] "A Boycott of the Revolutionary Government," *RG*, July 1, 1917 (no. 95), 1, and "A Challenge to Revolutionary Democracy," *RG*, July 2, 1917 (no. 96), 1–2.
[95] "A Challenge to Revolutionary Democracy," *RG*, July 2, 1917 (no. 96), 1–2.
[96] "The Crisis of Power," *RG*, July 4, 1917 (no. 97), 1.

not be against the implementation of the radical democratic reforms promised in the [May 6] declaration."[97]

Initially, this solution did not appear unrealistic. During a private meeting of all the ministers in Tereshchenko's apartment around noon on July 3, Nekrasov announced his decision to remain in the cabinet and leave the Kadet party, and he told of the considerable opposition the resignations of the Kadet ministers had caused within the party, especially among its Moscow members. His hope, shared by Tereshchenko, was that other Kadets would leave the party and join with Efremov's Party of Progressists to form a Radical Democratic party that could rally all the "nonsocialist democrats ready to cooperate with Soviet 'democracy' for the implementation of urgent democratic reforms."[98] Dan later assured the soviet's deputies that a split had occurred in Kadet ranks and "large groups within the bourgeoisie planned to join the socialist ministers in defense of the interests of the revolution."[99] It was only a few days later, in negotiating the reconstruction of coalition after the demonstration of July 3 and 4 had ended, that the Revolutionary Defensist leaders discovered how ill-founded their optimism had been.

At first, then, the Revolutionary Defensists did not see the Kadets' resignations as dangerous nor even without benefit to their strategy of coalition with the bourgeoisie. True, the event compelled some of them—though not yet Tsereteli and other believers in the "unity of the vital forces"—to follow Cherevanin's example at the recent trade-union conference in redefining the social groups whose cooperation in the revolution the Social Democrats could and should seek (see chapter 7). Yet none of them appeared ready to match the new perception of the revolution's social boundaries with a practical political program. They proposed tactical adjustments but saw no need to reconsider the coalition strategy. They believed that a coalition with the left wing of the bourgeoisie dedicated to radical reforms would be acceptable to

[97] Tsereteli again provides the only account of this meeting. The participants, besides himself, were Dan, Liber, Gvozdev, Vainshtein, Anisimov, and Ermolaev from the Menshevik party; Chernov, Gots, and Avksent'ev from the SRs; and Peshekhonov of the People's Socialist party: Tsereteli, *Vospominaniia o fevral'skoi revoluitsii* 2:259–62.

[98] Tsereteli gives the only firsthand account of the meeting, in *Vospominaniia o fevral'skoi revolutsii* 2:262–65, but the general thrust of Nekrasov's words is corroborated elsewhere, see esp. Rosenberg, *Liberals in the Russian Revolution*, 174–77.

[99] Quoted in Sukhanov, *Zapiski o revoliutsii* 4:419–20, from Dan's address to the soldiers' section on July 4.

the soviet's constituency, especially since the institutional structure of the soviets now allowed for the sentiment of workers and soldiers in Petrograd to be checked against that of the provinces.

Thus, on the afternoon of July 3, in comments about the crisis and its resolution to a combined meeting of the bureaus of the two all-Russian executive committees (that of the Soviet of Workers' and Soldiers' Deputies and that of the Peasants' Soviet), Dan and Tsereteli insisted that nothing be decided until the one hundred provincial deputies elected to the VTsIK during the Congress of Soviets could join, in emergency session, the two hundred deputies residing in Petrograd. In the meantime, the cabinet was to act as the supreme authority in the country, and any discussion of the coalition issue by the Petrograd soviet and the Petrograd-based executive committees was to be avoided.[100] But before the two bureaus could make any decisions, news came of unrest among the workers and soldiers of Petrograd, throwing the political tactics and the parliamentary manipulations of the Revolutionary Defensist leaders into disarray. They found themselves flung into a painful confrontation with a constituency which no longer subscribed to the moderates' portrayal of the social and political reality in the country and was now ready to challenge their policies.

OF THE TWO CRISES constituting the July Days, it was the street demonstrations by workers and soldiers that proved the most damaging to the Revolutionary Defensists' strategy. In retrospect, the demonstrations appear to have been the culmination of a process of embitterment and political radicalization that had been under way for most of the two months of coalition and that had accelerated with the offensive. Rabinowitch has shown that they were autonomous and largely spontaneous occurrences, neither begun on the orders of the Bolsheviks (whose Central Committee had in fact first attempted to dissuade workers from demonstrating) nor primarily concerned with the resignation of the Kadet ministers.[101]

The first call to workers and soldiers to demonstrate against the

---

[100] The meeting of the two bureaus is reported in Sukhanov, *Zapiski o revolutsii* 4:376–86, and Tsereteli, *Vospominaniia o fevral'skoi revoliutsii* 2:265–69. See Tsereteli, *Vospominaniia o fevral'skoi revoliutsii* 2:260–61, and Voitinskii, "God pobed i porazhenii," 185–87, on the leaders' intentions in calling the provincial deputies to Petrograd.

[101] Rabinowitch, *Prelude to Revolution*, 144–53. For a present-day Soviet perspective on the July Days, see Znamenskii, *Iiul'skii krizis*, esp. 45–77.

government came on July 3 from the First Machine Gun Regiment, stationed in Vyborg, after it had elected a "revolutionary committee" to plan the takeover of certain points in the capital in conjunction with the demonstrations. The regiment had a long history of contact with the Bolshevik military organization, and activists from that organization and from the Anarchist Communists were among the leaders of the insurrection. The machine-gunners' action followed two weeks of agitation and turmoil triggered by an order on June 20 that part of the regiment move to the front.[102]

In other units and factories in the Vyborg district, and later all over the city to which emissaries from the Machine Gun Regiment were sent with word of the planned demonstration, they found most workers and a large part of the soldiers eager to listen and follow (notwithstanding the Bolsheviks' advice to the contrary).[103] The most dramatic response came from the Putilov works. There, news of the Kadets' resignation had arrived on July 3 and had served to give clearer political definition to the workers' anger, which had been mounting during their month-long wage dispute with the Provisional Government. Thirty thousand Putilov workers responded to the summons with an armed march on the Tauride Palace to demand that the soviet assume "full power."[104] (Their forthrightness was particularly striking in comparison with their vague protest against "deceit" during the June 18 demonstrations barely two weeks earlier.) When they reached the Tauride Palace in the small hours of the morning of July 4, they joined the huge crowd that had already gathered in front of the gates, carrying banners of all sorts (many of them probably left over from June 18), exclaiming, among other things, "Down with All the Capitalist Ministers" and "All Power to the Soviets!"[105]

However well defined the workers' sentiment was, it did not produce anything resembling a program of action. Indeed, closer examination of the behavior and pronouncements of the workers and soldiers on July 3 and 4 shows a pattern of ambivalence. Although the workers who demonstrated seemed to have no doubt that government by the soviets was urgently needed, there were

---

[102] The regiment had threatened to demonstrate against the government and the offensive several times before: Rabinowitch, *Prelude to Revolution*, 135–40.

[103] See, for example, the reports from the Novyi Lessner and Russian Renault factories and from the Galernyi Island, in "Piterskie rabochie ob iiul'skikh dniakh," 28–35.

[104] *Khronika* 3:133–35; "Piterskie rabochie," 19–20.

[105] *Khronika* 3:135.

several contradictory elements in their attitude toward the soviet's leaders.[106] The demonstrators were united in wanting all of the bourgeois ministers—not merely the Kadets—out of the cabinet, for they held them directly responsible for the government's objectionable economic and war policies as well as the "distortions" of the revolution. As a worker representing a group of fifty-four factories at a meeting of the Central Executive Committee on July 4 put it in explaining his demand that the ten "capitalist ministers" resign: "We trust the soviet but not those whom the soviet trusts."[107] After two months of coalition, the workers no longer believed that the soviet could force the bourgeois ministers to do its will. Indeed, the issue was not really "soviet power" as such but rather the workers' desire to see realized the soviet's policies of peace, economic reconstruction, and democratization (to which the soldiers added the distribution of land) as well as their desire that their leaders acknowledge that these policies would not be realized in coalition: "Our comrades, the socialist ministers, entered into an agreement with the capitalists. But those capitalists are our sworn enemies. We demand that the land be seized immediately, that control over industry be seized immediately, and that a struggle be initiated immediately against the hunger that threatens us."[108] The repetition of "immediately" reflected the workers' desperation in seeking to resurrect the promises of the revolution to the point of challenging the soviet's leaders.[109]

This readiness to challenge and the workers' continued deference toward their leaders were brought into sharp focus in one of the more touching episodes of the July Days. A Putilov worker made his way into an executive committee meeting, climbed to the podium, rifle in hand, and declared the workers' determination not to disperse "until the ten capitalist ministers are arrested and the soviet takes power into its hands." When Chkheidze reproached him for having disturbed the meeting, he quietly left the hall, and later, outside the palace gates, he read the committee's order to his comrades that they return to their factories.[110] In sim-

[106] Mandel, *Petrograd Workers and the Fall of the Old Regime*, 158–66.

[107] *RD v iiule*, 21.

[108] Ibid.

[109] "Dispirited faces . . . like those of participants in a funeral procession" was Chernov's characterization of the demonstrators in front of the Tauride on the night between July 3 and 4, as quoted in Tsereteli, *Vospominaniia o fevral'skoi revoliutsii* 2:278.

[110] *Khronika* 3:137–38.

ilar ways, other workers demonstrated the contradictions born of their revolt against their moderate leaders, or more precisely, against the vision of the revolution these leaders sought to impose on them. The demonstrators wanted an end to the coalition government, yet they did not go to the government's offices in the Marinskii Palace, and only a few units (mostly from Kronstadt) presented themselves at Bolshevik headquarters in the Kshesinskaia mansion. Instead, the masses converged on the Tauride Palace, hoping to persuade, if need be to force, the soviet's leaders inside to act in their name, disband the coalition, and assume full authority.

Herein was the crux of the conflict that came to the fore during the July Days: The leaders refused to assume the authority that seemed to the workers within easy reach, and yet leaders and followers were reluctant to break openly with each other, and the conflict was thereby rendered emotionally explosive. Two of the many tragicomic episodes reported from these days exemplify the complexity of motives and reactions involved. In one case, Dan encountered a garrison unit on its way to the Tauride and asked the soldiers if they were ready to support the soviet "in fulfilling its duty and creating the conditions under which the representatives of all-Russian democracy might carry out their will without hindrance." To this the soldiers answered with a noisy affirmative, though their original intention had been to join the demand for soviet power.[111] What is evident is that the highly stylized formulas used by Dan had come to mean different things to leaders and followers. To the former, the proper "conditions" consisted of their ability to pursue the strategy approved by the Congress of Soviets without interruption from the masses of Petrograd; to the latter, the one essential condition was the exclusion of the bourgeoisie from participation in government. In early July, when the differentiation in rhetoric had not yet caught up with the evolving differences in attitude and strategy, it was often possible for both the Bolsheviks and the Revolutionary Defensists to lay claim to the loyalty of the same people. Meanwhile, the disagreement between the workers and the soviet's moderate leaders was leading to bitter frustration, even hostility toward formerly admired leaders. This was forcefully demonstrated in the second ep-

---

[111] Tsereteli, *Vospominaniia o fevral'skoi revoliutsii* 2:308–9, and Sukhanov, *Zapiski o revoliutsii* 4:419.

isode, in which a fist-waving worker shouted at Chernov, "Take power, you son of a bitch, when it's being handed to you!"[112]

The workers' new political mood did not change the leadership's strategy, though it affected their handling of the crisis in a number of important ways. First, the demonstrations had the effect of dividing society in Petrograd and isolating its working class. On July 3, and even more so on July 4, when more workers as well as twenty thousand Kronstadt sailors joined the demonstrations, armed confrontations took place between the radicalized soviet's constituency and the supporters of the Provisional Government which resulted in some four hundred deaths and revived earlier fears of civil war.[113] Second, the workers' behavior was viewed by most Revolutionary Defensists as symptomatic of their "confusion" and general political immaturity and strengthened the Revolutionary Defensists' determination to resist the pressure for a more radical policy.[114] Finally, the Bolsheviks' involvement in the July Days deflected the Mensheviks' attention from the change in working-class sentiment in Petrograd. After initially discouraging the demonstrations, the Bolshevik Central Committee yielded to the pressure of events and of the party's lower ranks and on July 4 issued an invitation to all workers and soldiers to exploit the cabinet crisis and press for soviet power.[115] As a result of these three factors, the street demonstrations of July 3 and 4 had the seemingly paradoxical effect of reinforcing the resolve of the Revolutionary Defensist leaders to see the coalition revived.

AT ABOUT THREE in the afternoon of July 3, when the two bureaus of the executive committees had just begun discussing the cabinet crisis, news reached the Tauride Palace of the movement developing in the streets. The mood immediately turned tense, and suspicions ran high. When a Bolshevik member, I. V. Stalin, rose to announce that the Bolsheviks had had nothing to do with the

[112] Miliukov, *Istoriia vtoroi russkoi revoliutsii* 1:244.

[113] Rabinowitch, *Prelude to Revolution*, 181–91, and Znamenskii, *Iul'skii krizis*, 77–107, have exhaustive accounts of the events on July 4. For examples of factories won over to the movement on July 4, see the accounts from Skorokhod and Sestroretsk in "Piterskie rabochie," 21–23, 36–41.

[114] This, for example, was Tsereteli's reaction on hearing of Chernov's short-lived "arrest" in front of the Tauride by the very Kronstadt sailors whom he was trying to pacify. See Tsereteli, *Vospominaniia o fevral'skoi revoliutsii* 2:306–8, and reports of the incident in *RG*, July 5, 1917 (no. 98), 3; Sukhanov, *Zapiski o revoliutsii* 4:422–26; and Trotsky, *History of the Russian Revolution*, 551–53.

[115] Rabinowitch, *Prelude to Revolution*, 161–66, 174–78, 180–81, 183–84, 201–5.

demonstration, Chkheidze commented tartly: "Peaceful people shouldn't have to insist on introducing a statement regarding their peaceful intentions." Then the meeting heard deputies from the Fifth Army complain about the antiwar propaganda carried in the Bolshevik newspapers *Pravda* and *Soldatskaia pravda*. Finally, the two bureaus adopted an appeal to the masses that they not heed the call of some "unknown people" to demonstrate, and the meeting adjourned.[116] By the time the plenary session of the two executive committees opened after midnight, thousands of demonstrators clamoring for "soviet power" had surrounded the palace, and many more (such as the Putilov workers) were on their way. By that time, too, Tsereteli's ministerial employees had gone on strike, and the workers' section of the soviet had adopted a resolution proposed by the Bolsheviks calling for a seizure of power by the soviets.[117]

The nature of the crisis had now changed. No longer was the issue merely the "desertion" of the cabinet by one subsection of the bourgeois partner in coalition but rather the unwillingness of both camps represented in the coalition to make the concessions that cooperation in the revolution would require. The Revolutionary Defensist leaders of the soviet were faced with three options: to insist on the principle of coalition, perhaps modified as a result of the cabinet crisis; to give in to the demonstrators' demand for "soviet power"; or to formulate an altogether new political arrangement. The choice among these options was arguably the most crucial decision of the eight months between February and October.

The ideological precepts militating against the second alternative had already been brought to the foreground by the cabinet crisis and had ended any disagreements between Dan and Tsereteli. But it was not ideology alone that made for the vehemence of Dan's, Tsereteli's, and some Internationalist Mensheviks' statements during the nightlong session of the executive committees as they spoke in opposition to the demand for soviet power. Their target was the radicalism of the masses both in its spontaneous form and in the political shape given it by the Bolsheviks: the "madly speeding cars and trucks from which soldiers and Red

[116] *NZh*, July 4, 1917 (no. 65), 3; Sukhanov, *Zapiski o revoliutsii* 4:385–86; Tsereteli, *Vospominaniia o fevral'skoi revoliutsii* 2:266–69. The appeal was printed in *IzvPS*, July 4, 1917 (no. 108), 1.

[117] For reports of the workers' section meeting, see *IzvPS*, July 4, 1917 (no. 108), 5; *Khronika* 3:135–36; and Sukhanov, *Zapiski o revoliutsii* 4:389–94.

Guards repeatedly opened fire on the peaceful population," and the Bolshevik victory in the workers' section, which the Revolutionary Defensists viewed as nothing less than an attempt to accomplish the transfer of power that they had failed to accomplish in early June.[118] Some of the Revolutionary Defensists believed that these manifestations of radicalism had become a political weapon as well as a factor in their inability to agree with Martov and other Internationalists on a new political arrangement to replace coalition.

When Dan opened the meeting of the two executive committees, he demanded that all those not willing to go "in the direction indicated by the congress" leave the meeting.[119] The Bolsheviks and Mezhraiontsy complied immediately, but the Menshevik Internationalists and the Left SRs are stayed behind to argue against Dan's demand. Nevertheless, it was approved by a vote of more than 300 in favor to 21 opposed. With their opponents absent or neutralized, Dan and Tsereteli began an attack against the Bolsheviks and the demonstrators. The actions taking place in the street, Tsereteli charged, were simply "counterrevolution," whereas the task of the executive committees was to "realize the will of Russian democracy." Dan contrasted the leadership's strategy, which had been endorsed by "the first parliament of the revolution," to the acts in the streets, which could cause a civil war at any moment. He too termed these actions "counterrevolutionary" and also as divisive, because they "separated one city from the rest of the country and the revolutionary army," and he added that the actions illustrated the wish of "some comrades" to deny the authority of the "central organs of revolutionary democracy" and "foist their will on democracy." These were the same accusations Tsereteli had hurled at the Bolsheviks in June, but now he was being seconded by Dan and, more surprisingly, by some Menshevik Internationalists. After "spontaneous" addresses to the meeting by a soldier from the First Machine Gun Regiment and by the Putilov representative, both carrying rifles, R. A. Abramovich, formerly a consistent critic of Revolutionary Defensism, joined Dan and Tsereteli in condemning the Bolshevik "plot" and the demonstrators'

---

[118] Tsereteli, *Vospominaniia o fevral'skoi revoliutsii* 2:300–4, 310–11. The Bolsheviks did make a special effort to have the resolution on soviet power passed on July 4, dispatching Zinov'ev, Kamenev, and Trotskii to speak to the workers' section.

[119] Reports of the meeting are in *RG*, July 5, 1917 (no. 98), 3; *IzvPS*, July 4, 1917 (no. 108), 3; *Khronika* 3:137–38; and Sukhanov, *Zapiski o revoliutsii* 4:401–4.

"irresponsible slogans" and their interruption of the "constructive revolutionary work" the meeting was attempting to accomplish.

In this atmosphere of fear of an outbreak of civil war and of anger toward the Bolsheviks and their followers, the political divisions in the soviet and within the Menshevik party were sharpened. The meeting of the executive committees ended early on the morning of July 4 with only an appeal to the workers and soldiers to end the street demonstrations, with further debate postponed until another meeting at six that evening.[120] When the committees reconvened, it was apparent that the Bolsheviks and Left SRs were no longer the only advocates of soviet power.[121] To most Internationalists, both Menshevik and Independent, the second, and more serious, day of demonstrations and unchecked clashes was proof that a radical departure from the strategy of the leadership was urgently required, both because this was the demand of the soviet's constituency and because it seemed the only way to prevent further bloodshed. Steklov, formerly an Independent SD but now affiliated with the Menshevik Internationalists, argued that a "socialist ministry" not only had been essential but also had been met with an "enthusiasm greater than that which had greeted the overthrow of the Romanov dynasty." The Menshevik Internationalists Kapelinskii and Lapinskii agreed; the latter declared that "any other solution would condemn the country to a state of chronic crisis."

It was Martov who offered the most innovative solution, a third alternative. All along, he had condemned coalition and had rejected a policy of soviet power for the same doctrinal reason: socialists should not hold political power in a revolution that could not accomplish a socialist transformation in the short run. Over the last two months, however, he had seen two long-standing threats to the revolution being realized: the bourgeoisie's refusal to "complete" the democratic revolution (now irrefutably shown in the Kadets' resignations) and the bourgeoisie's distortion of the policies of their socialist coalition partners in an effort to deprive them of the workers' support. He was now convinced that none of the traditional Menshevik arguments against the soviets' assumption of full power could outweigh the message of the demonstrators. Perhaps the masses lacked political consciousness, he

[120] *RG*, July 5, 1917 (no. 98), 1; *Khronika* 3:315–16.

[121] For reports of this meeting, see *IzvPS*, July 5, 1917 (no. 109), 2, and July 6, 1917 (no. 110), 3–6; *Khronika* 3:142–46; Tsereteli, *Vospominaniia o fevral'skoi revoliutsii* 2:322–27; and Sukhanov, *Zapiski o revoliutsii* 4:427–44.

conceded, but they, especially the workers of Petrograd, were the "active minority" whose support was essential to the soviet's leadership and could not be measured in simple numbers against the "passive majority." Martov proposed, then, a "purely democratic" government organized and dominated by the soviet (perhaps with a minority of nonsocialist democrats) and dedicated to a program of radical reforms: an immediate armistice and the democratization of the army; a struggle against counterrevolution, including a purge of all governmental agencies; the immediate preparation of agrarian reforms that would include the confiscation and redistribution of all large land holdings, subject to the approval of the Constituent Assembly; and extensive economic changes, such as new tax measures, central economic planning and regulation, and the sequestration of any plant shut down by the owners.[122] This was a preview of the strategy of a "homogeneous socialist government"—that is, a government drawn from among all the socialist parties represented in the soviets, which would be the principal alternative to coalition during the next few months.[123]

Martov's words must have been dismaying to his former comrades and followers, especially Dan, who was tied to him through friendship and familial relations. (The two men shared an apartment in Petrograd, where Lydia Dan, Martov's sister and Dan's wife, often served late-night tea to gatherings of Menshevik leaders that included Tsereteli as well.) But Dan's and Tsereteli's speeches that night did not betray a lessening of confidence in the correctness and feasibility of their own strategy. First, they pointed out that troops "loyal to the revolution" were on their way from the front to Petrograd and could physically deflect the pressure from the demonstrators.[124] Second, they argued that the preconditions for support of the coalition by the two camps still ex-

[122] *IzvPS*, July 6, 1917 (no. 110), 6, and July 7, 1917 (no. 111), 1.

[123] This "homogeneous government" was advocated repeatedly not only by Martov but also by Sukhanov and other Independent Internationalists. See, for example, "The Fall of the Coalition Ministry," *NZh*, July 4, 1917 (no. 65), 1.

[124] The dispatch of these troops from the northwestern front has been attributed to the soviet's two commissars there—Kuchin, a Menshevik, and Stankevich, a Trudovik: Tsereteli, *Vospominaniia o fevral'skoi revoliutsii* 2:315–22; Voitinskii, "God pobed i porazhenii," 207–8. The claim in Sukhanov, *Zapiski o revoliutsii* 4:450–51, that it was Tsereteli's idea is probably inaccurate. Dan and Tsereteli felt that their position was strengthened by the support they found on July 4 among the units of the Petrograd garrison when they were informed of the expected arrival of the troops from the front: Voitinskii, "God pobed i porazhenii," 261–66.

isted as it had at the time of the coalition's inception. As Tsereteli said:

The coalition does not mean a bloc with the Kadets alone, and their departure does not mean that a bloc is impossible. We form blocs not with parties but with all those who are ready to stand on our platform. . . .

Comrades! Don't forget that there is a difference between the attitudes expressed in Petrograd and the attitudes in the provinces and on the front. In those places, the events in Petrograd are regarded as attempts to foist the will of the minority on all of Russian democracy by force.[125]

Again, the leaders' perception that the Bolsheviks were attempting to gain politically from the masses' desperation at the failure to realize the promises of the revolution—especially peace and a higher living standard—added to their determined rejection of the solutions proposed by the soviet's left.

Another argument of the Revolutionary Defensists was that soviet power might well be used not for the realization of the May 6 program but to advance another set of policies, the most damaging of which would be a unilateral policy of immediate peace.[126] Peace, Dan argued, could not be unilaterally achieved, and because war was thus unavoidable, there were no "miraculous recipes for the economy or for other areas." To emphasize the duty not to mislead the soviet's followers by false intimations of easy solutions, Dan even declared that the leaders would rather see the Bolsheviks take power than do so themselves, though he did not appear to actually fear such an eventuality.[127]

In the short run, the Revolutionary Defensists' confidence proved well founded. When Dan and Tsereteli had finished their speeches, at about 1 A.M., the debate had been on for seven hours, during which time excited statements from regiments and factories had gradually been replaced by reports of looting, arson, and bloody fighting in the streets between demonstrators and Cossacks. But then the city grew quiet again, and the men in the Tauride could hear the orderly step of a military force marching toward the palace. A dramatic scene then took place in the Catherine Hall of the palace, where the executive committee was meeting. Again, Sukhanov describes it vividly:

Dan appears on the platform as though out of the ground. He is so filled with exaltation that he tries to conceal at least part of it . . . but does not

---

[125] *IzvPS*, July 6, 1917 (no. 110), 5.
[126] Ibid.
[127] Ibid., 6.

succeed. "Comrades," he announces, "be calm! There is no danger! Regiments loyal to the revolution have arrived to defend the Central Executive Committee!"

Just then a powerful "Marseillaise" thunders into the Catherine Hall. Enthusiasm in the hall, the faces of the Mamelukes [Sukhanov's derisive label for the Defensists and Revolutionary Defensists in the soviet] light up. Triumphant, looking asquint at the left, they take each other's hands in an outburst of emotion, and standing bareheaded they sing the "Marseillaise."

"A classic scene of counterrevolution!" Martov snaps angrily.[128]

When the excitement had died down, the executive committees voted on the three resolutions before them. The resolution submitted by Gots in the name of the SR and Menshevik Revolutionary Defensists won easily over those of Martov and Lunacharskii (only 40 nays out of more than 300 votes). Following the tactics worked out in the star chamber before the demonstrations had begun, the resolution recognized the reduced cabinet as the legitimate governmental authority and consigned a comprehensive discussion of political strategy to a plenary meeting of the All-Russian Central Executive Committee scheduled to meet in Petrograd two weeks later.[129] The meeting finally adjourned at 4 A.M. on July 5. The members of the star chamber were now free to dedicate their energies to repairing the damage done by the Kadets to the unity of the "vital forces" and to rectifying the havoc inflicted on democracy during the July Days.

EVEN FOR A PERIOD overburdened with ironies and rich in historical import, the scene in the Catherine Hall on the night between July 4 and 5 still ranks high. It contained the elements of the soviet leadership's immediate victory as well as some of the sources of its future defeat. The most significant message of the July Days was that of the workers and soldiers of Petrograd telling their leaders that coalition had become intolerable. Yet once the demonstrators were off the streets, the executive committees decided that coalition would continue. The leaders' confidence in their confrontation with the Petrograd demonstrators was based on the presumed support of the preponderance of revolutionary democracy

[128] Sukhanov, *Zapiski o revoliutsii* 4:440.

[129] *IzvPS*, July 7, 1917 (no. 111), 3; *Khronika* 3:319. Tsereteli had wanted the meeting to take place in Moscow, but that idea was rejected when Grinevich pointed out the similarity between the Petrograd-Moscow duality and that of the Paris Commune and Versailles: *IzvPS*, July 6, 1917 (no. 110), 5.

outside the capital. By early July, however, that support was rapidly declining at the fronts and in the industrial villages and towns of the central industrial region—a trend that was apparently underestimated by the Revolutionary Defensists in Petrograd, who depended for their information on the Menshevik committeemen in the army and the provincial Mensheviks from the towns of the Russian hinterland. As a result of that change, the political alignment of forces within the soviets would change rapidly in the following weeks and months. Although the Revolutionary Defensists' adherence to the strategy of coalition was founded on both their continued trust in its feasibility and their conviction that any increase in the soviet's share of power would be abused by the Bolsheviks, the coming months would see first the failure of acceptable coalitions and then a marked increase in the workers' sense of isolation, which would make them more receptive to Bolshevik slogans.

Within the Menshevik party, the summoning of loyal troops and, later, the measures against the Bolsheviks and their supporters would end any hope of a timely reconciliation between the Revolutionary Defensist leadership and the Internationalist wing led by Martov.[130] To be sure, Dan and many of the praktiki in Petrograd, who had formed the bulwark of the Revolutionary Defensist faction, had been growing increasingly uneasy with the party's coalition strategy, and at the start of the cabinet crisis they sought to alter the social definitions on which this strategy had been built. But they repressed their doubts and insisted that coalition could and should be maintained because intimations of a Bolshevik "conspiracy" had made it both easier to avoid the real import of the workers' message and riskier to replace the strategy of coalition with anything more radical.

The July Days brought to a head several developments that had influenced the relations between the soviet's leaders and its followers since the inception of coalition. For both leaders and followers, the two months of coalition had been a time of disillusionment, though they drew different conclusions from it. Whereas the workers believed that the coalition's failure lay chiefly in its inability to satisfy their own basic needs, which led them to the conclusion that the soviet should wrest "full power," the moderate

---

[130] Martov strongly opposed the application of punitive measures against workers and soldiers, because he viewed their excesses as the acts of misguided revolutionaries, not of criminals: L. Dan, interview no. 23, pp. 1–2.

leaders still believed that the soviets could and should cooperate in the implementation of their program with forces outside revolutionary democracy, be they the democratic representatives still thought to exist in census society or the intermediate social groups of urban democracy. Moreover, these differences of understanding turned into differences of mutual perception. The existence of a radicalized working class, especially when led by the Bolsheviks, was seen by the moderates to prove the necessity of cooperation between themselves and whatever other elements of "educated Russia" would consent to accept the minimum program of the soviet. Meanwhile, the moderates' participation in government, their shared responsibility for its failures, and the fundamental difference between the view of Russian society and the body politic they sought to impart to the workers and that which had taken shape in the workers' own minds, however vague—all these factors added to the workers' sense of alienation from the soviet's leadership and made their challenge to this leadership, on the basis of the political alternative formulated for them by the Bolsheviks, an easier step to take. Finally, the immediate outcome of the workers' spontaneous manifestation of their growing political radicalism was to make all these perceptual and attitudinal differences more intractable, because, as we shall see, the July demonstrations diminished the willingness of even the most democratic representatives of the propertied classes to meet the soviet's economic and political demands.

Clearly, the moderates' denial of a crisis in the coalition strategy contributed to the crisis itself as well as to the rift that opened between leaders and followers. Yet, as we have seen, it was not ideological rigidity alone that had guided the Mensheviks in their steadfast adherence to the strategy and in their support of government policies. Not only had the sense of usefulness, even power, been alluring, but the socialists in the cabinet had also become concerned with state interests that had often conflicted with the workers' aspirations and demands. The Revolutionary Defensists' assessment of the popular sentiment, on which their confidence in the strategy rested, clashed with a reality which seems compelling from a historical perspective, though it was easy enough to misapprehend at the time. In quantitative terms, and for the moment, the provinces' support for the moderate leadership did indeed outweigh the radicalism of Petrograd; the Duma elections, involving more workers than those for the district soviets, had given the Revolutionary Defensists a plurality; and the Menshevik Trade

Union Conference easily counterbalanced the Bolshevik factory committees. Above all, there was the belief that the workers were being manipulated into radical positions against their own best interest, for which the Bolsheviks were held responsible. All in all, then, considerations of state responsibility, an optimistic assessment of conflicting information, and the enmity born of a history of political-ideological struggle militated against the recognition that the strategy of coalition was in crisis.

In the short run, the outcome of the July Days was a Revolutionary Defensist victory over the opponents of coalition. But it was a shaky victory, and one built entirely on the premise that a new, more democratic coalition could be formed and be rededicated to the reforms demanded by the soviet's constituency. The extent to which this task could be accomplished or an alternative to coalition accepted will be examined in the next chapter.

Revolutionary Defensism at an Impasse

T HE PERIOD from early July to the Bolshevik seizure of power
on October 25 was one of mounting hopelessness for the Mensheviks. Developments in the economic sphere, labor relations,
the conduct of the war, and the alignment of political forces signaled the realization of the Mensheviks' worst fears about Russia's
economic and political backwardness and undermined the strategy of coalition. The socialists lost influence in the cabinet until
finally even the Revolutionary Defensists were forced to admit that
their political strategy had failed to safeguard the revolution. Yet
no Menshevik would support a seizure of power by the soviet,
because of both ideological principles and the suspicion that it
would merely be exploited by the Bolsheviks to further their political goals. This excruciating dilemma brought Revolutionary Defensism to an impasse. The Mensheviks' response alternated between attempts to forge new political solutions and periods of
meandering and paralysis. Meanwhile, the country was becoming
increasingly polarized, a development which limited the moderates' maneuverability and sharpened the inner contradictions of
their goals and strategies.

The Revolutionary Defensists' two principal guiding considerations remained essentially the same as those of the coalition's first
term in May and June: first, the necessity of effecting at least a
minimum degree of social change (accompanied by a rationalization of the economy, which was a precondition for any social betterment) while maintaining the support of the social and political
forces thought essential for the revolution's survival; and second,
the responsibility the Revolutionary Defensists had assumed for
national affairs, particularly the conduct of the war, which affected
the definition of both the social change that was possible and the
participants who were essential in any coalition. In the wake of the
July Days, each of these considerations became more urgent. The
sense of responsibility was heightened by the dangers of civil war
and anarchy which the July Days had made so real, by the Bolshevik challenge to the moderates' leadership of the soviets, and by
the workers' growing radicalism. But if responsibility had the ef-

fect of blunting the moderates' responsiveness to their constituency, the July crisis also spurred the Revolutionary Defensist leaders to rededicate themselves to the pursuit of democratic reforms, though they continued to insist that this was best done in the context of a coalition government. Even under the best of circumstances, it would have been difficult to reconcile these aims.

The moderates' problem was complicated further by the atmosphere of virtual civil war that resulted from the July Days. The political arena of the revolution was now to be dominated by two alternatives, both of them hostile to coalition, and though they developed contemporaneously and fed on each other, one can view them as played out in succession. The first of these was a right-wing dictatorship, which followed directly from the repressive measures taken against the Bolsheviks and their supporters in the wake of the July Days and ended in General Kornilov's attempted coup at the end of August. The second was a left-wing dictatorship of the soviet, advocated by the Bolsheviks since April but made far more plausible after Kornilov's failed adventure. These two alternatives, and the Mensheviks' response to them, will be examined successively in this chapter. In addition, before considering the second alternative, we will examine the social aspect of industrial relations between July and October, for without this dimension the workers' ultimate support for the Bolshevik seizure of power could not be explained.

As we shall see, in both the political and the social spheres the dichotomy between Petrograd and the provinces, which had been so important a factor in the Revolutionary Defensists' thinking during the months of May and June, now disappeared. Chastised by the experience of July, the Petrograd workers temporarily gave preference to less dangerous forms of struggle, whereas a mood of radicalism set in among the soviet's followers in the provinces. By the end of July, then, the Revolutionary Defensists' problem was no longer their misapprehension of the direction in which the sentiment of their followers in the provinces was developing but rather their failure to appreciate how deeply the July Days had affected the chances of accommodation between Russia's major social groups. Whether engendered by spatial or chronological change, Revolutionary Defensist misperceptions of the political attitudes among the groups essential to their political strategy were extremely damaging. This was so because timing was of crucial importance in the conditions of a rapidly evolving revolutionary situation. Between July and October, the Menshevik Revolutionary Defensists would find their overtures repeatedly rebuffed not only by their own constituency but also by the ever-diminishing groups whom they considered the natural allies of revolutionary democracy. Once missed, whatever opportunities might have existed were beyond retrieve.

THE AFTERMATH OF THE JULY DAYS

The July Days left three problems in their wake to which the Revolutionary Defensist leaders of the soviet immediately turned: the cabinet crisis, the legacy of disorder and unruliness, and a counterrevolutionary backlash directed against the Bolsheviks, against the workers in Petrograd, and indeed against the whole of revolutionary democracy. In Petrograd, bands of armed sailors from Kronstadt, prevented by government forces from returning to their base, continued to roam the streets, while in other parts of the city Bolsheviks and workers were arrested and lynched.[1] From the front, too, there was worrisome news: a German breakthrough in the Russian defenses at Tarnopol along the Galician front, and demoralization and mass desertion.[2] Meanwhile, it was becoming apparent that measures introduced in the army (with the Revolutionary Defensists' consent) to combat desertion and antiwar propaganda were being used against the soldiers' democratic organizations. These measures included the reinstitution of the death penalty, military censorship, and a ban on political association.[3]

As before, the Revolutionary Defensists were divided on the question of which of these dangers were the more serious. The problem, Tsereteli explained to an emergency session of VTsIK on July 17, was how to "strike at anarchy without striking at the revolution itself"—that is, how to ensure that the "revolutionary order" everyone agreed was necessary not be used by the "counterrevolution" to undermine the organizational strength of the soviet. His and the SRs' argument was that anarchy was the greatest danger—that, in fact, anarchy and counterrevolution "fed on each other" to the extent that the Provisional Government had to be given "unlimited powers" to fight anarchy "in all its manifes-

---

[1] Sukhanov, *Zapiski o revoliutsii* 5:457–61, 471–77.

[2] In both cases, the information came just as the executive committee was discussing the leadership's newest proposals on July 7 and 9: Tsereteli, *Vospominaniia o fevral'skoi revoliutsii* 2:455–56; Sukhanov, *Zapiski o revoliutsii* 4:496–507.

[3] *RD v iiule*, 293, 298–302; *RPG* 3:1359–61.

tations."[4] In contrast, Dan warned that the army generals had already begun to turn the disciplinary measures enacted after the July Days into instruments of counterrevolution so that Russia was now threatened with a "military dictatorship."[5] In *Rabochaia gazeta*, too, reports of unauthorized searches of the offices of Menshevik organizations, and other acts of repression, appeared frequently, with angry declarations about the danger of counterrevolution.[6]

The problem of Revolutionary Defensist strategy after the July Days, however, consisted not only of the need to balance the concurrent campaigns against anarchy and counterrevolution but also of the recognition that repressive measures alone could not be expected to stem the tide of disorder. That goal required the satisfaction of at least the most pressing of the workers' and soldiers' demands. In the days following the crisis, *Rabochaia gazeta* repeatedly called for making the program of "radical democratic reforms" the centerpiece of negotiations in the cabinet's reconstruction to the point where M. Panin accused the editors of having a "program fetish."[7] The same demand was placed by the Revolutionary Defensist leaders before the executive committee on July 7 and accepted. The program was one that had been drafted by Dan and had already been adopted by the Menshevik Organizational Com-

---

[4] *RG*, July 20, 1917 (no. 111), 2–3, and Tsereteli, *Vospominaniia o fevral'skoi revoliutsii* 2:395–99. See also the report of Avksent'ev's address to a VTsIK meeting on July 9, in *IzvPS*, July 11, 1917 (no. 114), 3–4, 6, and *RG*, July 11, 1917 (no. 103), 3–4.

[5] *RG*, July 11, 1917 (no. 103), 3–4. Dan's estimate of the danger posed by counterrevolution found support among the Menshevik Defensists who served as the soviet's commissars at the front; two of them, Kuchin and Vengerov, attended the VTsIK emergency meeting. Similar reports by Khinchuk of Moscow and Menshevik praktiki from the provinces were delivered at the meeting. Accounts of the meeting appeared in many newspapers, but they differed widely; probably the most reliable is in *Khronika* 3:187–88, which is based on unpublished protocols. Also see the accounts by Tsereteli, *Vospominaniia o fevral'skoi revoliutsii* 2:375–79; and Sukhanov, *Zapiski o revoliutsii* 5:58–59, 63.

[6] *RG*, July 16, 1917 (no. 108), 4; "Revolutionary Dictatorship and *Kontrol'* by Democracy," *RG*, July 18, 1917 (no. 109), 1; and *RG*, July 20, 1917 (no. 111), 3 (reporting "counterrevolutionary" food riots in the Peterhof district).

[7] M. Panin, "The Revolution's Program and the Class Struggle," *RG*, July 18, 1917 (no. 109), 2. Panin's was the only dissenting voice in *Rabochaia gazeta*; see also his article, "A Government for the Salvation of the Revolution," *RG*, July 14, 1917 (no. 106), 2–3. For articles demanding that the soviet dictate the government's program, see "How to Save the Country?" *RG*, July 13, 1917 (no. 105), 1; "The Moscow Conference," *RG*, July 15, 1917 (no. 107), 1; and "The Revolution's Program Cannot Be Discarded," *RG*, July 16, 1917 (no. 108), 1.

mittee.[8] It acknowledged that the use of repressive measures entailed the risk of counterrevolution, but it blamed the need for them on the Bolsheviks' "adventurist attempt at armed action" against the Provisional Government. On the other hand, it asserted that continued "revolutionary order" made necessary a series of steps, including the elimination of all "remnants" of the old regime; a declaration that Russia was a democratic republic; "immediate measures" in regard to the agrarian and labor questions; the development of self-government; the regulation of economic life, especially in the area of supplies; and the convocation of the Constituent Assembly without delay.[9] The program amounted to a blueprint for the most far-reaching domestic reforms that could reasonably be expected before the convocation of the Constituent Assembly, though the issue of war or peace was intentionally left vague.

However, given the Revolutionary Defensists' fundamental ambivalence about their role in the revolution, it was perhaps inevitable that their commitment to radical change was tempered by a search for agreement with other elements of educated Russia, just as the commitment against counterrevolution had been checked by worries about anarchy. Indeed, the July Days had heightened concerns about social and political polarization, even civil war, and for this reason, Revolutionary Defensist strategy now mandated the formation of the broadest possible coalition.[10] The experiences of 1905 and 1914 had taught the Mensheviks that the isolation of the proletariat would mean, as Panin phrased it, "the death of the revolution."[11]

But could a broad coalition be formed around the soviet's program? At first it seemed that while some liberals had succumbed to the atmosphere of intolerance that had arisen in the wake of the July Days, others stood firm by Nekrasov's and Tereshchenko's promises made in the early hours of the crisis (see chapter 8). On July 7, when the socialist ministers asked the cabinet to adopt the

[8] For details on the executive committee's meeting, see *IzvPS*, July 8, 1917 (no. 112), 4; *Khronika* 3:158–59; Sukhanov, *Zapiski o revoliutsii* 4:496–507; and Tsereteli, *Vospominaniia o fevral'skoi revoliutsii* 2:355–56.

[9] The organizational committee's resolution is in *RG*, July 8, 1917 (no. 101), 1. The attribution to Dan is made in Sukhanov, *Zapiski o revoliutsii* 4:485–87.

[10] See Dan's address to the VTsIK meeting on July 9, reported in *RG*, July 11, 1917 (no. 103), 3–4. For similar assessments among the provincial Mensheviks, see Denike, interview no. 11, p. 11; and Sukhanov, *Zapiski o revoliutsii* 5:58–59.

[11] Panin, "A Government for the Salvation of the Revolution."

soviet's program, now containing the additional demand that the Duma be immediately dissolved, Prince L'vov protested the attempt to "dictate" to the government and announced his resignation.[12] Not only did his resignation exemplify the widening rupture between democracy and the moderate liberals of the public organizations, but in practical terms it meant that the new prime minister would be Kerenskii, whom none of the Mensheviks trusted.[13] In any case, the cabinet accepted the soviet's program on July 8.[14] This apparent victory allowed the Revolutionary Defensists to secure the approval of the executive committee, and later of the full Petrograd soviet and of the workers' section, for investing the government with "unlimited power" for the "salvation of the revolution." After a provision by Dan was added to this resolution calling on the socialist ministers to report twice weekly to the executive committee, not even the Menshevik Internationalists voted against it.[15] On July 12, after I. N. Efremov, leader of the new Radical Democratic party, had joined the cabinet, the most controversial of the socialists' demands was decreed by the Provisional Government: the prohibition of all land transactions until the Constituent Assembly had discussed the agrarian issue. Efremov's decision to join the cabinet was celebrated as proof of the Revolutionary Defensists' contention that "reality" itself would lead the more enlightened representatives of the bourgeoisie to cooperate with revolutionary democracy.[16]

[12] Tsereteli gives the only account of this meeting of the cabinet and of L'vov's general opposition to reform: *Vospominaniia o fevral'skoi revoliutsii* 2:263–65, 281–82, 349–53. For L'vov's reasoning in his decision, see *RPG* 3:1388–89, and "Resignation from the Revolution," *RG*, July 9, 1917 (no. 102), 2.

[13] Tsereteli wrote (*Vospominaniia o fevral'skoi revoliutsii* 2:151–54) that Kerenskii "was the only candidate for that position who was acceptable to both socialist and nonsocialist democracy," but "he did not have consistent views on the questions dividing 'democracy' and the right-wing circles" and therefore could not "unflinchingly conduct a policy that was sure to provoke sharp assaults from the right-wing circles."

[14] *VVP*, July 9, 1917 (no. 100), 1.

[15] The meeting of the executive committee took place on July 9, that of the Petrograd soviet on July 10. See *RG*, July 11, 1917 (no. 103), 3–4, and July 12, 1917 (no. 104), 3; *IzvPS*, July 12, 1917 (no. 115), 7; and *Khronika* 3:169–70.

[16] "The New Government and the Bourgeoisie," *RG*, July 12, 1917 (no. 104), 1. See also *Khronika* 3:174; *IzvPS*, July 12, 1917 (no. 115), 4; and Tsereteli, *Vospominaniia o fevral'skoi revoliutsii* 2:360. The decree on land transactions is reported in *Khronika* 3:176, 330. Its purpose was to freeze the existing proprietary situation in relation to land so as to assure the peasants that the fund of land available for expropriation by the Constituent Assembly would not be reduced.

Nevertheless, although the Revolutionary Defensists would be slow to recognize it, this solution to the crisis—a broad coalition that would carry out radical measures—was in fact unworkable. The events of the July Days, especially the Bolsheviks' apparent complicity and the subsequent general disorder, had heightened and given political shape to the sense of injury and self-righteousness that the propertied and educated groups had increasingly felt over the past two months in regard to the economic and social demands of the have-nots. Now that even the leaders of the soviet were condemning Bolshevik "adventurism" and all forms of "anarchy," the public and commercial-industrial organizations gave free rein to their attacks both on the workers' specific demands and on the soviet as an institution. The Provisional Committee of the Duma described the soviet as a "socialist minority" seeking to subordinate the cabinet, and Riabushinskii described it as "a casual gathering of people, for the most part ignorant, nameless, unenlightened, irresponsible . . . , and unprepared to participate in state and social construction."[17] The Petrograd-based Union of Trade and Industry said the coalition cabinet was comprised of one wing (the socialist) that would not yield on its "narrowly partisan goals" and another (the nonsocialist) that had no real support among the "influential circles" of the country.[18] The general opinion of industrialists seemed to be that the government should break with the soviets.

The import of these charges was grave indeed. Whereas in practical terms the soviet now appeared to be stronger than ever before—the soviet's commissars to the fronts, for example, were able to say that it was only the soldiers' committees that still bore any respect with the rank and file in the army[19]—its public image was one of declining moral and political authority. This was true in part because the polarization of society had created more clearly defined boundaries between the soviets and even the most reform-minded elements in the rest of society: boundaries that were expressed in a new rhetorical distinction between "revolutionary democracy," identified with the soviets, and "democracy," which also included the nonsocialist intelligentsia, the cooperative movement, and local self-government. In addition, one result of the rhetoric was the distortion of the soviet's public image. In March

[17] *Rech'*, July 13, 1917 (no. 162), 3; *RV*, July 19, 1917 (no. 163), 6.
[18] *Rech'*, July 15, 1917 (no. 164), 1.
[19] *Khronika* 3:187.

and April, the intelligentsia had helped to articulate a desire for unity and to induce a spirit of compromise not only among those in the lower reaches of society who had just become conscious of their power to make demands but also among the upper levels who had to respond to such demands. Now, most of those who wrote and spoke for the propertied groups projected an image of Russian society as irrevocably divided between men of education and responsibility and an anarchic mob whose demands—and any concession to them—would destroy the country. The leadership of the soviet was presumed either to have acted as the manipulator of the masses or to have lost all influence among them. In either case, the effect was to deprive the moderate leadership of the soviet of its negotiating strength.[20]

In these circumstances, even Nekrasov and Tereshchenko, Tsereteli's strongest bourgeois supporters, began insisting that no reform be attempted by the cabinet until it could secure the support and participation of at least the more influential parties and organizations of the propertied classes.[21] Moreover, the socialist ministers were forced to give Kerenskii a free hand in negotiating the terms of such participation. When negotiations for a new coalition began on July 13—with the Kadets, the Moscow–based Union of Trade and Industry, and the Petrograd-based Association of Trade and Industry—the triumvirate of Kerenskii, Nekrasov, and Tereshchenko again played the leading role, as it had done when the first coalition had been negotiated in April. This time, however, the Kadets and the commercial-industrial organizations were dictating to the soviet the limits of its influence on government policy.[22] First, they demanded that on joining the cabinet the socialists relinquish their responsibility before the soviet. Then, on July 16, they made public an ultimatum that the government renounce the program that the soviet had "dictated" to it on July 8.[23]

[20] This assessment is based on the minutes of the Second Trade-Industrial Congress, the Conference of Public Activists, and the State Conference (to be discussed below).

[21] Tsereteli, *Vospominaniia o fevral'skoi revoliutsii* 2:366–67.

[22] Ibid., 372; *Khronika* 3:180; Sukhanov, *Zapiski o revoliutsii* 5:40–41. This situation should not have surprised the Revolutionary Defensist leaders, for they knew that, had the soviet not withdrawn its demands that a democratic republic be declared immediately and that the Duma be dissolved, the circles close to the Radical Democratic party would have prevented Efremov from joining the cabinet: Tsereteli, *Vospominaniia o fevral'skoi revoliutsii* 2:356–57.

[23] *Khronika* 3:188; *RPG* 3:1401–2; and Tsereteli, *Vospominaniia o fevral'skoi revoliutsii* 2:372–74. In contrast to their usual divisiveness, the three organizations involved

At this point, the Revolutionary Defensists' efforts to reconstruct the coalition took on an air of unreality, which their opponents attributed to rigid adherence to the doctrine of the two-stage revolution but which also owed much to the familiar factors of the experience of past revolutionary defeats and the sense of responsibility if not for Russian society at large then at least for the revolution. Tsereteli still argued that without "the united effort of revolutionary democracy and the vital forces of the country," neither the democratic promise of the revolution nor the state order needed to realize this promise could be secured.[24] Dan continued to insist that to implement "radical democratic reforms," it was necessary to have in the government "all those groups of the propertied classes capable of marching alongside revolutionary democracy," even though he had also accused the propertied classes of subverting the government's reforms.[25] The rejection of the July 8 program by the Kadets and the industrialists did not prevent the star chamber from attempting to implement it. Having secured the approval of the Petrograd executive committee and the VTsIK for a new coalition that would be prepared to carry out "radical democratic reforms," would be invested with "broad powers," and would be based on all the "vital forces of the country,"[26] they proceeded to persuade Kerenskii to initiate the formation of the kind of cabinet demanded by the soviet. The result was a decisive blow to Tsereteli's hopes.

On July 20, Kerenskii wrote to the Kadet negotiators to explain that any new government would have to be guided by the principles of all three programs adopted by previous cabinets, those of March 2, May 6, and July 8. The Kadets promptly informed Kerenskii that they would not join such a government, whereupon

in the negotiations apparently coordinated their positions, especially through contacts between Tret'iakov of the Moscow Union, N. M. Kishkin of the Moscow Kadets, and Kutler of the Petrograd Association: Laverychev, *Po tu storonu barikad*, 208–11.

[24] Address to the VTsIK on July 17, as reported in *RG*, July 20, 1917 (no. 111), 2–3, and reprinted in Tsereteli, *Vospominaniia o fevral'skoi revoliutsii* 2:395–99. Tsereteli threatened to resign from the government should unity prove impossible to achieve. For a full report of the meeting, see *RG*, July 19, 1917 (no. 110), 3, and *Khronika*, 3:191–92.

[25] These comments were made at meetings of the Menshevik Petrograd organization on July 15 and 16 and the Menshevik faction of the VTsIK on July 18, at which opposition to the Revolutionary Defensist strategy was considerable: *RG*, July 18, 1917 (no. 109), and Sukhanov, *Zapiski o revoliutsii* 5:65–67.

[26] *IzvPS*, July 18, 1917 (no. 120), and *Khronika* 3:338–39.

Kerenskii resigned and left for Finland in a huff.[27] This was followed by the resignation of all the nonsocialist ministers, and Russia found itself without a government.[28] If the socialist and nonsocialist camps of the revolution could at all have restored their cooperation on behalf of the necessary reforms and the revolution's survival, this was the time for it. At around 9 P.M. on July 21, the Revolutionary Defensist leaders convened the VTsIK to announce their decision to enter immediately into direct negotiations with all of the "big parties" except the Bolsheviks and the Octobrists.[29]

At the meeting with the "big parties," the soviet's representatives—Tsereteli, Dan, Chkeidze, and Liber—encountered unanimous rejection of their attempts to dictate the government's policies.[30] Even Nekrasov, the most radical of the Russian liberals, was unwilling to accept the soviet's claim to define the tasks and goals of the revolution. He was surely irritated by the impossibility of reconciling the conflicting demands placed on the government by revolution, war, and social polarization, but, as with many other liberal advocates of cooperation with the moderate socialists, his anger was vented at the leaders of the soviet:

I am withdrawing from the government. My political career will come to an end, and this enables me, finally, to tell you comrades from the soviet the whole truth. For you, too, are responsible for what is taking place now. Have you not held the socialist ministers in constant fear of a possible expression of no confidence? Have you not forced them to come to you twice a week and report on every one of their smallest steps . . . ? Could this contribute to the peace of mind in the work of the Provisional Government so necessary at the present critical time . . . ?

Take, then, this power into your own hands and bear the responsibility for the fate of Russia. But if you lack the resolve to do so, leave the power to the coalition government, and then do not interfere in its work.[31]

There followed a heated discussion: Tsereteli described the July 8 program as an "all-national program"; Liber termed it essential if the government were to have the support of the "working masses"; and Dan attempted to persuade Nekrasov and Tere-

[27] *RPG* 3:1405–6.

[28] *Khronika* 3:203.

[29] Ibid., 204, and Sukhanov, *Zapiski o revoliutsii* 5:94–97.

[30] *IzvPS*, July 22, 1917 (no. 124), 3–4, and July 23, 1917 (no. 125), 2; *Rech'*, as cited in *RPG* 3:1419–27; Sukhanov, *Zapiski o revoliutsii* 5:101–6; and Tsereteli, *Vospominaniia o fevral'skoi revoliutsii* 2:382–86.

[31] *RPG* 3:1423.

shchenko to rejoin forces with the soviet, characterizing them as "brave individuals" who alone could stand up to "Miliukov and company." Dan then threatened a soviet seizure of power, though in the end the official Menshevik response that he read instead invited Kerenskii to return and form a cabinet of all parties ready to work under him as prime minister.[32] Dan added a vague reference to the "program worked out by the government on July 8" but did not respond to the rejoinder from a Kadet leader, M. M. Vinaver, that this program was unacceptable to his party. If Nekrasov's speech had given an indication of the new political sentiment engendered by the July Days among the former progressive bourgeoisie, Dan's reply conceded the ineffectiveness of the moderate socialists in pressuring their presumed counterparts in census Russia.

THE CABINET established by Kerenskii on July 23 was the first to have come into being without a declaration of intentions, except that the ministers were "responsible to their consciences alone." Judging only from its composition, the new cabinet could not have been pronounced as dedicated to the program of social and political democratization that had been the declared goal of the three preceding cabinets in revolutionary Russia. The socialists were now a small minority, five out of fifteen ministers, and no longer included Tsereteli, the voice of Revolutionary Defensism and the soviet.[33] To the soviet's followers, the participation of socialists in this coalition must have seemed an ignominious concession to the right, though this was not how the Revolutionary Defensists saw matters.

Of all the Revolutionary Defensists, Tsereteli was the most honest about the impossibility of reconciling the tasks of reform and cooperation and the need to sacrifice the former to the latter. In presenting the new government to the VTsIK on July 24, he warned that henceforth the soviet should avoid any "interference" with the government's acts, be they social reforms or additional measures of repression, and he otherwise strived to make it plain

[32] The Menshevik resolution read by Dan is in RG, July 25, 1917 (no. 115), 1.

[33] The socialist ministers included four members of the star chamber: a Menshevik, Skobelev, minister of labor; two SRs, Chernov, agriculture, and Avksent'ev, interior; and one People's Socialist, Peshekhonov, food. The fifth was S. N. Prokopovich, a nonparty, nonsoviet figure with strong ties to the Moscow intelligentsia and only vague Menshevik connections, who took over the Ministry of Trade and Industry.

that his decision to remain outside the new cabinet should not be seen to cast doubt on the strategy of coalition.[34] Ideologically speaking, the compromise with the nonsocialists was a "lesser evil" when compared to the alternative of a government of the soviets that was isolated from Russia's propertied and "intermediate" classes.[35] Thus, he was still committed to the "unity of all the vital forces," but he now believed that large segments of the soviet's constituency lacked the political maturity he had ascribed to them at the outset of the revolution. To remedy that condition, he recommended that Social Democrats direct their efforts toward teaching the working class a proper understanding of the revolution, and he himself decided to make the soviet, "on whose conduct depended the fate of the revolution," his arena.[36]

In a surprising reversal of roles, it was now the more skeptical Revolutionary Defensists who insisted that coalition, even one so clearly weighted against its socialist members, still served the interests of revolutionary democracy.[37] They argued that the new government could be trusted to fight counterrevolution and advance the soviet's favored reforms, not only because the government still had to rely on revolutionary democracy for support but because the soviet had made clear its commitment to the July 8 program and its intention to recall the socialist ministers should that program not be implemented. The fact that the Kadet ministers were drawn mostly from the left wing of their party added considerably to the Revolutionary Defensists' confidence.[38] In-

[34] Tsereteli, *Rechi*, 159–64.

[35] Tsereteli, *Vospominaniia o fevral'skoi revoliutsii* 2:385.

[36] *RG*, August 20, 1917 (no. 138), 2, and August 23, 1917 (no. 140), 2; Tsereteli, *Vospominaniia o fevral'skoi revoliutsii* 2:360. Panin, "A Government for the Salvation of the Revolution," made a similar argument.

[37] Of the leading Revolutionary Defensists, only one, Rozhkov, repudiated the coalition strategy at this time. It is significant that his party affiliation prior to 1917 had been with the Bolsheviks, not the Mensheviks. Rozhkov resigned from his position as deputy minister of post and telegraph, in which he had served under Tsereteli, on July 28, citing as his reason that it was now time for a government responsible to the soviet alone: *RG*, July 29, 1917 (no. 119), 3.

[38] See Dan's address on July 24 to the VTsIK and the peasants' executive committee, in *RG*, July 26, 1917 (no. 116), 2; and *Khronika* 3:216; the resolution Dan drafted for that meeting, in *IzvPS*, July 25, 1917 (no. 126), 5; and *Khronika* 3:353; [Dan], "The Crisis of Government," *RG*, July 25, 1917 (no. 115), 1; N. Cherevanin, "On Concessions," ibid., 1–2; "Revolutionary Democracy and the Government," *RG*, July 26, 1917 (no. 116), 1–2; B. G[orev], "The New Government and Repression," ibid., 2; "The Kadets—Saviors of the Country," *RG*, July 27, 1917 (no. 117), 1; "Revolutionary Measures in the Army," *RG*, July 30, 1917 (no. 120), 1.

deed, when doubts were expressed, they concerned not coalition as such but rather the repression of the Bolsheviks and the radical workers, the leniency the new government showed toward the servants of the old regime, and the failure of the soviet's leaders to speak out against this conduct.[39] What made these Mensheviks, hitherto unenthusiastic about the prospects of national coalition, hold on to it so desperately now was the rising specter of a counterrevolutionary backlash, or, as formulated by the Internationalist Martynov (a consistent critic of coalition), the existence of only two alternatives in the aftermath of the July Days: that of a "premature attempt to realize socialism" and that of "reaction"—and even the former was likely to lead to the latter.[40]

What had been a sporadic campaign of vilification against the Bolsheviks, workers, and the soviets after the July Days turned, by the end of the month, into a more coordinated attack by the nonsocialist parties and organizations on the political autonomy and influence of revolutionary democracy. At the center of the antisocialist effort, giving it political unity and legitimacy, were the Kadets, whose own ranks in Petrograd and in many provincial towns had become determined to stand up to the soviets, the soldiers, committees, and those organizations they held responsible for the disorder in the country.[41] Having already brought several leading members of the Moscow bourgeoisie into the party—Tret'iakov, Konovalov, and P. A. Buryshkin had joined before the June elections to the Moscow city duma—the Kadets now moved to strengthen their ties to Riabushinskii's Trade-Industrial Union and established new contacts with the Union of Landowners, the Don Cossacks, the army's commanders, and the Republican Center, a group that advocated strong government and maintained ties with various antisoviet conspirators.[42]

Some voices of moderation were still heard in the publications and meetings of census society, though they were faint amidst the cacophony of antisoviet and antisocialist declamations that dominated three big conferences that met in Moscow during August: the Second Trade-Industrial Congress (August 3–5); the Conference of Public Activists (August 8–10); and the State Conference (August 12–14). Among the consistently moderate voices was that

[39] S. Ezhov, "What, Then, Is to Be Done?" *RG*, August 2, 1917 (no. 122), 2.

[40] *Vpered*, August 20, 1917 (no. 137).

[41] See the discussion of the Kadets' Ninth Congress in late July in Rosenberg, *Liberals in the Russian Revolution*, 200–5.

[42] Ibid., 196–200, 205–12.

of the Moscow-based journal, *The Productive Forces of Russia*, whose editors welcomed Kerenskii's new government as "a true coalition" with the "now sobered socialists."[43] At the Conference of Public Activists, a few of the speakers rejected the charge that the country's troubles were solely the fault of the socialists and the lower classes,[44] most of the other speakers, however, directed bitter complaints at the soviets, the soldiers' committees, the workers' and employees' committees, and even Tereshchenko and Kerenskii, whose indulgence toward socialist "dilettantes" was blamed for the desperate situation in the army, the railroads, industry, finance, and food supplies.[45] Moreover, they generally agreed on the necessity of a strong, authoritative government (meaning a government without socialists), and many called for a halt to all social reforms and the establishment of a military dictatorship.[46]

This conference demonstrated the deep cleavages that were splitting society and the determination of census groups to force their priorities on the democratic groups. The conference could also have been a warning that, even among those elements of educated Russia that the Mensheviks had considered most sympathetic to the ideals of Social Democracy, a process of realignment was under way that might preclude future attempts to restructure the coalition along more democratic lines. What was significant in this regard was that, alongside supporters of the old regime from among the landed nobility and the clergy, the conference had attracted representatives of the Union of Engineers, the Union of Junior University Instructors, the cooperative movement, and the Peasants' Union—that is, those groups that the Mensheviks had identified as rural and urban democracy. Indeed, among the most vociferous detractors of the workers and their organizations were

[43] *PSR*, July 30, 1917 (no. 11), 1–2.

[44] See the speeches by Ivanovskii, M. N. Sobolev, A. V. Rodionov, and Melikhor, in *Otchet o Moskovskom soveshchanii*, 28–29, 72–85, 109–22, 128–29.

[45] See the speeches on the general situation by Professor Ustinov; on the military situation by General Alekseev, General A. A. Brusilov, and Colonel A. E. Gruzinov (the commander of Moscow's military region and one of the conference's organizers); on the economy by P. B. Struve and S. V. Lur'e; on banking by A. I. Vyshnegradskii; on rail transport by Bublikov and A. A. Chamanskii; and on food supplies by G. Ia. Rakhovich, in ibid., 22–24, 30–51, 60–67, 86–100, 104–9, and 129ff.

[46] See the addresses by Professor Ustinov, V. S. Kuzmin-Karavaev, and Struve, in ibid., 22–24, 51–59, and 60–67; the resolutions adopted by the conference, in ibid., 132–36, and *Rech'*, August 12, 1917 (no. 188), 3; and a telegram sent by the conference to General Kornilov, in *RV*, August 10, 1917 (no. 182), 4.

several engineers, such as N. P. Nochevkin, who had supported Konovalov's progressive labor program.[47] The political implications of this shift in the attitudes of urban democracy would be most damaging to the Revolutionary Defensist search for an alternative political arrangement, though this did not become apparent for another month.

Shortly afterward, the antisoviet mood of the bourgeoisie proper manifested itself at the State Conference, the largest of the revolution's gatherings. This conference, attended by 2,500 delegates representing every social, professional, national, and political group, was meant to lend an appearance of unity and support to the Kerenskii regime.[48] Its effect, however, was to show how little authority the coalition government had among the mass following of revolutionary democracy and how mistrustful of its ability to maintain order were such elements of census society as the army commanders and the leaders of the Kadet party. Disregarding the advice of the soviet, Moscow's workers went on strike and demonstrated against the conference in numbers not seen since February, while inside the conference hall General Kornilov's call for "urgent" measures to restore order at the front and the rear (by extending the death penalty to the whole country) was greeted with applause bordering on adulation.[49] In general, the nonsocialist speakers, though disagreeing among themselves on almost every program discussed at the conference, followed the example of the Conference of Public Activists in devoting their statements to attacks on the socialists.

This wave of antisoviet feeling seemed to push the Revolutionary Defensists into a new initiative that would substantially alter the social basis and programmatic emphasis of coalition, while preserving the strategic principle. Dan, for example, now argued for an appeal to democracy at large to support the soviet's program, which addressed, as he emphasized, the interests of the revolution as a whole and not exclusively those of the working class.[50] If successful, this maneuver would have put the numerical weight

[47] See the addresses by Bublikov, Nochevkin, and Nauk, in *Otchet o Moskovskom soveshchanii*, 94–97, 122–28.

[48] *Gosudarstvennoe soveshchanie*, xxiv.

[49] Ibid., 61–66. For a discussion of the general strike, see Koenker, *Moscow Workers and the 1917 Revolution*, 124–28.

[50] "The Moscow Conference," *RG*, July 15, 1917 (no. 107), 1, and *Den'*, August 15, 1917 (no. 136).

of the intermediary democratic groups in the country behind the soviet's program and would have isolated the antisoviet forces.

Toward this end, the Revolutionary Defensist representatives of the soviet carefully sought to balance programmatic firmness and political compromise. They elaborated on the July 8 program and insisted that the revolutionary regime needed to implement measures for both social improvement and economic recovery, but they also indicated the soviet's readiness to accommodate census Russia's concern for law and order in the army and throughout the country.[51] (Tsereteli even embraced Bublikov in a well-recorded gesture.)[52] Finally, and only after long negotiations, the constituent elements of nonsoviet democracy—the cooperatives, city dumas, and zemstvos—were persuaded to subscribe to what came to be known later as the August 14 program. Yet neither the manifestations of national responsibility nor the parliamentary success of forming a "democratic front" could overcome the belligerent support of the bourgeoisie for a political solution that would absolve it altogether of having to consider the interests of revolutionary democracy. The State Conference was an omen of Kornilov's attack on the Provisional Government two weeks later.

IT WAS again time for the Revolutionary Defensists to reassess their coalition strategy, and the Unification Congress of Russian Social Democracy (in fact, of the Menshevik party), which opened in Petrograd on August 19, provided the opportunity, though in the end produced neither unity nor a clearer political direction. Instead, the debates underscored the party's splintering and the estrangement among its many factions and groups. On the extreme left was the group of former Independent Internationalists identified with the newspaper *Novaia zhizn'*. Together with them, forming an Internationalist faction, was Martov's group of Internationalist emigres, who were far closer to the traditions of Menshevism but no less extreme in their denunciation of coalition.[53] Close to them in opinion, though not in practice, were the Internationalist-Unifiers, praktiki from Moscow, Tula, Odessa, and Tver, whose Inter-

[51] See the speeches by Chkheidze, Tsereteli, and Kuchin, in *Gosudarstvennoe soveshchanie*, 77–86, 118–28, 212–22.

[52] Many newspapers reported the embrace, and it was also noted in the conference proceedings: ibid., 269.

[53] See Sukhanov, *Zapiski o revoliutsii* 5:184–87, for a discussion of the differences and similarities between Martov's group and the *Novaia zhizn'* group (of which Sukhanov was a member).

nationalism and critique of coalition were tempered by emphasis on the party's unity and by the fact that they often voted with the Revolutionary Defensists. At the center of the party stood the Revolutionary Defensist leadership, which for months had been carrying both the burden and the prestige of coalition negotiations and government work. To the right of the Revolutionary Defensists were most of the provincial Mensheviks, whose "statesman-like" concerns, born of governing Russia's localities and of their leadership of the provincial intelligentsia, were deepened in July by the precipitous rise in Bolshevik influence among the workers.[54] Finally, on the extreme right and largely excluded from the party's work during 1917, stood the Defensist Potresov, whose gloomy projections now closely resembled those of the provincials.[55]

The contrasts were startling. Tsereteli's boastful optimism that "at the head of future battles would stand those who had led the revolution from victory to victory" seemed hollow when compared to Potresov's profound pessimism about the proletariat's failure to "rise to the challenge of the all-national tasks" and the tendency of Social Democrats to "drag behind" the workers.[56] Bogdanov and Liber, like Tsereteli, warned against making the Social Democratic program of domestic reform too "radical" and alienating those elements of democracy that had seemed sympathetic to the soviet's position at the State Conference.[57] But the Internationalists Martov, Avilov, Semkovskii, and I. S. Astrov all called on Social Democrats to leave the coalition government, expose its counterrevolutionary nature, and make themselves the leaders of whichever elements (democratic as well as proletarian) could be won to a program of radical domestic and international policy. With opinions divided so sharply—the culmination of the Menshevik's long-standing ideological differences and their varying experiences in power and in opposition in the capital and the provinces—it was not surprising that the outcome was essentially a stalemate. The battered strategy of coalition did win majority approval, with 115 votes in favor, compared to 79 for Martov's posi-

[54] Denike, interview no. 11, pp. 1–4, 10.

[55] Ibid., p. 23, and Denike, "Mensheviki v 1917 godu," 37–39.

[56] The minutes of the congress have never been published, but a collection of press reports on it from *Rabochaia gazeta*, *Novaia zhizn'*, *Vpered*, and *Den'* is in the archives of the Project on Menshevik History.

[57] According to Denike, interview no. 11, pp. 31–32, any question addressed to the Revolutionary Defensist leaders on the possibility of doing something about the war or the land question was answered with an angry "Impossible!"

tion and 9 for Potresov's. But with the exception of Tsereteli, no one professed enthusiasm for it, and the congress itself offered no solution to the difficulties the Revolutionary Defensists had had since the July Days in their efforts to reinvigorate the Provisional Government's reform program. This sense of resignation afflicted the party as a whole as well as individual factions and in a curiously tragic way prevented the factions from even breaking away from the virtually paralyzed party.

The provincials, for example, offered no solution to the crisis except "strengthening oneself" in the fight against workers' radicalism, for in their localities they had done everything possible to have the soviets lead the "vital forces." Moreover, they could not believe, now that local alliances, like the national coalition, were being rejected by the soviet's constituency, that the soviet power for which the radicalized workers were calling would matter. On the contrary, they were certain that soviet power would destroy whatever goodwill there remained between the soviets and the educated groups in their towns. For their part, even the Internationalists appeared reluctant to advocate the solution of a "homogeneous socialist government," for which Martov had called during the July Days, in part because they had been repeatedly reminded by people to whom they were tied by family relations and a shared political past—i.e., Dan and Ezhov—of the dangers of isolation, defeat, and eventual counterrevolution. Indeed, the Bolsheviks' growing strength in the soviets and the likelihood of their manipulating a purely socialist government made these dangers seem even more real.[58]

Most significant, not even Tsereteli, for whom the dangers of soviet power were too apparent to require restatement, could now convey a sense of clarity and confidence about the soviet's partners in coalition. The progressive bourgeoisie had disappointed the moderate socialists and forced them into serving in a government that had defied every point on their social program, and the amorphous group of democracy had failed to emerge as an active political force capable of uniting with the soviet on a platform of truly democratic reforms and also participating in its realization. This must have been the reason why Cherevanin was hardly heard from at the August congress, for all along he had been the strongest proponent of urban democracy as a substitute for the progressive bourgeoisie in a coalition with the socialists. Yet de-

[58] Ibid., p. 32.

spite all these frustrations, the Menshevik Revolutionary Defensists made one last attempt to rescue their strategy of cooperation with other social groups.

Two WEEKS after the State Conference closed, General Kornilov attempted a coup against the Kerenskii government. During those two weeks, a sense of impending disaster spread among all groups, which seemed to call for the most decisive measures. The economy took a turn for the worse (as discussed later in this chapter); there was a haunting fear of renewed disorder in the cities; and with the fall of Riga on August 19, the German army came a step closer to Petrograd. A variety of nonsocialist organizations began planning for a radical shift in the nature of the provisional regime so as to be able to use the power of the state to curb the autonomy of revolutionary democracy—which they blamed for the disastrous conditions in the country—and to exclude it from organized participation in Russia's political life.

The web of conspiracy, misapprehension, and incompetence that brought about the Kornilov affair has been recounted elsewhere and need not be repeated here.[59] Whatever the intentions of those involved in it—a military coup against the Provisional Government itself or military support for a move by the government against the soviets, the soldiers' committees, and other "self-appointed organizations"—the goal uniting them was the political exclusion of the left.[60] It was, from the point of view of the workers, the soldiers, the peasants, and even the moderates among their leaders, a counterrevolutionary goal aimed not only at halting the advance of the revolution but at reversing its course. For that reason, the discovery of Kornilov's actions by a supposedly surprised Kerenskii on the night between August 26 and 27 produced a flurry of defensive activity by the soviet's supporters in Petrograd and on the railroads leading to the capital, and undermined the readiness of most soldiers in Kornilov's forces to carry out the ordered march on Petrograd. The coup attempt was quickly put down, but its very occurrence changed the political choices facing the Menshevik leaders in significant ways, closing off some possibilities as it seemingly opened others.

[59] See, for example, Ivanov, *Kornilovshchina i ee razgrom*; White, "Kornilov Affair"; and Ascher, "Kornilov Affair: A Reinterpretation," *Russian Review*, 29:3 [July 1970], pp. 286–300.

[60] The Kadets shared this goal as well. For a thorough and balanced discussion of their role in the affair, see Rosenberg, *Liberals in the Russian Revolution*, 221–33.

Coalition with the Kadets or the other elements of census society implicated in the Kornilov affair now became impossible. Instead, the Mensheviks decided to try to amalgamate the nonsocialist democratic groups with socialist revolutionary-democratic ones into a "homogeneous democratic government." Of course, the degree of social and political fragmentation so clearly reflected in the July Days, the State Conference, and the Kornilov affair made it unlikely that the amorphous elements of democracy would sever their ties to the census groups and align themselves with the socialists. Moreover, the lessons of Kornilov's assault on the soviets might lead workers and soldiers to a new surge of militancy and vindicate the Bolshevik view of Russian society and politics. The story of this final, tragic defeat of the moderates' strategy for the revolution must be viewed in the context of an unchecked economic crisis, a relentless industrial conflict, and the precipitous decline in the functioning of the state itself. It is to these aspects of the revolution's last months that we now turn.

The Agony of Russian Industry

"Crisis" is a term overused in describing Russia's economy during war and revolution. Crisis in the economy's capacity to meet the needs of war had been a principal element in the crystalization of public disaffection with the old regime and a major contributor to the February revolution. But the revolution did not remove the basic causes of the economic difficulties—the war and its effects on existing structural weaknesses—and these continued unabated under the Provisional Government. After a brief improvement in March and April, prompted by revolutionary patriotism and the dynamics of improved relations between labor and management, the production and supply of key products began declining again in May and June. Then, between July and October, a precipitous economic deterioration became evident from the growing number of closed factories and of temporary or terminal layoffs and the increase in unemployment. Although the situation in all these areas would become far worse after the Bolshevik seizure of power in October, both workers and employers felt the state of industry in the late summer and fall of 1917 was indeed one of "crisis."

That workers and industrialists differed on the causes of and political solutions for this crisis is not surprising. In the post-July period, as in May and June, "objective" economic factors inter-

357

acted with mutual hostilities to engender perceptions that in turn intensified the process of social and political polarization. The new political conditions and the changing industrial relations influenced each other. The politicization of social groups and the aggressive pursuit of political aspirations by one camp or another in the July Days and Kornilov's revolt affected the behavior of workers and employers on the factory floor and of both of them vis-à-vis the state's economic agencies. Conversely, the realities of industrial life in September and October and the decline in the effectiveness of labor's familiar forms of industrial struggle predisposed workers toward accepting as unavoidable the Bolshevik political solution of soviet power.

The examination of industrial relations during this final stage of the revolution will further demonstrate the crucial role of timing, especially during a rapidly evolving social revolution, in undermining political compromise and industrial accommodation. Relations among social classes in the post-July period did not leave much room for the kind of accommodation the Revolutionary Defensists sought to foster, so that their programs for labor and for the economy as a whole were becoming obsolete, and their efforts appeared uncoordinated, inconsistent, and contradictory.

THE ECONOMIC CRISIS of late summer was caused in part by the general problems that have already been described: the inability of Russian industry and economic infrastructures (especially rail transport) to meet the requirements of a prolonged war; the imbalance created by the channeling of all available resources into military production and related branches of industry; and in 1917, the impact of the revolution in undermining entrepreneurial confidence, in confusing lines of administrative oversight, and in failing to establish a more effective regulatory system.[61] Beyond these general causes, however, several new developments exacerbated the economic difficulties and the societal antagonisms. Escalating industrial conflict (to be discussed later) was both the result of economic deterioration and often its cause as production was disrupted by strikes and lockouts. In late summer, the railroads faced the added tasks of transporting multitudes of soldiers leaving the front and making the seasonal shift from the light summer load

---

[61] As Groman had predicted, a partial regulation of prices actually added to the difficulties; in September 1917, it was reported that this step had led to hoarding and speculation among metal producers: EPR 1:355–56.

(when river transport was possible and heating fuel was not needed) to the usually heavy fall and winter load. Meanwhile, a multifaceted labor struggle was raging in the railyards among the Ministry of Transportation, the Union of Railroad Workers, white-collar employees, and workers.[62] The production of coal and metals was also affected by a combination of factors: machinery that was idle because of mechanical problems; persistent labor conflicts in which management pleaded financial inability to meet the workers' demands; and the release of war prisoners from their work duties.[63] According to one report, only 50 percent of the railroads' rolling stock was in operation in late July, and fuel reserves were down to a one-week supply for industry and a two-week supply for the railroads.[64]

Another new phenomenon was the disastrous state of the treasury and financial markets. In the stock exchanges of Petrograd and Moscow, a veritable orgy of buying and selling stocks was taking place, which a financial journal attributed to the unscrupulous willingness of banks and entrepreneurs to benefit from the naivete of people wishing to invest their rapidly devaluating monetary notes in property they considered safe.[65] More generally, both private entrepreneurs and the new state monopolies were continuously short of operating capital because the new taxes, the Freedom Loan, and foreign loans had not obtained the necessary revenues, while the political instability and industrial conflict of

[62] Both the general nature of the crisis and the struggle against workers' demands were reflected in the journal of the SSPPiT; see "Railway Transport, 1916–17" and "How the Railroad Workers Want to Eat?" *PiT*, October 14, 1917 (no. 38/39), 208–13, 217–21. Also see Rosenberg, "Democratization of Russia's Railroads."

[63] See Priadkin's report on the production of coal at the Fourth Congress of Regional Commissioners of the Special Conference on Fuel, which took place from July 19 to 22: *IzvOS*, 1917, no. 5:141–69.

[64] *RG*, August 3, 1917 (no. 123), 1. Data collected by the Special Conference on Fuels show that the production of coal in the Donbas declined from 154,311 million puds in March to 127,000 in June and 119,000 in July: *Biulleteni statisticheskogo otdela*, supplement to *IzvOS*, 1917, no. 5:3.

[65] "The Resurrection of the Exchange," *FZh*, 1917, no. 23/25; 426–27. Another financial publication, a fiery defender of free enterprise, painted essentially the same picture, in spite of its praise of the stock exchange. The basic rule of the exchange, it said, was "the worse [the economy], the better [for the exchange]," and it added that stock prices were actually rising constantly, even of companies whose plants were known to be on the verge of closing down: "The State of the Exchange," *FG*, October 4, 1917 (no. 482), 5–6. A writer in this newspaper lamented the collapse of the ruble as a sign of "the beginning of the end" of the Russian economy: L. Eliasson, "On the Eve of the Crash," ibid., 4–5.

the period lowered the readiness of private banks to extend credit.[66]

Additional difficulties affected the supply of food to the industrial centers—a matter of immense political importance in the fall of 1917, as it had been the previous fall. Besides the problems in transporting grain from the countryside to the cities, there were few industrial goods to exchange for the grain, which prompted a major banking organization to recommend the armed requisitioning of grain.[67] Moreover, the state grain monopoly disrupted the old networks of grain purchasing, but the new public and state organs were as yet poorly organized and generally unable to obtain the necessary operating capital.[68] The banks and commercial organizations began to condition credit to these organs on certain governmental concessions, and such conditions led to the government's decision on August 27 to double bread prices and to allow private merchants to participate in grain purchasing alongside the cooperatives.[69] In late September, the bankers began conditioning credit on the complete dismantling of the state grain monopoly and then refused credit altogether, even to private merchants,

[66] Foreign loans not only were much lower than expected; they were also usually earmarked for particular war-related purposes: Lozinskii, *Ekonomicheskaia politika Vremennogo Pravitel'stva*, 112–19. The problems of state finances and entrepreneurial credit were discussed at length during the Conference of Public Activists; see especially statements by Vyshnegradskii and Lur'e in *Otchet o Moskovskom soveshchanii*, 86–97. G. D. Krasinskii, representing the Ministry of Labor, stated to the Special Conference on Defense that much of the special credit made available to war-related factories had gone to service their debts to the banks: *ZhOS*, September 9, 1917 (no. 192), 761–63. For a discussion of the difficulties with taxes and the Freedom Loan, see chap. 6.

[67] The recommendation was made by the Association of Joint-Stock Commercial Banks; see *Obzor deiatel'nosti . . . bankov*, 217.

[68] At the Conference of Public Activists, Rakhovich, an opponent of the state grain monopoly, reported that grain collections for April and May had been 150 million puds instead of the projected 440 million: *Otchet o Moskovskom soveshchanii*, 129.

[69] See the reports on the Congress of Commercial and Agricultural Exchanges, in *PiT*, September 2, 1917 (no. 32/33) 133, and on a meeting of the Association of Joint-Stock Commercial Banks, in *Obzor deiatel'nosti . . . bankov*, 217–19. Also see "The Fight against Hunger," ibid., 109–13, for an entrepreneurial interpretation of the doubling of food prices as a reflection of the government's admission that the "doctrinaire" principle underlying its monopoly on grain had been mistaken. As recently as August 4, the government had promised that bread prices would not be raised: *VVP*, August 5, 1917 (no. 123), 1; *RPG* 2:641–42; *EPR* 2:343–44. Also see the angry response of the "democratic organs in the Economic Council," in *IzvPS*, September 9, 1917 (no. 166), 8.

though the government had indicated a readiness to accommodate the bankers' demands.[70]

Indeed, to Mensheviks as well as workers, the failure to manage the economy effectively was perhaps the most serious shortcoming of the coalition government.[71] It will be remembered that in mid-May the government had rejected the soviet's program for the comprehensive regulation of entrepreneurial activity, and Konovalov had then been forced by a combination of economic difficulties and entrepreneurial opposition to resign. During the summer and fall of 1917, the soviet's efforts to revive its plan, albeit significantly modified, were again defeated by entrepreneurial opposition. Even the Provisional Government's establishment of a consultative Economic Council and an executive Main Economic Committee (MEC) on June 21, an apparent concession to Groman's plan, proved completely useless.[72]

The Economic Council did not meet until July 21, and by then the atmosphere of social conflict precluded consensus on any issue. The statements of industrialists and the soviet's economists in the council's public meetings served only to turn one class against another, and the council's projects for regulatory agencies came under severe criticism from both sides.[73] Meanwhile, the MEC eliminated the existing state and public agencies for central regulation. First, the Committee on the Development of the Productive Forces (which had been formed in early May) was disbanded, and then the MEC began to take over the regulatory functions of the Special Conference on Defense and its agencies, the regional factory conferences, and limited the Special Conference's jurisdiction to matters directly connected to state orders for war-related pro-

[70] Meetings between the bankers and representatives of the Ministry of Finance and the Ministry of Provisions took place on September 22 and 28; the bankers' decision was formulated in a meeting on October 2: *Obzor deiatel'nosti . . . bankov*, 220–23.

[71] "Facing the Threat of Bankruptcy," *RG*, August 3, 1917 (no. 123), 1, an editorial which contended that no improvement in productivity could occur, no matter how restrained the workers were, unless the state began to regulate industry and fight the effects of war and entrepreneurial selfishness.

[72] See Lozinskii, *Ekonomicheskaia politika Vremennogo Pravitel'stva*, 56–67, and Zagorsky, *State Control of Industry*, 187–89, for discussions of the problems of implementing regulatory measures in the summer of 1917.

[73] See, for example, the attacks of Bolshevik speakers at the All-Russian Congress of Regional Supply Committees on September 6 and at the Constituent Assembly of Ural Factory Conferences on September 23, and the statement of the Industry Section of the SSPPiT on September 26, all in *EPR* 1:296–305.

duction.[74] Yet the MEC itself never succeeded in establishing clear guidelines or in asserting its authority over the regional conferences—an understandable failure, given the level of entrepreneurial opposition, the administrative chaos, and the divisions within the cabinet.[75]

With the Special Conference excluded and the MEC virtually inoperative, whatever regulatory work was accomplished took place in some of the regional supply and regulatory agencies through the efforts of the economic sections of local soviets and usually at the initiative of Menshevik economic experts. In Petrograd, Groman had used the regional supply committee for such activity,[76] and the Ekaterinoslav soviet had been instrumental in setting up a Provisional Committee of the Donbas—a regulatory agency with equal representation for workers, industrialists, and the government.[77] In Moscow, two agencies under Menshevik influence has engaged in regulation: the "democratized" regional supply committee and the Factory Conference (which had played an important role in the government's decision to sequester Guzhon's factories in June).[78] However heroic or successful their efforts, these agencies could not achieve overall economic coordination because they did not exercise any governmental authority and because Pal'chinskii (the chairman of the Special Conferences on Defense, Fuels, and Metals, and the acting minister of trade and industry

[74] Ibid., 273–74; K. N. Tarnovskii, "Osoboe soveshchanie po oborone gosudarstva. 1917 g.," in ZhOS, 1014.

[75] Not until October 19 did the MEC take the first steps toward creating its own network of regional regulatory agencies: EPR 1:306–7.

[76] Volobuev, Ekonomicheskaia politika Vremennogo Pravitel'stva, 153.

[77] A. Sandomirskii, "The Struggle for the Organization of Industry," NZh, June 29, 1917 (no. 61), 1; minutes of the Constituent Congress on Supplying the Don Basin, in EPR 1:282–84; "The Kharkov Congress on Supplies," IzvMVPK, 1917, no. 41:4.

[78] EPR 1:279–81, 436–38, 446–48; Volobuev, Ekonomicheskaia politika Vremennogo Pravitel'stva, 150–53. Three Mensheviks were active in the Moscow Factory Conference: the engineers S. E. Veitsman (deputy chairman) and K. V. Shur (representative of the soviet), and L. M. Pumpianskii (representing the Ministry of Labor). Volobuev credits the regional regulatory agencies with having been prototypes of economic organization during the first year of Bolshevik power: Ekonomicheskaia politika Vremennogo Pravitel'stva, 133–34, 150–53, 158–59. For a favorable contemporary evaluation, see B. Avilov, "The Regulation of Supplies and Production," NZh, June 20, 1917 (no. 53), 1. The Moscow WIC also praised the work of the Moscow soviet's economic section and its cooperation with the technical intelligentsia in the supply committee; this, not the coalition government, was the "true cooperation of the vital forces," it stated: IzvMVPK, 1917, no. 41: 16.

in June and July) not only used every bureaucratic means to frustrate their efforts at regulating economic activity in their respective regions but eventually had the government redefine their membership to give the majority of seats in them to commercial-industrial interests.[79] Moreover, the regional agencies could have been effective only as long as entrepreneurial organizations had been willing to participate in their work or accept their decisions, and by August this was no longer the case.[80]

Underlying the government's inability to regulate economic activity was its failure to forge an authoritative national regime. As the gap between social groups widened, especially from July onward, the workers' and industrialists' perceptions of what was the state's appropriate role drew further and further apart. The workers demanded more state intervention and the takeover of privately owned plants and eventually of the whole economy. Meanwhile, private entrepreneurs began to view even the most circumspect regulation by the state as illegitimate intervention and to question the right of the intelligentsia in the economic ministries to exercise state power for which they were "unfit."[81] It is important to understand the reasons for the industrialists' position on matters of regulation and how this position affected the Mensheviks' ability to realize even those economic measures they deemed absolutely essential for the survival of the revolution.

[79] See, for example, the attack launched against the Moscow supply committee at the July 8 session of the Special Conference on Defense: ZhOS, July 8, 1917 (no. 176), 543–44. Also see the resolutions of the Congress of Provincial and District Committees on Fuel (July 29–August 1) for a critique of Pal'chinskii's work in the Special Conference on Fuels: EPR 1:294–95. When a congress of the regional commissioners of various economic agencies discussed the possibility of giving the factory conferences exclusive authority over the distribution of state orders, Pal'chinskii and others in the Special Conference on Defense opposed the idea for fear it would create a series of "democratic republics of supplies led by Groman and the other activists of democracy": ZhOS, September 6, 1917 (no. 191), 746–57. See Lozinskii, Ekonomicheskaia politika Vremennogo Pravitel'stva, 69–73, and Volobuev, Ekonomicheskaia politika Vremennogo Pravitel'stva, 121–25, 131–33.

[80] B. Avilov, " 'Ruin' in the Ministry of Trade," NZh, June 28, 1917 (no. 60), 1; Volobuev, Ekonomicheskaia politika Vremennogo Pravitel'stva, 158–59. A report from the Moscow WIC deplored the decision of the Moscow Commercial-Industrial Committee and the Union of United Industry to leave the regional supply committee: IzvMVPK, 1917, no. 41:11–16. Another example of entrepreneurial boycott of a public regulatory agency was the withdrawal by the Association of Leather Manufacturers of its representatives in the Main Committee on Leather: VVOKZ, August 15, 1917 (no. 38), 394–95.

[81] FG, July 16, 1917 (no. 473), 7–11; July 29, 1917 (no. 474), 6–8; August 5, 1917 (no. 475), 5–7; August 12, 1917 (no. 476), 8–12.

The first major economic statement by the Ministry of Trade and Industry after the July Days came on July 24, in Prof. Bernatskii's address to the Economic Council, and it reflected the reactions of entrepreneurial circles to the implications of the recent street demonstrations. Bernatskii declared that "Russia's near future belonged to capitalism, not socialism," and he blamed the country's economic difficulties on the workers and their "excessive" wage demands, which, according to him, had caused two-thirds of the decline in production (shortages accounting for the other third). Consequently, regulation was to be limited to state-owned or war-related industries; private enterprise was to be exempt.[82] The prospects for regulation were kept alive, however, by the appointment on July 23 of S. N. Prokopovich as minister of trade and industry, for he was a pillar of Moscow's democratic intelligentsia, with close ties to the Progressist industrialists and a longtime advocate of national reconciliation. Entrepreneurial circles bitterly criticized the appointment and intensified the attack on the two remaining elements of the soviet's projects: the tax law of June 12 and the plans for compulsory syndicalization.[83]

Prokopovich's appointment signaled a split between two elements within the technical intelligentsia which had in the past collaborated in advocating the rationalization of Russian economic life: the manager-engineers of the south, and Moscow's technical intelligentsia associated with Konovalov's Progressist view of society. Both groups had been active in the Ministry of Trade and Industry and the Special Conference on Defense; both saw themselves as representing a view of the national good that was above narrow class interests; and both condemned the backwardness of Russian society. Where the two groups differed was in their explanations of the polarization of industrial life; the manager-engineers tended to ascribe it to the workers' irresponsible quest for material gains, while the Muscovites blamed the industrialists' disregard for production.[84] This conflict had led on July 28 to the resignations

[82] *SOEZS*, July 24, 1917 (no. 3), 10–20.

[83] See P.P.N., "Instead of a Program," *PiT*, August 5, 1917 (no. 28/29), 71–74, for a denunciation of Prokopovich's appointment. The press and public attack on the June 12 tax was discussed in chap. 6. The attack on compulsory syndicalization began with a resolution adopted by the SSPPiT on July 14 and coincided with an effort by several Petrograd banks to organize metalprocessing factories in various industrial centers into nongovernmental trusts, possibly with the aid of foreign capital: *PSR*, August 15, 1917 (no. 11), 19.

[84] The manager-engineers' position was reflected during meetings of the Special Conference on Defense in Pal'chinskii's leniency toward entrepreneurs who ap-

from the Ministry of Trade and Industry of Pal'chinskii and Ia. D. Priadkin, two southern engineer-managers who were active in the wartime regulatory agencies and had been in effective charge of the ministry following Konovalov's resignation.[85] But more damaging had been the struggle Pal'chinskii had carried on against the efforts of the Moscow Factory Conference to sequester factories idled by their owners, impose wage agreements on employers who otherwise seemed content to see their workers strike indefinitely, and in general facilitate continued production amidst shortages of every kind and a raging industrial conflict.[86]

At the State Conference, the Menshevik leaders of the soviet made a last, though cautious, effort to save both the economy and the coalition. Chkheidze presented a program of economic measures in the name of "united revolutionary democracy" that barely exceeded what had already been done and in some cases constituted a retreat: a state monopoly on grains and other essential items (in the implementation of which he now saw a place for individual merchants); the immediate application of the June 12 tax proposals (to be complemented by indirect taxation on items of mass consumption); and state regulation of industrial activity

---

plied for large government loans and advances without providing proof of need or of the ability to produce and, on the other hand, in his insistence that workers must be forced to work on terms acceptable to the government. See, for example, the decisions on credit for the Moscow-based factories of Dinamo and Amo (owned by Riabushinskii) and for the Petrograd-based Russian-Baltic Society, A. A. Frolik woodfinishing factory, and Simmens and Shukert Company—all taken within one week: ZhOS, July 5, 1917 (no. 175), 526; July 8, 1917 (no. 176), 539–41; July 12, 1917 (no. 177), 556–62; and July 15, 1917 (no. 178), 568–71. See also the conference's recommended measures for the institution of military authority over all factories working for the war effort in order to "regulate" workers' intervention in management's functions and their wage demands: ZhOS, July 19, 1917 (no. 179), 586–89, and September 23, 1917 (no. 196), 811–17. Two of the factories that received credit returned to the conference in October, asked for more, and received it again, in spite of the concern that their production was insignificant or unnecessary: ZhOS, October 11 and 14, 1917 (no. 201 and 202). Also see the different evaluations offered by Pal'chinskii and Veitsman for the shutdowns at the A. V. Bari and Br. Bromel' factories in Moscow: ZhOS, July 8, 1917 (no. 176), 541–44, and July 29, 1917 (no. 181), 609–13.

[85] RG, July 29, 1917 (no. 119), 3.

[86] See, for example, the conference's discussions of difficulties at the Moscow capsule factory, at M. Tauber, M. Tsvetkov, and Co. (also in Moscow), and at the A. G. Smoliakov and Sons iron-copper foundry (in Smolensk), during which Pal'chinskii repeatedly accused the Moscow Factory Conference of overstepping its responsibilities: ZhOS, August 2, 1917 (no. 182), 625–27; August 19, 1917 (no. 186), 684–86; and August 28, 1917 (no. 188), 710–12.

"of even compulsory syndicates, trusts, and monopolies."[87] (Compulsory trusts and syndicates had actually been favored by the Moscow industrialists because they could neutralize the influence of the large Petrograd banks, though for the same reason the policy had been fought by the SSPPiT.)[88] But even this modest program was unacceptable—as was the Revolutionary Defensist plea for accommodation across class and political lines—to the representatives of commercial-industrial organizations, who were hoping at the time that the country's social and economic problems might find resolution in Kornilov's "strong hand."

After Kornilov's defeat, this hope was dashed, and as the disintegration of the state apparatus became more obvious than ever before, entrepreneurial organizations seemed disoriented, and their actions were often contradictory. Some intensified their demand to be completely free of state interference. On September 5, the newly established All-Russian Union of Societies of Industrialists adopted a resolution declaring that the distribution of raw materials should be placed under its purview, because the government was too ineffective. (Prokopovich and Savvin were said to have supported the resolution.)[89] Similarly, opposition to syndicalization became so strong that not only did the socialists have to drop it as a condition for the formation of a new coalition, but on October 20 the Ministry of Trade and Industry announced that the matter would be left to the discretion of the entrepreneurs concerned.[90]

However, other entrepreneurs, under the leadership of Konovalov, who returned to the Ministry of Trade and Industry in the coalition of September 25, seem to have concluded that a crisis might not work to their advantage and that whatever state authority still remained should be utilized to avert an impending catastrophe. But their concessions came too late, were too meager, and involved too much sacrifice on the workers' part to be credible. A declaration of intended policies published by the government on September 25 projected the continuation of state controls on certain prices, wages, and work time. It kept the June 12 tax on profit

---

[87] *Gosudarstvennoe soveshchanie*, 77–86.

[88] For a comparison of the two positions, see Reikhardt, "Russkaia burzhuaziia," 39–41, and Laverychev, *Po to storonu barikad*, 268.

[89] *EPR* 1:294–95.

[90] *FZh*, September 28, 1917 (no. 31/32), 509–10, and *EPR* 1:311–13. See Bor. R., "Socialism and Industry," *FG*, September 9, 1917 (no. 480), 10–12, for an example of entrepreneurial opposition to syndicalization.

(not to exceed 50 percent), called for higher indirect taxes, and reasserted the need for "state regulation of production," though offering no specific means of implementing this principle.[91] Then, as if to symbolize the failure of the Provisional Government to shape a broad consensus around the principle of state regulation, the consultative Economic Council recommended its own dissolution on October 11, and two days later the government decreed it.[92]

ALTOGETHER, the commercial-industrial interests emerge here as bearing the greatest share of responsibility for the regime's failure to regulate the country's economy, yet they commonly saw themselves as victims. In the weeks following the July Days, entrepreneurial circles sharpened the tone of their self-righteous complaint, already noticeable in May and June, that the workers were guilty of excessive material demands, arbitrary acts in the factories, and lack of concern for productivity and the right of private property. They railed against the soviets for their promotion of the workers' "narrow" interests and advocacy of "doctrinaire" remedies for the economy, and, perhaps most significant, they accused the government of indulging the soviets and of lacking authority and determination.

Confrontation had by now become the declared strategy of the Moscow industrialists, both those led by Riabushinskii in the All-Russian Trade-Industrial Union and those led by Guzhon in the Moscow Society of Industrialists (MSI). At the Second Trade-Industrial Congress, Riabushinskii had used the archaic appelation "trading men" (*liudi torgovye*) to rally his fellow entrepreneurs to the organizational work that would put them in a position to exploit the approaching economic "catastrophe."[93] In summing up the congress, a liberal newspaper had declared that the assembled merchants and industrialists had exhibited an "exclusiveness and intolerance" worthy of the Bolsheviks: they "did not grieve over the grave condition of the motherland but gloated over the mis-

---

[91] *VVP*, September 28, 1917 (no. 183), 1. An editorial in *Financial Life*, which had always been close to Konovalov, conceded the necessity of certain state monopolies and even syndicalization but insisted on the voluntary nature of these arrangements as well as their supplementation with the "regulation of labor" : "The Democratic Conference and the Economy," *FZh*, September 28, 1917 (no. 31/32), 509–10. Also, see Volobuev, *Ekonomicheskaia politika Vremennogo Pravitel'stva*, 83–84.

[92] *EPR*, 1:306–7.

[93] *EPR* 1:196–201.

takes of the Provisional Government."[94] Indeed, Riabushinskii seemed to be deliberately courting catastrophe in the hope that its outcome, "the bony hand of hunger," would teach the workers and members of "sundry committees and soviets" the lesson of submission to the "state interest" as defined by the commercial-industrial class. Meanwhile, the Moscow-based Union and the MSI were making every effort to restrain the government's regulatory efforts, to enforce on their member enterprises a strict code of resistance to workers' demands, and to undermine labor's strength by provoking lengthy strikes or locking the workers out.[95]

An even sharper shift in strategy, especially in regard to labor's demands, occurred during July and August among the industrialists of the south and Petrograd. Not only did the majority of strikes in the south end in the workers' full or partial defeat, but the industrialists now demanded that troops be sent to the Donbas mines to protect property and production.[96] In Petrograd, the July Days had the effect of hardening the employers' positions. Entrepreneurial circles were outraged as much by the soviet's attempt to dictate its program of reforms to the Provisional Government as by the demonstrators' disrespect for state order and legality. Moreover, the situation the July Days created, together with the insinuations of the Bolsheviks' complicity in German espionage and the punitive measures taken against them, were favorable for an attack on labor. During July and August, the Petrograd industrialists prepared themselves for a showdown with workers by adding industrial-branch sections to the PSI's district subdivisions, tightening the society's control over the settlements negotiated by

[94] "The Irreconcilable Ones," *RV*, August 5, 1917 (no. 178), 1.

[95] See, for example, the report of the meeting called by Guzhon to consider Prokopovich's appointment to a ministerial post, in *PiT*, August 5, 1917 (no. 28/29); the Moscow Society's July 18 circular concerning workers' requests for paid leaves, in *EPR* 1:527–28; the reports of shutdowns in the factories of Bromel', Bari, and M. I. Grigor'ev, in *RG*, July 16, 1917 (no. 108), 3; and the discussion of Tret'iakov's refusal to take over the Ministry of Trade and Industry until the Provisional Government had renounced its earlier promises to the soviet, in Laverychev, "Vserossiiskii soiuz torgovli i promyshlennosti," 46–47.

[96] Although the data are incomplete, the proportion of strikes ending in workers' victories seems to have declined much more sharply in the south than in the country as a whole: from 78.1 percent in May to 46.5 percent in July, according to an August 6 report in *Kharkovskii vestnik* cited in Gaponenko, *Rabochii klass Rossii v 1917 godu*, 386. On July 19, fon Ditmar requested of the Special Conference on Defense that the institution of military authority being proposed for factories producing for the war effort include all industry in the Donbas as well: *ZhOS*, July 19, 1917 (no. 179), 587–88.

these sections, and taking the initiative in organizing the All-Russian Union of Societies of Industrialists.[97] Member enterprises and the new sections were steadfast in resisting workers' demands during individual and collective bargaining, as noted earlier in discussing the collective agreements in the metalprocessing, woodworking, and printing industries (see chapter 6).[98]

This attack on labor was intended to actually reverse the workers' earlier gains in working conditions, organizational opportunities, and autonomy in the factory. In Petrograd, following the July demonstrations, the PSI and its sections instructed their members to renege on promises made during the crisis, to refuse payment for time spent by workers in the demonstrations, and to end "the procedure practiced hitherto" of submitting workers' demands to arbitration boards.[99] Later, the society and other entrepreneurial organizations began attacking the workers' right to be paid for time spent in the activities of the soviet, the trade unions, and the factory committees.[100] By September, entrepreneurs in Petrograd and elsewhere were assailing the eight-hour day and even the

[97] Shatilova, "Petrogradskaia krupnaia burzhuaziia," 48–50. The new industrial branch sections were in charge of negotiating and enforcing collective agreements with the appropriate unions, but the PSI claimed for itself the overall direction of such negotiations. The Typographic Section, for example, was disbanded on October 10 for having signed a collective agreement with the Union of Printers that limited the owners' competence in matters of hiring and firing, and in other instances fines were imposed on industrialists who violated the society's rules: EPR 1:542.

[98] In the case of the metalworkers, the PSI changed its team of negotiators after the July Days and rejected wage raises for unskilled workers, but it was finally forced to accept a compromise agreement under government pressure. When the coopers struck in mid-July in support of wage levels already accepted by many individual owners, the employers' representatives argued that those concessions had been granted under the pressure of "machine guns in the streets": RG, July 29, 1917 (no. 119), 4. A similar change in the employers' negotiating position led to a waiters' strike in late July after restaurant owners withdrew an offer they had made earlier: RG, July 28, 1917 (no. 118), 2–3, and August 1, 1917 (no. 121), 3.

[99] See the circulars issued by the PSI's Metalprocessing Section and by the PSI's chairman, in EPR 1:526, 527, and by its council, in Shatilova, "Petrogradskaia krupnaia burzhuaziia," 54.

[100] See the PSI's circular ordering that no payment be made for factory-committee work, in EPR 1:532, and the directives issued by the Main Committee of United Industry (a national entrepreneurial organization organized by Putilov in June) that no wages be paid to workers for time spent on factory-committee or soviet work, in VVOKZ, September 1, 1917 (no. 39), 433. Also see reports on efforts by the managements of the Skorokhod shoe factory and the Aivaz engineering works to stop payments to members of the factory committees: Stepanov, Rabochie Petrograda, 152.

workers' right to demand higher wages to compensate for the increased food prices.[101] One leather manufacturer who had previously taken a progressive view of labor relations now called on industrialists to do everything they could to break the workers' organizations: mechanize production, hire foreign workers, and shift from domestic production to imports.[102]

In the wake of Kornilov's defeat, the tone of the industrialists' public pronouncements took another turn, though their attack on labor would continue unrelieved up to the October overthrow of the Provisional Government.[103] Their sentiment became one of despair with the state's capacity to protect them. The mineowners of the Urals could hardly "gloat" over the government's shortcomings when they were told by Minister of Trade and Industry Konovalov on October 21 that the treasury could no longer help them meet the wage increases demanded by workers to compensate for higher food prices.[104] Entrepreneurial Russia was now desperately looking for the place "whence the genius of order might come," but in vain.[105] Yet underlying the despair was an element of entrepreneurial perception actually present since at least the July Days. From the point of view of the industrialists, the eight months of revolution could have been divided into three periods, each with its appropriate strategies: the bourgeois government of March and April, a time for concessions; the coalition government, leading to the entrenchment of May and June; and finally, the absence of any effective government following the July Days, producing entrepreneurial aggression even while it made such behavior futile.[106]

[101] For examples of the attack on the eight-hour day, see *EPR* 1:539–41. For statements on the necessity for a "strong government" to ensure higher productivity and stop wages from rising, see *Otchet o moskovskom soveshchanii*, 60–67, 72–85, 90–94. In a letter of September 19 addressed to the minister of labor, the Union of Societies of Industrialists asked that workers be prevented from demanding higher wages to compensate for the higher costs of food: *EPR* 1:534–35.

[102] V.T.T., "High Wages, Low Productivity, and Russian Industry," *VVOKZ*, October 1, 1917 (no. 40/41), 448–50.

[103] See *ZhOS*, September 13, 1917 (no. 193), 772–73, 777–82, for examples of entrepreneurial actions that were deemed harmful even by the Special Conference on Defense.

[104] *EPR* 1:542–44.

[105] *FG*, September 16, 1917 (no. 481), 1.

[106] See Bachmanov's statement at the September 5 meeting of the PSI's council on plans to add a political organization to the Union of Societies of Industrialists in view of the government's inability to protect entrepreneurial interests, and the September 15 letter of the Society of Textile Manufacturers to the Moscow Exchange Committee and the September 24 statement of the Third Conference of Southern

For the men entrusted with maintaining a semblance of industrial order, the period after the July Days was one of enormous pressures. The Mensheviks in the Ministry of Labor were often called on by other government agencies to intervene in industrial conflicts,[107] yet they found their mediation efforts snubbed or denounced by both workers and employers, as happened in the conflict in Moscow's leather industry, which had begun in mid-July and remained unresolved on October 25.[108] In addition, the ministry was under constant pressure from entrepreneurial organizations to limit the workers' right to struggle for improvement and to have autonomous organizations. Although the ministry did not relent on these matters and in numerous instances supported the workers' specific demands, the economic difficulties of late summer prompted the Mensheviks in government to define the boundaries of the possible and the permissible even more narrowly than in June.[109] Indeed, the ministry found itself in the paradoxical situation of insisting—as did other government agen-

---

Industry, both of which sounded a note of despair and called for a stronger government and the protection of proprietary rights, all in *EPR* 1:205–13. See also the editorial, "The Organization of Power and the Commercial-Industrial Class," *PiT*, September 16, 1917 (no. 34/35), 137–41.

[107] See the discussions of conflicts in the Shlissel'burg gunpowder works, the Tula iron foundry, the metallurgical and metalprocessing industry in the south, and the Central Industrial Region; of a scheduled evacuation of workers from Revel; and the conflict in the Respirator and Protivogaz factories of the Central WIC, in *ZhOS*, August 9, 1917 (no. 184), 654–56; August 30, 1917 (no. 189), 722–28; September 2, 1917 (no. 190), 733–36; September 6, 1917 (no. 191), 743–45; and September 9, 1917 (no. 192), 757–58.

[108] This conflict was one of the bitterest of the summer of 1917; see *VVOKZ*, October 1, 1917 (no. 40/41), 448–50, 489–90; and November 15, 1917 (no. 42/43), 526–28. Intransigence in these conflicts seems to have been greater among entrepreneurs judging from reports published in both the socialist and the entrepreneurial press and from the data described in Koenker and Rosenberg, "Limits of Formal Protest," 28. Also see reports on the conflict in Petrograd pharmacies, in *RG*, July 26, 1917 (no. 116), 4; and on the negotiations regarding the metalworkers' collective agreement, in *RG*, July 27, 1917 (no. 117), 3.

[109] Representatives of the Ministry of Labor in various public and state agencies fought constantly against attacks on the workers and against employer-initiated shutdowns. See, for example, Kolokol'nikov's statement to the Economic Council on August 4, in *IzvMVPK*, 1917, no. 41:15; Pumpianskii's statement to the MEC on September 23, in *EPR* 1:565–67; and the many statements by Krasinskii at the meetings of the Special Conference on Defense. Also see Skobelev's protest against infringements on the workers' freedom of association by the Provisional Government's commissar in the Kuban Region, in *RG*, July 22, 1917 (no. 113), 2. On the other hand, *Rabochaia gazeta* continued to exhort workers as well as employers to make "sacrifices": Kubikov, "A Painful Problem," *RG*, July 25, 1917 (no. 115), 2.

cies—that employers not grant wages higher than the state recommended, because that would trigger similar demands from the workers of other factories and cause a further depletion of the treasury or new industrial conflicts.[110]

It is easy to appreciate how disappointed the workers were with the ministry's attempts to hold down wages, the more so because they believed that the state could and should force industrialists to subject their private economic interests to those of the revolution. And yet the ministry's efforts fell far short of what industrialists saw as proper governmental responsibility for property and production.[111] Indeed, the work of the Mensheviks in the Ministry of Labor during the final weeks of the Provisional Government, however well intended, seems to have only further discredited them among both workers and industrialists. Nothing conveys both the Mensheviks' dedication and its futility as clearly as Schwarz's admission that he had spent the night of October 25—the very hours when the members of Kerenskii's last cabinet were being taken into custody by workers and sailors loyal to the Bolsheviks—editing an article on tuberculosis among workers that was scheduled for publication in *Workers' Insurance*.[112]

THE WORKERS were of course directly affected by the economic deterioration and the industrial conflicts. Inflation, particularly the steep rise in the cost of food that followed the August 27 doubling of grain prices, considerably diminished real wages.[113] Unemploy-

[110] During a cabinet meeting on July 29, Skobelev complained that the Ministry of War and the Navy was undermining his efforts to hold down wages by paying consistently higher wages than were paid in privately owned factories. On September 5, the Moscow WIC, having received a directive from Kerenskii that all wage changes were to be cleared with the Ministry of Labor, wrote to the ministry to ask for directions on how to respond to the workers' mounting demands: *IzvMVPK*, 1917, no. 43/44:9. See also the complaints about private owners made by Pal'chinskii and V. P. Litvinov-Falinskii during meetings of the Special Conference on Defense: *ZhOS*, July 19, 1917 (no. 179), 588, and July 26, 1917 (no. 180), 601–8.

[111] See, for example, the attacks on the ministry's work in *PiT*, September 16, 1917 (no. 34/35), 193, and in *EPR* 1:537–39, 542.

[112] Solomon Schwarz, interview no. 6, pp. 17–18.

[113] Overall, prices rose more slowly between July and October than they had in May and June: 14 percent in July, 4 percent in August, and 9 percent in September, according to Volobuev, *Proletariat i burzhuaziia*, 219. But the price of food, especially of grains, rose much more quickly; in Moscow, the price of bread and other grains increased by 21 percent in July, 17 percent in August, and 14 percent in September: "Tseny na produkty i zarabotnaia plata moskovskikh rabochikh," *Statistika truda* 1 (July 1918):9–19. Stepanov's data on Petrograd's unskilled workers show sharp

ment, too, was becoming a more widespread source of anxiety, because it now affected not only the seasonal construction and wood workers, and unskilled workers, but the relatively privileged metalworkers as well.[114] Moreover, even in factories in which operations had not stopped altogether, workers were often idled by temporary shortages and were frequently paid reduced wages or were not paid at all.[115] Above all, there was the prospect that, as the crisis worsened, workers would be let go in growing numbers and there would be food shortages, and outright hunger.

What made the situation particularly explosive was the way in which these difficulties interacted with the workers' perceptions of the employers and the Provisional Government. The industrialists' aggressive posture after July had raised the workers' mistrust to new heights, while the government's failure to deal with either the causes or the symptoms of economic deterioration had forced workers to rely more on themselves. In this atmosphere, conflicts between workers and management became a daily occurrence that further debilitated production. At the Putilov works, a whole month passed in conflict over machinery that management had ordered loaded on barges but that the factory committee had forbade moving until it was satisfied that the shipment was not a prelude to evacuating the factory from Petrograd.[116] At the Lebedev aircraft factory, actual preparations for evacuation in early September touched off an angry response from the workers, even though the plan had been approved by the Central Council of Petrograd Fac-

---

declines in the real wages between June and August and again between September and October: Stepanov, *Rabochie Petrograda*, 54–55. The situation was particularly difficult in the industrial centers of the Donbas and the Urals: Volobuev, *Proletariat i burzhuaziia*, 223–34. On the connection between wage demands and cost of bread, see *EPR* 1:534–35.

[114] "The Labor Market in Petrograd, January-July 1917," *PiT*, September 16, 1917 (no. 34/35), 157–62. On July 21, the Ministry of Labor held its first recorded meeting on unemployment with representatives of various government agencies and the soviet's economic section: *RG*, July 25, 1917 (no. 115), 3. At the Special Conference on Defense, the question of unemployment came up for the first time on August 13: *ZhOS*, August 13, 1917 (no. 185), 671–72.

[115] Under an agreement with the Union of Metalworkers, idled workers at the Putilov works were paid two-thirds of their wages during the first three days of idleness, one-half for the remainder of the first two weeks, and nothing after that. Similar terms were apparently common in private industry and were soon to be applied to state-owned enterprises. See *ZhOS*, September 13, 1917 (no. 193), 773–74.

[116] *RD nakanune*, 275–76. The conflict was prolonged by the management's refusal to prove that the machines did not belong to the factory.

tory Committees. The workers scoffed at the owner and the Provisional Government for their proposed "cure" of evacuation and added that "these 'doctors' were only capable of filling their already bulging bags with millions in subsidies given by the government."[117]

Although this period was one of heightened industrial conflict, it was not simply or even principally material conditions that provoked strike activity but rather a host of other factors, especially the workers' expectations of existing and future political structures. Workers in Petrograd seemed stunned by the sharpness of the counterattack from the government and the bourgeoisie following the July Days, and as if mindful of the danger of isolation that the soviet's had so often warned them about, they actually became more cautious in pressing their demands.[118] For a short while, mediation by the Ministry of Labor was again welcomed, and expressions of concern for productivity abounded. It appears that strikes actually diminished in both number and size.[119]

By the end of July, however, the trend was reversed once more. The antisocialist rhetoric, the attack on labor organizations, and the government's expressed preference for unrestricted capitalism over regulation indicated to workers that their relative restraint was not going to be rewarded with success or general economic improvement, as had been the case in the early weeks of the revolution. Thus, though the proportion of economic strikes ending in full or partial satisfaction of the workers' demands declined precipitously between July and October,[120] strike activity only rose

[117] EPR 1:414–15. In mid-July, these same workers had accepted a compromise on their wage demands negotiated by the Ministry of Labor: RG, July 13, 1917 (no. 105), 3.

[118] For instances of the initial retreat on the part of the workers in Petrograd, see the resolutions adopted between July 8 and 14 by workers of the Nevskii stearin works, the Promet, Staryi Parviainen, Obukhov, Putilov, and G. D. Rakovitskii machine-building plants, and the National, Ouf, Kamenskii, and Petrograd metal factories, in RG, July 13, 1917 (no. 105), 3; July 14, 1917 (no. 106), 3; July 15, 1917 (no. 107), 3; July 16, 1917 (no. 108), 3; and July 23, 1917 (no. 114), 3. For further discussion of the workers' actions after the July Days, see Mandel, Petrograd Workers and the Fall of the Old Regime, 166–76.

[119] The Factory Inspectorate's data show 66 economic strikes in July, averaging 163 strikers each, compared to 76 strikes averaging 230 strikers in June: RD v maeiiune, 324–27; RD v iiule, 388–91.

[120] Gaponenko, Rabochii klass v Rossii v 1917 godu, 386, has calculated the following proportions of successful economic strikes: June, 81.6 percent; July, 71.2 percent; August, 51.4 percent; and September, 38.5 percent. He also cites (ibid.) the

and continued unabated until the overthrow of the Provisional Government.[121] Moreover, the strikers' persistence, as measured in the length of strikes, increased, even though the strikes were taking place in conditions of grave economic difficulty.[122] In short, a major characteristic of the strike movement, when it revived in late July and August, was that workers often struck simply in protest and without hope of immediate success. This tendency became even more marked in the aftermath of the Kornilov affair.

In political terms, the strikes of September and October, all of them nominally economic in purpose, bore a remarkable similarity to the actions of the radicalized workers of St. Petersburg in the weeks preceding the outbreak of World War I. In both cases, strikes for better conditions undertaken in the knowledge that they were hopeless reflected an alienation from the existing order and a determination to destroy it.[123] The same destructive element in workers' attitudes was expressed in the numerous acts of coercion and violence reported during September and October. This point was made at a meeting of the Special Conference on Defense in late September by V. E. Varzar, who noted the unusually high incidence of physical destruction and threats against owners and management reported in the large centers of southern industry—Kharkov, Kiev, and Ekaterinoslav. Varzar explained that workers had ceased to view legal channels as an effective means of struggle and had therefore turned to the use of "force and terror."[124]

But if this element of workers' behavior resembles that of the St. Petersburg workers of 1914, another element that was on the rise

---

case of Kharkov, where workers had been successful in 78 percent of all strikes in May but only 46.5 percent in July.

[121] Gaponenko, ibid., counted 76 economic strikes in June, 73 in July, 109 in August, and 117 in September. The figures reported by the Factory Inspectorate, known to be incomplete, were: 61 economic strikes in August, averaging 330 strikers, and 60 strikes, all labeled "economic," in September, mostly in the last two-thirds of the month, after a lull in strike activity following the Kornilov affair: *RD v iiule*, 248–51, and *RD v sentiabre*, 350–53.

[122] The labor scene in the fall was dominated by a number of protracted strikes (for example, that of the Moscow leather workers), but the Factory Inspectorate figures only partially reflect this trend, showing strikes to have lasted an average of 4.4 days in July, 6.6 days in August, and 5.3 days in September: *RD v iiule*, 388–91; *RD v avguste*, 248–51; *RD v sentiabre*, 350–53.

[123] For a discussion of the 1914 strikes, see Haimson, "Social Stability in Urban Russia," 23.

[124] *ZhOS*, September 23, 1917 (no. 196), 811–17. Previously, Varzar had been responsible for the impressive statistical coverage of strikes in factories subject to the Factory Inspectorate.

on the eve of October, particularly in large metalprocessing plants, illustrates the changes that had occurred in the intervening years in the general political situation, the extent of workers' radicalism outside Petrograd, and the politicization of the Petrograd vanguard itself. In August, September, and October, the incidence of workers' intervention in the economic functions of management, including the (usually temporary) takeover of enterprises, rose rapidly in Petrograd. One source estimates that, by October, some form of workers' *kontrol'* was operative in ninety-six enterprises in Petrograd, which together employed nearly 300,000 workers—i.e., approximately three-quarters of the city's industrial work force, most of it employed in large metalfinishing factories.[125] This increase in intervention was chiefly the result of workers' desperate efforts to defend their jobs, though the owners may have perceived it as impermissible aggressiveness. When the management of the Russian Locomotive and Mechanical Society in Kharkov rejected the wage demands made by the factory's workers and threatened a shutdown, the factory was seized by the workers.[126] However, only a minority of committees took such drastic action.[127] Others appealed to the government to intervene, though less often in September than had been the case in June and July.[128] Still others, now more numerous, called for the establishment of a democratic state capable of maintaining production in the factories on conditions acceptable to the workers.[129]

[125] Itkin, "Tsentral'nyi sovet fabzavkomov Petrograda v 1917 g.," 179.

[126] *FG*, September 16, 1917 (no. 481), 20. According to an industrialists' newspaper, the "dream" of many of them was "to close their factories if only for a short time": *TPG*, October 1, 1917 (no. 213), 1.

[127] At the Nevskii shoe factory, the administration's withholding of committee members' wages led to a violent strike, followed by a shutdown and then a decision by the workers to seize the plant: *Rabochii put'*, September 10, 1917 (no. 7), 3–4; *RD nakanune*, 251. Frequently, a seizure by the workers raised the question of the state's taking over a factory in order to enable it to obtain operating credit; see the example of G. G. Brenner factory in Petrograd, in *ZhOS*, September 13, 1917 (no. 193), 777–800.

[128] Workers in the Bari and Bromel' factories in Moscow, both of which had been closed by the owners, appealed to the Provisional Government to pass a law declaring the disorganization of industry a treasonous crime: *RG*, July 28, 1917 (no. 118), 4. Workers in the Respirator and Protivogaz factories of the Central WIC asked the government to sequester those plants in order to keep them operating after they had been closed by management: *RD v sentiabre*, 284–85; *ZhOS*, September 6, 1917 (no. 191), 743–45; and September 13, 1917 (no. 193), 783–84.

[129] On September 23 the committee of the Vulkan machine-building factory appealed to the Central Council of Petrograd Factory Committees to establish a "truly

These actions implied a two-part position: first, that the state could and should take over the economy in order to regulate it, ensure production and jobs, and redress the imbalance in the apportionment of wealth between workers and employers; and second, that only under the guidance of a government dedicated to the interests of the revolution and democracy would the state perform these functions. That this was essentially the message of a pamphlet Lenin wrote in October 1917 ("The Impending Catastrophe and How to Combat It") helps explain why so many workers accepted the Bolshevik argument that power had to be seized even over the objections of the soviet's moderate leadership. The force of this argument was not lessened in cases where workers established their own *kontrol'* or management of a factory, for they recognized that their individual efforts would amount to nothing without the help of the state.[130] It is thus clear that the issue of industrial order raised that of political order, and the practice of *kontrol'*, whatever its origins, gave rise to a concept of what the new political order should be. Of course, the connection between the industrial and political orders did not appear with equal clarity to all workers; to some it was merely a dim perception, but the Bolsheviks were ready to articulate, legitimize, and exploit it.

In contrast, the Revolutionary Defensists did themselves great damage among workers by attacking the work of the factory committees. Under pressure from the industrialists and concerned about falling productivity, Skobelev issued two circulars: one on August 22 reminding the members of factory committees that their competence did not include matters of production (disagreements with management over such matters had to be referred to the regional factory conferences), and the second on August 28 condemning the practice of conducting the committees' affairs during working time.[131] These pronouncements reinforced the workers' sense of alienation from the moderate socialists in the government, because they were issued at the very time that workers felt compelled to expand the purview of the committees. The episode

---

democratic" government and workers' *kontrol'* over Vulkan and all other factories in which production was in danger (the management of Vulkan had stopped payment to committee members): *RD v sentiabre*, 326–27. For a fuller discussion of the situation in Vulkan, see Mandel, *Petrograd Workers and the Soviet Seizure of Power*, 269–73. Resolutions in the same vein were passed by conferences of Petrograd factory committees.

[130] Mandel, *Petrograd Workers and the Soviet Seizure of Power*, 275–84.
[131] *EPR* 1:555, 558.

gave workers another reason for disregarding the moderates' advice and following the Bolsheviks.[132]

For the Revolutionary Defensists, the period after the July Days was one of painful disappointment with the workers of Petrograd. The signs of an apparent return to workers' moderation—their initial retreat, their seeming heed of the warnings about isolation, and the few instances of workers' distancing themselves from the Bolsheviks[133]—suddenly turned in late July into renewed militancy. The Putilov workers, for example, had insisted in the most defensive language that their demonstration during the July Days should be understood as expressing support of the soviet—and then, within three weeks, they attacked the Revolutionary Defensist speakers who addressed them, leading the Menshevik I. Kubikov to describe his "sense of helplessness," comparing the situation with that of the doctors whose efforts to treat the peasants during cholera epidemics had been rewarded with blows.[134]

The Revolutionary Defensists might well have felt under siege. By the second half of August, the Bolsheviks appeared to have

[132] A resolution adopted by the Third Conference of Petrograd Factory Committees on September 10 condemned Skobelev's circulars and emphasized the critical need for worker *kontrol'* over industry: *EPR* 1:561–62. Skobelev was jeered when he tried to explain his decisions to the conference. When a worker expressed in an article his fear that declining productivity and higher wages were destroying industry and that "soon there would be nothing to control," the workers of Simmens and Shukert questioned his proletarian affiliation. He retorted that in 1916 he had worked as a lathe operator in their own factory and went on to say that he was attacking not the factory committees but the employers' disregard for industry and the government's failure to regulate it; then he added, in a sneering remark that appears characteristic of the attitude of the Menshevik worker-intelligents toward their more radical fellows, "You have to understand what you read, comrades": F. Mitin, "The Approaching Control," *RG*, July 22, 1917 (no. 113), 1–2; *RG*, August 1, 1917 (no. 121), 2–3; "Answering the Workers of Simmens and Shukert," *RG*, August 3, 1917 (no. 123), 3.

[133] In mid-July, the Bolshevik-dominated committee of the Petrograd metal factory voted to resign and to call for the resignation of the party's Central Committee and Petrograd committee pending the state's investigation of the July Days: *RG*, July 18, 1917 (no. 109), 4. For an expression of pleasure by one Menshevik at this development, see B. Mirov, "The Beginning of Enlightenment," *RG*, July 20, 1917 (no. 111), 2–3.

[134] I. Kubikov, "In the Crowd of Putilov Workers," *RG*, August 2, 1917 (no. 122), 3. Also see the resolutions in support of soviet power adopted by workers of the Westinghouse and Novyi Parviainen factories on July 22 and 25, respectively, in *RG*, July 26, 1917 (no. 116), 3, and July 27, 1917 (no. 117), 3; the reports from a special meeting of the Interdistrict Conference of Petrograd [District] Soviets on July 21, in *RG*, July 25, 1917 (no. 115), 3; and *RD v iiule*, 264–69.

recovered from the July debacle and to be increasing their strength among Petrograd's workers. They captured 33 percent of the vote in the elections to the city duma on August 20 (compared to 20 percent in early June); they did particularly well in the working-class districts, winning absolute majorities in Vyborg and Peter-hof.[135] Most district soviets had by then declared their opposition to the moderates, as had the Interdistrict Conference of Petrograd Soviets, which had become the radical counterpart of the Petro-grad soviet.[136] Similarly, among the trade unions of the capital only the printers and paperworkers remained loyal to the Men-sheviks, so that the Bolsheviks now held seventeen of the twenty-four seats on the Petrograd Trade Union Council.[137] Finally, among members of the factory committee there was nearly unan-imous support for the Bolsheviks. A Bolshevik resolution received 82 percent of the votes at the Third Conference of Petrograd Fac-tory Committees in early August.[138] In sum, the more active, better-organized workers in Petrograd (and increasingly else-where) had replaced the moderates' vision of the revolution with one offered by the Bolsheviks.

On the Eve of October

For the Revolutionary Defensists, the Kornilov affair was the sig-nal for a reconstruction of their political strategy. The question of an alternative to a coalition with the progressive bourgeoisie had hung over the party since June, when disappointment with that coalition had begun to be expressed by the praktiki in the soviet's labor section, the economists, and other skeptics among the Rev-olutionary Defensists. Cherevanin had repeatedly argued that it was among the intermediary social groups (the lower intelligen-

---

[135] Mandel, *Petrograd Workers and the Soviet Seizure of Power*, 220. See appendix 4 of the present work for district-by-district results.

[136] This conference was formed during the April crisis but became active only during the Kornilov affair: Wade, "Rajonnye Sovety of Petrograd," 237–40; Lur'e, "Petrogradskoe mezhraionnoe soveshchanie v 1917 godu," no. 3:13–14, and no. 4:30–50; and *Raionnye sovety Petrograda* 3:248–80.

[137] Shatilova, "Professional'nye soiuzy i oktiabr'."

[138] Amosov et al., eds., *Oktiabr'skaia revoliutsiia* 1:215. Since this conference took place barely a month after the July Days fiasco, the Bolshevik resolution did not call for a transfer of power to the soviets (as had the resolution introduced by Zi-nov'ev at the First Conference of Factory Committees in early June), but it did call for strict and extensive regulation of the economy by councils in which workers would hold "no less than half" of the seats.

tsia, the professionals, and the white-collar employees of public organizations) that the working class and revolutionary democracy could find the cooperation of which the bourgeoisie had proven incapable. It seems apparent that in his view neither Russia nor the revolution could weather the crisis unless served by a united effort of the intelligentsia—the nonsocialist technologists as well as the Social Democrats, whose goals he saw combined in his own person. Other Revolutionary Defensists, however, did not believe the intermediary groups were capable of replacing the progressive bourgeoisie in a coalition. Instead, they viewed these groups merely as a counterbalance to the more narrowly bourgeois elements in the coalition.

The Kornilov affair seemed to change this attitude by offering new possibilities, though these soon proved illusory, and by putting greater pressure on the Revolutionary Defensists to find some alternative. Among the Internationalists, there was a hope that the failed coup would force a decisive break between democracy and the "counterrevolutionary bourgeoisie"—the army command, the groups associated with the Conference of Public Activists, and the Kadets.[139] The Revolutionary Defensists believed that Kerenskii and his fellow champions of the "vital forces," Nekrasov and Tereshchenko, would now be prompted to resolve the cabinet crisis that had begun on the eve of the coup with the resignations of Peshekhonov and the Kadet ministers in a manner favorable to democracy and to democratic reforms.[140]

But there were also new constraints on the Revolutionary Defensists. First, the Kadets' complicity in Kornilov's coup attempt as well as their behavior after it was unmasked had done irreparable damage to their credibility and had undermined the Revolutionary Defensist concepts of the "progressive bourgeoisie" and the "vital forces."[141]

Second, the Kornilov affair had provoked a renewal of revolutionary militancy, which had quickly been brought under Bolshe-

[139] Denike, interview no. 11, p. 19; Sukhanov, *Zapiski o revoliutsii* 5:217.

[140] Peshekhonov resigned from the Ministry of Food Supply in protest over the doubling of food prices. On the Kadets' resignation and their intention to force Kerenskii and his triumvirate into like action, see Rosenberg, *Liberals in the Russian Revolution*, 229ff.

[141] Ibid., 234–39. Tsereteli himself, in a speech to a joint meeting of the VTsIK and the executive committee of peasant soviets on August 30, agreed that "that part of the coalition which had set itself in opposition to the interests of the whole country" had to be expelled, though he continued to assert that cooperation was still possible with the "real vital forces": *IzvPS*, August 31, 1917 (no. 158), 5.

vik direction through committees established everywhere for the "struggle against counterrevolution." Bolshevik influence in Petrograd was now ubiquitous both in the already militant Interdistrict Conference of Soviets and in the Petrograd soviet, in which on August 31 the Bolsheviks obtained an almost unanimous vote for their resolution favoring a government of the "revolutionary proletariat and peasantry." On September 9, the executive committee's challenge to this resolution was defeated, ending the moderates' leadership of the soviet. The Moscow soviet had meanwhile adopted the same resolution.[142] The moderates' claim to speak for the soviets now rested solely on their control of the VTsIK that had been elected by the First Congress of Soviets in June. New elections were to be held at the Second Congress, scheduled for late October.

Certain political conclusions were drawn from these new facts. The first and clearest point to emerge in Menshevik thinking concerned the exclusion of the Kadets from any future government, a point that had already been made during the VTsIK's first discussion of Kornilov's attack on August 27 by a new combination of the skeptics among the Revolutionary Defensists and the Internationalists in both the Menshevik and the SR parties. This point was adopted as official party policy by the Menshevik and SR central committees on August 31 and September 1, respectively.[143] Tsereteli's strategy of coalition with the progressive bourgeoisie was thus buried, and the soviet's moderates had to find an alternative.

Two alternatives had already been elaborated in the preceding months by the Revolutionary Defensists' opponents on the left: Lenin's "government of the soviets," which would function as a "dictatorship of the proletariat and the poor peasantry" and in practice would be dominated by the Bolshevik party; and Martov's

---

[142] In the August 31 vote in Petrograd, only fifteen delegates voted against the resolution, though on a subsequent roll call many Menshevik and SR delegates changed their vote, giving the moderates 135 to the Bolsheviks' 279 (with 51 abstentions). The vote on September 9 was 519 to 414, with 67 abstentions: *Khronika* 4:138–39, 186–89; Sukhanov, *Zapiski o revoliutsii* 4:28 and 5:291–92. In Moscow, the vote was 355 to 254: *Khronika* 4:270–72.

[143] The VTsIK meeting of August 27 was reported in *RG*, August 29, 1917 (no. 146), and *Khronika* 4:103–5. During that meeting, the same "coalition" insisted that the Provisional Government accept the soviet's July 8 program as well as several other hitherto rejected reforms, such as declaring Russia a republic, the immediate dissolution of the Duma, and the employment of existing land committees to effect further agrarian reforms. The resolutions of the Menshevik and SR central committees were reported in *RG*, September 1, 1917 (no. 149), and *Khronika* 4:143.

"homogeneous socialist government," which would preserve a multiparty democracy, albeit limited to the socialist parties represented in the soviets. As for the latter, though it appeared that workers and soldiers might support such a formulation, not even Martov was any longer actively advocating it. In September, the dangers of workers' excesses, anarchy, counterrevolution, and civil war loomed even larger than they had in July, and every Menshevik was convinced that these dangers would grow worse if a socialist government were established. In addition, the Revolutionary Defensists' participation in government had given a new dimension to the old fear about the fate of the revolution. Just as the success of the praktiki in managing labor relations in March and April had made them willing, if not eager, to take on governmental responsibilities, so the frustrations of their work in the cabinet and the Ministry of Labor since May had added to the despair they had all felt when contemplating a government in which they, the moderates, would have to stand alone against the radicalized workers and the Bolsheviks.[144]

The Bolsheviks, of course, were the most serious deterrent to a radicalization of Menshevik strategy. The two parties' history of competition for the workers' loyalties had brought about a divergence of their strategies and a mutual hostility. When the workers had become radicalized, the Bolsheviks had been held responsible—justifiably so, insofar as they had helped the workers to transform their disappointment in the revolution into a view of society which mandated a soviet dictatorship. Still more serious in Menshevik eyes was the suspicion that the Bolsheviks had not simply exploited the workers' deprivations but, if they came to power, would actually act on their promises and attempt to build socialism in Russia, something that no Menshevik, not even the Inter-

[144] Dan later recalled that Kamenev had declined to promise Bolshevik support for a democratic government established by the soviet's moderates and that the fear of Bolshevik "demagogic" attacks on such a government made it an even less appealing possibility: Dan, "K istorii poslednykh dnei Vremennogo Pravitel'stva," 166. An appeal by the Petrograd Menshevik committee (in which the Internationalists now dominated) to the workers of the capital condemned both the old Revolutionary Defensist majority of the soviet and the new Bolshevik majority. It warned that Bolshevik promises of socialism would turn not only the bourgeoisie but also rural and urban democracy against the proletariat: *Iskra*, October 17, 1917 (no. 4). Also see a resolution passed on October 7 by the Internationalist faction in the Preparliament (to be discussed below), condemning a Bolshevik walkout because of its potential for isolating the proletariat and dividing the revolutionary forces: *Vpered*, October 10, 1917 (no. 178).

nationalists, considered remotely possible. Indeed, this suspicion was especially strong among the Menshevik Internationalists because, of all Mensheviks, they were the least appreciative of the usages of state power. "Should power be transferred to the soviets," the Internationalist Abramovich had warned in July, "the Bolsheviks would demand that it be transferred to the Central Committee of the Russian Social Democratic Labor Party. . . . then, without taking anything into consideration, they would demand the socialization of the means of production."[145] For both Internationalists and Revolutionary Defensists, the Bolsheviks' hold over the soviets of Moscow, Petrograd, and a growing number of other towns and cities made either a "homogeneous socialist" or a soviet government an unpalatable prospect. This common negative view of the Bolsheviks had kept the Menshevik party from breaking apart, and it continued to do so even when Martov agreed in mid-October, under pressure from the *Novaia zhizn'* group, to establish the Internationalist faction as an autonomous organizational entity within the party.[146]

If neither a "homogeneous socialist government" nor a soviet government was possible, the only remaining alternative was cooperation with nonsocialist elements of Russian society. But with which such elements? At the very start of the Kornilov affair, during the VTsIK meeting on August 27, Dan had tied the expulsion of the Kadets from the coalition to a new initiative: the convocation of a "parliament of democracy" to oversee the Provisional Government. By the time the VTsIK convened again on September 1 to discuss the crisis, Bogdanov was ready to describe the concept more precisely. Its centrality to the evolution of Revolutionary Defensist strategy makes his presentation worth quoting at length:

The question before us is whether we can form a coalition. Of course, we cannot have a coalition with the Kadets; cruel facts have convinced us of this. . . . There can be no coalition with a party that provided ideological inspiration for the Kornilov revolt.

Some comrades raise the possibility at the present moment of a dictatorship of the poorest classes, i.e., the proletariat and the peasants. Those who speak of such a dictatorship . . . are following the course of the [Paris] Commune. Such a commune may be possible in Petrograd and in other cities but not in the rest of Russia. It will be crushed by the vacillating elements that will join the bourgeois bloc. . . . The course of a dicta-

---

[145] *IzvPS*, July 4, 1917 (no. 108), 3–4, reprinted in *RPG* 3:349.
[146] The Internationalists formed their own faction in the Preparliament: *RG*, October 11, 1917 (no. 183), and October 12, 1917 (no. 184).

torship of the proletariat into which the workers are being pushed is a perilous course.

But there is another course—the dictatorship of democracy, not of the soviets [alone] but of those democratic organizations whose cadres are working throughout the country, such as the cooperatives, the municipal dumas, and the new zemstvos. . . .

[The soviet] must immediately resolve that a congress of democratic organizations, municipal dumas, zemstvos, cooperatives, and so forth, be convoked in the nearest future, and this conference must decide the question of the organization of power.[147]

Bogdanov's "dictatorship of democracy," or, as it was better known in Dan's formulation, a "homogeneous democratic government," would be a government in which the soviets would take the initiative but would still cooperate with the intermediary social groups and the democratic public and self-governing organizations, without which a soviet government would be politically isolated and administratively helpless.[148]

This strategy became the party's official course in a resolution adopted at the September 1 meeting. But it remained to be seen whether democracy would agree to make a clean break with the Kadets and the organizations of census Russia. The problem was that although democracy, as defined by the Mensheviks, was as much an organizational as a social entity, it had never taken a clearly political stand, nor was it united. Thus, Dan's proposal for a "parliament of democracy" took on the added importance of providing not only a representative body to oversee the Provisional Government but also the means of unifying democracy and revolutionary democracy in the shaping of a new government. The first point in the VTsIK resolution called for the prompt convocation of a "congress of all democratic organizations and democratic organs of local self-government" for the purpose of forming a new government.[149] Meanwhile, in the star chamber, the Revolutionary Defensists began composing lists of candidates for the "homogeneous democratic government."[150]

[147] RPG 3:1662–69. The meeting was reported in IzvPS, September 2, 1917 (no. 160), 3–4. and September 3, 1917 (no. 161), 5–7.

[148] The democratic organizations were expected to bring to their collaboration with the soviets both the administrative experience and structure that were their essence and their ties to the very large intermediary and presumably neutral groups of the peasantry and meshchanstvo (or, in Social Democratic jargon, the rural and urban petite bourgeoisie): Dan, "K istorii poslednykh dnei Vremennogo Pravitel'stva," 164.

[149] IzvPS, September 3, 1917 (no. 161), 5–7.

[150] Dan, "K istorii poslednykh dnei Vremennogo Pravitel'stva," 164.

The Mensheviks' hopes, however, were dashed even before the Democratic Conference opened on September 14. The leading figures of nonsoviet democracy proved to be reluctant either to break with the political organizations of census Russia or to challenge these organizations by supporting the immediate implementation of the reforms called for by the August 14 program (to which the leaders had subscribed during the State Conference). At a meeting of the star chamber at Skobelev's apartment to which several of these figures had been invited—V. V. Rudnev, the Right-SR mayor of Moscow; A. M. Berkengeim, also a Right-SR and a member of the Central Union of Cooperatives; and the educator Dushkevich—"the idea of an all-democratic government was buried literally in ten minutes," as Dan later wrote, when the guests declared their refusal to join such a government and argued that it would not be acceptable to the population at large because it would only lead to anarchy and civil war.[151]

A month later, speaking before an audience of Georgian Social Democrats in Tiflis, Tsereteli complained that the Russian democratic intelligentsia, "unlike that of Georgia," had proven incapable of fulfilling its role in the revolution and had left the leaders of revolutionary democracy with the dismal choice of coalition or a soviet government.[152] Dan too blamed the intelligentsia leaders of nonsoviet democracy for his decision to support coalition during the Democratic Conference. Their position, he declared, had once again made coalition the only alternative to soviet power (dominated by the Bolsheviks) and civil war.[153] Perhaps Dan was recalling Martov's warnings at earlier Menshevik gatherings that Social Democracy's failure to uphold a "proletarian" policy would allow the bourgeoisie to dictate political developments to the petite bourgeoisie.[154] But this time Tsereteli's explanation was closer to the mark: the intelligentsia—a sociocultural formation to which most Mensheviks belonged but whose importance as a social and

---

[151] Ibid., 165.

[152] Tsereteli had gone to Georgia ostensibly for treatment of tuberculosis, but probably also to recover from the many disappointments he had suffered during the past few months. Reports of his speeches were published in *Golos kraevogo soveta* (Tiflis), October 7, 1917 (no. 94), and *Den' svobodu* (Batum), October 25, 1917 (no. 166), and are on file with Tsereteli's papers in the Nicolaevsky Collection.

[153] Dan, "K istorii poslednykh dnei Vremennogo Pravitel'stva," 165–66.

[154] See the reports of the May conference and the August unification congress in the collections of the Project on Menshevik History. A resolution adopted by the Moscow Menshevik organization on September 27 used the same language to analyze the outcome of the Democratic Conference: *Vpered*, September 29, 1917 (no. 169).

political force in Russia they generally belittled—had become thoroughly alienated from the radicalized revolutionary democracy and would have rejected its leaders' call for help even if the goals of these moderate leaders had not been in themselves antithetical to the goals of the intelligentsia at large.

In any event, the Democratic Conference foreclosed all hope the Mensheviks may still have had of averting a Bolshevik seizure of power.[155] At every level, the conference was divided nearly equally between supporters and opponents of coalition. The Menshevik faction first voted 59 to 55 in favor of coalition, then reversed itself (73 to 65, with 4 abstentions) after hearing Martov's and Zhordania's arguments in opposition and Tsereteli's defense.[156] When the conference divided itself up on September 19 into "curias," which voted separately on the question of coalition, the results were just as confusing: the military organizations, peasants' soviets, and municipal self-governments voted by a slight majority for coalition; the cooperatives and the zemstvos favored coalition more decisively; but the workers' and soldiers' soviets and the trade unions rejected coalition solidly. The conference as a whole voted 766 to 688 (with 38 abstentions) in favor of coalition, then amended its resolution to exclude those connected with Kornilov's conspiracy (798 to 139, with 196 abstentions); amended it a second time to exclude the Kadets explicitly (595 for the exclusion, 493 against, and 72 abstaining); and in the end voted to defeat the final resolution by 813 to 183, with 80 abstentions.[157]

Perhaps the greatest disappointment was the vote of the cooperatives, who the Mensheviks thought were close to the sentiments of the urban lower strata and therefore in favor of a determined reform policy. But the leaders of the cooperative movement had actually resented all along the presumptuousness of the Menshevik economists' grandiose plans for food supplies and in general had differed with the socialists over the proper approach to social transformation. The cooperatives had stressed gradual, "organic" change and had viewed the socialists' programs, especially

[155] According to Denike, interview no. 11, pp. 16–18, he, Liber, and others said at the VTsIK meeting on September 1 that the Kornilov episode had made a Bolshevik seizure of power unavoidable, and Tsereteli was rather unconvincing when he professed optimism. Also see the description of the same meeting, in Sukhanov, *Zapiski o revoliutsii* 5:364–66.

[156] *RG*, September 16, 1917 (no. 162), and September 17, 1917 (no. 163); *Den'*, September 16, 1917 (no. 165); and Sukhanov, *Zapiski o revoliutsii* 6:112–13.

[157] *IzvPS*, September 20, 1917 (no. 176), 5–7; and *Khronika* 4:239–41.

those of Social Democracy, as "mechanistic."[158] The Mensheviks, for their part, alienated the peasants of the rural cooperatives not only with their food-supply policies but also with their agrarian program, which called for the transfer of all land to the state.[159] Although at the State Conference, and amidst threats of counter-revolution, the urban cooperatives had pressed for acceptance of the soviet's August 14 program despite the objections of their rural counterparts, the cooperatives at the Democratic Conference united, when the danger was on the left, in rejecting a government under the tutelage of even the most moderate of Social Democrats.[160]

Hoping to break the stalemate, the Democratic Conference delegated the decision on a political solution to an enlarged presidium, but its daylong meeting on September 20 also ended in near-deadlock: fifty votes for coalition, sixty against. The presidium did agree, however, that the new government should work for the realization of the August 14 program and be accountable to a permanent Democratic Council that the Democratic Conference was to select. The possibility of continued coalition was implied in the provision calling for the addition of a bourgeois delegation to the new council, which would then become the Provisional Council of the Russian Republic, or Preparliament (*Predparliament*), if the new cabinet were joined by representatives of the propertied classes.[161] Yet the divided conference could not force even this modest program on Kerenskii, who saw the Kornilov affair as an opportunity to tighten his personal hold on the cabinet. In fact, exploiting the Kadets' departure, Kerenskii had already declared Russia a republic on September 1 and had thereby stolen the soviet's thunder.

[158] On the cooperatives' opposition to Groman's plans, see the discussion of the Congress of Supply Committees in chap. 6. For an example of their distaste for socialism, see A. E., "Party Tactics and Party Tactlessness," and A. Evdokimov, "The Cooperators' View," both in *VKS*, 1917, no. 6/7:1–19.

[159] See, for example, the statements made by P. P. Maslov and Cherevanin during the May conference of the Menshevik party on this question: *NZh*, May 12, 1917 (no. 21), 4; *RG*, May 12, 1917 (no. 54), 4, and May 13, 1917 (no. 55), 2.

[160] A. Evdokimov, "Peasant Cooperatives at the State Conference" and "The Organization of Power and the Cooperatives," *VKS*, 1917, no. 8:1–7 and 7–9; the resolution adopted on September 12 by the All-Russian Congress of Cooperatives, in *Khronika* 4:206; and the statements on September 17 of the leaders of the cooperatives' delegation to the Democratic Conference, Berkengeim and A. V. Merkulov, in ibid., 229.

[161] *IzvPS*, September 21, 1917 (no. 177), 2, 4; *Khronika* 4:245–47; and Sukhanov, *Zapiski o revoliutsii* 6:135–44.

He also took the first step toward reconstructing the cabinet in a form opposed by the VTsIK: that is, by creating a plenipotentiary "directory" of five members.[162] Then, just as the Democratic Conference was getting under way, Kerenskii began negotiating the formation of a new coalition in which the Kadets were to be represented. When the moderate leaders of the VTsIK (Tsereteli, Chkheidze, Gots, and Avksent'ev) joined the negotiations as representatives of the Democratic Conference, the minister-president closed ranks with the Kadets to force the socialists to give up the demand for government accountability to the Preparliament and accept the government's minimalist interpretation of the August 14 program.[163]

Whatever hopes had been raised by the unmasking of the counterrevolution in the Kornilov affair and the resulting initiative for a "homogeneous democratic government" had now been lost. Not only had democracy proven unable to see clearly the chasm dividing Russian society and align itself with the revolutionary democratic camp, but even its cautious support for the reforms advocated by the moderate leaders of the VTsIK seemed to count for naught among the representatives of the bourgeois camp who had taken the lead in forming the new cabinet. The defeat of the Revolutionary Defensists' initiative was not contained in the actual composition of the cabinet or its program; if anything, the last coalition was more "progressive" in makeup than its predecessors and even its Kadet members committed themselves to the August 14 program.[164] But in refusing to submit to the Preparliament, Ke-

---

[162] The VTsIK did adopt a resolution opposing the idea of a directory, but subsequently, when the extent of the Kornilov revolt became known, it rejected that resolution and instead, on the morning of August 28, resolved simply to express support for the government in its struggle against Kornilov: *RG*, August 29, 1917 (no. 146), and *Khronika* 4:103–5.

[163] The new government set out to concentrate its efforts on the search for peace, strengthening the army, and some vague measures to prevent the economy from collapsing: *IzvPS*, September 24, 1917 (no. 180), 3–4, and *Khronika* 4:250–51, 257–60, 263–64, 266–67.

[164] Rosenberg, *Liberals in the Russian Revolution*, 245, argues that in thus committing themselves, the Kadets had made "the greatest concessions of their political career," because they had accepted the immediate improvement of land relations through the existing land committees, the right of all nationalities to self-determination, and an active search for a democratic peace. Among the seventeen ministers in the new cabinet were Gvozdev (labor), Prokopovich (food), Konovalov (trade and industry), Smirnov (state controller), and the SR S. L. Maslov (agriculture). For the full composition and program of the new cabinet, see *VVP*, September 28, 1917 (no. 163), 1, and *RPG* 3:1715–17.

renskii's coalition had helped to further undermine the notion of a national revolutionary assembly—already greatly weakened by the inconclusive results of the Democratic Conference—through which contradictory social interests and conflicting visions of the revolution might have been at least partially reconciled and the revolution spared from a dictatorship of the right or the left.

The short history of the Preparliament demonstrated the futility of the concept underlying its existence. When it opened on September 23 as the Democratic Council, revolutionary democracy, with close to 200 of the 308 seats, had a comfortable numerical edge over nonsoviet democracy. However, when the Bolsheviks walked out, and when 156 representatives of census groups were added, what then became the Provisional Council of the Russian Republic was left almost evenly divided between the bourgeoisie, revolutionary democracy, and intermediary and indecisive democracy.[165] The debate on national defense, which took up most of the Preparliament's time, did not produce a majority for any resolution and proved all too clearly that no collaborative effort on behalf of the revolution's goals was now possible.[166] Not surprisingly, the workers of Petrograd voted through their deputies in the Petrograd soviet on October 9 to boycott the Preparliament.[167]

Meanwhile, the cabinet that had refused to recognize the Preparliament's authority was itself unable to check the disorder and disintegration. There were strikes on the railroads and in the Donbas mines and the Baku oil fields; factory shutdowns in Petrograd; an uprising in the fleet; mass desertions from the front; and perhaps most serious, an almost complete breakdown of grain sales in the countryside. Moreover, as memories of the Kornilov fiasco receded and the extent of Bolshevik popularity and confidence became clearer, census Russia again seemed bent on a strategy of confrontation. At the Kadets' Tenth Congress in mid-October, Miliukov's conservative wing of the party reasserted its strength against the more conciliatory leaders such as Nabokov, N. M. Kishkin, M. S. Adzhemov, and the new Kadet industrialists Smirnov and Konovalov.[168] A second Conference of Public Activists met in Moscow in mid-October with the aim of "uniting all statesmanlike and nationally thinking" people for a "reaction against

[165] Sukhanov, *Zapiski o revoliutsii* 6:239–51.

[166] *RV*, October 20, 1917 (no. 240), 3.

[167] *Khronika* 5:52–53.

[168] See Rosenberg, *Liberals in the Russian Revolution*, 246–54, for a discussion of divisions in the Kadet party during October 1917.

389

the revolutionary democratic organizations."[169] Indeed, there was talk in the halls of the Preparliament among delegates from the right of plans to exploit a Bolshevik attempt to seize power in order to rally the soldiers around the Provisional Government and enable it, where Kornilov had failed, to crush the organizations of the left.[170] Small wonder that in this atmosphere the cabinet hardened its stand. The ministers including Kerenskii and Tereshchenko, declined even unofficial contacts with the moderate leaders of the VTsIK; Tereshchenko, the minister of foreign affairs, now accepted the Kadet view of Russia's war aims; and General A. I. Verkhovskii, the minister of war, was summarily dismissed when he recommended to the Preparliament's Defense and Foreign Affairs committees that Russia enter into immediate peace negotiations to avoid military disaster.[171]

As the end drew near, and the Revolutionary Defensists' search for cooperation with at least some nonproletarian force of urban Russia proved hopeless, all that the moderate leaders of the VTsIK could do was to argue against the logic of the extremes on their right and their left. And it was again Dan, whose responses to the situation were emblematic of the Revolutionary Defensist approach, who illustrated the dilemma most vividly. On the one hand, he cautioned against "any careless step" by the soviets, for he was sure that would "kill the revolution," and in such times the duty of political parties was "not to follow the masses but to explain to them how disastrous was the road they wished to follow."[172] On the other hand, this didacticism, so reminiscent of Potresov's bitter words during the Unification Congress in August, did not either obscure Dan's understanding of the social underpinnings of the Bolshevik's appeal or interfere with his energetic pursuit of every practicable way of remedying old injustices. Al-

[169] *RV*, October 13, 1917 (no. 234), 5, and October 14, 1917 (no. 235), 5.

[170] Dan, "K istorii poslednykh dnei Vremennogo Pravitel'stva," 169–70.

[171] Ibid., 169, and "Nakanune oktiabr'skogo perevorota," 9–17, 28–41. Nabokov has said that in the weeks following Kornilov's attempted coup, Tereshchenko was inflamed with hatred for the socialists: Medlin and Parsons, eds., *Nabokov*, 96.

[172] From his speech to the Preparliament on September 23. A resolution proposed by Dan, which hailed the Preparliament as the "biggest step" in establishing a stable authority and realizing the August 14 program, was adopted by the Menshevik faction (with 109 voting for, 84 against, and 22 abstaining). Martov's resolution, calling the new government and its relationship with the Preparliament "unacceptable," was defeated, but the faction decided that both resolutions should be presented to the Preparliament; *RG*, September 24, 1917 (no. 169), and September 27, 1917 (no. 171).

though he supported Tsereteli's and Skobelev's contention that coalition was the only possible solution in the "tragic situation" created by the Democratic Conference, Dan and many praktiki also called on their party to voice its criticism of the new coalition openly.[173] In his statements to the Preparliament and its committees, Dan consistently pressed for government action on three points he considered essential in any effort to reclaim popular support for the regime: immediate peace talks; the transfer of all gentry-owned land to the land committees; and prompt convocation of the Constituent Assembly.[174] On October 24, a resolution on these points was narrowly approved by the Preparliament.[175] Dan improvised a "delegation" composed of himself, Gots, and the reluctant Avksent'ev, who was serving as chairman of the Preparliament, in the hope of persuading the cabinet to take last-minute action in conformity with the resolution. It was a last, desperate effort to force a "break in the sentiment of the masses" and prevent their supporting the seizure of power being planned by the Bolsheviks. But the cabinet took just a few minutes to reject the appeal, and once again the Mensheviks had failed to save the revolution and their own moderate strategies from destruction at the hands of the forces tearing society apart.[176]

By THEN, of course, the question of the Provisional Government's continued existence had been decided both in the hitherto divided Bolshevik party and in the soviets where the Bolsheviks held a majority.[177] For the Revolutionary Defensists, October 25 was a day of double tragedy: first, because they were removed from the leadership of the soviets through the votes of workers and soldiers all over Russia; and second, because their political strategy was dealt a final blow when sailors and workers loyal to

[173] *RG*, September 24, 1917 (no. 169).

[174] See the report on the meeting of the Foreign Affairs Committee on October 17, in "Nakanune oktiabr'skogo perevorota," 23–29; Dan's statement during the Preparliament's discussion of the approaching Bolshevik attack, in *Rech'*, October 25, 1917 (no. 205), 3–4; and Dan, "K istorii poslednykh dnei Vremennogo Pravitel'stva," 168, 170–71.

[175] The resolution was drafted by Dan and passed with the help of both the Revolutionary Defensist and Internationalist factions of the Mensheviks, the Left SRs, and part of the SRs: *RG*, October 25, 1917 (no. 195). The vote was 123 for and 102 against, with 26 abstentions: *IzvPS*, October 25, 1917 (no. 205), 3–4.

[176] Dan, "K istorii poslednykh dnei Vremennogo Pravitel'stva," 172–75.

[177] On the debates in the Bolshevik party and the preparation for a seizure of power, see Rabinowitch, *Bolsheviks Come to Power*, esp. chaps. 10–14.

the Bolsheviks arrested the members of the Provisional Government—an act which the Mensheviks strongly believed would lead to civil war. When the Second Congress of Soviets opened on October 25, the Menshevik faction was the smallest of the three major socialist factions, with about 50 seats for the Revolutionary Defensists (including the Bund) and 33 for the Internationalists, compared to over 300 Bolshevik delegates and nearly 200 SRs, of whom more than half were Left SRs (see appendix 5). According to the official proceedings, 505 delegates had come to the congress committed to vote for "all power to the soviets"; 86 for "all power to democracy"; and only 79 for a "coalition government," 21 of them for a "democratic coalition without the Kadets."[178] The soviets' constituency had turned decisively against the Revolutionary Defensist strategy of cooperation with the other elements of Russian society, and the congress's first act was to replace the Menshevik-SR presidium with a Bolshevik-Left SR one.[179] Early on the morning of October 26, the Second Congress of Soviets declared the Provisional Government deposed and assumed full authority in the country. By then, the SRs and Mensheviks had left the hall; this historic declaration was passed by vote of the remaining delegates, with two objections and twelve abstentions.[180]

The Mensheviks' statements during the long day of October 25 reveal not only the contradictory goals shaping Menshevik actions on the eve of the overthrow but also the reason for the party's nearly complete disappearance as a political force after October. The first statement, read out at a meeting of the Menshevik faction to the Second Congress in the small hours of October 25, was the result of a leftward move by Dan and many centrist praktiki which had begun in June, soon after the coalition had been established, and had then been checked by the July Days, but had grown in determination and political definition after the Kornilov affair. The cabinet's peremptory rejection of Dan's last-minute appeal finally forced these people to insist that a "homogeneous democratic government" was now an absolute necessity and should be established "immediately," presumably without waiting for the consent of democracy's more recalcitrant elements. A motion to that effect was made by Khinchuk, a veteran praktik and Revolutionary De-

[178] *Vtoroi vserossiiskii s'ezd sovetov*, 107–9. This account shows a total of 670 delegates when listing their policy mandates, but only 648 when giving their party affiliation.

[179] Ibid., 32–33.

[180] Ibid., 53–55; *IzvPS*, October 26, 1917 (no. 208), 3.

fensist from Moscow, and it was passed by the combined votes of Revolutionary Defensists and Internationalists.[181] A second statement, more openly radical, was contained in Martov's address to the Second Congress, delivered shortly after it opened; he urged that the fighting stop so that a civil war might be avoided and that the Bolsheviks negotiate with all other socialist parties the formation of a "united democratic government" acceptable to the whole of democracy. (A few minutes later, when he spoke again in favor of his proposal, Martov used the term "revolutionary democracy.")[182] This was, in other words, a revival of the idea of a "homogeneous socialist government."

Both statements suggested a remarkable departure from Revolutionary Defensist strategies during the past few months and could perhaps have affected the political outcome of the seizure of power even if the act itself could no longer be prevented.[183] Indeed, Martov's speech was received enthusiastically by the delegates, many of whom were desperate to avoid a split in the soviets at this grave moment,[184] and his proposals were even endorsed by Mstislavskii for the Left SRs and A. V. Lunacharskii for the Bolsheviks, and they were approved by the congress unanimously.[185]

This unanimity, however, was deceptive. Within minutes of the vote on Martov's proposals, a series of Menshevik speakers (Ia. Ia. Kharash and Kuchin from the army and the Muscovite Khinchuk) accused the Bolsheviks of conspiring to deprive the congress and the Constituent Assembly of their powers, threatened to mobilize the army on the front against this "adventure," and called on the congress to negotiate with the Provisional Government the formation of a cabinet to represent all elements of democracy.[186] Then, having provoked an explosion of hostility and bitterness by their attack on the Bolsheviks and their opposition to the seizure of power, the Menshevik, SR, and Bund factions left the congress amid shouts of "Deserters!," "Kornilovites!," and "Good riddance!"[187] But the Menshevik Internationalists remained, and Martov placed before the congress a more precise and binding resolu-

---

[181] *RG*, October 25, 1917 (no. 195), 2.

[182] *Vtoroi vserossiiskii s'ezd sovetov*, 4, 34.

[183] This point is made by Rabinowitch, *Bolsheviks Come to Power*, 292–98.

[184] Sukhanov, *Zapiski o revoliutsii* 7:199.

[185] *Vtoroi vserossiiskii s'ezd sovetov*, 4, 35.

[186] Ibid., 5, 35–37.

[187] Ibid., 38–40.

tion calling on "rebel democracy" to negotiate with the rest of "democracy."[188]

It was at this juncture that Trotskii hurled his famous imprecation at the departing delegates, which would henceforth haunt the Mensheviks: "To those who have left and who tell us to do this we say: Your role is played out; go where you belong—into the dustbin of history!"[189] But perhaps more telling of the effect the Revolutionary Defensists' conduct had on the congress was Lunacharskii's pronouncement, for he had endorsed Martov's proposal earlier: "We all accepted Martov's proposal to discuss peaceful ways of solving the crisis . . . but a systematic attack was launched at us. . . . Without hearing us out, without even discussing their own proposals, they immediately tried to separate themselves from us . . . to isolate us."[190] In any case, the Internationalists further obliged Trotskii when they, too, left the congress, and Martov's resolution was defeated.[191]

The Mensheviks, as Sukhanov later observed, had played into Lenin's and Trotskii's hands: The seizure of power by the soviets would eventually produce a "Bolshevik dictatorship," not a "soviet" one.[192] Yet the record of their activity on October 25 is a mixed one, and so were their motives. If their walkout was a tragic mistake, it should be remembered that even at that hour of misfortune they were resourceful enough to offer yet another heterodox solution: a socialist government committed to the broader aims of democracy. Although the formulation of a "homogeneous socialist government" had been Martov's, the Menshevik faction's vote on the night of October 24–25 to press for such a government immediately indicated that many Revolutionary Defensists now accepted the necessity for some radical alternative to coalition. Here again, their motives had been derived only partially from ideology. On the night of October 25–26, it was the sight of the radicalized delegates, the humiliation of being deposed once more by the Bolsheviks from the leadership of the working class, the realization of all the old suspicions about a Bolshevik "conspiracy" and "adventurism"—all that was reminiscent of the painful experiences of the past—that stood as an obstacle to the working out

[188] Ibid., 40–42.
[189] Ibid., 43–44.
[190] Ibid., 45–47.
[191] Ibid., 43–45, 47.
[192] Sukhanov, *Zapiski o revoliutsii* 7:200–1.

of a compromise. Even Khinchuk, a frequent critic of coalition, could not leave the formation of a new government to this congress, and even Martov could not stomach the sight of Trotskii, triumphant and spiteful, on the rostrum. The Mensheviks had once again been defeated.

Conclusions

SPECULATION is not supposed to be the historian's trade, yet only by asking whether the Russian Revolution of 1917 could have turned out differently can we see more clearly what elements determined some of the developments that came to pass. Among these determining elements, the most powerful and intractable one was the deep divisions within Russian society at large and urban society in particular. Russian urban society before 1917 had long been divided, and these divisions had produced attitudes of suspicion and intolerance on all sides. Mutual hostility was particularly strong between labor and the entrepreneurial class because of both the generally oppressive regime in the factories and the experience of failed revolutionary attempts. Yet for a time there was a distinct, if remote, possibility that such hostilities as existed might have been neutralized through some kind of modification in collective behavior or the satisfaction of the respective classes' most urgent demands and so might have led in turn to longer-lasting political cooperation between the classes. Under such conditions, the Mensheviks' self-assumed task of mediating the relations between workers and industrialists might have been more successful than it was.

A second determining factor of great importance was the war, which not only exacerbated societal divisions but also engendered the economic crisis that would ultimately destroy any possibility of satisfying the material demands of any of the classes and finally provoked irreconcilable conflict between workers and employers. War also contributed indirectly to the final outcome of the revolution by overburdening, fatally weakening, and virtually destroying the bureaucratic structure. Not only was the state in 1917 incapable of handling the enormously complex tasks of democratizing local government, reforming social legislation, and rationalizing economic performance, but it also lost the capacity of restraining the processes of social change because it could no longer command the instruments of order or coercion. The various police organizations disappeared literally overnight, while the soldiers—having declared their political allegiance to the soviets and the working class—could not be relied on to maintain social order. The war also played a role in providing the principal point in the political program around which the groups of revolutionary democracy united.

The third determining factor was the absence of parliamentary structures through which social groups might have gathered to work out their fundamental differences. The State Duma was too unrepresentative of the country and had discredited itself too thoroughly during the war years to fulfill the role of a national assembly or forum, and the Constituent Assembly was not convoked until after the fate of the revolution had been settled. The delay in convoking the assembly occurred precisely because of collective class suspicions: the representatives of the census groups in the Provisional Government feared its outcome and the disruptive effect it might have on the war effort, whereas the Mensheviks did not recognize its importance until the end, both because they had come to believe in their own capacity to mediate the urban social conflict and because they feared a confrontation with the peasantry that was sure to dominate the assembly.

Beyond these structural and otherwise impersonal determining factors, the outcome of the revolution was greatly influenced by ideologies and their articulators—that is, the various political groups into which Russia's radical intelligentsia had divided itself in the twenty years or so preceding the revolution. The revolution's rapid reworking of political structures, social relations, and attitudes immeasurably increased the power of those who could best exploit the complex realities. Eventually, it was the Bolsheviks' success in articulating a sense of working-class militancy—the workers' disappointment in the revolution, their anxiety about their livelihood, their growing hostility toward their employers and the Provisional Government, and a fear of counterrevolution and repression—that brought the constituency of the soviets to the conclusion that a "dictatorship of the soviets" was unavoidable. In short, the presence of a nationally organized militant party capable of articulating and legitimizing the anxieties and strivings of a desperate constituency was of critical importance.

Initially, however, it had been the moderate socialists, particularly the Mensheviks in the Revolutionary Defensist leadership of the soviet, who had given expression to the workers' ambivalence toward the bourgeoisie even as they fostered among the soviet's constituency a broad acceptance of their strategy for interclass cooperation. The Mensheviks' early success as leaders of the soviet and as national mediators was a result not only of their astute political sense but also of favorable conditions: the euphoria of the early days of the revolution, the workers' fear of isolation, their sense of power in the soviet, and the real opportunities for labor victories. Similarly, the eventual failure of this strategy must be attributed in part to the changes in these formerly favorable conditions.

The July Days were undoubtedly the great divide, and though there is general agreement on this point among historians of the Russian Revolution, few have focused on the interaction that occurred during May and June in two concurrent processes: first, the economic deterioration and its manifestations in the factories; and second, the moderates' loss of credibility through their participation in the coalition government. The expectations raised in the early months of the revolution were crushed during the first two months of the coalition, leading the workers of Petrograd to demand that interclass cooperation give way to a government of the soviets, though it seems clear that initially this government was conceived of as a multiparty democracy. The Menshevik leaders' refusal to take the path that seemed so inevitable to their followers created a rupture that proved irreparable.

The reasons for the Mensheviks' refusal to follow this lead and for the ultimate collapse of their strategy in 1917 are many. There would, of course, have been ideological difficulty in justifying a socialist government in a country that by all criteria was not ready for socialism and was indeed barely entering the stage of free capitalist development which was supposed to prepare the transition to socialism. But the Revolutionary Defensists had overcome similar ideological strictures in early May when they had decided to join a coalition government. Still, it was not until after Kornilov's attempted coup that they resolved on a "homogeneous democratic government" and not until the very eve of the Bolshevik seizure of power that they interpreted the refusal of nonsoviet democracy to join such a government as necessitating a "homogeneous socialist government." Even here, as the Revolutionary Defensists sought to explain reality in terms of a failing Marxist ideology, what emerged as the dominant Menshevik (especially Revolutionary Defensist) characteristic was their political practicality and their quest for political relevance.

Ideology had in fact proven quite flexible, but the emotional forces born of years of being the moderate and "responsible" rivals of a militant, "adventurist" party were deeper and less amenable to change. So also were the painful memories of the revolution's defeat in 1905 and the hopes developed in the intervening years of overcoming the forces that had made for that defeat. And the realities of July-October 1917 only reinforced the Mensheviks' image of themselves as the sole responsible voice in the country. Indeed, as the economy, civic order, and social peace were collapsing around them, the Revolutionary Defensists continued their work in the government and tried desperately to moderate the workers' collective behavior, even at the price of appearing to have forsaken the workers' cause. A militant solution that would have divided Russian society, have led to civil war, and given rise to a premature socialist experiment simply ran against their grain. As men committed to the realization of an ideal vision of society, they found themselves unable to change that vision for something else even if the vision had become impossible. And in the Russia of late 1917, the Menshevik vision of a society that combined social justice with pluralistic democracy had become quite impossible.

Appendixes

Glossary of Political Organizations and Groupings

Bolsheviks	Radical wing of Social Democracy; official name was Russian Social Democratic Labor Party (Bolsheviks).
bourgeois camp	Contemporary socialist term for the propertied classes, the intelligentsia groups that were close to them, and their parties and organizations.
democracy, democratic camp	*See* revolutionary democracy.
Independents	Social Democrats standing between the Menshevik and Bolshevik factions and not affiliated with either one.
Kadets	Constitutional Democrats, the largest of Russia's liberal parties.
Mensheviks	Moderate wing of Social Democracy, officially known as the Russian Social Democratic Labor Party (Mensheviks); divided both before and during 1917 into several factions (see appendix 2).
People's Socialists	A small, Defensist Populist party.
Populists	Non-Marxist socialist parties with a peasant constituency.
Progressists	Liberal party founded by the merchant-entrepreneurs of Moscow, which in 1917 was more conciliatory toward the socialists than were the Kadets.
Progressive bloc	Parliamentary bloc established in 1915 in the State Duma to unite the parties of the center, excluding the socialists and the extreme right wing.
public organizations	The unions of zemstvos and cities (united together in the Zemgor) and the War-Industrial Committees established by commercial and industrial groups, all intended to help the war effort and to unite the liberal opposition to the old regime.
Radical Democrats	Party founded in July 1917 by former Progressists and left Kadets to advance more liberal policies than the Kadets, especially toward the soviet.
revolutionary democracy	Term used by socialists to denote the lower classes and socialist intelligentsia organized in urban

	soviets (also referred to as the "democratic camp"); the term "democracy" was also used in this sense during the early months of 1917, but later, while "revolutionary democracy" continued to mean the urban soviets and their constituencies, "democracy" came to include the cooperative movement, the democratized self-governments, and the peasant soviets as well.
Social Democracy, Social Democrats	Used collectively to denote all the Marxist socialist parties with a working-class constituency.
Socialist Revolutionaries	Largest Populist party; along with the moderate Mensheviks, formed the Revolutionary Defensist bloc that dominated the soviets for much of 1917.
soviets	Local councils of deputies elected by workers, soldiers, and peasants; dominated by the socialist parties through the executive committees of the local soviets and the Central Executive Committee (VTsIK).
Trudoviki	The Groups of Toilers, a small, moderate Populist party on the Defensist wing of the soviets.
United Social Democrats	Local political groups in which Mensheviks, Bolsheviks, and Independents were represented together, reflecting a desire to bridge the old factional divides.

Glossary of Menshevik Factions and Groupings

Defensists	Advocates of socialist participation in defense efforts during World War I and of close cooperation with other educated groups in Russian society.
economists	Activists of the economic section of the Petrograd soviet; some were former Liquidationists, others were Independent Internationalists.
gosudarstvenniki	Mensheviks who held positions in the Provisional Government; they included many former praktiki-Liquidationists in the Ministry of Labor.
initsiatory	Members of the Menshevik Initiative Groups, founded after 1911 to combine legal labor organizing with underground work.
Internationalists	Mensheviks who felt socialists should not contribute to the war effort but should work toward a universal peace; also, in 1917, the opponents of any cooperation with the bourgeoisie.
laborists	Mensheviks who worked in the labor section of the Petrograd soviet, all former praktiki and most of them initsiatory.
Liquidationists	Mensheviks who wanted to "liquidate" the SD underground in the aftermath of 1905—some because they believed Russia's transformation to democracy might be possible without a revolution, others because they wanted to eliminate the "voluntarist" influence of the intelligentsia on the labor movement.
literatory	Menshevik publicists, identified during the interrevolutionary years with the Liquidationists.
praktiki	Mensheviks active in labor organizing, especially in the legal labor organizations of the post-1905 years; some were Liquidationists, others were initsiatory.
provincials	Mensheviks active in provincial town soviets, usually taking political positions similar to those of the former Liquidationists and the present gosudarstvenniki.
Revolutionary Defensists	Mensheviks who accepted the need for military defense after the February revolution and joined with the Socialist Revolutionaries to form the

Revolutionary Defensist bloc in the soviets, which
supported the policy of coalition; thus, the term
"Revolutionary Defensist" could refer either to the
Revolutionary Defensist faction within the
Menshevik party or to the Revolutionary Defensist
bloc of Mensheviks and Socialist Revolutionaries. In
this work, it is used mostly to denote the Menshevik
faction, but the term "Revolutionary Defensist
leadership of the soviets" is meant to include the
Socialist Revolutionaries as well.

Biographical Sketches of Menshevik Leaders

BATURSKII [*pseudonym of* Tseitlin], Boris Solomonovich (1879–1920). From wealthy Jewish family of Vitebsk; active in Jewish Bund while attending university (1897) but then shifted activities to Russian Social Democracy. After prison and exile, returned to Russia as Menshevik; completed university degree in Moscow during interrevolutionary years; contributed to legal labor press; after 1912, edited the journal *Workers' Insurance*. Liquidationist and Defensist; represented these views in Menshevik Organizational and later Central committees and on board of *Rabochaia gazeta*; belonged to the right wing of the party after October.

BOGDANOV, Boris Osipovich (1884–1956). Joined Mensheviks in Odessa in 1905; spent years from 1906 to 1917 in Petersburg; Liquidationist-praktik in the interrevolutionary period, active in both legal labor press and labor organizing. Defensist, secretary to the Labor Group at the Central WIC; among founders of Petrograd soviet in 1917; also founder of and activist in its labor section. Leader and defender of Revolutionary Defensist bloc; rejected any compromise with Bolsheviks after October; spent several decades in prison and exile.

CHEREVANIN, N. [*pseudonym of* Fedor Andreevich Lipkin] (1869–1938). Economist and publicist; led Marxist circles in Kharkov in the 1890s; joined Mensheviks in 1903; became leading Liquidationist literator during interrevolutionary period. Served as head of the Petrograd bureau of the Union of Cities' Economic Department during war; in 1917, among architects of economic planning in the Petrograd soviet's economic section; supporter of Revolutionary Defensism; editor of *Rabochaia gazeta* and frequent speaker on economic and political matters; joined Martov's wing of the party after October, represented it in VTsIK; arrested (1921), died in exile.

CHKHEIDZE, Nikolai Semenovich (1864–1926). From petty noble family of Georgia; participated in student circles while attending universities of Odessa and Kharkov; among founders of Georgian Marxism in 1892 and like most Georgian SDs chose the Menshevik wing (1903); elected as a Menshevik to the Third Duma (1907) and the Fourth (1912); chaired SD faction and, after its split in October 1913, Menshevik faction, which he led in denouncing the war (he was a moderate Internationalist) and in seeking cooperation with nonsocialist parties; also pursued such contacts through his membership in the "political" Free Masonry. Among founders of Petrograd soviet in 1917; was its chairman and that of the

VTsIK; belonged to the inner circle of the Revolutionary Defensist bloc. Fled to Georgia after October; worked for its Menshevik government until its collapse forced his departure (1921); committed suicide in Paris.

DAN [*pseudonym of* Gurvich], Fedor Il'ich (1871–1947). From assimilated Jewish family in Petersburg; educated as a physician; active in SD work in Petersburg (1895–1896) and Berlin (1901–1902); spent time in prison and exile. In 1903, married Martov's sister Lydia and became his close friend and collaborator and a leading Menshevik publicist and policy maker. After the dispersal of the First and Second Dumas (he was the Central Committee's contact with their SD faction), left Russia but continued to contribute to Menshevik publications, legal and otherwise; returned to Petersburg in 1913 to guide Menshevik's labor press and Duma faction; arrested at the start of the war; in Irkutsk with Tsereteli, with whom he formulated the principles of Siberian Zimmerwaldism. Active in the party and the soviet in 1917; served as organizational and political force behind Tsereteli's leadership of Revolutionary Defensist factions of both; parted ways with most Revolutionary Defensists after October in joining Martov's Internationalist faction and seeking accommodation with Bolsheviks; expelled from Soviet Union (1922); after Martov's death, led party's left wing in emigration.

DIUBUA, Anatolii Eduardovich (1882–1959). Attorney; a Bolshevik (1905), then a Menshevik Liquidationist (1906); contributor to legal labor press and union organizing. Wartime officer and Defensist; during 1917, served as soviet's commissar to Northern Front and deputy minister of labor. Participated in uprisings against the Bolsheviks in 1918; imprisoned, and then expelled from Soviet Union.

ERMOLAEV, Konstantin Mikhailovich (1884–1919). Menshevik organizer from 1904; elected to SD Central Committee in 1907 but refused to serve with Bolsheviks; after 1910, one of the most outspoken Liquidationists; grew close to Dan and Tsereteli in exile (1914–1917); contributed to Siberian Zimmerwaldist publications. On returning to Petrograd, represented Revolutionary Defensist views in the Menshevik Central Committee, the executive committee of the Petrograd soviet, and the VTsIK. Advocated armed opposition to Bolsheviks after October.

EZHOV [*pseudonym of* Tsederbaum], Sergei Osipovich (1879–1941). Brother of Martov and Levitskii (representing the left and right wings of Menshevism, respectively) and brother-in-law of Dan; involved in SD circles and labor organizing from early youth; served as underground agent for *Iskra*, smuggling in copies from Munich; after 1905, worked in legal trade unions, legal Menshevik press, and Initiative Group of which he was founder. Moderate Internationalist during war; supported Revolutionary Defensist leadership in 1917 but was often critical of coalition; active in workers' cooperatives in Moscow until imprisonment (1921) and banishment to Siberia; shot after German invasion (1941).

GARVI, P. [*pseudonym of* Petr Abramovich Bronshtein] (1881–1944). Joined SD activity in hometown of Odessa in 1899; became Menshevik while abroad in 1903. After 1905, studied for law degree in Petersburg University; also active in many Menshevik enterprises—labor organizing (of which he was a principal architect), labor press, and party affairs in Russia and abroad; Liquidationist, but participated in founding underground Initiative Group. Moderate Internationalist during the war; joined Revolutionary Defensists in 1917; served on editorial board of *Rabochaia gazeta*, in Petrograd soviet's labor section, and in organizing trade unions. Resigned from Menshevik Central Committee after October in protest over negotiations with Bolsheviks (as he had done in 1907 and 1910); was arrested (1921) and expelled from the Soviet Union (1923).

GOREV, B. [*pseudonym of* Boris Isakovich Gol'dman] (1874–?). Son of Hebrew scholar from Vilno; brother of Liber; began SD activity in 1895 while at Petersburg University; from then until 1917, alternately in prison and engaged in SD political organizing in Russia and abroad; Bolshevik sympathizer at first but became Menshevik in 1905; occupied a centrist position in party's policy-making bodies, congresses, and publications. Revolutionary Defensist in 1917; served on editorial board of *Rabochaia gazeta*; abandoned Menshevism in 1920, worked in Soviet publishing.

GRINEVICH, V. [*pseudonym of* Mikhail Grigor'evich Kogan] (1874–1943). SD from university days in Berlin (1897); Menshevik from 1903; organizer of Union of Printers (1905) and its delegate to Petersburg soviet; organizer and chairman of Second Conference of Trade Unions (1906); in following years, initiator and guide of various legal workers' organizations. Revolutionary Defensist in 1917; resigned from chairmanship of Central Council of Trade Unions after unions' delegates to Democratic Conference voted against coalition; remained active in Menshevik-led unions (1918–1919); later emigrated.

GROMAN, Vladimir Gustavovich (1874–?). Economist, statistician, and publicist; Social Democrat from the 1890s; supported liquidationism after 1905; worked as zemstvo statistician and published studies of the revolutionary movement. During war and revolution, promoted principle of economic planning as head of Economic Department of Union of Cities, which he represented in various public bodies and meetings; head of Petrograd soviet's economic section, of National Supply Commission, and of Petrograd regional supply committee (1917). Intensified Menshevik activity after October, but left it when party went underground; one of chief Soviet economic planners until arrest and conviction in "Menshevik trial" (1931); probably died in exile sometime after World War II.

GVOZDEV, Kuz'ma Antonovich (1883–?). Metalworker-intelligent of peasant origin; first followed SRs (1903–1905) but in interrevolutionary period, after arrest and imprisonment, came under influence of Menshevik praktiki; chairman of Petersburg Union of Metalworkers (1909–1911) until his second imprisonment. Active in workers' consumer cooperatives during the war, then chairman of Central WIC's Labor Group; among founders of Petrograd soviet in 1917 and its labor section; staunch Revolutionary Defensist; served in Ministry of Labor during coalition as deputy and minister. Favored compromise with Bolsheviks after October; left political activity when efforts at compromise failed and worked in Soviet economic organizations.

Isuv, Iosif Andreevich (1878–1920). Left rabbinical school to organize workers in Kiev and Ekaterinoslav; a founder of Moscow soviet (1905); organizer of open labor organizations in Petersburg; Liquidationist in subsequent years; one of founders of Petersburg Initiative Group (1911). Revolutionary Defensist in 1917; central figure in Moscow soviet; opponent of compromise with Bolsheviks (had resigned in 1907 and 1910 from SD Central Committee for this reason). Withdrew from party activity after October.

Kheisin, Minei Leont'evich (?–1924). Physician; active in SD circles in Siberia (1890s); joined Menshevik activities in Petersburg in 1906; contributor to party's press, its legal labor organizing, and contacts with its faction in the State Duma. Liquidationist, later Defensist; shifted from political activity to workers' consumer cooperatives, which he helped initiate in the prewar years; continued this work in 1917; supported Revolutionary Defensists; opposed Bolshevik seizure of power.

Khinchuk, Lev Mikhailovich (1868–?). Active in revolutionary circles from 1889; central figure among Moscow SDs and Mensheviks (1903); chairman of Moscow soviet (1905 and 1917); active in both legal labor organizations and underground Initiative Groups. Generally followed Revolutionary Defensist leadership in 1917. Resigned from party in 1920; joined Communist party and worked for Soviet government as an economist and diplomat.

Kolokol'nikov, Pavel Nikolaevich (1871–?). From manufacturing family in Moscow; did SD organizing among workers (1891–1892); foremost Menshevik theoretician and practitioner of unionism, labor legislation, and workers' cooperatives; after 1905, worked as economist and statistician in consumer cooperatives and other places. Served as deputy to the minister of labor (1917) for mediation, labor legislation, and contacts with the trade unions. Opposed negotiations with Bolsheviks after October; arrested (1922), exiled to Siberia.

Kol'tsov, D. [*pseudonym of* Boris Abramovich Ginzburg] (1863–1920). Active in Populist circles during gymnasium days in Mogilev and university years in Petersburg, where he discovered Marxism; emigrated in 1893; collaborated with founders of Russian Social Democracy abroad; became Menshevik in 1903, Liquidationist after 1905; important contributor to party's labor organizing in St. Petersburg and Baku and to its legal press and publications (wrote on history of European labor movement). In exile during war, became Defensist and then Revolutionary Defensist (1917); returned to Petrograd, worked in soviet's labor section, in trade union movement, and as Ministry of Labor's commissar for Petrograd province. After October, worked in archives of the revolution in Ufa.

KUCHIN, Georgii Dmitrievich. Lawyer and contributor to Menshevik press from at least 1912. Artillery officer when the revolution began; became chairman of the officers' soviet of the 12th Army and later of the Army Committee of the Northern Front; represented these organizations in soviet and Menshevik congresses and on VTsIK; Defensist. Joined right wing of Menshevism after October; organized workers against Bolsheviks, and, though he had volunteered to fight in the Soviet-Polish war, resumed underground Menshevik activity until arrested (late 1920s).

LIBER, M. [pseudonym of Mikhail Isakovich Gol'dman] (1880–1937). Brother of Gorev. Leader of Jewish Bund and its representative to many congresses and on SD Central Committee; Menshevik and Liquidationist (1907). Defensist during the war; chiefly a political organizer; served on governing bodies of Menshevik party and Petrograd soviet (1917); supporter of coalition. Opposed compromise with Bolsheviks after October; led underground Menshevik activity (1923–1924); imprisoned, exiled to Siberia, and executed.

MARTOV, L. [pseudonym of Iulii Osipovich Tsederbaum] (1873–1923). Brother of Ezhov, brother-in-law of Dan. From assimilated Jewish family of Petersburg; joined Marxist student movement (early 1890s); among the initiators (along with Lenin) of first SD organization in Petersburg (1895–1896) and of efforts to unify Russian Social Democracy (1900–1903); a leader of Menshevism after 1903; in emigration (1906–1917), he contributed to Menshevik publications, legal and otherwise; often criticized Liquidationists and later Defensists. Returned to Russia in May 1917; led Internationalist faction of Menshevism; strongly opposed to coalition until after October, when party's majority joined his faction in seeking accommodation with Bolsheviks; emigrated in 1920.

PANIN, M. [pseudonym of Mark Saulovich Makadziub] (1876–?). Joined SD circles in southern Russia (1901); identified with Menshevism from 1903; literator and Liquidationist. Wrote for Rabochaia gazeta in 1917; abandoned political activity after October. Represented Soviet lumber industry abroad until emigration (1931).

POTRESOV, Aleksandr Nikolaevich (1869–1934). From gentry family of some social standing; joined Marxist student movement in Petersburg (early 1890s); was one of founders of Iskra, with Martov and Lenin (1900); joined Mensheviks when SDs split (1903); sponsor and editor of important Menshevik legal publications, but gradually moved away from party's mainstream after 1905; championed unqualified liquidationism and defensism. Led a small group of right-wing SDs during 1917 and afterward; was not member of leading bodies of Menshevism either in Russia or in emigration (1925–1934).

ROZHKOV, Nikolai Aleksandrovich (1868–1927). Historian and university teacher; embraced Bolshevism (1905–1907) but subsequently rejected its tactics; supported use of legal opportunities for opposing autocracy; in Siberian exile (1908–1917), grew close to Tsereteli, contributed to Siberian Zimmerwaldist publications; on return to Petrograd joined Menshevik party. Member of the Revolutionary Defensist leadership; served as Tsereteli's deputy in Ministry of Post and Telegraph, but resigned to protest concessions forced on soviet. Left underground remnant of Menshevik party in 1923.

SCHWARZ [Shvarts], Solomon Meerovich (1883–1973). From Jewish merchant family of Vilno; a Bolshevik at first (1903–1906), but then joined Mensheviks (1907); after short imprisonment, left to study law in Germany (1907–1912, 1913–1914); in Russia (1912–1913), worked in Menshevik-led unions of printers and metalworkers and helped edit *Workers' Insurance*; became party's specialist on labor insurance; Liquidationist. During war, Defensist and then Revolutionary Defensist; secretary of Moscow Labor Group (1916); active in soviet's labor section (1917); head of Workers' Insurance Department in Provisional Government (May to October). Among organizers of a state employees' strike against Bolsheviks after October; joined left wing of Menshevism (1919), volunteered for Red Army; arrested (1921) for Menshevik activity and expelled from Soviet Union.

SKOBELEV, Matvei Ivanovich (1885–?). Son of Baku industrialist; SD organizer in Baku (1903–1906); in emigration (1907–1912); wrote for Trotskii's Vienna newspaper *Pravda*. Menshevik deputy from Baku to the Fourth Duma (1912–1917); one of organizers of Petrograd soviet; member of Revolutionary Defensist leadership group; minister of labor in Provisional Government. Joined Communist party (1922), served as Soviet commercial representative abroad.

TSERETELI, Iraklii Georgievich (1881–1959). Son of influential Georgian writer; began revolutionary activity at Moscow University (1900–1902); joined Menshevik wing of SDs during exile (1903); one of seven Mensheviks elected from Georgia to the Second Duma (February–June 1907), and headed its large SD faction; famous as orator and advocate of socialist collaboration with liberal opposition to autocracy; spent a decade (1907–1917) in prison and exile, where he was the central figure in the Siberian Zimmerwaldist group. Returned to Petrograd in March 1917 as leader of the Revolutionary Defensist bloc in soviets and Menshevik party; soviet's most prestigious representative in the Provisional Government and most powerful defender of coalition until October. Delivered scathing attack on the Bolsheviks at the short-lived Constituent Assembly (1918); returned to

Georgia; represented its independent Menshevik government abroad, but later withdrew from political life.

VAINSHTEIN, Semen Lazarovich (1879–1923). Joined SD circles as student in Kharkov (1899–1900) and Moscow (1902–1903); became revolutionary and underground labor organizer; arrested many times, eventually exiled to Irkutsk (1913–1917); follower of Siberian Zimmerwaldism. On return to Petrograd, elected to soviet's executive committee, in which represented Revolutionary Defensist bloc. Rejected any compromise with Bolsheviks after October; arrested (1921), expelled from Soviet Union (1923).

VOITINSKII, Vladimir Savel'evich (1885–1960). From academic family in Petersburg; economist; entered Bolshevik activity (1905); chairman of the soviet of the unemployed (1906–1907); spent a decade (1907–1917) in prison and exile in Irkutsk; supported use of legal opportunities for opposing autocracy and cooperation with other oppositional elements; collaborated with Tsereteli on Siberian Zimmerwaldist publications. Returned to Petrograd in March 1917; advocated unification of Social Democracy but, when this was rejected by Lenin, joined Mensheviks; chief editor of Petrograd soviet's newspaper and most effective propagandist of Revolutionary Defensism; soviet's commissar to Twelfth Army (August-October). Worked for the Menshevik government of Georgia (1918–1921); emigrated.

VOLKOV, Ivan Grigor'evich (1884–?). Metalworker of peasant origin; began political activity as SR (1902–1905); later a Menshevik and as such elected to leadership of Petersburg Union of Metalworkers. Active in workers' consumer cooperatives during war and 1917; among organizers of Petrograd soviet and its supply commission; followed Liquidationist praktiki before the war; resembled initsiatory in negative attitude to war; Revolutionary Defensist in 1917. Active in assemblies of factory deputies (1918); arrested, released, and worked as economic planner until conviction in "Menshevik Trial" of 1931.

Results of Elections to Petrograd Municipal Duma, May and August 1917

District	% Workers in Population[a]	% Metalworkers among Workers[a]	Moderate Socialists[d] N	%	Mensheviks[f] N	%	Bolsheviks N	%	Nonsocialists[g] N	%
						May 1917				
Admirality	1.8[b]	32.9[b]	11,105	58.7			2,983	15.7	4,843	25.6
Aleksandr Nevskii	7.9[c]	40.6[c]	49,891	73.0	(7,246	10.6)	8,737	12.8	9,690	14.2
Kazan	1.8[b]	32.9[b]	9,253	41.9			2,219	10.1	10,605	48.0
Kolomna	10.9	88.1	23,724	58.4			6,035	14.9	10,867	26.7
Liteinyi	7.9[c]	40.6[c]	30,583	51.5			5,085	8.6	23,755	39.9
Moscow	10.8	52.3	41,517	59.3			6,758	9.7	21,667	31.0
Narva	18.6	16.9	73,293	68.9			18,202	17.1	14,897	14.0
Petrograd	10.5	64.6	72,750	54.1			30,348	22.6	31,247	23.3
Rozhdestvenskii	6.2	20.2	37,671	63.4	(19,045	32.0)	2,944	5.0	18,743	31.6
Spasski	1.8[b]	32.9[b]	20,210	53.8			4,945	13.2	12,426	33.0
Vasileostrov	19.4	72.3	49,293	45.2			37,377	34.3	22,305	20.5
Vyborg	45.8	84.1	20,568[e]	34.9			34,303	58.2	4,071	6.9
Total			439,858	56.0	(26,291)		159,936	20.4	185,116	23.6

Sources: Percent workers in population and percent metalworkers among workers: Mandel, *Petrograd Workers and the Fall of the Old Regime*, 52–53. Election results: Rosenberg, *Liberals in the Russian Revolution*, 162 (May), 220 (August).

[a] Figures are based on number of workers employed in a district (January 1, 1917), not number residing in it.
[b] Figures for the Second City district, which included all three of these districts.
[c] Figures for the First City district, which included both of these districts.
[d] Includes votes for Mensheviks, SRs, Trudoviki, and People's Socialists. The Trudoviki and the People's Socialists ran on separate lists and received a total of 1.0% of the vote in May and 2.3% in August.
[e] Elections were held in early June.

August 1917[h]

District	Moderate Socialists[d]		Mensheviks[f]		Bolsheviks		Nonsocialists[g]	
	N	%	N	%	N	%	N	%
Admirality	4,763	40.1	(257	2.2)	4,233	35.7	2,869	24.2
Aleksandr Nevskii	24,894	57.1	(1,463	3.3)	12,180	28.0	6,478	14.9
Kazan	4,859	36.3	(471	3.5)	2,284	17.1	6,232	46.6
Kolomna	10,138	43.0	(543	2.3)	7,015	29.7	6,456	27.3
Liteinyi	13,169	42.2	(1,259	4.0)	5,293	16.9	12,774	41.0
Moscow	17,233	43.1	(1,784	4.5)	8,508	21.3	14,226	35.6
Narva	28,020	46.7	(2,218	3.7)	23,177	38.7	8,776	14.6
Petrograd	24,166	34.3	(3,785	5.4)	26,781	38.0	19,568	27.7
Rozhdestvenskii	16,278	47.5	(1,688	4.9)	5,321	15.5	12,688	37.0
Spasski	8,356	46.5	(650	3.6)	3,026	16.8	6,588	36.7
Vasileostrov	28,055	43.3	(5,281	8.2)	24,691	38.2	11,980	18.5
Vyborg	10,205	28.6	(1,264	3.5)	22,487	63.0	3,019	8.5
Total	241,955	44.0	(23,552	4.3)	183,624	33.4	123,771	22.5

[f] Where the Mensheviks ran on separate lists, their votes are reported in parentheses, though they are also included in the votes for moderate Socialists.

[g] Chiefly Kadets; other nonsocialist parties accounted for less than 2% of the total votes.

[h] Does not include the votes in six districts (Lesnoi, Nevskii, Novaia derevnia, Peterhof, and Poliustrovo-Porokhovskii) that were incorporated into the city of Petrograd subsequent to the May elections. Of these districts, only Peterhof (39.7% workers in population, 93.4% metalworkers among workers) gave the Bolsheviks a majority vote, 61.7%; the SRs received 31.5%, the Mensheviks 1.6%, and the nonsocialists 5.2%. Mandel, *Petrograd Workers and the Soviet Seizure of Power*, 220; Mandel, *Petrograd Workers and the Fall of the Old Regime*, 52–53.

Party Composition of Soviet Representational Bodies, June and October 1917

Party	First Congress of Soviets (convened June 3)		VTsIK (elected June 17)		Second Congress of Soviets (convened October 25	
	N	%	N	%	N	%
Mensheviks and affiliates	266[a]	32.4	104	40.5	80	12.3
Defensists and Revolutionary Defensists[b]					36	5.5
Internationalists[b]					33	5.1
Bund	10	1.2			11	1.7
SRs and affiliates	305	37.1	100	38.9	93	14.4
Bolsheviks	105	12.8	35	13.6	338	52.2
United and Internationalist SDs	42	5.1			16	2.5
Left SRs[b]					98	15.1
Other, unaffiliated, and undeclared	104	12.6	18	7.0	23	3.5
Total	822	100.0	257	100.0	648	100.0

Sources: First Congress of Soviets: *Pervyi s'ezd sovetov* 1:xxvii. VTsIK: *Khronika* 3:78. Second Congress of Soviets: *Vtoroi vserossiiskii s'ezd sovetov*, 107–9.

[a] Another source gives 333 as the number of Mensheviks, exclusive of the Bund: *PI*, July 1 1917 (no.1), 10.

[b] These factions did not exist at the time of the First Congress.

Bibliography

ARCHIVAL MATERIALS AND MANUSCRIPTS

Collections of the Project on Menshevik History, Harriman Institute, Columbia University

Collections of Menshevik articles, theses, and letters, 1903–1917.
Collections of press reports on Menshevik meetings and resolutions, 1917.
Dan, F. I. "Sotsial Demokratiia i rabochee dvizhenie za poslednie 5 let." Report written for the Second Socialist International. 1914.
Dan, L. O. Interviews, nos. 16–23.
Denike, Iu. P. Interviews, nos. 6–11.
———. "Men'sheviki v 1917 godu (v strane)."
Departament politsii. "Obzor politicheskoi deiatel'nosti obshchestven-nykh organizatsii za period vremen s 1 marta po 16 aprelia 1916 g."
Garvi, P. A. "Rabochaia kooperatsiia v pervye gody russkoi revoliutsii, 1917–1921."
———. "Unpublished Memoirs, 1906–1912."
———. "Unpublished Memoirs, 1915–1916."
———. "Unpublished Memoirs, 1917."
Nikolaevskii, B. I. "RSDRP (Men'sheviki) v pervye gody revoliutsii, 1914–17."
Nikolaevskii, B. I., and Bourguina, Anna M. *Biographical Dictionary*.
Schwarz, S. M. Interviews, nos. 4–6.
———. "Materialy o razvitii programm ekonomicheskoi politiki v 1917–18 godakh."

Collections of the Hoover Institution on War, Revolution, and Peace, Stanford University

NICOLAEVSKY COLLECTION
Correspondence between Iu. O. Martov and A. N. Potresov, 1907–1909.
Grinevich (Kogan), M. G. "Avtobiograficheskie zametki (kak material dlia S. M. Shvartsa)."
Nikolaevskii, B. I. "Gruppa 'Sibirskikh Tsimmervaldistov'."
Tsereteli, I. G. "Souvenirs sur la révolution russe" (fifty-seven articles written in French and published between 1927 and 1929 in the Swedish newspaper *Ny Tid*).
Voitinskii, V. S. "God pobed i porazhenii" (intended as the third volume of *Gody pobed i porazhenii*, Berlin, 1923).
———. Letter to I. G. Tsereteli, January 4, 1930. No. 15, box 2, #20.

BIBLIOGRAPHY

Manuscript Collection
Rodichev, F. I. "Vospominaniia o 1917 g."
Serebrennikov, I. I. "Vospominaniia, 1917–1922." 3 vols.
Shvarts, S. M. "Fabrichno-zavodskie komitety i profsoiuzy v pervye gody revoliutsii."
Vinavera, Rosa G. "Vospominaniia."

Collections of the Axelrod Archive, International Institute on Social History, Amsterdam

Dan, F. I. Letters to P. B. Akselrod, 1913.
————. Letters to Iu. O. Martov, February 12 and May 12, 1913.
Ezhov, S. O. Letter to Iu. O. Martov, ca. October 19, 1916.
Maiskii, I. Letter to P. B. Akselrod, August 8, 1916.
Tsereteli, I. G. Letter to P. B. Akselrod, June 2, 1914.

Collections of the Bakhmetev Archive, Columbia University

Gurevich, B. A. "Krasnyi sfinks (Povest' o sud'be russkoi revoliutsii i russkikh evreev)."

Newspapers and Journals (dates refer to runs actually consulted)

Biulleten' komiteta iugo-zapadnogo fronta. Kiev, 1917.
Biulleteni statisticheskogo otdela Upravleniia delami Osobogo soveshchaniia po toplivu. Petrograd, 1917.
Delo. Moscow, 1916.
Delo naroda. Petrograd, 1917.
Delo zhizni. Moscow, 1907.
Den'. Petrograd, 1917.
Edinstvo. Petrograd, 1917.
Finansovaia gazeta. Petrograd, 1915–1917.
Finansovaia zhizn'. Petrograd, 1917.
Finansovoe obozrenie. Petrograd, 1917.
Golos (Nash golos; Golos truda). Samara, 1915–1916.
Iskra. Geneva, 1905.
Izvestiia Glavnogo komiteta po snabzhenii armii. Moscow, 1916.
Izvestiia Moskovskogo voenno-promyshlennogo komiteta. Moscow, 1915–1917.
Izvestiia Osobogo soveshchaniia po toplivu. Petrograd, 1917.
Izvestiia Petrogradskogo soveta rabochikh i sol'datskikh deputatov. Petrograd, 1917.
Izvestiia revoliutsionnoi nedeli. Petrograd, 1917.
Izvestiia Soveta s'ezdov predstavitelei promyshlennosti i torgovli. Petrograd, 1917.
Izvestiia Tsentral'nogo voenno-promyshlennogo komiteta. Petrograd, 1915–1917.

Izvestiia Vremennogo komiteta Gosudarstvennoi Dumy. Petrograd, 1917.

Izvestiia Vserossiiskogo soiuza gorodov. Moscow, 1916–1917.

Izvestiia zagranichnogo sekretariata Organizatsionnogo komiteta RSDRP. Geneva, 1915–1917.

Letopis'. Petrograd, 1916–1917.

Letuchii listok Men'shevikov-Internatsionalistov. Petrograd, 1917.

Nasha zaria. Petersburg, 1910–1914.

Nashe slovo. Paris, 1915–1916.

Novaia zhizn'. Petrograd, 1917.

Otkliki sovremennosti. Petrograd, 1906.

Partiinye izvestiia. Petersburg, 1906.

Partiinye izvestiia. Petrograd, 1917.

Pravda. Petrograd, 1917.

Professional'nyi vestnik. Petrograd, 1917.

Proizvoditel'nye sily Rossii. Moscow, 1916–1917.

Promyshlennaia Rossiia. Petrograd, 1915–1916.

Promyshlennost' i torgovlia. Petrograd, 1917.

Rabochaia gazeta. Petrograd, 1917.

Rabochii put'. Petrograd, 1917.

Russkiia vedomosti. Moscow, 1917.

Sibirskii zhurnal. Irkutsk, 1914.

Sibirskoe obozrenie. Irkutsk, 1915.

Sotsialisticheskii vestnik. Berlin, Paris, and New York, 1921–1963.

Stenograficheskii otchet zasedanii Ekonomicheskogo soveta pri vremennom pravitel'stve. Petrograd, 1917.

Strakhovanie rabochikh i sotsial'naia politika. Petrograd, 1917.

Tifliskii listok. Tiflis, 1917.

Torgovo-promyshlennaia gazeta. Petrograd, 1917.

Torgovo-promyshlennyi iug. Odessa, 1916–1917.

Vestnik kooperativnykh soiuzov. Moscow, 1917.

Vestnik kustarnoi promyshlennosti. Petrograd, 1915.

Vestnik Ministerstva truda. Petrograd, 1917.

Vestnik Vremennogo pravitel'stva. Petrograd, 1917.

Vestnik Vserossiiskogo obshchestva kozhevnykh zavodchikov. Petrograd, 1917.

Vpered. Moscow, 1917.

Vserossiiskii vestnik torgovli i promyshlennosti. Petrograd, 1915–1917.

Zhurnaly zasedanii Osobogo soveshchaniia po oboronu gosudarstva. Petrograd, 1917. (Reprint edited by L. G. Beskrovnyi et al. 13 vols. Moscow, 1975–1982.)

CONTEMPORARY MATERIALS (publications, collections of documents, stenographic reports, chronologies)

Amosov, P. N., et al., eds. *Oktiabr'skaia revoliutsiia i fabzavkomy: Materialy po istorii fabrichno-zavodskikh komitetov*. 2 vols. Moscow, 1927–1928.

Avdeev, N.; Vladimirova, V.; Riabinskii, K.; and Liubimov, I. N., eds. *Revoliutsiia 1917 goda: Khronika sobytii.* 6 vols. Moscow and Leningrad, 1923–1930.

Browder, R. P., and Kerensky, A. F., eds. *The Russian Provisional Government, 1917.* 3 vols. Stanford, Calif., 1961.

"Chastnoe soveshchanie chlenov Gosudarstvennoi Dumy 27 fevralia 1917 g." *Volia Rossii,* March 15, 1921 (no. 153).

Chetvertyi (ob'edinitel'nyi) s'ezd RSDRP (aprel'-mai) 1906 goda. Moscow, 1959.

Drezena, A. K., et al., eds. *Burzhuaziia i pomeshchiki v 1917 godu.* Moscow and Leningrad, 1932.

Fabrichno-zavodskie komitety Petrograda v 1917 godu: Protokoly. Moscow, 1982.

"Fevral'skaia revoliutsiia i okhrannoe otdelenie." *Byloe,* 1918, no. 1(29)(7): 158–76.

"Fevral'skaia revoliutsiia 1917 g." *Krasnyi arkhiv,* 1927, no. 2(21):3–78, and no. 3(22):3–70.

Golder, F., ed. *Documents of Russian History, 1914–1917.* New York, 1927.

Gosudarstvennoe soveshchanie. Moscow and Leningrad, 1930.

Grave, B. B., ed. *Burzhuaziia nakanune fevral'skoi revoliutsii.* Moscow, 1927.

Gvozdevshchina v dokumentakh. Kazan, 1929.

"Iz dnevnika Gen. V. G. Boldyreva." *Krasnyi arkhiv,* 1927, no. 4(23):251–56.

Kakurin, N. E., ed. *Razlozhenie armii v 1917 godu.* Moscow, 1923.

"K istorii 'Rabochei gruppy' pri Tsentral'nom voenno-promyshlennom komitete." *Krasnyi arkhiv,* 1933, no. 57:48–84.

Konferentsii rabochikh i promyshlennikov iuga Rossii. No. 1. Kharkov, 1917.

L'vov-Rogachevskii, V. L., ed. *Sotsialisty i tekushchii moment: Materialy velikoi revoliutsii 1917 g.* Moscow, 1917.

Miller, V. A., and Pankratova, A. M., eds. *Rabochee dvizhenie v 1917 godu.* Moscow, 1926.

Milonov, Iu., ed. *Putevoditel' po rezoliutsiiam s'ezdov i konferentsii professional'nykh soiuzov.* Moscow, 1924.

"Nakanune oktiabr'skogo perevorota: Vopros o voine i mire." *Byloe,* 1918, no. 6(12):28–41.

Obzor deiatel'nosti s'ezdov predstavitelei aktsionernykh kommercheskikh bankov i ikh organov (l iiulia 1916 g.–1 ianvaria 1918 g.). Petrograd, 1918.

Otchet o moskovskom soveshchanii obshchestvennykh deiatelei 8–10 avgusta 1917 goda. Moscow, 1917.

Pervyi vserossiiskii s'ezd sovetov rabochikh i soldatskikh deputatov. 2 vols. Moscow, 1930–1931.

Pervyi vserossiiskii torgovo-promyshlennyi s'ezd v Moskve, 19–22 marta 1917 goda: Stenograficheskii otchet i rezoliutsii. Moscow, 1918.

Petrogradskii sovet rabochikh i soldatskikh deputatov: Protokoly zasedanii Ispolnitel'nogo komiteta i Biuro ispolnitel'nogo komiteta. Moscow, 1925.

Piatyi (londonskii) s'ezd RSDRP: Protokoly. Moscow, 1963.

"Politicheskoe polozhenie Rossii nakanune fevral'skoi revoliutsii v zhandarmskoi osveshchenii." *Krasnyi arkhiv*, 1926, no. 4(17):3–34.

Rabochii kontrol' i natsionalizatsiia promyshlennykh predpriiatii Petrograda v 1917–1919 gg. 2 vols. Leningrad, 1949.

Raionnye sovety Petrograda v 1917 godu. 3 vols. Moscow and Leningrad, 1964–1966.

Revoliutsionnoe dvizhenie v Rossii nakanune oktiabr'skogo vooruzhennogo vosstaniia (1–24 oktiabria 1917 g.). Moscow, 1962.

Revoliutsionnoe dvizhenie v Rossii posle sverzheniia samoderzhaviia. Moscow, 1957.

Revoliutsionnoe dvizhenie v Rossii v aprele 1917 g.: Aprel'skii krizis. Moscow, 1958.

Revoliutsionnoe dvizhenie v Rossii v avguste 1917 g.: Razgrom kornilovskogo miatezha. Moscow, 1959.

Revoliutsionnoe dvizhenie v Rossii v iiule 1917 g.: Iiul'skii krizis. Moscow, 1959.

Revoliutsionnoe dvizhenie v Rossii v mae-iiune 1917 g.: Iiunskaia demonstratsiia. Moscow, 1959.

Revoliutsionnoe dvizhenie v Rossii v sentiabre 1917 g.: Obshchenatsional'nyi krizis. Moscow, 1961.

Sbornik materialov komiteta moskovskikh obshchestvennykh organizatsii. 2 parts. Moscow, 1917.

Shecheglov, P., ed. *Padenie tsarskogo rezhima.* 7 vols. Moscow and Leningrad, 1924–1927.

Tret'ia konferentsiia promyshlennikov iuga Rossii, 20–24 sentiabria 1917 g. Kharkov, 1917.

Tret'ia vserossiiskaia konferentsiia professional'nykh soiuzov: Stenograficheskii otchet. Moscow, 1927.

Trudy pervogo s'ezda predstavitelei metalloobrabatyvaiushchei promyshlennosti (29-go fevralia–1-go marta 1916 goda). Petrograd, 1916.

Trudy Vserossiiskogo prodovol'stvennogo s'ezda v moskve, 21–26 maia 1917 goda. 2 vols. Moscow, 1917–1918.

Trudy vtorogo s'ezda predstavitelei voenno-promyshlennykh komitetov. 2 vols., paginated continuously. Petrograd, 1916.

"V ianvare i fevrale 1917 g.: Iz donesenii sekretnykh agentov." *Byloe*, 1918, no. 13(7):91–123.

Volobuev, P. V., et al., eds. *Ekonomicheskoe polozhenie Rossii nakanune velikoi oktiabr'skoi sotsialisticheskoi revoliutsii.* 3 vols. Moscow and Leningrad, 1957.

Vserossiiskii s'ezd upolnomochennykh predstavitelei Obshchegosudarstvennogo prodovol'stvennogo komiteta v g. Petrograd, 5–7 maia 1917. Petrograd, 1917.

Vserossiiskoe soveshchanie sovetov rabochikh i soldatskikh deputatov. Moscow and Leningrad, 1925.

Vtoroi vserossiiskii s'ezd sovetov rabochikh i soldatskikh deputatov. Moscow and Leningrad, 1928.

Works by Mensheviks and Affiliated Social Democrats

Akselrod, P. B. *Istoricheskoe polozhenie i vzaimnoe otnoshenie liberal'noi i sotsialisticheskoi demokratii v Rossii.* Geneva, 1898.

Aronson, G. Ia. *Rossiia nakanune revoliutsii: Istoricheskie etiudy.* New York, 1962.

———. *Rossiia v epokhu revoliutsii: Istoricheskie etiudy i memuary.* New York, 1966.

[———.] "Sud'ba V. G. Gromana, I. I. Rubina, i N. N. Sukhanova." *Sotsialisticheskii vestnik*, 1956, no. 7/8:1–2.

Bazarov, V. A. "Gromanovskaia kontseptsiia narodnokhoziaistvennogo tselogo." *Planovoe khoziaistvo*, 1927, no. 6:162–66.

Bulkin, F. A. *Soiuz metallistov, 1906–1918 gg.* Moscow, 1926.

Dan, F. I. "Die Sozialdemokratie Russlands nach dem Jahre 1908." In *Geschichte der russischen Sozialdemokratie*, edited by L. Martow. Berlin, 1926.

———. "K istorii poslednykh dnei Vremennogo Pravitel'stva." *Letopis' revoliutsii*, 1922, no. 1:163–75.

Dubnova-Erlikh, S. *Obshchestvennyi oblik zhurnala "Letopis'."* New York, 1963.

Ermanskii, O. A. *Iz perezhitogo (1887–1921).* Moscow and Leningrad, 1927.

———. *Marksisty na rasput'ia: O sbornik "Samozashchita."* Petrograd, 1916.

Garvi, P. A. "Iz vospominanii o fevral'skoi revoliutsii." *Sotsialisticheskii vestnik*, 1957, no. 2/3:46–49.

———. *Kapital protiv truda: Chto takoe lokauty?* Petrograd, 1917.

———. "Pamiati pionera rabochego dela v Rossii (M. G. Grinevich)." *Sotsialisticheskii vestnik*, 1942, no. 19/20:254–56.

———. *Professional'nye soiuzy: Ikh organizatsiia i deiatel'nost'.* Petrograd, 1917.

———. *Professional'nye soiuzy v Rossii v pervye gody revoliutsii (1917–21).* New York, 1958.

———. *Revoliutsionnye siluety.* New York, 1962.

———. *Zapiski sotsial demokrata (1906–1921).* Newtonville, Mass., 1982.

Gol'dman-Liber, M. *Zadachi rabochego klassa v russkoi revoliutsii: Rech' proiznosennaia 9 maia 1917 goda na narodnom sobranii v Moskve.* Moscow, 1917.

Maevskii, Evg. *Kanun revoliutsii: Iz istorii dvizheniia nakanune 1917 g. Deiatel'nost' predstavitelei rabochikh pri Tsentral'nom voenno-promyshlennom komitete.* Petrograd, 1918.

Nikolaevskii, B. I. "I. G. Tsereteli: Stranitsy biografii." *Sotsialisticheskii vestnik*, 1959, no. 6:119–22; no. 7:141–43; no. 8/9:159–64; no. 10:196–200; no. 11:219–23; no. 12:243–45.

———. "V. S. Voitinskii." *Sotsialisticheskii vestnik*, 1960, no. 8/9:165–69.

Nikolaevskii, B. I., ed. *Potresov, A. N.: Posmertnyi sbornik proizvodenii.* Paris, 1937.

Pervaia obshcherossiiskaia konferentsiia partiinykh rabotnikov. Supplement to *Iskra* (Geneva), May 15, 1905.

Pis'ma P. B. Akselroda i Iu. O. Martova. Berlin, 1924.

Rafes, M. "Moi vospominaniia." *Byloe*, 1922, no. 19:177–97.

Samozashchita. Petrograd, 1916.

Sapir, B. "Theodor Dan und sein letztes Buch." In Th. Dan, *Der Ursprung des Bolschewismus*. Hanover, 1968.

Shvarts, S. M. *Sotsial'noe strakhovanie v Rossii v 1917–1919 godakh*. New York, 1968.

Skobelev, M. I. "Gibel' tsarizma: Vospominaniia." *Ogonek*, 1927, no. 11(207) (unpaged).

Sokolov, N. D. "Kak rodil'sia Prikaz no. 1." *Ogonek*, 1927, no. 11(207) (unpaged).

Sukhanov, N. N. *Pochemu my voiuem?*

———. *Zapiski o revoliutsii*. 7 vols. Berlin, Petrograd, and Moscow, 1922–1923.

Tsereteli, I. G. "Lecture Delivered [October] 23 by I. G. Tsereteli." *Den' svobodu* (Batumi), October 25/26, 1917 (no. 166/67).

———. "Arrival of I. G. Tsereteli." *Golos kraevogo soveta* (Tiflis), October 7, 1917 (no. 94).

———. *Rechi (proizvedeny v 1917)*. Petrograd, 1917.

———. *Vospominaniia o fevral'skoi revoliutsii*. 2 vols. Paris and The Hague, 1968.

Voitinskii, V. S. *God pobed i porazhenii*. 2 vols. Berlin, 1923.

Zhordania, N. *Moia zhizn'*. Stanford, Calif., 1968.

Works by Other Participants

Auerbakh, V. A. "Revoliutsionnoe obshchestvo po lichnym vospominaniiam." *Arkhiv russkoi revoliutsii*, 1924, no. 14:5–38.

Buchanan, Sir George. *My Mission to Russia and Other Diplomatic Memoirs*. 2 vols. London, 1923.

Buryshkin, P. A. *Moskva kupecheskaia*. New York, 1954.

Chernov, V. *The Great Russian Revolution*. New Haven, 1936.

Denikin, A. T. "Ocherki russkoi smuty." In *Fevral'skaia revoliutsiia*, edited by S. A. Alekseev. Moscow and Leningrad, 1925.

Guchkov, A. I. "Iz vospominanii." *Poslednye novosti*, August 9, 1936–September 30, 1936.

Iurenev, I. *Bor'ba za edinstvo partii*. Petrograd, 1917.

———. "Mezhraionka, 1911–1917 gg." *Proletarskaia revoliutsiia*, 1924, no. 1(24):103–39; no. 2(25):114–43.

Jasny, N. *Soviet Economists of the Twenties*. Cambridge, 1972.

———. *To Live Long Enough*. Wichita, Kans., 1976.

Kaiurov, V. "Shest' dnei fevralia." *Proletarskaia revoliutsiia*, 1923, no. 13: 157–70.

Kerensky, A. F. *The Catastrophe: Kerensky's Own Story of the Russian Revolution*. New York, 1927.

Kirpichnikov, T. "Vosstanie l.-gv. Volynskogo polka v fevrale 1917 g." *Byloe*, 1917, no. 5/6 (27/28):5–16.

Kondrat'ev, K. "Vospominaniia o podpol'noi rabote peterburgskoi organizatsii RSDRP(b) v period 1914–17 gg." *Krasnaia letopis'*, 1922, no. 5:227–43; 1923, no. 7:30–72.

Lomonosov, Iu. V. *Vospominaniia o martovskoi revoliutsii 1917 g.* Stockholm and Berlin, 1921.

Lukomskii, A. "Iz vospominanii." In *Fevral'skaia revoliutsiia*, edited by S. A. Alekseev, 210–15. Moscow and Leningrad, 1925.

Mansyrev, S. P. "Moi vospominaniia o Gosudarstvennoi Dumy." In *Fevral'skaia revoliutsiia*, edited by S. A. Alekseev. Moscow and Leningrad, 1925.

Manuilov, A. A. "Shingarev vo Vremennom Pravitel'stve." *Russkiia vedomosti*, March 6(19), 1918 (no. 39), 5.

Marochkin, G. I. "Na Vasileostrove v 1917 g.: Iz vospominanii o Vasileostrovskom sovete." *Krasnaia letopis'*, 1927, no. 1(22):93–102.

Medlin, V. D., and Parsons, S. L., eds. *V. D. Nabokov and the Russian Provisional Government*. New Haven, Conn., 1976.

Miliukov, P. N. *Istoriia vtoroi russkoi revoliutsii*. 2 vols. Sofia, 1921–1923.

———. *Vospominaniia (1859–1917)*. 2 vols. New York, 1955.

Mstislavskii, S. *Piat' dnei*. 2d ed. Berlin, Petrograd, and Moscow, 1922.

Ol'minskii, M. *Iz epokhi "Zvezdy" i "Pravdy" (1911–1914)*. Moscow, 1921.

Perets, G. G. *V tsitadeli russkoi revoliutsii: Zapiski komendanta Tavricheskogo dvortsa, 27 fevralia–23 marta 1917 g.* Petrograd, 1917.

Peshekhonov, A. V. "Pervye nedeli: Iz vospominanii o revoliutsii." *Na chuzhoi storone*, 1923, no. 1:255–319.

"Piterskie rabochie ob iiul'skikh dniakh." *Krasnaia letopis'*, 1924, no. 9:19–41.

Rodzianko, M. V. "Gosudarstvennaia Duma i fevral'skaia 1917 goda revoliutsiia." *Arkhiv russkoi revoliutsii*, 1922, no. 6:5–80.

Shidlovskii, S. I., *Vospominaniia*, 2 vols. Berlin, 1923.

Shliapnikov, A. G. *Kanun semnadtsatogo goda*. 2 vols. Moscow and Petrograd, 1923.

———. *Semnadtsatyi god*. 4 vols. Moscow, 1923–1931.

Shul'gin, V. V. *Dni*. Leningrad, 1927.

Stankevich, V. B. *Vospominaniia 1914–1919*. Berlin, 1920.

Taras-Rodionov, A. *February 1917*. New York, 1931.

Trotsky, L. *The History of the Russian Revolution*. New York, 1977.

Zalezhskii, V. N. "Pervyi legal'nyi Pe-ka." *Proletarskaia revoliutsiia*, 1923, no. 1(13):135–56.

Zenzinov, V. "Fevral'skie dni." *Novyi zhurnal*, 1953, no. 34:188–221, and no. 35:208–40.

Secondary Works

Andreev, A. M. *Mestnye sovety i organy burzhuaznoi vlasti, 1917 g.* Moscow, 1983.

Anweiler, O. *The Soviets: The Russian Workers, Peasants, and Soldiers Councils, 1905–1921.* New York, 1974.

Ascher, A. Introduction to *Zapiski sotsial demokrata (1906–1921),* by P. A. Garvi. Newtonville, Mass., 1982.

————. "The Kornilov Affair: A Reinterpretation." *Russian Review* 29 (July 1970):286–300.

————. *Pavel Axelrod and the Development of Menshevism.* Cambridge, Mass., 1972.

Avrich, P. "The Russian Revolution and the Factory Committees." Ph.D. diss., Columbia University, 1961.

Bailes, K. E. *Technology and Society under Lenin and Stalin: Origins of the Soviet Technical Intelligentsia, 1917–1941.* Princeton, 1978.

Basil, J. D. *The Mensheviks in the Revolution of 1917.* Columbus, Ohio, 1978.

Berlin, P. A. *Russkaia burzhuaziia v staroe i novoe vremia.* Moscow, 1922.

Blok, A. "Poslednie dni starogo rezhima." *Arkhiv russkoi revoliutsii,* 1922, no. 4:5–54.

Boll, M. M. *The Petrograd Armed Workers Movement in the February Revolution (February–July, 1917): A Study in the Radicalization of the Petrograd Proletariat.* Washington, D.C., 1979.

Bonnell, V. E. *Roots of Rebellion: Workers' Politics and Organizations in St. Petersburg and Moscow, 1900–1914.* Berkeley and Los Angeles, Calif., 1983.

"Bor'ba za tarif derevoobdelochnikov." *Materialy po statistike truda,* 1919, no. 7:28–42.

"Bor'ba za tarif rabochikh pechatnogo dela." *Materialy po statistike truda,* 1919, no. 7:14–28.

Burdzhalov, E. N. *Vtoraia russkaia revoliutsiia: Vosstanie v Petrograde.* Moscow, 1967.

Devlin, R. "Petrograd Workers and the Workers' Factory Committees in 1917." Ph.D. diss., State University of New York at Binghamton, 1976.

Diakin, V. S. *Russkaia burzhuaziia i tsarizm v gody pervoi mirovoi voiny, 1914–1917.* Leningrad, 1967.

Dmitriev, N. "Petrogradskie fabzavkomy v 1917." *Krasnaia letopis',* 1927, no. 2(23):77–79.

Duggan, W. L. "The Progressists and Russian Politics, 1914–1917." Ph.D. diss., Columbia University, 1984.

Fallows, T. "Politics and the War Effort in Russia: The Union of Zemstvos and the Organization of Food Supplies, 1914–1916." *Slavic Review* 37 (March 1978):70–90.

Ferro, M. *The Russian Revolution of February 1917.* Englewood Cliffs, N.J., 1972.

————. "The Russian Soldier in 1917: Undisciplined, Patriotic, and Revolutionary." *Slavic Review* 30 (September 1971):483–512.

Fleer, M. "K istorii rabochego dvizheniia 1917 g." *Krasnaia letopis',* 1925, no. 2(13):239–43.

Galili y García, Z. "The Origins of Revolutionary Defensism: I. G. Tsereteli and the 'Siberian Zimmerwaldists.' " *Slavic Review* 41 (September 1982):454–76.

Gaponenko, L. S. *Rabochii klass Rossii v 1917 godu*. Moscow, 1970.

Getzler, I. *Martov: A Political Biography of a Russian Social Democrat*. London, 1967.

Gleason, W. E. "The All-Russian Union of Towns and the All-Russian Union of Zemstvos in World War I." Ph.D. diss., Indiana University, 1972.

Gol'denberg, M. "Sotsial'no-politicheskoe soderzhanie likvidatorstva." *Proletarskaia revoliutsiia*, 1928, no. 6/7 (77/78):222–64.

Grave, B. B. *K istorii klassovoi bor'by v Rossii v gody imperialisticheskoi voiny: Proletariat i burzhuaziia*. Moscow, 1926.

Haimson, L. H. Introduction to *The Making of Three Russian Revolutionaries: Voices from the Menshevik Past*, edited by L. H. Haimson, Z. Galili y García, and R. Wortman. New York, 1987.

———. "Menshevism and the Evolution of the Russian Intelligentsia." In *The Making of Three Russian Revolutionaries: Voices from the Menshevik Past*, edited by L. H. Haimson, Z. Galili y García, and R. Wortman. New York, 1987.

———. Preface to *The Russian Revolution of 1905*, by S. Schwarz. Chicago, 1967.

———. "The Problem of Social Stability in Urban Russia, 1905–1914." *Slavic Review* 23 (December 1964):619–42; 24 (March 1965):1–22.

Haimson, L. H., and Brian, E. "Three Strike Waves in Imperial Russia (1905–7, 1912–14, 1915–16): Findings and Interpretation of a Comparative Analysis." Paper presented at the International Colloquium on Strikes, Social Conflict, and World War I, Cortona, Italy, June 1986.

Hasegawa, Tsuyoshi. *The February Revolution: Petrograd, 1917*. Seattle, Wash., 1981.

Iakovleva, K. N. "Zabastovochnoe dvizhenie v Rossii za 1895–1917 gody." *Materialy po statistike truda*, 1920, no. 8:3–83.

Itkin, M. L. "Tsentral'nyi sovet fabzavkomy Petrograda v 1917 g." *Oktiabr'skoe vooruzhennoe vosstanie v Petrograde*, 172–81. Moscow, 1980.

Ivanov, N. Ia. *Kornilovshchina i ee razgrom*. Leningrad, 1965.

Katkov, G. *Russia, 1917: The February Revolution*. London, 1967.

Keep, J. L. H. *The Russian Revolution: A Study in Mass Mobilization*. New York, 1976.

Kin, D. "Bor'ba protiv 'ob'edinitel'nogo ugara' v 1917 godu." *Proletarskaia revoliutsiia*, 1927, no. 6(65):3–71.

"K istorii tarifa metallistov." *Materialy po statistike truda*, 1919, no. 7:3–13.

Koenker, D. *Moscow Workers and the 1917 Revolution*. Princeton, 1981.

Koenker, D. P., and Rosenberg, W. G. "The Limits of Formal Protest: Worker Activism and Social Polarization in Petrograd and Moscow, March to October 1917." Paper presented at the International Colloquium on Strikes, Social Conflict, and World War I, Cortona, Italy, June 1986.

————. "Strikes in Revolution: Russia, 1917." Paper presented at the Conference on Russian Labor History, New York, 1983.

Kondrat'ev, N. D. *Rynok khlebov i ego regulirovanie vo vremia voiny i revoliutsii*. Moscow, 1922.

Korbut, M. "Strakhovaia kampaniia 1912–14 gg." *Proletarskaia revoliutsiia*, 1928, no. 2(73):90–118.

Laverychev, V. Ia. *Po tu storonu barikad*. Moscow, 1967.

————. "Vserossiiskii soiuz torgovli i promyshlennosti." *Istoricheskie zapiski*, no. 70 (1961):35–60.

Leiberov, I. P. "O revoliutsionnykh vystupleniiakh petrogradskogo proletariata v gody pervoi mirovoi voiny i fevral'skoi revoliutsii." *Voprosy istorii*, 1964, no. 2:63–77.

Levin, Sh. M. "Sotsialisticheskaia pechat' vo vremia imperialisticheskoi voiny." *Krasnyi arkhiv*, 1922, no. 2:200–225.

Liebman, M. *The Russian Revolution*. New York, 1970.

Lozinskii, Z. *Ekonomicheskaia politika Vremennogo Pravitel'stva*. Leningrad, 1929.

Lur'e, M. L. "Petrogradskoe mezhraionnoe soveshchanie v 1917 godu." *Krasnaia letopis'*, 1932, no. 3(48):13–43; no. 4(49):30–50.

Mandel, D. M. "The Development of Revolutionary Consciousness among the Industrial Workers of Petrograd between February and November 1917." Ph.D. diss., Columbia University, 1977.

————. *The Petrograd Workers and the Fall of the Old Regime*. New York, 1983.

————. *The Petrograd Workers and the Soviet Seizure of Power*. New York, 1984.

Mel'gunov, S. P. *Martovskie dni 1917 goda*. 2d ed. Paris, 1961.

————. *Na putiakh k dvortsovomu perevorotu*. Paris, 1931.

Miller, V. I. "Nachalo demokratizatsii staroi armii v dni fevral'skoi revoliutsii." *Istoriia SSSR*, 1966, no. 6:26–43.

————. *Soldatskie komitety russkoi armii v 1917 g*. Moscow, 1973.

Mindin, E. "Rabochee vremia i zarabotnaia plata na predpriiatiakh moskovskoi oblasti za 1914–1918 gody." *Statistika truda*, 1919, no. 8/10:8–14.

Mints, I. I., et al., eds. *Sverzhenie samoderzhaviia: Sbornik statei*. Moscow, 1970.

Owen, T. C. *Capitalism and Politics in Russia: A Social History of the Moscow Merchants, 1855–1905*. Cambridge, 1981.

Pearson, R. *Russian Moderates and the Crisis of Tsarism, 1914–1917*. New York, 1977.

Pushkareva, I. M. *Zheleznodorozhniki Rossii v burzhuazno-demokraticheskikh revoliutsiiakh*. Moscow, 1975.

Rabinowitch, A. *The Bolsheviks Come to Power: The Revolution of 1917 in Petrograd*. New York, 1976.

Rabinowitch, A. *Prelude to Revolution: The Petrograd Bolsheviks and the July 1917 Uprising.* Bloomington, Ind., 1968.

Radkey, O. H. *The Agrarian Foes of Bolshevism.* New York, 1958.

Reikhardt, B. B. "Russkaia burzhuaziia v bor'be za sokhranenie ekonomicheskogo gospodstva, fevral'-oktiabr' 1917 g." *Krasnaia letopis',* 1930, no. 1(34):5–47.

Rieber, A. J. *Merchants and Entrepreneurs in Imperial Russia.* Chapel Hill, N.C., 1982.

Roobol, W. H. *Tsereteli: A Democrat in the Russian Revolution: A Political Biography.* The Hague, 1976.

Roosa, R. A. "Russian Industrialists and 'State Socialism,' 1916–1917." *Soviet Studies* 23 (January 1972):395–417.

Rosenberg, W. G. "The Democratization of Russia's Railroads in 1917." *American Historical Review* 88 (December 1981):983–1008.

———. *Liberals in the Russian Revolution: The Constitutional Democratic Party, 1917–1921.* Princeton, 1974.

———. "Russian Labor and Bolshevik Power after October." *Slavic Review* 42 (1985):213–38.

Ruckman, J. A. *The Moscow Business Elite: A Social and Cultural Portrait of Two Generations, 1840–1905.* De Kalb, Ill., 1984.

Sanders, J. "The Union of Unions: Economic, Political, Civic, and Human Rights Organizations in the Russian Revolution of 1905." Ph.D. diss., Columbia University, 1985.

Shatilova, T. I. "Petrogradskaia krupnaia burzhuaziia mezhdu dvumia revoliutsiiami 1917 g." *Krasnaia letopis',* 1926, no. 6(2):47–67.

———. "Professional'nye soiuzy i oktiabr'." *Krasnaia letopis',* 1927, no. 2(23):179–88.

Siegelbaum, L. *The Politics of Industrial Mobilization: A Study of the War-Industries Committees in Russia, 1914–1917.* New York, 1983.

Smith, S. A. *Red Petrograd: Revolution in the Factories, 1917–1918.* Cambridge, 1983.

Sobolev, G. L. "Pis'ma v petrogradskii sovet rabochikh i soldatskikh deputatov kak istochnik dlia izucheniia obshchestvennoi psikhologii v Rossii v 1917 g." In *Vspomogatel'nye istoricheskie distsipliny,* 159–73. Leningrad, 1968.

Stepanov, A. V. *Rabochie Petrograda v period podgotovki i provedeniia oktiabr'skogo vooruzhennogo vosstaniia, avgust–oktiabr' 1917 g.* Moscow and Leningrad, 1965.

Strumilin, S. G. *Zarabotnaia plata i proizvoditel'nost' truda v russkoi promyshlennosti za 1913–1922 g.* Moscow, 1923.

Struve, P. B., ed. *Food Supply in Russia during the World War.* New Haven, 1930.

Suny, R. G. "Toward a Social History of the October Revolution." *American Historical Review* 88 (February 1983):31–52.

Tal', L. S. *Ocherki promyshlennogo rabochego prava.* 2d ed. Moscow, 1918.

Taniaev, A. *Ocherki dvizheniia zheleznodorozhnikov v revoliutsii 1917 g.* Moscow and Leningrad, 1925.

Tarnovskii, K. N. *Formirovanie gosudarstvenno-monopolisticheskogo kapitalizma v Rossii v gody pervoi mirovoi voiny.* Moscow, 1958.

Tokarev, Iu. S. *Petrogradskii sovet rabochikh i soldatskikh deputatov v marte-aprele 1917 g.* Leningrad, 1976.

Vanag, N. N. "K metodologii izucheniia finansovogo kapitala v Rossii." *Istorik-Marksist*, 1929, no. 12:5–46.

Volobuev, P. V. *Ekonomicheskaia politika Vremennogo Pravitel'stva.* Moscow, 1962.

―――. "Politika burzhuazii i Vremennogo Pravitel'stva v rabochem voprose (mart-aprel' 1917 g.)." *Istoricheskie zapiski*, no. 73 (1963):127–55.

―――. *Proletariat i burzhuaziia v Rossii v 1917 g.* Moscow, 1964.

Wade, R. A. "The Rajonnye Sovety of Petrograd: The Role of Local Political Bodies in the Russian Revolution." *Jahrbucher für Geschichte Osteuropas* 20 (June 1972):226–40.

―――. *Red Guards and Workers' Militias in the Russian Revolution.* Stanford, Calif., 1984.

―――. *The Russian Search for Peace, February-October 1917.* Stanford, Calif., 1969.

White, J. D. "The Kornilov Affair." *Soviet Studies* 20 (October 1968):187–205.

Wildman, A. K. *The End of the Russian Imperial Army: The Old Army and the Soldiers' Revolt (March-April 1917).* Princeton, 1980.

Zagorsky, S. O. *State Control of Industry in Russia during the War.* New Haven, 1928.

Zmeul, A. *Ot fevralia k oktiabriu: Profsoiuzy i fabzavkomy v 1917 g.* Moscow, 1934.

Znamenskii, O. N. *Iiul'skii krizis 1917 goda.* Moscow, 1964.

Index

Italicized numbers denote glossary entries.

jected by, 207, 208. *See also* Arbitration

Lapinskii, P., 199n, 331

Larin, Iu., 33, 133n, 134, 191n, 192; on war, 133

Left Kadets, *403. See also* Kadets

Left Socialist Revolutionaries (SRs), 391n; continue to oppose coalition, 177; in July Days, 330, 331. *See also* Socialist Revolutionaries (SRs)

Lena goldfield massacre, 256

Lenin, 27, 38, 60, 193, 206, 251, 253, 306, 377, 381; advocates economic regulation, 236; "The Impending Catastrophe and How to Combat It," 377; "liquidationist"coined by, 32, 32n; returns to Petrograd, 157, 157n

Letopis, 38

Levin, V. M., 248, 249

Levitskii, V. O., 34, 35, 38

Liaison committee of soviet, 132, 138, 145

Liber, M. I., 27, 159, 276, 347, 354, 386n, *411*; against coalition, 170; at Congress of Soviets, 307, 307n, 309, 313; dictum of self-restraint, 276; in July Days, 323n; supports coalition, 179; on war, 136

Liquidationism: Menshevik critique of, 36; origin and definition of, 32, 32n, *405*

Liquidationists, 144, *405. See also* Menshevik Liquidationists

Lisetskii, A. M., 204

Literatory, *405*

Litvinov-Falinskii, V. P., 372n

Lunacharskii, A. V., 334, 393, 394

Lur'e, S. V., 351n, 360n

L'vov, Prince G. E., 23, 239, 343; on coalition, 168, 169, 171, 176, 178

Maevskii, E., 34

Main Committee on Leather, 363n

Main Economic Committee (MEC), 237, 361, 362, 362n

Maiskii, I. M., 259, 283n

Mandel, D., 211, 297

Manikovskii, Gen. A. A., 78n

Manuilov, A. A., 23, 82n, 321n

Martov, Iu. O., 33, 354, 381–82, 385,

386, 390n, 395, *411*; against coalition, 191; against liquidationism, 33, 36; concept of revolution after 1905, 36–37; at Congress of Soviets, 306, 310, 312; in July Days, 331, 332, 334, 335n; at May Conference, 199n, 200; origin of internationalism, 37–38; at Second Congress of Soviets, 393–94; on seizing power, 37

Martynov, A. S., 36, 199n, 350

Maslov, P. P., 82n, 387n

Maslov, S. L., 388n

May Conference. *See* Menshevik May Conference

May Day, 160, 160n, 161, 162

Menshevik August Congress (Unification Congress of RSDRP), 353–56, 390

Menshevik Defensists, 38–39, *405*; on danger of counterrevolution, 341n; in soldiers' committees, 128, 146n

Menshevik Internationalists, 38, 136, 343, 391n, *405*; accept coalition, 183; affected by Bolshevik danger, 382–83, 382n; at August Congress, 354–55; and Bolshevik seizure of power, 392–95; conception of revolution, 43; defeated at May Conference, 199, 199n, 200; on economic regulation, 251n; in emigration, 191, 191n, 200; in July Days, 329, 330, 331; and Kornilov affair, 380, 381; for Menshevik unity, 190n

Menshevik Liquidationists, *405*; against workers' *kontrol'*, 250–51, 253; defensism of, 38–39; rethinking revolution after 1905, 32, 34–35. *See also* Ministry of Labor

Menshevik May Conference (All-Russian Conference of RSDRP), 301n, 387n; composition of, 194, 195n, 196n; debate on coalition, 192, 192n–93n; debate on war, 193–94, 193n; division and unity at, 199, 200; impact of provinces at, 198, 199; on labor legislation, 258; victory of Revolutionary Defensism, 191, 194, 200, 201

Menshevik Organizational Committee, 301n, 307, 308n, 341–42; composition of, 200, 200n; reservations about coa-

Studies of the Harriman Institute

Soviet National Income in 1937 by Abram Bergson, Columbia University Press, 1953.

Through the Glass of Soviet Literature: Views of Russian Society, Ernest Simmons, Jr., ed., Columbia University Press, 1953.

Polish Postwar Economy by Thad Paul Alton, Columbia University Press, 1954.

Management of the Industrial Firm in the USSR: A Study in Soviet Economic Planning by David Granick, Columbia University Press, 1954.

Soviet Policies in China, 1917–1924 by Allen S. Whiting, Columbia University Press, 1954; paperback, Stanford University Press, 1968.

Literary Politics in the Soviet Ukraine, 1917–1934 by George S. N. Luckyj, Columbia University Press, 1956.

The Emergence of Russian Panslavism, 1856–1870 by Michael Boro Petrovich, Columbia University Press, 1956.

Lenin on Trade Unions and Revolution, 1893–1917 by Thomas Taylor Hammond, Columbia University Press, 1956.

The Last Years of the Georgian Monarchy, 1658–1832 by David Marshall Lang, Columbia University Press, 1957.

The Japanese Thrust into Siberia, 1918 by James William Morley, Columbia University Press, 1957.

Bolshevism in Turkestan, 1917–1927 by Alexander G. Park, Columbia University Press, 1957.

Soviet Marxism: A Critical Analysis by Herbert Marcuse, Columbia University Press, 1958; paperback, Columbia University Press, 1985.

Soviet Policy and the Chinese Communists, 1931–1946 by Charles B. McLane, Columbia University Press, 1958.

The Agrarian Foes of Bolshevism: Promise and Defeat of the Russian Socialist Revolutionaries, February to October, 1917 by Oliver H. Radkey, Columbia University Press, 1958.

Pattern for Soviet Youth: A Study of the Congresses of the Komsomol, 1918–1954 by Ralph Talcott Fisher, Jr., Columbia University Press, 1959.

The Emergence of Modern Lithuania by Alfred Erich Senn, Columbia University Press, 1959.

The Soviet Design for a World State by Elliot R. Goodman, Columbia University Press, 1960.

Settling Disputes in Soviet Society: The Formative Years of Legal Institutions by John N. Hazard, Columbia University Press, 1960.

Soviet Marxism and Natural Science, 1917–1932 by David Joravsky, Columbia University Press, 1961.

449

Russian Classics in Soviet Jackets by Maurice Friedberg, Columbia University Press, 1962.

Stalin and the French Communist Party, 1941–1947 by Alfred J. Rieber, Columbia University Press, 1962.

Sergei Witte and the Industrialization of Russia by Theodore K. Von Laue, Columbia University Press, 1962.

Ukranian Nationalism by John H. Armstrong, Columbia University Press, 1963.

The Sickle under the Hammer: The Russian Socialist Revolutionaries in the Early Months of Soviet Rule by Oliver H. Radkey, Columbia University Press, 1963.

Comintern and World Revolution, 1928–1943: The Shaping of Doctrine by Kermit E. McKenzie, Columbia University Press, 1964.

Weimar Germany and Soviet Russia, 1926–1933: A Study in Diplomatic Instability by Harvey L. Dyck, Columbia University Press, 1966.

Financing Soviet Schools by Harold J. Noah, Teachers College Press, 1966.

Russia, Bolshevism, and the Versailles Peace by John M. Thompson, Princeton University Press, 1966.

The Russian Anarchists by Paul Avrich, Princeton University Press, 1967.

The Soviet Academy of Sciences and the Communist Party, 1927–1932 by Loren R. Graham, Princeton University Press, 1967.

Red Virgin Soil: Soviet Literature in the 1920's by Robert A. Maguire, Princeton University Press, 1968; paperback, Cornell University Press, 1987.

Communist Party Membership in the U.S.S.R., 1917–1967 by T. H. Rigby, Princeton University Press, 1968.

Soviet Ethics and Morality by Richard T. De George, University of Michigan Press, 1969; paperback, Ann Arbor Paperbacks, 1969.

Vladimir Akimov on the Dilemmas of Russian Marxism, 1895–1903 by Jonathan Frankel, Cambridge University Press, 1969.

Soviet Perspectives on International Relations, 1956–1967 by William Zimmerman, Princeton University Press, 1969.

Krondstadt, 1921 by Paul Avrich, Princeton University Press, 1970.

Class Stuggle in the Pale: The Formative Years of the Jewish Workers' Movement in Tsarist Russia by Ezra Mendelsohn, Cambridge University Press, 1970.

The Proletarian Episode in Russian Literature by Edward J. Brown, Columbia University Press, 1971.

Labor and Society in Tsarist Russia: The Factory Workers of St. Petersburg, 1855–1870 by Reginald E. Zelnik, Stanford University Press, 1971.

Archives and Manuscript Repositories in the U.S.S.R.: Moscow and Leningrad by Patricia K. Grimsted, Princeton University Press, 1972.

The Baku Commune, 1917–1918 by Ronald G. Suny, Princeton University Press, 1972.

Mayakovsky: A Poet in the Revolution by Edward J. Brown, Princeton University Press, 1973.

Oblomov and his Creator: The Life and Art of Ivan Goncharov by Milton Ehre, Princeton University Press, 1973.

German Politics Under Soviet Occupation by Henry Krisch, Columbia University Press, 1974.

Soviet Politics and Society in the 1970's, Henry W. Morton and Rudolph L. Tokes, eds., Free Press, 1974.

Liberals in the Russian Revolution by William G. Rosenberg, Princeton University Press, 1974.

Famine in Russia, 1891–1892 by Richard G. Robbins, Jr., Columbia University Press, 1975.

In Stalin's Time: Middleclass Values in Soviet Fiction by Vera Dunham, Cambridge University Press, 1976.

The Road to Bloody Sunday by Walter Sablinsky, Princeton University Press, 1976; paperback, Princeton University Press, 1986.

The Familiar Letter as a Literary Genre in the Age of Pushkin by William Mills Todd III, Princeton University Press, 1976.

Russian Realist Art. The State and Society: The Peredvizhniki and Their Tradition by Elizabeth Valkenier, Ardis Publishers, 1977.

The Soviet Agrarian Debate by Susan Solomon, Westview Press, 1978.

Cultural Revolution in Russia, 1928–1931, Sheila Fitzpatrick, ed., Indiana University Press, 1978; paperback, Midland Books, 1984.

Soviet Criminologists and Criminal Policy: Specialists in Policy-Making by Peter Solomon, Columbia University Press, 1978.

Technology and Society under Lenin and Stalin: Origins of the Soviet Technical Intelligentsia by Kendall E. Bailes, Princeton University Press, 1978.

The Politics of Rural Russia, 1905–1914, Leopold H. Haimson, ed., Indiana University Press, 1979.

Political Participation in the U.S.S.R. by Theodore H. Friedgut, Princeton University Press, 1979, paperback, Princeton University Press, 1982.

Education and Social Mobility in the Soviet Union, 1921–1934 by Sheila Fitzpatrick, Cambridge University Press, 1979.

The Soviet Marriage Market: Mate Selection in Russia and the USSR by Wesley Andrew Fisher, Praeger Publishers, 1980.

Prophecy and Politics: Socialism, Nationalism, and the Russian Jews, 1862–1917 by Jonathan Frankel, Cambridge University Press, 1981.

Dostoevsky and the Idiot: Author, Narrator, and Reader by Robin Feuer Miller, Harvard University Press, 1981.

Moscow Workers and the 1917 Revolution by Diane Koenker, Princeton University Press, 1981; paperback, Princeton University Press, 1986.

Archives and Manuscript Repositories in the USSR: Estonia, Latvia, Lithuania, and Belorussia by Particia K. Grimsted, Princeton University Press, 1981.

Zionism in Poland: The Formative Years, 1915–1926 by Ezra Mendelsohn, Yale University Press, 1982.

Soviet Risk-Taking and Crisis Behavior by Hannes Adomeit, George Allen and Unwin Publishers, 1982.

Russia at the Crossroads: The 26th Congress of the CPSU, Seweryn Bialer and Thane Gustafson, eds., George Allen and Unwin Publishers, 1982.

The Crisis of the Old Order in Russia: Gentry and Government by Roberta Thompson Manning, Princeton University Press, 1983; paperback, Princeton University Press, 1986.

Sergei Aksakov and Russian Pastoral by Andrew A. Durkin, Rutgers University Press, 1983.

Politics and Technology in the Soviet Union by Bruce Parrott, MIT Press, 1983.

The Soviet Union and the Third World: An Economic Bind by Elizabeth Kridl Valkenier, Praeger Publishers, 1983.

Russian Metaphysical Romanticism: The Poetry of Tiutchev and Boratynskii by Sarah Pratt, Stanford University Press, 1984.

Ruling Russia: Politics and Administration in the Age of Absolutism, 1762–1796 by John LeDonne, Princeton University Press, 1984.

Insidious Intent: A Structural Analysis of Fedor Sologub's Petty Demon by Diana Greene, Slavica Publishers, 1986.

Leo Tolstoy: Resident and Stranger by Richard Gustafson, Princeton University Press, 1986.

Workers, Society, and the State: Labor and Life in Moscow, 1918–1929 by William Chase, University of Illinois Press, 1987.

Andrey Bely: Spirit of Symbolism, John Malmstad, ed., Cornell University Press, 1987.

Government and Peasant in Russia, 1861–1906: The Prehistory of the Stolypin Reforms by David A. J. Macey, Northern Illinois University Press, 1987.

The Making of Three Russian Revolutionaries: Voices from the Menshevik Past, edited by Leopold H. Haimson in collaboration with Ziva Galili y García and Richard Wortman, Cambridge University Press, 1988.

Revolution and Culture: The Bogdanov-Lenin Controversy by Zenovia A. Sochor, Cornell University Press, 1988.

A Handbook of Russian Verbs by Frank Miller, Ardis Publishers, 1988.